Researching the Culture in Agri-*Culture*

Social Research for International Development

Researching the Culture in Agri-*Culture*

Social Research for International Development

Edited by

Michael M. Cernea

and

Amir H. Kassam

CABI Publishing

338.1072
R4323

CABI Publishing is a division of CAB International

CABI Publishing
CAB International
Wallingford
Oxfordshire OX10 8DE
UK

CABI Publishing
875 Massachusetts Avenue
7th Floor
Cambridge, MA 02139
USA

Tel: +44 (0)1491 832111
Fax: +44 (0)1491 833508
E-mail: cabi@cabi.org
Website: www.cabi-publishing.org

Tel: +1 617 395 4056
Fax: +1 617 354 6875
E-mail: cabi-nao@cabi.org

A catalogue record for this book is available from the British Library, London, UK.

Library of Congress Cataloging-in-Publication Data

Researching the culture in agri-culture : social research for international
   agricultural development / edited by Michael M. Cernea and Amir H.
   Kassam.
     p. cm.
   Based on papers from a conference of social scientists, mainly from
   within the CGIAR (consultative group on international agricultural re-
   search) held in CIAT, Colombia.
   Includes bibliographical references and index.
   ISBN-13: 978-0-85199-003-3 (hardcover : alk. paper)
   ISBN-10: 0-85199-003-7 (hardcover : alk. paper)
   ISBN-13: 978-0-85199-026-2 (pbk. : alk. paper)
   ISBN-10: 0-85199-026-6 (pbk. : alk. paper)
   1. Agriculture--Research--Sociological aspects--Congresses. 2. Con-
   sultative Group on International Agricultural Research--Congresses.
   I. Cernea, Michael M. II. Kassam, Amir H.
   S540.S63R47 2006
   338.1'072--dc22   2005019032

Paperback ISBN   0 85199 026 6
978 0 85199 026 2
Hardback ISBN   0 85199 003 7
978 0 85199 003 3

Typeset by SPI Publisher Services, Pondicherry, India
Printed and bound in the UK by Biddles Ltd, King's Lynn

In memoriam

Robert K. Merton

This volume is dedicated to the memory of one of the foremost sociologists of our times – Robert K. Merton, who made enduring contributions to many fields of sociological thinking and research and has been recognized as the founding father and tireless architect of the sociology of science and scientific research.

Robert Merton's profound insights into the nature and functioning of human society, and his research on the endeavours of science and scientists, have inspired many of the contributors to this volume.

Merton knew of the preparation of this book, which is largely a study in the sociology of research and research institutions, and he would have surely introduced it to the readers, had he not left us, sadly, just a few months before this volume was completed.

The ideas he developed and imparted remain vital and will continue to guide the efforts of social scientists and researchers throughout the world.

Contents

Part I
Social Research for Agricultural Policies

Part II
The Insiders' Views: Social Research in the CGIAR System

Part III
The Outsiders' View:
Issues, Expectations and Agendas

Foreword

Emil Q. Javier and Per Pinstrup-Andersen

Research in sociological or anthropological disciplines represents an important, although relatively small, segment in the broad research agenda of the Consultative Group on International Agricultural Research (CGIAR) System. The expressions of this research, influenced by CGIAR's goals, have varied over the years. During its first two decades, CGIAR's technical research styles and approaches were generally 'top down' and the farming communities were seen mainly as beneficiaries rather than as 'partners', to be engaged in the research process of all CGIAR centres. The importance of direct beneficiary participation and of socio-cultural variables in CGIAR research, emphasized tenaciously by the system's social researchers, began to permeate more seriously in most centres only in the late 1980s and the 1990s when the CGIAR incorporated sustainable food security into its goals.

As the mission of the CGIAR is now expanding beyond food production to assist in sustainable poverty reduction, social and economic research are becoming increasingly functionally relevant for enhancing the quality and effectiveness of research and for achieving impact. In recent years, various policy and strategy documents in the CGIAR have repeatedly stated and stressed the need to strengthen and expand social, economic and policy research, consistent with the CGIAR's overall mandate, and to integrate it more organically with biophysical, economic and technical research.

During the preparation of the new CGIAR vision and strategy, adopted in 2000, social scientists from many countries were invited to incorporate into the system's strategy the social and cultural areas thought essential for achieving the CGIAR mission. The response was very encouraging, and many of the proposals were incorporated in the final vision and strategy document approved by the entire CGIAR. Thus, the CGIAR family and the international donors supported a stronger investment of human talent and material resources in social research within the CGIAR centres. Since this increased social emphasis is one of the new elements brought by the current CGIAR strategy into the system's current agenda, the challenge now is to ensure its translation in actual research processes and creative products of all CGIAR centres and of their partners in the national research systems of developed and developing countries.

In this context, at the behest of the CGIAR interim Science Council (iSC), an international CGIAR Social Research Conference was initiated and took place in September 2002 at CIAT, Cali, Colombia. The conference brought together a large group of scholars from CGIAR centres and the wider international academic community. The many specialties represented at the conference helped to place its central focus on social research well within its interdisciplinary linkages and development perspectives on agricultural issues.

Given the importance of this research area, the CGIAR management and iSC appointed Prof. Michael Cernea and Dr Amir Kassam to prepare, as editors, a book as an outgrowth from the conference deliberations and materials. The iSC also recommended that the book should not be in the form of conference proceedings, but take a rather distinct, independent form. Therefore, the editors selected the best material from the conference and also invited additional world-level scholars from outside the CGIAR system to contribute new studies and reflections about the state-of-the-art, the future directions and the challenges to international and national social research in the areas of agriculture, forestry, fisheries, land and water management and related development policy.

By placing 'the culture in agri-*culture*' on the book's masthead, the authors explore not only the knowledge, behaviour and values of farmers, fisher folk and forest dwellers but also, in the larger sociological and anthropological sense of culture, the institutional structures in agriculture and in research, the patterns of social organization in natural resource management, the cultural and organizational premises of collective action, behavioural variables, gender, the participation of farmers in research and the nature of social science research products as international public goods. This way, the volume tackles some of the most central themes on the international and national agendas in social science and links the relevance of social research to the main paradigm in development today – the sustainable poverty reduction paradigm.

Both the CGIAR system, and many people and institutions outside the CGIAR, have cooperated during recent years to advance the intellectual and scientific base of social research for development, through regular research programmes, challenge programmes, and to rekindle the involvement of rural sociologists and social anthropologists with different backgrounds in social science in the CGIAR mainstream research.

However, as this volume indicates, social research in the CGIAR is still incompletely and insufficiently institutionalized and financed to fully meet the demands of our system's new strategy and assignments. Many ideas and recommendations are put forward in this book's studies to intensify and mainstream this research, and bring its needed products to bear upon agricultural programmes and policies. We therefore consider this volume to be timely and helpful, and we hope that it will make a significant contribution towards strengthening social science research in the CGIAR in the coming years.

We express our appreciation to the CGIAR Chair and to CGIAR donors, who have supported the preparation of this volume. Particular thanks are due to the book's editors, Prof. Michael M. Cernea, member of the former TAC and of the interim CGIAR Science Council and Dr Amir H. Kassam, Senior Officer in the CGIAR Science Council Secretariat, for their tenacious work in conceiving and preparing this massive reference volume, and to all the contributing authors from within and outside the CGIAR, for making this publication possible.

We hope that the valuable and innovative experiences in social research recorded in these pages, and the volume's timely critical messages, will be shared and heard widely, inside and beyond the CGIAR proper, helping international agricultural research diversify and improve its indispensable contributions to a food-secure world.

Stock Taking and New Challenges in Social Research
Editors' Preface

Michael M. Cernea and Amir H. Kassam

After being a largely spontaneous process for uncounted millennia, agricultural development has increasingly become science-based and planned. Historians would probably place the turning point for this shift somewhere in the 19th or early 20th century. What matters more than the exact timing, though, is that due to this revolutionary shift to professionally generated scientific and technical knowledge and to knowledge about improved social organization patterns, agriculture can now feed additional billions of people, more than ever in the past, and prove wrong the dire Malthusian prediction.

It is on this path that agriculture continues in the new century. Its basic characteristic is that the role of scientific research in maximizing agriculture's productivity is growing exponentially.

This historical shift vastly enhances the expectations from, and the global importance of the huge scientific effort deployed within the Consultative Group on International Agricultural Research (CGIAR) network – 15 autonomous international research centres with over 8500 scientists and staff – co-sponsored by major development agencies, by some 50 countries of the North and the South and by other international and regional organizations and foundations.

Social science research, as a specialized and distinct domain, is an integral part of CGIAR's activities. Although the social research domain is far outranked by the extent, staffing and financing of research in the agro-bio-physical sciences, it is none the less a key and irreplaceable domain, indispensable to reaching CGIAR's declared developmental, nutritional and socio-political objectives. It is also indispensable to conducting state-of-the-art work in biological and natural sciences.

Social research began in CGIAR's centres shortly after CGIAR's establishment and by now has over 30 years of important achievements. But these have also been years of incessant struggle to affirm its potential and contributions against institutional obstacles, intellectual narrowness, under-financing and prejudices of various sorts. This struggle still continues.

This book is devoted to a collective stock-taking of the storehouse of social knowledge and knowledge-generating methods amassed in three decades of multi-sided and committed social research. It is a collective product of a large number of scientists working in CGIAR research centres and, some, in academic settings outside CGIAR. Beyond its direct authors, this volume also builds on the creativity of numerous other CGIAR researchers who contributed to the projects the book describes and who should share in the credit. Most of the book's co-authors are sociologists, social anthropologists and economists, and some are biological and natural resources scientists.

This book was put together interactively across the entire CGIAR through a collaborative process of over 30 months. The editors have aimed to build an enduring and documented tribute to the innovative and consequential research contributions of CGIAR's social researchers and to offer various outside audiences a reference volume, conveying valuable experiences and enriching knowledge. As we look at the final product with some amazement ourselves, this collective product appears now to be the most comprehensive record to date of social research in CGIAR's existence.

Yet, this is not a simple 'festive' volume, recording only successes and turning the eye away from problems that are unresolved. The book's co-authors do not only passionately advocate the relevance of social research but critically examine their own achievements and weaknesses. They are not shy in raising thorny institutional and methodological issues lingering unresolved within various CGIAR centres and hampering their work.

The volume benefits from both the wisdom of hindsight analyses and the intellectual stimuli of foresight and anticipation of future research. The authors discuss substantially not only what has been accomplished but also the major research themes and methodological challenges facing social research in light of the new 'vision and strategy' of CGIAR, adapted in 2000. Many of the lessons from past research – such as the issues of weak institutionalization, of one-sided or top-down research strategies, of depleted staffing, underestimation, under-financing and others – raised in the volume will, we hope, be departure points for further discussion, organizational improvements and expanded, new creative research.

The volume has three main parts. Part I is devoted to some general issues of the place and functions of social research in the CGIAR system and to the system's receptivity to social science findings, methods and messages. The Foreword to the volume comes from two scholars – chairmen of CGIAR Technical Advisory Committee and CGIAR Science Council, whose tenures span the book's preparation period – Emil Javier and Per Pinstrup-Anderson, with decades of experience in CGIAR and international agriculture. The two opening studies, written by the book's editors, examine fundamental challenges and issues: the content of social research and the concept of the 'culture of agri-*culture*' as a field of scientific study; the not fully resolved problems of durably institutionalizing the socio-cultural and behavioural research within a scientific group focused mainly on biological and natural sciences; the unaddressed and worrisome issues of decreased staffing capacity for social and cultural research; the need for both interdisciplinary and autonomous social research; and the demand for 'knowledge conveyor-belts' as an institutional function of social researchers, not only for disseminating the knowledge developed within CGIAR externally but also for bringing inside and promoting within CGIAR the knowledge achieved by 'outside' social research in university-based academic research and in national agricultural research systems (NARS).

This part concludes with a report of findings from a special demographic and sociological survey undertaken within CGIAR's research community itself. It answers empirically the questions: '*Who are CGIAR's social scientists and how do they perceive their activities?*' This is perhaps the first study of this kind and brings to light, as readers will notice, many surprising findings.

Part II and Part III of the volume are organized along an idea stressed by Robert Merton's dialectic analysis of complementarities inherent in the 'perspectives of "insiders" and "outsiders"',[1] despite their belonging to different systems and communities, each with its culture. We thought that inviting a larger number of scholars from outside CGIAR's centres would foster much-needed healthy debate about the potentials of, and the expectations from, CGIAR's social research, and would gain wider resonance for the book's analyses. Indeed, we hope that this volume will catalyse and encourage such debate further, to be continued by other scholars inside and outside CGIAR's centres, by donors, development aid agencies and practitioners and by public officials interested in the production of international public goods.

Part II includes the contributions of CGIAR 'insiders' studies each contributed by a group of researchers from different CGIAR centres, taking stock of the social research done so far by each centre, highlighting constraints and outlining the path ahead. One additional study is devoted to the systemwide social research programme of rural institutions – property rights and collective action mechanisms.

These studies' richness of facts and issues defies any attempt to summarize them. They offer not only vast information about past and ongoing scientific work, but also substantial 'food for thought' for revisiting and rethinking institutional arrangements, social research strategies or thematic priorities in those specific centres, as seen by CGIAR and centres' insiders.

Conversely, Part III gives voice to a number of highly respected so-called 'outsiders' – university-based scholars, or representatives of donor agencies such as USAID and the Rockefeller Foundation, or development specialists (some of these authors had also been CGIAR 'insiders', and can comment from both perspectives). The dialogue between the two perspectives illuminates multiple aspects rarely addressed, not only about successes, but also about dysfunctions in the CGIAR system.

Altogether, the social study and understanding of farmers' behaviour, knowledge and forms of social organization have immeasurably enriched and corrected the knowledge generated by biophysical scientists for over three decades. They have resulted in better targeted breeding and the creation of new cultivars and in farther-reaching dissemination and marketing strategies.

The uncounted numbers of farmers assisted throughout the world by CGIAR owe a deep debt of credit to the hard research work, innovativeness and creativity of social researchers for their contribution to the system's performance over three decades.

The fundamental question, however, that comes up repeatedly in the book's studies, is whether the vast needs for social research have been fully recognized and internalized, and whether the current difficulties and bottlenecks confronted by social researchers are adequately dealt with by CGIAR as a system and by the centres' managers.

The message to managers and donors from the Cali Conference on Social Research (September 2002), the largest in CGIAR history, and the assessments by social researchers themselves, was that the CGIAR system is still far from doing what it should, and from benefiting as much as it could, from the research on the 'culture of agri-*culture*' and on farmer behaviour and potential.

CGIAR still has a number of unacceptable weaknesses in its social research activities, staffing and financing. The community of social researchers in the centres has not expanded over the last decade. In fact, in several centres it has significantly diminished – a trend that is contrary to the increasing emphasis placed on social issues in CGIAR strategy and position papers. Some senior research positions have been lost in attrition and have not been replaced.

In the judgement of the co-authors of this volume and of the colleagues whom they represent, social research in CGIAR is still far from reaching the weight that it should, and producing the products that the system needs and could, ideally, produce. This is because the intellectual human capacity of the system for social research has been dysfunctionally decreasing over the previous several years, despite public calls to the contrary. The total number of social researchers has dropped by about 24% and a centre-by-centre examination shows that the total number of social scientists has fallen below critical mass in several CGIAR centres. This runs contrary to the orientation and tasks that result from the Millennium Development Goals for CGIAR and the tasks explicitly defined in CGIAR's formally adopted 'vision and strategy': both documents call for intensified social research on farmers' needs and their capacities to use and manage natural resources in a sustainable manner.

Social researchers' mission is to produce knowledge usable as an international public good by farming communities throughout the developing world. This is and must be their contribution to CGIAR's overall research for agro-ecological intensification in areas of both low and high-potential, in research to increase water productivity, to improve income opportunities for the poor through changed farming behaviour and expanded cultivation of higher-value commodities, through better organized collective actions and gender-specific analyses on capacity-enhancing technologies, through promotion of equity and gender equality and empowerment of women and through many other specific research paths. However, fully effective research on these priorities is simply impossible, and will be incomplete and hobbled without intensified and integrated social-cultural research in CGIAR.

This is what this volume's authors argue, suggesting many different and mutually complementary ways of improving and expanding this research area.

It is hoped that this book will directly help in this worthwhile, collective scientific effort.

Notes

[1]Robert K. Merton 'The Perspectives of Insiders and Outsiders', in Merton, R.K. *The Sociology of Science. Theoretical and Empirical Investigations.* University of Chicago Press: Chicago and London. 1973. pp. 99–136.

Acknowledgements

The publication of this volume has been made possible through the scientific, moral and financial support of the Consultative Group on International Agricultural Research's (CGIAR) senior management and of the Technical Advisory Committee (TAC), the interim Science Council (iSC) and the current Science Council of CGIAR.

We express our thanks to Ian Johnson, the Chairman of CGIAR and to Francisco Reifenschneider, the CGIAR Executive Director, to Emil Javier, the former Chair of TAC and the interim Science Council and to Per Pinstrup-Andersen, the Chair of the current Science Council; as well as to members of the Science Council who took part in this book's review process, particularly Alain de Janvry, Hans Gregersen and Richard Hardwood, and to Shellemiah Keya, Ruben Echeverria, Tim Kelley and Sirkka Immonen in the Council Secretariat. Special thanks are also due to USAID for its generous partial contribution toward the cost of publishing this volume. Our thanks go also to Ismail Serageldin, the former Chairman of CGIAR, who has given particularly strong encouragement to social research in CGIAR and to initiatives which led to this volume as well.

The preparation of this volume was recommended and stimulated by the Conference on Social Research in CGIAR, initiated by the iSC, which took place at CIAT in September 2002, although by its content and its expanded authorship this book is not a 'proceedings' volume and has exceeded the initial goal. We express our appreciation to Joachim Voss, anthropologist, former 'Rocky doc' and now CIAT Director General, and to Jacqueline Ashby and Ruth Meinzen-Dick, who together with the editors were members of the Conference Organizing Committee. Our thanks go also to Andres Palau, Uwe Nagel and Julia Efremova, who contributed significantly to the preparation, unfolding and success of the Social Research Conference. A group of professionals and young researchers contributed to the technical preparation and repeated processing of this volume's many chapters. A technical copy editor, Muriel Ordoñez worked on the chapters before their submission to the publisher and Fidel Rillo kindly helped in preparing the book's graphs. In turn, Marie Leon, Maya Silver, Maria Weir and Andrea Berardi assisted skilfully with the repeated processing of studies. Their contributions helped bring the volume to its present form, for which the authors and editors publicly express their thanks to them.

Finally, the editors express their heartfelt appreciation to their families for the invaluable support, tolerance and encouragement they received throughout the long period of the preparation of this book. Michael expresses his most grateful thanks to his wife Ruth, his children, and particularly to Sarah, Rebecca, Evan, Elena and Dylan, and to Zachary, Alex, Jane, Natalie and Eve, for their love, patience and good humour, and for allowing him to take a substantial part of 'their time' for working on this book. Amir conveys his special thanks to his wife Parin and to his children Zahra, Shireen, Laila and Salman for all their kindness, care and love, which allowed him to continue to work on his book assignment during his life-threatening illness.

Part I   Social Research
for Agricultural Policies

Rites of Entrance and Rights of Citizenship

1

The Uphill Battle for Social Research in CGIAR

Michael M. Cernea

'The CGIAR's focus on poverty reduction will entail
an increased role of socioeconomic research to build up the body
of knowledge on understanding people.'

'Behavioural and socio-cultural variables
of resource management are no less important for sustainability
than physical parameters. These variables require
the use of social science research methods...'

'There are important developments in sociology, social geography,
anthropology and economics relevant to the future strategy
and research priorities of the CGIAR.'

From *CGIAR: A Food Secure World for All.*
Towards a new vision and strategy for the CGIAR (2000)

Within the vast total research portfolio of the Consultative Group on International Agricultural Research (CGIAR), the size of social research is unexpectedly small and under-resourced. This is paradoxical, because the strategic and policy relevance of social research to CGIAR's overall research for food security and poverty reduction is necessarily high. Such inverse proportionality is therefore abnormal. As with any inside abnormality, the effects are dysfunctional to the system's operations and performance.

©CAB International 2006. *Researching the Culture in Agri-*Culture:
Social Research for International Development
(eds M.M. Cernea and A.H. Kassam)

Perceived Discrepancies

In fact, this discrepancy has been growing for a while, getting deeper. On the one hand, CGIAR recently adopted a new strategy statement (CGIAR, 2000), which lists verbatim key social research themes and recommends them to CGIAR's centres. This strategy does this more explicitly and forcefully than any prior CGIAR programme document. On the other hand, however, evidence accumulates to show that the practice of many CGIAR centres contradicts the system's public commitments on this matter. The actual human capacity for social research in the system at large, and in some of its 15 centres, is either long stagnant or has severely shrunk. And despite the new strategy, it is not growing again. Surely, this is a most serious issue. This reduction of capacity affects not only current performance but also the future of social science research[1] as part of CGIAR's activities and products.

In this chapter I will present a broad discussion and personal reflections on the issues outlined above, informed by my decades of experience in the World Bank and lately within CGIAR, as well as relying directly on the collective analysis undertaken at the Conference on Social Research in CGIAR held in 2002 in Cali at Centro Internacional de Agricultura Tropical or the International Center for Tropical Agriculture (CIAT). I have been following the work of social researchers in the CGIAR for some 30 years, since I joined the World Bank in the mid-1970s as its first anthropologist/sociologist and was located in its central agricultural department. More recently, I had the privilege to be appointed and worked for 6 years (1998–2003) as a member of CGIAR's high-level science bodies: the Technical Advisory Committee (TAC) and the interim Science Council (iSC). This enabled me to gain added insights into the workings of CGIAR, and also gave me an in-depth view on social research in all of its centres. The 2002 systemwide conference on social research in CGIAR was among the culminating events of my activities in this capacity, as was TAC's intense effort in 1999–2000 to prepare and write CGIAR's new strategy statement.

The observations and analysis that follow owe, therefore, much to what I learned during these years of work in CGIAR's leading scientific committees. However, as the usual disclaimer says, this chapter voices personal reflections: it neither engages, nor does it necessarily express the views of, the institutions with which I am or have been associated.[2]

Along these lines, this chapter will address several matters crucial for the status and performance of social research in CGIAR today: a brief retrospective of major social research successes; the institutionalizing of social research in CGIAR, its structural weaknesses and the risks of marginalization; the severe erosion and contraction of CGIAR's body of social researchers and the imperative need to restore its capacities;

the role of social research in policy elaboration in CGIAR, along and jointly with economic research; the 'knowledge-conveyor belt' function and the relationship between CGIAR and outside social researchers who work within academic institutions and in national agricultural research systems (NARS).

Every relevant review undertaken recently[3] has signalled unevenness between various centres in social research (Kassam *et al.*, 2002). Therefore, no identical characterization can apply equally to all centres' capabilities and output. But the sum total of social research at the system level justifies serious concern. The discrepancy signalled above should, therefore, be addressed at all the levels of the CGIAR system, and counteracted at all levels, because it is structural and programmatic. Receptivity to social research, as another study (Kassam, 2003, Chapter 2 this volume) strongly argues, needs to exist and be examined *at every level* of the system. Because the crucial links in CGIAR's systemic chain are the centres' management teams and the director general, it is upon them primarily that responsibility rests and resolution depends. The system's overall success and scientific fertility and its pursuit of policy impact require concordance between its declared strategy on social research and its actual capacity and dedication for performing and delivering it.

The Key Concept: Culture in Agri-*Culture*

Over about three decades, CGIAR social researchers have built a record of many indisputable achievements, making tangible contributions to the sum of international public goods generated by CGIAR. They started from the very bottom, as intruders in an organization created initially, as Groenfeldt and Moock wrote, for 'managing agricultural technology' (1989), one that was dominated by biological scientists. Historically, social research has paid for its 'rites of entrance' with the golden coin of creativity, innovations and tenacious work, gradually acquiring rights to citizenship in the system's citadels. Despite obstacles and often a marginalized status, their productive efforts have harvested many successes and travelled an amazing uphill ascent from their initial intruder status. However, this ascent is now, unexpectedly and unnecessarily, at risk.

The most comprehensive and up-to-date stock taking, as well as self-analysis, of social research in CGIAR was carried out by the 2002 conference in Cali, initiated by the iSC (see Cernea 2001a,b). Its main results are reflected in the present volume.[4] The conference participants, coming from 13 of CGIAR's 15 centres and from outside academic institutions, have prepared centre-by-centre historical and content analyses of staffing, current standing and past and ongoing research.[5]

While the recount of accomplishments during the conference was at times elating, a hallmark of the conference was also the candid revelation of difficulties, past and current. The perceived erosion of capabilities was documented and analysed with great concern. Overall, the sum of these analyses points to a downward trend in the system's capacity for social research (see details in Kassam, Chapter 2 this volume, and the studies from various centres). This conclusion was stressed, together with the recognition that substantial work and good results continue in a few centres. In those centres social researchers maintain a minimum critical mass and are enabled to carry on specialized work on major social topics, that is, on the heartland area of the culture of agriculture.

This concept of *culture in agriculture* covers not some elusive elements of peripheral importance, as some simplistically believe, perhaps because in the common language the concept of *culture* is used in innumerable confusing or undefined ways. On the contrary, in its social science meaning the concept of culture, considered here in the context of agricultural research, comprises a cluster of fundamental building blocks of agricultural production processes, rural life and their actors, whose understanding is indispensable for grasping the deeper essence of agriculture.

Among these, the primary components of 'culture' are diverse *patterns and forms of social organization* within which people practice agriculture and forestry, fish or raise livestock. Many of these are crystallized into institutions and organizations while others are informal and proteic; the tissues of relationships that give content and structure to these patterns of social organization and association, all of which are eminently socio-cultural constructs, and upon which agricultural production and productivity decisively depend; peoples' behavioural rationales, either individual or collective, and their shifting characteristics;[6] the storehouses of knowledge and beliefs, which are so diverse in different populations, indigenous or mainstream, and which trigger and shape practice; as well as aspirations, motivations; and value systems. Each of these elements can in turn be further described and specified in detail.

These foundational socio-cultural building blocks – tangible and intangible, visible or invisible to the naked eye – are indispensable for human existence and practice, and are part and parcel of the complex edifice of agriculture (and of course, in other different forms, of other human activities).

To come back now from this working definition of 'culture in agri-culture', the argument that I want to stress in this chapter is *the ontological* one: because these fundamental building blocks of agriculture *do exist* in real life, and are hugely important, they must be the object of scientific social research in CGIAR as well.

Anybody who does not recognize this, and does not understand their actual weight in real-life processes, misperceives reality. Any centre manager or scientist in an international research centre who, either in public documents or in his or her own mind, downgrades or leaves out from research agendas the study of these fundamental social-cultural components, ends up with an incomplete grasp on reality and undermines his individual, and his institution's performance.

Scientific social research on the cultural building blocks of the agricultural edifice supplies *cognitive* value added, deepening the understanding of agriculture's social organizational structures and functions. This indispensable scientific contribution[7] comes uniquely from the social sciences, because no biophysical discipline systematic-ally studies these constituent building blocks of agriculture and there-fore, does not supply knowledge about them. In fact, the biophysical sciences intrinsically need this supply of specialized knowledge from social research to more accurately understand and socially contextual-ize the variables and processes they study.

In addition to supplying analytical knowledge and descriptive ethnographies, the social research of these components is irreplaceable because it also charts the path to transforming and improving these forms of social organization of production and exchange activities. Social research is not just a contemplative exercise; it has an action-oriented finality. It serves to transform reality. State agricultural policies that aim at agricultural development vitally need this kind of know-ledge as their stepping stone, because without it they cannot leap from what exists today to what such policies prescribe for the future. There-fore, social research is at its best when it is able to generate, in addition to bodies of analytical and descriptive knowledge, also action-oriented recommendations to modify and improve existing patterns of social organization, making them better able to serve their actors.

Work of this kind on the culture of agriculture is apt to be an impact multiplier to the tremendous scientific effort deployed by the CGIAR system for the cause of a food-secure world and poverty reduction. I strongly believe that the purpose of scientific research for all of CGIAR is not only to produce new high-yielding crop varieties but also to help develop high-yielding human systems, to use William Foote Whyte's felicitous term (1983).

How to foster and continuously perfect such high-yielding human systems is the ultimate challenge – for science, for policies, for development work. The kind of research that exemplifies most fittingly this understanding of the study of the culture of agriculture is the impressive body of research generated by the school of thinking created by Elinor Ostrom (see Chapter 16 and its References in this volume) on alternative human systems for managing natural resources, and also some of the products of social research in CGIAR.

Fostering High-yielding Human Systems: Achievements in Social Research

The past accomplishments in social research in CGIAR are the bedrock demonstration that the social research (SR) domain holds promise for the future as well (given space and support) to produce scientific public goods belonging to two key broad categories: (i) substantive in-depth knowledge about farming populations and their social organization, needs, aspirations; and (ii) methodology tools to better research agricultural processes. These two bodies of knowledge are nothing less than vital, indispensable for CGIAR's success. Along these two categories we may, most briefly, recall:

- The early International Potato Center (CIP, i.e., Centro Internacional de la Papa), which charted and incorporated a new path – 'from farmer back to farmer' – into the centre's formal research strategies (Werge, 1977; Rhoades and Booth, 1982; Rhoades, 1984; Prain *et al.*, Chapter 8 this volume), enabling them to solve postharvest potato storage problems.
- The early CIAT, with its advocacy for research experiments on farmers' fields, instead of in-laboratory only, moving afterwards to farmer-managed experiments and to farmer-led participatory plant breeding (see Holland *et al.*, Chapter 11 this volume).
- The push to conceptualize, introduce and expand farming system research (Tripp, 1991) championed by CYMMIT (i.e., International Maize and Wheat Improvement Center), International Service for National Agricultural Research (ISNAR) and other centres, which had to confront, among other adversities, the in-your-face denial by some biological scientists of anthropologists' contribution (see Cernea and Guggenheim, 1985).
- The pioneering research on water users associations and on farmers' management of irrigation systems carried out in the International Water Management Institute (IWMI) for years, with impacts on numerous public sector projects for irrigation development (Merrey, 1997; Samad and Merrey, Chapter 7 this volume).
- The original social research on forestry and agroforestry management and sustainable use, highlighting cultural diversity and gen-

der in forest management, mainly at the Center for International Forestry Research (CIFOR) (see Colfer *et al.*, Chapter 5 this volume; Colfer, 2000; Colfer and Byron, 2001) and in earlier years at the International Centre for Research in Agroforestry (ICRAF).

• The social and ethno-botanical research at the International Plant Genetic Resources Institute (IPGRI) on farmers' culture and knowledge systems on how plants behave when used or disturbed by people, on farmers' management of genetic diversity and varietal selection, on how agrarian communities classify plants, preserve genetic material, intervene in biodiversity through plant domestication (see Eyzaguirre, 2001; and Chapter 13 this volume).

There are many other examples, of which this book is full.

In addition to the substantive research findings, the methodological contribution that social researchers have made – and keep making – to the research methods of CGIAR's entire scholarly family is enriching and has the most impact. This kind of contribution is what Robert Merton defined as 'the basic process of transfer of research procedures from one scientific specialty to another' (Merton, 1979: 25). The best-known example of such 'transfer of procedures' is the introduction by social scientists of participatory research methodologies into the work of CGIAR biological scientists who have not previously used such procedures. The pioneers of this effort were the sociologists working at CIAT, led by Ashby (see Ashby, 1986) and social scientists in other CGIAR centres. The 'value added' became obvious. The extent to which such procedures have 'transferred' inside various CGIAR centres testifies to an important change in the research behaviour of non-social scientists as a result of absorbing methodology and conceptualizations from social sciences.[8]

In terms that readily apply to 'emerging' (social) and 'established' (biophysical) disciplines in CGIAR as well, Merton observed that 'little is known about the vectors of such transfer between more or less established specialties and emerging ones' and called for mastering the 'cognitive and organizational facilitators and inhibitors of inter-specialty transfers of theories, models and concepts, as well as research procedures' (Merton, 1979; see also Merton, 1973).[9] Following this insightful observation, it would be surely worthwhile to do a sociology of science study on the 'cognitive and organizational facilitators and inhibitors' that accounted for the spread[10] of participatory methodologies inside CGIAR's centres, not least because, once understood, such mechanisms and processes can be purposively promoted within research communities in the future.

The chapters of this volume give a richer image of the social research accomplishments on record, centre by centre, than any summary

I could compile, or any adjective I could use, to describe this contribution. But a careful reading of the studies also shows that the contributors critically reveal a series of institutional obstacles, constraints, discrepancies and conceptual biases (or mind-set barriers) that adversely affect the standing, staffing and social research performance in numerous CGIAR centres.

Issues in the Institutionalization of Social Research in CGIAR

Perhaps the most adequate sociological concept through which I can begin to examine these systemic discrepancies is *institutionalization* (Cernea, 2002). Among the concept's many available definitions, the most detailed is the one offered by Edward Shils and embraced by Merton:

> By institutionalization of an intellectual activity I mean the structured and relatively dense interaction of people who perform that activity. The more intense the interaction, the more its structure makes place for authority which makes decisions regarding assessment, admission, promotion, allocation. The high degree of institutionalization of an intellectual activity entails its teaching and administered organization. The organization regulates access through a scrutiny of qualification, provides for organized assessment of performance – for example, study, teaching, investigation, publications, appointment and so forth. It also entails the organized support of the activity from outside the particular institution and the reception of the results of the activity beyond the boundaries of the institution.
>
> (Merton, 1979)

This definition gives us key criteria for assessing how well or how insufficiently social research is institutionalized within CGIAR.

My personal observations, confirmed by numerous independent external reviews of the centres submitted to and discussed in TAC and iSC, indicate that despite many years of in-house presence, social research is still unsteadily or weakly institutionalized in CGIAR – certainly not at the level that is possible and required by the system's mission (Kassam *et al.*, 2002). This is a matter of both organizational structures and research paradigm.

The manifestations of weak institutionalization are visible, for instance, in the unsteady and insecure place of social research and social researchers on the 'organizational charts' of many centres and within their institutional structures; in centres' depleted staffing patterns, falling below critical mass and diluting scientific interaction; in the auxiliary, non-core or 'service' roles into which social research is pushed; in the ways social research is often left out of policy elaboration work; in funding and resource allocations. On several of these indicators of institutionalization the vectors are worryingly pointing downward. These downward trends inevitably affect the agenda, weight, contribution and influence of social research, both inside and outside an international research centre.

In its formal self-definitions as an association of scientific centres, CGIAR characterizes itself not as just a technical but rather as a development research institution, dedicated to promoting agricultural science in the service of sustainable development and poverty reduction. Its technical (agro-biological) scientists are the core, the numerically predominant group of scholars. However, by the importance of their function, the social scientists are also vital to the aims of the system. Social scientists are trained to enable CGIAR to better know its ultimate clients – the world's farmers and their communities – and are tasked to identify the socio-structural, cultural and behavioural variables of agri-cultural processes. They could and should be first in line to help empower the poor farmers with the weapons of knowledge from science and research. The importance of these functions, however, is understood differently at various levels of the system, and within each of the system's centres.

To examine this understanding, I will consider four fundamental dimensions of institutionalization:

- the system's human capacity for social research, staffing size and distribution, critical mass and recent trends;
- interdisciplinary work as research strategy and its autonomous research complement;
- policy elaboration: does social research participate in it?
- interactions in social research – knowledge transmission-belts between CGIAR, NARS and academic research.

Staff Depletion: Diminishing Social Research Capacity

The system's capacity for doing state-of-the-art social research is, first but not only, a matter of adequate staffing. But staffing size is a dependent variable, a function of at least two other, independent variables: resource allocation and the paradigm that guides the scientific work.

A brief appeal to history may help remind us that when CGIAR was established in 1971, the leading paradigm in agricultural research was not exactly calling for social research, and financial resources were scarce. The four international agricultural centres pre-existing CGIAR were staffed by competent biophysical scientists, who had not been

exposed during their own academic training to social and economic
sciences and had little way of anticipating the value added from social
research. Therefore, the institutional culture and personal attitudes were
not receptive to social research. But donor governments, development
agencies and the foundations supporting CGIAR financially did advocate from CGIAR's beginning the incorporation of social and economic
research capacities into its institutional structures, as they incessantly
continue to do today (see Bode and Rubin, Chapter 19 this volume;
Conway *et al.*, Chapter 18 this volume; Dalrymple, Chapter 22 this
volume).

The Rockefeller Foundation's Programme: To short-circuit the obstacles
and jumpstart acceptance, the Rockefeller Foundation took an extra-
ordinary initiative. In 1974, it offered to finance a 'social science fellowship programme' to bring young PhDs in anthropology, rural sociology
and other social sciences as researchers into CGIAR centres, enabling
them to interact with biophysical researchers (Conway *et al.*, Chapter 18
this volume). The premise was that interaction among researchers
would foster institutionalization enduringly. It might be more persuasive than abstract arguments about the need for social research. These
researchers, it was assumed, would generate findings on farmers and
their cultural practices that would demonstrate in convincing scientific terms how these disciplines enriched traditional biophysical
research.

Along these lines, a significant number of the famous 'Rocky docs'
landed in almost all centres and started to work.[11] The Rockefeller
Foundation assumed that once the researchers demonstrated legitimacy and usefulness, each centre's management would 'get the message' and recognize that it paid to regularize social researchers and
would finance their slots as regular positions.

What were the results? Year after year, the Rockefeller Foundation
financed some of the best and brightest PhD graduates who, in turn,
came with enthusiasm and new ideas to work in the CGIAR centres.
Because of their contributions, the span of social and cultural variables
addressed by the centres expanded. The minds of biophysical
researchers were exposed to new ideas and methods. Most of the new
researchers performed admirably and their contributions gained recognition. The Rockefeller Foundation's initiative proved its case and was
a remarkable success. The 'Rocky docs' who stayed longer, becoming
real pillars of the centres' activities, and those who pursued work in
other places after their fellowships, have convincingly made the point
for which they came into CGIAR. Towards the mid-1990s, the Rockefeller Foundation concluded this programme.

What was the follow-up on the CGIAR side? There is wide consensus
on two points. First, that the CGIAR system has substantially benefited

from the programme and that the programme 'won the bet'. Second, CGIAR has not consistently carried out its part of the deal in the long term. True enough, during the Rockefeller programme a number of research positions were regularized, and some centres took in social researchers from outside the programme. But the follow-up never reached a level commensurate with the success of the experimental programme, let alone expanding on it as was to be expected. Several 'Rocky docs', who were welcome in the centres as long as the Rockefeller Foundation paid their costs, were not regularized when the centres had to take over the financing of their research.

Sadly, indeed, 4–5 years after the end of the Rockefeller programme, not only has each year's 'infusion' of young social researchers been closed down, but a gradual process of shrinking resources for this research area has also set in. The trend is even more visible in the first years of the current decade. Normal scientist turnover, combined with departures caused by unsatisfactory conditions and routine attrition, vacated the slots for social scientists, but were often not filled with scholars of the same profile.[12]

The failure of several major CGIAR centres to maintain and expand a credible staff capacity for social research appears starkly by examining social research staffing centre by centre (see the following four graphs Figs 1.1–1.4). In about half the CGIAR centres, the proportion of social researchers to total research staff has dropped below a reasonable critical mass needed to exercise intellectual institutional influence and effective scholarly interaction. In some centres, the absolute staff numbers of social specialists may be as low as two, one or even zero.

Staffing Trends and Curves at CIP, ICARDA, ILRI and IRRI. CIFOR, CIP and CIAT, are among the centres with better social research capacity. In CIP (Fig. 1.1), for instance, social researchers represent about 10% of all internationally recruited scientists (IRS), and the economists represent 15% (Prain *et al.*, Chapter 8 this volume). The curve indicating the presence of social researchers in CIP has been generally ascendant, close to the curve for economists. Together, they form an impressive and substantial 25% segment of all international researchers.

Such substantial presence, however, characterizes only a minority of the 15 CGIAR centres. At the opposite end of the spectrum are centres with a weak or decreasing social research staffing, among them ICARDA, ICRAF, ICRISAT, IITA, ILRI, IRRI, WARDA, even CYMMIT, as their researchers themselves have documented.

At ICARDA, for instance, once much stronger in social research, the social researchers have left one after the other (the last two anthropologists left in 2002), and the graph falls to zero (see Fig. 1.2,

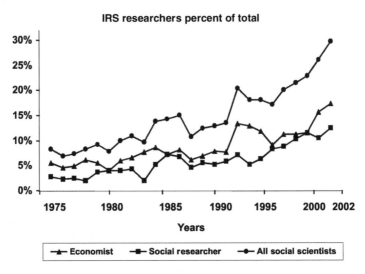

Fig. 1.1. CIP social scientists compared to all IRS, 1975–2002. Percent of total IRS researchers.

compiled by Aw-Hassan and Martini, based on ICARDA personnel statistics for 1978–2002). When the social researchers left, ICARDA's management reallocated their positions, filling them with researchers of other specialties.

ICRISAT has one recognized social researcher, while CYMMIT, where for decades anthropologists were a forceful presence and carried the flag for farming systems research, has today just one researcher – defined as a 'human ecologist'.

At ILRI, the decrease has been constant over the last two decades, and staffing has not improved even after the recent merger of the previous two livestock centres (see Fig. 1.3. prepared by Romney and Minjauw, Chapter 9 this volume). This capacity loss was allowed despite the need to systematically study the complex web of social relationships of ownership, custodianship and usufruct rights over livestock, and the particular cultures of herding, which characterize pastoral and agropastoral activities in many developing countries, especially in Africa.

Without a correct understanding of the power systems and of the customary property and custodianship relationships, any intervention in the livestock sector is at risk of almost certain failure. This graph marks on the staff curve the years spent under the centre's four general directors (Brumby, Walsh, Fitzhugh and Sere) and shows that in

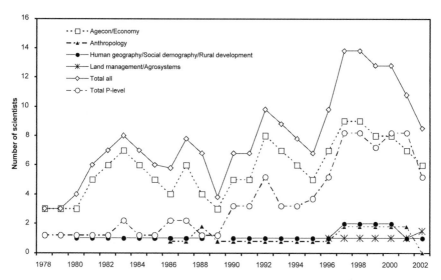

Fig. 1.2. ICARDA trends in social science research, 1978–2002.

1993–2002, the number of social researchers has oscillated between one and two, with zero in the year of the Cali conference.

Located in the Philippines, IRRI is virtually surrounded by a large cohort of local rural sociologists and anthropologists and could easily recruit and employ a strong group of social researchers. But as the graph in Fig. 1.4 shows, it only has one individual (Paris *et al.*, Chapter 5 this volume) (*Mutatis mutandis*, the same is true for ICRISAT in India, another country with a rich tradition in social research). WARDA, in West Africa, does not have on its staff even one stable social researcher, and IITA is in a similar poor situation.

The extensive, in-depth World Bank OED 2003 study on CGIAR led by Uma Lele, has sounded the alarm bell, signalling an aggregate loss of CGIAR social research capacity over the last 8 years. Since 1995/1996, OED concluded that the corps of non-economist social researchers has suffered a shocking 24% loss. In relative terms, this heavy loss means even more than the number suggests: conversely, in the same period, CGIAR's total number of scientists increased by 2.2%. Clearly, other specialties have grown at a fast rate due also to the decreased number and proportion of social researchers.

The loss in institutionalization caused by these downtrends has been accompanied by the loss of a clear and steady place of social

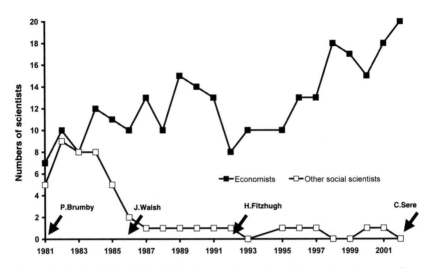

Fig. 1.3. ILCA–ILRI, 1981–2002: change in numbers of social science staff.

researchers in the centres' organizational structures. Amir Kassam (Chapter 2 this volume) correctly argues that 'receptivity' and 'voice' must be present at all the system's levels, not just punctually or by happenstance. But he and others have found that social research is

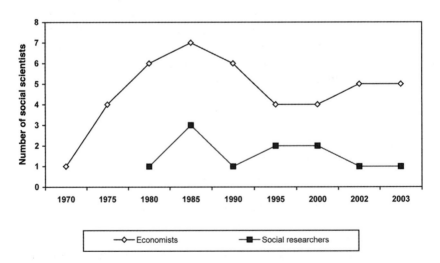

Fig. 1.4. IRRI 1965–2003: number of social scientists.

underrepresented at various key levels of research decision making and strategic orientation.

I have dwelt much above, with hard data, on the reality of CGIAR's shrinking capacity for two reasons.

First, without commensurate human capacity it is unrealistic to expect state-of-the-art social research and knowledge across CGIAR. The delivery of public goods in this area inevitably suffers. Rhetoric discourse alone, declaring the relevance of social objectives, cannot substitute for reduced scientific capability inside the system.

Second, all facts must be brought together into an overall picture because the diminished capability of the CGIAR system is sometimes denied or explained away. Some of the system's donors are not adequately informed about it.

From my experience in creating human capacity for social analysis inside the World Bank, I learned that having specialized staff in each major compartment[13] (the regional vice presidencies) was the indispensable condition to get tangible results at the level of investment/ development projects, by professionally and competently addressing the socio-cultural dimensions of those projects. The same can be said, beyond the obvious differences, for CGIAR, as well. But as an organizational system, CGIAR is far behind, in proportionate terms, the level of staffing by social specialists achieved in the World Bank, both in its centre and in the decentralized country offices. This concern should be present on the CGIAR system's, and on each centre's, agendas.

Important as well for success is not only the number of researchers but also the culture of research, the institutional culture surrounding this part of the centres' activities. Again, no generalization is possible, because situations are very different (as they were discussed in Cali, and in my own perception as well) from one centre to another. But in some centres, social researchers have an uncertain institutional and professional status and career path, are too transient, and are financed in too high a proportion with soft money.

The practice of issuing employment contracts only for a year or two at a time fosters a sense of job insecurity and prompts some of the most senior social researchers to seek more secure careers outside our system. Surveys done by social scientists themselves have found that career prospects inside CGIAR are perceived as poor. Some of these cultural and institutional issues are common for other researchers, as well.

All this needs to be changed through systematic, institutional systemwide and centre-by-centre measures.

With concern for the present and the future, the Cali conference collectively concluded that the downward trends affecting staffing and research capacity have diminished CGIAR's capability to fine-tune its work to meet the needs of its ultimate clients – the broad spectrum of diverse farming populations – and will have further adverse effects.

This staffing decrease, as studies in this book stress, goes contrary to the reorientation of the CGIAR strategy adopted in 2000 toward poverty reduction objectives. The findings of the Cali conference have been communicated to all CGIAR's centre managements and boards, together with the conference's specific and well targeted recommendations. So far, however, in the 2 years that have passed since the Cali conference, little corrective action has been undertaken.

Interdisciplinary and Autonomous Research Strategies

Beyond staffing patterns, another factor determining systemwide institutionalization of social research is the theoretical rationale adopted to ground its presence in the system and to define its functions. From this rationale may result two important courses of action:

1. Its relationship with the system's other research areas; and
2. The role given to social research in translating findings into policy recommendations.

The basic rationale that currently justifies the presence and functions of social research within CGIAR is the commandment of interdisciplinarity. Cooperation with other disciplines in joint research projects has become the mantra repeated at every juncture. This rationale is legitimate and unimpeachable.

However, limitation to it is not equally justified. It is warranted, I believe, to re-examine this rationale and it is necessary to broaden and strengthen it.

The footing on which social research was initially introduced in CGIAR was by necessity narrow, giving it a role auxiliary to CGIAR's 'leading' disciplines, but not the function of independent social research. An example of how contortedly narrow was its rationale is the first CGIAR meeting of anthropologists convened in 1981 at IRRI, which limited anthropologists only to a role within interdisciplinary teams and to basically one topic – 'technology management'.[14]

Things have changed much since those early definitions of rationale and role. But despite broader wordings, the basic postulate – an ancillary function – has survived and is affirmed alone, with insufficient recognition of its normal counterpart: the need for *independent social research* on those major topics that are *par excellence* social, behavioural, cultural.

Social research has a place in CGIAR because the research on agriculture needs to be integrated, covering all variables, not only the technical ones. But the necessary integration can be achieved in several ways and at different junctures of the knowledge generation process.

In the practice of planning research projects, the role of social research is seen too narrowly as just an auxiliary, a complement to biological or technical research,[15] which is apt to play only the part of a second or third violin in an interdisciplinary project.

In many research projects, the role of, metaphorically, 'second violin' is perfectly fine. This justified and necessary strategy has been practised, with remarkable achievements, and should be continued. But at the same time, it is warranted to ask: is this the only strategy for social research? Is this the only entrance point, the only way in which social research can generate and maximize its knowledge contribution, useful for CGIAR's objectives?

An old saying suggests that the best way of killing a good idea is to push it beyond its normal limits and reduce it to the absurd. Complementarity within the same project has become such an unquestioned slogan that it is seen as virtually the *only* 'passport to acceptance' for social research. But while the advocacy of complementarity helps force the door open to integrating social research in other programmes, this exclusive advocacy also has a downside. It forgos the options of fully exploring social and cultural variables and processes, which, by their content, require comprehensive social research on their own.

In other words, social research needs room to identify and address the topics, variables and relationships in which social research can contribute even more to CGIAR as the lead discipline. This argument holds that the potential of social research may not be fully achieved if it is always limited to an ancillary role.

Some topics require full-scale programmes in sociological and anthropological research, concomitantly with other programmes in which social research is a necessary auxiliary to other lead disciplines. Within the edifice of agriculture and its processes there are components ('building blocks') of paramount importance that are what we defined earlier as the culture of agri-*culture*, whose understanding requires full and focused social research for which the main charge will be in the social researchers' camp. This orientation is of strategic importance for expanding in new ways the contribution of social research inside CGIAR, now and in the future. Research programmes in which a social (non-economics) science is the lead science would often require, in their turn, the wisdom and tools of biologists or agro-technical researchers,[16] but will open new vistas of inquiry and pathways to new knowledge.

To pre-empt misinterpretations, it must be said that this is in no way an argument for 'hegemonic' purposes but one for using the comparative advantages of each scientific discipline in turn in fully studying its specific variables, an argument for deriving added benefits from the full cognitive and methodological potential of social research.

Incipient steps have been taken inside CGIAR towards this kind of focused social research, which involves other disciplines but whose main theme is sociological and the lead research charge is of a socio-organizational and cultural nature. One example of this alternative strategy is the multi-centre research programme on collective action, whose premises and process are described in Chapter 14 of this volume (Meizen-Dick), and another example is the systemwide research programme on participation (PRGA, 1996, 1999, 2001). Yet, there is more potential for this strategy inside each centre that must be exploited to understand and help transform the social structures of the developing world's agriculture.

Examining current international agricultural research we can also see that such *primarily social* research is taking place increasingly, mostly outside the CGIAR network, in university settings. The eminent research carried out by the group of scientists led by Elinor Ostrom and centred at Indiana University (with vast international ramifications), which I mentioned earlier, has produced a most valuable body of knowledge on the 'culture of agriculture' in its broad sense defined earlier, explicitly dedicated to understanding *the patterns of social organization* of farmers' agricultural, pastoral, fishing and sylvicultural activities, their modes of functioning and their potential. This is primarily social–cultural and political/institutional research that pursues a research strategy different from the kind of complementarity favoured in CGIAR, with important findings and vast international audiences. It generates substantial knowledge of the kind directly usable in crafting macro-level agricultural policies on natural resources management and localized development projects in agriculture. Ostrom's study in Chapter 16 of this volume persuasively illustrates some excellent results of this kind of research strategy which should be emulated in CGIAR centres as well.

Priority Themes for Social Research in CGIAR's Strategy

The new strategy prepared by TAC and adopted in 2000 by the entire CGIAR system forcefully recommended elevating and broadening the social and economic research of all centres. It emphasized not only complementary work, but also specialized themes for expanded social research efforts. The future social science research agenda, including economic and social research, was subject to broad outside consultations and substantial preliminary discussions in TAC. Scholars in economics – Alain de Janvry and Joachim von Braun, as members of TAC at that time – spoke primarily for

CGIAR's research needs in economic sciences, with consistent emphasis on the benefits of joint socioeconomic research. Iterative drafts and proposals for the new strategy occasioned vigorous discussions about, among other issues, the extent of social research and of economic research necessary for CGIAR's new agenda.[17] Added emphasis was included in the new strategy on joint socioeconomic research projects.

Adopted at the beginning of the century and looking to the future, the 2000 strategy calls CGIAR's full attention to the fact that *'there are important developments in sociology, social geography, anthropology and economics relevant to the future strategy and research priorities'* (CGIAR, 2000). It also explicitly spells out a series of priority researchable themes, recommended verbatim in the 2000 strategy:

> *'Better understanding of the decision-making process of individuals and groups in rural communities'*
> *'Identifying the characteristics and needs of the ultimate clients/beneficiaries, poor farmers and poor urban food consumers'*
> *'The institutional arrangements needed to foster social capital creation and activation'*
> *'Improved property rights and custodianship regimes and their management and distributional implications'*
> *'The factors of collective action in agricultural, forestry and fish production and marketing'*
> *'Patterns of community and group resource management'*
>
> *(CGIAR, 2000: 7).*

No other major document of CGIAR, in the past, has defined with such clarity and directness the social and cultural variables for which social research is needed in the CGIAR. A common denominator in several of these themes is the issues of natural resources management and sustainability. But beyond one or other theme, this legitimization of a full agenda of researchable social processes is the most important message in this area for crafting CGIAR centres' future research plans.

Social Research for Policies: How to Overcome Marginalization?

Doing policy-relevant research is a basic demand in CGIAR to virtually all its researchers. When it focused on evaluating policy research in CGIAR, however, the World Bank's OED study (2003: 88) pointed to a perception of economic one-sidedness and to a 'problematic' disconnect between macro-economic research and micro-household focused social-research:

> Policy research in the CGIAR is largely perceived as the province of economists and addresses mostly sector, macroeconomic and international issues. Social science research (research by sociologists, anthropologists and so forth) is considered to focus on household and community-level issues and is to help plant breeders... The distinction is important, but not without problems.

The analysis done at the Cali conference has pointed to the same disconnect and revealed some mechanisms of how it occurs. One is to push social research too much 'downstream', towards collecting data on impacts, at the expense of upstream research and knowledge generation on the social and cultural parameters of farming, agropastoral strategies and natural resources management. This is described in the CGIAR vernacular as pushing or limiting social research to 'service research', which ends up 'taking precedence over strategic research' and reflects the kinds of underestimation and marginalization discussed earlier. As mentioned before, social research is seen as 'a poor cousin to economics'.

By definition, policy elaboration must meet at least three requirements: it must be comprehensive in considering independent and dependent variables; must be focused on the actors' and stakeholders' actions; and must anticipate long-term consequences. Integrated knowledge is needed because no single discipline, economics included, can suffice to translate diversified agricultural research findings into recommended policy. Fundamental social knowledge and up-to-date findings of social research are indispensable for meeting each requirement for good policy development. But social researchers are seldom included in the teams tasked to develop policies, and the policy products are poorer for this reason.

The tendency to see policy formulation as 'the province of economists' and to marginalize other bodies of knowledge was once dominant in the World Bank as well. But practice has proved the fallacies of such economic reductionism, and the World Bank has largely moved away from narrow 'econocentric' approaches. Social scientists inside the World Bank, together with other non-economics specialists (e.g. technical experts), have carried on a sharp dialogue with their economist colleagues to de-legitimize monopoly over policy development (see Cernea, 1996) and, as a result, World Bank policies have become better balanced, more integrated, including social considerations and prescriptions. Explicit policy planks and statements, or formal social policies, have also been developed. This experience has much to speak for it and much that needs to be emulated in CGIAR's policy research and policy development activities.

During the preparation of CGIAR's 2000 strategy, the awareness of previous one-sidedness and insufficiencies in policy research and policy recommendations has led to blindingly clear statements prescribing a 'putting people first' focus for social, economic and biophysical research, as the grounding for policy elaborations:

> *CGIAR's greater focus on poverty reduction will entail increasingly the role of socio-economic research to augment the understanding of people and their agricultural and technological needs... A highly selective socio-economic and policy research agenda is needed to focus on the CGIAR centres' new responsibilities in addressing both poverty reduction and sustainable food security.*

(p. xviii)

The ultimate success of all CGIAR's work on productivity-enhancing technologies decisively depends on the embrace and practice of these technologies by CGIAR's ultimate clients – the world's farmers. No policy research can omit, therefore, the behavioural characteristics of farmers' productive activities.

For policies with a clear focus on the actors (and oriented not only to what states and governments must necessarily do) and with a long-term perspective, the social research on patterns of natural resources management is of paramount importance. By definition, the forms of social organization for production and exchange, their establishment, structures of roles, rules, incentive, penalties, etc. are subjects in which disciplines such as sociology and anthropology have a high comparative advantage (although, it must be stressed, no monopoly either). This is why both economists and biophysical researchers cannot do well without major social research contributions of high quality. If they ignore the understanding produced by such research, their own research outputs will be of lesser quality.

CGIAR has called, in its open self-assessment, for:

> understanding why existing information and knowledge has not been used more effectively to improve NRM (natural resources management) practices... Much research-generated information on NRM is readily available but not being put to use at present... This is a promising area of research and the CGIAR Centres are well positioned to undertake this.

(CGIAR, 2000: 36)

The CGIAR strategy unambiguously charted the way towards overcoming the neglect of such available information, emphasizing the critical relevance of social dimensions:

> The management of natural resources *clearly has social and behavioural components, the understanding of which is indispensable* for orienting

biophysical research to these resources. *Behavioural and socio-cultural variables of resource management are no less important* for resource sustainability than physical parameters. These variables require in-depth exploration through the use of social science research methods.

(CGIAR, 2000: 21; emphasis added)

An inevitable question emerges: these robust directives are certainly encouraging, but is the CGIAR able at this time to fulfil them?

The system's diminished capacity for social research was examined earlier, and the answer imposes itself: unless the staff depletion is corrected, a number of centres are unequipped to take on these key issues substantively within their research domains.

Despite the clear guidance offered, during the first 2–3 years after adopting the new strategy, no significant steps have been taken at the system level, or at the level of most centres, to reverse social research understaffing and under-resourcing. The Cali conference reported not increases but reductions in social research staff. It does not appear that the management teams of the centres with low or absent capacity have so far followed the call of CGIAR, by taking effective measures in their research domain. However, positive exceptions exist, and they demonstrate that this can be done within CGIAR. Such positive examples are CIFOR, CIAT, CIP and, to a certain extent, IWMI due to its new challenge programme on water that includes relevant socio-cultural variables and possibly others. In these centres, the abilities of their stronger in-house groups of social scholars to do policy- and strategy-relevant research generates valuable knowledge on these themes and reflects favourably on the output and overall standing of those centres within the CGIAR family.

In sum, the CGIAR strategy does give a clear road map for the social component of policy research. This road map remains as important and necessary as ever. To assist and guide this process, CGIAR's Science Council (appointed in 2003) has initiated, at the request of the system's Executive Committee and of the former interim Science Council, a process of system-level priority setting.[18] The social research priority themes recommended in the CGIAR strategy must be included explicitly and internalized in these general priorities. There is no reason to regard policy research in CGIAR as only 'the province of economics'. Integrated policy research – economic, social, biophysical – remains essential, and the centres' implementation of the 2000 strategy must now

pursue more vigorously and consistently an integrated and high quality social and biophysical research approach... A stronger capacity in modern social and economic sciences will amplify CGIAR research and policy effectiveness.

(CGIAR, 2000: 21–22)[19]

Linkages: Social Researchers as 'Knowledge-conveyor Belts'

Even if CGIAR as a system would in the short term expand and consistently prioritize social research across its centres, it will continue to need for its work *much more social knowledge and social research findings than it can produce itself.*

It is an unfortunate fact that the system's core funding has declined in recent years, while certain resource dispersion results from selective funding of a number of specific projects negotiated directly with donors. This is in itself a reason for initiating wider collaborative relationships with social researchers in organizations outside CGIAR. But even with improved resources for social research, CGIAR will need to access and use in its work state-of-the-art social information and knowledge that is generated and available outside its in-house-produced knowledge (as is true for other scientific domains as well).

These circumstances require CGIAR's social researchers to increase their efforts and role not only as direct producers of knowledge but also as 'knowledge-conveyor belts', by bringing into the system the products of agricultural and social research carried out by other research providers – for instance, academic research centres and NARS. There are important and promising new scientific developments outside CGIAR, not only in natural sciences such as molecular biology and genomics, but also in sociology, anthropology and political sciences (for example, research on the social systems for resource management of rural institutions, research on capacity building, on livelihood strategies, on risks, on farmers' motivations for product-diversification, on gender and empowerment of women farmers, on social capital mobilization, etc.).

Current weaknesses of international agricultural research in studying 'the culture of agri-culture' reside not only, and perhaps not primarily, inside CGIAR. The problem is much more severe in developing countries, whose NARS, by and large, still pay little attention to social and cultural dimensions. This is yet another paradox: many developing countries have a large number of sociologists trained by the countries' academic system, who nevertheless remain unemployed in their specialty (India, for instance). However, NARS that chronically lack such expertise – for various reasons that have to be examined in detail in public analyses – are not able to employ them.

In essence, this situation is caused not only by financial constraints but also by misconceptions and a persistent lack of understanding of the relevance of social, cultural and organizational variables for agricultural research and policies. Social researchers inside CGIAR realize increasingly that they themselves have not built strong and sufficiently wide relationships with powerful external centres of excellence in social science[20] that exist in some of the European universities, or in some major US universities. As a result, the social researchers are often on their own when it comes to making a stand over the scientific importance of their contribution. Partnerships on substantive research between CGIAR social scientists and university-based strong groups of cultural and economic anthropologists or sociologists, must be much extended.

In turn, the input of social research and knowledge from developing countries' NARS to the international agricultural research centres is clearly insufficient. CGIAR as a system, and not only its group of social researchers, has a major stake in anything that NARS could do to overcome the disregard of social research.

Perhaps a more systematic collaborative effort between CGIAR and the NARS in this respect, comparable to the type of relationships in other fields of science, would be not only warranted and timely, but would substantially enhance both sets of institutions' impacts at the grass-roots farm level. Current CGIAR strategy does not include such an effort and it would be useful to explore its feasibility.

In more than one way, CGIAR is still defining its ways and agendas for the beginning of this new century. While the needs for CGIAR's contributions are increasing, its resources, including financial means, are under strong pressures. But social research and its costs are not a liability for CGIAR: on the contrary, social research is a multiplier for all that CGIAR does and aspires to do, it helps increase CGIAR's direct effectiveness and its overall standing in the world.

The Millennium Development Goals for CGIAR, which are a mandate for CGIAR as well, demand such an increase, and as I argued in this chapter, CGIAR's formally adopted 'vision and strategy' does the same, convergently.

Social researchers' mission is to produce knowledge usable as an international public good by farming communities throughout the developing world.

Because the strategic tasks have been defined, 'the ball is now in the court' of the centres' management teams and researchers for translating the strategy in priority research programmes for each centre. Within CGIAR's total programme, intensified social research on farmers' needs and their capacities to use and manage natural resources in a sustainable manner must be placed in its mainstream. Effective research on CGIAR's priorities is simply impossible, and will be incomplete and hobbled, without intensified and integrated social-cultural research in CGIAR.

Notes

[1]Like many other studies in this volume, this one frequently uses three concepts with the following working meanings: 'social science research', to designate the overall body of research in economics and other (non-economics) social sciences such as sociology, anthropology, political science, social geography, etc.; 'social research', to designate the body of research carried out by non-economics social sciences such as anthropology, sociology, social geography and political science; and 'socio-economic research', particularly to describe joint economic and social research.

[2]A brief background 'disclosure' comment may also be in order. My connection of almost three decades with the social researchers in CGIAR was along professional lines and emerged from the parallelism and similarities between our activities in the two organizations. Beyond many differences, there are pronounced cultural similarities between the World Bank and CGIAR as organizations, and even some overlapping activities. My primary sector of work during the first 10–12 years as the World Bank's first rural sociologist was the same as that of my CGIAR colleagues – agriculture and rural development. In many World Bank-assisted projects on which I worked directly – particularly in agricultural extension and research, irrigation, livestock and forestry – I often crossed paths and collaborated with CGIAR colleagues. The few anthropologists in CGIAR and the even fewer, for a while, in the World Bank were engaged in comparable causes. From the outset I had a feeling of 'shared destiny' with my peers in CGIAR, the sense of significant commonalities in status, purpose and encountered challenges, beyond the obvious differences in work content.

The conceptual roots of our main argument were the same: at the Bank, my argument was the famous call for *'Putting People First'* in development projects' concept and design (Cernea 1987, 1991); in the CGIAR, the social researchers called for the study of *the actors* of farming, not just the seeds and genes, and militated for including them as participants in research. Intellectually, our goal was similar: to bring the bodies of knowledge from sociology and anthropology into our organizations and to make them relevant to their activities. We had not just personal tasks; we also had some kind of meta-mission – to be 'ambassadors' for our scientific disciplines, presenting their credentials to organizational empires still intellectually sceptical about accepting us. Within both organizations, we were newcomers with untested ideas and without established 'rights of citizenship'. We first had to go through rites of entrance and confirmation, to struggle for a place under the organizational roof and to gain the privilege of making a contribution.

The reason I am evoking those challenges of 'entrance' and 'citizenship' is not for the sake of reminiscing: it is because I want to clarify my starting position and also because challenges and adversities of a similar nature, surely less crude in form but comparable in content, are still to be fought today as well by new generations of social researchers.

[3]Particularly, the periodic EPMR – External Programme and Management Reviews – commissioned by TAC/the Science Council from outside independent scholars on each one, in turn, of CGIAR's centres.

[4]Previously, only two comparable stock-taking conferences on social research were held in the entire history of the CGIAR, in 1981 and 1992. Each, however, was much smaller than the Cali conference. The first was organized by Grace Goddell (see IRRI, 1982) and the second by Michael Collinson (see Collinson and Platais, 1992).

[5]Often such rationalities may appear 'irrational' when compared to what, in market terms, would be 'economically rational', if the criterion were profit maximization only for an individual market actor. This is precisely a typical instance in which cultural analysis explains farming behaviours that otherwise would remain not understood through economic analysis alone, and thus would remain hard to influence as well.

[6]For a vast reference list of the published research outputs, the interested reader may consult and consolidate the references at the end of all centre-focused studies in this volume.

[7]This kind of cognitive contribution made by CGIAR researchers is a 'public good'. See the discussion and definition of social science research products as public goods in the study by Dana Dalrymple, this volume. See also Vernon Ruttan's (2003) fundamental analysis of social science knowledge as a component of economic development and a tool for crafting and introducing institutional innovations.

[8]This can also be seen as a particular case of what, in development anthropology, is defined generally as the elaboration of 'methodologies and patterns of social action' (Cernea, 1987). Such methodologies for action as social instruments are a type of 'product' of development anthropology of a more general value and applicability than applied, case-based social work on one or another specific development intervention.

[9]Offering an example from biological sciences, Merton quoted the case of discovery of sexual recombination in bacteria, which laid the foundations for the new specialty of bacterial genetics, and referred to the studies of Zuckerman (1974).

[10]Despite overall success, Merton's 'organizational facilitators and inhibitors' were at work in the CGIAR as well during this methodological transfer process. The acceptance curve went up and down: see a pertinent analysis in the provocatively titled study *What Happened to Participatory Research at the International Potato Center?* by Thiele *et al.* (2001).

[11]Several contributed to this volume. See in particular the discussion of the 'Rocky docs' programme in the chapters by Scott Guggenheim and by Robert Rhoades.

[12]This issue became a regular point of discussion during the External Programme and Management Reviews (EPMR) in TAC and iSC sessions. My TAC colleagues and I repeatedly used the opportunity to highlight the diminishing capacity for social research in one or another CGIAR centre. Yet, the post-EPMR follow-up by centres' managements was often absent.

[13]This has required years of advocacy and tenacious fighting against technocentric or econocentric reductionisms in the World Bank, but the results have exceeded many people's expectations in terms of both staffing capacity and firm institutionalization of specialized social development units in the World Bank's

organizational structures. That process also had temporary setbacks and may still have others in the future, but enduring foundations have been laid. The elaboration and enactment of explicit social policies on a spectrum of issues has, in turn, institutionalized the need and demands for the professional contribution of social specialists in the World Bank and helped adopt the broader social development paradigm pursued now by the World Bank (Cernea, 1996).

[14]The first CGIAR conference of social researchers circumscribed this role very narrowly, phrasing its title as follows: 'The role of anthropologists and other social scientists in interdisciplinary teams developing improved food production technology' (IRRI, 1981).

[15]During the systemwide electronic discussion that preceded the 2002 Cali conference, Jaqueline Ashby, a senior social scientist with decades of experience in CGIAR characterized this narrow role poignantly: *'Social science in the CG has been a servant to the biological sciences, and a poor cousin to economics. As a result, social science has relied heavily on applying "known" social science and is not, as far as I can tell, closely in touch with new ideas and thinking in social and political sciences.'*

[16]The same way in which various ongoing economic research programmes involve joint multidisciplinary participation from biological sciences, soil sciences, technical disciplines, etc.

[17]I owe it to my colleagues to give great credit to TAC as a group, and to geneticist Emil Javier as its chair at the time, for giving their full support – after due examination and argument, not necessarily free of controversy – to the numerous recommendations I had the chance to make, on behalf of social scientist colleagues in CGIAR, to more explicitly specify in the new strategy the broad span of social research issues to be addressed in CGIAR's new phase. The same solid support was given by all biophysical scientists of TAC to the specific recommendations made by Alain de Janvry and Joachim von Braun for economic research.

[18]This process led by the Science Council is ongoing, as this volume goes to press.

[19]It is worth quoting the constructive recommendation made by the World Bank's OED 2003 study: *'There is a critical need for an independent external review of social science and policy research in the CGIAR, not only to examine the system's comparative advantages, but also the allocation of resources among various systemwide programmes'* (World Bank OED, 2003: 89).

[20]Jacqueline Ashby, personal communication.

References

Ashby, J. (1986) Methodology for participation of small farmers in design of on-farm research. *Agricultural Administration* 22.

Cernea, M.M. (1987) The 'production' of a social methodology. In: Eddy, E.M. and Partridge, W. (eds) *Applied Anthropology in America.*

Columbia University Press, New York, pp. 237–262.

Cernea, M.M. (ed.) (1991) *Putting People First: Sociological Variables in Rural Development*, 2nd edn. Oxford University Press, New York/London.

Cernea, M.M. (1992) A sociological framework: policy, environment and the social actors for tree planting. In: Sharma, N.P. (ed.) *Managing the World's Forests: Looking for Balance between Conservation and Development.* Kendall/Hunt Publishing Co., Dubuque, Iowa, pp. 301–335.

Cernea, M.M. (1996) Social Organization and Development Anthropology. The Malinowsky Award Lecture. SfAA, World Bank, Washington, DC.

Cernea, M.M. (2001a) *The Role of Social Research in the CGIAR – Supporting the Strategy–Achieving Development Impact* (SDR/TAC:IAR01/25). TAC Secretariat, FAO, Rome.

Cernea, M.M. (2001b) Outline Paper: Proposal for a Social Research Conference in the CGIAR. Presented at the CGIAR Annual General Meeting, Washington, DC, October 2001. (SDR/TAC:IAR/ 01/25). TAC Secretariat, FAO, Rome, 8 pp.

Cernea, M.M. (2002) The Institutionalization of Social Research within the International Agricultural Research System. Opening address at the CGAIR Social Research Conference. Cali, September.

Cernea, M.M. and Guggenheim, S. (1985) Is anthropology superfluous in farming system research? *Farming Systems Research. Kansas State University Research Series* 4(9).

CGIAR (2000) *A Food Secure World for All: Towards a New Vision and Strategy for the CGIAR.* FAO, Rome.

Colfer, C.P. (2000) Cultural Diversity in Forest Management. Keynote Address, Twenty-first International Union of Forestry Research Organizations Congress. Kuala Lumpur, Malaysia.

Colfer, C.P. and Byron Y. (eds) (2001) *People Managing Forests.* Resources for the Future, Washington, DC, and CIFOR, Bogor.

Collinson, M. and Wright Palatais, K. (eds) (1992) Social Science in the CGIAR. *Proceedings of a Meeting of CGIAR Social Scientists held at ISNAR. CGIAR Study Paper 28.* The World Bank, Washington, DC.

Eyzaguirre, P.B. (2001) People and plant genetic resources. *Handbook Sources for Applying Ethnobotany to Conservation and Community Development.* Issue 7, September 2001, UNESCO, 1–2.

Groenfeldt, D. and Moock, J.L. (eds) (1989) *Social Science Perspectives on Managing Agricultural Technology.* IWMI, Sri Lanka.

IRRI (International Rice Research Institute) (1981) *The Role of Anthropologists and Other Social Scientists in Interdisciplinary Teams Developing Improved Food Production Technology.* Philippines.

Kassam, A.H. (2003) An overview of social science research in the consultative group on International Agricultural Research. *The International Social Science Journal* 177, 441–462.

Kassam, A.H., Barat, S. and Moreddu, E. (2002) Summary of Excerpts from TAC Commissioned External Reviews of Centres and Systemwide Programmes since 1995. CGIAR interim Science Council Secretariat, FAO, Rome. A background document prepared for the Social Research Conference, 10–12 September 2002. CIAT, Cali, Colombia.

Kassam, A.H., Gregersen, H.M., Fereres, E., Javier, E.Q., Harwood, R.R., de Janvry, A. and Cernea, M.M. (2004) A framework for enhancing and guarding the relevance and quality of science: the case of the CGIAR. In: *Experimental Agriculture*. Cambridge University Press, Cambridge, UK, vol. 40, pp. 1–21.

Merrey, D.J. (1997) *Expanding the Frontiers of Irrigation Management Research*. IIMI, Colombo, Sri Lanka.

Merton, R.K. (1973) The perspectives of insiders and outsiders. In: Merton, R.K. (ed.) *The Sociology of Science. Theoretical and Empirical Investigations*. University of Chicago Press, Chicago and London, pp. 99–136.

Merton, R.K. (1979) *The Sociology of Science. An Episodic Memoir*. Southern Illinois University Press, Carbondale, Feffer and Simons, London and Amsterdam.

PRGA (Participatory Research and Gender Analysis) (1996) New Frontiers in Participatory Research and Gender Analysis. *Proceedings of the International Seminar on Participatory Research and Gender Analysis for Technology Development*. CIAT, Cali, Colombia.

PRGA (1999) *Crossing Perspectives: Farmers and Scientists in Participatory Breeding*. PRGA, CIAT, Cali, Colombia.

PRGA (2001) An Exchange of Experiences from South and South-East Asia. *Proceedings of the International Symposium on Participatory Plant Breeding and Participatory Plant Genetic Resources Enhancement*. 1–5 May 2000. PRGA, CIAT, Pokhara, Nepal.

Rhoades, R.E. and Booth R. (1982) Farmer-back-to-farmer: a model for generating Acceptable Agri-

cultural Technology Lima, Peru. International Potato Center.

Rhoades, R.E. (1984) *Breaking New Ground: Agricultural Anthropology*. International Potato Center, Lima, 84 pp.

Rhoades, R.E. and Booth, R. (1982) *Farmer-back-to-farmer: a Model for Generating Acceptable Agricultural Technology*. International Potato Center, Lima, Perú.

Ruttan, V.W. (2003) *Social Science Knowledge and Economic Development. An Institutional Design Perspective*. University of Michigan Press, Ann Arbor, Michigan.

Thiele, G., Fliert, E.V. and Campilan, D. (2001) *What Happened to Participatory Research at the International Potato Center?* Kluwer Academic Publishers, Dordrecht, The Netherlands.

Tripp, R. (1991) *Planned Change in Farming Systems: Progress in On-Farm Research*. Ebenezer Baylis & Son Ltd, The Trinity Press, Worcester, UK.

Werge, R.W. (1977) *Anthropology and Agricultural Research: the Case of Potato Anthropology*. CIP socio-economic unit, Lima, Peru.

World Bank OED (Operations Evaluation Department) (2003) *The CGIAR at 31. An Independent Meta-evaluation of the CGIAR*. Report carried out by a team led by Uma Lele. Report nr.25926, Washington, DC.

White, W.F. and Boynton, E. (eds) (1983) *Higher Yielding Human Systems For Agricultural Development*. Cornell University Press, Ithaca, New York.

Zuckerman, H. (1974) Cognitive and Social Process in Scientific Discovery: Recombination in Bacteria as a Prototypal Case. Paper presented at the ASA Annual meetings, Montreal, Canada.

Agricultural Institutions and Receptivity to Social Research: the Case of the CGIAR

2

Amir H. Kassam

The Consultative Group on International Agricultural Research (CGIAR) system is a large and complex multilayered organization comprising donors, centres and their research partners, and advisory bodies that promote and implement multidisciplinary agricultural research to produce international public goods, consistent with its mission and goals. This structure of interconnected layers – from the political (donors) to the strategic (advisory bodies), to the operational (research centres), to the ultimate clients and beneficiaries (farmers) – is an institutional voluntary construct in which dialogue, field work, laboratory work and collective interdisciplinary collaboration, generate and deliver research products, knowledge, technologies and policies.

Within this propitious context, one would expect that social and cultural research on agriculture and farmers is a 'natural' and should thrive unimpeded. However, the situation is not quite so. Many independent external reviews show that CGIAR's receptivity to sustain a critical mass of social research[1] capacity and programmes has been poor.

A Look Back

During the 1970s and 1980s, CGIAR's technology-generation research principally aimed to increase the production of CGIAR-mandated food commodities, with success or impact at the farm level, measured largely through the adoption of improved varieties of crops. The purpose of the accompanying social science research effort was to complement the biophysical effort to help increase the proverbial 'pile of rice' through improved production technologies. The social science research 'agenda' at each centre was defined and implemented mainly by production economists, working under the label of socioeconomics but generating mainstream economics research. The emergence of CGIAR's interest in farming systems research took researchers closer to the ultimate clients – the farmers – and their production, livelihoods and community environments, but even in this sound orientation, some biased scientists denied that anthropologists could make a contribution (Cernea and Guggenheim, 1985).[2] Farming systems research soon led to more sophisticated village-based socioeconomic studies, on-farm research and research on common property resources management, particularly as off-station and regional research programmes expanded.

CGIAR research styles and approaches during the 1970s and part of the 1980s were mostly 'top down', and beneficiaries did not systematically identify needs and research planning or subsequently engage in technology research and development or beyond, technology delivery and dissemination. Some centres began to appreciate more deeply the importance of direct beneficiary[3] participation and sociocultural variables for CGIAR's technology research and development process (so-called R&D) only towards the latter part of the 1980s and the early 1990s. However, they generally lacked a deep and effective two-way engagement with the beneficiary communities (see Baum, 1986[4] for a historical review of the CGIAR system, and Collinson and Platais, 1992[5] for a review of the state of the art in social science research in the CGIAR at that time).

In the mid-1990s, the CGIAR formally incorporated poverty alleviation and sustainable food security into its goals and began orienting itself to become an output- and impact-driven system. The 1997 Technical Advisory Committee (TAC) review of CGIAR priorities and strategies stated:

> The activities carried out by the CGIAR are undertaken in order to fulfil its mission: to contribute, through its research, to promoting sustainable agriculture for food security in developing countries; and its goals: to alleviate poverty and protect natural resources so as to achieve sustainable food security.
>
> (TAC, 1997)

This signalled a deep change in outlook and vision, not easy to accomplish. There was an increasing recognition of the importance of both the 'context' of farming, physical and sociocultural, and of the variability and diversity of sociological factors, in fighting rural poverty through improved agricultural productivity.

The involvement of rural sociologists and social anthropologists from different backgrounds in social research, moving to the 'mainstream' of agricultural and social science research in the CGIAR was signalled by the conceptualization and implementation of two systemwide programmes in the mid-1990s: Participatory Research and Gender Analysis (PRGA) and Collective Action and Property Rights (CAPRi).[6] PRGA, led by Jacqueline Ashby, focused on developing methods and organizational innovations for gender-sensitive participatory research on plant breeding and natural resources (e.g. PRGA, 1996, 1999, 2001). CAPRi, led by Ruth Meinzen-Dick, aimed to focus on collective action and property rights institutions as tools for empowering rural people in agricultural improvements and in natural resource use (e.g. CAPRi, 2002).

Recent Social Research in the CGIAR

Excerpts about CGIAR social science research were extracted from the reports of the TAC-commissioned external reviews of the CGIAR centres and systemwide programmes since 1995 and compiled by Kassam *et al.* (2002).[7] The brief overview presented here draws on the excerpts given in Kassam *et al.* (2002) and Kassam (2003). The Organizing Committee of the Social Research Conference[8] called for a survey of social science staff capacity in CGIAR, and the results were posted on the conference website. The extracted information on social science research in CGIAR was sorted into eight domains of activities along the research-to-development (R-to-D) continuum: (i) from baseline characterization and *ex-ante* studies to research and research-related activities in the five CGIAR output categories; (ii) germplasm conservation; (iii) germplasm improvement; (iv) sustainable production systems and natural resources management; (v) policy analysis and management; (vi) enhancing national institutions; (vii) output-related activities of technology adoption and information dissemination; and (viii) *ex-post* impact assessment on outcomes (Kassam, 2003). The data were also broadly categorized as predominantly social,[9] or predominantly economic[10] or a mixture of both, i.e. socioeconomic.[11]

Policy analysis and management is the dominant area of the social science effort (21% of the total CGIAR social science effort, of which 29% is social research). The second most important social science effort is *ex-post* impact assessment (19 and 32%). The next set of social science activities that are at about equal level are characterization (14 and 38%), enhancing national institutions (12 and 50%) and technology adoption research and information dissemination (12 and 29%). Trailing behind are production systems and integrated natural resource management research (9 and 54%), germplasm improvement research (7 and 70%) and germplasm conservation (6 and 67%).

More than half the social science activities in germplasm conservation, germplasm improvement and production systems/natural resources management (NRM) are of a social research nature. However, these three domains receive the least amount of social science attention (22% of the total effort). On the other hand, social science research dealing with characterization, policy analysis and management, enhancing national institutions, technology adoption and information dissemination and *ex-post* impact assessment collectively account for 78% of the total social science effort but this is mainly economic or socioeconomic in content.

We conclude that social science research and social research have unevenly permeated the CGIAR research agenda. The bulk of the social science research effort is being directed toward policy, *ex-post* impact measurements and *ex-ante* characterization activities, which account for some 67% of all social science research *per se,* although with relatively low social research content (Kassam, 2003). The rest of the social science effort is split among germplasm conservation, germplasm improvement, production systems/NRM and technology adoption/information dissemination. Similar patterns reveal themselves with the distribution of social research efforts across the eight domains of activity in the CGIAR research cycle, although the social research content in germplasm enhancement and production systems/NRM domains appears to be greater than in the others. Thus, the overall balance of social science research is still significantly tilted away from the core germplasm enhancement, production systems/NRM and technology adoption work – the 'bread and butter' of technology generation and development effort – towards *ex-ante* and *ex-post* activities.

The staff survey showed that there were 124 social scientists, including economists, in the CGIAR system, out of a total of 958 researchers. This is 39 fewer than in 1995, when there were 163 social scientists out of 937 researchers (TAC, 1996), although the total number of scientists has increased by 21 (2%) since 1995. This is a severe decrease of 24% in total social science staff capacity. Social science staff members make up 13% of the total but were 17.4% in 1995 (TAC, 1996) and close to 15% in 1991 (Collinson and Platais, 1992).

TAC's and External Review Panels' Views about Social Science Research in CGIAR

How receptive the CGIAR system is to social research is a question that needs to be asked about all layers of the system, starting with the centres, their boards and their executive and senior managements, including TAC (Mow Science Council) itself as an important institutional link of the CGIAR system and other central units of the system. The history of TAC in that respect is significant. While it would be hard to say that at any point TAC explicitly denied the need for socio-cultural research, it is accurate to state that for a long time TAC did not proactively or effectively promote such research, either. The historical examination of TAC documents (Kassam *et al.*, 2002) has not revealed a strong message to the centres to expand this kind of research, except perhaps the stripe review report of 1996 prepared by a team led by Alain de Janvry.

However, an important change occurred after 1997, when for the first time in TAC's history, an experienced sociologist was appointed as a member (Michael M. Cernea, formerly rural sociology advisor of the World Bank's Agricultural Department and then general senior advisor for social policies of the World Bank). For those watching from inside TAC, the difference was immediate and tangible, and it became obvious outside TAC as well throughout Cernea's 6-year tenure in TAC and the interim Science Council. Social research and the small community of social researchers working in the system gained a forceful voice in all deliberations of TAC about CGIAR strategies, centres, programmes, resource allocations, performance, etc. That also became manifest in the setting-up of the external reviews of centres, in the terms of reference for such reviews and in the composition of the teams appointed by TAC: sociologists and anthropologists started to be appointed almost regularly to external review panels. Explicit requirements were included for assessing the presence, quality and relevance of social research in the centres. As a result, TAC and afterwards, the interim Science Council helped produce a crop of external programme and management reviews that paid more attention than ever to this domain. These reviews examined unresolved issues and unaddressed areas in various centres. Based on external reviews now guided to examine the social research more closely, TAC and the interim Science Council regularly sent out clear messages to the entire system that such research was indispensable. Interest in social research was clearly stronger and the argument for intensifying it gained weight (Kassam *et al.*, 2002).

It was a decisive moment when TAC was asked to prepare a new strategy for the CGIAR. TAC's new recognition and advocacy of the importance of social research was stated repeatedly in the new strategy document. This new emphasis on the social and cultural variables in agricultural research was highlighted also at the CGIAR Annual General Meeting 2000, which discussed and adopted the new 'vision and strategy' prepared by TAC. Today, the CGIAR has a formal strategy that legitimizes the intrinsic need and creates the institutional room for its centres to expand rather than reduce social research. It even explicitly defines some of the topical areas of priority for socio-cultural and behavioural research for sustainable agricultural development and poverty reduction (Cernea, Chapter 1 this volume). The ball was put squarely and is now in the centres' court.

Based on the information about TAC and the external review panel recommendations (Kassam *et al.*, 2002), there were some 60 documented calls from TAC, the interim Science Council and the external review panels to strengthen the centres' social science capacity (Kassam, 2003). Each centre was encouraged to strengthen its social science research, to address particular themes and overall staff numbers. Some 60% of the time, TAC and the panels proposed strengthening the *social* component of social science research capacity, which appeared to be the best supported and staffed by the centre's managers; 30% of the time, the *economics* component; and 10% of the time, the *socioeconomic* component. About 94% of the time devoted to strengthening social research was for increasing social research capacity *per se* by adding staff members, because the few existing ones did not amount to a critical mass and/or to improve the type of research work. All the time devoted to strengthening economic and socioeconomic research capacity was aimed at improving the type of research work.

Some of the main concerns about and criticisms of the state of social science capacity raised by TAC and the panels in external reviews in the last 6–8 years, or recommendations to address specific topical social issues, are listed below.

Center for International Forestry Research (CIFOR)
- Conduct more in-depth research of the social, institutional and tenurial dimension of forests and reforestation.
- Consider social diversity in policy recommendations.
- Link quantitative data familiar to biophysical scientists and economists with qualitative and interpretative data generated by sociologists and anthropologists.
- Continue to recruit women and social scientists in multidisciplinary approaches to the rural poor's problems.

International Center for Tropical Agriculture (CIAT)
- Exert a greater effort to incorporate users' preferences in breeding programmes.
- Expand the range of social indicators.

International Maize and Wheat Improvement Center (CIMMYT)
- Gradually broaden and re-establish the Economics Programme as a social science programme.

International Potato Center (CIP)
- Increase the social science capacity employed in research and decrease the emphasis on administrative functions.

International Center for Agricultural Research in the Dry Areas (ICARDA)
- Integrate socio-anthropological variables (human and cultural ecology) into its natural resources research, which had not been done despite several years of anthropology input.
- Improve its field investigative capacity in the non-economics social sciences, which had decreased by attrition and non-replacement of staff members.
- Develop an internationally recognized and specific dry-area focus.
- Conduct more and improved impact studies of its major technologies, particularly by improving the quality and capacities of its social science programme.

WorldFish Center (ICLARM)
- Translate its recognition that social science research must be on par with technology research into changes in its programmes and staff.
- Solve the shortage of social and policy scientists, particularly at the senior research level, to meet multiple demands.
- Increase the sociological and anthropological orientation of the Integrated Aquaculture–Agriculture Systems Programme.
- Hire staff members who are qualified to research the social and economic conditions that influence integrated agriculture and agricultural systems.

International Centre for Research in Agroforestry (ICRAF)
- Reintegrate sociological and economic research into its programmes and quality control to regain its social research capacity.
- Evaluate these variables distinctly rather than only in a wholesale manner under 'socioeconomic research'.
- Deepen its understanding of the appropriateness of varied dissemination and adoption pathways under different social, cultural and environmental conditions.

International Crops Research Institute for the Semi-Arid Tropics (ICRISAT)
- Address the problem that all scientists in the socioeconomics programme are economists.
- Reflect the gender findings from *ex-post* adoption and impact studies in *ex-ante* technology design and interpret them – a task deemed 'vital'.
- Develop critical mass in social research and greater interdisciplinarity within on-farm research. Improve the integration of social science and biological science.

- Collect farmers' assessments and opinions to evaluate it's – the centre's – outputs and to shape its research and policy priorities.

International Food Policy Research Institute (IFPRI)
- Address the problem that the staff has too many economists and too few sociologists in a centre mandated to do multisided social science research.
- Expand its understanding of impacts of social science and policy research.

International Institute for Tropical Agriculture (IITA)
- Address the problem that there is no senior scientific leadership to guide and integrate social science research into the centre's overall programme.
- Immediately strengthen research staff capacity in social sciences.

International Livestock Research Institute (ILRI)
- Revise its strategic plan, specifying explicitly the proposed allocations for social science research, in view of the importance of social and cultural variables in animal husbandry.
- Address the problem that sociological research is virtually absent. The centre made a commitment to incorporate sociological capacity into its research staff soon.

International Plant Genetic Resources Institute (IPGRI)
- Garner more international support to research the socioeconomic factors influencing small farmers' participation in rehabilitation and planting.
- Use a need-driven approach to set objectives and formulate programmes through closer involvement of partners (farmers, non-governmental organizations, conservationists, national and international organizations, policymakers).
- Establish a documentation advisory and support group to facilitate documentation on farmers' data and cultural practices.
- Ensure that regional strategies emphasize more farmers' training for *in situ* conservation.

International Rice Research Institute (IRRI)
- Hire a sociologist and a gender specialist to strengthen its Social Science Department, which has been gradually depleted as staff members leave.

International Water Management Institute (IWMI)

• Expand research on irrigation management transfer, particularly on equity in access to water and on the private sector's capacity to manage water resources.

IWMI has integrated staff members with socioeconomic and biophysical disciplinary backgrounds. Its interdisciplinary approach is held out as one of its major strengths and as a model for other institutes.

West Africa Rice Development Association (WARDA)
- Strengthen its socioeconomic research component, which lacks continuity.
- Focus less on fields and more on the actors – farming households and communities – and more deeply integrate biophysical with socio-economic research, as required by the nature of irrigated systems in West Africa.
- Focus a new strategic research agenda on technology transfer on the major social and institutional constraints on adopting new rice technologies. Understand existing knowledge and social systems to speed the diffusion of new rice technologies. Create a disciplinary mix of scientists, including sociologists and anthropologists.

Systemwide Genetic Resources Programme (SGRP)
- Given the lack of knowledge on gender and the role of women in biodiversity conservation and use, develop methodologies for diagnostic and participatory research; develop criteria for conservation after production, which is often a woman's domain; and improve the linkage between social science and 'technical' disciplines influencing genetic resources conservation.
- Develop participatory breeding methodologies to support on-farm crop improvement.

Systemwide Programmes with an Ecoregional Approach (SPEA)
- Strengthen social science research, which has been inadequate, to improve the disciplinary balance between it and technical research.
- Revise the conceptual framework for NRM research to redefine the research domain, as a set of biophysical, socioeconomic, market and policy variables, as key to designing and executing research and to extrapolating results.
- Raise the exceedingly low social science research capacity within the national agricultural research system (NARS), which hampers balancing technical and social science research.
- Recognize that, aside from inadequate expertise in economics, sociology and anthropology, major weaknesses persist in strategic research on patterns of community decision making in managing natural resources.

Despite the strong push by TAC and the external review panels for centres to strengthen their social science capacity, most have not been able to do so and remain understaffed, particularly in the sociological and anthropological disciplines, which have never sustained a critical mass. Such obvious weaknesses in social analysis for research on technological and social innovation, social policy and institutional and organizational reform can only lead to missed opportunities as well as research of questionable relevance and poor quality.

The 2000 CGIAR Strategy and Social Research

In 2000, the CGIAR adopted the new vision and strategy elaborated by TAC (TAC, 2000) – 'A food-secure world for all'. The overall goal was defined as 'To reduce poverty, hunger and malnutrition by sustainably increasing the productivity of resources in agriculture, forestry and fisheries'. The CGIAR's mission was defined as 'To achieve sustainable food security and reduce poverty in developing countries through scientific research and research-related activities in the fields of agriculture, livestock, forestry, fisheries, policy and natural resources management'.

Pointing to scientific opportunities in the social sciences, and specifically social research, TAC directly guided the new CGIAR strategy in developments in sociology, social geography, anthropology and economics seen as bearing directly upon the CGIAR research priorities:

> These include planning and priority setting, a better understanding of the decision-making process of individuals and groups in rural communities, bioeconomic modelling and the new institutional economics. Primarily, social science research in the CGIAR needs to focus more on: identifying the characteristics and needs of the ultimate clients/beneficiaries, i.e. poor farmers and urban food consumers; the institutional arrangements needed to foster social capital creation and activation; improved property rights and custodianship regimes and their management and distributional implications; the motivation behind poor farmers' cropping strategies; the factors of collective action in agricultural, forestry and fish production and marketing; and patterns of community or group resource management. The increased interest in social sciences is an important way of expanding knowledge-partnerships in the CGIAR. Research in sociology and anthropology should complement economic research in the CGIAR, and this socioeconomic research must be linked better, both upstream and downstream, to that in the biological and physical sciences. The CGIAR social researchers also facilitate bringing into the system the new social research and knowledge on poverty worldwide that is needed by the CGIAR to determine its strategy, priorities and research agenda and to assess its impact.

> (TAC, 2000)

The new CGIAR vision and strategy stresses:

> Additional socio-economic research by the CGIAR, in collaboration with others, should focus on the socio-cultural and agricultural dimensions of rural and urban poverty.

> (TAC, 2000)

TAC went further in justifying and specifying these strategic research directions in the CGIAR. The TAC strategy preparation document (Cernea and Kassam, 2002) argued that social research needs more explicit support in the CGIAR centres in order to reach the following objectives:

- Improve the socio-economic understanding of household and community behaviour by considering the heterogeneity of farming actors, their differential demands and their potential for technological and institutional innovations.
- Clarify the extent and location of poverty, its causes, risks of further impoverishment and resulting needs within the target populations and agroecosystems of each CGIAR centre.
- Integrate poverty mapping with farming systems mapping, spatially and with relation to markets, using geographic information services and other research tools, to increase the responsiveness of biophysical research to the locations of the poorest farmers and to the issues related to their cropping and farming systems.
- Intensify the study of efficient patterns of social organization for better use and sustainable management of key natural resources, water, soil and trees. Study collective action patterns, gender and participation.
- Analyse policy-triggered constraining effects on productive rural populations, and research improved policy options and solutions.
- Improve the use of conceptual and methodological advances in social research to develop knowledge to fight the causes of poverty and lack of assets.

The CGIAR vision and strategy call for a socially oriented, pro-poor research agenda with a strengthened social research input. But the trend is in the opposite direction, with social research capacity having decreased over recent years in most centres, and social science research, including social research, being of variable quality and relevance.

The CGIAR Social Research Conference

TAC repeatedly expressed disappointment that, despite strong encouragement – from TAC itself and the TAC-commissioned external reviews – to strengthen social research capacity and content, the centres did so unevenly and showed little progress (TAC, 2001). Consequently, TAC initiated[12] a systemwide Conference on Social Research in the CGIAR in September 2002 at Centro Internacional de Agricultura Tropical (CIAT), Cali, and occasioned a much-needed critical analysis of the 'state of the art' in the CGIAR's social research. Following up on the conference, TAC (renamed in the meantime as the interim Science Council of the CGIAR) decided to commission a strategic 'stripe review' of social science research. Such a review across the system would aim to recommend priorities, strategies and scientific capacity in social science research, with particular attention to social research. The conference endorsed TAC's proposal for a stripe study (Cernea and Kassam, 2002), and the new Science Council appointed in 2003/04 is mandated to carry it out.

The 2002 conference made a detailed and documented collective analysis of social research as an important component of the CGIAR's overall research agenda. The focus was on the status of social research in the system, capacity, issues, achievements, resources, weaknesses, difficulties, understanding and new tasks. The substance was provided by 'centres' papers' containing an extensive analysis of these issues in centre after centre (see selected chapters in Part II of this volume).

Major problems regarding the recent decline in the system's capacity, depletion of intellectual capital and decrease of social research staff below critical mass in several centres were highlighted in the papers and discussions. The conference debates confirmed and documented the critical signals given by TAC and the TAC-commissioned external reviews, again and again over several years, about the insufficient non-economics research in many centres, in sharp contrast to the increasing demand for social analysis.

The report on the Cali Conference to the interim Science Council distilled the main content, messages and recommendations (Cernea and Kassam, 2002). It was submitted to the CGIAR's chair along with recommendations on how to address the dysfunctional situations highlighted in the conference, and how to build upon achievements and potentials in the CGIAR. It was emphasized that the CGIAR offers important comparative advantages for pioneering social research: such advantages are the continuous intra-centre and intra-system interaction between social researchers and biophysical researchers; the opportunities for immediate field-testing; the incentives for and legitimacy of applied research, more than in many other settings, etc. Various models of integrating biophysical with social research are successfully practised and encouraged. Interaction between economists and non-economics social researchers proves most fertile when they work in the same centre. The 'socioeconomic' label in itself does not add value and remains hollow unless skills and social and economic concepts are integrated. When social issues are addressed with quality social science, the results can make – and have made – an important difference in the centres' work. But the CGIAR system was found to be still far from using the guidance and opportunities provided by the vision and strategy adopted in 2000.

However, at the same time, the Science Council and CGIAR management learned from the conference about major problems and dysfunctional drawbacks in the state of, and resource allocation for, some research in the CGIAR system. Conference papers reported that the capacity for social research has severely declined in the last 5 years in several CGIAR centres. This erosion shows in the decrease in number of social researchers in several centres; in composition change, such as decrease in PhD-level researchers and increase in below-PhD-level researchers; disappearance – total or near total – of social researchers, other than economists, in several commodity or natural resources CGIAR centres; at best, prior staff is maintained. Some centres once known for their strong presence of social researchers now have none (e.g. CIMMYT, which had four or five anthropologists and sociologists in the past, now has none, except for one 'human ecologist'; ILRI and ICARDA have none, as well). WARDA, similarly, had none. The pseudo-remedy often proposed in such situations – making better use of existing resources – can hardly be done when such resources are sub-minimal or absent. Some centres, directors general, or directors of research, while paying lip service to the importance of social research, systematically deny it resources and use attrition as a means to replace anthropologists with economists, conveniently re-labelled 'socio-economists', or with other professionals.

Regarding staffing, no single centre participating in the conference reported any increase in social researchers during the previous 2 years, notwithstanding the emphasis in the 2000 CGIAR strategy on poverty orientation, participation and other social variables in research. Several centres reported a worrisome drop 'below critical mass' level. This further diminishes the ability to intellectually influence the centres' agenda. Skill-mix impoverishment in centres discourages interdisciplinarity and partnerships.

The census of social researchers (economists and non-economists), carried out before the conference through centre directors general, TAC and CIAT, revealed the following 'human capital' for social research:

- Economists dominate social science staff, making up over 60%.
- For every three-and-a-half economists in the CGIAR, there is one sociologist or anthropologist.
- Some economists undoubtedly have a strong social orientation, but for the CGIAR as a specialized research system this is not seen as a substitute for the trained theoretical and methodological professionalism required for scientific research.
- Some 27% of the researchers listed by centres' management as social researchers and included in the survey turned out to be neither sociologists nor anthropologists nor economists. Yet they are

considered participants in social research. They only increase the appearance of social research but not its quality.

- Compared with 1995/96, when the last TAC-commissioned stripe study of social science was conducted, there had been a massive 24% drop in social science staff numbers in the CGIAR, while the total number of scientists had increased by 2.2%.
- Economists from several centres (e.g. ICARDA, ILRI), attending the Cali conference, reported that they did not have sociological counterparts in their centres, and described and deplored the declining curve, nearing a zero curve, for non-economics researchers.

The conference identified the following six areas with major opportunities for social value-adding research that would contribute to implementing the 2000 CGIAR vision and strategy for substantive research:

- Sharpen the poverty perspective on social research in the CGIAR.
- Promote culturally informed methodologies in the CGIAR's biophysical, technological and policy research.
- Study how innovation is done.
- Carry out more research on social organization patterns of farmers and institutional analysis and promote institutional learning.
- Study how policy and power relations affect technology adoption by producers and produce social policy and strategy recommendations.
- Research the social impact of the CGIAR's outputs.

During the conference, considerable criticism replaced discussion on internal organizational difficulties faced by social researches in various centres and more broadly, in the CGIAR system. Researchers' expectations are that, having endorsed the new CGIAR strategy, the donors, centre boards and directors general should proactively facilitate changes in the culture and skill-mix of the CGIAR governance and management bodies, to strengthen and sustain an intellectually robust social research capacity. The expectation at the 'grass-roots' is that the boards and senior managers must raise the status of social research in each centre, providing adequate funds for interdisciplinary social research based on centre policy and providing opportunities to social researchers for strategic research and resource mobilization. The mind-set in many CGIAR centres must be changed regarding farmers and cultural and behavioural factors in agricultural development. Values that do not support social research must be proactively altered. This requires that board membership include social researchers, and that social research be explicitly included in the development of research proposals from the very beginning, as well as in the peer review process, calling upon eminent social researchers.

The conference concluded, *inter alia*, that:

- There is a large potential for integrating social research into the CGIAR agenda not only in the centre-based core programmes but also in systemwide and challenge programmes. Each of these opportunities should be seized and the system's commitment can best be demonstrated by visibly placing social research at the core of the programmes.
- Each centre board and management must formulate a clear position regarding social research within the centre. This should include establishing and safeguarding the critical mass for social science research and social research competence, and managing an effective balance between the service research function of social researchers and the longer-term social research topics.
- In particular, there is a need for a more effective balance between economics and non-economics social scientists as recommended by virtually all TAC-commissioned external reviews since 1995, often without consistent follow-up from the reviewed centres. Social research must regain its prestige within the centre and be put in a position to deliver cutting-edge products. This concerns two professional groups within the centre: social scientists and non-social scientists doing social research. To ensure quality research, some training of non-social scientists in social science research methodology is indispensable and of high priority. Social researchers themselves must head this process of institutional learning and change. They should lead reflection groups on socio-cultural issues in agricultural research, networking between centres.

Social scientists must be given the opportunity to upgrade their knowledge and competence through sabbaticals, exchange programmes, write-shops, etc. as part of their professional skill-maintenance needs. The decline in the number of social scientists in the CGIAR and in social scientists holding PhDs must be reversed. Equally in protest is the strengthening of the extremely weak social research capacity in NARS. The CGIAR's social researchers must contribute more substantially to developing social research in NARS. The successful Rockefeller Foundation programme to place post-doctoral anthropologists and sociologists in the CGIAR centres functioned for some 20 years, but was not mainstreamed. The CGIAR should assess the outcomes of this programme. Together with the World Bank, the conference recommended that a group of donors under the Rockefeller Foundation's leadership consider co-sponsoring a new comparable programme, with commitments for mainstreaming successful post-doctoral fellows as social research staff. In turn, the Science Council should commission a strategic stripe review of social research in the CGIAR system to deepen the critical analysis of priorities and assess on a centre by centre basis, the potential, needs and work patterns.[13] Many other constructive recommendations were made at the conference, but so far CGIAR's managers have not considered or implemented them.

Concluding Remarks

Despite its achievements, the CGIAR has not been successful in sustaining a critical mass of social research effort in all its centres. Given the recent negative trend in social research capacity in many centres, a systematic effort is needed to expand and implement a credible and sustainable social research agenda. Following the broad strategic framework for social science research in the 2000 CGIAR vision and strategy, a research culture and ethos in CGIAR must be fostered to unambiguously broaden the agenda for social research that directly pursues poverty reduction by increasing agricultural productivity and integrating biophysical and human sciences.

The CGIAR Conference on Social Research and its analytical assessments are a step toward mainstreaming social research, but this depends not only on social researchers: it depends largely on the CGIAR senior managers and on centres' managers and boards. Such mainstreaming is both a matter of mind-set change and of resource allocation. Action is now imperative. To begin with, the positive momentum generated by the conference needs to be followed up soon with a comprehensive Science Council stripe study of social science research, complemented by centre management analyses, to chart definite steps and actionable measures.

Notes

[1]For the purpose of this chapter, the term 'social research' refers to research in sociological or anthropological disciplines, not to research in economics, without implying in any way that economics, for instance, or other related disciplines, are not social disciplines as well (Technical Advisory Committee (TAC), 2001). Sociological research aims to study the society or community and how individuals relate among themselves and organize their social existence and productive activities. Anthropological research aims to study individuals in the context of their culture. Hence, rural sociology and social anthropology are two disciplines most relevant to scientific social research, sometimes called socio-cultural research. However,

CGIAR scientists from other disciplines – economics, politics, management, geography, communications, law, statistics and geographic information services – have also contributed in varying degrees to what we term here, as indicated above, 'social research' in the CGIAR.

[2]An internal tension inside the CGIAR and the opposing views around the substance and orientation of farming systems research surfaced in the mid-1980s in connection with the assessment study carried out by Norman Simmonds for the World Bank on farming systems research studies across the entire CGIAR. Simmonds minimized the social and cultural elements in farming systems research and the role of CGIAR's anthropologists but ran into opposition at the World Bank. Simmonds reflected some of the biased views held then within the CGIAR, while not fairly representing the argument of social researchers. Writing in support of CGIAR's anthropologists, Michael M. Cernea, who at the time was the rural sociology advisor of the World Bank, and Scott Guggenheim, who became later a post-doctoral fellow in CGIAR, responded with a severe rebuttal to Simmonds's study, titled 'Is anthropology superfluous in farming system research?' (Cernea and Guggenheim, 1985).

[3]The term includes not only the ultimate beneficiaries but also other actors in the public and private sectors that may help enable or create the conditions for desired change.

[4]For example, in Baum (1986), socioeconomics is mentioned only twice and rural sociology only once.

[5]For example, poverty alleviation is hardly mentioned by Collinson and Platais (1992) although some attention was paid to the topic of 'Users' Perspectives: Factoring Farmers' Needs into the Research Agenda'. According to Collinson and Platais (1992), the relationship between natural and social scientists was still evolving. Within the CGIAR, a number of centre programmes had promoted the use of social scientists who, according to a 1991 survey, comprised close to 15% of the senior science staff, of whom the vast majority were economists. 'Promotion arose from a conviction that understanding the priorities, circumstances and decision-making processes of resource-poor farmers was vital to the development of innovative techniques attractive to them'.

[6]Ideas underlying the importance of participatory research as well as of collective action and property rights began to take shape in the 1980s and early 1990s, when some centres conducted such research.

[7]The information was extracted from the following 16 TAC-commissioned external programme and management review reports of centres: IITA (2001), IWMI (2000), WARDA (2000), ICARDA (2000), CIAT (2000), ILRI (1999), ICLARM (1999), CIFOR (1998), ICRAF (1998), IRRI (1998), IFPRI (1998), CIMMYT (1997), IPGRI (1997), ICRISAT (1996), International Service for National Agricultural Research (ISNAR) (1996), CIP (1995); and from three external review reports of systemwide programmes: SGRP (1998), Systemwide Livestock Programme (SLP) (2001) and SPEA (1999).

[8]The Conference Organizing Committee comprised Jacqueline Ashby, Michael M. Cernea, Amir H. Kassam and Ruth Meinzen-Dick.

[9]The 'S' category refers to either the social research activity itself or to the social research process used to undertake the research in which sociological and anthropological variables and issues are addressed in the context of CGIAR goals. These variables deal with farming patterns, traditional ownership, gender, equity, empowerment, common property resources management and social structures and institutions – all of which are pertinent to the management and productivity of resources, who owns and controls them, who benefits from their use, who is accountable, etc. These variables occur in activities related to indigenous knowledge, farming system and household characterization, *ex-ante* rural livelihood needs assessment, common property resources management, gender, participatory research, etc.

[10]The 'E' category indicates activities in which the key variables are primarily related to economics: for instance, to the economics of production systems, input-output economic analyses, cost of water or other resources, economic rates of return studies, *ex-post* adoption assessments and counterfactual economic analysis.

[11]The 'SE' category refers to social science activities that include both types of variables – social and economic – and are described under the broad term 'socio-economic', with no clear distinction in either category possible from the information given in the external review documents surveyed.

[12]See details in the proposal submitted to the CGIAR Annual General Meeting 2001 (Cernea, 2001).

[13]Commissioning such a strategic stripe review of social research in the CGIAR System was one of the most explicit recommendations of the conference.

References

Baum, C.W. (1986) *Partners Against Hunger: The Consultative Group on International Agricultural Research*. The World Bank, Washington DC, 337 pp.

Cernea, M.M. (2001) Outline Paper: Proposal for a Social Research Conference in the CGIAR. Presented at the CGIAR Annual General Meeting, Washington, DC, October 2001. TAC Secretariat, FAO, Rome, Italy, 8 pp.

Cernea, M.M. and Guggenheim, S. (1985) Is anthropology superfluous in farming system research? In: Flora, C. (ed.) *Farming Systems Research*. Kansas University Press University Research Series, vol. 4 (9), pp. 504–516.

Cernea, M.M. and Kassam, A.H. (2002) Brief Report on the Social Research Conference to the interim Science Council. September 2002. iSC/TAC Secretariat, FAO, Rome, Italy, 10 pp.

Collective Action and Property Rights (CAPRi) (2002) *The First External Review of CAPRi*. iScience Council/Technical Advisory Committee (iSC/TAC) Secretariat, Food and

Agriculture Organization of the United Nations (FAO), Rome, Italy.

Collinson, M. and Platais, K.W. (eds) (1992) Social Science in the CGIAR. *Proceedings of a Meeting of CGIAR Social Scientists held at ISNAR, The Hague, The Netherlands, August 1992.* CGIAR Study Paper 28. Washington, DC, 141 pp.

Kassam, A.H. (2003) An overview of social science research in the Consultative Group on International Agricultural Research. *The International Social Science Journal* 177, 441–462.

Kassam, A., Barat, S. and Moreddu, E. (2002) Summary of Excerpts from TAC Commissioned External Reviews of centres and systemwide programmes since 1995. CGIAR interim Science Council Secretariat, FAO, Rome. (A background document prepared for the Social Research Conference, 10–12 September 2002, International Centre for Tropical Agriculture (CIAT), Cali, Colombia).

Participatory Research and Gender Analysis (PRGA) (1996) New Frontiers in Participatory Research and Gender Analysis. *Proceedings of the International Seminar on Participatory Research and Gender Analysis for Technology Development.* CIAT, Cali, Colombia.

PRGA (1999) *Crossing Perspectives: Farmers and Scientists in Participatory Breeding.* PRGA, CIAT, Cali, Colombia.

PRGA (2001) An exchange of experiences from South and South East Asia: Proceedings of the International Symposium on Participatory Plant Breeding and Participatory Plant Genetic Resources Enhancement. Pokhara, Nepal, 1–5 May 2000, PRGA, CIAT, Cali, Colombia.

TAC (1996) Perspectives on Policy and Management Research in the CGIAR (SDR/TAC:IAR/95/26.1). TAC Secretariat, FAO, Rome, 70 pp.

TAC (1997) Review of CGIAR Priorities and Strategies (AGR/TAC: IAR/96/6.1 and 6.2). TAC Secretariat, FAO, Rome, Italy, 86 pp.

TAC (2000) A Food Secure World for All: Towards a New Vision and Strategy for the CGIAR (SDR/TAC:IAR/00/14.1/Rev.2). TAC Secretariat, FAO, Rome, Italy, 50 pp.

TAC (2001) The Role of Social Research in the CGIAR 'Supporting the Strategy – Achieving Development Impact' (SDR/TAC: IAR/ 01/25). TAC Secretariat, FAO, Rome, 190 pp.

Who are the Social Researchers of the CGIAR System? 3

Eva Rathgeber

When the Consultative Group on International Agricultural Research (CGIAR) system was formally established in 1971, early efforts were focused on the development and spread of new varieties of wheat, rice and other technologies. As new technologies were developed, they were disseminated through top-down mechanisms. Although economists were part of the CGIAR from its early days, other social scientists, when they existed at all, provided primarily a service function and did little independent research. In the late 1970s, participatory research methods that emphasized the involvement of small-scale farmers in agricultural research began to be more widely accepted (Gladwin *et al.*, 2002) and they started to be integrated slowly into some of the work of the CGIAR. The International Potato Center (CIP) in Peru was the first CGIAR centre to request an anthropologist from the Rockefeller Foundation in the late 1970s (Thiele *et al.*, 2001), and in the 1980s, the CIP became known as a strong proponent of participatory research. However, although the non-economic social sciences now enjoy wider recognition, they continue to have a limited function within the research activities of the CGIAR system, where social scientists are under-represented as a group. This is surprising and even inexplicable, given the CGIAR strategy and its definition of goals and priorities, which place major importance on the socio-economic elements of poverty reduction through food security and improved agricultural production and productivity.

©CAB International 2006. *Researching the Culture in Agri*-Culture:
Social Research for International Development
(eds M.M. Cernea and A.H. Kassam)

Overview and Methodology

This chapter presents findings from a 2002 sociological survey to explore the composition, background, experiences and perceptions of work by male and female scientists employed in the CGIAR system. Although most large research organizations develop detailed databases about the educational experiences, working conditions, aspirations, work/life balance, etc. of their scientists, almost nothing is known about scientists employed within CGIAR. The present study – and the larger report from which it originates[1] – can only begin to fill this gap, but certainly the CGIAR must undertake a much more in-depth 'sociology of science' analysis to know and better understand its own valuable body of human resources.

The 2002 survey tested 12 hypotheses that were developed based on an extensive review of the literature. These focused on issues ranging from family and educational backgrounds, disciplinary concentration, promotion and job security, interaction with colleagues and networking, professional competence, work/life balance, management styles to future career plans.

By 2001, the CGIAR system had 7851 scientific staff members, of whom 6829 were nationally recruited and 1022 were internationally recruited; 73% were male (Acosta and Wilde, 2001). The disciplines represented by scientific staff in the CGIAR system are concentrated in the agricultural, natural and life sciences. The number of non-economist social scientists working in the CGIAR centres continues to be small and some centres have none.

Overall, the 2002 survey was based on a stratified sampling strategy, designed to reach all women scientists and an equal number of randomly selected male scientists (stratified by centre and recruitment status). The survey was piloted with scientists from several centres, and then posted in April–May 2002 to a web-based survey programme. Only a very few responses were unusable, for inadequate or late completion. The total of 368 valid responses included 183 females and 185 males. A slight bias towards internationally recruited scientists may have been introduced because they had a higher response rate than other categories of scientists. Table 3.1 shows the breakdown of responses across various position categories.

The survey comprised 82 questions within nine broad analytical categories. Most were close-coded, although some were open-ended to allow respondents to provide comments or insights. To assure confidentiality, all responses were anonymous and respondents were not asked to identify their centres, although some felt at liberty to do so in their commentary answers. Results of the quantitative study were analysed using the Statistical Package for the Social Sciences (SPSS) program.

Table 3.1. Breakdown of responses by recruitment status.

Recruitment status	Female	Male	Total
Nationally recruited	77	41	118
Regionally recruited	7	9	16
Internationally recruited	79	121	200
Postdoctoral fellows	9	8	17
Secondment	5	6	11
Postgraduate students	3	0	3
Other	3	0	3
Total	183	185	368

To probe and supplement some of the information collected in the survey, in-depth telephone interviews were undertaken with 19 randomly selected scientists: Center for International Forestry Research (CIFOR) (2), International Maize and Wheat Improvement Centre (CIMMYT) (1), West Africa Rice Development Association (WARDA) (1), International Rice Research Institute (IRRI) (2), International Center for Agricultural Research in the Dry Areas (ICARDA) (1), International Livestock Research Institute (ILRI) (2), International Food Policy Research Institute (IFPRI) (3), Centro Internacional de Agricultura Tropical (CIAT) (2), International Agroforestry Research Centre (ICRAF) (2), International Center for Living Aquatic Resources Management (ICLARM) (1), International Water Management Institute (IWMI) (1) and CIP (1).

For the purposes of this chapter, the data were re-analysed to focus on the role and status of social scientists within the CGIAR. Because social scientists were not specifically targeted in the original survey, some of the data are less precise than they would have been had questions been phrased differently. For example, the respondents were asked to indicate the discipline in which they received their highest degree. They were also asked to identify the disciplinary areas in which they work. A slightly abridged version of the CGIAR standard list of disciplines was provided and respondents were asked to check the appropriate disciplines.

Unfortunately, the CGIAR standard list allows for insufficiently distinctive identification of social science disciplines. Based on the list, the analytical category 'social sciences', used in this chapter was constructed to include anthropology, education, geography, political

science, social science and rural development and planning. The inclusion of the broadly termed 'social science' and 'rural development and
planning' as subsets of the larger social science category is problemat-
ical, but we cannot correct that because these disciplinary categories
were used in the classification extant at the time in the CGIAR system.
Particularly, 'rural development and planning' creates a residual category that gives license to include unrelated disciplinary specialties. In
our view, the net effect on our survey of this very imperfect standard
list of disciplines is to inflate the proportion of social scientists with a
number of researchers who, under a more accurate recording, would be
counted under other unrelated specialties. Thus, the actual number of
bona fide social scientists working in the CGIAR system may be less
than what is reflected in our tables. This upward bias should be kept
in mind in discussing the data presented here.

A more detailed study, focused specifically on social scientists,
should be undertaken by the CGIAR not only to confirm and refine the
findings reported here, but also for more general purposes, in order to
develop a better database about employees of the centres. It is also
worth observing that the CGIAR's standard categories for the biological
and agricultural sciences have been more precisely defined than those
for the social sciences.

The Social Researchers: Demographic Profile

The figures and tables below reflect key demographic characteristics of
the study sample.

Region of origin

Figure 3.1 reveals the region of origin of the respondents. The largest
number ($n = 90$, $f = 52$, $m = 38$) came from Western Europe; followed
by South-east Asia ($n = 50$, $f = 27$, $m = 23$); North America ($n = 48$,
$f = 21$, $m = 27$) and South America ($n = 44$, $f = 27$, $m = 17$).

Eleven percent of the respondents had their highest degree in a
social sciences discipline (anthropology, education, geography, political science, social science or rural development and planning).
However, 34% indicated that they considered at least some of their
work to be on social science-related topics. Respondents were permitted to identify themselves as working in more than one disciplinary
area. Table 3.2 indicates the region of origin of researchers who said
they did at least some work on social science-related topics. Again, the
largest number came from Western Europe, followed by North America

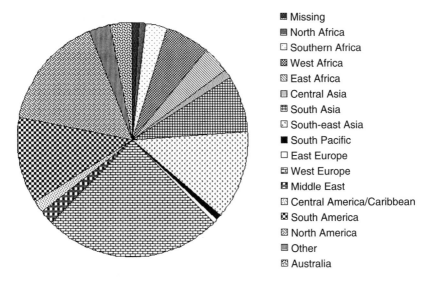

Legend:
- Missing
- North Africa
- Southern Africa
- West Africa
- East Africa
- Central Asia
- South Asia
- South-east Asia
- South Pacific
- East Europe
- West Europe
- Middle East
- Central America/Caribbean
- South America
- North America
- Other
- Australia

Fig. 3.1. Region of origin of respondents.

and South-east Asia. Almost 47% ($n = 59$) of scientists working in social science-related areas originated from Western Europe or North America.

As Fig. 3.2 shows, most of the scientists with their highest degree in a social sciences discipline (60%) also originated from North America or Western Europe.

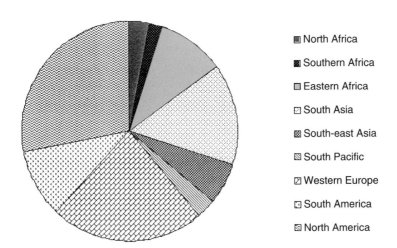

Legend:
- North Africa
- Southern Africa
- Eastern Africa
- South Asia
- South-east Asia
- South Pacific
- Western Europe
- South America
- North America

Fig. 3.2. Region of origin of scientists with highest degree in the social sciences.

Table 3.2. Region of origin of researchers working on social science-related topics.

	Anthropology	Geography	Policy analysis	Political science	Social science	Education	Total
N.Africa*		1	1		1		3
S.Africa			3		4		7
W.Africa		1	1		3		5
E.Africa		1	2		2		5
S.Asia	1		2	2	7		12
SE Asia		4	4	1	10		19
S.Pacific		1					1
E.Europe						1	1
W.Europe	5	7	5	2	14	3	36
C.America/Caribbean					1		1
S.America	1	2	1	1	5	1	11
N.America	3	3	4	2	10	1	23
Total	10	20	23	8	57	6	124

*N.Africa = Northern Africa, S.Africa = Southern Africa, W.Africa = West Africa, E.Africa = Eastern Africa, S.Asia = South Asia, SE Asia = South-east Asia, S.Pacific = South Pacific, E.Europe = Eastern Europe, W.Europe = Western Europe, C.America/Caribbean = Central America and Caribbean, S.America = South America, N.America = North America.

Discipline of highest degree

Table 3.3 provides information on the discipline of highest degree of all respondents, most of whom hold more than one degree. The breakdown indicates that out of the sample of 356 scientists under study, 41 had their highest degree in a social science discipline (anthropology, education, geography, political science, social science or rural development and planning). Twelve scientists did not answer the question (therefore, 11% of social scientists did not answer the question). We recall, however, that in the general survey an unexpectedly large proportion (34% of the total population) indicated that, in their view, at least some of their work was of a social science nature. This suggests that many scientists, untrained or only slightly trained in social sciences, are none the less engaged in some kind of social science work across the CGIAR system.

Among all CGIAR scientists, a far higher proportion of males than females have achieved more advanced training. Seventy percent of males held PhD degrees, compared with 44% of females. Thirty-nine percent of females held MSc or MA degrees, compared with 19% of

Table 3.3. Discipline of highest degree of all respondents.

Discipline	Frequency	Percent
Agricultural engineering	11	3.0
Agronomy	23	6.2
Animal sciences	5	1.4
Aquatic resources	15	4.1
Anthropology	10	2.7
Biochemistry	5	1.4
Biology	22	5.9
Botany	9	2.4
Biotechnology	3	0.8
Climatology	1	0.3
Computer sciences & modelling	3	0.8
Crop physiology	1	0.3
Economics	63	17.0
Education	3	0.8

Table 3.3. *(continued)*

Discipline	Frequency	Percent
Entomology	7	1.9
Epidemiology	3	0.8
Food science/nutrition	4	1.1
Forestry science	15	4.1
Genetic resources	30	8.1
Geography	8	2.2
GIS	2	0.5
Horticulture	4	1.1
Hydrology	1	0.3
Immunology	3	0.8
Information management	3	0.8
Irrigation engineering	1	0.3
Management	6	1.6
Microbiology	5	1.4
Molecular genetics	9	2.4
Natural resources management & ecology	12	3.2
Phytopathology	4	1.1
Plant pathology	29	7.8
Political science	8	2.2
Rural development & planning	6	1.6
Social science	6	1.6
Soil science	9	2.4
Statistics/biometrics	4	1.1
Systems research	1	0.3
Zoology	3	0.8
Other	3	0.8
Total	360	

males. Internationally recruited males were the most likely to hold PhD degrees: 88% held PhDs compared with only 22% of nationally recruited males. Internationally recruited women were also more likely to hold PhDs than nationally recruited women (76% vs.11%).

Among scientists who perform work on social science-related topics, 56% held PhD degrees, as seen in Table 3.4. Almost equal numbers of male and female scientists worked in social science-related areas (49.5% males and 50.5% females), but male scientists were more likely to hold PhD degrees. Sixty-five percent of all male scientists who worked on social science-related topics held PhD degrees, in comparison with only 47% of female scientists who worked on social science-related topics.

Overall, the profile for economists was somewhat different. There were 63 economists, comprising 17% of the total sample. Forty percent of the economists were female and 60% male. Seventy percent of the economists held PhD degrees and 41% originated from Western Europe or North America, with a further 19% coming from South-east Asia. The remaining 40% were drawn from other regions (with a substantial 13% from West Africa).

Age and sex of respondents

As is seen in Table 3.5, most of the scientists working on social science-related topics were evenly spread among three main age categories: 25–34 (32%); 35–44 (30%) and 45–54 (31%). This is slightly different than the age spread of the entire sample of 368 scientists: 25–34 (23%), 35–44 (37%) and 45–54 (28%). This may suggest that younger scientists are more likely to be open to and interested in the social science aspects of agricultural research.

Table 3.6 shows that scientists working on social science-related topics were almost evenly distributed between males and females. Males were slightly more likely to be found in the area of policy analysis, while females dominated anthropology.

In terms of location, about two thirds of all scientists who worked on social science-related topics were based at their centre headquarters. Similarly, 65% of all scientists in the 2002 survey reported that they were based at their centre headquarters.

Recruitment status and contract length

Table 3.7 provides information on the recruitment status of scientists working in social science-related areas. Forty-nine percent, who said

Table 3.4. Highest degree of scientists working on social science-related topics (%).

Degree	Anthropology		Geography		Policy analysis		Political science		Social science		Education		Total
	M	F	M	F	M	F	M	F	M	F	M	F	
PhD	1.7	4.3	4.3	2.6	7.0	3.5	2.6	0.9	15.6	11.3	0.9	0.9	55.6
MSc/MA	0.9	0.9	2.6	6.0	3.5	3.5	0.9	1.7	4.3	9.6			33.9
BSc/BA			1.7		0.9	0.9	0.9		1.7	2.6		0.9	9.6
Other										0.9			0.9
Total	2.6	5.2	8.6	8.6	11.4	7.9	4.4	2.6	21.6	24.4	0.9	1.8	100.0

Table 3.5. Age of all scientists working on social science-related topics (%).

| Discipline of work | Age of scientist | | | | |
	Below 25	25–34	35–44	45–54	55–64
Anthropology		2.6		3.4	1.7
Geography		6.9	6.0	4.3	
Policy analysis		4.3	7.8	6.0	0.9
Political science		2.6	2.6	1.7	
Social science		13.8	12.9	15.5	3.4
Education	0.9	0.9	0.9	0.9	
Total	0.9	31.1	30.2	31.8	6.0

Table 3.6. Sex of scientists working on social science-related topics (%).

Discipline of work	Female	Male
Anthropology	5.6	2.8
Geography	9.3	9.3
Policy analysis	8.3	12.0
Social sciences	25.9	23.1
Education	2.8	0.9
Total	51.9	48.1

Table 3.7. Type of contract held by scientists working in social science-related areas (%).

Discipline of work	NRS[1]	RRS	IRS	Post-doc	Second-ment	Post-grad	Other
Anthropology	0.9	0.9	3.4	0.9	1.7		
Geography	6.0	0.9	5.2	0.9	2.6	0.9	0.9
Policy analysis	4.3	0.9	12.0	0.9	0.9	0.0	0.0
Political science	2.6	0.9	1.7	0.9	0.9	0.0	0.0
Social science	14.7	1.7	24.1	2.6	2.6	0.0	0.0
Education	0.9	0.0	2.6	0.0	0.0	0.0	0.0
Total	29.4	5.3	49.0	6.2	8.7	0.9	0.9

[1] NRS, nationally recruited staff; RRS, regionally recruited staff; IRS, internationally recruited staff.

that they spent at least some of their time working on social science-related topics, identified themselves as internationally recruited staff. This is slightly lower than the proportion of scientists in the total sample who said that they were internationally recruited (54%). However, as shown in Table 3.8, among scientists with a highest degree in social sciences, 55% identified themselves as being internationally recruited. Nationally recruited staff are somewhat less likely to be trained social researchers. Since nationally recruited staff are likely to bring with them in-depth knowledge of local cultures and conditions, it would seem particularly efficacious for the centres to ensure that at least some nationally recruited staff have analytical skills in the social sciences.

The 2002 survey revealed that contract lengths vary substantially for scientists in the CGIAR system. Figure 3.3 shows contract lengths for all scientists in the 2002 survey.

Most scientists (78%) working on social science-related topics had contracts of only 1–3 years, as shown in Fig. 3.4. This is too short to develop a personal sense of job security, or to make family arrangements for work in remote locations and not least, to ensure continuity of research projects. Economists had even less job security, with 82% reporting that they had contracts of only 1–3 years.

For scientists who had their highest degree in social sciences, the length of contract is shown in Table 3.9. Again, most had contracts of 1–3 years, although a few had indeterminate contracts.

Table 3.8. Type of contract held by scientists with highest degree in a social science-related discipline (%).

Discipline of highest degree	NRS[1]	RRS	IRS	Post-doc	Second-ment	Post-grad	Other
Anthropology	2.5	2.5	17.5				
Education	2.5	2.5	2.5				
Geography	2.5		10.0	2.5	2.5	2.5	
Political science	7.5		12.5				
Social science	5.0		7.5	2.5			
Rural development and planning	7.5		5.0		2.5		
Total	27.5	5.0	55.0	5.0	5.0	2.5	0

[1]NRS, nationally recruited staff; RRS, regionally recruited staff; IRS, internationally recruited staff.

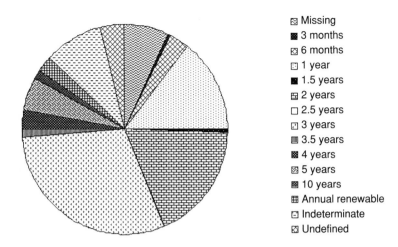

▨	Missing
▦	3 months
▨	6 months
⊡	1 year
■	1.5 years
⊞	2 years
□	2.5 years
⊡	3 years
▥	3.5 years
▩	4 years
▨	5 years
▩	10 years
⊞	Annual renewable
⊟	Indeterminate
▨	Undefined

Fig. 3.3. Contract lengths, all scientists.

However, when contract lengths were analysed by sex, there were major differences. As shown in Fig. 3.5, men tended to have longer contracts than women. The average length of contract for all males was 32.4 months, and for females, 26.5 months.

The average length of contract for scientists working in social science-related areas was 29.3 months. The difference between males and females was highly significant: 24.3 months for females, 34.2 months for males.

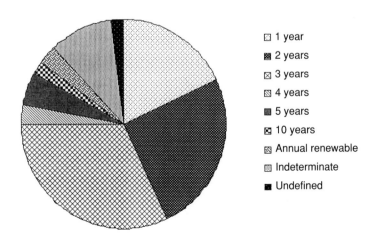

⊡	1 year
▩	2 years
▨	3 years
▨	4 years
▦	5 years
▨	10 years
▨	Annual renewable
▦	Indeterminate
■	Undefined

Fig. 3.4. Contract lengths of scientists working on social science-related topics.

Table 3.9. Length of contract of scientists trained in the social sciences (%).

Discipline of training	Length of contract (years)					In-det*	Undef*
	1	2	3	4	5		
Anthropology	5.0	5.0	10.0	0.0	5.0		
Education	2.5	0.0	2.5	0.0	2.5		
Geography	2.5	5.0	7.5	0.0	0.0	2.5	
Political science	2.5	5.0	7.5	0.0	2.5	2.5	
Social science	0.0	5.0	7.5	0.0	0.0	2.5	
Rural development and planning	2.5	2.5	5.0	2.5	0.0		2.5
Total	15.0	22.5	40.0	2.5	10.0	7.5	2.5

*An ren, annual renewable; Indet, indeterminate; Undef, undefined.

Professional Profile of the Respondents

There were some important differences among the demographic profile of scientists trained in the social sciences, those working in the social sciences and the broader sample in the 2002 survey. Below, we provide

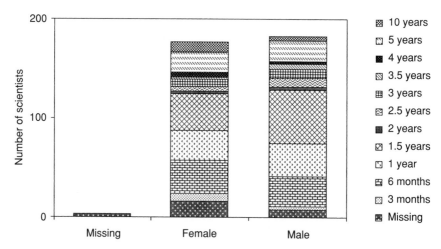

Fig. 3.5. Contract length for all scientists, by sex.

some details about the work experiences of social scientists in the CGIAR system.

Time allocation to research

A series of questions aimed to establish how scientists spend their time during a typical work week. Very few (less than 6%) spent almost all their time (90–100%) on research, but women composed 60% of this number. This proved to be a consistent finding.

An analysis of how male and female scientists spend their time reveals interesting differences. Most significantly, for the overall sample of scientists, women spend more of their time engaged in scientific research. Figure 3.6 compares time spent by men and women on scientific research. More women than men spent 60% or more of their time on research.

This may be explained by the fact that more men are in supervisory positions. Further analysis of the time data reveals that men spend more time fundraising and proposal writing, promoting partnerships, networking and on official travel and conferencing. Men and women

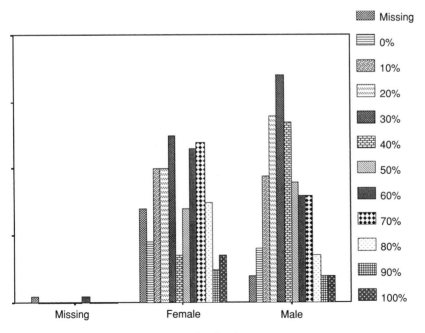

Fig. 3.6. Time spent on research, all scientists.

spend approximately equal amounts of time mentoring junior staff, although men report themselves to be slightly more engaged in general team building.

Figure 3.7 below shows the amount of time spent weekly on research by scientists working on social science-related topics. Most spent less than 50% of their time engaged in research activities. Only 28% spent from 50–80% of their time on research, compared with 38% of non-social scientists.

Table 3.10 provides information on the proportion of time spent weekly on research by scientists who had their highest degree in a social sciences discipline. The table reveals that these scientists spent even less time on research: 73% spent less than 50% of their time on research and 78% spent 50% or less of their time on research. Only 23% spent from 50–80% of their time on research. For economists, only 13% spent 70% or more of their time on research, and 70% spent 50% or less of their time on research. These figures suggest that the CGIAR system may not be making the most efficient use of its trained human resources.

Since agricultural research is at the centre of the work of the CGIAR system, it is surprising that so few staff members spend more than half their time on research.

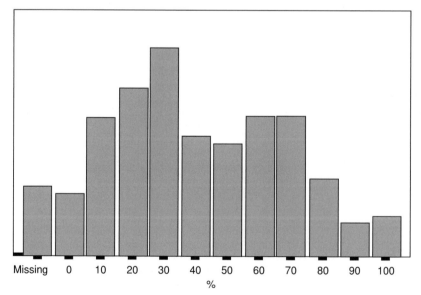

Fig. 3.7. Time spent weekly on research, all scientists working on social science-related topics.

Table 3.10. Proportion of time spent weekly on research by scientists with highest degree in a social sciences discipline.

Discipline of highest degree	Proportion of time spent on research (%)										
	0	10	20	30	40	50	60	70	80	90	100
Anthropology	2	2	4	1				1			
Education				1							
Geography		1		2	1	1	1		2		
Political science	1	1	1	2		1					
Social science			2	2			2				
Rural development and planning		1	2		1			1		1	
Total	3	5	9	8	2	2	3	2	2	1	0
Percentage	8	14	24	22	5	5	8	5	5	3	0

Perceptions of competence

Several questions dealt with self-perceptions of competence, with the expectation that scientists who worked squarely within the discipline of their training would have a higher sense of competence than those who worked in completely unrelated areas (Table 3.11). The 2002 survey found that both male and female scientists tended to rate their own competence quite highly. However, many more men than women rated themselves as 'well above average'.

Nationally recruited males tended to give themselves the highest ranking. Almost two thirds (65%) considered their ability to be 'well above average', compared with only 30% of nationally recruited females. Regionally recruited male staff members similarly tended to consider their abilities to be 'well above average', with 44% selecting this choice, as compared with 14% of women. Among international recruited staff, 40% of men and 29% of women considered their own ability to be 'well above average'.

Table 3.11. Self-ranking of scientific ability by sex, all scientists (%).

	Female	Male	Average
Well above average	28.6	40.3	34.6
Slightly above average	40.6	33.1	36.8
About average	24.6	24.3	24.4
Slightly below average	2.3	1.1	1.7
Well below average	0.6	0.0	0.3
No idea	3.4	1.1	2.2
Total	100.0	100.0	100.0

Males also tended to rate their colleagues' perception of their own scientific ability more highly (Table 3.12). In general, the most interesting observation from Table 3.12 is that women tend to think that their colleagues perceive their scientific ability to be somewhat lower than they themselves do. Males tend to think that their colleagues perceive their ability to be slightly higher than they themselves do. Moreover, while one quarter of all women think their colleagues consider them to be only average, only 17% of men think that they are perceived in this way. Also, women are more likely to say that they have no idea how their ability is perceived by others.

Again, nationally recruited men were most likely to think that others perceive their ability as 'well above average'. More than two thirds

Table 3.12. Colleagues' perception of scientific ability by sex, all scientists (%).

	Female	Male	Average
Well above average	25.1	45.9	35.7
Slightly above average	32.6	27.1	29.8
About average	25.1	17.1	21.1
Slightly below average	3.4	2.2	2.8
Well below average	1.1	0.6	0.8
No idea	12.6	7.2	9.8
Total	100.0	100.0	100.0

(72%) felt this way, compared with only 25% of nationally recruited women. In contrast, 44% of regionally recruited males and 40% of internationally recruited males state that their colleagues perceive their ability as 'well above average'. The comparable rates for regionally and internationally recruited females are 43 and 24%.

Among scientists working on social science-related topics, 63% considered their scientific ability to be well or slightly above average, and only 2.1% considered it to be slightly below average (Table 3.13).

It is noteworthy that 60% of female scientists working on social science-related topics considered their competence to be 'well above or slightly above' average. For all scientists, 69% of female scientists considered themselves to fall into these categories. For males working on social science-related topics, 67% considered themselves to be 'well above or slightly above' average, compared with 73% of males in the total sample. It is possible that scientists working on social science-related topics, but without a highest degree in the social sciences, may feel slightly inadequate because of their lack of formal training in the social sciences. Scientists with their highest degree in a social sciences discipline had a much higher perception of their own abilities (Table 3.14).

When the data in Tables 3.13 and 3.14 are compared, it is evident that scientists with a highest degree in a social science discipline have a higher perception of their own ability than scientists without a highest degree in social sciences and working in social science-related areas (73 vs. 63%). This may suggest that scientists engaged in social science work without appropriate training feel somewhat disadvantaged and uncertain of the quality and performance on these tasks. It

Table 3.13. Self-ranking of scientific ability by sex, all scientists working on social science-related topics (%).

	Female	Male	Average
Well above average	29.8	28.2	29.0
Slightly above average	29.8	38.5	34.1
About average	27.7	33.3	30.5
Slightly below average	4.3	0.0	2.1
Well below average	0.0	0.0	0.0
No idea	8.5	0.0	4.2
Total	100.0	100.0	100.0

Table 3.14. Self-ranking of scientific ability by sex, scientists with highest degree in the social sciences (%).

	Female	Male	Average
Well above average	42.8	21.0	31.9
Slightly above average	28.6	52.6	40.6
About average	23.8	26.3	25.0
Slightly below average	4.7	0.0	2.3
Well below average	0.0	0.0	0.0
No idea	0.0	0.0	0.0
Total	100.0	100.0	100.0

further suggests that if they are assigned to undertake work in the social sciences, although trained in another discipline, their CGIAR centre is probably not getting the best value for its investment in human capital.

Although all scientists working in social science-related areas generally have relatively high perceptions of their own abilities, they are less likely to think that their colleagues and supervisors share this opinion. Only 54% think that they are perceived as slightly or well above average, compared with 65% of other CGIAR scientists. Table 3.15 provides information on how scientists working on social

Table 3.15. Perceived ranking of ability by colleagues and supervisors, all scientists working in social science-related topics (%).

	Female	Male
Well above average	22.0	18.2
Slightly above average	32.2	36.4
About average	33.9	29.0
Slightly below average	1.7	5.4
Well below average	0.0	0.0
No idea	10.2	10.9
Total	100.0	100.0

science-related topics think others perceive their abilities. For all scientists, the difference in the perceptions of males and females of how others rate their abilities is considerable: 58% of females and 73% of males think that their supervisors and colleagues perceive their abilities as being well or slightly above average. However, among scientists working on social science-related topics, there is little difference: 54% of women and 55% of men think their abilities are perceived as well or slightly above average. This does not hold true for scientists with their highest degree in the social sciences: 67% of women and 62% of men think that their colleagues and supervisors rank their abilities as 'well or slightly above average' (Table 3.16). This further supports the idea that untrained social scientists working on social science-related topics may feel – understandably – outside their area of expertise. That they nonetheless, have to carry out such tasks points to problems in the CGIAR system that need to be solved by various centres by hiring professionally trained specialists for social science topics. Among economists, 75% felt that their competence was well or slightly above average and 22% perceived themselves as average. In contrast, 73% of economists said they thought their colleagues and supervisors regarded them as above average and 17% thought they perceived them as average. These generally higher rankings of competence among the economists could be related to the fact that their discipline is well established and well regarded within the CGIAR system.

Table 3.16. Perceived ranking of ability by colleagues and supervisors, scientists with highest degree in social science discipline (%).

	Female	Male
Well above average	38.0	28.6
Slightly above average	28.6	33.3
About average	14.3	9.5
Slightly below average	0.0	14.3
Well below average	4.8	0.0
No idea	14.3	14.3
Total	100.0	100.0

Career perspectives and perceptions of the role of social scientists

Few scientists working on social science-related topics (3%) aspired to join senior management in the CGIAR system: 22% aspired to become managers, but most planned to pursue such careers in the private sector, government and/or national agricultural research systems or in NGOs. Among scientists who had their highest degree in a social sciences discipline, 17% wanted to become senior managers, but only 3% wanted to achieve this status within the CGIAR system. This is an important finding that requires further exploration by the CGIAR system. If a substantial number of staff aspire to become senior managers but do not wish to do so within the CGIAR system, it suggests a perception that it is difficult for social scientists to become managers within the CGIAR system or that it does not value the skills and expertise of social scientists.

A small group of randomly selected scientists were interviewed by telephone and asked to comment on the perceived importance of social sciences in the work of the CGIAR system. An overview of some of their responses is presented below:

'Yes. In a CGIAR centre there is research and administration. For the administration (e.g. human resources), it is good to have people who have studied social sciences. A researcher cannot do good research and administration at the same time.' (Translated from French)

Female nationally recruited physical scientist

'Both science and social science are equally important. Working with people is the most important. But I think my centre gives greater credibility to people who can work with ecology and high technology.'

Female nationally recruited life scientist

'Yes, agriculture is by its very nature a mixture of hard science (development of technology) and social science (adoption and use).'

Male internationally recruited economist

'Life science is the most important aspect of research, not social sciences. I have no thoughts about social science research but I am not informed.'

Female nationally recruited life scientist

'No. The CGIAR system has a definite bias towards biophysical science. Social science is just seen as that "mushy stuff" ... It is not very macho. Guys don't really want to talk about gender. My last centre was worse than my current one in this regard. The economists have a belief that it is only valid if it can be quantified. It was a real battle between economists and anthropologists and sociologists.'

Female internationally recruited economist

'My centre does not do much on the social side except for economics. We do not have the staff for this so it has not taken on great importance from an institutional perspective. Since we do not have social scientists, all our social analysis is done by non-specialists.'

Female nationally recruited agricultural scientist

'Hard science should be slightly favoured. It should be 60–70% hard science. Social science is necessary because it feeds back into the loop. However, national partners should conduct the social science components. The CGIAR system should focus solely on nutritional needs.'

Female internationally recruited economist

It seems that there are many different understandings, including some conflicting ones, among CGIAR scientists about the role of social research within the CGIAR. While diversity of views in itself is positive, what may be of concern for the system is the seeming absence of a stronger common core understanding of the main functions of socio-cultural research within the CGIAR. To the extent that some of the above comments are typical of the views of scientists within the system, it seems clear that the centres as a whole may not have paid sufficient attention to ensuring that staff fully understand the importance of the 'human' dimensions of research. Significant work has to be done to introduce a better understanding of multidisciplinary approaches within the centres. Some of the comments in the 2002 survey suggested that for many scientists the idea of 'multidisciplinary research' meant the utilization of other branches of their own core discipline in their research.

Discussion

Social science disciplines have had a mixed reception within the CGIAR system. Graham Thiele *et al.*'s (2001) discussion of the use of participatory research at CIP provides insights into the slow processes through which social science research was accepted by biological scientists, despite the demonstrated success and value of early interventions by anthropologists. CIP was an early advocate of social sciences research and the process of acceptance within other centres has undoubtedly been even more problematic.

The data presented in the 2002 survey confirm that the social sciences still have a mixed reception within the CGIAR system. Although the value of working directly with farmers and developing knowledge of their attitudes, perceptions, values, etc. is widely recognized, most of this work appears to be done by scientists who do not have specialized training in social sciences.

Almost half the people who say they work on social science-related topics are of Western European or North American origin. This is somewhat higher than the representation of these regions within the overall sample (37%). The over-representation of Western Europeans and North Americans may reflect processes of self-selection or the choices of managers who asked certain scientists to include a social science perspective in their work. The reasons for this bias are not immediately evident. Further research needs to be done to assess whether this prevalence is to be associated with the origin of the training of these scientists. Many scientists from other regions received their highest degree in Western Europe or North America but did not describe themselves as working on social sciences.

Job security is a problem for many scientists, but the difference in average contract lengths for male and female scientists working on social science-related topics is astounding (24.3 months for females, 34.2 months for males.) This needs further examination and ultimate redressment.

In general, most CGIAR scientists in the 2002 survey spend surprisingly little time on research activities, but social scientists seem to spend marginally less. Scientists who spend at least some of their time on social science-related activities tend to spend less of their time on research activities than other scientists, but scientists with their highest degree in the social sciences spend the least amount of time on research. For the total sample, 38% of all scientists spent 50–80% of their time on research; for scientists working on social science-related topics, 28% spent 50–80% of their time on research; for scientists with their highest degree in a social sciences discipline, only 23% spent 50–80% of their time on research. This suggests that those scientists who do have specialized training in social sciences may not be able to significantly contribute to the social research being done within the CGIAR system. Further research is needed to establish how they do spend their time and to determine whether they are being relegated to a service capacity.

The data about perceptions of ability are revealing. Respondents who hold their highest degree in the social sciences have a higher perception of their own abilities than scientists who work at least part of the time on social science-related topics but do not have their highest degree in social sciences. They are also more likely to think that their supervisors and colleagues have a higher opinion of their abilities. Overall, the data strongly suggest that scientists who work on social science-related topics without having training in that area have a lower sense of personal competence. They also tend to feel that their colleagues and supervisors have a negative view of their competence.

Although many scientists – those working on social science-related topics and those with their highest degree in social sciences – aspire to become senior managers, few hope to do so within the CGIAR system. Economists have greater interest in pursuing senior management positions within the CGIAR system. Almost 12% said that they aspired to this, while an equal number said that they aspired to become senior managers outside the CGIAR system. This may reflect the fact that economics has been integrated more thoroughly into the core work of the CGIAR system, and economists perceive better chances of upward mobility into the ranks of senior management.

Interviews with a small sample of scientists revealed considerable lack of understanding about the function and purpose of research in the social sciences. Many scientists who were asked whether social research had a role to play in the CGIAR system had only a minimal understanding of the work done by social scientists and clearly were biased towards technology development. This suggests that the CGIAR system, despite some successes in this respect, has not been fully effective in defining the areas for specified, distinct social research or in developing integrated, multidisciplinary approaches to research. While in recent years the policy and management level of the CGIAR system has focused on 'alleviation of poverty', some of the interviews with scientists working within the system suggest little understanding and grasp of the potential socio-cultural and economic implications of poverty issues for their biophysical research.

Finally, the presence of large numbers of scientists doing work on social science-related topics indicates growing receptivity within the system to the need to include social science analysis in its work. However, the fact that few scientists who work in social sciences actually have their highest degree in a social science discipline gives cause for concern. It suggests that the CGIAR may not be making optimal use of its human resources. Most of the researchers working on social science topics are highly trained in other disciplines and divert part of their time to working on social science-related issues for which they feel they have no comparative advantage derived from an advanced level of academic training. At the same time, some of those who do have training in the social sciences appear to be diverted into non-research activities.

The importance of social scientists in the CGIAR system is not recognized, partly due to a lingering belief that the social aspects of the centres' research programme is being handled by economists, who are well represented within the system. While some economists bring a high level of social, cultural, political and gender sensitivity to their work, few have been trained in the more detailed qualitative methodologies commonly used by anthropologists and rural sociologists. To burden economists with the need to gather information and undertake analyses that they have not been trained to do is unlikely to be in the best interests of the CGIAR system. This approach may reduce the effectiveness of economic analysis, as economists are diverted from their main areas of interest and expertise, and at the same time produce less-than-satisfactory social analysis.

Essentially, the findings of the 2002 survey lead to two important sets of issues. First, a large number of scientists within the CGIAR system are not being utilized most effectively, i.e. in the disciplinary area in which they have training and high levels of expertise. No doubt there are 'good' reasons for each individual misuse of trained human resources (often linked to lack of funding to hire more social science expertise), but in the final analysis, the net results are unsatisfactory for the CGIAR system and certainly not conducive to helping the centres meet their core objectives: food security and poverty alleviation.

The second set of issues has to do with the job satisfaction and well-being of CGIAR science staff. The 2002 survey revealed that the most satisfied staff members were those who worked within their own area of expertise. The fact that few scientists working on social science-related topics or trained in the social sciences aspired to become managers within the CGIAR system, although many had the ambition to reach this level outside the system, is revealing, suggesting that they do not believe that they can advance within the system. This provides further urgency to the need for the CGIAR system to undertake an in-depth human resources analysis of its scientific staff and to develop policies that recognize and utilize all scientific expertise.

Over the past four decades, the CGIAR system has contributed to the development of thousands of technologies to improve food security and alleviate poverty. Without underestimating the significance of this work, it is evident that much still remains to be done to improve the lives of the poor in developing countries. There has been an obvious gap between the development of CGIAR technologies and their effective utilization by poor farmers. Given this continuing lacunae, it is highly appropriate for the CGIAR system to give serious attention to the use of social science research to identify the bottlenecks in technology development, adoption and utilization.

Notes

[1] The initial study was carried out as an activity of the Gender and Diversity Programme of the CGIAR system. The present chapter develops certain aspects of the study that were not addressed in the initial version of the full report, posted on the programme's web site and as such, some of the information contained in the present chapter is brought out publicly for the first time. Full details on survey methodology are included in the web version and are not repeated here. http://www.genderdiversity.cgiar.org/resource/working_papers.asp. The author is indebted to Michael Cernea for comments on the present work and to Vicki Wilde for comments on the original study.

References

Acosta, A.S. and Wilde, V. (2001) Updated analysis of future harvest centre demographics. Working Paper No. 33. CGIAR Gender and Diversity Programme, Nairobi.

Gladwin, C.H., Peterson, J.S. and Mwale, A.C. (2002) The quality of science in participatory research: a case study from Eastern Zambia. *World Development* 30(4), 523–543.

Thiele, G., van de Fliert, E. and Campilan, D. (2001) What happened to participatory research at the International Potato Centre? *Agriculture and Human Values* 18, 429–446.

Part II   The Insiders' Views: Social Research in the CGIAR System

Rice for the Poor: the Call and Opportunity for Social Research

4

Thelma R. Paris, Stephen Morin, Florencia G. Palis and Mahabub Hossain

Rice is one of the world's most important crops. Approximately 90% of the world's rice is grown and consumed in Asia, which is home to most of the poor. In countries where per capita income is US$500 or less, rice accounts for 20–30% of gross domestic product, 30–50% of agriculture value added and 50–80% of consumed calories. Feeding the poor and helping them work their way out of poverty means increasing the production, yield and profitability of rice and improving access to it at affordable prices. Rice production and processing provide livelihoods to millions of poor and landless men, women and children, who are also net buyers of rice (IRRI, 2000).

Fear of famine and penury in Asia in the 1950s motivated the Rockefeller Foundation and Ford Foundation, in cooperation with the government of the Philippines, to establish the International Rice Research Institute (IRRI) in 1960. Its goal is to 'improve the well-being of present and future generations of rice farmers and consumers, particularly those with low incomes'. Its objectives are to generate and disseminate rice-related knowledge and technology of short- and long-term environmental, social and economic benefits and to help enhance national rice research systems.

Social science research is, therefore, functionally necessary and will become increasingly important in reducing the poverty of rice-growing and -consuming populations. However, compared with economists, social researchers occupy a small place in IRRI and in most Consultative Group on International Agricultural Research (CGIAR) centres. The anthropologist's position was not renewed in 2002 due to drastic budget cuts, exacerbating the situation at IRRI. Can it achieve its goals and objectives without a full-time anthropologist or rural sociologist? How can social research be effectively integrated with bio-physical sciences and make a positive impact on the poor in the absence of a minimum critical mass of specialized researchers?

We show how social science research evolved in IRRI and then highlight the important contributions of social researchers in achieving its research thrusts. We also discuss the difficulties and constraints faced by social researchers and identify opportunities and needs for new social research in IRRI's programmes.

Evolution of Social Science Research at the IRRI

The evolution of social research at the IRRI has been linked to shifts in research focus, changes in research organization structure and in disciplinary mix, as well as in the dynamic of external forces. IRRI has gone through major research phases. While the first economist was hired in IRRI in 1965, it was only 13 years later, in 1978, that the first anthropologist came on board to work with a team of scientists on integrated pest management (IPM) for rice. The roles of IRRI anthropologists have been less defined and their methodologies less understood and accepted than those of agricultural economists. In 1981 the anthropologists organized a workshop, and published its results, on the role of anthropologists and other social scientists in interdisciplinary teams developing improved food production technology. Social researchers from other CGIAR centres also participated (IRRI, 1982).

From the mid-1960s until 1989, the IRRI's economists were based in the Agricultural Economics Division and different technical divisions. In 1990, however, rural sociologists, anthropologists, political scientists, gender specialists and geographers joined with agricultural economists to deal with a wide range of socio-economic issues and were housed in what is now called the Social Sciences Division (SSD). With the fusion of Geographic Information Services (GIS) with SSD, four agronomists are officially under this division, apart from five economists and one socio-economist–gender specialist. Historically, economists have outnumbered social researchers at the IRRI. The number of economists peaked in 1985, gradually declined in 1995 and then rebounded and stayed stable (Fig. 4.1). Yet, while the number of core-funded economists has been maintained, the number of social researchers has declined with the departure of the anthropologist (Stephen Morin) in 2002. The policy economist position added in 1999 was also dropped in 2003. In 2005, an impact assessment specialist (economist) was hired. Now IRRI has only two internationally recruited

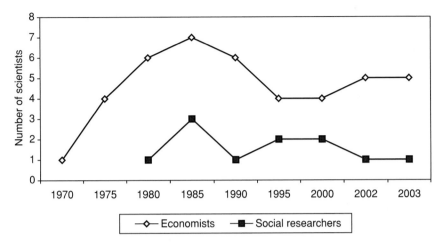

Fig. 4.1. Number of social scientists in IRRI, 1970–2003.

social researcher staff members – below any definition of a 'critical mass'. One socio-economist–gender specialist remains in SSD, while the communication development specialist is based in the Crop and Water Science Division. A nationally recruited staff member with a PhD in anthropology conducts research on socio-cultural concerns in technology development and dissemination. For the past years, Gelia Castillo, an internationally known rural sociologist, has been a consultant to the director general and other scientists.

Contributions of Social Research

The roles of social researchers at the IRRI can be described under several headings:

Analysing the socio-cultural and economic characteristics of groups, including those that may be adversely affected by some developments. Social scientists greatly help identify and explain the socio-cultural and economic characteristics of rice farmers, including groups that may be adversely affected by some developments, such as the poor, landless, women and children. Social scientists conduct baseline studies to assess social impact and help identify potential agents of change who can accelerate technology dissemination.

Identifying farmers' needs and constraint, and solutions to problems. Biological scientists have become increasingly convinced that social scientists' work is important in getting feedback from intended users of proposed technologies, or for initial problem diagnosis, technology design, identification of options to overcome constraints, monitoring and evaluation of adoption rates, or adaptation and diffusion of new technologies. Eliciting farmers' perceptions and understanding their knowledge, beliefs and farming practices have helped biological scientists identify early on the technology features needed to accelerate acceptability, thus increasing opportunities for social researchers to work with biological scientists rather than in isolation. To make this interaction work, social researchers must learn the technical aspects of farmers' problems and accept that both perspectives are needed to solve them. The interaction between social and biological scientists is increasing through joint activities such as preparing proposals and conducting stakeholders' meetings, field visits and research with farmer participation.

Assessing the social and cultural impact of technologies. Social researchers have examined the *ex-post* social and cultural impact of specific technologies on different categories of end users, particularly women engaged in rice farming. Specific rice technologies – whether yield increasing or labour saving – have a differential impact on the employment of men and women and on women belonging to landless families and other social subgroups (Paris *et al.*, 1996; Paris, 1998). In the Philippines, the demand for labourers for transplanting (mostly women from poor and landless families) was reduced by the direct seeding method of crop establishment (Res, 1985). The study of the employment or dismissal of female labourers due to the introduction of postharvest machinery such as threshers and reapers (Ebron *et al.*, 1983; Polak, 1985) also considered social and cultural variables. Juarez *et al.* (1988) revealed that some farmers did not adopt mechanical reapers, fearing that many poor and landless women would be displaced and lose their main source of livelihood. Social scientists also established that injudicious and frequent spraying of pesticides hindered women from gathering food in the rice fields. Price (1995) found that farmers in intensive rice cultivation systems consume fauna and flora that naturally thrive in the rice field environment. However, their use is curtailed by intensive over-application of insecticides and possibly other pest-control chemicals. Women's roles as marketers and gatekeepers of family nutrition are severely hampered by the scarcity or destruction of these foods.

The social and cultural dimensions of adopting IPM technology and other pest management strategies for rice have been an important research interest of anthropologists in collaboration with economists and entomologists. Palis (1998) showed that liberating farmers from purely chemical-control technology can be achieved by changing farmers' perceptions via experiential learning – through the farmer field school. Palis and Hossain (2003) revealed that IPM empowers farmers with knowledge and changes some behavioural patterns in rice farming – from insecticide spraying to no insecticide spraying. However, Palis *et al.* (1990) attributed the rice farmers' non-adoption of IPM in the 1980s based on single insect pest focus to technological complexity, location specificity of economic threshold level (single or multiple pests) and complicated computation of threshold levels. Similarly, Palis *et al.* (2003) assessed the social, cultural and economic factors that constrain and support the adoption of a community trap barrier system (CTBS) in South Vietnam. CTBS is an ecologically based rodent management strategy introduced to rice farmers in the Mekong Delta, Vietnam, for adaptation by them and eventually, large-scale adoption.

Facilitating farmers' participation in the innovation process. An important role of social researchers – which also differentiates them from economists – is facilitating farmers' participation in the innovation process as well as developing partnerships between scientists and farmers. Anthropologist Godell *et al.* (1982) developed replicable ways for scientists and farmers to work together as partners, described the premises for collective action in IRRI and the role of community organizers in organizing farmers to test IPM technology and developed techniques to evaluate the structural effectiveness of farmers' groups in managing crops.

In the 1990s, entomologists joined IRRI with a new approach to rice pest management and sought the help of communication specialists to spread simple messages to farmers (Heong *et al.*, 1994). An anthropologist working within an interdisciplinary team facilitated farmers' experiments to test the need for insecticide during the early stages of rice growing and demonstrated that simple and inexpensive farmer experiments could introduce IPM practices or other technologies (Fujisaka, 1994). Morin *et al.* (2002a) and Palis *et al.* (2002a) explored the feasibility of community management of CTBS in managing rodent damage in South Vietnam and the Philippines.

Social researchers included biological scientists and agricultural engineers as collaborators in testing and evaluating income-generating technologies to meet women's technology needs (Diaz *et al.*, 1998, 1999; Paris 2000a; Paris and Diaz, 2001) and facilitated feedback from farmer to farmer and from farmer to scientist on upland soil conservation (Fujisaka, 1993a).

How farmers manage rice diversity became an important component of the germplasm research porfolio at IRRI in the late 1990s. Anthropologists at the Genetic Resources Centre compared genetic diversity and its management by farmers in different rice ecosystems. Results demonstrated the need to define on-farm conservation strategies based on a thorough assessment of agronomic, genetic and socioeconomic criteria, and led to participatory experiments to make diversity an option for farmers and increase their access to it (Bellon *et al.*, 1997; Morin *et al.*, 1998, 2002a). Germplasm specialists, breeders, an anthropologist and an economist are working together under a unique project to enhance the conservation and use of traditional Lao rice varieties by integrating farmers' indigenous knowledge in managing agro-biodiversity (Sackville-Hamilton *et al.*, 2003). This innovative project was built on an earlier project conducted in 1995–2000 to protect and safeguard rice biodiversity in Laos, under which germplasm samples were collected for *ex-situ* conservation. Acknowledging the co-evolution of genetic with cultural diversity, the current research focuses on documentation and analysis of indigenous knowledge of traditional rice varieties and facilitates *in-situ* conservation. The project's long-term aim is to improve the Lao rice economy by building upon, rather than by replacing, traditional farmers' methods, relying on the valuable knowledge base and maintaining the high quality and rich diversity of rice.

Introducing social research methodologies and frameworks in monitoring and comprehending social change. Social researchers should continue to make advances in theory and break new ground in research methodology while making their work distinct from that of economists, who conduct large household surveys with the use of structured questionnaires. Polak and Acena (1986) recommended the case study method as a useful and cost-effective addition to the range of research tools used in multidisciplinary farming systems research (FSR). Fujisaka (1993a,b, 1994) used ethnographic methods and diagnostic surveys to understand farmers' practice. Price's (2001) study on farmers' (groups and individuals) entomological and rice pest management knowledge combined qualitative and quantitative analysis. She tested several methods such as free listing, triad testing and consensus analysis from multiple-choice testing instruments among rice farmers in Central Luzon, Philippines. The triad groupings used were generated by the ANTHROPAC program to document farmers' knowledge before intervention (IPM, farmer field school and no early spraying) and changes in that knowledge after intervention. The knowledge base data were then linked to behaviour: number of insecticide applications, hazard class of insecticide used, number of days after transplanting that insecticide was applied and cash expenditures on insecticides.

In South Asian countries, where women's illiteracy rate is high, other creative methods of collecting information are necessary. Paris *et al.*'s (2001a) study on rain-fed rice varietal improvement in eastern India used graphic illustrations apart from open-ended questionnaires to elicit male and female farmers' perceptions of desirable traits of rice varieties according to land type. The study also analysed farmers' preferences by size of landholdings, gender and caste, and complemented these methods with narratives to make women's voices heard.

In facilitating the up-scaling of IPM technology, Palis (2000) and Palis *et al.* (2002b) introduced a new perspective by employing the concept of social capital. Her study used the ego-centred network approach to explore farmers' social network and employed quantitative and qualitative techniques to collect information. Social capital operates on many levels in the village, particularly in agriculture and rural life. One cultural avenue in building social capital in the Philippines in relation to technology sharing and learning is through *huntahan* – Filipino for a group of two or more people holding a conversation or informal discussion. *Huntahan* in the house neighbourhood is generally wide in scope, and the common topics discussed are family affairs, politics, 'hot' events in the village and gossip. Conversation in the farm neighbourhood focuses more on rice farming and other on- and off-farm livelihood prospects. Farmers commonly discuss the growth and development of their rice crop, rice production problems and possible solutions and other rice production issues. The farmers compare the 'health' of their respective crops and seek advice from one another in handling symptoms caused by pests.

Palis's study revealed that the major sources of social capital among Filipino farmers are kin networks, house neighbourhood, farm neighbourhood and membership in a farmers' association. Kinship holds primacy among social relations and is characterized by strong ties, mutual trust and norms, which promote coordination and cooperation for mutual benefit. Kinship reduces transaction costs in IPM sharing. Secondary to kinship is the farm neighbour relationship. The geographical dimension of farmers' activities is a major factor in determining where social interactions take place. The farm is the community space where kin and non-kin share and learn technologies such as IPM.

Palis's study further revealed that kinship ties and farm location are the two most important factors to consider in developing a sampling scheme to identify IPM participants. Kinship is the radius of spontaneous sharing, whereas the farm is the radius of sharing and learning, resulting in fast and spontaneous diffusion of IPM technology. Palis concluded that social capital is a way to make farmer-to-farmer IPM extension more efficient as well as to facilitate cooperation, coordination and action in adopting technologies.

Social researchers continue to combine quantitative and qualitative methods for data collection and analysis but focus more on the human perceptions and behaviour that are crucial to understanding the acceptance or rejection of any technology.

Social researchers have integrated their knowledge from social science into existing frameworks to address concerns about women and gender in technology development and dissemination. Sociologists, for example, employed action research within the FSR framework (Castillo, 1986; Dey, 1985). Guidelines for applying gender analysis in the project cycle were also developed for agricultural researchers and extension workers who deal with rice-based farming systems (Paris, 1988a,b). Gender analysis is applied within the farming and livelihood system framework to characterize the social, cultural and economic circumstances of farming families in rain-fed rice environments and to meet the technology needs of women farmers (Paris *et al.*, 2000). With increasing male labour migration from rural to urban areas, women are becoming *de-facto* heads of households, which has far-reaching implications of technology design, training and extension programmes. Biological scientists are increasingly aware that they should consult women farmers at the onset of project development and include them as much as possible as collaborators in activities where they have direct influence.

Morin *et al.* (2002a) define CTBS (to control rodents) as a common property resource, and thus subject to many of the same constraints and opportunities as other common property resource systems, which allow understanding of CTBS social relations.

Enhancing capacities for social research within the national agricultural research and extension systems (NARESs). A major reason for the neglect of social concerns in technology development is the lingering problem of lack of NARES social researchers who are trained to work in an interdisciplinary manner with farmers and to conduct participatory research. Anthropologists, sociologists and other non-economist social researchers lack basic training in agriculture and have no experience in applied social research. Anthropologists and sociologists are generally associated with or based in non-agricultural universities, which are far from research stations, making logistical arrangements difficult. To solve this problem, IRRI organized several training programmes. Formal and informal training researchers and extension workers from NARES were provided with skills and tools to collect and analyse quantitative and qualitative information at each stage of the technology development and dissemination process as well as in farmer participatory research. These training courses are: (i) socioeconomic perspectives in farming systems research; (ii) gender analysis and its application in FSR; (iii) problem-based training courses for rain-fed rice environments; and (iv) qualitative and quantitative methods in agricultural research. Most SSD research is collaborative, providing on-the-job training to NARES social scientists in research methodology and augmenting their capacity to conduct social science research. NARES social scientists spend 1–2 months at a time in SSD under close supervision of its staff, analysing data from ongoing projects and writing reports. Social researchers are now more in demand to provide NARES collaborators and biological scientists with skills to conduct participatory rural appraisal (PRA) for initial problem diagnosis and technology impact assessment.

Difficulties and Constraints Facing Social Researchers

Over the years, the role and activities of IRRI's social scientists have changed with IRRI's research thrusts, paradigm shifts, organizational change and culture. Social scientists are often perceived to be the 'bearers' of bad news rather than the 'drivers' of research for technology development and diffusion, and were only called on to do impact studies. Biological scientists, particularly those working in rain-fed environments, have realized that social scientists greatly help to identify problems and assess needs until the technology is diffused, and act as the bridge between farmers and biophysical scientists, making research more relevant to farmers' needs. Yet, social researchers have faced difficulties and constraints that have affected the sustainability of non-economist social scientists within IRRI.

Maintaining social researchers' independence and objectivity in reporting results while keeping the team's credibility and harmonious relationships. When they join the project in the middle or at the end when the technologies or products are almost fixed, social researchers have difficulty independently and objectively assessing their impact. Criticizing the way the project was designed and managed by biological scientists has often led to social researchers' unpopularity or eventual departure from the team. Biological scientists expect social researchers to provide services – participatory rural appraisal (PRA), facilitate farmers' field days, organize participatory varietal selection, etc. to 'sell' or 'distill' technologies into products and to ensure that farmers adopt them. To maintain harmonious relationships with the other team members, the social researcher may be obliged to stay and please them rather than objectively assess the project, thus losing credibility.

Biological scientists' perception of social researchers' methods of data collection and analysis as non-rigorous, invalid and inconclusive. While economists traditionally do extensive household surveys using structured questionnaires for conventional economic analysis, social researchers use qualitative methods such as ethnography, rapid rural appraisal, PRA, case studies, participant observation, games, role-playing etc. which biological scientists, and sometimes also economists, perceive as non-rigorous, too micro and unable to be subjected to statistical analysis. Thus, the results are seen as invalid and inconclusive. To please the biological scientists and economists, social researchers have also begun to do household surveys. In the process, social researchers tend to lose their unique contribution and expertise: providing qualitative information and in-depth understanding of the historical, social, cultural, political and institutional perspectives, which may affect the adoption and diffusion of technologies.

Biological scientists saw participatory action research activities with women farmers, which were conducted within FSR projects, as more developmental than research, and thus did not see the use of gender analysis. Feldstein (1997) cited men's resistance as a difficulty she faced as a former programme leader of the CGIAR Gender Analysis Programme:

> However reasoned the argument for using gender analysis to improve the efficiency of research, many male scientists are still inclined to laugh, to ignore or to not listen. Often, the question, 'Will it make a difference to what I am working on?' reflects their reluctance even to read the basic texts and consider the applications to their own work.

Economists also resisted disaggregating data on labour (family, exchange and hired) by gender to make women's contributions to rice production visible (Paris, 2000). Poats (1990) explained the reasons for the difficulty in addressing gender issues within CGIAR: (i) confusion between gender analysis and affirmative action; (ii) lack of experienced social scientists who go beyond gender analysis; (iii) lack of interaction between scientists and women farmers; (iv) lack of senior scientists' involvement in gender issues; (v) the view that gender issues should be addressed by NARES and not by international agriculture research centres (IARCs); (vi) the perception that gender issues are a special project; and (vii) lack of mechanisms to implement action goals. The gender specialist confronted the resistance of male scientists by using the following strategies: (i) talking to scientists about their technology rather than about women; (ii) going to the fields and talking to male and female farmers with scientists and agricultural engineers; (iii) hands-on testing of agricultural machinery for women-specific tasks; (iv) co-authoring technical papers and presenting research findings on gender issues in male-dominated technical forums; (v) establishing allies with male scientists and mentors; and (vi) including women without excluding men. The resistance to, and scepticism about the value of, addressing gender issues in research and technology development have changed through the years due to external and internal influences on IRRI and CGIAR.

Faster rate of turnover of anthropologists than economists. Over the years, the turnover of anthropologists has been faster than that of economists. Anthropologists stayed a shorter time in IRRI than economists, except for one who has been with IRRI for nine years (Fig. 4.2). Most anthropologists joined the project when the problem had already been identified by biological scientists, or had left the project before the farmers had adopted the technologies. Thus, the anthropologists failed to see the completion of the project and make an impact on the end users. Anthropologists ought to be visibly active at all stages of the project, particularly at inception. After all, anthropologists, particularly applied anthropologists, are trained to use anthropological knowledge to solve practical problems.

Balancing the resource allocation between socioeconomic and policy research per se, *versus helping address socioeconomic issues in the Medium-term Plan projects.* IRRI's Medium-term Plan organizes research by programme and project. While the plan offers a good opportunity for social scientists and biophysical scientists to work together, its structure has advantages and disadvantages. Working with biological scientists enables social scientists to address the immediate needs of farmers in the target environment, secure financial support for projects and get technical inputs from biophysical scientists. Biological scientists come to understand the social, cultural and economic constraints that they tend to overlook in technology development. Social researchers, who are based in SSD rather than in the technical

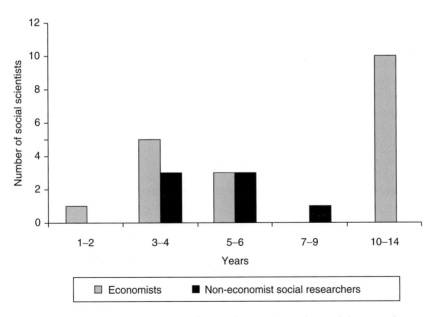

Fig. 4.2. Duration of stay of economists and non-economist social researchers at IRRI.

division where the project is based, have more independence while maintaining high-quality disciplinary research and credibility. However, social scientists may be spread too thinly, which raises the question of balancing the resource allocation between socio-economic and policy research and helping address socio-economic issues in the Medium-term Plan projects. Some agricultural economists spend more time in interdisciplinary research or providing service than doing independent research (Table 4.1).

Table 4.1. Allocation of core resources for independent social research and interdisciplinary research. (Proportion of individual scientist's time per year.)

Social scientists	Independent social research	Interdisciplinary research
Economist	0.40	0.60
Agricultural economist	0.20	0.80
Agricultural economist	0.40	0.60
Agricultural economist	0.60	0.40
Socio-economist– gender specialist	0.50	0.50

Opportunities for Social Researchers

While social researchers have faced difficulties and constraints, they also have exciting opportunities to play a key and proactive role in achieving IRRI's goals and impact positively on poor rice-farming communities.

Social researchers as the process drivers toward integration

Social researchers need to lead in facilitating integration – not just become involved in, but also drive the process. They are the 'brokers' between farmers and biological scientists to develop appropriate technologies and accelerate their spread using natural and cultural pathways of reaching rice farmers. As one biological scientist at the IRRI said,

> We biological scientists are stuck in our own domain, but social
> scientists are not. They tend to see the big picture, farmers, communities,
> societies, rituals etc. and can thus act as 'brokers' to integrate scientific

information bits and participation. At the same time, biological scientists want their work to have impact, but see it in a different perspective. Almost like emic-etic between social science and biological science. In other words, social researchers can act as the 'distillers' to accelerate the impact of technology adoption (Heong (2003), personal communication).

Biological scientists also need the help of social scientists who can simplify technologies for farmers and lead discussions with various stakeholders on community-based projects. However, this requires orienting social scientists toward an interdisciplinary team approach in solving problems as well as doing action-oriented and applied social research. As Cernea (2003) emphasizes:

> In carrying out action-oriented applied research work, sociologists and anthropologists must go outside the academic cocoon of their disciplines. They must undertake policy-oriented social inquiry and must re-structure their research work to fit operational frameworks and practical demands.

Continuing problem-oriented research management

IRRI's research structure has strengthened the interaction between biological and social scientists. IRRI's Medium-term Plan organizes research into several programmes and outputs, and social and biological scientists into teams to address a common problem in specific rice environments. Several consortia such as the Consortia for Unfavorable Rice Environments and Irrigated Rice Research Consortia require validation of technologies and promote effective delivery mechanisms to accelerate impact on the poor. Thus, demand is high for social researchers whose time allocation cuts across different programmes and outputs. Social researchers should be given a fair share in funding support to produce quality applied social research while providing service roles to problem-oriented research.

Including social research from the onset when developing research proposals

Funders' requirement that research projects have a positive social, apart from economic and environmental, impact legitimizes social researchers' inputs as well as allocation of separate funds for social issues that are often overlooked in technology-driven proposals. For example, funding agencies such as the Swiss Agency for Development and Cooperation, Department for International Development – UK, Australian Council for International Agricultural Research (ACIAR), Danish

International Development Agency, Canadian International Development-ment Agency, Asian Development Bank, International Fund for Agricul-tural Development, and others concerned with poverty reduction, as well as the CGIAR Global Challenge Programmes, require proposals to explicitly state that social (including gender) concerns be addressed in the process as well as by the impact of the research project.

The CGIAR Global Challenge Programmes have made a good start in changing the system by integrating social science research needs and by tapping the social science competence of IARCs. Pre-proposal development, review process and requirements for social impact (including gender concerns) of the programmes have enabled IRRI social researchers to help develop proposals rather than be merely 'add ons' or 'tokens'. The anthropologist and socio-economist–gender spe-cialist, apart from an economist and GIS specialist, will be involved in the research projects on water and productivity, bio fortification and genetic resources. The non-economist social scientists will address the social and cultural issues in technology development, adoption and dissemination, and facilitate participation of farmers and other stake-holders such as non-governmental organizations.

Strengthening the internal capacity of the CGIAR system to undertake social research

The CGIAR system should continue to strengthen its internal capacity to undertake social research and to make it more visible. For example, IRRI sustained its commitment to address gender issues in rice research technology and development by developing a gender strategy plan for 2001–2003 (Paris, 2001a,b) and to build capacities of NARES partners to replicate this process in their institutions.

To strengthen intellectual capital in social research at the institute level, system management should provide opportunities for social researchers to upgrade their knowledge and competence through sab-baticals, exchange programmes and write-shops. System management should also strongly encourage and reward inter-centre exchange and networking activities. System initiatives such as the Participatory Research and Gender Analysis (PRGA) have provided a vehicle to improve exchange of information, experiences and methodologies as well as highlight the value of participatory research in plant-breeding programmes among IARCs (Bellon and Reeves, 2002). However, more has to be done to revive the gender working group under the PRGA to address gender concerns in technology development, design and dis-semination within IARCs.

Conclusions

Social researchers working with interdisciplinary teams should be involved in project preparation and given the same amount of time and weight as researchers from other disciplines to make an impact on development. Bringing social researchers in only at the end of the project, to do impact studies or to sit temporarily in an agricultural research institute is window dressing and will not impact on the poor. Anthropologists and other social researchers who work in interdisciplinary research can best contribute by driving the process of integration by providing methodologies to analyse farmers' knowledge systems, which are likely to be complex, culturally specific and only partly articulated by the farmers. Their inputs are necessary to understand the social, cultural and economic environment, and its dynamics, and to use this information to identify interventions that can increase production and reduce poverty. Feedback should be elicited from men and women farmers, and the social and cultural consequences of introducing technology for food production and consumption systems identified.

The IRRI and CGIAR offer exciting opportunities for social research to make a difference. These depend on the institutions' support for social research and on social researchers articulating how they can best help IRRI reduce the poverty of millions of rice-producing and -consuming populations in Asia.

References

Bellon, M.R. and Reeves, J. (eds) (2002) *Quantitative Analysis of Data from Participatory Methods in Plant Breeding.* International Maize and Wheat Improvement Centre (CIMMYT), Mexico, 143 pp.

Bellon, M.R., Pham, J.L. and Jackson, M.T. (1997) Genetic conservation: a role of rice farmers. In: Maxted, N., Ford-Lloyd, B.V. and Hawkes, J.G. (eds) *Plant Genetic Conservation: the In Situ Approach.* Chapman & Hall, London, pp. 263–285.

Castillo, G. (1986) Filipino women in rice farming systems: some empirical evidence. In: International Rice Research Institute (IRRI), Small Farm Equipment for Developing Countries. *Proceedings of the International Conference on Small Farm Equipment for Developing Countries: Past Experiences and Future Priorities,* 2–6 September 1985. IRRI, Los Baños, Philippines, pp. 584–621.

Cernea, M. (2003) *Using Knowledge from Social Science in Development Projects.* World Bank Discussion Papers No. 114. World Bank, Washington, DC, 66 pp.

Dey, J. (1985) Proposals for women in rice farming network research. In:

IRRI, Report of the Project Design Workshop on Women in Rice Farming Systems. IRRI, Los Baños, Philippines, 143 pp.

Diaz, C.P., Hossain, M., Merca, S. and Mew, T. (1998) Seed quality and effect on rice yield: findings from farmer participatory experiments in Central Luzon, Philippines. *Philippine Journal of Crop Science* 23(2), 111–119.

Diaz, L., Hossain, M. and Paris, T. (1999) Appropriate technology for improving women's welfare: a case study of farmer participatory evaluation of a micro rice mill in Central Luzon, Philippines. *Philippine Sociological Review* 47, 68–80.

Ebron, L., Castillo, B. and Kaiser, P. (1983) Changes in harvesting–threshing arrangements and landless labourers. In: IRRI, *Proceedings of the Workshop on the Consequences of Small Farm Mechanization in the Philippines*, 1–2 December 1983. Development Academy of the Philippines, Tagaytay City, Philippines, 433 pp.

Feldstein, H. (1997) *Gender Analysis: Making Women Visible and Improving Social Analysis.* Gender Analysis Programme, Consultative Group on International Agricultural Research, Washington, DC, 13 pp.

Fujisaka, S. (1993a) A case of farmer adaptation and adoption of contour hedgerows for soil conservation. *Experimental Agriculture* 29, 27–105.

Fujisaka, S. (1993b) Were farmers wrong in rejecting a recommendation? The case of nitrogen in transplanting for irrigated rice. *Agricultural Systems* 43, 272–286.

Fujisaka, S. (1994) Bringing together rice farmers' science and formal agricultural science. Social Sciences Division (SSD), IRRI, Los Baños, Philippines (unpublished).

Godell, G.E., Kenmore, P.E., Litsinger, J.A., Bandong, J., De la Cruz, C.G. and Lumaban, M.D. (1982) Rice insect pest management technology and its transfer to small-scale farmers in the Philippines. In: IRRI, Report of an Exploratory Workshop on the Role of Anthropologists and Other Social Scientists in Interdisciplinary teams Developing Improved Food Production Technology. Sponsored by the IRRI and the Division for Global and Interregional Project United Nations Development Programme. IRRI, Los Baños, Philippines, pp. 25–41.

Heong, K.L., Escalada, M.M. and Mais, V.O. (1994) An analysis of insecticide use in rice: case studies in the Philippines and Vietnam. *International Journal of Pest Management* 40(2), 173–178.

IRRI (1982) *Report of an Exploratory Workshop on the Role of Anthropologists and Other Social Scientists in Interdisciplinary Teams Developing Improved Food Production Technology.* IRRI, Los Baños, Philippines, 101 pp.

IRRI (2000) *Medium-Term Plan 2001–2003.* IRRI, Los Baños, Philippines, 136 pp.

Juarez, F., Te, A., Duff, B., Crissman, L., Stickeny, R.E., Manaligod, H.T., Salazar, G.C. and Fernandez, C.P. (1988) The Development and Impact of Mechanical Reapers in the Philippines. Agricultural Economics Paper No. 88–23. IRRI, Los Baños, Philippines, 25 pp.

Morin, S.R., Pham, J.L., Sebastian, L.S., Abrigor, G., Erasga, D., Bello, M.R., Calibo, M. and Sanchez, P. (1998) The role of indigenous technical knowledge in on-farm conservation of rice genetic resources in the Cagayan Valley, Philippines. In: Philippine Council for Agriculture, Forestry and Natural Resources Research and Development (PCAFNRRD) *People, Earth and Culture. Readings in Indigenous Knowledge Systems on Biodiversity Management and Utilization.* Book Series No. 165/1998. PCAFNRRD, Department of Science and Technology, National Commission for Culture and the Arts, Los Baños, Philippines, pp. 137–150.

Morin, S.R., Palis, F., Chien, H.V., Chi, N.T., Magsumbol, M. and Papag, A. (2002a) A sociological perspective on community-based trap barrier system. In: Singleton, G., Hinds, L., Krebs, C. and Spratt, D. (eds) *Rats, Mice and People: Rodent Biology and Management.* Australian Council for International Agricultural Research (ACIAR), Canberra, Australia, pp. 380–388.

Morin, S., Calibo, M., Belen, M., Phan, J.L. and Palis, F. (2002b) Natural hazards and genetic diversity in rice. *Agricultural and Human Values* 19, 133–149.

Palis, F.G. (1998) Changing farmers' perceptions and practices: the case of insect pest control in Central Luzon, Philippines. *Crop Protection* 17(7), 599–607.

Palis, F.G. (2002) The impact of social capital in technology sharing and learning on integrated pest management in Central Luzon, Philippines. PhD dissertation, College of Social Sciences and Philosophy, University of the Philippines, Quezon City, Philippines, 202 pp.

Palis, F.G. and Hossain, M. (2003) Impact of integrated pest management on rice farmers: a case study in Central Luzon. Paper presented

at the annual meeting of the Society for Applied Anthropology, 19–23 March 2003, Portland, Oregon.

Palis, F.G., Pingali, P.L. and Litsinger, J.A. (1990) A multi-pest economic threshold for rice production: a case study in the Philippines. In: Teng, P. (ed.) *Crop Loss Assessment in Rice.* IRRI, Los Baños, Philippines, pp. 229–242.

Palis, F.G., Morin S., Chien, H.V., Chi, T.N. and Hossain, M. (2002) Farmer participatory research in rodent pest management. Paper presented at the First World Rice Congress, 15–20 September 2002. Bejing, People's Republic of China.

Palis, F.G., Morin S., Chien, H.V., Chi, T.N. and Hossain, M. (2003) Socio-cultural and economic assessment of community trap barrier system adoption in South Vietnam. In: Singleton, G., Hinds, L., Krebs, C. and Spratt, D. (eds) *Rats, Mice and People: Rodent Biology and Management.* ACIAR, Canberra, Australia, pp. 422–425.

Paris, T.R. (1988a) Women in a crop-livestock, farming systems project in Sta. Barbara, Pangasinan. In: Poats, S., Schmink, M. and Spring, A. (eds) *Gender Issues in Farming Systems and Extension.* West View Press Inc., Boulder, Colorado, pp. 269–286.

Paris, T.R. (1988b) A methodology for integrating women's concerns into rice-based farming systems research: an IRRI case study. Presented at the International Conference on Appropriate Agricultural Technologies for Farm Women, 30 November–4 December 1988, New Delhi.

Paris, T. (1998) Technology and policy needs of poor women in Asian rice farming. *Gender Technology and Development* 2, 187–217.

Paris, T. (2000) Bringing women from the margin to the mainstream of rice research and technology development: strategies and lessons learned. PhD dissertation, Faculty of Social Inquiry (Social Ecology), University of Western Sydney, Hawkesbury, Australia.

Paris, T.R. (2001a) *Addressing Gender Concerns in Rice Research Technology Development: Opportunities to Improve Rural Livelihood – IRRI's Gender Strategy Plan for 2001–2003.* SSD, IRRI, Los Baños, Philippines, 10 pp.

Paris, T.R. (2001b) *Gender Strategy for PETRRA-Funded Project in Bangladesh.* SSD, IRRI, Los Baños, Philippines, 29 pp.

Paris, T. and Atlin, G. (2002) Farmers and scientists – building a partnership for improving rain-fed rice in eastern India. In: Bellon, M.R. and Reeves, J. (eds) *Quantitative Analysis of Data from Participatory Methods in Plant Breeding.* CIMMYT, Mexico, 143 pp.

Paris, T. and Diaz, L. (2001) Adding value in rice production: a case study of women's participatory evaluation of rice flour mill in Central Luzon, Philippines. *Philippine Engineering Journal* 22 (1) June, 1–14.

Paris, T., Singh, A. and Hossain, M. (1996) Social consequences of stress environments. Physiology of stress tolerance in rice. In: Singh, V.P., Singh, R.K. and Zeigler, R.S. (eds) *Proceedings of the International Conference on Stress Physiology of Rice.* Lucknow, Eastern Uttar Pradesh. IRRI and Narendra Deva University of Agriculture and Technology, Faizabad, Uttar Pradesh; and IRRI, Los Baños, Philippines, pp. 207–220.

Paris, T., Singh, A., Hossain, M. and Luis, J. (2000) Using gender analysis in characterizing and understanding farm-household systems in rain-fed lowland rice environments. In: Tuong, T.P., Kam, S.P., Wade, L., Pandey, S., Bouman, B.A.M. and Hardy, B. (eds) *Proceedings of the International Workshop on Characterizing and Understanding Rain-Fed Environments,* 5–9 December 1999, Bali, Indonesia. IRRI, Los Baños, Philippines, pp. 339–370.

Paris, T., Singh A. and Luis, J. (2001a) Listening to farmers' perceptions through participatory varietal selection: a case study in villages in eastern Uttar Pradesh, India. In: CGIAR Systemwide Programme on Participatory Research and Gender Analysis for Technology Development and Institutional Innovation (PRGA Programme), *An Exchange of Experiences from South and Southeast Asia. Proceedings of the International Symposium on Participatory Plant Breeding and Participatory Plant Genetic Resource Enhancement,* Pokhara, Nepal, 1–5 May 2000. Centro Internacional de Agricultura, Cali, Colombia, pp. 179–192.

Paris, T.R., Singh, A., Luis, J., Hossain, M., Singh, H.N., Singh, S. and Singh, O.N. (2001b) Incorporating gender concerns in participatory rice breeding and varietal selection: preliminary results from eastern India. In: Lilja, N., Ashby, A. and Sperling, L. (eds) *Assessing the Impact of Participatory Research and Gender Analysis.* Participatory Research and Gender Analysis Programme,

Coordination Office, CIAT, Cali, Colombia, pp. 117–121.

Paris, T., Singh, A., Luis, J. and Hossain, M. (2005) Labour out-migration livelihood of rice farming households and women left behind: a case study in Eastern Uttar Pradesh. *Economic and Political Weekly* 70, 25.

Poats, S. (1990) Gender issues in the CGIAR system: lessons and strategies from within. Paper presented at the 1990 CGIAR Mid-Term Meeting, 21–25 May 1990. The Hague, The Netherlands, 43 pp.

Polack, A. (1985) *Does Growing Modern Varieties Expel Women from Harvesting Rice?* IRRI, Los Baños, Philippines; and Wageningen Agricultural University/KIT, Amsterdam, 13 pp.

Polack, A. and Acena, L. (1986) *Social Anthropological/ Sociological Contribution to Farmer-Oriented Agricultural Research: Outline of an Approach.* IRRI, Los Baños, Philippines; and Wageningen Agricultural University/KIT, Amsterdam, 99 pp.

Price, L.L. (1995) IPM – no early spray – farmer practice: farmer attitudes toward natural resources and exploitation on rice field flora and fauna in the Philippines. Paper presented at the workshop on Reducing Early Season Insecticide Use for Leaf Folder Control in Rice: Impact, Economics and Risks, 1995. IRRI, Los Baños, Philippines.

Price, L.L. (2001) Demystifying farmer's entomological and pest management knowledge: a methodology for assessing the impact on knowledge from IPM – FFS and NES Interventions. *Agriculture and Human Values* 18(2), 153–176.

Res, L. (1985) Changing labour allocation patterns of women in rice farm households: a rain-fed rice village in Iloilo province, Philippines. In: IRRI, *Women in Rice Farming.* Grower Publishing Co. Ltd, Aldershot, UK; and IRRI, Los Baños, Philippines, pp. 91–118.

Sackville-Hamilton, R., Appa Rao, S., Bounphanousay, C., Douangsila, K., Palis, F.G., Atlin, G. and Pandey, S. (2003) Community-based *in situ* conservation and utilization of rice genetic resources in the Lao PDR. Poster presented at the CAPRi workshop on Property Rights, Collective Action and Conservation of Local Genetic Resources, 29 September–2 October 2003, Rome.

Understanding Forests–People Links: the Voice of Social Scientists $\quad$ 5

Carol J. Pierce Colfer, Edmond Dounias, Marina Goloubinoff, Citlalli Lopéz and William Sunderlin

At the Center for International Forestry Research (CIFOR) the receptivity to and atmosphere for social scientists have been much better than in many CGIAR centres, judging from what we have heard from colleagues over the years. Anthropology, sociology and economics were intended to be part of CIFOR from its inception. Although the first director general, Jeff Sayer, was of an ecological bent, he strongly supported the centrality of social science research and the importance of interdisciplinary cooperation. Some of his earliest hires were fairly junior, most had interdisciplinary degrees and had mandates to perform social research functions. Throughout CIFOR's 10-year history, researchers have been roughly evenly divided between social and biophysical scientists, although many are a little hard to pigeonhole.

In 2002, the new director general, David Kaimowitz, and CIFOR's board of trustees decided to reorganize the institution. It is now divided into three major research areas: Environmental Services and Sustainable Use of Forests Prgramme, Forests and Livelihoods Programme, and Forests and Governance Programme. Much of the work discussed here was done under previous organizational structures.

The first two and last two sections of the chapter contain a detailed case study based on my experience. The first two sections are followed by a patchwork of views and contributions invited from social scientists working in two other programmes. William Sunderlin, another 'old-timer' and a sociologist, writes about CIFOR's Underlying Causes of Deforestation (UCD) Programme. Edmond Dounias and Citlalli Lopéz, anthropologists and more recently employed staff members, explore CIFOR's experience in the Forest Products and People (FPP) Programme (previously Nontimber Forest Products (NTFP)), supplemented by some

©CAB International 2006. *Researching the Culture in Agri-*Culture:
Social Research for International Development
(eds M.M. Cernea and A.H. Kassam)

observations by Marina Goloubinoff, a recurrent anthropological consultant in that programme. We also represent some diversity of nationality
(American, French and Mexican). In this way, we hope to convey some of
the interdisciplinary dynamics, roles of various disciplines and a work-
able approach to teamwork. However, the account below should in no way
be taken to describe fully the breadth of CIFOR's social science work.
There is other social science work under way in and from the home office
and CIFOR's philosophy of being a 'centre without walls' means that much
of our research is done with partners in the countries where we work.

Criteria and Indicators for Sustainable Forest Management

In late 1994, forest economist Neil Byron asked me to join CIFOR. As I
have a background in Indonesian ethnography (specifically East Kalimantan, where the Indonesian government had urged CIFOR to work),
he wanted me to join a new project, headed by forester Ravi Prabhu, to
test criteria and indicators (C&I) for sustainable forest management.
I was to write a concept note outlining the role of human well-being in
sustainable forest management, as a starting point from which we
could test and/or develop C&I to assess human well-being (an integral
part of sustainable forest management).

After developing the concept note (revised for Colfer and Byron
2001), I joined an interdisciplinary international team to test existing
C&I in a forest concession in East Kalimantan. The five-person core
team (two Indonesians – an anthropologist and a forester – a Malaysian
forester, a British botanist and an Australian ecologist) interacted
intensely for a month in an area where I had done considerable
research. The testing process was stimulating, difficult and involved a
great deal of sharing of perspectives among the participants, who were
trying to identify the most feasible C&I for their topics (production
forestry, ecology, social issues and policy).

Over the next few years, Prabhu and I developed an excellent working relationship, which was carried over to Côte d'Ivoire, Brazil, Austria,
Cameroon, Gabon and the USA (see Prabhu, *et al.*, 1999). Our research
allowed us to put together a series of manuals designed to help forest
managers, as well as certifiers, project managers, funding agencies, non-
governmental organizations (NGOs), etc., assess the sustainability of
management in a particular forest (see the CIFOR C&I Toolbox, consisting
of nine manuals translated into French, Indonesian, Spanish, Chinese and,
some, in Portuguese; or Prabhu *et al.*, 1996, 1998). We regard such manuals as important 'methodologies for social action', the concept proposed
by Cernea (1987) to define one of the distinct 'types of social research

products' generated by CGIAR anthropologists as 'public goods'. Our efforts to develop such manuals for (social) knowledge-based action in forestry clearly contain some of the components called for by Cernea. These manuals respond to the need for social science applied methodologies and guidelines for action, dealing with institutional and socio-cultural issues ('software'), to complement the more usual focus on development 'hardware'. We continue the production of such methodologies, in various forms, as and when our research projects reach the point of articulating recommendations for social action and policies.

Several other research efforts spun off this initial effort. Funds were secured and personnel hired to look at C&I for community-based forest management following a format similar to that of the original research. Field tests by international and interdisciplinary three-person teams were undertaken in Brazil, Cameroon and Indonesia (Burford de Oliveira, 1999; Burford de Oliveira *et al.*, 2000; Ritchie *et al.*, 2000). Field tests were conducted in India and Indonesia to develop C&I for plantation forestry (Muhtaman *et al.*, 2000; Sankar *et al.*, 2000). Another body of research developed a computer program, Criteria and Indicators Modification and Adaptation Tool (CIMAT), to allow users to adapt the C&I sets to their own environment (Purnomo *et al.*, 2000). All these efforts addressed biophysical and social issues.

While research was under way, we realized that the social C&I we designed were too vague and difficult to assess. We examined in more detail two of the three social principles, which in a hierarchical framework, are above the levels of criteria, indicators and verifiers: (i) maintenance or enhancement of intergenerational access to natural resources; and (ii) acknowledged rights and means to manage forests in a cooperative and sustainable manner. We did not have the time or money to address the third principle – maintenance or improvement of human, cultural and forest health – which we expect to do soon. This process involved collaboration with social scientists – local and international – in Brazil, Cameroon and Indonesia, and resulted in several manuals of the C&I Toolbox (Colfer *et al.*, 1999a–c; Salim *et al.*, 1999), as well as more academic treatment in Colfer and Byron (2001).

Local People, Devolution and Adaptive Collaborative Management of Forests

In 1997 and 1998, as the last of these efforts was drawing to a close, Prabhu and I were troubled to realize that even if C&I were perfected (and we were already convinced that any C&I would have to be adapted to local conditions), forest conditions or human well-being would not improve unless conditions specified in the C&I were obtained in the real world. After reading *Compass and Gyroscope*

(Lee, 1993), we first considered adaptive management, and then 'adaptive co-management'. At the same time and unknown to us, Eva Wollenberg and Louise Buck, an anthropologically oriented natural resources management specialist and a sociologist in another CIFOR programme, were struck by the adaptability of the populations they were working with and began thinking along similar lines.

By the spring of 1998, at the suggestion of CIFOR's board of trustees and with our concurrence, we decided to put our thoughts together into one programme: Local People, Devolution and Adaptive Collaborative Management (ACM) of Forests. I led the development of this programme, which involved a great deal of collaborative writing. We discussed what we wanted to do; I wrote a draft; we circulated it; team members, administrators and external colleagues critiqued it; and I wrote again. We went through no less than 17 rounds of this process, finally coming up with a statement of what we wanted to do. We were concerned about empowerment, as the people living in tropical forests had little control over the resources that had been theirs and little say over what was done with them. We were convinced that forests and cultures were complex, adaptive systems, meaning that surprise was inevitable and prediction impossible. We were also convinced of the capacity of rural peoples to act on their own behalf and on behalf of their children's future and the environment.

> CIFOR defines adaptive collaborative management as a value-adding approach whereby people who have 'interests' in a forest agree to act together to plan, observe and learn from the implementation of their plans (recognizing that plans often fail to fulfill their stated objectives). ACM is characterized by conscious efforts among such groups to communicate, collaborate, negotiate and seek out opportunities to learn collectively about the impacts of their actions.[1]

We were trying to catalyze processes of social learning and collaboration that would empower communities and allow them to adapt better to the rapidly changing circumstances they were facing.

Since 1999 we have had research under way at 30 sites in 10 countries (Bolivia, Brazil, Cameroon, Ghana, Indonesia, Kyrgyzstan, Malawi, Nepal, Philippines and Zimbabwe), working closely with partners from government, NGOs and research and academic institutions. Researchers have brought together knowledge from diverse disciplines and levels of expertise.

Our efforts focused on three dimensions. The first was a horizontal one, emphasizing local interaction and collaboration among the important stakeholders. We reasoned that the different management systems that characterize particularly tropical forest contexts suggested a need for coordination and management that recognized the diverse uses of forests. Considerable effort was put into getting different groups within communities and between communities and other stakeholders to understand each other's perspectives and ideally, to work together. We developed a number of tools for this process. We used the social science methods suggested in the CIFOR C&I Toolbox, and the C&I themselves to improve communication (Tiani *et al.*, 2002). We developed a manual on future scenarios, which is now widely used and translated into Spanish and Indonesian (Wollenberg *et al.*, 2000).

The second dimension was a vertical one, strengthening the links between community members and other actors on a broader scale (e.g. with government, timber companies, conservation groups) as in the long run, communities would need the support of government and other powerful stakeholders if success was to be sustainable. We did formal studies on topics such as policy contexts (e.g. Colfer and Resosudarmo, 2002; Sarin *et al.*, 2003), pluralism in forest management (Wollenberg *et al.*, 2001) and the creation of political space (Contreras, 2003). We found funding to train local communities in 'legal literacy' in East Kalimantan, where decentralization was under way (CIFOR, 2000). We organized multi-stakeholder workshops of various kinds in Indonesia (Hakim, 2002); Cameroon (Diaw and Kusumanto, 2005) and Bolivia (Cronkleton, 2005). We arranged Training for Transformation in Zimbabwe (Nyirenda *et al.*, 2001) to strengthen local groups' self-confidence.

The third dimension was a diachronic one. We were convinced that effective management of complex systems, where surprise is frequent and prediction difficult, requires effective feedback mechanisms. Some mechanism was needed to allow community groups to recognize when their plans were going astray. An early study of the topic was done (Anderson, 2001). Our initial plan was to use adapted C&I as monitoring tools, and that was effective in some locations (McDougall *et al.*, 2002 for Nepal; Hartanto *et al.*, 2002a,b for the Philippines; Pokorny *et al.*, 2001 in Parà, Brazil; and Kamoto, 2002 in Malawi). In other areas, a more open-ended, qualitative approach to social learning was preferred (Yuliani *et al.*, 2002 for Indonesia; Mutimukuru *et al.*, 2005 in Zimbabwe; Cunha dos Santos, 2002 for Acre; Cronkleton, 2005 in Bolivia).

From the beginning, with our emphasis on empowerment, we were concerned about equity in forest management. We wanted to catalyse a process that would involve relevant forest users and other stakeholders in a cooperative way that would result in benign collective action. Although we specified no standardized method for dealing with equity, its pertinence was reiterated routinely and many researchers opted to address it directly (see *The Equitable Forest: Diversity, Commumity and Resource Management* (Colfer 2005), with 14 contributions).

At the beginning, we identified a series of issues that we anticipated might affect the conduct of ACM: devolution status, management type, forest type, population pressure, human diversity, level of conflict and level of social capital. We used these dimensions to select field sites along the various continua or types. CIFOR exerted considerable pressure on us to complement our planned participatory action research with a more conventional, positivist approach, which we did.

We also developed a series of broad research steps for use by ACM facilitators of whatever discipline (a 'social methodology' in terms of Cernea, 1987), with a strong emphasis on eliciting local definition of goals. These steps began with a series of context studies on policy, stakeholder identification, historical trends, degree of collaboration and adaptability and biophysical and social contexts using C&I. The researchers began participatory action research once they felt they had: (i) gained sufficient understanding of the local context; and (ii) established sufficient rapport with community members. This was the heart and soul of ACM, involving collaborative and cyclical problem identification, planning, implementation, monitoring and reflection. To the degree that we have been able to keep the funds flowing, this process has continued.

We have begun assessing this process. The most systematic assessment has been an attempt to examine the issues listed above (devolution status, management type, etc.) in combination with impacts on the 30 sites (Colfer, forthcoming). But a number of other regional analyses are in the offing (e.g. by Chimere Diaw, Ravi Prabhu, Frank Matose, Robert Fisher and others).

A number of manuals have also come out, building on these experiences (e.g. Hartanto *et al.*, 2003; Sithole, 2002; Nemarundwe *et al.*, 2003); as well as software such as CO-VIEW (Haggith *et al.*, 2002) and CO-LEARN.

We have struggled with how best to capture the impacts of this kind of approach, which is so responsive to local conditions and thus so different from place to place. Increased confidence and negotiation skills among community members have been common outcomes. In a number of sites, women and/or minority groups have become more involved in local decision making. More interaction between community members and stakeholders operating on a wider scale has meant greater understanding within district governments, conservation projects and timber company offices, of local priorities and concerns. In some countries such as Nepal, the Philippines and Cameroon, the national governments are interested in our results, so that the potential to extrapolate the process to other locales is significant. In other countries such as Indonesia and Zimbabwe, where the political system is in disarray, interest is greater at the district level where we work. In Pasir, East Kalimantan, for instance, workshops involving various stakeholders resulted in agreements about priorities for forest management, although we cannot yet say whether these will result in concrete action. Experimentation has been significant with various mechanisms for social learning such as C&I monitoring, routine reflection meetings to assess plans and learn from failures and successes and study trips. The acquisition of related skills reflects capacity building that should lead to greater empowerment and more rational forest management (and improved human well-being). But the process has only been under way for about 2 years. We anticipated that we would need longer than that to assess our results, and we still believe that to be the case.

The projects described above reflect only one part of CIFOR's social science. The next two sections focus on two other CIFOR programmes that have had significant social science input: UCD and FPP. The programme described briefly below by Sunderlin focuses on policy issues, with a nearly exclusive socioeconomic orientation (led over the years by various individuals, including Neil Byron, David Kaimowitz, Ida Aju Pradnja Resosudarmo, Sunderlin and Sven Wunder). Although this programme has been more oriented toward economic issues than ACM, still there was consistent and serious attention to social concerns and clearly, there was and is cooperation between sociologists and economists.

FPP's central orientation has been on economic and to a lesser extent, ecological concerns. But they too have included a considerable amount of social science. Edmond Dounias and Citlalli López provide a recent perspective on this programme. We do not tackle here the lesser but still significant attention paid to social issues in CIFOR programmes addressing biophysical issues (plantations, biodiversity and sustainable forest management). My own work on C&I, for instance, was under the programme on sustainable forest management.

CIFOR's internal organization has also changed over the last couple of years, and there are now three larger programmes: livelihoods, governance and environmental services. I confess to some malaise about the apparent shift from a 50–50 balance to what looks like a 66–33 balance, a malaise shared by some of our colleagues. Several foresters and ecologists have left, and jokes about marginalization of biophysical scientists are not uncommon. Some biophysical scientists have expressed feelings of vulnerability, with some hard evidence to support their concerns. The fact that none of the four non-social scientists I invited to contribute to this chapter wanted to do so may reflect such feelings. I think it would be a shame if we repaid our biophysical colleagues' open-mindedness with the kind of marginalization experienced by social scientists in many Global Change centres. What the ultimate effects of the recent organizational changes will be on interdisciplinary collaboration and openness to scientific diversity, however, remain to be seen.

Underlying Causes of Deforestation Programme

William Sunderlin

CIFOR's UCD programme, which existed in various incarnations since CIFOR's founding in 1994 through early 2002,[2] merits attention because it was comprised almost entirely of social scientists and economists. UCD developed an approach to understanding forest problems that reflected its strong social science orientation and made an imprint on the overall *modus operandi* of CIFOR as an institution. In 1994, UCD coined the term 'extra-sectoral influences' (ESI) to describe the belief that the causes of deforestation and forest degradation lie mainly *outside* the forestry sector and not mainly within the sector itself. Specifically, this philosophy underscores the point of view that we must give much more attention to society-wide and macro-level processes (such as economic growth, exchange rates, indebtedness, population growth and migration, resettlement programmes, infrastructure development, economic crisis, structural adjustment programmes and currency devaluations) to understand the disappearance of forests and the consequences of forest cover change for people's well-being in forest communities. Implicit in the ESI perspective is a critique of placing too much importance on forest policies to solve forest problems. Why tinker with stumpage rates and the length of concession contracts, the reasoning goes, if such policy measures stand little chance of making a significant difference against overwhelming forces lying outside the reach of forest policy?

UCD took an international comparative approach and focused its attention on country case studies in Latin America (Bolivia), Africa (Cameroon) and Asia (Indonesia). The programme also devoted considerable attention to the Miombo woodlands of southern Africa and Central America. The key cross-country comparative topics were the following:

- analysis of the causes of deforestation and degradation,
- impact of structural adjustment programmes,
- effects of economic crisis (Cameroon and Indonesia),
- population and migration,
- effects of decentralization on forests,
- political economy of the formulation of forestry laws,
- role of traditional forestry policies and
- impact of infrastructure and roads.

UCD also produced global background and thematic studies on the underlying causes of deforestation, macroeconomic Dutch disease and the effects of oil and mineral extraction and the effects of technological change in agriculture on forests.

UCD's achievements include a strong publication record internationally and in case-study countries. Among UCD's more notable publications for international dissemination were those giving attention to economic models of deforestation (Kaimowitz and Angelsen, 1998); oil wealth, Dutch disease and forest cover change (Wunder, 2003); effects of technological change in agriculture (Angelsen and Kaimowitz, 2001); the fate of people in tropical forests (Byron and Arnold, 1999); forestry research capacity (Kowero and Spilsbury, 1997); municipal laws and forests in Bolivia (Pacheco and Kaimowitz, 1998); macroeconomic causes of deforestation in Cameroon (Ndoye and Kaimowitz, 2000); integration of social science and satellite imagery to specify the causes of deforestation in Cameroon (Mertens *et al.*, 2000); effects of economic crisis on forest cover change in Indonesia (Sunderlin *et al.*, 2001); effects of corporate debt in Indonesia (Barr *et al.*, 2002); and forestry laws in Indonesia (Resosudarmo, 2002). UCD has also had a strong emphasis on policy dialogue and media outreach, which has produced especially good results in Indonesia (e.g. Setiono and Barr, 2003).

UCD was the home base of Polex, an influential international listserve with 10,000 subscribers, which continues to thrive at CIFOR. UCD had a detectable influence on the international community, for example, helping shape the World Bank's recent outlook and policies on forests. UCD had an overall positive but uneven record in research capacity building.

Two consequences of UCD's disciplinary make-up are noteworthy. First, UCD's strong social science and economics orientation, while entirely logical given its ESI philosophy, did not always favour collaboration with researchers at CIFOR in the biophysical sciences, and this may have had negative consequences.[3] Given the privileged attention to social science and economics at CIFOR, and given also the strong grip of ESI thinking on the institutional character of CIFOR, some foresters and other biophysical scientists in the organization felt they were out of favour and looked down upon. This dynamic took on considerable significance when David Kaimowitz, former leader of UCD, became director general of CIFOR in August 2001. Differences of outlook between Kaimowitz and Kenneth MacDicken, a forester by training and director of research at CIFOR from 1999 to 2002, led to overt friction and MacDicken's resignation. Kaimowitz has stated that his ascent to the position of director general should in no way be interpreted as a threat to foresters and other biophysical scientists at CIFOR. He strongly affirmed the relevance of the biophysical sciences at CIFOR and called for greater collaboration among researchers in various disciplines. As of this writing, past tensions appear to have decreased markedly.

Second, it is important to note that the collaboration within UCD among social scientists was not only friction-free but also showed a degree of unconscious hybridization between social science and economic approaches. As a sociologist working in UCD, I found that over time I gave much more attention to economic themes than my training prepared me for. I have published in economics journals but not in sociological journals. Conversely, the economists in UCD (Byron, Kaimowitz, Kowero, Ndoye and Wunder) have steered clear of traditional quantitative economics and instead have leaned toward a qualitative approach. These theoretical and methodological preferences are in part a reflection of the extremely poor quality of worldwide data on forest cover change for purposes of quantitative analysis.

Forest Products and People
(previously Nontimber Forest Products)

Edmond Dounias and Citlalli López

Another programme, initially on NTFP, focused on the entire process from growth of plants, through harvesting, processing and sale at various levels. That programme was initially led by ecologist Manuel Ruiz-Pérez, and then by natural resource economist Brian Belcher. Although economic analyses were perhaps more central than social ones, the programme paid considerable attention to social issues.

Its concern about social issues is reflected in the social topics that many non-social scientists addressed. Belcher, an economist, wrote, for instance, about cultural considerations in oil palm, rubber and rattan cultivation (Belcher *et al.*, 2004); Ruiz-Pérez, an ecologist and Ndoye, an economist, wrote about African women traders (Ruiz-Pérez *et al.*, unpublished). De Jong, a forester by training, examined local people's management of the production and use of honey in Kalimantan (de Jong, 2000). Shanley, an ecologist, is proposing work on the impacts of logging on women (CIFOR, 2003).

This programme, aware of the shortage of social scientists, also drew on other programmes. Eva Wollenberg produced a collection on forest incomes, drawing on the work of many researchers from the NTFP programme (Wollenberg and Ingles, 1998). The group also contracted work out to others with more social science skills (e.g. Campbell *et al.*, 2001).

Recently, López, an anthropologist, has tried to 'translate' the results of the large multi-country comparative study of NTFPs that formed the core of the FPP Programme, from the rather dry, economic orientation into more user-friendly and culturally relevant language. The objective of this multiyear comparison project, led by Belcher and Ruiz-Pérez, has been to analyse the effects of commercialization of NTFPs on development and forest conservation. One of the objectives is to extract key lessons learned and set out recommendations for project- and policy-level interventions. Sixty-one research collaborators from Africa, Asia and Latin America with different backgrounds (ecologists, foresters, agronomists and anthropologists) have been involved in this analysis.

During recent regional meetings, the collaborators in this project discussed the use and impact of traditional research products such as statistical analyses, technical surveys and research reports, which are normally more oriented to the scientific community and donors than to communities and the public in general. Some collaborators (mainly ecologists and economists) emphasized the limited impact through usual research products; others (mainly collaborators experienced in and concerned about alternative uses of research information) stressed the importance of giving back information to communities and the

general public. Within CIFOR the commitment to reaching a larger
audience beyond scientists has strengthened over time, based on the
experience and work of Patricia Shanley (see e.g. Shanley *et al.*, 1998)
on tree resources in the Brazilian Amazon for rural peoples; or Shanley and Gaia, 2002; Shanley and Laird, 2001), and reinforced by
forester Michael Spilsbury's impact analyses.

After considerable discussion, the collaborators in the comparative
NTFP cases decided that their information provided an excellent basis
for a popular publication to improve public knowledge about forests'
commercial as well as cultural benefits (often overlooked in economic
surveys and ignored by consumers). In response to these inputs, the
coordinators of the case comparison project supported the preparation of
three region-specific volumes (Asia, Africa, Latin America). These were
published in 2004, in English, with the hope that Portuguese, Spanish
and other languages can be added (López and Shanley, 2004a–c).

Starting in 1996, however, a team of French anthropologists from
the French Research Institute for Development (formerly Institut
Français de Recherche Scientifique pour le Développement en
Coopération (ORSTOM)) has been developing a partnership with the
FPP Programme. This team focuses on the changing perceptions, uses
and values of the forest among forest people in Sumatra and East
Kalimantan. The team also tries to assess how local economic growth
and regional autonomy, which have negative ecological and social
consequences but also offer new economic opportunities, may affect
the availability and accessibility of forest resources.

Anthropologists Esther Katz and Marina Goloubinoff looked at
benzoin management, use and marketing in Sumatra and Java (e.g.
Michon *et al.*, 1997; Goloubinoff, 1998; Katz, 1998), and at other non-
wood forest products in Kalimantan (Katz, 1997). These studies were
often done in collaboration with biophysical scientists (Katz *et al.*,
2002; García-Fernández *et al.*, 2003; García-Fernández, 2001). Katz also
maintained her interest in Central Africa (Katz and Nguinguiri, 1999).

With the help of the Yayasan Adat Punan (Punan Customary Association), ethnoagronomist Patrice Levang undertook a systematic census of all the Punan communities of Kalimantan (a hunter-gatherer
group). His surveys of 254 households reveal that the contribution of
agriculture to household income appears very similar, regardless of
type of economy and settlement. He thus contradicts the general belief
among economists that forest products serve as a safety net, arguing
instead that from the most accessible to the remotest settlements, agriculture is, in fact, the safety net (Levang *et al.*, 2003).

Agni Klintuni Boedhihartono recently finished a doctorate in
visual anthropology at the University of Paris 7. As a member of this
team, she studied the complex interactions between traditional healing
and modern medicine among different Dayak and Punan communities

of the Bulungan research forest (Boedhihartono, 2004). Nicolas Cesard, another French graduate student in anthropology, studied the changing contribution of forest products to interethnic relationships, and focused on the decreasing contribution of NTFPs to bride-wealth payments and compensations.

Ethnoecologist Edmond Dounias, who also has extensive experience in Central Africa (Dounias, 2000), arrived at CIFOR in 2001, and began studying mobility among the Punan of the Tubu River (Dounias and Loutrel, 2002; Dounias and Leclerc, forthcoming). Even though these Punan have now all become swidden agriculturalists living in permanent villages, they have still preserved their high mobility. It is a major characteristic of hunting and gathering societies, motivated not only by the search for NTFPs for subsistence and trade but also driven by social reasons (visits to relatives, kinship obligations, intermarriage alliances, etc). The extent of the interactions in space and time between the Punan and their biological and social environments have become a crucial issue, as the Tubu River seems likely to become the scene of severe conflicts of interest between a growing number of stakeholders in the coming years.

Since early 2003, Dounias has oriented his research toward the anthropology of food and is analysing the interactions between the Punan diet and health status. One of his study's key objectives is to assess the contribution of NTFPs to the food and health integrity of the Punan, and to determine to what extent differences in access and use of NTFPs can explain the gap in health conditions between remote and peri-urban settlements.

The research rests on a quantitative approach that was proven efficient with Cameroonian forest populations (see CD-ROM devoted to research in Cameroon, Dounias, 2003). The Kalimantan research consists of analysing Punan food behaviour from several interacting perspectives:

- social: relationships among food consumers via food-sharing rules, meal distribution and festive, ritual, ostentatious and curative dishes;
- cultural: habits, perceptions and representations concerning medicinal and food resources;
- ethno-ecological: knowledge, know-how and access modalities concerning the spatial and seasonal availability of resources; and
- anthro-biological: nutritional value of food and the influence of diet on physiological and epidemiological status.

By comparing the diet and health situations of the Punan in two contrasted social and ecological environments (remote villages versus recent settlements close to Malinau town) and with reference to their recent past as nomadic hunter-gatherers, Dounias questions the health consequences of development. In the process of adaptation, every population develops defenses against the predators, parasites and pathogens in its environment. However, social change such as settling near a city may not necessarily have positive effects on people's well-being. Social change may even sometimes destroy or invalidate defense mechanisms or present new challenges for which there are no defenses, thus precipitating an increase in disease and adding to the population's adaptation load. Social change – as generally observed among hunter-gatherers when they shift from nomadic life to settling in permanent villages – may also threaten nutritional status in various indirect ways (Dounias, 2003).

From time to time, some social scientists within this programme have felt marginalized, particularly those focusing on the qualitative and symbolic aspects of NTFP use (see Box 5.1). The programme tended to emphasize quantitative analyses and economic interpretations, with qualitative social scientists having to defend their approaches repeatedly. However, this feeling of marginalization was moderated by the insertion of a number of French anthropologists with public funding from the French Ministry of Research. They were thus in a more 'independent' financial position to pursue their methodological preferences to analyse cultural factors that are so difficult to quantify (Dounias *et al.*, 2004).

Box 5.1. Anthropologists or Rural Economists?

Marina Goloubinoff

There is a fundamental misperception among many at CIFOR about sociology and anthropology. Some people tend to see us as rural or forest economists and expect us to act accordingly. For sure we can generally make some basic calculations about income, profitability and such things. However, we often use these data only as a 'background', not as our main focus. Of course, we may use some tools such as questionnaires when we have to systematically collect specific data that can fit in matrices and lists. This is also convenient when we have to interview many people in a short time. But most of us do not consider questionnaires (even the best) as a privileged way of communicating with and understanding people.

Anthropological research relies on much more than that. It includes all kinds of observations we make – on surroundings; perceptions of relationships among people; the environment; practices (techniques, rituals, social life); symbolic speech and non-verbal communication and links.

In short, we listen to people, we observe what they do, and we try to understand what they think and what they feel. This is a long process and the reason why anthropologists want to spend a long time in the field, which is discouraged for CIFOR scientists.

Socioeconomic data alone gives a flat picture of a multidimensional structure. We can feel, somehow 'misused', and 'real' rural economists

Box 5.1. (contd)

would probably do a much better job since they have their own knowledge and tools, which are much more suitable for the kind of data expected.

The trouble is that we are often not very good at explaining what we are, what we do and how we do it to other disciplines. We look with annoyance or pity at those who 'blindly' believe in numbers (magical thinking, according to the anthropological literature), while others do not take seriously our 'qualitative' data (anything qualitative is considered bad!).

CIFOR has promoted a multidisciplinary approach from the beginning. As sociologists and anthropologists, we have made a big effort trying to integrate tools from other disciplines into our work. We have also tried to find a common language by integrating more numbers, figures and tables into our products. This has resulted in recognition and respect for some individual social scientists. However, even they acknowledge that they had sometimes to censor themselves, avoiding words or topics such as 'symbol', 'representation' and so on. Anthropological and sociological research has also often taken a more economic approach. This is not necessarily bad, but it is maybe the right moment for anthropologists to face a new challenge: to try to bring out what they left behind (or unsaid) from their own unique potential contributions and find ways to share it with colleagues from other disciplines and thus enrich debates and open new perspectives.

Organizational Aspects

CIFOR has reorganized fairly regularly. Programmes have changed size, leaders were given different names, office locations were rearranged, but I'm not sure that has made much difference in our ability either to do our work or to collaborate with one another.

However, several things have made a difference – at the institutional level.

- There has been strong and consistent support from the top for social science and interdisciplinary efforts. The board of trustees and both directors general believed strongly that forest problems were closely linked to socioeconomic and policy issues and were adamant that these should be addressed as a central part of our mandate. Hiring patterns have been consistent with this interest (roughly half social scientists and half biophysical scientists).[4] CIFOR boards have consistently been interdisciplinary, always including professional anthropologists and sociologists as well as foresters and environmental scientists.
- An effort has been made to keep CIFOR's structure comparatively flat, a pattern we understand is not so common in other CGIAR centres. Scientists were welcome to communicate with administrators at all levels at any time, within reason,[5] and forums were created to

allow for in-depth discussion of serious issues (periodic meetings, retreats, even performance appraisals).
- Scientists and programmes were carefully put in a position of not competing with one another. An atmosphere of cooperation, of working toward common goals, was explicitly encouraged. When programme leaders met with administrators to discuss budgetary issues, for instance, it was not uncommon for one programme leader to volunteer to share resources with another programme that was considered underfunded or that encountered an unexpected problem.[6]
- Scientists were granted considerable freedom to pursue topics of interest. Small interest groups on 'hot topics' were encouraged. One such spontaneous group developed into Forest Land-Oriented Resource Envisioning System (FLORES) (Haggith *et al.*, 2003; Prabhu *et al.*, 2003; Vanclay *et al.*, 2003), a series of systems analyses of forest ecosystems, including significant social components. Some hot topics cooled down and died out, but there was an explicit attempt to keep the staff intellectually alive and to share perspectives through periodic facilitated retreats, routine lecture series, drop-in visits by the director general and so on.
- Interdisciplinary groups spent time in the field together, which allowed each to see the skills and knowledge of the other and to better understand how the other's knowledge pertained to real-world problems.

The first three people involved in ACM were Prabhu (a forester), Wollenberg (a natural resources management specialist, with strong anthropological leanings) and me (an anthropologist). We were merging two existing projects, which included people with training in political science, ecology, economics, geography, sociology and philosophy.

Once we decided what we wanted to do, we organized several retreats and training exercises together to fill in gaps in our knowledge (on participatory action research, teamwork, decision support systems plus planning meetings). We made ample use of the facilitation and group dynamics skills within the team and occasionally brought in outside facilitators.

One area where we needed routine facilitation was the tendency for some of us to dominate in group discussion at the expense of the Indonesian staff. A successful technique was the use of a talking stick: one could only talk when one had the stick. In this way, quiet team members could be encouraged to speak and verbose ones could be gently (and humourously) reminded to share the floor.

We were self-conscious in our efforts to ensure good teamwork. We began with a desire to succeed at interdisciplinary collaboration, and had some idea of how difficult it could be. Part of our definition of success included the degree to which we managed to work together effectively. We also explicitly recognized and tried to build on the strengths represented by our diversity, which included differences in ethnicity, nationality, gender, religion, race and discipline. All of this took some effort: group discussion of how to make it work, one-on-one discussion when problems arose, facilitated retreats addressing issues and increasing our skills, use of Myers-Briggs and other team self-assessment instruments and so on.

We also instituted a very flat administrative structure. Although I was programme leader, our official and shared view was that each team member was as important as any other. We needed drivers as much as we needed administrators. Each individual had a part to play, a significant potential input to the overall process, and we felt that we were trying to do something difficult. We needed everyone's wholehearted involvement. If we did not have it, we needed to figure out why and what we could do to obtain it.

Professionally, we also took some care. We did a lot of exchanging of draft manuscripts and getting inputs from other team members, but we tried to make our critiques gently, with concern for the authors' feelings. This did not mean whitewashing a bad job but simply thinking a little before writing and phrasing our critiques with care. We reminded each other that different scientific fields have different traditions of scholarship, different understandings of 'data', different meanings for words. We knew we had to take care also in trying to communicate verbally with each other.

We also made an explicit, written policy on authorship. I drafted one that made sense to me and circulated it for the team's comments. In the end, we accepted it as our policy. Team members felt much freer to share their ideas and their drafts because they knew the philosophy. Most fundamentally, our policy recognized 'sweat equity' (the one who did the most work was the primary author) and 'the more the merrier' (we explicitly approved of joint authorship).

Although we only recently learned of 'the Matthew Effect', we were trying to counter this tendency for the 'famous to get famouser',[7] and the unknown to remain so (Merton, 1968). Merton also noted some self-fulfilling prophecy elements of relevance to CGIAR research teams (note additions in brackets):

> Judged ordinary by comparison with their precocious 'age-peers' (or in the CGIAR system, 'International Research Staff'), they are treated as youth (researchers) of small capacity. They slip through the net of our institutional sieves for the location of ability, since this is a net that makes chronological age (or national origin) the basis for assessing relative ability. Treated by the institutional system as mediocrities with little promise of improvement, many of these potential late bloomers (or 'National Research Staff') presumably come to believe it of themselves and act accordingly. At

least what little we know of the formation of self-images suggests that this is so...our self-image – our image of potentiality and of achievement – is a reflection of the images others make plain they have of us.

(Merton, 1962, quoted in Merton, 1988)

Returning to our team strategy in ACM, perhaps most importantly, we became friends with each other. Viewing your colleagues as whole people – who need time off, enjoy having fun, have bad days, need and can provide help – makes the process of interdisciplinary communication more of a joy than a pain.

In Sum

In this short piece, we have used a historical case study approach by describing my experience from the beginning to the present. We have supplemented my experience with that of four other CIFOR social scientists to lend breadth to the description. We have tried to convey some sense of the kinds of research social scientists do at CIFOR. We have considered how the institution has contributed to effective interdisciplinary collaboration and acceptance of social science research efforts and analysed the elements of one programme that seemed to contribute to our own success at working together. Our hope is that our largely positive experience can serve as a model for other centres where interdisciplinary collaboration may be more stressful.

Notes

[1]This definition was initially crafted by Prabhu *et al.* (2001), and modified by the team in conjunction with a meeting of the programme's International Steering Committee, in Manila, Philippines, October 2001.

[2]The full name of the programme was Causes of Deforestation, Forest Degradation and Changes in Human Welfare. Its early manifestation was as the 'extra-sectoral influences' project in CIFOR's Policy and Social Sciences Division (1994–1995) before being a full-fledged programme at CIFOR in 1996–2001. In October 2001, UCD became CIFOR's Forests, Society and People (FSP) Programme. It lasted until late 2002, when a major reorganization at CIFOR brought to a close, formal attention to the causes of deforestation in CIFOR's research portfolio.

[3]In spite of a tendency of social sciences and economics to be insular, there were several instances of productive collaboration with researchers in the biophysical sciences.

[4]As mentioned above, I see some worrying signs that this healthy balance may be in danger, with the apparent hegemony of economics and macro-level policy research at this time. Only time will tell.

[5]This freedom was technically available to everyone, but international scientists felt much freer to avail themselves of this opportunity than did national staff. This was partly related to Indonesian ideas about appropriate behaviour with bosses.

[6]This was probably more feasible than in some centres because of a fairly generous supply of funds until recently.

[7]Provided in more stately fashion from the biblical Matthew himself (quoted in Merton, 1988): 'For unto everyone that hath shall be given, and he shall have abundance; but from him that hath not shall be taken away even that which he hath'.

References

Anderson, J. (2001) On the edge of chaos – crafting adaptive collaborative management for biological diversity conservation in a pluralistic world. In: Buck, L., Geisler, C.C., Schelhas, J. and Wollenberg, E.W. (eds) *Biological Diversity: Balancing Interests through Adaptive Collaborative Management*. CRC Press, Boca Raton, Florida, pp. 171–185.

Angelsen, A. and Kaimowitz, D. (eds) (2001) *Agricultural Technologies and Tropical Deforestation*. CAB International, Wallingford, UK, 422 pp.

Barr, C., Brown, D., Casson, A. and Kaimowitz, D. (2002) Corporate debt and the Indonesian forestry sector. In: Colfer, C.J.P. and Resosudarmo, I.A.P. (eds) *Which Way Forward? People, Forests, and Policymaking in Indonesia*. Resources for the Future, Centre for International Forestry Research, and Institute for South East Asian Studies, Washington, DC, pp. 277–292.

Belcher, B., Rujehan, N.I. and Achdiawan, R. (2004) Rattan, rubber or oil palm: cultural and financial considerations for farmers in Kalimantan. *Economic Botany* 58(Suppl.), 577–587.

Boedhihartono, A.K. (2004) Dilema à Malinau, Bornéo: Être ou ne pas être un chasseur-cueilleur Punan. Évolution et transformation d'une communauté de chasseurs-cueilleurs. Thesis, Université Paris 7, Paris, 252 pp.

Burford de Oliveira, N. (1999) *Community Participation in Developing and Applying Criteria and Indicators of Sustainable and Equitable Forest Management*. CIFOR, Bogor, Indonesia, 37 pp.

Burford de Oliveira, N., McDougall, C., Ritchie, B., Hartanto, H. and Setyawati, T. (2000) *Developing Criteria and Indicators for Community Managed Forests as Assessment and Learning Tools: Objectives, Methodologies, Results*. CIFOR, Bogor, Indonesia, 303 pp.

Byron, R.N. and Arnold, M. (1999) What futures for the people of the tropical forests? *World Development* 27, 789–805.

Campbell, B., Mandondo, A., Nemarundwe, N., Sithole, B., de Jong, W., Luckert, M. and Matose, F. (2001) Challenges to proponents of common property resource system: despairing voices from the social forests of Zimbabwe. *World Development* 29(4), 589–600.

Cernea, M.M. (1987) The 'production' of a social methodology. In: Eddy, E.M. and Partridge, W.L. (eds) *Applied Anthropology in America*. Columbia University Press, New York, pp. 237–262.

CIFOR (2000) Responsive policy research and development for sustainable and equitable forest system management. Proposal to Ford Foundation, Jakarta, Indonesia.

CIFOR (2003) Vulnerability and Resilience: Response of women and forest products to escalating logging in Eastern Amazonia. Proposal submitted to International Development Research Centre (IDRC), Sustainable Use of Biodiversity (SUB), Jakarta, Indonesia.

Colfer, C.J.P. (ed.) (forthcoming) *The Complex Forest: Communities, Uncertainty and Adaptive Collaborative Management*. Resources for the Future/CIFOR, Washington, DC.

Colfer, C.J.P. (ed.) (2005) *The Equitable Forest: Diversity, Community and Resource Management*. Resources for the Future/CIFOR, Washington, DC.

Colfer, C.J.P. and Byron, Y. (2001) *People Managing Forests: The Links between Human Well-Being and Sustainability*. Resources for the Future/CIFOR, Washington, DC, 447 pp.

Colfer, C.J.P. and Resosudarmo, I.A.P. (eds) (2002) *Which Way Forward?: People, Forests, and Policymaking in Indonesia*. Resources for the Future/CIFOR, Washington, DC, 433 pp.

Colfer, C.J.P., Brocklesby, M.A., Diaw, C., Etuge, P., Gunter, M., Harwell, E., McDougall, C., Porro, N.M., Porro, R., Prabhu, R., Salim, A., Sardjono, M.A., Tchikangwa, B., Tiani, A.M., Wadley, R., Woelfel, J. and Wollenberg, E. (1999a) The BAG (Basic Assessment Guide for human well-being). In: Prabhu, R. (ed.) *C&I Toolbox*, Vol. 5. CIFOR, Washington, DC, 79 pp.

Colfer, C.J.P., Brocklesby, M.A., Diaw, C., Etuge, P., Gunter, M., Harwell, E., McDougall, C., Porro, N.M., Porro, R., Prabhu, R., Salim, A., Sardjono, M.A., Tchikangwa, B., Tiani, A.M., Wadley, R., Woelfel, J. and Wollenberg, E. (1999b) The grab bag: supplementary methods for assessing human well-being. In: Prabhu, R. (ed.) *C&I Toolbox*, Vol. 6. CIFOR, Bogor, Indonesia, 64 pp.

Colfer, C.J.P. with Prabhu, R., Gunter, M., McDougall, C., Miyasaka Porro, N. and Porro, R. (1999c) Who counts most? Assessing human well-being in sustainable forest management. In: Prabhu, R. (ed.) *C&I Toolbox*, Vol. 8, CIFOR, Bogor, Indonesia, 62 pp.

Contreras, A.P. (ed.) (2003) *Creating Space for Local Forest Management in the Philippines*. LaSalle Institute of Governance and Antonio Contreras, Bogor, Indonesia, 228 pp.

Co-View: Collaborative Vision Exploration Workbench (negotiating/visioning tool). CIFOR, Bogor, Indonesia.

Cronkleton, P. (2005) Gender, participation and the strengthening of indigenous forestry management. In: Colfer, C.J.P. (ed.) *The Equitable Forest: Diversity, Community and Resource Management*, pp. 256–273. Resources for the Future/CIFOR, Washington, DC pp. 256-273.

Cunha dos Santos, M. (2002) *Adaptive Co-Management, a Case Study: PAE Porto Dias, Acre, Brazil*.

PESACRE/University of Florida/ CIFOR, Gainesville, Florida, 67 pp.

de Jong, W. (2000) Micro-differences in local resource management: the case of honey in West Kalimantan, Indonesia. *Human Ecology* 28(4), 631–639.

Diaw, M.C. and Kusumanto, T. (2005) Scientists in social encounters: the case for an engaged practice of science. In: Colfer, C.J.P. (ed.) *The Equitable Forest: Diversity, Community and Resource Management.* Resources for the Future/CIFOR, Washigton, DC, pp. 72–109.

Dounias, E. (ed.) (2000) *Rewiew of Ethnobotanical Literature for Central and West Africa.* AETFAT – People and Plants Initiative-Unesco–WWF-Royal Botanical Gardens Kew, Bulletin of the African Ethnobotany Network 2, 117 pp.

Dounias, E. (ed.) (2003) *Cameroon's Forest and People. A collection of publications, maps, pictures, hyperlinks and references.* (CD-ROM). CIFOR, Bogor, Indonesia.

Dounias, E. and Loutrel, G. (2002) Swidder fallows among the Punan of upper Tubu river (East Kalimanton). What do they tell us about agroecosystem dynamics? http://www.capri.cigiar.org/ projects/project020.asp

Dounias, E. and Leclerc, C. (forthcoming, 2005) In, out, in, out: shift in space and time scales of migration among the Baka pygmies of Cameroon and the Punan of Borneo. In: de Jong, W. and Ichi, A. (eds) *Migration and the Social Ecology of Tropical Forests.* UN University Press, Tokyo.

Dounias, E., Kishi, M., Selzner, A., Kurniawan, I. and Levang, P. (2004) No longer nomadic.

Changing Punan Tubu lifestyle requires new health strategies. *Cultural Survival Quarterly* 28(2), 15-20.

García-Fernández, C. (2001) Sistemas tradicionales de gestión del bosque tropical en Indonesia: ecología y prácticas silviculturales. Doctoral thesis, Ecology, Universidad Complutense de Madrid, Madrid, Spain.

García-Fernández, C., Casado, M.A. and Ruiz-Pérez, M. (2003) Benzoin gardens in North Sumatra, Indonesia: effects of management on tree diversity. *Conservation Biology* 17, 829–836.

Goloubinoff, M. (1998) Senteurs de miel et d'encens. Le benjoin à Java Centre. In: Guillot, C. (ed.) *Historie de Barus. Le Site de Lobu Tua.* Cahier d'Archipel no 30 Association Archipel-EHESS, Paris, France.

Haggith, M., Purnomo, H. *et al.* (2002) Co-view Collaborative Vision Exploration Workbench. CIFOR, Bogor, Indonesia.

Haggith, M., Prabhu, R., Colfer, C.J.P., Ritchie, B., Thomson, A. and Mudavanhu, H. (2003) Infectious ideas: modelling the diffusion of ideas across social networks. *Small-Scale Forest Economics, Management and Policy* 2 (2), 225–240.

Hakim, S. (2002) District-level workshop, Paser District, East Kalimantan, Indonesia. *ACM News* 3(3), 6–8.

Hartanto, H., with Arda-Minas, L., Burton, L.M., Estanol, A., Lorenzo, M.C. and Valmores, C. (2002a) *Planning for Sustainability of Forests through Adaptive Co-Management: Philippines Country Report.* CIFOR, Bogor, Indonesia, 68 pp.

Hartanto, H., Lorenzo, M.C. and Frio, A.L. (2002b) Collective action and learning in developing a collaborative monitoring system. *International Forestry Review* 4(3), 184–195.

Hartanto, H., Lorenzo, C.M., Valmores, C., Arda-Minas, L., Burton, E.M. and Prabhu, R. (2003) *Learning Together: Responding to Change and Complexity to Improve Community Forests in the Philippines.* CIFOR, Bogor, Indonesia, 166 pp.

Kaimowitz, D. and Angelsen, A. (1998) *Economic Models of Tropical Deforestation: A Review.* CIFOR, Bogor, Indonesia, 139 pp.

Kamoto, J. (2002) Chimaliro, Malawi context study – ecology and production C&I. Internal report, CIFOR, Harare, Zimbabwe.

Katz, E. (1997) NWFPs in Bulungan, East Kalimantan, Indonesia. In: Mittelman, A.J., Lai, C.K., Byron, N., Michon, G. and Katz, E. (eds) *Non-Wood Forest Products Outlook Study for Asia and the Pacific: Towards 2010.* FAO Regional Office for Asia and the Pacific, Bangkok, Thailand, pp. 39–46.

Katz, E. (1998) L'exploitation du benjoin dans les hautes terres batak. Situation actuelle. In: Guillot, C. (ed.) *Histoire de Barus. Le Site de Lobu Tua.* Cahier d'Archipel, Association Archipel-EHESS, Paris, pp. 243–264.

Katz, E. and Nguinguiri, J.C. (1999) Clans, ethnies et etat: partage et conflict dans l'appropriation de l'espace au Kouilou (Congo). In: Bonnemaison, J., Cambrezy, L. and Quinty-Bourgeois, L. (eds) *La Nation et Le Territorie – Le territoire, lien ou frontièr?* L'Harmattan, Paris, pp. 149–162.

Katz, E., Garcia, C. and Goloubinoff, M. (2002) Sumatra benzoin (*Styrax* spp.). In: Shanley, P., Pierce, A.R., Laird, S.A. and Guillen, A. (eds) *Tapping the Green Market: Certification and Management of Non-Timber Forest Products.* Earthscan, Bangkok, Thailand, pp. 246–256.

Kowero, G.S. and Spilsbury, M.J. (1997) Evaluation of forestry research capacity in Eastern and Southern Africa. *Journal of World Resource Management* 8, 159–182.

Lee, K.N. (1993) *Compass and Gyroscope: Integrating Science and Politics for the Environment.* Island Press, Washington, DC, 243 pp.

Levang, P., Dounias, E. and Sitorus, S. (2003) Out of forest, out of poverty? *Proceedings and Documentation of the International Conference on Rural Livelihoods, Forests and Biodiversity.* Bonn, May 19–23, 2003. (CD-ROM). CIFOR, Bogor, Indonesia.

Lópéz, C. and Shanley, P. (2004a) *Riches of the Forest: Food, Spices, Crafts and Resins of Asia.* CIFOR, Bangkok, Thailand.

Lópéz, C. and Shanley, P. (2004b) *Riches of the Forest: For Health, Life and Spirit in Africa.* CIFOR, Bangkok, Thailand.

Lópéz, C. and Shanley, P. (2004c) *Riches of the Forest: Fruits, Oils, Remedies and Handicrafts in Latin America.* CIFOR, Bogor, Indonesia.

McDougall, C., Kaski ACM Team, New ERA ACM Team, and Forest Action (2002) Planning for the sustainability of forests through adaptive co-management: Nepal country report. ACM Project/MoFSC Internal Research Report, CIFOR, Bogor, Indonesia, 162 pp.

Mertens, B., Sunderlin, W.D., Ndoye, O. and Lambin, E.F. (2000) Impact of macroeconomics change on deforestation in South Cameroon: integration of household survey and remotely sensed data. *World Development* 28(6), 983–999.

Merton, R.K. (1962) 'Recognition' and 'excellence': Instructive ambiguities. In: Yarmolinsky, A. (ed.) *Recognition of Excellence: Working Papers.* Free Press, New York, pp. 419–438.

Merton, R.K. (1968) The Matthew effect in science. *Science* 159 (3810), 56–63.

Merton, R.K. (1988) The Matthew effect in science, II: cumulative advantage and the symbolism of intellectual property. *ISIS* 79, 606–623.

Michon, G., Katz, E. and de Foresta, H. (1997) From extraction to production: building on indigenous inspiration or using conventional agricultural models. Paper read at International Workshop on Sustainable Management of Non-Wood Forest Products, 14–17 October, at Serdang, Selangor, Malaysia.

Muhtaman, D.R., Siregar, C.A. and Hopmans, P. (2000) *Criteria and Indicators for Sustainable Plantation Forestry in Indonesia.* CIFOR, Bogor, Indonesia, pp. 63.

Mutimukuru, T., Nyirenda, R. and Matose, F. (2005) 'Learning amongst ourselves'. Adaptive forest management through social learning, in Zimbabwe. In: Colfer, C.J.P. (ed.) *The Equitable Forest Diversity, Community and Resource Management.* Resources for the Future/CIFOR, Washington, DC, pp. 188–204.

Ndoye, O. and Kaimowitz, D. (2000) Macroeconomic, markets, and the humid forests of Cameroon,

1967–1997. *Journal of Modern African Studies* 38(2), 225–253.

Nemarundwe, N., de Jong, W. and Cronkleton, P. (2003) *Future Scenarios as an Instrument for Forest Management: Manual for Training Facilitators of Future Scenarios.* CIFOR, Bogor, Indonesia, 29 pp.

Nyirenda, R., Mutimukuru, T. and Matose, F. (2001) *Overcoming Inertia: Stimulating Collective Action Among Forest Users in Mafungautsi Forest, Zimbabwe.* Internal Report, CIFOR, Bogor, Indonesia.

Pacheco, P. and Kaimowitz, D. (eds) (1998) *Municipios y Gestion Forestal en el Tropico Boliviano.* Serie Bosques y Sociedad, No. 3. Centre for International Forestry Research, Centro de Estudios para el Desarrollo Laboral y Agrario, Taller de Iniciativas en Estudios Rurales y Reforma Agraria, Bolivia Sustainable Forest Management Project, La Paz, 489 pp.

Pokorny, B., Cayres, G., Nunes, W., Segebart, D. and Drude, R. (2001) *Final Report, Pilot Project: Adaptive Co-Management in Pará.* CIFOR, Bogor, Indonesia, 63 pp.

Prabhu, R., Colfer, C.J.P., Venkateswarlu, P., Tan, L.C., Soekmadi, R. and Wollenberg, E. (1996) *Testing Criteria and Indicators for the Sustainable Management of Forests: Phase 1 Final Report.* CIFOR, Bogor, Indonesia, 217 pp.

Prabhu, R., Maynard, W., Atyi, R.E., Colfer, C.J.P., Shepherd, G., Venkateswarlu, P. and Tiayon, F. (1998) *Testing and Developing Criteria and Indicators for Sustainable Forest Management in Cameroon: The Kribi Test, Final Report.* CIFOR, Bogor, Indonesia, 122 pp.

Prabhu, R., Colfer, C.J.P. and Dudley, R.G. (1999) Guidelines for developing, testing, and selecting criteria and indicators for sustainable forest management: a C&I developer's reference. In: Prabhu, R. (ed.) *C&I Toolbox*, Vol. 1. CIFOR, Bogor, Indonesia, 186 pp.

Prabhu, R., Colfer, C.J.P. and Diaw, C. (2001) *Sharing Benefits from Forest Utilisation: Trojan Horses, Copy Cats, Blind Mice and Busy Bees.* Cropper Foundation, Georgetown, Guyana.

Prabhu, R., Haggith, M., Mudavanhu, H., Muetzelfeldt, R., Standa-Gunda, W. and Vanclay, J. (2003) ZimFlores: a model to advise co-management of the Mafungautsi Forest in Zimbabwe. *Small-Scale Forest Economics, Management and Policy* 2(2), 185–210.

Purnomo, H., Rizal, A., Haggith, M., Yasmi, Y., Simarmata, J.P.P., Zacharias, T.Y. Taylor, J., Yulianto, E., Sukardi, D., Helianthy, G.E., Sartika, E. and Indriatmoko, Y. (2000) CIMAT 2 (C&I Modification Adaptation Tool) CD-ROM, CIFOR, Bogor, Indonesia.

Resosudarmo, I.A.P. (2002) Timber management and related policies. In: Colfer, C.J.P. and Resosudarmo, I.A.P. (eds) *Which Way Forward?: People, Forests, and Policymaking in Indonesia.* Resources for the Future, Centre for International Forestry Research, and Institute for South East Asian Studies, Bogor, Indonesia, pp. 161–190.

Ritchie, B., McDougall, C., Haggith, M. and Burford de Oliveira, N. (2000) *An Introductory Guide to Criteria and Indicators for Sustainability in Community Managed Forest Landscapes.* CIFOR, Bogor, Indonesia, 104 pp.

Salim, A., Colfer, C.J.P. and McDougall, C. (1999) The scoring and analysis guide for assessing human well-being. In: Prabhu, R. (ed.) *C&I Toolbox*, Vol. 7. CIFOR, Bogor, Indonesia, 140 pp.

Sankar, S., Anil, P.C. and Amruth, M. (2000) *Criteria and Indicators for Sustainable Plantation Forestry in India.* CIFOR, Bogor, Indonesia, 64 pp.

Sarin, M., Singh, N., Sundar, N. and Bhogal, R.K. (2003) *Devolution as a Threat to Democratic Decision-making in Forestry? Findings from Three States in India.* Overseas Development Institute, London, 66 pp.

Setiono, B. and Barr, C. (2003) Using anti-money laundering laws to fight forestry crime in Indonesia. Policy memo prepared for the Indonesian Working Group on Forest Finance. June 5, Bogor, Indonesia.

Shanley, P. and Gaia, G. (2002) Equitable ecology: collaborative learning for local benefit in Eastern Amazonia. *Agricultural Systems* 73, 83–97.

Shanley, P. and Laird, S. (2001) Giving back: making research results relevant to local groups and conservation. In: Laird, S. (ed.) *Biodiversity and Traditional Knowledge: Equitable Partnerships in Practice.* Earthscan, London, pp. 102–124.

Shanley, P., Cymerys, M. and Galvão, J. (1998) *Frutíferas da Mata na Vida Amazônica.* Editora Supercores, Belém, Brazil.

Sithole, B. (2002) *Where the Power Lies: Multiple Stakeholder Politics over Natural Resources: A Participatory Methods Guide.* CIFOR, Bogor, Indonesia, 70 pp.

Sunderlin, W.D., Angelsen, A., Reso-sudarmo, I.A.P., Dermawan, A. and Rianto, E. (2001) Economic crisis, small farmer wellbeing and forest cover change in Indonesia. *World Development* 29(5), 767–782.

Tiani, A.M., Nguiébouri, J. and Diaw, C. (2002) Criteria and indicators as tools for adaptative and collabora-tive forest management: a guide. Internal report, CIFOR, Yaoundé, Cameroon, 34 pp.

Vanclay, J.K., Sinclair, F.L. and Prabhu, R. (2003) Modelling interactions among people and forest resources at the landscape scale. *Small-Scale Forest Economics, Management and Policy* 2(2), 117–120.

Wollenberg, E. and Ingles, A. (eds) (1998) *Incomes from the Forest – Methods for the Development and Conservation of Forest Products for Local Communities*. CIFOR, Bogor, Indonesia, 227 pp.

Wollenberg, E., Edmunds, D. and Buck, L. (2000) *Anticipating Change: Scenarios as a Tool for Adaptive Forest Management (a Guide)*. CIFOR, Bogor, Indonesia, 38 pp.

Wollenberg, E., Anderson, J. and Edmunds, D. (2001) Pluralism and the less powerful: accom-modating multiple interests in local forest management. *International Journal of Agricultural Resources, Governance and Ecology* 1(3/4), 199–222.

Wunder, S. (2003) *Oil Wealth and the Fate of the Forest: A Comparative Study of Eight Tropical Countries*. Routledge, London and New York, 432 pp.

Yuliani, L., Kusumanto, Y., Indri-atmoko, Y. and Hakim, S. (2002) *Indonesia Country Report – ACM PAR Main Case Studies*. CIFOR, Bogor, Indonesia, 37 pp.

Humanizing Technology Development in the Green Revolution's Home

6

Mauricio R. Bellon, Michael Morris, Javier Ekboir, Erika Meng, Hugo De Groote and Gustavo Saín

The International Maize and Wheat Improvement Center (CIMMYT) holds a global mandate to develop improved maize and wheat production technologies, to ultimately improve productivity in maize- and wheat-based farming systems, reduce poverty and enhance the natural resource base. CIMMYT has mostly been, first and foremost, a plant-breeding institute. Most of its researchers have thus been biological scientists, mainly plant breeders and agronomists, who research crop improvement. CIMMYT's technology development efforts are supported by a small team of social scientists – primarily agricultural economists, but also (at one point or another) one or two researchers from non-economics social disciplines such as anthropology, sociology, human ecology, geography and political science.

Social science research at CIMMYT is carried out by staff of the Economics Programme. Its principal role is to ask and answer impact-relevant questions about CIMMYT's maize and wheat research activities. Are our research programmes targeting the right set of technologies? Do the products of our research programmes reach poor farmers in developing countries? If so, do such products help improve productivity, reduce poverty and increase the sustainability of the natural resource base? Do we conduct our research efficiently? Does our portfolio of research activities require adjustment? Should we undertake new research activities not on the agenda? Should we abandon some activities?

History of Social Science Research at CIMMYT

Institutional history[1]

Officially established in 1966, CIMMYT traces its origins to a special-ized research programme on maize, wheat and other crops initiated 25 years earlier by the government of Mexico and the Rockefeller Foun-dation. CIMMYT's original mandate was 'to assist nations throughout the world to increase the production of wheat and maize'. During its early years, CIMMYT functioned without any social scientists. Its research focused narrowly on genetic improvement of wheat and maize, and its staff consisted exclusively of crop genetic improvement specialists, mainly plant breeders and other biological scientists (e.g. physiologists, pathologists, entomologists). As the green revolution set in and semi-dwarf wheat varieties originating from Mexico spread throughout developing countries, CIMMYT soon gained a reputation as one of the world's premier plant-breeding organizations.

Social science research at CIMMYT started in 1971 with the hiring of its first economist, which appears to have been motivated by three considerations. First, management wished to improve CIMMYT's in-house capacity to respond to growing criticism that green revolution technologies were widening income disparities between rich and poor farmers. Second, certain second-generation problems of the green revo-lution demanded economic and social analysis. Third, social scientists were thought to be able to help extend the green revolution to maize, which had not enjoyed as much success as wheat.

CIMMYT did not recruit a second social scientist until 1976. After that, social scientists began to increase steadily. By 1980, ten social sci-entists were on the staff – nine economists and the first non-economist, Robert Tripp, an anthropologist. In 1986, the Economics Programme was recognized as a full research programme, making it CIMMYT's third research programme after the wheat and maize programmes. It peaked in size during the mid-1980s, when it swelled to include 16 full-time pro-fessional social scientists, of which two were anthropologists and one a geographer. Subsequently the programme contracted, as its staff had to leave gradually because of budget reductions. The Economics Programme now includes ten full-time professional staff, virtually all economists, with only one human ecologist, plus a number of part-time collaborators and affiliated scientists. It should be pointed out that, of the approxi-mately 91 scientists[2] who have ever been affiliated with the Economics Programme, only seven have been non-economists: three anthropologists, one sociologist, one geographer and two human ecologists.

Partly because of the presence of non-economists, and partly because of the pragmatic and applied nature of the research agenda, the work of the Economics Programme has never had a rigid disciplinary 'economics' perspective.

Evolution of the social science research agenda

Throughout its existence, the Economics Programme has concentrated primarily on technology design and impact evaluation, reflecting primarily the desire of management to measure the impact of modern varieties of wheat and maize on the size and distribution of farmers' incomes. Early critics of the green revolution alleged that most varieties required high levels of purchased inputs, especially fertilizer, and that modern varieties therefore, were adopted mainly by wealthy farmers who could afford these inputs. CIMMYT thus commissioned a series of country case studies that explored the relationship between farm size (a proxy for wealth) and the adoption of seed–fertilizer technology. These case studies found that although large-scale farmers were often first to adopt modern varieties and associated technologies, small-scale farmers eventually followed. Over the long term, farm size was not a major factor in accounting for the use of modern varieties (Perrin and Winkelmann, 1976).

While they downplayed the importance of farmers' wealth as a determining factor in the adoption of modern varieties, the early country case studies did turn up evidence of a strong interaction between adoption and agro-climatic conditions. The early studies on the influence of agro-climatic and socioeconomic factors on technology adoption gave rise to a new phase of economic research, when it became more relevant to particular sets of farmers' circumstances.

A particular concern of social scientists was that the choice of technology or the input levels proposed by researchers for on-farm experiments often were not relevant to, or appropriate for, farmers' needs and circumstances. These social scientists soon became heavily involved in planning on-farm trials, stressing the need to carry out initial diagnostic surveys to collect information on farmers' circumstances – information that could be used to plan relevant experiments and formulate management recommendations. Initially, agronomists and social scientists were suspicious of each other, but as their disciplinary perspectives became obviously complementary, disciplinary barriers gradually broke down, leading to a marriage of on-farm surveys and controlled experimentation.

By the beginning of the 1980s, a well-defined paradigm had emerged for on-farm research (OFR). The paradigm was based on the idea of using information derived from surveys to design experiments of relevance to farmers, i.e. those that would be carried out in farmers' fields, under farmers' management. For some time a debate raged over whether the focus should be on individual commodities or on the entire farming system (farming systems research (FSR)). These two approaches gradually converged. Researchers working under commodity mandates came to appreciate the critical importance of system interactions, while those claiming allegiance to FSR learned that developing focused, stepwise interventions targeted at individual cropping activities was often more effective than introducing entire new cropping systems.

As CIMMYT social scientists became known as leaders in OFR/FSR, requests mounted for assistance to institutionalize these methods within national agricultural research systems (NARS). CIMMYT social scientists became active in training NARS researchers in OFR/FSR and in helping set up OFR/FSR units in NARS. While economists played an important role in OFR/FSR – and some controversies arose about the role and contribution of non-economist social scientists in this line of work – there is no question that anthropologists and other social scientists made important contributions, particularly due to their understanding of local culture and the social contexts in which technological interventions had to be applied (Cernea and Guggenheim, 1985).

By the late 1980s, some research managers had begun to raise questions about the cost-effectiveness of OFR/FSR. Concerns that their impacts were modest for their considerable cost motivated CIMMYT and some of its partners to launch a number of studies to determine whether farmers were adopting on a large scale the technologies developed through OFR/FSR (e.g. Tripp *et al.*, 1987). For example, these studies showed that many farmers adopted recommended practices and tested their components carefully and in steps, rather than suddenly switch to the complete set. Differences in farmers' circumstances helped explain patterns of adoption. Although little evidence suggests that these studies swung the debate decisively one way or another, gradually OFR/FSR fell out of favour mainly because it was considered to require large investments for low pay-offs. The great strength of OFR/FSR – developing technologies for well-defined groups of farmers – was also a key explanation for their failure: location specificity. This meant that benefits accrued to a small number of farmers, while investment needed in research resources was high (Tripp, 1991). By the early 1990s, attention had shifted to a new set of issues: the efficiency with which technology was used, forces in the policy environment that affected technology use and the effectiveness of different extension methods to disseminate technologies.

When CIMMYT was doing a lot of OFR/FSR, most of the collaboration between the Economics Programme and NARS took place with economists or agronomists. Every now and then, not often, a NARS sociologist or anthropologist would be a collaborator. The main reasons for the lack of collaboration with non-economist social scientists were that: (i) CIMMYT social scientists were mainly economists, who naturally gravitated towards working with other economists; and (ii) because CIMMYT was a commodity centre, CIMMYT social scientists tended to collaborate with counterparts lodged in NARS maize and wheat programmes, which even if they had some sort of social science unit, tended to be light on non-economists.

Although OFR/FSR is no longer prominent in the research lexicon, it would be a mistake to conclude that the concepts developed under these paradigms have vanished. On the contrary, OFR/FSR has left a lasting impression on how technology design and evaluation research is carried out. Today we take for granted the importance of seeking farmers' perspectives when setting breeding priorities or defining problems for strategic crop management research. Diagnostic surveys and farmers' assessments are viewed as necessary starting points for technology development research. The 'bottom-up' perspective that formed the core of OFR/FSR is solidly embodied in many tools that share the premise that farmers' perspectives are fundamental. Participatory methods routinely used today are designed to tap into sources of information that before OFR/FSR were often ignored: local knowledge systems, social networks and collective action.

During the 1990s, funding for international agricultural research began to contract in real terms, bringing pressure on research administrators to raise funds to maintain research programmes. CIMMYT management increasingly called upon social scientists, who had already established a reputation for adoption and impact studies, to generate more compelling evidence that the centre's maize and wheat research programmes were continuing to produce significant benefits. The primary focus of social science research consequently shifted from technology design and evaluation back to impact assessment. However, unlike earlier studies, which did little more than document the adoption and diffusion of modern varieties and associated technologies, the new wave of impact studies encompassed an expanded set of impact measures, including on people and the environment.

The evolving research agenda has been paying increasing attention to poverty. While the Economics Programme has always been interested in analysing the impact of modern varieties on income distribution and poverty, initially the focus was mainly on identifying factors that influence the adoption of modern varieties and on testing for the existence of possible scale biases in the technology. More recently, attention has centred on how poverty is affected by such adoption, requiring a broader definition of poverty, one that recognizes its multiple dimensions.

The research agenda has also been paying more attention to gender. Past technology development efforts focused predominantly, if not exclusively, on male farmers. The farmers involved in research were mainly men. Male and female farmers were implicitly assumed to share the same goals, have the same access to resources and outputs and face similar constraints. Now we know that this view is incorrect. Household members do have diverse responsibilities, perform different activities and have varying work loads and access to resources. They may also have conflicting interests. Clearly, gender matters. CIMMYT social scientists are working hard to ensure that gender variables are not overlooked.

From *ex-post* to *ex-ante*

The latest shift in the Economics Programme research agenda commenced during the past few years. While CIMMYT has a long tradition of close collaboration between social scientists and agronomists, collaboration between social scientists and plant breeders has been much less common. While welcoming the work of social scientists, CIMMYT plant breeders were mainly interested in having social scientists carry out *ex-post* impact studies to validate the success of the breeding programmes. Breeders rarely felt the need to involve social scientists in an *ex-ante* capacity, i.e. breeders were not often motivated to enlist the help of social scientists at the beginning of the breeding cycle to identify breeding priorities and define target environments. This attitude has started to change as more evidence shows that many farmers still have not adopted modern varieties. Breeders now understand that one reason is that those available do not always have the desired combination of traits. Many plant breeders thought that identifying traits desired by farmers was easy. Now they know that traits considered important by farmers may not be considered important by breeders and vice versa. It has also become clear that farmers' preferences often involve 'subjective' traits that are difficult to measure quantitatively, such as taste, smell and appearance.

While social scientists traditionally played a minor role in crop genetic improvement research in CIMMYT, this role has been gradually changing. The plant-breeding community has realized that farmers' preferences do matter and that information about them must be obtained directly from farmers themselves, generating interest in participatory plant-breeding methods. These require close collaboration among plant breeders, social scientists and farmers (Morris and Bellon, 2004). While plant breeders continue to perform crossing and selection based on well-established principles of crop genetic improvement, social scientists who are trained to study human perceptions and preferences, have a comparative advantage in interacting systematically with farmers, particularly in identifying their preferences and constraints. Recognizing the importance of these skills, plant breeders have become much more receptive to participatory breeding methods carried out in collaboration with social scientists.

Current Focus of Social Science Research at CIMMYT

Principal social science research themes

The research agenda of the Economics Programme, carried out by a group of several economists and one human ecologist, encompasses five major themes:

Technology adoption and impact assessment studies. Researchers and research managers need to know whether improved technologies are being taken up and used by farmers. Economics Programme staff design and implement studies on the adoption and diffusion of improved technologies developed by CIMMYT and its partners. Complementing these studies are those on impact assessment designed to shed light on what happens when improved technologies are successfully taken up. Challenged to go beyond traditional measures of impact – the more easily measurable productivity measures, such as gains in yield or production increases – the Economics Programme has launched a series of targeted case studies to link technology adoption to improvements in broader measures of welfare (e.g. reduction in poverty, improvement in health and nutrition).

Economics of emerging technologies. Technology assessment can be backward or forward looking. To complement their *ex-post* studies on technology adoption and impact assessment, Economics Programme staff also engage in *ex-ante* studies to explore the economics of emerging new technologies that are not yet being used. These include production technologies intended for use by farmers (e.g. plants with novel traits, new types of agricultural machinery), as well as research technologies intended for use by scientists (e.g. biotechnology-assisted plant-breeding methods). Since this work involves technologies that are not yet in use, many parameters must be projected based on experimental data.

Economics of crop genetic diversity. Although crop genetic diversity is widely acknowledged to be important, assigning an economic value to its importance is difficult. The fact that the benefits of genetic diversity are difficult to measure poses a problem because maintaining genetic diversity is costly. *Ex-situ* conservation requires investment in the construction and operation of gene banks, and *in situ* conservation requires that incentives be maintained for farmers to continue growing and managing traditional cultivars. To invest in a socially optimal level of genetic resource conservation, the costs must be related to expected benefits. Economics Programme staff study the economics of genetic resource conservation and use.

Setting research priorities. Economics Programme staff generate information that can be used by research managers to set research priorities and manage ongoing research programmes, such as about the cost of doing research and the likely size and distribution of research benefits. With the help of a formal research priority-setting model, specific areas have been identified in which CIMMYT's maize and wheat improvement programmes can be expected to have the greatest impact.

Sector and policy analysis. To make sound decisions, agricultural policymakers and research managers need accurate information about international commodity markets to set research priorities. Consistent with its mandate to serve these two important constituencies, the Economics Programme monitors developments in global maize and wheat markets and tracks changes in the global policy environment likely to affect the supply and demand of these and other major cereals.

Selected social science research initiatives

Much of the Economics Programme's research under the five themes above is grounded in traditional economics concepts and methods. Yet, not all of it is economics research. A considerable amount consists of non-economics social science research, or abbreviated 'social research', of which we highlight several examples from our current research.

Conservation and valuation of genetic resources

In recent years, *in situ* conservation has attracted increased attention as a way to complement the work of gene banks. *In situ* or on-farm conservation occurs when farmers continue to cultivate and manage a diverse set of landraces within the agroecosystem where they were developed. CIMMYT social scientists have been studying how farmers conserve maize and wheat genetic resources, analysing incentives for farmers to continue to do so and assessing possible types of interventions to support them (Bellon *et al.*, 2003; Smale *et al.*, 2003). This work has involved close interaction among genetic resources specialists, plant breeders and plant population geneticists. A related area of research is the valuation of genetic resources and genetic diversity, in the gene bank as well as in farmers' fields (Meng and Brush, 1998; Smale, 1997; Gollin and Smale, 1999).

FARMER MANAGEMENT OF GERMPLASM. Most adoption and impact studies on modern varieties implicitly assume that when a particular one is taken up by farmers, its genetic composition remains essentially unchanged. Any change is likely to be seen as negative and characterized as 'contamination'. Once a modern variety has become 'contaminated', plant breeders usually recommend that the farmer replace the seed. Studies carried out by CIMMYT social scientists and others suggest that this recommendation is often inappropriate, especially for crops with high rates of outcrossing, such as maize. Research done in Mexico shows that many small-scale maize farmers take up modern varieties and through management strategies, deliberately transform them to suit their own needs. Known as 'creolization' or 'rustication', this process can be seen as the 'middle way' by which improved technology is adapted to local farmers' conditions (Morris *et al.*, 1999; Bellon and Risopoulos, 2001). This work has important implications for measuring impacts of germplasm improvement programmes, particularly among the poor, and has generated valuable information needed to assess the potential environmental risks of introducing genetically modified maize varieties into areas where farmers recycle and exchange seed (Bellon and Berthaud, 2004).

SEED SYSTEMS. For plant-breeding research to be successful, seed systems must be in place that can effectively deliver improved, affordable germplasm to farmers on time. CIMMYT social scientists analyse the organization and performance of national seed industries and track their evolution over time (Morris, 1998). Seed-industry studies require a broad social science perspective to understand the incentives and constraints that participants face and to interpret the 'rules of the game' that must be negotiated. Complementing the work being done on formal seed systems is that on local or informal seed-exchange systems, through which farmers acquire seed from other farmers. Understanding local systems is important to assess the diffusion of seed from farmer to farmer, which in turn, has implications for the conservation and use of local genetic resources in farmers' fields. Of particular interest is how big a role collective action plays in the local maize seed systems (Badstue *et al.*, 2003).

HUMAN NUTRITION. The Global Challenge Programme recently approved by CGIAR on biofortification involves breeding nutritionally enhanced plants containing elevated levels of protein or essential micronutrients lacking in the diets of the poor. The best-known research at CIMMYT along these lines is the work on quality protein maize, which has elevated levels of the essential amino acids – lysine and tryptophan. Less well known are ongoing efforts to develop maize with elevated levels of beta carotene (metabolized by humans into vitamin A), as well as efforts to develop wheat varieties that are rich in iron and zinc. CIMMYT's biofortification work has consisted mainly of breeding, but the plan is to complement it with strong social research.

Input from social scientists will be needed to assess the potential nutritional impact of biofortified varieties, identify target populations that could most benefit from them and evaluate the cost effectiveness of delivering improved nutrition through plant breeding versus traditional fortification or supplementation. Once the efficacy of biofortification can be demonstrated, additional social science research will be needed to assess farmers' varietal preferences and consumers' preferences. Breeders need this information to develop nutritionally enhanced varieties that farmers will be willing to grow and consumers to eat.

INSTITUTIONAL INNOVATION. With the increasing intensification of many agricultural systems, technologies are becoming increasingly complex. The integration of local product and factor markets with international markets is increasing the complexity of farmers' decisions. Yet, complex technologies cannot be generated by isolated agents, because no individual agent can muster all the financial and technical resources required to develop and evaluate such technologies. Complex technologies must thus be generated by networks of agents, the nature of which depends partly on the characteristics of the technology and partly on historical accident. CIMMYT social scientists are studying the dynamics of innovation networks to improve the ability of public research organizations and private firms with whom we partner to generate new knowledge or adapt knowledge generated by others. Innovative system concepts are being used to analyse the development and diffusion of zero-tillage technology in Latin America, sub-Saharan Africa and South Asia (Ekboir, 2002).

Outlook for Social Science Research at CIMMYT

Social science research has come a long way at CIMMYT since the days when a single economist spent all his time organizing adoption studies. While the role and activities of social scientists in the centre have changed over the years, the general trend has been to integrate social science methods and perspectives into the biological research agenda. Perhaps the most significant development has been the realization that social scientists have an important contribution to make early in the technology development process and, by serving as an effective interface with the intended end users of new technologies, can significantly improve the effectiveness of the research process.

How can the role of social scientists in CIMMYT be expected to change? As the entire CGIAR system enters a period of uncertainty, projection is risky. At the same time, certain constraints on, and opportunities for, the evolution of social science research can be discerned.

Constraints

DONOR-DRIVEN AGENDAS. The sources and nature of CIMMYT's funding have changed significantly in recent years. Core unrestricted funding has declined, leaving management increasingly dependent on special-project funding to implement the research agenda. Many traditional donors have been replaced by new funding sources, including foundations and individuals. These changes have had a number of undesirable consequences, not least on social research. To begin with, the decline in core unrestricted funding has significantly reduced the ability of management to make long-term plans, while the increase in special-project funding means that the research agenda is increasingly influenced by donors' wishes and demands. While research organizations must be accountable to those who pay the bills, one unfortunate by-product of increased dependence on donors' subject selection is that management is less able to pursue research problems that may be important but not necessarily fashionable. Donors, after all, are neither omniscient nor infallible and their interests and priorities shift. Donors also operate under many constraints that restrict their ability to make sound funding decisions. For example, many donors are under pressure to be 'innovative' in their grant making, which makes them willing to consider 'new subjects' and reluctant to fund long-term, mainstream research activities such as plant breeding, which are considered routine and unexciting. Donors may be constrained by the need to satisfy political constituencies, which means that their funding decisions are often dictated by considerations that have little to do with actual research needs and priorities. This is a fact of life, and while they may try to engage and educate donors about research issues and their policy and political implications, researchers can do little about political processes beyond their sphere of influence.

On the face of it, the long-term changes in the nature of CIMMYT's funding do not necessarily help or hurt social science research. To the extent that donors may be interested in questions that social scientists are uniquely qualified to address, the rising importance of special-project funding could actually help strengthen the role of social scientists in CIMMYT. Clearly, however, the declining importance of core unrestricted funding has necessarily shortened the planning horizon of CIMMYT management and reduced its ability to respond to temporary disequilibria in the centre's budget, particularly affecting smaller research programmes such as the Economics Programme, which have less room to manoeuvre in the short term.

DISCIPLINARY BLINKERS. Consistent with its historical focus on plant breeding and crop improvement research, CIMMYT has traditionally been managed by plant scientists, who continue to exert an important intellectual influence on the organizational culture and disciplinary orientation even today, when the research agenda has expanded far beyond its original focus on modern-variety development. Natural sciences have their own paradigms, body of knowledge, accepted assumptions and methods. These define the lens through which biological scientists perceive and understand the world. However, because these elements are so ingrained, sometimes they limit the ability of scientists from one discipline to see other perspectives, understand other sets of assumptions and accept the validity of other methods.

CIMMYT's organizational culture and disciplinary orientation is characterized by an ideological mindset that emphasizes 'hard' over 'soft' science, controlled experimentation over sampling, objectively measurable 'facts' over subjectively determined perceptions. This disciplinary bias has worked to the detriment of social sciences in CIMMYT, since much social science research is based on data that are qualitatively different from those with which biological scientists are most comfortable.

LACK OF CREDIBILITY AMONG NATURAL SCIENTISTS. Closely related to the problem of disciplinary blinkers is lack of credibility. If one cannot perceive the lens through which others see the world, one is unlikely to accept the validity of their data, analysis and results. Partly because of the strong 'biological science perspective' that dominates the maize- and wheat-breeding programmes, social scientists at CIMMYT have sometimes had to struggle to have their work and perspective accepted.

The problem has been particularly acute for non-economists and compounded by their lack of 'critical mass' and diminishing numbers. Biological scientists are often willing to accept the results of conventional economic analysis (e.g. cost–benefit analysis) but tend to be sceptical of data about behaviour, culture, farmers' preferences and knowledge and other 'subjective' aspects; and data produced using other social science methods, particularly those regarded as 'non-rigorous'. For example, a small minority of 'old school' plant breeders still think that verbal information provided by survey respondents is so unreliable that any data generated using participatory methods are not amenable to rigorous statistical analysis. We know, in fact, that even some social scientists do not accept each others' methods and evidence. Fortunately, this has not been a problem within the Economics Programme, as its scientists, despite their different disciplinary backgrounds, have been open to different perspectives and methods.

SERVICE ROLE OF SOCIAL SCIENCE. Since plant scientists make up most of the staff, it is not surprising that a strong biological science perspective prevails within CIMMYT's research programmes. An unfortunate consequence, however, is that social scientists at CIMMYT are sometimes seen to play only a service role in support of the (primary) plant-breeding function. At times this attitude appears to have rubbed off on management, judging from the large number of requests for information and analysis routinely directed by CIMMYT's administration to the Economics Programme. While it is flattering that social scientists are appreciated for being able to generate information valued by management, the Economics Programme must be careful to avoid being relegated to a full-time service role. Economist Carl Eicher once famously remarked that 'the trouble with working as a social scientist at CIMMYT is that one risks becoming a handmaiden to the breeders'. The fact that social scientists are housed at CIMMYT within a separate programme and have not been assimilated into the crop programmes remains a positive institutional feature, since it has allowed social scientists to maintain an independent presence. It should be maintained, as it provides them with leverage to balance their service role with an ability to produce high-quality disciplinary research, but it could also gain from a more substantial presence of non-economist social scientists.

Opportunities

SUPPORT FROM DONORS. The fact that donors now have a louder voice in setting the CGIAR research agenda can have positive consequences for the social sciences. Donors' demands for increased accountability have required us to more clearly focus our research, comprehensively analyse the cost effectiveness of our activities, systematically think through the projected impact pathways for our products and convincingly document the impact of our efforts. In all these areas, social scientists are being asked to play a major role. Happily, many donors are willing to fund methodological work to improve our ability to do solid social science research. Support and encouragement by these donors has allowed us to test approaches and methods that might not be considered relevant or useful by others within the organization. For example, targeted support from donors has been important in fostering our participatory technology development work, as well as in allowing us to explore the sustainable livelihood approach, which defines poverty not only by income or consumption, but also other dimensions such as health, nutrition and empowerment. This approach also recognizes that farmers' livelihoods depend on multiple activities that interact and are heavily influenced by institutions and policies, leading to outcomes that enhance or worsen farmers' well-being (Adato and Meinzen-Dick, 2003).

NEW WILLINGNESS OF BIOLOGICAL SCIENTISTS TO COLLABORATE. Economics Programme staff have increasingly been able to convince their colleagues that a social science perspective is important for their work. Many biological scientists now recognize the importance of including an end-user perspective in developing technology, assessing the appropriateness and acceptability of new technologies, monitoring and evaluating the adoption and diffusion of new technologies and assessing their impacts on peoples' livelihoods and on society. Biological scientists' greater demand for the services of social scientists has led to increased collaboration across disciplinary boundaries, which has helped biological and social scientists recognize the value of alternative points of view and, thus, remove their disciplinary blinkers.

PROBLEM-ORIENTED RESEARCH MANAGEMENT. Changes in research design and management at CIMMYT have helped strengthen interaction between social and biological scientists. CIMMYT's Medium-term Plan organizes research into a series of projects[3] that bring together scientists from different disciplines to address well-defined problems (CIMMYT, 1997). The project-based management system has done much to institutionalize a collaborative, multidisciplinary approach to research and to solidify the place of social scientists alongside biological scientists. Institutionalization of multidisciplinary approaches is also taking place at the CGIAR level. The Global Challenge Programme[4] is intended to create a research environment that requires and values cooperation across disciplines to address complex issues of global or regional importance.

Conclusions

The social science research agenda at CIMMYT has expanded from a narrow focus on technology adoption to encompass technology design and evaluation, technology targeting, adoption and impact assessment, research priority setting and many other issues. While much of the Economics Programme's work is grounded in traditional economic analysis, not all of it is 'economics research'. A considerable amount has been based on methods drawn from social sciences other than economics, including anthropology, human ecology and political science.

Three lessons can be drawn from this brief review of social science research at CIMMYT:

- Successful technology development requires participation by social scientists, because they deal with human perceptions and behaviour that must be understood if technology development efforts are to be effective.

- Social science research cannot be conducted in isolation, separate from research done by biological and physical scientists.
- Close collaboration between all branches of the social sciences helps define more comprehensive and relevant messages, increasing their usefulness to plant scientists and to crop and resource management specialists.

Notes

[1]This section draws heavily on Byerlee (1991).

[2]This number includes full-time staff as well as visiting scientists and pre- and post-doctoral fellows, but not consultants.

[3]Medium-term Programme projects should not be confused with special projects. The former, which may include a number of special projects, encompass broad areas of research organized around a well-defined problem or theme such as conservation of genetic resources, crop improvement or impact assessment.

[4]The CGIAR Global Challenge Programme consists of time-bound, independently governed, high-impact research projects and requires partnerships with a wide range of institutions.

References

Adato, M. and Meinzen-Dick, R. (2003) Assessing the impact of agricultural research on poverty and livelihoods. *Quarterly Journal of International Agriculture* 2, 149–166.

Badstue, L.B., Bellon, M.R., Juárez, X., Manuel, I., and Solano, A.M. (2003) Social relations and seed transactions among smallscale maize farmers in the Central Valleys of Oaxaca, Mexico. CIMMYT Economics Working Paper No. 02–02. CIMMYT, Mexico DF, 15 pp.

Bellon, M.R. and Berthaud, J. (2004) Transgenic maize and the evolution of landrace diversity in Mex-ico: the importance of farmers' behaviour. *Plant Physiology* 134(3), 883–888.

Bellon, M.R. and Risopoulos, J. (2001) Small-scale farmers expand the benefits of improved maize germplasm: a case study from Chiapas, Mexico. *World Development* 29, 799–811.

Bellon, M.R., Berthaud, J., Smale, M., Aguirre, J.A., Taba, S., Aragón, F., Díaz, J. and Castro, H. (2003) Participatory landrace selection for on farm conservation: an example from the Central Valleys of Oaxaca, Mexico. *Genetic Resources and Crop Evolution* 50, 401–416.

Byerlee, D. (1991) The CIMMYT Economics Program: A brief history. Draft paper. CIMMYT internal document.

Cernea, M.M. and Guggenheim, S.E. (1985) Is anthropology superfluous in farming systems research? *Farming Systems Research* 4, 504–517.

CIMMYT (1997) *People and Partnerships: Medium-Term Plan of the International Maize and Wheat Improvement Centre (CIMMYT), 1998–2000*. CIMMYT, Mexico DF, 95 pp.

Ekboir, J. (2002) Developing no-till packages for small-scale farmers. In: Ekboir, J. (ed.) *World Wheat Overview and Outlook*. CIMMYT, Mexico DF, 66 pp.

Gollin, D. and Smale, M. (1999) Valuing genetic diversity: crop plants and agroecosystems. In: Collins, W.W. and Qualset, C.O. (eds) *Biodiversity in Agroecosystems*. CRC Press, Boca Raton, Florida, pp. 238–265.

Meng, E. and Brush, S.B. (1998) Farmers' valuation and conservation of crop genetic resources. *Genetic Resources and Crop Evolution* 45, 139–150.

Morris, M.L. (ed.) (1998) *Maize Seed Industries in Developing Countries*. Lynne Rienner, Boulder, Colorado, 401 pp.

Morris, M. and Bellon, M.R. (2004) Participatory plant breeding research: opportunities and challenges for the international crop improvement system. *Euphytica* 136(1), 21–35.

Morris, M.L., Risopoulos, J. and Beck, D. (1999) *Genetic Change in Farmer-Recycled Maize Seed: A Review of the Evidence*. CIMMYT Economics Working Paper 99–07. CIMMYT, Mexico DF, 62 pp.

Perrin, R.K. and Winkelmann, D.L. (1976) Impediments to technical progress on small versus large farms. *American Journal of Agricultural Economics* 58, 889–894.

Smale, M. (1997) The green revolution and wheat genetic diversity: some unfounded assumptions. *World Development* 25, 1257–1269.

Smale, M., Bellon, M.R., Aguirre, A., Manuel, I., Mendoza, J., Solano, A.M., Martínez, R. and Ramírez, A. (2003) The economic costs and benefits of a participatory project to conserve maize landraces on farms in Oaxaca, Mexico. *Agricultural Economics* 29, 265–276.

Tripp, R. (1991) The limitations of on-farm research. In: Tripp, R. (ed.) *Planned Change in Farming Systems: Progress in On-Farm Research*. John Wiley and Sons, Chichester, UK, pp. 247–256.

Tripp, R.K., Marfo, A., Dankyi, A. and Read, M. (1987) *Changing Maize Production Practices of Small-Scale Farmers in the Brong-Ahafo Region, Ghana*. CIMMYT/Ghana Grains Development Project, Mexico DF, 30 pp.

Water to Thirsty Fields: How Social Research Can Contribute

7

Madar Samad and Douglas J. Merrey[1]

Four basic features shape the research agenda of the International Water Management Institute (IWMI). First, the primary focus of its research is on issues relating to the management of irrigation and water resources.[2] Management is fundamentally a social process. Second, the research centres on relationships between water and people: farmers, irrigation agency personnel, women, the rural and urban poor and other water users and stakeholders. Better water management is believed to increase the productivity of land and water and empower poor people to improve their lives. Third, because of the emphasis on people-centred research, a key research method employed is interacting with people who are a major source of data and information and the beneficiaries of our research. Finally, IWMI's research laboratories are 'real' – the irrigation systems and river basins of the world. These features make it imperative to take an explicitly interdisciplinary approach and to integrate concepts and methods from social sciences with those of other disciplines in the institute's research strategies and methodologies.

We highlight the applications of social science concepts and methods at IWMI to analyse water sector problems and issues, particularly in irrigation management, which has been a dominant component of IWMI's research agenda since the institute's inception. We demonstrate that the transformation of the International Irrigation Management Institute (IIMI) into IWMI, with a broader mandate, has reinforced the need for social science applications.

©CAB International 2006. *Researching the Culture in Agri-*Culture: *Social Research for International Development* (eds M.M. Cernea and A.H. Kassam)

IWMI's Programme Themes: Past and Present

By the early 1980s it was becoming increasingly clear that the heavy investments in irrigation construction in developing countries in the 1960s and 1970s had, in many cases, not yielded benefits on the scale anticipated. The poor performance of irrigation systems, especially the large schemes owned and managed by government agencies was attributed to poor management. The 'management gap' was perceived in terms of erratic and unequal distribution of irrigation water, poor maintenance of physical facilities, increasing incidence of water-related conflicts among farmers and between farmers and officials, information gaps, negative environmental impacts and lack of trained irrigation managers. IIMI was set up in 1984 to find solutions to these problems. Most of the work during the first decade sought to find ways to improve the productivity and equity of canal irrigation schemes.

At the inception of the institute, three research themes were defined: system management, system rehabilitation and improvement and farmer-managed irrigation systems. The first Medium-term Plan for 1994–1998, prepared after IWMI joined the Consultative Group on International Agricultural Research (CGIAR), proposed five major research themes and four cross-cutting themes. The focus was primarily on the irrigation sector, which continued to be considered a high priority in water resource development.

By the mid-1990s, the understanding of water resource issues had changed dramatically within the institute and among the world's scientists, policymakers and leadership. They had a greater appreciation of the problems posed by growing scarcity and competition for water. Investments by international agencies and national governments steadily declined in irrigation infrastructure, operation and maintenance of irrigation systems and research for irrigated agriculture. Given the long gestation period for most irrigation improvements, under-investment could lead to a crisis in food supply and in the quantity and quality of water in many regions of the developing world. The emerging trends required new policies, technologies, institutions and management systems. The institute's mission and name were changed to reflect the new realities and problems arising as we enter an era of water scarcity. Since 1995 the research focus has undergone a major shift – a 'paradigm shift'.

The salient features of the new IWMI paradigm are the following:[3]

- While irrigation will continue to be the dominant user of water, irrigation and irrigated agriculture cannot be analysed in isolation from other water uses and users. There is a growing need for policies and institutions based on integrated water resource management (IWRM).

- Closely related to IWRM, a basin-level approach to measuring water-use efficiency is needed to take into account the multiple uses and reuses (recycling) of water for irrigation and other purposes.
- Basin- and system-level analyses must consider both groundwater and surface water irrigation and the links between the two.
- Increasing pressure on water resources, including the need to recycle waste water, leads to major deterioration in water quality, although in some instances agriculture may benefit.
- Water scarcity is associated with growing problems of poverty, gender inequity and environmental degradation. Attention must be given to productivity, equity and sustainability in the use of water resources.
- Poverty persists in chronically water-scarce and marginal areas. To reduce it, rainfall and limited water supplies must be used more effectively.

These features of the new research paradigm are reflected in the current research themes and projects, which will continue to evolve. The major research themes and their goals are as follows:[4]

1. *Integrated water management for agriculture.* Develop and apply new research methodologies to assess and improve irrigation water management performance in an IWRM framework and identify key methodologies, processes and actions that will help reduce poverty and increase food and environmental security.

2. *Smallholder water and land management systems.* Identify and promote smallholder water and land management systems that will help improve the livelihoods of poor rural men and women and drive increases in water productivity while conserving the environment.

3. *Sustainable groundwater management.* Develop and disseminate an accurate and refined understanding of the socio-ecological value of groundwater and highlight the nature and scale of the consequences of its unsustainable use. Identify promising technologies and management approaches with potential to help achieve sustainable use of groundwater.

4. *Water resource institutions and policies.* Identify policies, legal and institutional frameworks and organizational options that will best enhance and sustain high productivity of water and land resources and help eradicate rural poverty. Develop research-based guidelines for water policy reform, design of river basin management institutions that give poor people a voice and support systems for local management of irrigation that will lead to more effective management of water in river basins.

5. *Water, health and the environment.* Incorporate health and environmental safeguards in water resource planning and management by scientifically documenting the relationships among water, human health and ecosystems, and by developing practical solutions to mitigate adverse health impacts and sustain ecosystems while obtaining optimum agricultural production. Reuse of urban waste water for agriculture and agro-ecological approaches to malaria are two important thrusts.

Each research theme has a separate focus but complements the work of the others. Most of the research projects under each theme adopt a multidisciplinary approach; many straddle themes. The second, third and fourth themes have more substantial (non-economics) social science input than the others.

A sixth area is the Comprehensive Assessment of Water Management in Agriculture, which is not a research theme *per se* but an international (inter-centre) programme supporting research, capacity building and knowledge sharing to find ways to address the perceived conflicts between agricultural and environmental uses of water.

IWMI's mission is to improve water and land resource management for food, livelihoods and nature.

Role of Social Science Research at IWMI

IWMI scientists have always recognized the complexity of water management issues: no single discipline has adequate tools and concepts to solve problems. Scientists of different disciplines must collaborate by defining and understanding the core causes of problems. This has required scientists to achieve a reasonable understanding of their colleagues' disciplines and also led IWMI's social scientists to be eclectic and practical in choosing theoretical frameworks and methodologies. In its first decade, IWMI's research programme largely consisted of donor-funded applied research and capacity-building activities, in cooperation with government departments. Nevertheless, application of concepts and methods from various branches of social sciences has always been central to achieving IWMI's mandate. The following sections summarize some of the key findings of research projects that involved substantial application of concepts and methods from the social sciences.

Farmer-managed irrigation systems

Research on farmer-managed irrigation systems (FMISs) has been an important component of the research agenda since the institute's inception. The main objective of the research was to understand the organization and functioning of these systems to find ways to help them improve their performance and to test the notion that FMIS principles could be transferred to government-built irrigation schemes. IWMI's work in this area builds on important work of other scholars carried out over the past several decades, notably studies of Edmund Leach, Clifford Geertz, Walter Coward and, more recently, Elinor Ostrom and the Workshop in Political Theory and Policy Analysis at Indiana University[5]. Three key research questions have been addressed:

- What kinds of institutional arrangements and management practices have proven effective and sustainable in traditional FMISs?
- What internal and external stresses interfere with the performance and sustainability of FMISs?
- What lessons from FMISs can be used to improve performance of government-built irrigation schemes?

Field work was done primarily in Nepal and Sri Lanka, complemented by some empirical investigations in the Philippines, Indonesia and Pakistan. Social scientists worked with engineers to assess the performance of FMISs and to understand the underlying social principles that explained their performance. Some of the salient findings are as follows (see Merrey, 1997b: 131–142, for a synthesis and references):

- Traditional FMISs develop rules gradually over periods of negotiation and experimentation.
- Rule compliance and leadership are more effective when rules are established by the irrigators themselves.
- Socioeconomic differentiation within the community weakens rule compliance.
- FMISs generally use less formal sanctions (e.g. public shame) for rule breakers.
- Water laws and policies related to FMIS are poorly developed and in some cases, counterproductive, undermining the viability of FMIS.
- The most common threats to institutional viability of FMISs are socio-economic differentiation and non-participatory public interventions.

IWMI has also developed information systems based on farmers' knowledge and perceptions. IWMI scientists drew eclectically from rural sociology, social anthropology and economics in analysing FMIS. Participatory rural appraisal techniques and methodologies for socioeconomic profiling have been developed and applied to action research programmes to strengthen support services (Gosselink and Strosser, 1995; Jinapala *et al.*, 1997).

Institutional reforms in the irrigation sector

Research under this theme has covered a wide range of topics; including farmer participatory irrigation management and irrigation management transfer (IMT). The early work was heavily influenced by Robert Chambers, Robert Wade and Norman Uphoff[6] – again showing the eclectic nature of IWMI's work. IWMI's social scientists were driven by a belief that by supporting the transfer of irrigation systems to farmers' organizations, they were also empowering rural people. Studies on IMT dominated IWMI's research agenda for about a decade, and the volume of work done in this field is substantial. It is a topic that consumed the time of most IWMI social scientists. The research focused on four broad areas:

- the process of management transfer,
- preconditions for viable management transfer,
- appropriate organizational models for water-users' organizations and
- impacts of transfer on the performance of irrigation and irrigated agriculture.

Much of the work on IMT consists of country-specific studies in Asia, Latin America and Africa (see, e.g. Vermillion and Johnson, 1995; Vermillion, 1997, 1998; Vermillion and Garcés-Restrepo, 1998; Vermillion *et al.*, 2000; Kloezen *et al.*, 1997; Johnson, 1997, 2002; Samad, 2002). While the earlier studies varied in conceptual design, later ones adopted a common methodology to facilitate comparative analyses. Most studies use a 'before-after transfer' and 'with-without transfer' framework and various farm- and system-level indicators to assess the impact of IMT on equity, efficiency, cost recovery and sustainability of irrigation systems. Reports of stakeholders and *post facto* assessments of single cases have also been used.

The results from the various cases suggest that, with the exception of Mexico and Colombia, unequivocal evidence of the extent of change due to IMT is insufficient. The main change has been a gradual decline in government financing of the operation and maintenance of irrigation systems. Water-users' associations also contribute only modestly to maintenance, raising concerns about the long-term sustainability of irrigation systems in the absence of adequate investments to keep systems functional. Again, with a few exceptions, evidence of broad impacts of IMT on system operations and agriculture production is not discernible. Evidence relating to agricultural productivity is mixed – neither improving negative performance nor detrimental where performance is positive. In Mexico, an assessment of performance of two transferred modules in the Lagunera region revealed that water users have successfully implemented water allocation and crop plans without any head–tail or other biases (Levine *et al.*, 1998). In Colombia, IMT improved management efficiency and accountability of agency personnel to water users but did not have a positive or detrimental effect on agricultural productivity (Vermillion and Garcés-Restrepo, 1998). However, evidence shows that even where impacts on agricultural or water management performance were not spectacular, farmers' organizations and the associated changes in government irrigation departments have helped achieve the broader empowerment goals of reform (see Uphoff, 1992).

Brewer *et al.* (1997) suggest that three basic provisions needed for successful transfer are recognition of water-users' associations and joint management committees, transfer of legal authority to these associations and legalization of changes in water allocation procedures. The case of the Tambraparani Irrigation System in Tamil Nadu, India, shows that water allocation rules conflict with farmers' interests, resulting in dissatisfaction among the associations' members. Farmers, through their water-user association, use various tactics such as demonstrations, political pressure and even illegal means to ensure the cooperation of the irrigation agency staff to authorize allocation of more water or with regard to special issues for their areas. In extreme cases, they take their water problems to courts (Brewer *et al.*, 1997). The problems at Tambraparani apply to other large scale irrigation schemes. Increasing demands for water from both farmers and other users make it essential to modify water distribution rules over time. The involvement of users in making the changes is essential to ensure that distribution rules serve their needs and that users accept the limitations in uses imposed by water availability. Bandaragoda (1998) finds similar evidence from selected canal command areas in Pakistani Punjab. The study documents that inflexibility in water allocation rules, despite management transfer, coupled with high inter-temporal and spatial variations in canal irrigation supplies, results in serious inequity for small, poor and tail-end farmers.

Sakthivadivel *et al.* (1993) show in a Sri Lankan scheme, what can be achieved through participatory action research even in the absence of favourable government policies. The first phase of research in two major schemes in southern Sri Lanka was only partly carried out in a participatory manner. In the second phase IWMI scientists adopted the basic principles of 'participatory action research' (Whyte, 1991), and guided a process that involved Irrigation Department and Mahaweli Authority officials and farmers in designing and assessing interventions. The process was not at all neat and straightforward but did lead to significant changes in how the schemes were managed, including a stronger and legitimate role for farmers in decision making and to better performance.

Merrey (1997c) addressed the question of how to design institutions that are accountable, to manage large-scale irrigation schemes. Based on a review of selected case studies and drawing largely on work by Ostrom (1992, 1993) and Coward (1980), he argues that where each irrigation scheme is managed by an autonomous organization accountable to its customers, performance will be better than if the scheme is managed by agencies dependent on the government or by agencies such as irrigation departments managing large numbers of systems (the norm in Asia).

In Africa, IWMI has worked on IMT issues in Niger, Nigeria and Sudan. In Niger, IWMI investigated the institutional and financial viability of systems transferred to farmers' cooperatives (Abernethy *et al.*, 2000). In Nigeria, IWMI worked with a river basin management authority to pilot-test a participatory action research approach to organizing farmers based on experiences in Asia. IWMI's work in Sudan focused on the transfer of pump irrigation schemes along the White Nile to farmers (Samad *et al.*, 1995). The study found that policy implementation was flawed. The government had concentrated its efforts exclusively on the divestiture of the parastatal agency and had been lax about enacting complementary policies and institutional reforms that would encourage alternative management systems to function effectively. The withdrawal of parastatal support was abrupt. Farmers were unprepared to face the new situation. They lacked the skill, resources and organizational capacity to manage the schemes.

In contrast to Sudan, Bangladesh's privatization policy entailed the transfer of equipment and inputs from the public to the private sector, liberalization of equipment imports, withdrawing subsidies on equipment and the sale of publicly owned pumps to users' groups. The first of these policy changes has led to the rapid growth of shallow tube wells and to some extent, low lift pumps. Liberalization has made irrigation equipment more available and significantly reduced prices. Small farmers form a growing proportion of pump owners as the availability of inexpensive equipment in a range of sizes has enabled them to increase their purchases. Male and female rural workers seem to have benefited from jobs resulting from irrigation expansion (Mandal and Parker, 1995).

Research and practitioners' reports suggest that the success of management transfer programmes depends on certain prerequisites (Vermillion and Sagardoy, 1999; Merrey, 1997b,c), the most common of which are the following:

- clearly recognized and sustainable water rights and water service;
- infrastructure that is compatible with the water service, water rights and local management capacities (Perry, 1995);
- well-specified management functions and assignment of authority;
- effective accountability and incentives for management;
- arrangements for viable and timely conflict resolution; and
- adequate resources that can be mobilized for irrigation.

Despite the uncertainties of its benefits, IMT continues to be a major component of institutional reform programmes worldwide. Andhra Pradesh state in India is implementing an ambitious programme to transfer management of the bulk of the state's irrigated area to water-users' groups. South Africa has recently launched a programme to transfer publicly managed irrigation schemes to farmers' organizations. A key question is, 'Can IMT experiences in Asia and elsewhere be successfully replicated in Africa?' This formed the central theme of a recent study by Shah *et al.* (2002). Based on a comparative study of the experience of several countries and drawing on economics and sociology, the authors point out that nowhere in Africa does a significant body of positive experience suggest that straightforward IMT will work in smallholder irrigation as it has in the USA, Mexico, Turkey, New Zealand and Colombia. In many respects, the sub-Saharan African smallholder context differs from the situations where IMT has proven successful. African smallholders need broad-based multi-sectoral institutional reforms, credit, input and output markets, land tenure and extension services because only such broad multi-sectoral institutional reforms will make smallholders' farming viable. The study argues that even if basic 'process' preconditions (supportive legal policy framework, secure water rights, local management capacity building) are met, IMT is unlikely to work for African smallholders. They need a set of institutional alternatives that address the whole complex set of constraints facing them. IWMI's study also shows that institutional alternatives that have the best chance for success are those that help smallholders move to a substantially higher trajectory of productivity and income from where they can bear the additional cost and responsibility of managing their irrigation system. The first step must be to enhance the income-creation potential of smallholder irrigated farming by strengthening market access, promoting high-value crops and improving systems that provide extension and technical support to smallholder irrigators. This approach, rather than focusing exclusively on the direct transfer of irrigation management, will help create the right climate for it in these regions.

Beyond IMT: Institutional Reform Imperatives

To set the scene, Vermillion and Merrey (1998) argue that water management institutions require radical reform if they are to meet the challenges facing them in the next few decades. The challenges include increasing food production from irrigated agriculture to meet growing demand, coping with escalating water demand in other sectors, sustaining the quality of soils and water and improving the equity of water distribution. The five most important institutional changes required are: (i) replacement of administrative with service delivery organizations; (ii) conversion of irrigation systems into multi-use water service systems; (iii) transcending the infrastructure dependency-deterioration trap; (iv) establishing legal and regulatory frameworks for sustainable water management; and (v) implementing integrated water basin management. The central challenge will be to design institutions that ensure that water service providers are accountable to users. Effective, sustainable and integrated water management requires putting in place new institutions to ensure that the world can meet the twin imperatives of dramatically increasing water productivity and halting water-related environmental degradation.

The next two sub-sections examine IWMI's work on government agency and river basin institutional reforms.

Reform of government agencies

Reforming public irrigation management has been a priority area of IWMI's research since the institute's inception. Bandaragoda and Firdousi (1992) make an important contribution to contextualizing and understanding the reasons for this gap in an institutional context. Building on earlier work of Merrey and Wolf (1986), they adopt a broad definition of 'institutions' to include not only 'organizations' but also irrigation 'rules' – both formal (laws, regulations) and informal (customs, norms). A complex and strong institutional milieu has evolved in Pakistan. Established irrigation rules and organizations exist simultaneously with an intricate set of informal social institutions, which are often in conflict with the formal system. For example, 'actual' and 'operational' *warabandi* (rotational system of allocating canal irrigation turns) continue to co-exist in most canal command areas of Punjab province. This dualistic, uncoordinated and increasingly ineffective institutional framework is poorly articulated with Pakistan's physical infrastructure. Emerging requirements to improve irrigation performance are incompatible with institutions' capacities.

Raby and Merrey (1989) applied concepts from business management to analyse the performance of the Mahaweli Authority of Sri Lanka during a severe drought and found that the authority did a good job of allocating water at higher levels to sub-systems, but failed to support the efforts of field staff and farmers to apply more entrepreneurial approaches at lower levels. In a later paper, Merrey (1995) addressed the question, 'What is the potential for decentralization of decision making and control given the scale, complexity and hierarchical organization of the Mahaweli Authority of Sri Lanka?' The paper argued for restructuring of the authority long before the World Bank forcefully pressed the case.

In 1994, IWMI collaborated with the US Agency for International Development (USAID) and the Ministry of Public Works and Water Resources of Egypt to carry out an institutional analysis of the ministry's experience in implementing a multi-component 15-year project. Building on a successful approach used in Sri Lanka (Merrey *et al.*, 1992), IWMI followed a highly intensive and participatory approach for this analysis to enable the ministry to accept the results as its own, i.e. to feel a sense of ownership and commitment to the results. Detailed results are summarized and interpreted by Merrey (1997), who documented the high degree of hierarchy and fragmentation and duplication of programmes and functions among ministry units. This is amplified by the creation of special units to implement various donor-assisted projects. Inter-unit cooperation and sharing of information are also problematic. The study concluded that while the ministry is meeting current needs, it will have to make major improvements in its overall framework, management processes and human resource policies if it is to make good use of technical innovations.

A study by Kikuchi *et al.* (2001) analyses compensation levels of irrigation engineers in the Philippines, Sri Lanka and Pakistan to understand promotion policies and their relationship to performance. The study compares the level of irrigation engineers' compensation to that in other professions. In the Philippines and Sri Lanka, irrigation engineers' compensation has declined continuously, reaching a 1995 low that is 50% of what they received in 1965 in real terms. Irrigation engineers' compensation in these countries was also considerably less than for engineers working in private firms and even in other government agencies. In contrast, irrigation engineers in Pakistan's Water and Power Development Authority (WAPDA) have enjoyed a significant increase in their compensation, largely because of the high levels of benefits. Trends in the performance of the three agencies studied are consistent with trends in engineers' compensation, suggesting the plausibility of a relationship but not proving it. The study found that none of the agencies maintain adequate long-term records (two other agencies were dropped from the study because the data were not adequate). The crudeness of the data and the analysis is such that no causal relationship is established, but there is a plausible case for increasing compensation of irrigation professionals as part of a programme to increase irrigation agency performance in developing countries.

River basin institutions

Beginning in about 1998, IWMI initiated research on the design and effectiveness of institutional arrangements to manage river basins. This complemented work on irrigation performance in a river basin context – work that demonstrated that 'efficiency' of irrigation is very much a matter of perspective: while an irrigation scheme may be 'inefficient' if water is reused effectively downstream, then 'basin efficiency' may be very high, raising questions about the efficacy of interventions to improve scheme efficiencies in many contexts (Seckler, 1996; Keller *et al.*, 1996).

Many donors assume that river basins must have 'river basin organizations' for effective management, and promote various models throughout the developing world (such as the 'French model' or the 'Australian model'). In these initial years, IWMI researchers have asked two questions:

- Accepting that institutional arrangements are required to manage river basins as they are increasingly developed, what kinds of institutions are most effective at different stages of basin development?
- Where river basin organizations are needed, how can they be designed and implemented to enable the full range of stakeholders, including poor women and men water users, to have access to water and a voice in decisions?

IWMI researchers have argued that the history of river basin development can be seen as usually proceeding through three states: (i) a development phase when infrastructure is created to make water available; (ii) a management or 'utilization' phase as it becomes more efficient to improve management of existing infrastructure than to create new ones; and (iii) an 'allocation' phase, when demand for water exceeds the sustainable supply, and allocation among different uses must be managed (Molden *et al.*, 2001). In the first phase, the focus is on construction. A single entity such as the Tennessee Valley Authority or the Mahaweli Development Authority of Sri Lanka may be effective. But as water becomes increasingly scarce, leading to pollution, conflict, environmental damage, etc., institutional arrangements become increasingly necessary to manage these new issues.

Shah *et al.* (2001) argue strongly that it is a mistake to try to transfer successful experiences from developed to developing countries – that there are 'limits to leapfrogging'. The issues and problems faced by rich industrialized countries are not at all the same as the huge numbers of smallholders and high rates of poverty in poor developing countries. Rich countries' capacities – funds, human resources, information systems – are not present in developing countries. Therefore, developing countries must develop their own models for river basin management, building on their own histories, cultures and experiences. Developing countries can learn much from each other but cannot borrow wholesale from rich ones.

Many developing countries are radically reforming their water institutions. For example, Mexico and South Africa are introducing river basin management institutions as part of comprehensive water sector reforms to decentralize and democratize water management institutions and make them self-financing. Using a perspective on water institutions as imbedded arenas for contesting water resources, drawn from political science, Wester *et al.* (2003) assess emerging forums for river basin management in the two countries and conclude that the pace of democratization in both is slow. Mexico is characterized by continued government dominance and attempts to include already organized stakeholders in decision making, while substantive stakeholder representation is lacking. South Africa emphasizes social mobilization and transformation, leading to slower implementation and struggles over redistribution of resources. The authors conclude that, while not a panacea, moving from stakeholder participation to substantive stakeholder representation in river basin management holds more promise of achieving equitable water management. IWMI continues to work with South Africa to help make the new institutional arrangements more 'pro-poor', i.e. representative of the rural poor who form the majority in many water-stressed basins but find it difficult to compete with wealthy commercial farming and mining interests.

Closely linked to these studies was one supported by the Asian Development Bank – Developing Effective Water Management Institutions. It used a similar analytical framework to examine river basin institutions and their interactions with local irrigation management in river basins in five Asian developing countries (China, Indonesia, Nepal, Philippines and Sri Lanka) as well as supporting case studies of river basin management in Japan and Australia. The framework was based on institutional economics literature, especially North (1990), and is described in Bandaragoda (2000); some of the findings are in Bruns *et al.* (2002). The most significant finding of this study is the urgent need for clearly defined water rights. Without clear understanding of water rights and effective enforcement, the poor and disadvantaged groups are vulnerable to losing access to water. Effective mechanisms are urgently needed to consult stakeholders and enlist their cooperation in implementing programmes to develop and manage water resources. Well-designed stakeholder-driven institutions are more likely to have positive outcomes.

Some of this river basin institutional work is synthesized in Svendsen (2005). The case studies in this book test and apply a framework based on the idea that a minimum set of functions must be fulfilled for sustainable, effective river basin management, but that a wide variety of institutional arrangements may fulfil them. The idea is an argument against prescriptive river basin institutional designs. As river basins face more competition for water, smallholder agriculture will come under increasing pressure as it is perceived to be a 'lower-value' water consumer. However, given the importance of agriculture in rural livelihoods in most developing countries, measures are needed to improve the productivity of smallholder irrigated agriculture and strengthen the 'voice' of poor farmers in the newly created river basin management institutions (Wester *et al.*, 2005).

Mainstreaming Gender Issues

Gender studies at IWMI began in a modest way in 1993, with a junior professional staff member leading the research programme. The research was carried out mainly by other junior professionals and students and confined mostly to case studies on gender issues in irrigation under various socioeconomic settings. These studies generated useful insights into women's contribution to irrigated agriculture (e.g. Zwarteveen 1994, 1995a,b, 1997a). Two early studies, one in Nepal and the other in Burkina Faso, demonstrated the potential significance of gender analysis, overcoming initial scepticism among IWMI staff and management. Zwarteveen and Neupane (1996) report a case study of Chhattis Mauja Irrigation System, a large FMIS in the Terai region of Nepal, previously studied by Yoder (1994). The case study focuses on the intra-household organization of production to identify water users, the nature of participation of men and women in water-users' organizations and their implications for system performance. Chhattis Mauja is generally managed by the 'users' through several levels of organization

(Yoder, 1994). However, women never participate in any of the top levels – the general meeting, executive committee or area-level committees. Women do sometimes attend village-level irrigation meetings only if their husbands are not available, but rarely participate. Given that women are highly involved in managing irrigated farms, women's lack of participation in irrigation management organizations could potentially lead to discrimination against women irrigators. The study points out that non-involvement of female water-users, rather than being a disadvantage to women, enables them to become free riders (Zwarteveen and Neupane, 1996). Female-headed households pay less irrigation fees, are among the first to receive water, and are not penalized for water theft.

A study (Zwarteveen, 1997b) of the Dakiri irrigation system in Burkina Faso, one of the few where some women (in addition to men) obtained irrigated plots as individuals, also analysed the impact of women receiving an irrigated plot on agricultural productivity, labour contribution patterns and intra-household distribution of agricultural incomes. The study finds that where a man and woman each has a plot, labour productivity is more than twice that in households where only men do. In households with female plot holders, women are able to contribute more to the household's welfare. Having an individual plot sharply increases the efficiency of labour use and clearly enhances women's economic well-being, contribution to their household and bargaining position.

Apart from its empirical contribution to the gender-irrigation nexus, Zwarteveen's pioneering work and networking led to IWMI organizing an important workshop on irrigation and gender (Merrey and Baviskar, 1998), and hiring a senior gender specialist. The workshop brought together some of the best researchers in gender and water issues from around the world and significantly contributed to IWMI's decision to emphasize a gender and water programme in the Medium-term Plan for 1998–2001, initiate new field research programmes to address gender issues and build gender analysis into several ongoing projects.

Research on gender has continued to be a prominent feature of IWMI's research agenda in Asia and Africa (e.g. van der Molen, 2001; Saini and van Koppen, 2001) and helped raise awareness of gender issues among irrigation managers, policymakers, farm leaders and researchers. Yet, the gap remains considerable between positive intentions and concrete action. An important but hitherto ignored reason for this is the lack of adequate generic concepts and tools that are policy relevant and can accommodate the vast variation in irrigation contexts worldwide. The gender performance indicator for irrigation developed by IWMI aims to fill this gap (van Koppen, 2002). This sociological tool diagnoses the 'gendered' organization of farming and gender-based inclusion or exclusion in irrigation institutions, informs irrigation agencies what they can do for effective change (if necessary) and identifies gender issues beyond a strict mandate to provide irrigation water. The indicator was applied and tested in nine case studies in Africa and Asia (van Koppen, 2002). This is one of the few gender studies that offer a practical tool to guide the interventions of policymakers, non-governmental organizations (NGOs) and senior irrigation managers wishing to achieve greater gender equity in their development projects.

Recent research focuses largely on gender and poverty issues in the context of river basin management, mostly in Africa. Early findings are from experiences designing catchment management agencies in South Africa as required by the National Water Act. The findings show that achieving 'enough for all forever' through decentralized IWRM that helps eradicate poverty requires careful design and implementation of new pro-poor water institutions from local to basin level. The government's ability to steer this process will be crucial to its success (see Schreiner and van Koppen, 2002).

Water and poverty

Poverty alleviation through sustainable development is the central goal of CGIAR and its partner institutions and members. Historically, irrigation has played an important role in alleviating poverty and sustaining rural livelihoods by providing food security through increased production and lower food prices, protection against famine and expanded opportunities for on- and off-farm employment. Development of large-scale canal irrigation has been an engine of economic growth and poverty reduction in Asia. However, growing scarcity and competition for water and conflicts among people using the water for many different purposes and between stakeholders, pose a major threat to advances in poverty reduction (Barker *et al.*, 2000). Against this backdrop, IWMI has argued for adopting a comprehensive strategy for holistic management of water: a 'from bucket to basin' paradigm has been articulated as a front-end response mechanism for managing river basins to alleviate water deprivation, assure efficiency and equity in the use of basin water resources, protect the interests of the poor and marginalized gender and ethnic groups and harness environmental sustainability (van Koppen, 2000). 'Water deprivation' is primarily human made, not the inevitable result of natural scarcity. Water deprivation is conceptualized as 'asset related' (limited technological, institutional and financial capacity of the society to deliver water) as well as 'direct deprivation' (richer people depriving the poor of easy access to water). To ensure that *all* people receive the water they need for basic well-being, policies need to address both aspects of water deprivation (van Koppen, 2000).

Empowering poor women through access to irrigation and other production resources for their own farm businesses is an effective way to alleviate poverty. Customary practices and social norms in most parts of South Asia, for example, do not provide women with an equal and direct access to irrigation water. Likewise, some irrigation agencies exclude women categorically from access to irrigation water, although recently some have developed approaches based on a sound under-standing of irrigation–gender relations. Poor men and women stake-holders must be included early on in planning infrastructure development, defining access rules and establishing water-users' asso-ciations (van Koppen, 2000).

Ongoing IWMI studies show that access to land and water resources is an important determinant of poverty, and institutional reforms and interventions in water and non-water sectors to improve poor people's access to these resources offer considerable scope to enhance agricultural productivity and catalyse growth for effective poverty alleviation (see Hussain and Biltonen, 2001).

Treadle pumps in South Asia's 'poverty square'

In recent years, there has been an upsurge in the adoption of irrigation technologies for smallholders such as low-cost pumps, treadle pumps, low-cost bucket and drip lines, sustainable land management prac-tices, supplemental irrigation, recharge and use of groundwater and water-harvesting systems. Recent IWMI research suggests that the trea-dle pump has tremendously improved the livelihoods of the poor in eastern India, the Nepal Terai and Bangladesh (the heartland of the Ganga–Brahmaputra–Meghna basin) – South Asia's so-called 'poverty square' (Shah *et al.*, 2000). This region, which contains 500 million of the world's poorest people and is characterized by tiny landholdings, has underlying it, one of the world's best groundwater resources, 1.5–3.5 m deep (see Shah *et al.*, 2003).

The treadle pump is a pro-poor technology. It is affordable at US$12–30 in South Asia; is easy to install, operate and maintain; and has no fuel costs. Treadle-pump technology has the unique property of self-selecting the poor and positively impacting their livelihoods. Shah *et al.* (2000) suggest that treadle-pump technology augments land, enabling poor smallholders to raise crops in summer and winter, thereby increasing overall cropping intensity. Treadle-pump technol-ogy enables farmers to grow high-yielding and high-value crops such as 'china boro' rice and vegetables. In Uttar Pradesh and North Bihar, treadle-pump users had average potato yields of 16–17 t/ha, 60–70% higher than those of diesel-pump users (Shah *et al.*, 2000). As a result of improvements in these intermediate variables, the study estimates that farms using treadle-pump technology see an average increase of US$100 per year in annual net income, with gross incomes of US$750–1000/ha being quite common. However, net incomes do vary across households and regions. International Development Enterprises (IDE), a US-based NGO that developed and promoted the technology, claims to have sold 1.3 million pumps in Bangladesh since the mid-1980s and 200,000 in eastern India and the Nepal Terai since the mid-1990s. IDE indicates that eastern India and the Nepal Terai are potential markets for some 10 million treadle pumps. If and when IDE does saturate these markets, it will have accomplished one of the world's biggest and best-targeted poverty-alleviation interventions by increasing the net annual income of South Asia's poorest rural households. During the past 2 years IWMI, with IDE and other partners, has turned its attention to the possibility of replicating this impact in sub-Saharan Africa, where treadle pumps are more than twice as expensive as in South Asia (Inocencio *et al.*, 2003).

Conclusions

We have highlighted some of the conclusions emerging from IWMI social science research. Most of it has been interdisciplinary and highly eclectic in concept, theory and methodology, which we regard as a strength. The highlighted research outputs indicate the wide range of topics to which social science concepts and methods have been applied. These include household-level analyses of issues relating to gender and water; community-level studies on FMIS; and studies on the management of large-scale irrigation schemes that applied principles from sociology, institutional economics, anthropology and management science to the analysis of institutional reforms in the irrigation sector, macro-level issues relating to cost recovery and trends in irrigation investments, basin-level institutions, gender issues at various levels and to global-level analyses of future supply and demand for water. Because of the interdisciplinary nature of this research, most of it has been published in multidisciplinary journals on water resources, irrigation management and development, not in discipline-specific journals.

Clearly, social scientific research has been at the core of much of IWMI's work since its inception. In the early 1990s, 40% of IWMI's internationally recruited staff were social scientists (Merrey and

Bandaragoda, 1994). The ratio of social to non-social scientists has been fairly stable throughout IWMI's existence, except briefly in the late 1990s when some of the more technical issues dominated the institute's research agenda. As IWMI has broadened its mission and interests, new disciplines have been added, somewhat diluting the percentage of staff who are social scientists. They account for around 35% of the internationally recruited research staff (Wright *et al.*, 2003). Economists account for half the number, and the rest have formal training in other social science disciplines: there are two anthropologists and two sociologists and others with formal training in various combinations of social sciences. Many nationally recruited social scientists are employed for various country-specific assignments. In its recruitment policies, IWMI has often explicitly sought candidates with degrees in more than one discipline.

IWMI's social science work has identified the scaling-up of institutional interventions as a challenging area of research. Previous studies focused on institutional and policy aspects of establishing water-users' associations for irrigation management and their subsequent scaling-up to water-users' federations. IWMI envisions extending the domain of its social analysis to issues related to establishing private water companies, vendors' associations and federations of water supply agencies soon. The recognition that the river basin is the most appropriate geographical unit for developing and managing water resources not only broadens the physical domain in which research is conducted, but also requires dealing with a larger and more diverse group of water users and stakeholders. This is especially so in Africa, where most river basins are shared by two or more countries and therefore, international cooperation is essential to develop these water resources (Sadoff *et al.*, 2002). How to design transboundary basin institutions that build on and give voice to local institutions is likely to be an important research topic over the next 5 years in Africa.

The high priority given to poverty eradication is a major challenge, especially in the light of growing scarcity of water, which in many developing countries, severely burdens the poor. Demand is growing for the institute to play an important role in clarifying and solving water scarcity issues and thereby helping improve food security and the welfare of the poor living in water-stressed, poverty-stricken environments. Increasing the physical supply of water is only part of the solution. Effective institutional mechanisms are needed to improve access of the poor and disadvantaged to safe water. These requirements will prompt a greater need to apply social science research methods to analyse problems in the water sector. More than ever, social scientists must work with professionals of many disciplines as part of research teams to address the complex water issues of the 21st century. This is an important challenge for the next generation of IWMI social scientists.

Other changes in CGIAR and IWMI add further complexity to the research programme. For example, IWMI, like other centres, now carries out most of its work through partnerships with national institutions and through regional networks. However, too few social scientists are among our partners, a problem that will take years to overcome. The CGIAR Challenge Programmes are an attempt to restructure CGIAR centres to work effectively in partnerships on long-term global issues. IWMI is the lead partner in the CGIAR Challenge Programme on Water and Food. It is at an early stage – the first set of projects was announced only in November 2003 – but early evidence suggests that social scientists will play significant roles in the research to be supported. The programme has been proactive in encouraging participatory methodologies involving a wide range of stakeholders and addressing gender and other equity issues. The programme is not designed to address specific sociological or institutional problems but rather those such as improving food security, reducing poverty and making water and other natural resources more productive through interdisciplinary and inter-institutional partnerships. The proposed Sub-Saharan Africa Challenge Programme has a similar thrust. These new Challenge Programmes will provide important opportunities to social scientists and demand much of them for over the next decade and beyond.

Notes

[1]The authors gratefully acknowledge the assistance rendered by Munir Hanjra, IWMI, Colombo, in preparing this chapter.

[2]In April 2001, IWMI absorbed the programme and staff of the International Board for Soil Research and Management, adding land management to IWMI's mission. However, this has not yet significantly affected IWMI's social science work.

[3]For details, see Seckler (1995, 1996).

[4]With effect from January 2005, IWMI redefined its research themes. The current research themes are as follows: (i) basin water management; (ii) land, water and livelihoods; (iii) agriculture, water and cities; and (iv) water management and environment.

[5]See for example, Leach (1971, 1980), Coward (1980), Geertz (1969, 1972), Ostrom (1989, 1992, 1993), and http://www.indiana.edu/~workshop/

[6]For example, Chambers (1988); Chambers *et al.* (1989); Wade (1982, 1985); Wade and Chambers (1980); and Uphoff (1986, 1991, 1992).

References

Abernethy, C.L., Sally, H., Lonsway, K. and Maman, C. (2000) *Farmer-Based Financing of Operations in the Niger Valley Irrigation Schemes.* IWMI Research Report No. 37. International Water Management Institute (IWMI), Colombo, Sri Lanka, 35 pp.

Bandaragoda, D.J. (1998) *Design and Practice of Water Allocation Rules: Lessons from Warabandi in Pakistan's Punjab.* IWMI Research Report No. 17. IWMI, Colombo, Sri Lanka, 25 pp.

Bandaragoda, D.J. (2000) *A Framework for Institutional Analysis for Water Resources in a River Basin Context.* IWMI Working Paper No. 5. IWMI, Colombo, Sri Lanka, 45 pp.

Bandaragoda, D.J. and Firdousi, G.R. (1992) *Institutional Factors Affecting Irrigation Performance in Pakistan: Research and Policy Priorities.* Country Paper – Pakistan No. 4. IIMI, Colombo, Sri Lanka, 81 pp.

Barker, R., van Koppen, B. and Shah, T. (2000) *A Global Perspective on Water Scarcity/Poverty: Achievements and Challenges for Water Resource Management.* IWMI, Colombo, Sri Lanka, 17 pp.

Brewer, J.D., Sakthivadivel, R. and Raju, K.V. (1997) *Water Distribution Rules and Water Distribution Performance: a Case Study in the Tambraparani Irrigation System.* IWMI Research Report No. 12. IWMI, Colombo, Sri Lanka, 34 pp.

Bruns, B., Bandaragoda, D.J. and Samad, M. (eds) (2002) Integrated water-resources management in a river basin context: institutional strategies for improving productivity of agricultural water management. *Proceedings of the Regional Workshop*, 15–19 January 2001, Malang, Indonesia. IWMI, Colombo, Sri Lanka, 315 pp.

Chambers, R. (1988) *Managing Canal Irrigation: Practical Analysis from South Asia.* Oxford and IBH Publishing Co. Pvt. Ltd., New Delhi, 279 pp.

Chambers, R., Saxena, N.C. and Shah, T. (1989) *To the Hands of the Poor: Water and Trees.* Intermediate Technology Publications, London, 273 pp.

Coward, E.W. Jr (1980) Management themes in community irrigation systems. In: Coward, E.W. Jr (ed.) *Irrigation and Agricultural Development in Asia: Perspectives from the Social Sciences.* Cornell University Press, Ithaca, New York, pp. 203–218.

Geertz, C. (1969) *Agricultural Involution: The Processes of Ecological Change in Indonesia.* University of California Press, Berkeley, California, 176 pp.

Geertz, C. (1972) The wet and the dry: traditional irrigation in Bali and Morocco. *Human Ecology* 1(1), 23–39.

Gosselink, P. and Strosser, P. (1995) *Participatory Rural Appraisal for Irrigation Management Research: Lessons from IIMI's Experience.* Working Paper No. 38. IWMI, Colombo, 67 pp.

Hussain, I. and Biltonen, E. (eds) (2001) Managing water for the poor. *Proceedings of the Regional Workshop on Pro-Poor Intervention Strategies in Irrigation Agriculture in Asia*, 9–10 August 2001, Colombo. IWMI, Colombo, 220 pp.

Inocencio, A., Sally, H. and Merrey, D.J. (2003) *Innovative Approaches to Agricultural Water Use for Improving Food Security in Sub-Saharan Africa.* IWMI Working Paper No. 55. IWMI, Colombo.

Jinapala, K., Brewer, J.D., Sakthivadivel, R. (1997) Multilevel participatory rural appraisal: an experience from Sri Lanka. In: Shivakoti, G., Varughese, G., Ostrom, E., Shukla, A., and Thapa, G. (eds) *People and Participation in Sustainable Development: Understanding the Dynamics of Natural Resource Systems. Proceedings of the International Conference*, 17–21 March 1996, Institute of Agriculture and Animal Science, Tribhuvan University, Rampur, Chitwan, Nepal. Workshop in Political Theory and Policy Analysis Indiana University, Bloomington, Indiana, pp. 251–272.

Johnson, S.H. III (1997) *Irrigation Management Transfer in Mexico: a Strategy to Achieve Irrigation District Sustainability.* IWMI Research Report No. 16. IWMI, Colombo, Sri Lanka, 31 pp.

Johnson, S.H. III (2002) Irrigation management transfer: decentralizing public irrigation in Mexico. *Water International* 22(3), 159–167. In: German Association for Water Resources and Land Improvement (ed.) *Deregulation, Decentralization and Privatization in Irrigation: State Functions Move to the Free Market.* Wirtschafts und Verlagsgesellschaft Gas und Wasser, Bonn, Germany, pp. 437–445. Also published in: Saleth, R.M. (ed.) *Water Resources and Economic Development.* Edward Elgar Publishing, Cheltenham, UK, pp. 40–63.

Keller, A., Keller, J. and Seckler, D. (1996) *Intergrated Water Resource Systems: Theory and Policy Implications.* IWMI Research Report No. 3. IWMI, Colombo, 15 pp.

Kikuchi, M., Merrey, D.J. and Dassenaike, L. (2001) Compensation of irrigation professionals: three Asian irrigation agencies. *Irrigation and Drainage* 50(1), 65–74.

Kloezen, W.H., Garcés-Restrepo, C. and Johnson, S.H. III (1997) *Impact Assessment of Irrigation Management Transfer in the Alto Rio Lerma Irrigation District, Mexico.* IWMI Research Report No. 15. IWMI, Colombo, 33 pp.

Leach, E.R. (1971) *Pul Eliya: A Village in Ceylon – A Study on Land Tenure and Kinship.* Cambridge University Press, London, 346 pp.

Leach, E.R. (1980) Village irrigation in the dry zone of Sri Lanka. In: Coward, E.W. Jr (ed.) *Irrigation and Agricultural Development in Asia: Perspectives from the Social Sciences.* Cornell University Press, Ithaca, New York, pp. 91–126.

Levine, G., Cruz Galvan, A., Garcia, D., Garcés-Restrepo, C. and Johnson, S. III (1998) *Performance of Two Modules in the Lagunera Region of Mexico.* IWMI Research Report No. 23. IWMI, Colombo, 15 pp.

Mandal, M.A.S. and Parker, D.E. (1995) *Evolution and Implications of Decreased Public Involvement in Minor Irrigation Management in Bangladesh.* Short Report Series on Locally Managed Irrigation No. 11. IIMI, Colombo, 22 pp.

Merrey, D.J. (1995) Potential for devolution of management to farmers' organizations in an hierarchical irrigation management agency: the case of the Mahaweli Authority of Sri Lanka. In: Muller,

H.P. and Hettige, S.T. (eds) *The Blurring of a Vision – The Mahaweli: Its Social, Economic and Political Implications.* Sarvodaya Book Publishing Services, Ratmalana, Sri Lanka, pp. 222–243.

Merrey, D.J. (1997a) *Governance and Institutional Arrangements for Managing Water Resources in Egypt.* The Liquid Gold Series. Wageningen University and International Livestock Research Institute, The Netherlands, 28 pp.

Merrey, D.J. (1997b) *Expanding the Frontiers of Irrigation Management Research: Results of Research and Development at the International Irrigation Management Institute, 1984 to 1995.* IWMI, Colombo, 228 pp.

Merrey, D.J. (1997c) *Institutional Design Principles for Accountability in Large Irrigation Systems.* IWMI Research Report No. 8. IWMI, Colombo, 26 pp.

Merrey, D. and Bandaragoda, T. (1994) The role for social sciences in International Irrigation Management Institute's (IIMI) mandate to strengthen institutions and link research to policy. In: Collinson, M.P. and Platais, K.W. (eds) Social Science Research in the CGIAR. *Proceedings of the Meeting of CGIAR Social Scientists held at International Service for National Agricultural Research,* 17–20 August 1992, The Hague, Netherlands. CGIAR Study Paper No. 28. CGIAR, Washington, DC, pp. 27–28.

Merrey, D. and Baviskar, S. (eds) (1998) Gender Analysis and Reform of Irrigation Management: Concepts, Cases, and Gaps in Knowledge. *Proceedings of the Workshop on Gender and Water,* 15–19 September 1997, Habarana, Sri Lanka. IWMI, Colombo, 268 pp.

Merrey, D.J. and Wolf, J.M. (1986) *Irrigation Management in Pakistan: Four Papers. Digana Village, Sri Lanka.* IIMI Research Paper No. 4. IIMI, Colombo, 66 pp.

Merrey, D.J., de Silva, N.G.R. and Sakthivadivel, R. (1992) A participatory approach to building policy consensus: the relevance of the irrigation management policy support activity of Sri Lanka for other countries. *IIMI Review* 6(1), 3–13.

Molden, D., Sakthivadivel, R. and Samad, M. (2001) Accounting for changes in water use and the need for institutional adaptation. In: Abernethy, C.L. (ed.) *Intersectoral Management of River Basins. Proceedings of the International Workshop on Integrated Water Management in Water-Stressed River Basins in Developing Countries: Strategies for Poverty Alleviation and Agricultural Growth,* 16–21 October 2000, Loskop Dam, South Africa. IWMI and Deutshe Stiftung Für internationale Entwicklung (DSE), Colombo, pp. 73–87.

North, D.C. (1990) *Institutions, Institutional Change and Economic Performance.* Cambridge University Press, New York, 52 pp.

Ostrom, E. (1989) Governing the Commons: The Evolution of Institution for Collective Action. Workshop in Political Theory and Policy Analysis, Bloomington, Indiana, pp. 390.

Ostrom, E. (1992) *Crafting Institutions for Self-Governing Irrigation Systems.* ICS Press, San Francisco, California, pp. 111.

Ostrom, E. (1993) Design principles in long-enduring irrigation institutions. *Water Resources Research* 29(7), 1907–1912.

Perry, C.J. (1995) Determinants of function and dysfunction in irrigation performance, and implications for performance improvement. *Water Resources Development* 11(1), 25–38.

Raby, N. and Merrey, D.J. (1989) *Professional Management in Irrigation Systems: A Case Study of Performance Control in Mahweli System H, Sri Lanka*. IIMI Country Paper, Sri Lanka, No. 1. IIMI, Digana, Sri Lanka, 95 pp.

Sadoff, C., Whittington, D. and Grey, D. (2002) *Africa's International Rivers: An Economic Perspective*. World Bank, Washington, DC, 82 pp.

Saini, H. and van Koppen, B. (2001) Gender in Lift Irrigation Schemes in East Gujarat, India. Working Paper No. 11. IWMI, Colombo, 17 pp.

Sakthivadivel, R., Brewer, J.D. and Wijayaratna, C.M. (1993) Participatory action research in irrigation management: an example from Kirindi Oya. In: IIMI, *Advancements in IIMI's Research 1992: A Selection of Papers Presented at the Internal Programme Review*. IIMI, Colombo, pp. 189–208.

Samad, M. (2002) Impact of irrigation management transfer on the performance of irrigation systems: a review of selected experiences from Asia and Latin America. In: Sally, H. and Abernethy, C.L. (eds) *Private Irrigation in Sub-Saharan Africa. Proceedings of the Regional Seminar on Private Sector Participation and Irrigation Expansion in Sub-Saharan Africa*, 22–26 October 2001, Accra, Ghana. IWMI, Food and Agricultural Organization of the United Nations (FAO); and African,

Caribbean, Pacific (ACP) – European Union (EU) Technical Centre for Agricultural and Rural Cooperation, Colombo, pp. 139–149.

Samad, M., Dingle, M.A. and Shafique, M.S. (1995) Political and economic dimensions of privatization and turnover of irrigation schemes in Sudan. In: Johnson, S.H., Vermillion, D.L. and Sagardoy, J.A. (eds) *Irrigation Management Transfer: Selected Papers from the International Conference on Irrigation Management Transfer, 20–24 September 1994, Wuhan, China*. FAO, Rome, pp. 211–223, 457–476.

Schreiner, B. and van Koppen, B. (2002) Catchment management agencies for poverty eradication in South Africa. Paper presented at the Second Water Research Fund for Southern Africa (WARFSA)/WaterNet Symposium on Integrated Water Resources Management: Theory, Practice, Cases, 30–31 October 2001, Cape Town, 11 pp.

Seckler, D. (1995) New era of water resource management. *CGIAR News* 2(2), 11–12.

Seckler, D. (1996) The New Era of Water Resources Management: From 'Dry' to 'Wet' Water Savings. IWMI Research Report 1. IWMI, Colombo, 17 pp.

Shah, T., Alam, M., Kumar, M.D., Nagar, R.K. and Singh, M. (2000). *Pedaling Out of Poverty: Social Impact of a Manual Irrigation Technology in South Asia*. IWMI Research Report 45. IWMI, Colombo, 36 pp.

Shah, T., Makin, I. and Sakthivadivel, R. (2001) Limits to leapfrogging: issues in transposing successful river basin management institutions in the developing world. In:

Abernethy, C.L. (ed.) *Intersectoral Management of River Basins. Proceedings of the International Workshop on Integrated Water Management in Water-Stressed River Basins in Developing Countries: Strategies for Poverty Alleviation and Agricultural Growth,* 16–21 October 2000, Loskop Dam, South Africa. IWMI and DSE, Colombo, pp. 89–114.

Shah, T., van Koppen, B., Merrey, D., de Lange, M. and Samad, M. (2002) Institutional Alternatives in African Smallholder Irrigation: Lessons from International Experience with Irrigation Management Transfer. Research Report No. 60. IWMI, Colombo, 24 pp.

Shah, T., Roy, A.D., Qureshi, A.S. and Wang, J. (2003) Sustaining Asia's groundwater boom: an overview of issues and evidence. *Natural Resources Forum* 27(2), 130–141.

Svendsen, M. (ed.) (2005) *Irrigation and River Basin Management: Options for Governance and Institutions.* CAB International, Wallingford, UK and IWMI, Colombo, 258 pp.

Uphoff, N. (1986) *Improving International Irrigation Management with Farmer Participation: Getting the Process Right.* Westview Press, Boulder, Colorado, 215 pp.

Uphoff, N. (1991) *Managing Irrigation: Analysing and Improving the Performance of Bureaucracies.* Sage Publications, New Delhi, India, 263 pp.

Uphoff, N. (1992) *Learning from Gal Oya: Possibilities for Participatory Development and Post-Newtonian Social Science.* Cornell University Press, Ithaca, New York, 448 pp.

van der Molen, I. (2001) *An Assessment of Female Participation in Minor Irrigation Systems in Sri Lanka.* Working Paper No. 8. IWMI, Colombo, 38 pp.

van Koppen, B. (2000) *From Bucket to Basin: Managing River Basins to Alleviate Water Deprivations.* IWMI, Colombo, 48 pp.

van Koppen, B. (2002) *A Gender Performance Indicator for Irrigation: Concepts, Tools and Applications.* IWMI Research Report No. 59. IWMI, Colombo, 42 pp.

Vermillion, D.L. (1997) *Impacts of Irrigation Management Transfer: A Review of the Evidence.* IWMI Research Report No. 11. IWMI, Colombo, 35 pp.

Vermillion, D.L. (1998) Impacts of irrigation management transfer: Results from IIMI's research. *INPIM* 7 (1–3), 12–13, 21.

Vermillion, D.L. and Garcés-Restrepo, C. (1998) *Impacts of Colombia's Current Irrigation Management Transfer Programme.* IWMI Research Report No. 25. IWMI, Colombo, 38 pp.

Vermillion, D.L. and Johnson, S.H. (1995) Globalization of irrigation management transfer: A summary of ideas and experiences from the Wuhan Conference. In: Johnson, S.H., Vermillion, D.L. and Sagardoy, J.A. (eds) *Irrigation Management Transfer.* Selected papers from the International Conference on Irrigation Management Transfer, 20–24 September, Wuhan, China. FAO, Rome, pp. 1–14.

Vermillion, D.L. and Merrey, D.J. (1998) What the 21st century will demand of water management institutions. *Journal of Applied Irrigation Science* 33(2), 165–187.

Vermillion, D.L. and Sagardoy, J.A. (1999) *Transfer of Irrigation Management Services, Guidelines.* FAO Irrigation and Drainage Paper No.

58. IWMI, Gesellschaft für Technische Zusammenarbeit (GTZ), FAO, Rome, 98 pp.

Vermillion, D., Samad, M., Pusposutardjo, S., Arif, S.S. and Rochdyanto, S. (2000) *An Assessment of Small-Scale Irrigation Management Turnover Programme in Indonesia,* IWMI Research Report No. 38. IWMI, Colombo, 36 pp.

Wade, R. (1982) The system of administrative and political corruption: canal irrigation in South India. *Journal of Development Studies* 18(3), 287–328.

Wade, R. (1985) The market for public office: why the Indian state is not better at development. *World Development* 13(4), 467–497.

Wade, R. and Chambers, R. (1980) Managing the main system: canal irrigation's 'blind spot'. *Economic and Political Weekly* 15(39), A107–A112.

Wester, P., Merrey, D.J. and de Lange, M. (2003) Boundaries of consent: stakeholder representation in river basin management in Mexico and South Africa. *World Development* 31(5), 797–812.

Wester, P., Shah, T. and Merrey, D.J. (2005) Providing irrigation services in water scarce basins: representation and support. In: Svendsen, M. (ed.) *Irrigation Water Scarce Basin: Options for Governance and Management.* CAB International, Wallingford, UK and IWMI.

Whyte, W.F. (ed.) (1991) *Participatory Action Research.* Sage Publications, Newbury Park, California, 247 pp.

Wright, A., del Rosario, B. and Vaidyanathan, A. (2003) Unpublished draft consolidated report on external HQ programme and management review. IWMI, Colombo.

Yoder, R. (1994) Organization and Management of Farmers in Chhattis Mauja Irrigation System, Nepal. IWMI Research Paper No. 11. IIMI, Colombo, 149 pp.

Zwarteveen, M.Z. (1994) Gender Issues, Water Issues: A Gender Perspective to Irrigation Management. IIMI Working Paper No. 32. IIMI, Colombo, 62 pp.

Zwarteveen, M.Z. (1995a) Gender aspects of irrigation management transfer: rethinking efficiency and equity. In: Johnson, S.H., Vermillion, D.L. and Sagardoy, J.A. (eds) *Irrigation Management Transfer. Selected Papers from the International Conference on Irrigation Management Transfer, 20–24 September, Wuhan, China.* FAO, Rome, pp. 87–100.

Zwarteveen, M.Z. (1995b) *Linking Women to the Main Canal: Gender and Irrigation Management.* IIED Gatekeeper Series No. 54. International Institute for Environment and Development, Sustainable Agriculture Programme, London, 27 pp.

Zwarteveen, M.Z. (1997a) Water: from basic need to commodity: a discussion on gender and water rights in the context of irrigation. *World Development* 25(8), 1335–1349.

Zwarteveen, M.Z. (1997b) A Plot of One's Own: Gender Relations and Irrigated Land Allocation Policies in Burkina Faso. IWMI Research Report No. 10. IWMI, Colombo, 13 pp.

Zwarteveen, M.Z. and Neupane, N. (1996) Free riders or victims: women's nonparticipation in irrigation management in Nepal's Chhattis Mauja Scheme. IIMI Research Report No. 7. IIMI, Colombo.

Rootcrops in Agricultural Societies: What Social Research has Revealed

8

Gordon Prain, Graham Thiele, Oscar Ortiz and Dindo Campilan

A defining moment in the history of social research at the International Potato Center (CIP) was the radical proposal presented to it in the late 1970s and early 1980s for the conduct of agricultural research. Anthropologist Robert Rhoades and biophysical scientist Robert Booth argued that farmers themselves are innovators in their use of agricultural technology and that their innovativeness is conditioned by their social-cultural and economic circumstances as well as their physical environment (Rhoades and Booth, 1982). Therefore, technology development should begin and end with the farmer. This was an important and distinct new perspective. It does not begin and end with an understanding of the farmers' (changed) circumstances, or a description of the 'social context' through a diagnostic study at the beginning and an impact assessment at the end. Technology development means that research must engage with the 'social arena' – that complex of social actions, power relations and negotiations, decision making and innovation where agriculture takes place. Technology development also means that farmer innovation can be promoted by putting new ideas at farmers' disposal and following up to see how these ideas are adapted to the farmers' context.

This perspective contrasts strongly with the dominant model guiding most international agricultural research centres (IARCs) then and to some extent, now, which sees the centres as the main source of innovation in the mandated area, with technologies being channelled through national programmes and extension services and feedback on appropriateness (and priorities) returning via the same route. The recently renewed discourse within CIP and other IARCs on 'products' and 'delivery processes' seems, to some extent, a restatement of the model, once again failing to distinguish between centres as sources *of* innovation and as producers of information or *for* innovation (concepts, principles, 'rules of thumb', etc.).

The new proposal was a major contribution by social science to technological research and development. The question this chapter addresses is to what extent and in what way social research in CIP has subsequently transformed and elaborated that model, or whether it has moved in a different direction. A paper by Thiele *et al.* (2001) recently reviewed participatory research in CIP and covered some similar ground. Whilst this chapter draws on that earlier review, the focus here is specifically on the contribution of social research to CIP's programme, including, but not limited to participatory research.

Social Research Staffing in CIP

CIP has been one of the most consistent hirers of social researchers in the Consultative Group on International Agricultural Research (CGIAR) system. By social researchers we refer to non-economist social scientists, whereas 'social scientists' generally refer to economists and social researchers. The separation of a category of 'social researcher' is relevant, given the way that agricultural economics has dominated the hiring of social scientists over much of CGIAR's history. The dominance of economics was graphically highlighted in the Technical Advisory Committee (TAC) external review of CIP in 1976, which negatively commented on the 'complications' of a concern with 'broader social issues' that went beyond 'strictly economic methodologies'. The review stated the following:

> The Panel feels that in the future, the core of CIP's socio-economic work should remain in the realm of agricultural economics. However, to the extent that special funding and fellowships will permit...the participation of other social scientists...is encouraged.
>
> (TAC, 1977)

Yet, social researchers have had an unbroken presence since 1975, when anthropologist Robert Werge was hired as the first social researcher, just 3 years after CIP's founding. This early diversification of social science capacity occurred because of the commitment of the then Director General, Richard Sawyer, to a broad disciplinary mix in the Center and to the determination of the first CIP economist, Michael Twomey in having an anthropologist on the social science team. One way CIP was able to deflect TAC's recommendation was via a series of social science planning conferences, which made their own recommendations. David Norman, an economist and early pioneer of farming systems research, noted during the first social science planning conference two factors that help explain CIP's early commitment to social research:

> there is already a complete socio-economic team in CIP and '..' technology development on potatoes is only commencing at the present time...therefore there is a unique opportunity for the socio-economic group to play an *ex-ante* role rather than *ex-post* role, which often has destructive criticism connotations.

(Norman, 1977: 124)

The 1977 social science planning conference supported the plans put forward by the two economists and anthropologist making up the Social Science Department staff: to focus on field-level research with biological scientists. The conference strongly counselled the Social Science Department against becoming involved in a service role within the regional and training programme. The adoption of this recommendation set the stage for a strong field orientation within the department, a mixing of social science disciplines and a commitment to interdisciplinary research. Anthropologist Robert Werge was particularly influential in building an interdisciplinary style of working with biological scientists, especially postharvest researchers and plant breeders. Most social researchers have been social, cultural or agricultural anthropologists, but sociologists, extension scientists, human ecologists and a geographer have also worked at CIP (Table 8.1). The general pattern of CIP funding of social research positions as compared to economics and other staff from 1975 to the present is shown in Fig. 8.1. An average of 1.5 social researcher person-years per year have received unrestricted

Table 8.1. Person-year contribution of different social research disciplines, 1975–2002.

Social research disciplines	Person-years, core funds	Person-years, special projects
Anthropology	32	30
Sociology	2.5	5
Extension sciences	4	8
Human ecology	0	8.5
Geography	0	3
Total	38.5	54.5

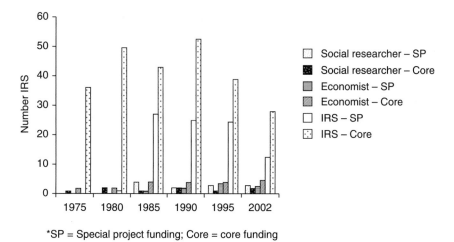

*SP = Special project funding; Core = core funding

Fig. 8.1. CIP staff by funding type*.

core funding. The centre has obtained restricted funds for 2–4.5 positions annually since 1984, averaging 2.9 person-years per year, in contrast with the funding of economist positions, which have averaged 3.3 person-years over the past 27 years using unrestricted funds and 1.7 person-years using restricted funds since 1981. Although the centre has relied more on restricted funds for social researchers, their overall strength is comparable with that of economists (Fig. 8.2).

The strengthening and consolidation of social research and economist positions over the years contrasts with the situation of other

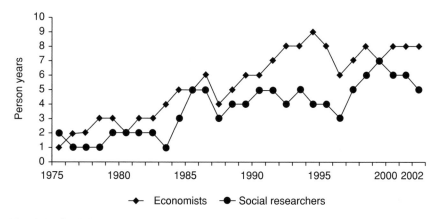

Fig. 8.2. Social researchers and economists, 1975–2002.

disciplines in the institution. From 1990 to 2002, for example, social scientists increased from 13 to 30% of total international recruited research staff (Fig. 8.3). The reasons for this 'staying power' are diverse, but three factors can be highlighted:

- Whereas CIP's regional programme[1] started off by locating generalist agronomists as regional representatives and liaison officers, this role has been increasingly taken over by social scientists, who have become 'networkers' as well as researchers.
- Demand for quantitative *ex-ante* support for research priorities and impact assessments of research results has been increasing.
- Funders are becoming more interested in participatory and gender-sensitive research, where social researchers have been active.

Patterns of Research and Deployment of Social Researchers, 1975–2002

The pattern in social researchers' activities during the past 27 years was initially linked to social science planning conferences in 1977, 1982 and 1988.[2]

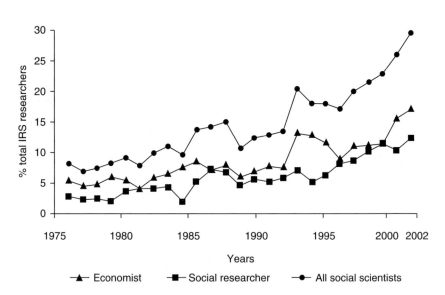

Fig. 8.3. Social scientists compared to all IRS, 1975–2002.

Social research skills developed early in CIP, up to about 1983, thanks to a supportive intellectual environment within the Social Science Department, which prioritized field-level research and gave importance to non-economic variables. Social researchers also had the chance to concentrate on a specific research field – postharvest.[3] CIP had already identified postharvest management as strategically important for a perishable and bulky crop such as the potato and this offered fertile ground for using social research skills.

The second period, up to about 1990, saw the consolidation of interdisciplinary micro-level research of headquarters staff and its expansion in regional settings and with National Agricultural Research Institutes, helping resolve the earlier conflict between the need for direct farm research experience among social science staff and the pressure to provide a service or backstopping role for the regional programme. This period saw continued postharvest research by social researchers, but also growing attention to seed and to more general characterization of potato-based cropping systems (Fig. 8.4). The period from 1990 to 1997 saw diversified research activities, including characterization of farming systems involving the newly mandated sweet potato crop, growing attention to genetic resources conservation and the beginnings of networking.[4] Diversification was driven largely by the systematic decentralization of social research staff from

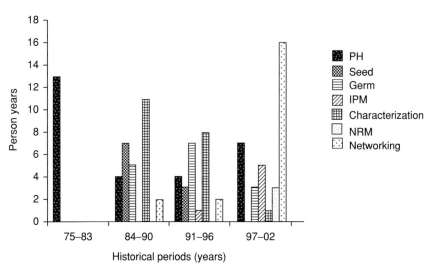

Note: PH, Postharvest; IPM, Integrated pest management;
NRM, Natural resource management

Fig. 8.4. Research fields of social researchers by 'historical periods'.

headquarters, which started in the late 1980s. Social researchers continued their postharvest work, linked to the increased use of sweet potato. Potato and sweet potato integrated pest management (IPM) also emerged as an important area of work, especially linked to farmer field school (FFS) methodology,[5] but the dominant activity is clearly 'networking'.

The regionalization of social researchers on staff in the past 20 years was a deliberate policy formalized during the second and third CIP social sciences planning conferences in 1981 and 1998. The second recommended placement of social scientists in regional settings through special project funding (CIP, 1982: 19). The third recommended 'one and perhaps two of CIP's senior social scientists be regionally based' (CIP, 1988: 13). Three social researchers were regionally located on special funding during the 1980s, and all social researchers were regionalized during the 1990s (Fig. 8.5). This contrasts with CIP economists who have remained predominantly and consistently headquarters-based whilst being supplemented with a regional presence in the 1990s.

Contribution of Social Research to CIP's Research and Innovation Processes

Modernization theory and the theory of a central source of innovation have been the two major development models dominating CIP's intellectual environment over the past 25 years, as they have other IARCs' (Biggs, 1990; Biggs and Farrington, 1991). This is not the place to elaborate these models in detail, but it is useful to recall that modernization theory, in its cruder formulations, posits a linear development from a 'traditional' and homogenized baseline characterized by technological inefficiency and conservatism and a largely subsistence-oriented, inward-looking production system. Modern technology is meant to liberate traditional societies and allow 'take-off' into economic development. This was the philosophical framework in which most CIP biological scientists were trained.

Put crudely, farmers' plots were the fields of tradition, while the IARC laboratories and experiment stations were the fields of modernity. Interactions with local farmers were structured in ways that derived from this philosophy and obviously tended to reinforce this model. Thus, a farmer in the Andes interviewed about crop genetic diversity during the mid-1980s would only mention her four 'modern' potato varieties to the researcher, not her 35 native varieties. She had received the message that 'traditional' potatoes were not important to *ingenieros*.

HQ/regional location of economists

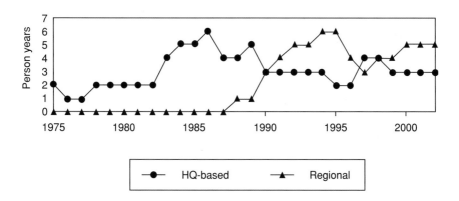

HQ/regional location of social researchers

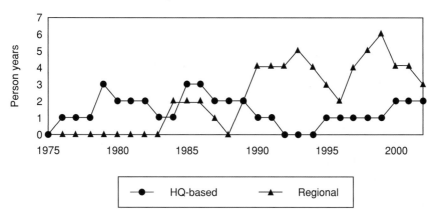

Fig. 8.5. Regionalization of social scientists, 1975–2002.

Meanwhile, the central-source model reinforces modernization theory with the notion of centres of excellence, pushing out modern innovations to national programmes, thence to extension services and to early-adopting farmers and driving out traditional practices. The model includes feedback mechanisms to IARC researchers but emphasizing the uppermost links in the chain.

Models, however, are simplifications of reality and all centres experienced differences in the playing-out of these models and their mix. Personalities, organizational structure and crop characteristics, among other factors, have been influential. At CIP the personality of the founding director general was important. Although trained in, and in many respects an exponent of, the central-source model of technology generation, he was also committed to disciplinary diversity and to close working collaboration with national research systems. He was also able to see the benefits – and funding opportunities – in currents of thought and opinion quite far removed from the technocratic, linear aspects of the orthodox model of international agricultural research. The useful role of anthropology and sociology was one unorthodox perception at that time. Gender was another. Whatever the complex motives involved, the appointment of rural sociologist Gelia Castillo, an outspoken professor of sociology from the Philippines, as the first female CIP board member in 1978, brought the issues of gender and social research more firmly into CIP's research discourse.

Crop characteristics were also important, especially the diversity of potato production ecologies and the problems of seed multiplication for a tuber crop. These factors largely dictated the need for a decentralized, regional organization with a close interface with users, quite different from the requirements of spreading new varieties of rice or wheat, for which a central-source model worked well enough. It led to a relatively lean and mean headquarters and the biggest network of regionally posted scientists linked to National Agricultural Research Institutes in the CGIAR system. The perishable nature of the potato crop also underlined the importance of postharvest research, including household storage and processing. As will be discussed below, postharvest and seed, and also IPM, are knowledge-intensive and 'socially intensive' technologies – their management is complex and penetrates deeply into the social arenas of agricultural communities – underlining the inadequacies of central-source thinking and making greater demands on the contribution of social research.

Breaking New Ground: Social Research 1975–1983

Early social research at CIP drew on several ideas current in farming systems research, such as the need to understand the ecological, physical and socioeconomic milieu and the 'customs', attitudes and personal constraints of farmers, as well as the institutional and policy setting and economic development aspects (Rhoades, 1984: 40). However, the research also drew on a longer anthropological history that involves 'getting inside' farmers' situations. The special strength of social research proved to be understanding the way technical issues are linked to social and cultural phenomena and how decision making about and the use of technologies are inseparable from this social arena.[6] But social research went further than this. It identified the social arena where agriculture is practised as an action space of innovation and thus connected with the action research ideas of sociologist William Foot Whyte, who was another important influence at that time (Whyte, 1984). The attention given to local innovation in this approach was also a major challenge to the central-source model. A third key element has been the way social research has been tethered to a technical perspective through strong interdisciplinary teamwork with biological scientists, ensuring that the emic vision of the social researcher – the view from the inside, from the local producer's or consumer's point of view – has been focused in scope and duration. The approach yielded a model that prioritized the farmer's social arena yet was a practical tool for on-farm research – farmer-back-to-farmer (Rhoades and Booth, 1982).

The farmer-back-to-farmer model was developed through research on postharvest issues affecting potato, especially improved use of a perishable crop through processing and the need to reduce postharvest losses in storage. One of the earliest and starkest illustrations of the need to understand the way technology is embedded in a social arena concerned the conservation of potato through cooking and drying for use in a traditional Andean potato dish (Werge, 1984). Whereas for the postharvest specialists, with a vision shaped by developed-country experience, the research issue was increased efficiency of solar dehydration (CIP, 1976: 61), the social researcher found that the farmers' real constraint was the time taken to peel the potatoes, when other agricultural tasks needed to be completed. Farmers needed better peeling equipment, not faster drying.

The experience with storage was equally striking. Whereas the initial focus of the postharvest team was reducing storage losses of table potatoes, the social researcher's informal survey revealed that local perceptions of 'waste' and 'loss' were different from the 'marketable' assessments familiar to the physiologists. Shrivelled, sweeter old potatoes have a role in the domestic food system of Andean farmers. However, farmers were greatly concerned with severe deterioration of seed potatoes. The solution was interdisciplinary and participatory. It was based on a social understanding of seed storage as embedded in the domestic domain, usually under the control of women, and a physiological understanding that the principle of diffused light to reduce sprout growth can be applied by farmers in 'stores' of their own choosing. The solution avoided the 'hardware' of separate storage structures favoured by conventional storage physiology as potentially conflicting with social dynamics. The solution favoured a 'software' encouraging farmers' innovation.

Four 'building blocks' of incremental social knowledge and strategic approaches proposed and built into CIP's overall knowledge contributions and research programmes can be identified:

- understanding and documenting the social arena where agriculture is practised and farmers make decisions on technologies;
- identifying the capacity of farmers for innovation in agricultural 'hardware', based on access to technological principles, such as diffused light storage;
- as part of engagement with the farmers' social arena, shifting emphasis to a different 'social unit' – from the individual, often male, farmer – to the domestic household involved in agriculture; and
- formalizing the focus on postharvest and consumption issues as well as production in the concept of the food system, a farmer-derived perspective where decisions and practices from production to consumption are interconnected.

Social Research in National Programmes, 1984–1990

These contributions to CIP's research were further elaborated following the 1982 planning conference, which recommended integration of an on-farm research approach in national programmes, especially by hiring additional social research staff on special funding. Three post-doctoral social researchers joined CIP and research activities became more diverse (Fig. 8.4). Some work on postharvest continued, but greater attention was given to seed and germplasm and especially later, to characterization work associated with the inclusion of sweet potato into the CIP mandate.

The idea of harnessing farmers' capacity for innovation by sharing new technological principles was systematically evaluated in Indonesia with true potato seed (TPS) technology (Potts *et al.*, 1992). Initial work was carried out by an interdisciplinary team consisting of national and CIP social and biological researchers and more detailed studies were undertaken as a sociology PhD (Sinung-Basuki, 1994).

Through working with two groups of farmers, the study examined the interest and capacity of farmers to innovate on the basis of concepts and principles of TPS use, provided in a spirit of collegiality by researchers, as compared to receiving more explicit extension-type instructions associated with technology packages in a formal manner.

The positive lesson was that creative involvement of farmers' capacity to innovate shortens the time needed to evaluate technologies – encountered as principles or as hardware – and eliminate those that are ill-adapted to the environment as turned out to be the case with TPS in Indonesia. Farmers exposed to extension-type instructions and packages had to go through the required steps of the 'package' to understand the concepts and principles of the technology, before they were able to change, adapt and ultimately reject the technology.

Unfortunately – and somehow surprisingly – the lesson learnt rather quickly by innovative farmers took much longer to be digested by the research community. TPS research and development continued for another 8 years, with two further efforts to evaluate their feasibility in Indonesia (Chilver, 1997; Suherman *et al.*, 2001). Despite changed progeny and better targeting of 'best bet' locations, the original judgement of the innovating farmers was not overturned and nowhere in Indonesia has TPS been adopted.

Seed research in the Andes involving social and biological researchers from CIP and the Peruvian national programme also elaborated a research strategy based on recognition of the socially embedded character of potato seed use and the important role of farmer innovation (Scheidegger *et al.*, 1989; Thiele, 1999).

To meet the needs of the 90% of potato farmers outside the formal seed system, the project adopted was to work with two major components of indigenous seed systems: self-supply systems, where farmers maintain their own seed from season to season through careful seed selection and storage; and seed renewal systems, where farmers in higher, healthier environments sell or barter seed in lower, more disease-affected zones. In this system, farmers obtain a small quantity of good seed and multiply it under carefully monitored conditions to obtain the necessary quantity of good seed. The 'certification scheme' for this informal seed system is the good name of seed-producing areas and the trust – often kinship based – between barter partners or buyer and seller. The formal government programme supplied subsidized clean seed to small producers in these strategic seed-producing regions to 'insert it' into the informal system. The programme also made directly available 25-kg lots of seed to farmers in other zones through multiple outlets to start off individual multiplication sequences.

The close working relations with farmers, and their social setting brought to light problems with some of the varieties that national programme agronomists had selected for inclusion in the clean-seed programme. A complementary activity, therefore, involved participatory variety selection with farmers in a wide range of locations to determine which varieties should be included in the seed programme and in what quantities (Prain *et al.*, 1992). The activity was taken one step further in Bolivia, where social researchers and breeders worked with farmers to select potato clones for varietal release (Thiele *et al.*, 1997) and then trained farmers to make crosses to produce their own clones (Gabriel *et al.*, 2000).

Another area of social research activity was linked to the inclusion of sweet potato in CIP's mandate. Because knowledge of sweet potato production systems and utilization patterns was limited, characterization studies were undertaken in Latin America, Africa and Indonesia, which drew on and further developed earlier social analysis tools. These were particularly important given the nature of the sweet potato crop and the systems where it is found. Although widely grown, sweet potato is often a secondary crop, planted in limited areas in different production systems of the same household, for example, as a home garden crop, an intercrop in upland fields and a dry-season crop in lowland rice paddies (Watson *et al.*, 1991). The diversity of production systems is also matched by a wide range of social uses, including different types of food preparation, as animal feed and as a raw material for processed products (Watson *et al.*, 1991; Fonseca *et al.*, 1994).

In summary, social research:

- showed that concepts and principles can stimulate local innovation, lower long-term risks and shorten farmers' learning curves;
- demonstrated that local social networks can provide a framework for technical solutions, and local or informal seed systems can form a part of a national strategy on seed quality – a contribution incorporated into CIP strategy and adopted by a number of countries as a national strategy;
- validated the evaluation of new clones or progeny with farmers to ensure inclusion of appropriate varieties in seed programmes, leading to 'standard procedure' of participatory variety selection in CIP and increasingly, in national systems and to explore options for Participatory Plant Breeding with CIP partners; and
- gained recognition for the approach requiring the characterization of social and gender dimensions of agricultural systems as an integral component of diagnostic studies aimed at technical interventions.

Regionalization of Social Research, 1991–1996

The social science planning meeting of 1988 called for moving senior social scientists out of Lima and into the regions, partly to develop more participatory and food systems-type methods through direct involvement in fieldwork and partly to introduce social science methods and approaches into regional networks (CIP, 1988: 13). Viewed through the lens of participatory research, Thiele *et al.* (2001) see this regionalization as a fragmentation of the major gains made with participatory research in the 1980s, when CIP became world-renowned as a centre of participatory methods innovation. Thiele *et al.* (2001) also see a fragmentation of on-going effort because little interaction took place among the regionally based exponents of participatory research, mainly social researchers during the early 1990s.

Both Center leadership of, and actual involvement in the practice of social research in CIP's headquarters research activities certainly declined, when no internationally recruited social researchers were present.[7] Cross-regional interaction was also limited, at least until the end of the decade. However, along with fragmentation at the core, there was also a positive reorientation towards key issues and opportunities in the new regional settings: continued development of participatory methods through contacts with, and learning from, other practitioners; and also a new networking role, which ranged from representing CIP in meetings with national research managers to supporting the inclusion of participatory, socially sensitive methods and tools in the national system where the social researcher was based, or across national systems. Asia and Latin America made significant gains in stimulating technology innovation and development in local social arenas.

In Asia, a novel research and development network sponsored by CIP and coordinated by CIP social researchers was established: Users' Perspectives with Agricultural Research and Development Network (UPWARD). It used a small-grant mechanism, method development and diffusion, training and an egalitarian publishing strategy to build a cadre of national scientists across the region capable of conducting participatory research on rootcrop agriculture (Prain *et al.*, 1993). Households and food systems were fundamental concepts, and tools were developed to permit a detailed understanding of the social arena within which rootcrops are grown (Rhoades, 1990). It was also UPWARD's work that helped highlight the importance of targeting diverse user groups, beyond farmers, and to orient research to their particular needs and circumstances (Prain, 1995). The network linked national researchers and development workers from non-governmental organizations (NGOs) and government, in collaboration with CIP scientists, to pursue specific research activities through small-grant support and mentoring (Castillo and Campilan, 1999). An external review of UPWARD (Horton and Guzman, 1997) concluded that the programme had significantly influenced the research agenda of CIP's regional programme in South-east Asia, notably through the agenda's integration in CIP's postharvest research. The same review cited the dynamic, flexible, non-bureaucratic and supportive programme operations that have resulted in UPWARD functioning more like a team than a network.

UPWARD social researchers developed methods to collect and document indigenous knowledge associated with rootcrop genetic diversity (Nazarea-Sandoval, 1992; Prain *et al.*, 1995). The method of memory banking developed by Nazarea-Sandoval documented in detail not only the cultural meanings of present and past varieties, but also the cultural and social arena that gives rise to that diversity. The method was the entry point for exploring *in situ* conservation, as an indigenous process as well as a way for researchers to work with a local arena of innovation (Prain, 1993; Prain and Bagalanon, 1998). Studies of the way local communities dynamically manage local genetic diversity, selecting and deselecting materials as local circumstances and demands vary led to a more general model of local innovation, referred to as 'local R&D' (UPWARD, 1997a).

In Latin America, the programme 'Promoción e Investigación de Productos Andinos' (PROINPA) was established in the early 1990s. A CIP social researcher, previously involved in participatory TPS research in Indonesia, was brought in to PROINPA to help institutionalize innovative research approaches in the Bolivian potato programme. Working with national plant breeders, the team sought to involve farmers as experimenters in the programme and provided groups of men and women with disease-resistant clones for evaluation under their own management (Watson *et al.*, 1992). However, the interests of breeders and social scientists diverged as the latter began to emphasize understanding processes of varietal diffusion among farmer networks. A later evaluation indicated limited impact (Thiele *et al.*, 1997). With the arrival of a replacement social research advisor, a new more institutionally sensitive strategy was devised, giving a central role to the Bolivian plant breeders and a methodological support role to social researchers (Torres *et al.*, 1999).

The team also sought a more institutionalized mode for working with farmer innovators, adopting the farmer experimenter committees or comité de investigación agrícola local (CIAL) model developed in the region by Centro Internacional de Agricultura Tropical (CIAT) (Thiele *et al.*, 2001: 435).

In the early 1990s, with special funding from the Kellog Foundation, the first experience of participatory IPM development was initiated in Huatata, Cusco, to control the Andean potato weevil. In the following years, similar experiments were carried out in other parts of Peru. The involvement of social researchers in this process allowed the collection and analysis of farmer opinions about IPM and the realization that for it to work, not only efficient practices were needed but also methods to facilitate farmer understanding of pest control (Ortiz *et al.*, 1997). This experience facilitated the design of a collaborative project between CIP and CARE-Peru to disseminate IPM to Andean communities (Fano *et al.*, 1996). This project confirmed the need to develop appropriate training methods to facilitate farmer learning of IPM, which was the beginning of the search for participatory research and training methods (Ortiz, 1997).

In summary, social research:

- established the importance for CIP of decentralized innovation emanating from close links with regional and local partners;
- facilitated the adoption of models of local research teams involving farming households, researchers and local change agents among national partners in Asia and Latin America;
- provided participatory research methods for biological researchers, including documentation of indigenous knowledge associated with crop germplasm, participatory plant breeding and IPM components; and
- contributed directly to institutional strengthening of national programmes.

Social Research Since 1997

The most significant developments in CIP social research since 1997 seem to be a greater sharing of the lead role in participatory research with biological scientists and a vastly increased role in 'networking' – an area where social researcher skills have become evident and have been tapped by the Center.

The most widespread participatory research conducted in CIP since the mid-1990s has been connected to IPM, including, in many cases, its inclusion within FFS methodology (Ortiz *et al.*, 1996; van de Fliert and Braun, 1999). Biological researchers primarily introduced and championed FFS in CIP, strongly supported by social researchers. This effort included a methodological debate with other entomologists involved in an alternative 'pilot unit' approach to field-based IPM with local communities.[8] Two CIP ecologists first adapted FFS to rootcrops from its use in rice agriculture in Asia, and a plant pathologist who had experience with rice FFSs in Asia before being hired by CIP introduced FFS into the headquarters research programme. FFS has more recently been further strengthened in headquarters, and the role of social researchers increased with a multi-country project funded by International Fund for Agricultural Development, now led by a social researcher (Ortiz and Forbes, 2003). Social research involvement in adapting FFS to potato-related problems highlighted the importance of not only developing technical principles for pest control but also of transforming them into discovery-based learning activities. Social researchers with a background in extension sciences made an essential contribution to this process in Peru, Bolivia and Ecuador. The refinement of the FFS method to work on potato late blight in the Andes has resulted in important benefits for farmers. An assessment of the contribution of the learning derived from involvement in the field schools – as distinct from the contribution of the improved technology – showed yield improvements valued at around US$236/ha (Zuger, 2003).

This most recent period has also seen a resurgence of social research involvement in, and contribution to, postharvest issues in CIP, especially linked to the use of sweet potato in Asia. This resurgence is a response to continuing recognition that family decisions about crop storage and use and the multitude of relationships in which crop-processing households engage are in a social arena of roles, power and rights over resources, beliefs, obligations and expectations that need to be analysed sociologically as well as agriculturally or economically. Gender sensitivity has been especially important in this field, because of the mix of household, production and marketing activities. Social researcher-led work in Asia has analysed household-based rootcrop processing, pig-raising enterprises and flour and candy producers. This work highlighted not only the need to increase income through improved efficiencies in local livelihoods (Campilan, 1998) but also looked at the environmental and social impacts of rootcrop processing (Peters *et al.*, 2002a). Recognizing the importance of social networks in local, household-based enterprises, social researchers and biological science colleagues have adapted the business concept of industrial clusters to understand better the synergies among micro-enterprises in Asia and their contribution to livelihoods (Peters *et al.*, 2002b). Action research associated with improved feed processing for pigs has bene-fited farmers by increasing the numbers of pigs they can manage and reducing cooking time and costs (Peters *et al.*, 2002c).

The second development has been formal network positions[9] which has accounted for the increase in time devoted by social researchers to networking: 16 person-years or about 43% of social research time during the period (Fig. 8.4). These 'networks' include regional programme coordination and country liaison positions; country development programme participation and the coordination of regional and global partnership initiatives and programmes. Different tasks are associated with these different positions:

- local institutional support and platform-building, including facili-tating local research and development ownership of projects among farmers, change agents of different kinds, local decision makers and researchers from different levels;
- national and regional knowledge sharing, planning, organizing and capacity building among traditional agricultural research institu-tion partners and public sector development agencies and also with non-traditional NGO and private sector organizations; and

- at the global level, linking with other IARCs, convening stakeholder meetings and building alliances with other international organizations.

At least three factors help explain why social researchers have gravitated towards networking responsibilities. Social researchers tend to have a rather broad and integrative outlook on agricultural research and development, which takes in perspectives of farming families as well as policy concerns at the national and international levels. Second, this outlook includes technical interests and awareness. The strong tradition of interdisciplinary research has particularly involved social researchers, who have been expected to become familiar with biophysical concepts and approaches while maintaining their own sphere of expertise in the social and cultural aspects of agricultural practices. This is helpful in building relationships and linkages with different types of organizations represented by different specializations, from molecular biologists to NGO community organizers. A third factor is the affinity between building networks and understanding social networking, a key area in the social research agenda.

Although the large amount of time dedicated to networking activities by social researchers is time not spent in field-level research, these activities have made an important contribution to CIP's mission. Networking is a process of building social and human capital in partner institutions and in CIP itself. Networking also locates the Center within an agricultural knowledge and information system, as one of a number of actors (individuals and institutions) who generate knowledge and exchange agricultural information (Röling, 1990).

At the local level, platform building aims to strengthen the linkages, trust and understanding between different stakeholder groups to enable them to work together and complement their skills and perspectives to achieve sustainable development. This is the goal of 'local R&D' pioneered by CIP's UPWARD network in Asia. Similar platform building has been achieved in Latin America at local and national levels through the activities of PROINPA in Bolivia and more recently, regionally, through PAPA ANDINA and the project Innovación Tecnológica y Competitividad de la Papa en el Perú (Devaux and Thiele, 2002).

The strengthening of relationships among research and development institutions in the regions facilitates the flow of knowledge and skills that is a major part of CIP's mission. Social researchers have contributed to this not only in terms of process (building social capital for the partner institutions and CIP) but also of content (building human capital through increased awareness of the social aspects of agriculture; better understanding and application of participatory approaches and methods; and greater gender sensitivity in national priorities, plans and research activities). For example, participation in the

UPWARD network by Chinese research institutions led to major changes in attitudes to field-level, participatory and gender-sensitive research. Chinese national and provincial governments gave awards to an UPWARD project in Zheijang province and promoted the local counterpart (UPWARD, 1997b). In the Philippines, an UPWARD project involving a regional research centre and the government's health and education departments was given a national award in recognition of outstanding inter-agency partnerships (Perez *et al.*, 2001).

In summary, the contributions of social research since 1997 have:

- helped institutionalize FFS within CIP as the major tool for farmer innovation in integrated management of pests and diseases; and quantified income impact demonstrated in Peru through the effects of the learning component of FFS, distinct from the effects of the technology (Zuger, 2003);
- established the centrality of a livelihood approach to agriculture in general and as the entry point to postharvest agro-enterprise improvement and sustainability (examples of pig-raising in Vietnam and sweet potato processing in the Philippines);
- helped strengthen institutional capacities, knowledge and information sharing and technology dissemination through networking responsibility: e.g. participatory methodologies, marketing chain approach, FFS; and
- helped build social capital in CIP through networking.

Institutionalization of Social Research Results and Approaches

Institutionalization of social research can be looked at across a number of dimensions:

- **technical**, involving the inclusion of social research approaches in policies and actions, in the structuring of tasks and responsibilities and in the extent of expertise present in the institution;
- **socio-political**, involving the influence of social research over policy, decision making and the availability of 'space' for social research innovation; and
- **cultural**, the extent to which social research is present in the organizational culture, evident in cooperation between staff and expressed in attitudes.

In the technical dimension, institutionalization of social research in CIP has been increasing since the early 1980s. A number of successful interdisciplinary 'double acts' over the years have helped to embed interdisciplinary research within the centre's strategy and to make it a cornerstone of team-based project structure. Douglas Horton, an economist and head of the Social Science Department from 1977 to 1990, contributed importantly to this institutionalization. He was the architect of a major field-based project in the late 1970s (Horton, 1984), where economist-led surveys and agronomist-led trials were compared with an interdisciplinary, participatory team approach involving a social researcher (Horton, 1986). The success of the latter approach helped establish diversity in social science disciplines and interdisciplinary collaboration as CIP strategies (Horton, 1991). The establishment in 1999 of a small-budget working group on participatory research by CIP management seemed to indicate further institutional recognition of approaches strongly linked to social research. Unfortunately, this working group was an early victim of financial difficulties in 2002 and continues as a scientist-led initiative outside CIP's formal structure.

Other 'technical' indicators of institutionalization include the currency enjoyed by concepts and frameworks that were developed primarily through social research approaches. Gender analysis and sensitivity in research was especially pioneered by female social researchers such as Susan Poats and Angelique Haugarud in the early and mid-1980s; Greta Watson, Adihambo Adaga and Virginia Nazarea in the late 1980s and early 1990s; and more recently, Sonia Salas and Diana Lee Smith. Despite their efforts, gender mainstreaming is still a work in progress in CIP, especially to define a gender focal point in the institution to assist with and improve gender analysis in projects.

The concept of 'indigenous knowledge' has been central to several social research-led projects in the CIP, but remained marginal and contested well into the 1990s. The idea of collecting associated indigenous knowledge at the time of collecting crop germplasm when CIP took on a sweet potato mandate in the late 1980s, took several years to become accepted. In the 1990s, the term increasingly became part of formal presentations by non-social researchers and became a key component of a major project on Andean roots and tubers within CIP headquarters. Nevertheless, indigenous knowledge is still not incorporated into the institutional database for CIP's genetic resources. The idea of working with informal potato seed systems progressed from a minor social research project to the main component of a centre-wide project in the 1990s. Participatory plant breeding has very rapidly moved from a small, specially funded activity within PROINPA to a part of the Bolivian national agricultural research programme and is now part of CIP's plant-breeding strategy. Integrated crop management and FFS (thanks to strong lobbying by biological as well as social researchers) now make up the content and approach of a major division in CIP's research structure. *In situ* conservation has shifted from a tentative and exploratory approach to crop genetic resources in social research-led special projects in the early 1990s (Prain and Bagalanon, 1994), to incorporation by 2000 in the research structure of CIP's genetic resources conservation project. The livelihood systems framework, influenced in part by UPWARD's earlier pilot activities in Asia (Campilan, 1999), has become a major feature in CIP's ongoing visioning and strategic planning activities.

Of course, many of these concepts were gaining acceptance in the wider research and development environment during the past decades. Their institutionalization cannot therefore be attributed uniquely to social research in CIP. But the fact that such concepts were being assiduously if marginally cultivated in CIP over several years has surely helped them to be more easily incorporated.

There was less social research influence during the 1990s in the socio-political dimension, on policy and decision making. This was the period of regionalization of social research staff, of a stronger presence in headquarters of mainstream economics, a reassertion of farming systems approaches with a strong quantitative component and an external review in 1995 that criticized the level of 'science quality' in the institution and the excessive involvement in downstream, 'technical assistance'-type activities. These factors may explain why, at the same time as regionalized social researchers were developing methods and working to incorporate participatory research into regional networks in Africa, Asia and Latin America, CIP headquarters did not appear to build on social research experiences as it incorporated natural resource management into its research programme and to assume leadership of CONDESAN, a multi-institutional, cross-sectoral natural resources management consortium in the Andes. In some ways it seemed like a lost opportunity to continue innovative social research undertaken in the 1980s through incorporation in CIP's natural resources management activities.

Despite the external review and other wider pressures to go 'upstream', CIP continued to provide plenty of 'institutional space' for its social and biological researchers in the regions. This has ultimately resulted in approaches such as participatory plant breeding, FFS, *in situ* conservation and livelihoods approaches, feeding back from their regional elaboration into policy formulation within the institutional mainstream. More recently, social researchers have had increasing opportunities to influence the formation of policy in headquarters and to contribute to decision making through membership of the Programme Management Team.[10]

Organizational culture and attitudes have shifted enormously in the past decade, reflected in the acceptance of many of the concepts and approaches mentioned above. To cite just one indicator, one third of the main articles featured in CIP's *Annual Report* from 1994 to 2002 related to projects with a strong social research component.

Until the beginning of the 1990s, interdisciplinary research in CIP, although institutionally supported through policy and staffing, involved social researchers working with maverick biological scientists outside the mainstream. They were often young, and either low in their disciplinary hierarchy or working in a disciplinary area such as postharvest physiology or field agronomy, considered less central to the institution's main concerns. Considerable scepticism existed at the scientific core of the institution – among senior plant breeders and pathologists.

Paradoxically, it was during the 1990s, when the socio-political institutionalization of social research at CIP was weaker than in the 1980s, that the organizational culture began to change along with attitudes. Part of the explanation for this was certainly the feedback of CIP's activities in the regions. But other factors are also important. The composition of CIP's research staff changed significantly during that period, with older, more traditionalist biophysical scientists leaving and younger staff, with stronger interests in interdisciplinary research and involvement of social science, joining. The changing external environment began to legitimate certain cultural notions and attitudes that were already part of the social research agenda, creating 'buzz words' that no proposal should be without: participation, bottom-up, women, indigenous knowledge and so on. Sometimes, however, opportunism is the mother of assimilation. Increasing use of the terms in proposal preparation has combined with greater exposure to the ideas behind the terms in presentations by and informal interactions with social researchers. This has helped to transform these terms into operational concepts with wide currency in the CIP community.

Conclusions

This brief history has shown CIP to be mostly an enabling environment for social research in the CGIAR system. The bottom line has been that social researchers have received subsidized special projects and occasionally, core funding over an extended period. This has occurred for several reasons, internal and external. Internally social research has made some successful contributions to CIP goals, especially through interdisciplinary double acts that have highlighted the value of combining technical with socio-cultural as well as economic perspectives. The characteristics of rootcrops have probably favoured the strong relevance of socio-cultural factors, especially in relation to managing planting materials and addressing postharvest issues. Another internal factor has been the gradual change in the composition of biophysical research staff, especially with the arrival of younger scientists with a greater sense of the complexity of food systems and the need for multiple perspectives to solve problems.

Externally, the development paradigm underpinning international agricultural research has undergone important changes, including a softening of the central-source model as actual and potential impacts of agricultural science become more complex to analyse and to attribute, although not all centres have responded to these changes by deploying social research skills. How should CIP respond to agriculture in a globalizing world, to farming that is increasingly part of a more complex set of livelihoods and social relations? The conference on which this volume is based spent a good deal of time discussing CGIAR's goal of poverty eradication under the changing conditions of agriculture. CIP is reorienting its own research programme towards an alignment with the Millennium Development Goals, which have a strong focus on poverty, hunger and vulnerable groups such as young children, women and the urban poor. The social arenas in which poor people pursue their livelihoods must be understood to clarify the social meaning of poverty, and most crucially, to define how agriculture can impact on the livelihoods of the poor. These are areas where social research has much to do.

Notes

[1]CIP's organizational structure was originally based on a headquarters research programme and a regional programme based on eight regional offices, each headed by a regional representative.

[2]Reference has already been made to the contrary positions adopted by the planning conference and the TAC external review in 1978. At least until the 1990s, planning conferences seem to have had more influence than External Programme Management Reviews on the direction of the social sciences in CIP.

[3]A recent paper on participatory research at CIP (Thiele *et al.*, 2001), suggested four major periods of participatory research: emergence, implementation with National Agricultural Research Institute, fragmentation and recent work involving farmer field schools. The present chapter benefits from the insights of the review although they have somewhat different objectives.

[4]Social research 'networking' responsibilities began towards the end of the 1980s with the Users' Perspectives with Agricultural Research and Development Network (UPWARD) in Asia.

[5]Viewed as the dominant mode of participatory research in CIP by Thiele *et al.* (2001).

[6]The emphasis given to the social arena is not to suggest that the biological and physical environments are unimportant, rather that social research has been able to bring these other elements together in the social arena.

[7]Oscar Ortiz, then a nationally recruited social researcher, however, made an important contribution to the development of the headquarters IPM programme.

[8]The main difference between pilot units and FFS had more to do with working style than purpose. Whereas FFS-related activities aimed to adapt or develop learning activities for IPM, working with small groups of farmers, pilot units focused on providing information to farmers, with no systematic attention given to innovative communication means, trying to reach as many farmers as possible (Nelson *et al.*, 2001; Ortiz *et al.*, 2005).

[9]As distinct from the normal 'networking' all scientists do as part of research implementation.

[10]A group of senior CIP scientists who advise the deputy director general for research on strategic research issues.

References

Biggs, S. (1990) A multiple source of innovation model of agricultural research and technology promotion. *World Development* 18(11), 1481–1499.

Biggs, S. and Farrington, J. (1991) *Agricultural Research and the Rural Poor. A Review of Social Science Analysis.* International Development Research Centre (IDRC), Ottawa, Canada, 139 pp.

Campilan, D. (1998) Livelihood issues in rootcrop research and development: Preface. In: *UPWARD, Sustainable Livelihood for Rural Households, Contributions from Rootcrop Agriculture.* Los Baños, Laguna, Philippines, pp. ix–xii.

Campilan, D. (1999) Introducing a livelihood systems framework in participatory agricultural research. In: *UPWARD, Learning to Manage Livelihoods: New Challenges for Rootcrop R&D.* Los Baños, Laguna, Philippines, pp. 13–22.

Castillo, G. and Campilan, D. (1999) Nurturing a network: lessons in the evolution of the UPWARD program. In: Niehof, A. and Terp-stra, P. (eds) *Households in an Interdisciplinary Perspective.* H&C Publication Series No. 2. Wageningen University, Wageningen, Netherlands, pp. 37–46.

Chilver, A.S. (1997) Innovation paths in developing country agriculture: true potato seed in India, Egypt and Indonesia. PhD thesis, University of East Anglia, Norwich, UK.

CIP (1976) Annual Report 1976. International Potato Center, Lima, Perú, 129 pp.

CIP (1982) Social Science Research at the International Potato Center. Report of the Second Social Science Planning Conference. International Potato Center, 7–11 September 1981. Lima, Peru, 196 pp.

CIP (1988) The Social Sciences at CIP. Report of the Third Social Science Planning Conference. International Potato Center, Lima, Peru, 355 pp.

Devaux, A. and Thiele, G. (2002) Papa Andina: apoyando la innovación tecnológica de la papa en Bolivia, Ecuador y Perú. In:

Devaux, A. and Thiele, G. (eds) *Papa Andina, logros y experiencias de la primera fase: 1998–2002.* Centro Internacional de la Papa, Lima, Perú.

Fano, H., Ortiz, O. and Walker, T. (1996) Peru: inter-institutional cooperation for IPM. In: Thrupp, L.A. (ed.) *New Partnerships for Sustainable Agriculture.* World Resources Institute, Washington, DC, pp. 85–98.

Fliert, E. van de and Braun, A.R. (1999) *Farmer Field School for Integrated Crop Management of Sweet Potato: Field Guides and Technical Manual.* Bogor (Indonesia); International Potato Center (CIP); Research Institute for Legume and Tuber Crops; User's Perspective with Agricultural Research and Development (UPWARD), Bogor, Indonesia, 265 pp.

Fonseca C., Daza, M., Aguilar, C., Bezençon, N., Benavides, M., Fano, H., Goyas, H., Prain, G., Roncal, H. and Tafur, S. (1994) El Camote en los Sistemas Alimentarios de la Yunga Norte del Perú. Social Science Department Working Paper 1994–4. CIP, Lima, Peru, 40 pp.

Gabriel, J., Torrez, R. and Thiele, G. (2000) Participatory approaches in potato improvement: Experiences of PROINPA in Bolivia. In: Almekinders, C. and de Boef, W. (eds) *Encouraging Diversity. The Conservation and Development of Plant Genetic Resources.* Intermediate Technology Publications, London, pp. 194–199.

Horton, D. (1984) *Social Scientists in Agricultural Research. Lessons from the Mantaro Valley Project, Peru.* IDRC, Ottawa, 67 pp. (Also available in Spanish and French.)

Horton, D. (1986) Farming systems research: twelve lessons from the Mantaro Valley projects. *Agricultural Administration* 23, 93–107.

Horton, D. (1991) Social scientists in international agricultural research. In: Whyte, W.F. (ed.) *Participatory Action Research.* Sage, Newbury Park, California, pp. 218–236.

Horton, D. and Guzman, R. (1997) Networking with Users, Report of an External Review of the UPWARD Program 1994–97. UPWARD, Los Baños, Laguna, Philippines, 81 pp.

Nazarea-Sandoval, V. (1992) *Memory Banking Protocol.* UPWARD, Los Baños, Laguna, Philippines, 22 pp.

Nelson, R.J., Orrego, R., Ortiz, O., Mundt, M., Fredrix, M. and Vien, N.V. (2001) Working with resource-poor farmers to manage plant diseases. Invited Featured Article. *Plant Disease* 85(7), 684–695.

Norman, D. (1977) Comments on Farm Level Constraints Study at CIP. In: CIP, *Report of the Planning Conference on Social Science Research and Training.* CIP, Lima. pp. 122–130.

Ortiz, O. (1997) The information system for IPM in subsistence potato production in Peru: experience of introducing innovative information in Cajamarca Province. PhD thesis. Agricultural Extension and Rural Development Department, The University of Reading, Reading, UK.

Ortiz, O. and Forbes, G. (2003) Fighting a global problem: managing potato late blight through partnership. Poster presentation at the GFAR Conference, Senegal, 30 May.

Ortiz, O., Alcázar, J., Catalán, W., Villano, W., Cerna, V., Fano, H. and Walker, T. (1996) Economic impact of IPM practices on the Andean Potato Weevil in Peru. In: Walker, T. and Crissman, C. (eds) *Case Studies of the Economic Impact of CIP – Related Technology.* CIP, Lima, Peru, pp. 95–113.

Ortiz, O., Alcázar, J. and Palacios, M. (1997) La enseñanza del manejo integrado de plagas en el cultivo de la papa: La experiencia del CIP en la Zona Andina del Perú. *Revista Latinoamericana de la Papa* 9/10(1), 1–22.

Ortiz, O., Garret, K., Heath, J., Orrego, R. and Nelson, R. (2005) Management of potato late blight in the Peruvian highlands: evaluating the benefits of farmer field schools and farmer participatory research. Accepted for publication in *Plant Disease.*

Perez, J., Sim, J., Campilan, D. and Boncodin, R. (2001) Participatory agricultural research in the Philippines: summary of evaluation case study. In: Horton, D. (ed.) *Learning About Capacity Development Through Evaluation.* ISNAR, The Hague, The Netherlands, pp. 14–16.

Peters, D., Ngai, D.D. and Prain, G. (2002a) Agro-processing waste assessment and management in peri-urban Hanoi. Paper presented at the Conference on Wastewater Use in Irrigated Agriculture: Confronting the Livelihood and Environmental Realities. IWMI, Hyderabad, India, 11–14 November.

Peters, D., Wheatley, C., Prain, G., Slaats, J. and Best, R. (2002b) Improving agroenterprise clusters: root crop processing and piglet production clusters in peri-urban Hanoi. Presented at the Symposium on Local Agrifood Systems: Products, Enterprises and the Local Dynamics. 16–18 October. CIRAD, Montpellier, France, 21 pp.

Peters, D., Nguyen, T.T. and Pham, N.T. (2002c) Sweet potato root silage for efficient and labor-saving pig raising in Vietnam. *AGRIPPA Peer Reviewed Electronic Journal – FAO* (Rome), 1–12 June.

Potts, M.J., Watson, G., Sinung-Basuki, R. and Gunadi, N. (1992) Farmer experimentation as a basis for cropping systems research: a case study involving true potato seed. *Experimental Agriculture* 28, 19–29. International Potato Center and Lembang Horticultural Research Institute, West Java, Indonesia.

Prain, G. (1993) Mobilizing local expertise in plant genetic resources research. In: de Boef, W., Amanor, K., Wellard, K. and Bebbington, A. (eds) *Cultivating Knowledge. Genetic Diversity, Farmer Experimentation and Crop Research.* Intermediate Technology Publications, London, pp. 102–110.

Prain, G. (1995) Sweet potato in Asian production systems: an overview of UPWARD's first phase research. In: *UPWARD, Taking Root, Proceedings of the Third UPWARD Review and Planning Workshop.* Los Baños, Laguna, Philippines, pp. 1–35.

Prain, G. and Bagalanon, C. (eds) (1994) *Local Knowledge, Global Science and Plant Genetic Resources: Towards a Partnership.* UPWARD, Los Baños, Laguna, Philippines, 267 pp.

Prain, G. and Bagalanon, C.P. (1998) *Conservation and Change: Farmer*

Management of Agricultural Bio-diversity in the Context of Development. UPWARD, Los Baños, Laguna, Philippines, 267 pp.

Prain, G., Uribe, F. and Scheidegger, U. (1992) The friendly potato: farmer selection of potato varieties for multiples uses. In: Moock, J.L. and Rhoades, R. (eds) *Diversity, Farmer Knowledge and Sustainability.* Cornell University Press, Ithaca, New York, pp. 52–68.

Prain, G., Sandoval, V. and Rhoades, R. (1993) Networking for low-external-input and sustainable agriculture: the case of UPWARD. In: Alders, C., Haverkort, B. and van Veldhuizen, L. (eds) *Linking with Farmers.* ITP, London, pp. 215–228.

Prain, G., Gin Mok, Il., Sawor, T., Chadikun, P., Atmodjo, E. and Relwaty Sitmorang, E. (1995) Interdisciplinary collecting of *Ipomoea batatas* germplasm and associated indigenous knowledge in Irian Jaya. In: Guarino, L., Ramanatha Rao, V. and Reid, R. (eds) *Collecting Plant Genetic Diversity: Technical Guidelines.* CAB International, Wallingford, UK, pp. 127–137.

Rhoades, R.E. (1984) *Breaking New Ground. Agricultural Anthropology.* CIP, Lima, Peru, 84 pp.

Rhoades, R.E. (1990) Coming revolution in methods for rural development research. In: *UPWARD, Proceedings of the Inaugural Planning Workshop on the User's Perspective With Agricultural Research and Development.* Los Baños, Philippines, pp. 196–210.

Rhoades, R.E. and Booth, R.H. (1982) Farmer back to farmer: a model for generating acceptable agricultural technology. *Agricultural Administration* 11, 127–137.

Röling, N. (1990) The agricultural research-technology transfer interface: a knowledge systems perspective. In: Kaimowitz, D. (ed.) *Making the Link: Agricultural Research and Technology Transfer in Developing Countries.* ISNAR, Washington, DC, pp. 1–43.

Scheidegger, U., Prain, G., Ezeta, F. and Vittorelli, C. (1989) *Linking Formal R&D to Indigenous Systems: a User-Oriented Seed Programme for Peru.* Network Paper 10. ODI, London, 16 pp.

Sinung-Basuki, R. (1994) Farmer-led experimentation as the basis of new technology development: a case study of TPS technology in Indonesia. PhD thesis, Department of Agriculture, University of Reading, Reading, UK, 354 pp.

Suherman, R., Ameriana, M., Sinung-Basuki, R. and Fuglie, K. (2001) Marketing of true potato seed in Indonesia. In: Fuglie, K. (ed.) *Performance and Prospects of Hybrid True Potato Seed in South and Southeast Asia.* CIP-ESEAP and AARD, Indonesia, pp. 209–220.

TAC (1977) Report of the TAC Quinquennial Review Mission to the International Potato Center, 1976. TAC Secretariat, Food and Agriculture Organization of the United Nations, Rome, 93 pp.

Thiele, G. (1999) Informal potato seed systems in the Andes: why are they important and what should we do with them? *World Development* 27(1), 83–99.

Thiele, G., Gardner, G., Torrez, R. and Gabriel, J. (1997) Farmer involvement in selecting new varieties: potatoes in Bolivia. *Experimental Agriculture* 33, 275–290.

Thiele, G., Van de Fliert, E. and Campilan, D. (2001) What happened to participatory research at the International Potato Center? *Agriculture and Human Values* 18, 429–446.

Torres, R., Veizaga, A., Macias, E., Salazar, M., Blajos, J., Gandarillas, A., Navia, O., Gabriel, G. and Thiele, G. (1999) Capacitación a agricultores en el manejo integrado del tizón de la papa en Cochabamba. Documento de Trabajo 12. Proinpa Foundation, 30 pp.

UPWARD (1997a) Local R&D: *Institutionalizing Innovations in Rootcrop Agriculture*. UPWARD, Los Baños, Laguna, Philippines, 223 pp.

UPWARD (1997b) UPWARD faces. *Fieldnotes Newsletter* 6(1), 14.

Watson, G., Dimyati, A., Bahagiawati, A.H.M. and Wargiono, J. (1991) Sweet potato production, utilization, and marketing in commercial centres of production in Java Indonesia. In: *UPWARD, Sweet Potato Cultures of Asia and South Pacific*. Los Baños, Laguna, Philippines, pp. 361–381.

Watson, G., Estrada, N. and Bejarano, C. (1992) Andean farmers' evaluation of late blight resistant clones. *CIP Circular* 19(2), 6–7.

Werge, R. (1984) Evaluation of solar dehydration techniques. Annex 3. In: Rhoades, R. (ed.) *Breaking New Ground. Agricultural Anthropology*. CIP, Lima, Peru, pp. 59–64.

Whyte, W. (1984) *Learning from the Field. A Guide from Experience*. Sage Publications, Newbury Park, London/New Delhi, 295 pp.

Zuger, R. (2003) Impact assessment of farmer field schools in Cajamarca. An economic evaluation. Social Sciences Working paper No. 2004–1. CIP, Lima, Peru, 38 pp.

Why the 'Livestock Revolution' Requires Research on People   9

Dannie Romney and Bruno Minjauw[1]

Social science research has a chequered history at the International Livestock Research Institute (ILRI), not unlike that of social research in other Consultative Group on International Agricultural Research (CGIAR) centres, but with sharper peaks and drops. These patterns reflect an unusual institutional history being created from two original CGIAR institutes – the International Livestock Centre for Africa (ILCA) and the International Laboratory for Research on Animal Diseases (ILRAD), which had very different research approaches which will be discussed further. Given the complex social and cultural issues surrounding livestock ownership and the contribution of livestock to sustainable livelihoods, a multi-disciplinary approach incorporating sociological and anthropological analysis might be expected. Our review covers the development and changes since the early years of ILCA and ILRAD, in representation of scientists trained in the biological and social sciences as well as the use of non-economics social research. We emphasize current trends and directions within ILRI and the challenges it faces as it starts to implement a new strategy. For the international and national institutes much remains to be learned to ensure that biological and social scientists work together to ensure that research supports development and helps alleviate poverty.

Two Discordant Staffing Curves

In 1993, CGIAR requested a Rockefeller Foundation-appointed task force to develop a unified strategy for a global livestock research

©CAB International 2006. *Researching the Culture in Agri-Culture:*
Social Research for International Development
(eds M.M. Cernea and A.H. Kassam)

institute by integrating the programmes and resources of two centres: ILCA and ILRAD. The resulting organization, ILRI, began operating in January 1995 with a global mandate to address livestock health and production. To analyse the state of social science research in ILRI, developments in all three institutes must, therefore, be considered.

Figure 9.1 shows how the number of social scientists has changed over the last 20 years. Numbers were high in the early days of ILCA, representing almost 30% of all scientific staff, but dropped or remained constant during the early 1980s as non-economists virtually disappeared. From 1988 on, the institute had only one non-economist researcher and at times none. When ILRI was established, the very high number of biological scientists coming from ILRAD reduced even more the proportion of social scientists to only 7% despite the sustained increase in economists recruited since 1991. ILRI's 2002 annual report (ILRI, 2003) shows that the social scientists were all economists. Since 1987 none of the institutes ever had more than one full-time non-economist social scientist, and in some years not even one. From 1973 to 1993 the contribution of social science research at ILRAD was minimal, and so Fig. 9.1 does not represent it.

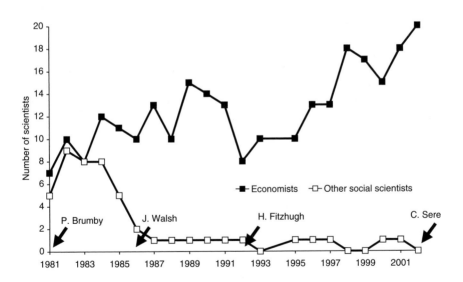

Fig. 9.1. Change in numbers of social science staff in ILCA–ILRI, 1981–2002 (under four of the centre directors (Brumby, Walsh, Fitzhugh and Sere)). (Source: ILCA 1982–1994a; ILRI 1996–2000a, 2001, 2002a and 2003.)

Social Science Research in ILRAD

ILRAD was established in 1973 in response to the belief that an institute was needed to initially emphasize haemoprotozoal parasites and immunological aspects of African animal diseases, and that focusing on two diseases and on developing vaccines to prevent them would afford greater chance of success than ranging widely over many problems of cattle production. As a result, for 20 years the main focus of ILRAD's animal parasitic disease programme was strategic research on East Coast fever and trypanosomosis, with little attention paid to the implications of the research on rural livelihoods or to the potential for delivery or use of new vaccines.

In the late 1980s, however, a Rockefeller Foundation-funded 'socio-economics programme' was established, consisting of one economist, one anthropologist and one epidemiologist responsible for evaluating the impact of the diseases and the control strategies being developed. Unfortunately, support from ILRAD management was limited. By the early 1990s, when funding cuts forced significant redundancies, the anthropologist position in ILRAD was one of 12 eliminated. An ecologist position, again funded by the Rockefeller Foundation, was added to the group to study the environmental impacts of trypanosomosis control. When discussions of combining ILRAD and ILCA commenced, impact assessment was considered to be an important area of focus for the new institute.

Social Science Research in ILCA

In contrast to ILRAD, ILCA has had a long and initially rich tradition of recognizing the importance of social science issues and incorporating non-economist social scientists into its research programme. ILCA's establishment was based on recommendations from two Rockefeller Foundation-funded task forces (1971 and 1972) to examine the need for and possible role of a livestock centre for Africa. The second task force concluded:

> A considerable fund of knowledge has resulted from several decades of work at numerous research centres... (But) the primary cause of the disappointing growth in animal productivity in tropical Africa has been the failure to integrate the biological, economic and sociological components of research and development programmes.

> (ILCA, 1994b)

During its first years, ILCA attempted to redress this imbalance. The zonal research programmes in Mali, Kenya, Ethiopia, Botswana and Nigeria put considerable effort into describing systems. A highly active systems research team, initially identified problems based on literature review and field surveys, then described selected production systems and identified possible development paths. Technical solutions were tested at the field and station levels, with models used to evaluate alternatives at a system level. ILCA gave monitoring of pastoral development projects high priority, with substantial involvement of both social scientists and ecologists.

ILCA's first quinquennial review in 1981 considered that, with the baseline surveys completed or near completion, emphasis should move away from system description towards component research to overcome constraints identified. Although system description continued, the numbers of non-economist social scientists in the field programmes started to decline as component research was emphasized. Only economists were represented at the headquarters in Addis. The period of decline coincided with the directorship of Peter Brumby, who was less supportive of system description than the previous director, David Pratt. Some technical scientists felt that the sociology studies did not directly link to what they were doing. Although the teams were multidisciplinary, biological and social scientists did not work in an integrated manner and their studies were carried out in parallel.

As the emphasis on system description declined, the importance of policy research increased and looked at the institutional framework in which the farming systems operated. In the late 1980s, a new strategy was developed identifying six research thrusts: (i) cattle meat and milk; (ii) small-ruminant meat and milk; (iii) animal traction; (iv) animal feed resources; (v) trypanotolerance[2]; and (vi) livestock policy and resource use. Of these, (i) to (iii) were considered commodity thrusts, in that they aimed to increase production of the three outputs (milk, meat and traction), with the other three strategic thrusts providing information and technology. Economic inputs were provided in all the thrusts, mainly focusing on identifying factors affecting production, marketing and technology uptake. Many of these activities were carried out through the field programmes, while at headquarters research focused on cross-country comparisons of critical policy issues affecting technology uptake and the sustainability of crop and livestock production.

Social Science Research in ILRI

IMPACT ASSESSMENT. As the process of establishing ILRI from the two institutes began, impact assessment research was increasingly emphasized, partly due to the changing nature of funding for agricultural research and the increased expectations of the research community to demonstrate impact. *Ex-ante* and *ex-post* studies can provide information to help allocate scarce research resources and to determine the impact of past investment.

ILRI is involved in three main areas related to impact assessment: adoption studies, economic impact assessment and modelling activities (Thornton and Odero, 1998). Adoption studies have been used to provide information on farmers' adoption of innovations and the factors that facilitate uptake. Yet, of the 53 impact assessment studies carried out in 1982–1998, only a few have been adoption studies, largely because only a limited number of specific and well-defined interventions could be identified that had been used in the field for some time and for which scaling-up strategies had been followed. Such prerequisites were essential to allow a comprehensive evaluation of factors affecting adoption to be undertaken. Methods used have been largely farmer surveys, data collection through formal questionnaires and informal interviews with key informants and farmers' groups. Economic impact assessments have prevailed, representing more than half the studies carried out, and have been used to evaluate interventions' economic benefits to the targeted users and to evaluate the potential benefits of research against costs. Methods have included economic surplus models, scoring techniques, cost–benefit analysis and simulation models. Social and environmental impact assessments have examined the broad effects of research projects on, for example, soil erosion and human welfare and nutrition, using formal economic valuation methods together with a wide range of modelling techniques. ILRI's System Analysis and Impact Assessment Group recognizes the importance of non-economic social factors in determining whether farmers will or will not adopt an intervention, and the likely impact it will have at the household and community level. Although the main inputs so far have come from agricultural economists, efforts are increasing to understand farmers' perceptions and decision-making processes and to develop multi-objective models apt to consider non-economic objectives.

RESEARCH PRIORITIZATION. Impact assessment is part of a broader goal of research prioritization. To realize the livestock sector's full potential to reduce poverty, donors and researchers need to know where livestock are important for the poor, which livestock species are most important in any community or system and what the most severe constraints are on enhanced livestock productivity. Where the greatest returns to research investments, in terms of impact on the poor, are likely to occur must also be identified. At the research project level the needs of local clients must be met while contributing to the institute's global mandate. ILRI's research tools include the following:

- *Cross-sectional and longitudinal household surveys* to understand the variability in resource endowment and farmers' practice between households and within and across regions and systems. The data are used to understand the complex interrelationships between crops and livestock and, by comparisons across regions, the effects of intensification. The data can be used to set parameters of predictive system models such as those employed in some impact assessments to predict impact of technological intervention and identify options. Development of statistical relationships between spatial parameters and point data is being used to study factors affecting adoption and to predict where particular systems and practices are likely to prevail or be suitable (e.g. Staal *et al.*, 2002, 2003).
- *Contingent valuation and conjoint analysis* approaches to understand how farmers value their environment and animals, to guide the conservation and sustainable development of animal genetic resources (Drucker *et al.*, 2001). Outcomes are intended to inform policymakers as well as the genetic resource programme at ILRI. The same methods are also being used to assess the potential demand for vaccines to guide the vaccine development programme and assess the potential impact of vaccine introduction.
- *Participatory approaches for problem diagnosis and constraint identification.* These are being used to support formal-survey data to understand farmers' practices, constraints, perceived priority problems and interrelationships between households and the external environment at various spatial scales (household, community area etc.). These approaches are sometimes used at the start of projects to better understand the issues.
- *Mapping.* This technique is used increasingly to collect spatially defined information to help map geographically defined areas where particular conditions are expected to exist. In turn, these techniques have been used to map poverty and livestock globally and predict trends (Thornton *et al.*, 2002). Predictive relationships are being developed between household-level data from geo-referenced households and spatially defined parameters to produce maps predicting where particular systems are likely to occur and where specific interventions are likely to be appropriate.
- *Policy research.* The key foci of ILRI's policy research are the following:
  - global livestock policy issues, including trends;
  - policies and institutions to improve sustainable livelihoods;
  - policies to improve the competitiveness of smallholder livestock systems, market access and trade;

- policies to improve livestock technology adoption, nutrition and food security; and
- policies for the sustainable delivery of animal health services.

While the Livestock Policy Analysis Programme is too broad to describe here, we mention two activities that will highlight the work of multidisciplinary teams and research, based on a broader use of social science methodologies than typically found in standard economic analyses. The first example is a collaborative research and development project in the smallholder dairy sector in Kenya, where a wide range of stakeholders identified the inappropriate regulatory environment as a key constraint to enterprise development. Another example is the wide-ranging work undertaken on policies for sustainable land management. A number of projects have focused on such policies for the East African highlands, but work has also been undertaken in the Sahelian region of West Africa. Research teams generally include social scientists and biophysical scientists. Although often led by agricultural economists at ILRI, this work has benefited from strategic partnerships with other institutions, where collaborators include rural sociologists, political scientists and anthropologists. Key government policymakers, with different disciplinary backgrounds, also sit on an advisory board for the research undertaken in the East African highland countries (Kenya, Ethiopia and Uganda), and have been actively involved in identifying their research needs, as well as engaging in local-level stakeholder workshops highlighting the needs of local peoples. The more typically *social* methods we successfully use in our research include participatory mapping, analyses of timelines, networks and local-level organizations and institutions. More important, the information generated through these procedures has been combined with more conventional survey information on households, markets and agro-ecological conditions to generate knowledge that captures the impact of local institutions and of social customs and norms on natural resource use and sustainable land management. This is particularly important as many governments are developing decentralization and devolution strategies, but implementation has often stalled for lack of information on local-level institutions and management.

Economists in the policy analysis group at ILRI have also undertaken a wide range of studies on marketing, technology adoption and food security and international and regional trade. Innovative work on the role of livestock as a key asset base of many poor rural households and the potential to improve livelihoods through livestock was highlighted in work to capitalize on the potential benefits of the 'livestock revolution'.

A New Strategy for ILRI and the Use of 'Action-research'

In January 2002, Carlos Sere took over ILRI's leadership, opening the way for a change in institutional culture and practices. A first step was to build upon *ILRI's Strategy to 2010: Making the Livestock Revolution Work for the Poor* (ILRI, 2000b). The revised strategy was finally agreed on in 2002 (ILRI, 2002b) and commits to focus livestock research and capacity building on reducing poverty and making sustainable development possible for the poor. Livestock provide three main pathways to alleviate poverty: (i) securing key livestock assets and improving nutrition; (ii) allowing for improved and, in many cases, intensified production; and (iii) opening market opportunities. In assessing the research challenges posed by this vision and commitment, five research themes that focus attention on key outcomes have been developed:

- *Targeting opportunities.* Target research for sustainable livestock development to ensure that research has the largest benefits among the world's poorest people.
- *Enabling innovation.* Link innovation processes more tightly to key stakeholders through their direct involvement and consultation in those processes.
- *Market opportunities.* Improve market access for poor livestock keepers and marketers.
- *Biotechnology.* Make use of revolutionary advances in the biosciences to protect smallholder livestock from disease and improve livelihoods of the poor.
- *People, livestock and the environment.* Sustain lands and livelihoods through better use of close links among human, animal and environmental health issues.

While ILRI and its partners have been involved in adapting and delivering technologies to poor livestock keepers, the coordinated effort to enable and foster innovation is new and will require strengthening ILRI's social science capacity, partnerships and interdisciplinary teamwork. From the beginning, ILRI wished to consult widely in gathering ideas and advice to guide the development of this research theme. A task force was set up to initiate the process and prepare a concept paper incorporating comments from external reviewers. In February 2003, a workshop was held to develop a draft strategic plan, key concepts, outcomes and a *modus operandi* for the theme together with partners and advisors. Partners came from ILRI field projects while advisors were largely drawn from people with experience in livestock innovations.

The 'enabling innovations' theme recognizes that the linear paradigm of basic to strategic to adaptive research, leading to extension and diffusion of innovations, does not address poverty effectively because the paradigm does not embrace the circumstances and realities of farmers and other private and public stakeholders. The conventional paradigm's basic principle is that only one objective truth can be elucidated through the application of scientific methodology (Röling, 1996). Gibbons *et al.* (1994) describe this as a 'mode 1' type of knowledge production in which problems are set and solved in a context governed by the interests – largely academic – of a given community. The same author promotes a 'mode 2' type of production of knowledge, carried out in an application context, characterized by heterogeneity rather than homogeneity. Gibbons *et al.* (1994) propose that, to implement 'mode 2' research, groups should be less firmly institutionalized and come together in temporary work teams and networks that dissolve or change when a problem is solved or redefined and where an individual may have different roles in a team depending on the problem. One of the objectives of ILRI's reorganization was to allow for such flexible problem-solving teams. However, a major challenge being addressed is how to implement such an approach given the conservative belief that clearly defined hierarchies are required to ensure accountability and effective personnel management and budgeting.

One of the key characteristics of the new research paradigm is that innovation should be the result of interaction among different actors with complementary contributions (Röling, 1996). Researchers should no longer remain exclusively external actors but need to engage themselves in action-research to develop solutions (Campbell, 2003). Agricultural innovation should be viewed as a continuous learning process involving all actors, including biological and social scientists (Engel and van den Bor, 1995).

Within ILRI, however, concerns still persist that such modes of operation are not compatible with its primarily research mandate. Some ILRI scientists fear that generating knowledge for application, or 'action-learning', will convert scientists into development agents, for which the institution has no mandate and no comparative advantage. This fear, in our view, ignores the fact that an extended research paradigm does not discard the original paradigm but builds on it, expanding activities and integrating different actors, at different spatial and social scales, to ensure that the new knowledge is incorporated into the development of a new, socially constructed reality (Röling, 1996; Sayers and Campbell, 2001). Laboratory-based science and upstream research will continue to play a major role in the research agenda. However, incorporating action-learning as a key element of ILRI's research profile will help allay concerns of development practitioners and target clients that researchers are not involved in practical work (Campbell, 2003).

Expanding ILRI's research profile to include action-research and place greater emphasis on working with a wider range of research and development partners is a response to changes in the external environment, including increased donor demand to show that poverty at the grass-roots is being reduced. ILCA forged strong partnerships with NARS through its research networks and emphasis on capacity building. In the new environment the partner base will be expanded to include the private sector as well as public sector partners such as state extension services, farmers' groups, non-governmental organizations, national agricultural research services (NARS) and other CGIAR centres. Some ongoing ILRI activities contribute to, or conform to, the philosophy of the extended research paradigm:

- Participatory technology development is used to focus on specific problems, including the use of legumes for soil fertility and food and feed crops in West Africa, and testing of woody and herbaceous legumes and smut-resistant Napier accessions in Kenya.
- The Farmer Field School project adapts and tests the methodology for application to animal health and production issues, representing an innovative and participatory learning approach (Minjauw *et al.*, 2003). Development partners are showing considerable interest in the outcomes of this project, and the potential is great for scaling-up and testing of the approach in other systems and for other livestock species.
- In Kenya and Uganda, approaches to agroecosystem health integrate farmers' and scientists' perceptions of it. Community participation is a key element, and studies to generate information and knowledge are linked to action plans expected to have direct impact.
- The Rapid Appraisal of Agriculture Knowledge Systems methodology is being used in a study of actors, linkages and processes in the Kenyan dairy sector. The outcome will be identification of constraints and an action plan to address them drawn up by the actors themselves (Hooton *et al.*, 2003).

Some scientists view the use of participatory approaches with suspicion, particularly when they lead to qualitative and not quantitative information. Inclusion and participation of stakeholders as equal partners require scientists to yield some control, and lead to heterogeneous data, which they cannot analyse using conventional techniques. However, data analysis using methods such as conjoint analysis and contingent evaluation, matrix ranking or scoring captures some elements of the farmers' decision-making process and contribute significantly to knowledge. The advantage of participatory tools designed to capture knowledge and information informally by facilitating dialogue between actors should not be lost. Pragmatically, choosing between quantitative or qualitative approaches is unnecessary, as both contribute different and complementary information to the innovation process.

Another criticism often levelled at the implementation and study of diverse livestock innovation processes using action-research is that it generates site-specific outputs. For the international research community and to some extent, the donors, who have global mandates, such specificity has a negative connotation. The challenge, therefore, is to analyse the process leading to local impact to generate generic lessons and methodologies that can be tested and adapted for application to other sites. At the same time, given the depth of research, unexpected results, information and new research questions with international value and relevance may be generated. Involvement in case studies often leads to valuable links with existing platforms and networks of a broader range of partners, including non-governmental organizations and others that would not normally be accessed. Recognition by these networks helps ILRI be recognized as a credible partner not only academically but also as one with a strong understanding of field realities.

Institutional Change

Chambers (2003) describes institutional learning and change as:

> part of an emerging redefinition of good professional practice in agricultural science. It entails and requires continuous learning, unlearning and learning-about-learning. Elements may include frequent exposure to field realities, co-learning with poor farmers and changing priorities and programmes through continuous monitoring and evaluation.

The 'Enabling innovation' theme proposes to be a driving force within ILRI to change its research culture, behaviour and attitudes, and to take responsibility for catalysing and documenting the process of institutional change within ILRI. Not all members of ILRI recognize the role of scientists in institutional change, and some feel this should be the reserve of senior managers rather than of scientists. Some of these fears appear to arise because of the failure to distinguish between organizational and institutional change. Organizational change is considered by the authors to be that affecting structural systems such as those governing staff reporting, or finance, while institutional change pertains also to the behaviour and attitudes of the staff and how research is implemented. One definition of the institutional context of research and development is given by Hall *et al.* (2003) as the:

> rules and norms governing: the role of various actors involved in the production, transfer and use of knowledge; the relationship between these different actors; the way research priorities emerge and are promoted and executed; the way research performance is evaluated and rewarded and by who; and the way research and development are held accountable to different interest groups.

This does not mean that organizational and institutional changes do not overlap. Creation of a motivating environment where individuals or groups have the freedom and incentive to be creative is the responsibility of managers and scientists.

ILRI is changing the reward system for its international scientists. In the new salary structures, ILRI values development recognition (for dissemination of technology and impact on improving livelihoods) as well as scientific recognition and will reward those able to build multiple and complex partnerships. These structures should help change the attitudes of scientists so that they feel they are able to seek funds and implement research conforming to the extended research paradigm where participatory approaches and direct impact are components and where broader stakeholder partnerships, beyond the traditional ones with NARS, are key.

Conclusion

As elsewhere in CGIAR, agricultural economics has dominated social sciences at ILCA since the mid-1980s and subsequently, at ILRI. Economists ascended to senior positions when CGIAR was under close scrutiny along 'value for money' criteria, and when evaluation research emerged as a prestigious area of specialization within the discipline of agricultural economics (Hall *et al.*, 2003). Although the reasons for the long decline of non-economics social research and the drop in the number of social scientists at ILCA are not fully clear and have not yet been sharply analysed, indications are that contributing factors included the following:

- lack of integration between biological and social scientists;
- lack of support from ILRI's senior management; and
- predominance of the view that, although social science can help characterize systems and identify problems, its role in developing solutions is not clear.

The 1999 external review initiated by the Technical Advisory Committee (TAC), expressed concern 'about a virtual absence of sociological capacity'. This issue became a central point of discussion that stressed the need for socio-cultural research and in-house capacity to address the highly important issues of social and cultural characteristics in ownership, custodianship and management of herds in various regions of the world, particularly in Africa (Michael Cernea, personal communication).

Despite ILRI's commitment to building sociological capacity among its research staff, which was welcomed by TAC, ILRI management did not take immediate corrective action, and the contribution of sociologists remains low. This is not to say that exclusively 'hard science research' is carried out. Biological scientists and economists, using some methods advocated by sociologists, have been responsible for implementing the activities described above. In some cases, these have been carried out in collaboration with anthropologists and sociologists from other CGIAR centres and advanced research institutes in Europe and America. Their contribution, however, is small. ILRI now has a unique opportunity to change its history of social science as ILRI's strategy emphasizes the importance of such social research.

With the commitment of ILRI senior management and the energy and initiative of scientists who believe in the value of a new research culture, the institute will be able to change and embrace an extended research paradigm, including a stronger role for social sciences.

Notes

[1]We would like to thank all those who contributed to this chapter by providing background documents and information and by outlining their perceptions and understanding of institutional history. In particular, we would like to acknowledge Carlos Sere, Phil Thornton, Ralph von Kaufmann, Brian Perry, John McDermott, Adam Drucker, Simeon Ehui, Nancy McCarthy and Susan MacMillan.

[2]Capacity to recover from trypanosomosis.

References

Campbell, B.M. (2003) Rising to the challenge of poverty and environmental sustainability: Towards a conceptual and operational framework for INRM. Keynote paper presented at the Sub-Saharan Africa Challenge Programme formulation workshop, 10–14 March 2003. Accra, Ghana.

Chambers, R. (2003) Preface. *Agricultural Systems* 78(2), 119–121.

Drucker, A., Gomez, V. and Anderson, S. (2001) The economic valuation of farm animal genetic resources: a survey of available methods. *Ecological Economics* 36(1), 1–18. Available online: http://www.elsevier.nl/cas/tree/store/ecolec/sub/2001/36/1/1163.pdf

Engel, P.G.H. and van den Bor, W. (1995) Agricultural education from a knowledge systems perspective: from teaching to facilitating joint inquiry and learning. *Journal of Agriculture Education and Extension* 1(4), 1–24.

Gibbons, M., Limoges, C., Nowotny, H., Schwartzman, S., Scott, P. and Trow, M. (1994) *The New Production of Knowledge: the Dynamics of Science and Research in Contemporary Societies.* Sage, London, 192 pp.

Hall, A., Rasheed Sulaiman, V., Clark, N. and Yoganand, B. (2003) From measuring impact to learning institutional lessons: an innovation systems perspective on improving the management of international agricultural research. *Agricultural Systems* 78(2), 213–241.

Hooton, N., Kinyanjui, H., Agili, G., Nyangaga, J. and Larsen, C.E.S. (2003) Understanding the effect of commercialisation on knowledge and information flow in the Kenyan dairy sub-sector. Presented at the *Tanzanian Society of Animal Production Annual Scientific Conference*, 28–30 October 2003, Tanga, Tanzania.

International Livestock Centre for Africa (ILCA) (1982) *Annual Report 1981.* ILCA, Addis Ababa, Ethiopia, 34 pp.

ILCA (1983) *Annual Report 1982. A Year in the Service of African Livestock Improvement.* ILCA, Addis Ababa, Ethiopia, 62 pp.

ILCA (1984) *Annual Report 1983: Improving Livestock and Crop-Livestock Systems in Africa.* ILCA, Addis Ababa, Ethiopia, 79 pp.

ILCA (1985) *Annual Report 1984: Livestock Research and Food Production in Africa.* ILCA, Addis Ababa, Ethiopia, 87 pp.

ILCA (1986) *Annual Report 1985/86: Serving African Agriculture.* ILCA, Addis Ababa, Ethiopia, 88 pp.

ILCA (1987) *Annual Report 1986/87: A Year of Progress and Change.* ILCA, Addis Ababa, Ethiopia, 82 pp.

ILCA (1988) *Annual Report 1987.* ILCA, Addis Ababa, Ethiopia, 103 pp.

ILCA (1989) *Annual Report 1988.* ILCA, Addis Ababa, Ethiopia, 156 pp.

ILCA (1990) *Annual Report 1989.* ILCA, Addis Ababa, Ethiopia, 144 pp.

ILCA (1991) *1990 Annual Report and Programme Highlights.* ILCA, Addis Ababa, Ethiopia, 84 pp.

ILCA (1992) *1991 Annual Report and Programme Highlights.* ILCA, Addis Ababa, Ethiopia, 81 pp.

ILCA (1993) *1992 Annual Report and Programme Highlights.* ILCA, Addis Ababa, Ethiopia, 86 pp.

ILCA (1994a) *1993/94 Annual Report and Programme Highlights.* ILCA, Addis Ababa, Ethiopia, 106 pp.

ILCA (1994b) *Improving Livestock Production in Africa: Evolution of ILCA's Programme 1974–94.* ILCA, Addis Ababa, Ethiopia, 233 pp.

International Livestock Research Institute (ILRI) (1996) *ILRI 1995: Building a Global Research Institute* ILRI, Nairobi, Kenya, pp. 66.

ILRI (1997) *ILRI 1996 Out of Africa, Into a Global Mandate.* ILRI, Nairobi, Kenya, 54 pp.

ILRI (1998) *ILRI 1997 Livestock, People and the Environment.* ILRI, Nairobi, Kenya, 61 pp.

ILRI (1999) *ILRI 1998 Linking Livestock and Natural Resources Management.* ILRI, Nairobi, Kenya, 58 pp.

ILRI (2000a) *ILRI 1999 Making the Livestock Revolution Work for the Poor.* ILRI, Nairobi, Kenya, 75 pp.

ILRI (2000b) *ILRI's Strategy to 2010: Making the Livestock Revolution Work for the Poor.* ILRI, Nairobi, Kenya, 112 pp.

ILRI (2001) *ILRI 2000–2001: Deciphering the Code of Life to Benefit the Poor.* ILRI, Nairobi, Kenya, 85 pp.

ILRI (2002a) *ILRI 2001 Annual Report. The Poor and Livestock Mapping: Targeting Research for Development Impact.* ILRI, Nairobi, Kenya, 77 pp.

ILRI (2002b) *Livestock: A Pathway out of Poverty. ILRI's Strategy to 2010.* ILRI, Nairobi, Kenya, pp. 23.

ILRI (2003) *ILRI Annual Report 2002.* ILRI, Nairobi, Kenya, 68 pp.

Minjauw, B, Muriuki, H.G., and Romney, D. (2004) Development of farm field school methodology for small-holder dairy farmers in Kenya. In: Owen, E., Smith, T., Steele, M.A., Anderson, S., Duncan, A.J., Herrero, M., Leaver, J.D., Reynolds, C.K., Richards J.I. and Ku-Vera, J.C. (eds) *Responding to the Livestock Revolution – The Role of Globalisation and Implications for Poverty Alleviation*, British Society of Animal Science Publication No. 33, Nottingham University Press, Nottingham, UK, pp. 299–314.

Röling, N. (1996) Towards an interactive agricultural science. *Journal of Agricultural Education and Extension* 2(4), 35–48.

Sayers, J.A. and Campbell, B. (2001) Research to integrate productivity enhancement, environmental protection, and human development. *Conservation Ecology* 5(2), 32. Available online: http://www.consecol.org/vol5/iss2/art32

Staal, S.J., Baltenweck, I., Waithaka, M.M., de Wolff, T. and Njoroge, L. (2002) Location and uptake: integrated household and GIS analysis of technology adoption and land use, with application to smallholder dairy farms in Kenya. *Agricultural Economics* 27, 295–315.

Staal, S.J., Romney, D., Baltenweck, I., Waithaka, M., Muriuki, H. and Njoroge, L. (2003) Spatial analysis of soil fertility management using integrated household and GIS data from smallholder Kenyan farms. Paper presented at the 25th International Conference of the International Association of Agricultural Economists, 16–20 August 2003, Durban, South Africa.

Thornton, P.K. and Odero, A.N. (eds) (1998) *Compendium of ILRI Research Impact and Adoption 1975–98.* ILRI Impact Assessment Series 1. ILRI, Nairobi, Kenya, 134 pp.

Thornton, P.K., Kruska, R.L., Henninger, N., Kristjanson, P.M., Reid, R.S., Atieno, F., Odero, A. and Ndegwa, T. (2002) *Mapping Poverty and Livestock in Developing Countries.* ILRI, Nairobi, Kenya, 132 pp.

Aquatic Resources: Collective Management Patterns and Governance for the World's Fish Wealth

10

K. Kuperan Viswanathan,
Mahfuzuddin Ahmed,
Paul Thompson, Parvin Sultana,
Madan Dey and Magnus Torell

The widespread failure of governments to regulate and manage fisheries has resulted in the continued overexploitation of fisheries the world over – another instance of the failure of the state going it alone in managing natural resources. Strong pressure has developed to radically change the approach to managing fisheries. Important research focuses on the role of fisher communities in managing and sustainably exploiting this resource. This chapter will discuss the social research programme, developed and carried out at the WorldFish Center since 1996, focusing on community approaches to managing aquatic resources.[1] This programme may be relevant to more than the aquatic environment. Many of the conceptual and methodological problems we address in researching community-led natural resources management, for example, are also present in the management of other resources such as social and community forestry, community wildlife and community-based irrigation.

Theoretical Considerations

The new approach is centred on the proposition that the resource users – fisher communities – must become more involved in management and regulatory decision making. Users possess knowledge based on their production experience. Social research, among other things, studies, designs and recommends patterns of social organization that can

©CAB International 2006. *Researching the Culture in Agri-*Culture: *Social Research for International Development* (eds M.M. Cernea and A.H. Kassam)

bring this knowledge to bear on production and conservation. Users'
participation in research, in turn, can help solve problems effectively
and equitably and enhance the legitimacy of regulatory regimes, thus
reducing enforcement costs. Users' involvement encourages voluntary
compliance with fishery regulations (Viswanathan *et al.*, 2003). A
range of concepts is used to describe this approach: community-based
resource management, participatory resource management, devolution,
co-management and cooperative management.

The study of co-management and community management of
aquatic resources is a study of social organizations and institutions. It
involves understanding the basis for developing cooperative and non-
cooperative institutions. The cultural qualities of human communities
underpin economic action and self-organization, influencing how they
respond to common challenges of declining natural resources such as
fisheries. Pollnac (1991), for example, convincingly argues for understanding the peculiar social-organizational characteristics of fishing
communities and for designing development interventions to remove
constraints on fishing. These characteristics should be used as a development resource to carry out informed social engineering to promote
changes that can fit, strengthen and develop fishing communities'
social and cultural systems.

Social scientists researching fisheries contribute a distinct
'knowledge platform' to the research of fishing and fishing populations, consisting of a body of theory about patterns of social organization, and a body of ethnographic information about fisher
communities from prior research. Both remain largely ignored or
unused in the absence of specialized social scientists from research
institutions and their research teams, but have been and are important intellectual tools to further the general research programme at
the WorldFish Center. These bodies of theory and information should
also become a building block of knowledge in the various national
research centres dealing with aquatic resources in developing countries, yet socially specialized researchers in these centres are usually
scarce, if they exist at all.

Many coastal sea areas are subject to 'sea tenure systems', much
like land tenure systems, but these are not well studied or documented as they are often invisible. Sea tenure arrangements, however,
are well known and respected by coastal populations, themselves
divided into tribes, clans and groups, with distinct claims of tenure on
different sections of coastal waters and following full sets of rules
about ownership, entitlement, access rights, use rights and rental payment. A number of anthropological and sociological studies have
described these sea tenure systems (Emmerson, 1980; Ruddle and
Johannes, 1985; Ruddle, 1989). This body of accumulated knowledge

is important to the WorldFish Center and the Consultative Group on International Agricultural Research (CGIAR) for understanding human impact on the marine environment. Opportunities to blend sea tenure systems with co-management arrangements (a system of shared responsibility and authority between a local group of fishers and different levels of government) are important considerations in the research on social organizations that manage aquatic resources. Such opportunities are useful entry points to introduce the knowledge emerging from non-economics social sciences and to address key problems of managing aquatic resources. This is why 'putting people first' in agricultural research, similar to 'putting people first' in development programmes, is both formidable and rewarding for social sciences (Cernea, 1991).

The WorldFish Center's social research programme recognizes that fishery management must place people at the centre of research and not, as conventional fishery management often does, at the periphery. Cernea (1996) notes that 'social analysis must be used to explain the social fabric, design the social goals, and chart the path of collective action'. In developing countries, institutional weakness and constraints are pervasive in fisheries and coastal resource management (Torell and Salamanca, 2002). Social analysis of these institutions and crafting innovative institutions is thus central to solving the governance problems of the aquatic resource sector.

Social Research Programme

Social research at the WorldFish Center takes place within the Policy Research and Impact Assessment Programme (PRIAP), which was created in 1996. PRIAP's goals are to: (i) examine the policy environment and provide policy options to ensure wider adoption of technologies and resource management policies to enhance nutrition, reduce poverty and improve food security; (ii) ensure benefits to poor people in the developing world from production, management and conservation of aquatic resources; and (iii) provide measures to set research priorities and assess the impacts of aquatic resource research and development. The programme research activities are organized around three thematic areas: (i) economic and social analysis and valuation of aquatic resources in developing countries; (ii) aquatic resource planning and impact assessment; and (iii) legal and institutional analysis of fishery management. Social research plays a major role in all. The most important research area is community participation and collective action.

Community Participation and Collective Action

It is in community participation and collective action that the World-Fish Center has contributed significantly to social research (Pomeroy, 1994; Pomeroy and Williams, 1994; Viswanathan *et al.*, 2003). The continued deterioration of aquatic resources in the developing world, coupled with governments' inability to arrest the decline of resource conditions or provide alternatives to an increasing population spurred communities and non-governmental organizations (NGOs) to actively manage natural resources, basically through institutional changes such as within fishery co-management, which changed the rules determining access to resources. The process, however, goes beyond just changing rules: it involves a communicative and collaborative process through which rules are formed and determines who is allowed to participate and how conflicts are addressed and agreements made. Scot's (1995: 33) broader definition of institutions is used here: they consist of cognitive, normative and regulative structures and activities that provide stability and meaning to social behaviour. The WorldFish Center's research on co-management is discussed further by looking at two major research projects: the Community-based Fisheries Management Project, phases 1 and 2, in Bangladesh; and the Global Fisheries Co-management Project, phases 1 and 2 in the Philippines.

Community Involvement in Fishery Management in Bangladesh

The 4 million ha of open waters in Bangladesh are among the world's richest and most complex fisheries. The rivers, *beels* (permanent and seasonal lakes and wetlands), *baors* (oxbow lakes), *haors* (large, deeply flooded depressions) and floodplains support some 260 fish species. About 80% of rural households catch fish for food or to sell, and fish contributes about 60% of animal protein consumed. However, the many 'miscellaneous' small fish caught from the floodplains by poor people have been neglected in official statistics and policies, yet are the accessible and preferred food of the poor.

Construction of roads and embankments, drainage and flood control and natural siltation, along with overfishing, are commonly cited as major causes of deterioration of fishery resources. Bangladesh has over 12,000 *jalmohals* (inland water bodies generating government revenue). These are leased to the highest bidder. While fisher cooperatives are preferred, very often, either directly or by bidding through a cooperative, control ends up in the hands of rich and influential lessees.

Fishermen suffer not only from declining catches but also from exploitation under this leasing system.

Social research intervention

The approach developed from the concept of co-management was to help fisher groups organize, or be represented in, local management bodies to cooperate, take collective decisions and develop local rules to regulate fishing. Indicators of co-management include the establishment of management committees, level of participation of fishers in fishery decision making and rules and decisions made.

The complexity of inland fisheries and the usually strong competition for control over their resources and benefits (income and resource rent) often give rise to various conflicts. The WorldFish Center's Community-based Fisheries Management Project helped develop local management committees that improve cooperation among the fishers and the community, ensuring that conflicts are mediated before they become widespread and uncontrollable.

Models of cooperation

Different models of cooperation have evolved. Four, shown in Fig. 10.1, resulted from the process of working with communities and NGOs, government agencies and research organizations. The first model is an NGO-led strategy for target groups to establish fishery rights in publicly owned water bodies (*jalmohals*). The second reflects a government-led strategy to establish a direct relationship between the state and fisher communities. The third involves collaboration between the government, NGOs and researchers, working together and interacting with fishing communities. The fourth involves fisher communities assuming co-management responsibility and becoming partners of the government, NGOs and research agencies (Ahmed *et al.*, 1997). The benefits of community-based fishery management are realized from: (i) fishers cooperating in planning to increase and conserve fish stocks; (ii) fishers sharing the costs and benefits of improved management; (iii) fishers managing conflicts among themselves; (iv) enhanced position of organized fishers in dealing with other stakeholders; (v) sharing of data on fishery conditions between the government and fishers; and (vi) emergence of more effective and enforceable rules with a high level of acceptance by the different stakeholders (Thompson, 1999).

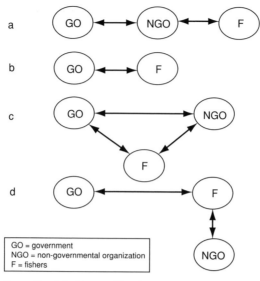

Fig. 10.1. Models of cooperation. Source: Ahmed, Capistrano and Hossain, 1997.

Key lessons

The complexities of managing inland fisheries makes imperative a more cooperative model for NGOs, fishing communities, government and research agencies. In 1991, with funding from the Ford Foundation, the WorldFish Center, in partnership with the Department of Fisheries and a number of local NGOs (Bangladesh Rural Advancement Committee, Proshika, Caritas and Friends in Village Development Bangladesh) implemented a 5-year project, Improved Management of Open-water Fisheries, which emphasized testing different arrangements to involve stakeholders in managing open-water fisheries by drawing in NGOs to develop local institutions with communities. A key feature of the project was providing credit to poor fishing households to help them develop more sources of livelihood to compensate for the loss of access to fishery resources during closed seasons or in sanctuaries. The main impact of the project is bringing poor fishers into decision making, ensuring fair and equitable distribution of benefits and enhancing poor fishers' overall incomes. The large development NGOs have also offered skills in credit training for additional livelihood and an enhanced partnership with the Department of Fisheries to lease water bodies to communities for 10 years. The World-Fish Center, in partnership with NGOs and the government, designed a larger project in 2000 to fill the gaps in the first project. Under phase 2, the project works with NGO partners to systematically generate evidence of the impacts and effectiveness of local institutions in managing open-water inland fisheries.

Phase 2 fills the key gaps in knowledge identified by Campbell and Thompson (2002):

- sustainability of institutional arrangements for community involvement in fishery management;
- potential for government policy (particularly regarding fisheries and land) and the legislative environment to respond to the work and to support those arrangements;
- attribution of benefits to community involvement in fishery management rather than to wider development efforts taking place in the location;
- extent to which the very poor benefit from the work;
- effectiveness of alternative income-earning opportunities in the long run;
- potential threat of future fishers (especially the young, who are excluded from fisheries) to management stability;
- how effective it will be to increase the number of water bodies and including larger water bodies in an effort to scale up co-management;
- cost-effectiveness of such arrangements; and
- understanding the implications of community involvement for gender roles.

Phase 2, which was initiated in 2000 with Department of International Development, UK funding will consider a number of approaches to deal with these gaps.

Fishery Management in San Salvador Island, Philippines – Organizing Communities

Key problems and issues

San Salvador is a 380 ha island that forms part of Masinloc municipality, Zambales province, Philippines, on the western coast of Luzon, about 250 km from Metro Manila. In 1996, the island had about 1620 people consisting of 284 households. Rampant illegal fishing activities began to take their toll in the 1980s in the form of depletion of fisheries and unabated destruction of coral reefs. The highly centralized national government was too distant to control the situation while the San Salvador fishers were too fragmented to act collectively to avert resource degradation.

Co-management process

Initiated by a Peace Corps volunteer, with the cooperation of resource users and stakeholders and the participation of a local NGO, a marine sanctuary and reserve was conceived in 1998. The Marine Conservation Project of San Salvador sought to enhance institutional capabilities, develop and implement a marine resource management plan and establish a coral reef fish sanctuary and a marine reserve. Central to doing so was organizing the community to collectively solve resource management problems by launching intensive information campaigns to help residents realize the consequences of unsustainable resource use and heighten their concern for nurturing the natural environment for their continued survival and livelihood. A core group of residents participated in project activities. It spearheaded a campaign to support the 127 ha marine sanctuary reserve of San Salvador. In consultation with the fishers and the community, the core group drafted a local ordinance that banned fishing within the sanctuary and allowed only non-destructive fishing methods in the marine reserve. The Masinloc municipal council passed the ordinance in July 1989. The ordinance banned the *kunay*, traditional fishing gear that uses a long scare line of coconut fronds for herding fish from the reef flat into a fine-mesh net. Led by the municipal government, law enforcement is now the collective responsibility of the coast guard, fishers' organization and village police. In 1991, policy and legal support from the national government came through the passage of the Local Government Code, which gave the municipal government jurisdiction over municipal waters. The national government declared Masinloc Bay a protected seascape in 1993 under Presidential Proclamation 231. In July 1996, the San Salvador sanctuary won a prestigious national award for its achievement in coastal resource management and local governance, providing a source of pride to all partners and reinforcing the incentive to protect the sanctuary. The strength of this success was due in part to the involvement of resource stakeholders in project planning and implementation, well-defined objectives, supportive leadership, strong linkages with the municipal government and sources of technical expertise and funds and generation of tangible project benefits. Decision making was participatory, marked by consultations, dialogues and public hearings to thrash out issues and conflicting interests, as well as to encourage interaction among partners.

Outcomes

Resource assessment surveys conducted in San Salvador in 1998, 10 years after the establishment of the marine sanctuary, showed that living coral cover improved from an average of 23% for the whole island in 1988 to 57% in 1998. Fish species increased from 126 belonging to 19 families in 1988 to 138 belonging to 28 families in 1998 (Katon *et al.*, 1999). These changes appear to have resulted from the control of destructive fishing practices and vigilant law enforcement by the community with the support of the municipal government. Fishers perceived gains in equity and in fair allocation of access rights, household well-being and household income. These outcomes are encouraging, given how degraded the resource base was in the late 1980s.

Conclusions

These two examples show how users' participation in resource management can promote resource sustainability and reduce poverty. However, the processes to realize the benefits of community participation are not simple and involve substantial investment in innovative institution building. The WorldFish Center's social research programme is studying these processes to link theory with field evidence to design effective social interventions. A number of new approaches are now available in developing countries, including new governance regimes such as community-based management and co-management, which use community development as an integral part of fishery resource management.

Note

[1]This chapter benefits from discussion at the Cali conference and from comments on an earlier version offered by Michael M. Cernea.

References

Ahmed, M., Capistrano, A.D. and Hossain, M. (1997) Experience of partnership models for the co-management of Bangladesh fisheries. *Fisheries Management and Ecology* 4, 233–248.

Campbell, J. and Thompson, P. (2002) *An Overview of Community Involvement in Inland Fisheries Management in Bangladesh*. Community-Based Fisheries Management Phase 2 (CBFM-2) Project. WorldFish Center, Dhaka, 42 pp.

Cernea, M.M. (ed.) (1991) *Putting People First – Sociological Variables in Rural Development*. 2nd edn revised and expanded. Oxford University Press, London/New York, 458 pp.

Cernea, M.M. (1996) *Social Organization and Development Anthropology – The 1995 Malinowski*

Award Lecture. Environmentally Sustainable Development Studies and Monographs Series No. 6. World Bank, Washington, DC, 52 pp.

Emmerson, D.R. (1980) *Rethinking Artisanal Fisheries Development: Western Concepts Asian Experiences.* World Bank, Washington, DC, 238 pp.

Katon, M.B., Pomeroy, R.S., Garces, L.R. and Salamanca, A.M. (1999) Fisheries management of San Salvador Island, Philippines: a shared responsibility. *Journal of Natural Resources* 12, 777–795.

Pollnac, R.B. (1991) Social and cultural characteristics in small-scale fishery development. In: Cernea, M.M. (ed.) *Putting People First – Sociological Variables in Rural Development.* Oxford University Press, London/New York, pp. 259–299.

Pomeroy, R.S. (ed.) (1994) Community management and common property of coastal fisheries in Asia and the Pacific: concepts, methods and experience. *International Centre for Living Aquatic Resources Management (ICLARM) Conference Proceedings 45.* Manila, Philippines, 115 pp.

Pomeroy, R.S. and Williams, M.J. (1994) *Fisheries Co-Management and Small-Scale Fisheries: A Policy Brief.* International Center for Living Aquatic Resources Management (ICLARM), Manila, Philippines, 15 pp.

Ruddle, K. (1989) The organization of traditional inshore fishery management systems in the Pacific. In: Neher, P.A., Arnason, R. and Mollet, N. (eds) *Rights-Based Fishing.* Kluwer Academic Publishers, Dordrecht, The Netherlands, pp. 73–85.

Ruddle, K. and Johannes, R.E. (eds) (1985) *The Traditional Knowledge and Management of Coastal Systems in Asia and the Pacific.* UNESCO, Jakarta, Indonesia, 105 pp.

Scot, F.R. (1995) *Institutions and Organisations.* Sage Publications, Thousand Oaks, California, 202 pp.

Thompson, P.M. (1999) Theoretical basis for community-based fisheries management in Bangladesh. In: Middendrop, H.A.J., Thompson, P.M. and Pomeroy, R.S. (eds) *Sustainable Inland Fisheries Management in Bangladesh.* ICLARM, Danida, and the Ford Foundation, Manila, Philippines, 198 pp.

Torell, M. and Salamanca, A.M. (eds) (2002) *Institutional Issues and Perspectives in the Management of Fisheries and Coastal Resources in South-east Asia.* ICLARM Technical Report 60, Penang, Malaysia, 212 pp.

Viswanathan, K.K., Nielsen, J.R., Degnbol, P., Ahmed, M., Hara, M. and Abdullah, N.M.R. (2003) Fisheries Co-Management Policy Brief: Findings from a Worldwide Study. WorldFish Center, Policy Brief 2, Penang, Malaysia, 26 pp.

Tropical Agriculture and Social Research: an Analytical Perspective

11

Dean Holland, Jacqueline Ashby, Mariano Mejía and Joachim Voss

The Centro Internacional de Agricultura Tropical (International Center for Tropical Agriculture) (CIAT) is based in Cali, Colombia and is one of 15 international agricultural research centres of the Consultative Group on International Agricultural Research (CGIAR). This chapter outlines the history of CIAT's social science research and explains how it went from zero to forming a key part of CIAT's organization, work and vision. CIAT is a 34-year case study on the effectiveness of different approaches to integrating social and biophysical sciences for development.

CIAT, like other CGIAR centres, is also a social community, albeit one with peculiar dynamics due to the large proportion of 'displaced' (expatriate) members. Interviews with research staff showed that social and interpersonal relationships are a key to understanding CIAT's activities.

Social sciences are defined in this chapter as the academic and practical activities traditionally associated with anthropology, sociology, geography and community development, irrespective of the formal training of the person carrying them out. To make this study consistent with simultaneous studies at the other CGIAR centres, economics is not addressed in detail here.

This chapter comprises: (i) an outline of the study's methodology; (ii) an overview of CIAT's history; (iii) an outline of several models in the evolution and use of social sciences in CIAT; and (iv) themes and lessons from the application of social sciences in CIAT.

©CAB International 2006. *Researching the Culture in Agri-Culture: Social Research for International Development* (eds M.M. Cernea and A.H. Kassam)

Methods

Data for this study were collected in three ways:

- convergent interviews (Dick, 1998) with 12 current and former CIAT social and natural scientists and directors general, together representing over 124 person-years of experience of working at CIAT;
- a review of key literature relating to CIAT, particularly the annual reports and selected research publications;
- circulation of the study's arguments to all social scientists in CIAT and former directors general and a review of an earlier draft of this manuscript.

Interviews were semi-structured, allowing participants to raise what they saw as key issues during their time at CIAT, their interpretations of the causes of these issues and their recommendations about what should be done in CIAT. Participants' explanations generated a list of issues and theories, which were discussed with subsequent respondents. With each interview, some of the emergent theories gained more support while others were refined, replaced or discarded. Biases are inevitable in this process. As CIAT employees and colleagues of the participants in the study, we recognize that there are some limits on what we can say.

When participants were asked for the reasons underlying events and activities in which they had participated, the replies frequently included not only descriptions of people's roles but also their personalities, friendships and alliances. As in any community (Argyris, 1999), some of the reasons behind peoples' actions were portrayed as being driven by such relationships. For confidentiality, these views are not included here, but they have reinforced our conclusion that such issues are important to understand what has happened.

The interviews and literature do not give a single, united story of social sciences in CIAT. Different projects, different commodity programmes and different outposted sites have created a mosaic of coexisting approaches to integrating social sciences. Each person brings his or her own perspectives and interpretations to the events. The interpretations in this chapter are largely those given by the actors themselves in the story, to try to harvest the best wisdoms from the last 30 years. Where possible, we have tried to present the diversity of their viewpoints.

The CIAT annual reports (1970–2001) have been used to show changes over time in staff, projects and organization, key changes in direction, interpretations of events and trends affecting the centre. Total numbers of staff are reported, but records from the annual reports will overestimate the number of staff where there is a turnover, as incoming and outgoing staff are recorded in the same year.

A Brief History of the International Center for Tropical Agriculture

CIAT was founded in 1968 to take a systems approach to agricultural development in the neotropical lowlands. CIAT initially covered seven target systems, which included swine and maize production systems, which were soon felt to be too broad, and in 1976 the structure was focused around four commodity programmes: rice, beans, cassava and forages. This commodity-based structure remained largely unchanged for 16 years, during which social sciences gained a firm niche in the organization. From 1992, three new ecoregional programmes and a fourth on land use were added, and CIAT was divided into two research streams: germplasm and natural resources management (NRM). Most of the social scientists went to the NRM division, which started with 42% of its budget dedicated to socio-economic studies. A CIAT-wide budget decline in 1989–1996 caused large changes in staff and organization, and in 1996 CIAT closed its programmes, adopting project-based management of its research, with 16 projects, including the former programmes. CIAT is reorienting itself to focus on sustainable rural livelihoods, based on the foundations of competitive agriculture, agroecosystem health and collective rural innovation.

Figure 11.1 outlines the changes over time in the number of CIAT's social scientists and staff members, and in the organization of research at headquarters.

Results and Analysis

CIAT before social scientists

From the earliest days, CIAT's mission statements have recognized social dimensions. For example, the 1968 Programme and Budget Document, which outlined the rationale for CIAT, stated the following:

> (CIAT is) a research and training institution specifically designed to engage decisively – in both the technological and social dimensions – with the closely related problems of economic development, food production, and adequate diets... In the developing nations, particularly, these new approaches must involve and influence every segment of society – the policy makers in government, within industry and business, in the market place, in the laboratory and experimental plot, in the community, and on the farm.

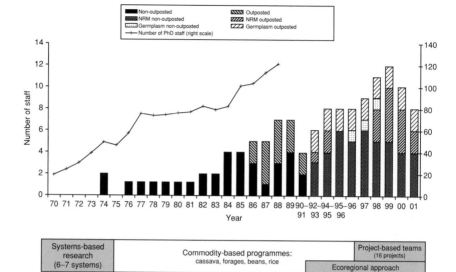

Fig. 11.1. Number of CIAT research staff members with a Master's degree or above in anthropology, sociology or geography; and number of staff members with a PhD in any discipline, 1970–2001.

At first, these social dimensions were felt to fall outside the mandate of the institution and seen as a job for CIAT's partners. The institution had been born out of a focus on breeding and green revolution strategies, with an implicit focus on large-scale producers and a trickle-down model of development. For example, the 1976 CIAT Report defines CIAT's mission objectives as the following:

> To generate and deliver, in collaboration with national institutions, improved technology which will contribute to increased production, productivity and quality of specific basic food commodities in the tropics...thereby enabling producers and consumers, especially those with limited resources, to increase their purchasing power and improve their nutrition. (List of countries omitted)

It was not until 1974 that funders pushed the first social scientists onto a generally reluctant CIAT. Until this time the social dimensions of CIAT's mission had been handled exclusively by economists.

Models of Integrating the Social and Biophysical Sciences

CIAT has integrated social with biophysical sciences in three ways:

1. In separate programmes or projects that specialized in social issues: Small Farm Systems Programme, 1973–1975; Participatory Research Programme from 1987 onward; Inter-centre Participatory Research and Gender Analysis Programme from 1996 onward; and the Rural Innovation Institute from 2002;
2. In commodity-based programmes through multidisciplinary teams: the cassava programme from 1984 and the bean programme from 1986; and
3. In ecoregional NRM projects from 1992, particularly the hillsides and forest margins ecoregions and the Land Management Project.

Social sciences started in CIAT in a separate programme. Following pressure from the Ford Foundation, in 1973 the Small Farm Systems Programme was started in CIAT to understand small farming systems 'in order that the impact of new technology on farm family welfare be understood' (CIAT, 1973: 217). This was the first experiment in integrating social sciences into CIAT, and while it produced work that would be difficult to distinguish from what today we define as participatory rural appraisal (PRA), the programme was disbanded after 2 years. Its brief history is outlined below.

The Small Farm Systems Programme brought the first social scientists to CIAT and housed them in a multidisciplinary team that included a visiting PhD anthropologist, an MSc rural sociologist, a PhD economist, a PhD agronomist, a systems engineer and a programmer. At the time, distrust reigned between the social and biological sciences. 'Green revolution varieties were going to save the world', said a member of the programme, but social scientists were perceived as leading a campaign to reveal the lack of impact of green revolution varieties on the poorest farmers. 'Social scientists were seen in the institute as troublemakers', said the member, 'likely to go off-station and generate criticism of station research'. The then director general described the atmosphere between social and biological sciences as 'conflictual'.

The Small Farm Systems Programme had multiple goals: (i) to provide guidelines to (a) identify factors limiting production, (b) select research alternatives, (c) assess probable adoption and (d) evaluate impacts on food availability and income; and (ii) to suggest novel approaches. The programme's principal 'clients' were CIAT commodity teams and national agricultural development agencies. 'The ultimate clients are, of course, farm families and the consumers of Latin America that benefit from the implementation of the process by national agencies' (CIAT, 1973: 220). The programme clearly recognized that farmers' own goals should be the central focus of this research approach:

> An intrinsic feature of the systems approach is that it requires that the farmer's objectives be made explicit. For the farm family these objectives probably include income, nutrition, cash flow, security, health and education. There is no clear nor explicit understanding of these objectives as yet.
>
> (CIAT, 1973: 219)

The programme conducted anthropological surveys to rank and compare farmers' and national agricultural researchers' perceptions of key production constraints at five sites across South America. The comparative research found strong differences between the perceptions of farmers and national researchers. It also found a broad diversity in farmers' goals at different sites. An agronomic and economic model was built from farm interview data in La Maquina, a 1954 settlement in Guatemala. These findings were a challenge to commodity research programmes, suggesting that farmers' practices were close to optimal, with little additional benefit to be gained from the use of available technologies such as herbicides, improved seeds, credit or more land. The model also suggested that government requirements for fertilizer use to obtain farm credit had 'forced adoption' of fertilizers above optimal levels. A parallel study at Cacoatal, a village on Colombia's north coast, investigated the impact of the adoption of improved rice varieties, finding positive and negative effects.

In 1975, CIAT's new director general disbanded the project and the multidisciplinary research team for several reasons. One team member reported that teamwork had been poor, with staff retreating to their professional disciplines and not integrating their approaches. The project was said to have lacked focus on its goals and clients, with different team members pushing in different directions. The director general also saw flaws in the very model of having a separate social science research programme focused on social and behavioural variables, independent of the powerful and relatively autonomous commodity programmes. Given the conflict between social scientists and breeders, the director general felt that integration would be better achieved by locating the social scientists within the commodity programmes. The team was disbanded and its members dispersed among the six commodity-based programmes.

In 1976, reorganization reduced the number of commodity programmes to cassava, beans, beef (with forages) and rice. These programmes were relatively autonomous, creating in effect four separate CIATs, each with their own approaches dictated by the nature of their crop. Each programme would eventually develop its own way of integrating social sciences. CIAT was still expanding its staff rapidly, but not its complement of social scientists. From 1975 to 1979, the number of senior staff, visiting scientists and postdoctoral fellows jumped from 34 to 72, but they did not include any social scientists. In 1980, the first long-term social scientist, a rural sociologist, Jacqueline Ashby, arrived at CIAT, but she was located in a separate 'special project', outside the mainstream commodity programmes.

It was the Rockefeller Foundation programme that introduced social science into the heart of CIAT – the commodity programmes. From 1984 to 1986, three anthropologists joined CIAT's commodity programmes in beans and cassava, two of them Rockefeller Foundation appointees. By 1990, half of CIAT's social scientists would be assigned by the Rockefeller Foundation. They arrived at a CIAT very different from the present one. 'It felt strange not being a breeder in CIAT', said a contemporary. At least two did not call themselves anthropologists at first, choosing instead titles such as 'cropping systems specialist', with which biophysical scientists could easily identify.

The institutional role of these early social scientists was to bring 'social science *in* development' (DeWalt, 1988), using social science to help define the target of agricultural technologies and to help 'sell' new technologies more effectively to farmers. In the early 1980s social scientists were mainly involved in surveys, interviewing farmers to gain insights into their perceptions of technologies. However, this institutionally defined role formed only a small part of what the social scientists actually did. Eventually, it was the success of their additional activities that created legitimacy for broader involvement of social sciences in CIAT.

Three separate projects are widely acknowledged as having blazed a trail for social sciences in CIAT: (i) cassava cooperatives in Colombia and Ecuador from 1984; (ii) bean research in Africa from 1984; and (iii) farmer-participatory research on the hillsides of Colombia from 1986. The projects display how biophysical and social scientists have achieved various degrees of integration and jointedness in their research. These projects are discussed separately below, and commonalties are drawn out in the conclusions.

Cassava cooperatives

Until the early 1980s, CIAT's cassava research had been driven by the goal of increased productivity. However, economic analyses prompted by an external review found demand for fresh cassava to be inelastic: greater production would depress prices and not ease poverty. The cassava programme was reoriented to look for a new product with an expanding market, help farmers establish marketing channels and eventually increase cassava production to meet the created demand. A pilot project in Colombia identified dried cassava chips for animal feed as a product with such market potential. The pilot was successful (Gottrett and Raymund, 1999) but its impact constrained by difficulties of organizing farmers to operate the processing equipment and market the produce (Romanoff, 1993). What was missing was a better *social technology* to complement and enhance the existing biophysical technologies.

The research was extended into Ecuador, where the social aspects of farmers' organization were addressed by a series of PhD anthropologists. Working in Ecuador gave them the 'luxury of more time to do the work' and freedom from headquarters to follow innovative approaches such as linking closely with the private sector rather than with agricultural researchers. The anthropologists facilitated the formation of a second-order union of cassava-drying organizations, and this social technology became a technical and commercial success, elements of which endure today. Yet, Romanoff (1993) stresses that the social technology itself was not innovative; the concept of cooperatives could not be considered new. We argue that the key was the existence of the practical developmental skills to facilitate the formation and maintenance of the association, allowing the establishment of an effective and functional social group. It offered a showcase within CIAT of a social technology able to complement biophysical research and increase its benefits.

Bean research

A contrasting approach to integrating social science research comes from CIAT's Great Lakes Bean Project in Africa (Voss, 1989). Here, teamwork and a close integration of social sciences with the development of biophysical technologies were reported to be the key. The project brought together a plant breeder, plant pathologist, anthropologist, agronomist and nutritionist to increase the productivity of common beans (*Phaseolus vulgaris*) in the Great Lakes region. As in the cassava cooperatives, the team had a large amount of freedom in their remote site. Contemporaries reported that this multidisciplinary team became close-knit and highly effective in working together.

In collaboration with national programmes, the team surveyed bean production and consumption, identifying farmers' goals, preferences, views of their production constraints and practices in experimenting with new bean varieties. Subsequent on-farm trials produced more detailed information about farmers' preferences. Farmers preferred risk-reducing strategies such as planting mixtures of bean varieties and using early-maturing varieties. The study also found that the farmers making decisions about household bean production were women. These findings changed the design of bean breeding so that many factors in addition to yield were considered in producing and testing new varieties.

The Great Lakes project was an example of well-integrated team research and teamwork between social and biophysical sciences, and it produced an integrated understanding of the farmers' situation and a technology response that drew on germplasm and social sciences.

Early participatory research

The third and final example of pioneering research in CIAT that legitimized social sciences is another social technology, but one that integrates biophysical research. By 1990, the role of farmer participation in evaluating technologies was widely acknowledged in CIAT and was promoted to the commodity programmes by the Participatory Research Project established in 1987, which later became the Participatory Research in Agriculture (IPRA) Project. With support and pressure from the Kellogg Foundation, IPRA first researched and then helped farmers to organize and build their capacity to research and produce their own technologies and make demands on formal agricultural research systems. A social technology known as the local agricultural research committee (CIAL) was constructed through work with the El Diviso farmer association in Cauca, Colombia, in 1990 (Ashby *et al.*, 1997). The approach is a methodological development that helps a small group of farmers organize themselves into a research circle, accountable to their local community, that develops and tests new practices, crop varieties, marketing initiatives or whatever is of pressing interest locally. The success of the approach has been dramatic, with 249 CIALs in eight Latin American countries by 1999. Participating and neighbouring farmers reported increased income and better food security (Ashby *et al.*, 2000). These benefits accrue disproportionately to poor participants.

Mainstream social theory provided frameworks and entry points through which social scientists with practical skills could experiment with social technologies in agriculture. However, practical developmental and facilitation skills were paramount to form the first CIALs and ensure active participation of the poor community members without domination by local elite (Ashby *et al.*, 2000).

Social research gained additional legitimacy in CIAT through the impact of these and other projects. In 1992, a social scientist was made programme manager for the first time, and the complement of social scientists in management positions has continued to increase since then.

In 1991, the CIAT mission statement was reformulated to include 'preserving the natural resource base' as a guiding principle, and in 1992 CIAT accordingly reorganized its research programmes into the NRM and germplasm divisions. Most of the social scientists went to the NRM division (Fig. 11.1) facing a new challenge: how to integrate social and biophysical sciences for research based on NRM, not commodities.

Social sciences in the CIAT headquarters started to coalesce into social science-rich programmes; the Land Management Programme with geographers, participatory research in IPRA, and the Hillsides Programme with mixed social scientists. Individual social researchers now had the freedom to create specialist 'niches' and to develop new 'social technologies' as complements to biophysical technologies. Social research flourished. In Colombia, Honduras, Nicaragua and Peru, watershed-level consortia were created to provide a platform for land users to negotiate collective NRM, on the hypothesis that greater social capital and collective action would broaden the types of technical change that could be achieved. Action research investigated how to organize farmers to make use of decision-support tools and to form agro-enterprises. A second-order federation of CIALs was created in Colombia.

Impact from these initiatives was mixed. In many cases the organizations were effective and outcomes for the poor spectacular (Ashby *et al.*, 2000; Lundy *et al.*, 2002), building income and food security, reducing inequality and building capacity for sustained and collaborative action. However, in other situations similar farmer organizations struggled just to survive and achieved little impact. A cross-country analysis in 1999 found that similar approaches had been used to promote collective action in each CIAT reference site, and concluded that the approach being used was a '*social* high-yielding variety'. This social organization of farmers' activities proved very effective under the right conditions. Specifically, it relied on the existence of certain minimum levels of local human and social capital; in other words, certain skills and quality of relationships among the participants that allowed them to work creatively, together. Where these did not obtain, the high-yielding organizations failed. Field skills to develop and implement novel strategies for collective action were identified as a key constraint.

These organizational models and approaches were promoted within CIAT by the social science-rich programmes but encountered resistance from some biophysical scientists. 'Scientists wanted participatory approaches but not the recipes', said one. Another argued that 'scientists didn't want a social-science packet...they wanted components'. To address this, IPRA shifted its emphasis to developing approaches specifically for biophysical researchers.

Additional social research was initiated to understand farmer decision making on NRM and to investigate the nature and location of poverty through geographic information system (GIS) mapping and on-ground participatory evaluations. Knowledge about these issues could not accrue within CGIAR but through its social researchers. Some projects marshalled social sciences around researchable chunks of NRM, such as soils or integrated pest management, creating what one respondent called 'NRM commodities' for research. On another level, in 1996 CGIAR agreed to start the inter-centre Participatory Research and Gender Analysis Programme to advance the state of the art of participatory and gendered research and to institutionalize such approaches within CGIAR and partner centres.

Theory-led or Practice-led Development of Social Sciences?

The acceptance of new social science technologies in CIAT has grown out of the development of practical field skills and the demonstration of impact, rather than *a priori* theoretical concepts. For example, the determining factor in the creation and evolution of CIALs, cassava cooperatives and watershed-level consortia has been the practical skills to create such associational structures and demonstrate their impact, not just the ability to conceive of them. That also demanded applied work in the field from CIAT's social researchers. CIAT only recognized the theoretical underpinnings of these approaches (such as the role of power in development and concepts of social capital) after the approaches proved successful.

As in the 17th century, when the most effective physics researchers were often those with the best carpentry skills to build the apparatus to test their conjectures (Bragg, 1998), now effective social action research requires the skills to build the social structures to meet new challenges. You can only test the types of organizations and relationships that you have the practical skills to build. Cernea (1991) argues that this is a characteristic of a young and evolving field, and that practical approaches and applied 'social work' are needed, as well, to be contemplated with systematization and effective integration with the theoretical.

This situation, however, is supposed to evolve and change and by now it may be changing. During the mid-1990s CIAT's participatory research project had a major role in training, but from 1998 the project was reoriented toward research on the effectiveness of CIALs, with experienced practitioners systematizing their skills. CIAT has recruited additional staff skilled in practical approaches to community development in Africa and at headquarters, strengthening the links between the practical and the theoretical. CIAT's new approach, focused on the concept of livelihood (broader than income), is driven by a theoretical framework but has a practical orientation.

The Trade-off for Social Scientists: a Career in CGIAR or in the Discipline?

'If you want to be a top-flight social scientist, CGIAR is maybe not the place to be. If you're willing to sacrifice your disciplinary career, CIAT is dynamite'. So one participant introduced the issue of career paths for social scientists in CGIAR.

Several social scientists we interviewed felt that their work in CIAT was in some way 'watered-down' social science. A common concern was that little of their work includes novel social research hypotheses and therefore, contributes little to social science theory. CIAT's focus on demonstrated impact was seen to encourage the application of established knowledge, rather than research to deepen understanding of issues. 'There is not much call in CIAT for writing weedy social science papers', said one respondent. 'What gets recognition is impact, such as enhancing adoption of technologies, or opening new opportunities for local communities... You can't expect a pure social scientist to come here and thrive'. This statement expressed the tension between the career path of the social scientist as an academic, striving to push the theoretical or practical edge of knowledge and the more action-oriented role and career within CGIAR. Most social scientists work at CIAT for 1–4 years (Fig. 11.2).

The trade-off between the academic role and practitioner role centres around the function of peer support and critical feedback. CIAT was said to lack a critical mass of social scientists and established mechanisms to support social science research. Frequently, lone social scientists are attached to a project, often posted in remote sites (Fig. 11.1). In as much as the driving force behind scientific thought is debate and discussion, having just one social scientist on a project may limit the advances possible in social theory and practice. There are not enough colleagues to give alternative viewpoints.

We asked the participants how they get the critical feedback they need. Half the responding social scientists commented that they sought their alliances principally outside CIAT. Partly to get more contact with

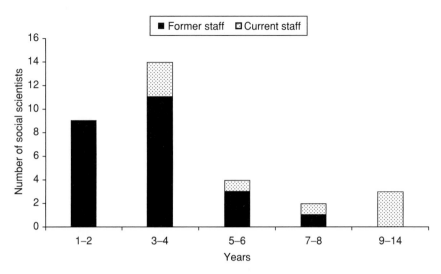

Fig. 11.2. Duration of employment of research social scientists (excluding consultants) at CIAT, 1970–2001.

colleagues, most of CIAT's social scientists choose not to be located at CIAT headquarters. Six of CIAT's current (2002) eight social scientists (who are actively researching, and are not directors) are based outside of CIAT and four are affiliated with other institutions. CIAT projects provide a platform for the practical fieldwork, and the outside affiliations provide much of the peer support.

Blurring the Boundaries

Figure 11.1 captures only part of the growth of CIAT's social science research. The boundaries between social and biophysical research have been blurring over time. Several respondents highlighted that researchers with training in biophysical sciences are increasingly taking on research activities that were traditionally associated with social scientists. The spread of participatory research activities encourages such blurring of disciplinary boundaries: for example, CIAT's project on participatory research approaches was managed from 1998 to 2000 by a researcher with formal training in ecology and entomology.

Social scientists have also been changed by interaction with biophysical scientists. 'I knew very little about working with biophysical sciences at first', said one, 'and learned most of it on the job'. Some social scientists have become 'apprentice' agronomists or plant breeders, and have reported that this has been a key to the success of their inter-actions with biophysical sciences: 'Social scientists must be well versed biophysically in order to work well with biophysical scientists', said one.

Opinion was divided on how broadly this co-option of social sci-ence activities has spread or should spread through CIAT. Many saw it positively as a sign that social science considerations are helping shape biophysical research and orienting it toward the poor.

From 1992, social scientists started moving into managerial posi-tions within CIAT's organizational structure, creating greater space and legitimacy for social science activities.

Personalizing or Institutionalizing Social Sciences?

One interview respondent stated, 'It's *personalization* instead of *insti-tutionalization* of social sciences that counts'. All but one interview participant argued that personal relationships are at least as important as institutional roles for effective integration of social scientists and biophysical scientists. Three suggested that working together in the field can be a key part of generating this: 'It's personality-based. We went to the field together, and built up trust'; 'It's about getting that 'Aha' experience in the field. It's necessary to be together in the field'; and '(Strong working relationships are formed) when people go to the field together, not just writing articles together'.

Two respondents suggested that as social scientists moved into more specialized programmes, it was personal relationships outside those programmes that maintained effective bridges with biophysical scientists.

Conclusions

Funding agencies induced and promoted the initial rise of social sci-ences in CIAT. As impact became more visible, however, more social scientists were brought on board and more arrangements for integrat-ing social and biophysical sciences tested.

Social sciences have come to be involved earlier in the project and technology cycle. During the 1970s and early 1980s, social science knowledge was seen as useful for 'selling' technologies to farmers. A programme that claimed a broader mandate for social sciences was not viable under that approach and was closed. Through the 1980s, how-ever, the role of social sciences expanded, including, first, a targeting role through understanding farmers' needs and goals. By demonstrating success, social sciences reached back to the goals of breeding programmes in beans and cassava. From the late 1980s, CIALs brought part of the research function under the control of farmers, speeding up the traditional technology development process.

The examples of early pioneering social research in CIAT – cassava cooperatives, bean research and CIALs – suggest some common principles for developing new social science approaches. The researchers had freedom to operate in new ways: two of the three projects were in sites considered as outposts, and the other was in a separate, externally funded project – a rarity at the time. The projects were all field-based and multidisciplinary. The researchers brought advanced practical field skills, allowing new forms of farmer organization and relationship to be created and hence, researched.

Social scientists' practical skills often come from experience as well as from formal training. This poses new challenges to an organization traditionally structured around levels of scientific qualification, as people with the practical skills may not always be the PhD holders.

How can we organize social sciences to integrate them with biophysical sciences and to maximize their impact on poverty reduction? Effective projects have taken place when the social scientists work relatively independently of biophysical scientists on complementary topics (such as for the cassava cooperatives or IPRA), and also when the social scientists are deeply integrated into a multidisciplinary team for biophysical and social research such as bean research in Africa. The benefits and risks of integrating and separating the social and biophysical sciences seem similar to those of integrating researchers and farmers. Separate social scientists have been able to generate new 'high-yielding' social technologies that have sparked advances in the field, but at the cost of lower 'adoption' of the technologies by biophysical scientists. Close-knit multidisciplinary teams lead to changes in social and biophysical scientists, but may make an academic career path in the social sciences difficult to follow.

This is only part of the story. The interviews suggest that CIAT could be considered a *gemeinschaft* community, in which people relate to each other as people first and then by their institutional roles. By considering just the institutional roles we may miss a large part of the story of integrating social and biophysical scientists into teams. Perhaps the lesson here is that CIAT is not so dissimilar to the communities in which we work.

Some of the most dramatic impacts of the early social science work on biophysical research are now less visible, precisely because the impacts have been so widespread and are now internalized as routine practice. As the debate on new approaches settles and they become accepted, it will be easy to forget their once controversial origins. Consideration of farmers' goals, priorities, production constraints and markets are now almost universal and do not have the novelty value they once held in the condensed research highlights of the CIAT annual reports. Initiatives such as the Forages for Smallholders Project are now routinely built around these considerations. Participatory approaches have, to varying degrees, infiltrated all of CIAT's research, and the role of farmer as the key to evaluating biophysical technologies is now unquestioned. Farmers are understood to be men and women. A social scientist who joined CIAT in the mid-1990s commented:

> When I arrived, the biophysical scientists themselves saw the need for social scientists and social science inputs... All of my work was tied in with the work of biophysical scientists, and I never had any feeling of being a bolt-on.

CIAT is moving toward a sustainable rural livelihood framework for its research, based on multidisciplinary research on the foundations of competitive agriculture, agroecosystem health and rural innovation. The Rural Innovation Institute, established in 2002, will study how rural innovation works, investigate collective organization to scale-up technology change, look for new ways to combine local and exotic knowledge and develop rural policy.

What are the options to maximize the impact of social sciences?

- Social sciences could be left mostly to partner organizations (as at CIAT, 1968–1980). This would have implications for the choice of partner, and type of relationship with partners and would go against current orientation.
- Natural scientists could be up-skilled in social sciences. This has been happening informally at CIAT, leading to changes in the ways that biophysical research is conducted. This option would have implications for the supervision and mentoring of the social aspects of the work by an experienced social scientist.
- Social sciences could be handled mostly within CIAT. This strategic option would also have implications for the choice of partners and type of relationship with partners. The perception that social scientists face a trade-off between developing a career in CGIAR and in their discipline may need to be changed, and hinges on successful peer support and mentoring.

To maintain an effective career path for social scientists we should ask not only what social sciences can do for CGIAR but what CGIAR can do, more than it has, for social sciences.

Acknowledgements

It has been a humbling experience researching this chapter. In a curious Doppler effect, decisions and situations rushing toward you sound very different to those receding into the past (Stegner, 1971). The authors would like to thank the participants for sharing the unrecoverable 'high-pitched' note of past decisions as they were being made. We have not been able to do justice to the richness of the descriptions given but we hope to have shown the relevance of past decisions to the future.

Notes

[1]International Center for Tropical Agriculture, Apartado Aéreo A 6713, Cali, Colombia.

References

Argyris, C. (1999) *On Organizational Learning*, 2nd edn. Blackwell, Oxford, UK, 560 pp.

Ashby, J., Gracia, T., Guerrero, M.P., Patiño, C.A., Quirós, C.A. and Roa, J.I. (1997) Supporting local farmer research committees. In: Veldhuizen, L., Water-Bayer, A., Ramirez, R., Johnson, D.A., and Thompson, J. (eds) *Farmers' Research in Practice.* Intermediate Technology Publications, London, pp. 245–261.

Ashby, J., Braun, A., Gracia, T., Guerrero, M.P., Hernández, L.A., Quirós, C.A. and Roa, J.I. (2000) *Investing in Farmers as Researchers.* International Center for Tropical Agriculture (CIAT), Cali, Colombia, 200 pp.

Bragg, M. (1998) *On Giants' Shoulders.* Hodder and Stoughton, London, 365 pp.

Cernea, M. (1991) *Using Knowledge from Social Sciences in Development Projects.* World Bank Discussion Paper 114. Available online: http://www-wds.worldbank.org

CIAT (1970–2001) *Annual Reports.* CIAT, Cali, Colombia. (In 1970–1991, these were titled *CIAT Report*; in 1992–1993, *CIAT at the Threshold of Sustainable Development*; and from 1994 to date, *CIAT in Perspective.*)

DeWalt, B. (1988) Halfway there: social science in agricultural development and the social science of agricultural development. *Human Organization* 47(4), 343–354.

Dick, B. (1998) *Convergent Interviewing: A Technique for Qualitative Data Collection.* Available online: http://www.scu.edu.au/schools/gcm/ar/arp/iview.html

Gottret, M.V. and Raymond, M. (1999) An analysis of a cassava integrated research and development approach: has it really contributed to poverty alleviation? Paper presented at the International Workshop on Assessing the Impact of Agricultural Research on Poverty Alleviation, 14–16 September 1999, San José, Costa Rica.

Lundy, M., Ostertag, C.F., and Best, R. (2002) Value adding, agroenterprise and poverty reduction: a territorial approach for rural business development. Paper presented at the First Henry A. Wallace Inter-American Scientific Conference, Globalization of Agricultural Research, CATIE, 25–27 February 2002, Turrialba, Costa Rica.

Romanoff, S. (1993) Farmers' organization, research and diffusion of technology. In: Dvorak, D.A. (ed.) *Social Science Research for Agricultural Technology Development.* CAB International, Wallingford, UK, pp. 51–64.

Stegner, W. (1971) *Angle of Repose.* Doubleday, Garden City, New York, 569 pp.

Voss, J. (1989) Integrating social science research into the development and testing of new agricultural technology: the case of CIAT's Great Lakes bean project. In: Groenfeldt, D. and Moock, J.L. (eds) *Social Science Perspectives on Managing Agricultural Technology.* International Irrigation Management Institute, Colombo, Sri Lanka, pp. 57–68.

Dry Areas and the Changing Demands for Social Research

12

Aden A. Aw-Hassan and Malika Abdelali-Martini

International agricultural research faces as great a challenge today as it did when it began some four decades ago. At that time, increased food production was the main goal, given the threat of mass starvation due to food shortages and growing populations in developing countries. The remarkable increase in food production in developing and developed countries has diminished this threat. However, recent developments such as increased global trade, global climate change and concerns over food safety, degradation of the environment and natural resources and persistent poverty pose new challenges. As international agricultural research has shifted its focus from production to use and impact of agricultural research outputs, demand for social science research has been changing in response to the increasing need to understand more complex issues.

We present an overview of the changes in social science research at the International Center for Agricultural Research in the Dry Areas (ICARDA) in the last 25 years. We analyse trends in, and the status of, social science research at ICARDA and assess research trends since the early 1980s in agricultural economics, anthropology, geography, sociology, rural development, nutrition and related fields, analyse the themes dealt with by scientists at the centre and the implications for research outputs. Demand for social science research is increasing, driven by the need to understand the complex systems that affect poverty and natural resources management (NRM). This is all part of the international agricultural research community's evolved awareness, which has had an important effect on the type and quality of research. Clear prioritization of social science research is critical.

©CAB International 2006. *Researching the Culture in Agri-Culture: Social Research for International Development* (eds M.M. Cernea and A.H. Kassam)

When established in 1977, ICARDA had little documented information about the farming systems of dry areas at its disposal. Not many studies were conducted on the agricultural systems of West Asia and North Africa (WANA) where the centre is located. The region was going through great political instability – revolutions and counter-revolutions, civil wars and armed conflicts between countries. Agriculture was affected by the socialist political thinking that led to extensive land reform and nationalization of large estates. National agricultural research programmes gave low priority to social science research as economies were centrally planned. As a result, social science research in the region was very weak and not fully integrated into the national agricultural research systems (NARS).

During the last 25 years, many political and economic changes have taken place in the region. Countries are increasingly becoming more open; the command economy has been largely rejected; and countries are experimenting with aspects of the market economy and in some cases, fully adopting it. The oil boom of the 1970s, which led to the migration of mostly male workers to more affluent Arabian Gulf countries, has brought huge economic benefits and transformed many rural areas.

During those years, development thinking among policymakers also changed. Issues such as rural poverty; gender and sustainability of natural resources (land, water and biodiversity) have recently been put at the top of the agenda. Participation of clients (users) in the research process is considered essential to increase the likelihood of technology adoption. For example, Ashby *et al.* (1996) assert that users' participation in the early stages of technology design ensures that new technologies can be adopted rapidly.

Social science research at ICARDA has evolved as a result of increased awareness of the role of social sciences in agricultural research and the changes in research and development regionally and globally and in particular, at the centre. Its 2000 External Programme and Management Review (EPMR[1]) raised a number of issues concerning the role and performance of social science research. The panel recommended the following:

> ICARDA should reduce its scope and concentrate on fewer issues,
> selected in close collaboration with the Center's physical and biological
> scientists and the national programmes – that are central to the
> operational mandate of the Center; and seek to improve the quality of
> output by among others, (a) judicious recruitment or designation of a
> lead social scientist, (b) recruitment of high-quality support staff and
> (c) entering into more cooperative arrangements like those existing with
> IFPRI (International Food Policy Research Institute).

> (Consultative Group on International Agricultural Research
> (CGIAR), 2001)

We analyse how ICARDA's social science research has evolved since the centre's establishment and the lessons learned and suggest ways to prioritize the research, keeping in mind EPMR's recommendations. We do this analysis in light of ICARDA's focus on poverty and sustainable management of natural resources and of EPMR's recommendations. We consider three important aspects deemed necessary for international agricultural research aimed at generating global public goods: (i) the framework of agricultural research as a tool for poverty reduction; (ii) key characteristics that such agricultural research needs to be successful; and (iii) general benefits offered by social science research. We analyse the institutional evolution of ICARDA's agricultural research programmes that have shaped social science research. We then describe the development of social science research, including human resources, research activities, outputs and impacts and how these have changed as the centre evolved, and some of the research impacts. We discuss the challenges and how they affect the priorities of social sciences. Finally, we draw some conclusions.

Evolution of ICARDA's Research Programmes

The changing demands for social science research at ICARDA largely reflected institutional changes. Originally the centre comprised four research programmes: Cereals, Food Legumes, Pasture Forage and Livestock Programme (PFLP) and Farming Systems Research (FSR) Programme. In the beginning, the main concerns of the first three were technology development, particularly germplasm development, with little need perceived for social science research. Hence, no social science input was included in those research activities. However, the need for social science research was seen as crucial for FSR and ICARDA's first social scientists were placed there. Social scientists were members of multidisciplinary research teams of researchers in the programme, which covered crop and cropping systems, soil fertility, livestock and socioeconomics.

In 1986, FSR became the Farm Resource Management Programme, with greater emphasis on managing and conserving natural resources (water, soil and natural vegetation), thus creating demand for new social science research but retaining the production system perspective and farmer orientation. The concept of sustainable production systems has become part of the programme's mission statement.

In 1984, the Technical Advisory Committee (TAC) of CGIAR recommended that the capacity of livestock research at ICARDA be increased. Consequently, in 1990 the livestock research component of

FSR was transferred to the PFLP to increasingly integrate its pasture, forage and livestock research while maintaining collaboration with FSR (Nour, 2002). In 1994, as a result of the 1993 EPMR, Cereals and Food Legumes were merged into the Germplasm Improvement Programme to take advantage of the synergy and efficiency resulting mainly from sharing support activities in plant protection, physiology and agronomy and biotechnology (CGIAR, 1993).

As new varieties became increasingly available from the Germplasm Improvement Programme, researchers needed to understand and monitor the diffusion of these crop varieties, document farmers' preferred characteristics and identify the constraints on adoption of modern varieties. Farmers' access to good-quality seed was considered critical to such adoption. As a result, the Seed Production Unit was formed in 1985 to support national seed systems and recommend policies to improve them, generating the need for research on seed economics, small-scale seed enterprises and seed policy.

Another factor that shaped demand for social science research was the establishment of ICARDA's regional programmes – North Africa, Nile Valley and Red Sea, West Asia, Highlands, Arabian Peninsula and Central Asia and the Caucasus – and intensification of collaboration with national programmes. Most of the centre's adaptive research, such as testing and evaluation of technologies under farm conditions and field research, has been carried out through these regional programmes in collaboration with NARS partners, creating demand for social science research in technology evaluation, adoption and impact studies, analysis of farmer preferences and capacity building of NARS partners.

In 1997, Farm Resource Management and Pasture, Forage and Livestock were merged to form the Natural Resources Management Programme (NRMP), offering advantages from efficient deployment of limited resources and facilitating the integration of ICARDA's research activities into a cogent research programme on crop and livestock production within a framework of natural resource conservation (CGIAR, 1993). This has brought new dimensions to the centre's research agenda: integrated resource management, the need to understand determinants of rural livelihoods and characterization of rural households to target technologies to the needs of the poor. The need to simultaneously address short-term livelihood objectives of rural households and the long-term implications of NRM required greater understanding of the role of socioeconomic factors in determining different options' outcomes and their trade-offs. The analysis of poverty and typologies of rural households in terms of their capabilities, assets and vulnerability came to the forefront of the social science research agenda. The strategy has been to couple crop and livestock productivity improvement research with NRM research and to integrate them with socioeconomic research that provides the perspectives of producers and end users. At the same time, application of participatory methods in NRM research has generally increased, and demand for social scientists' skills in applying participatory tools and gender analysis has become critical for biophysical sciences. The methods for incorporating user participation and perspectives and indigenous knowledge were fundamental in this research. Social scientists were, therefore, required to support it. As all projects were required to demonstrate their impacts, demand for impact assessment research increased.

In 1998, ICARDA's research became organized on a project basis according to the 19 research projects of the Medium-term Plan. Seven fall within the Germplasm Improvement Programme and ten within NRMP (production system management, NRM and socioeconomics and policy). The Genetic Resources Unit and Seed Production Unit each cover one Medium-term Plan project.

The increasing shift from unrestricted core to restricted project funding at ICARDA, and the increased emphasis on linking research with development to demonstrate impact has also changed how research projects are formulated. With a few exceptions, all restricted-funding projects have socioeconomic dimensions and require information on impacts, in most cases with specific reference to poverty and to communities' and farmers' participation in the research. More information is demanded on the characteristics of the beneficiaries of research and the pathways through which research is expected to impact upon them. This demand is clearly expressed in the 2001 EPMR, which stated that

> changes in the CGIAR and ICARDA missions and priorities call for increases in research focused upon poverty alleviation, with an emphasis on beneficiaries, especially rural women, as well as increased attention to on-farm participatory approaches in the whole ICARDA research agenda.
>
> (CGIAR, 2001)

Development of Social Science Research at ICARDA

Human resources

Social science research has always been part of ICARDA's research agenda. Data on all categories of social science staff, including senior scientists, postdoctoral fellows, visiting scientists and research associates since the centre's establishment are shown in Fig. 12.1. The data reveal a steady growth of ICARDA's social science staff from 1978 until 1997, most being non-senior scientists. However, since then the number has dropped markedly. Overall, agricultural economics was the dominant field of specialization among social scientists. The non-economist social science disciplines included anthropology, agricultural extension, human geography, rural development and gender analysis and land management, but were less represented than economics. Figure 12.1 also shows that the centre employed an average of one senior social scientist in 1978–1998, with the rest of the staff being postdoctoral fellows, visiting scientists and research associates. The number of senior social scientists has increased significantly and peaked at eight in 1997, mainly agricultural economists, dropping to five in 2002.

The social science staff can be further analysed by taking into account the full-time equivalent of senior scientist person-years dedicated to research and the changes in the research agenda over the years (see the next section). This analysis is presented in Table 12.1 and shows that the human resource capacity in social science research has been changing in terms of full-time senior scientist person-years and discipline mix. However, full-time social science research staffing has declined markedly for the last 5 years (Table 12.1).[2]

On average, ICARDA's investment in social science research during 1978–1982 was about 1.3 staff-years[3] working full-time in research, increasing to 2.7 person-years during 1982–1987 and dropping slightly to 2.4 during 1988–1992. A significant number of social science research staff members are assigned to restricted projects. The number of these

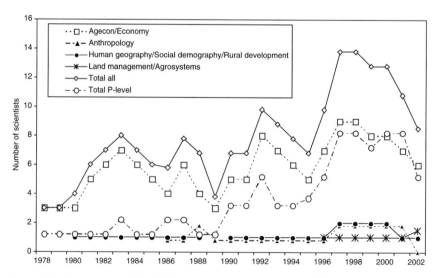

Fig. 12.1. The trend of ICARDA social science research, 1978–2002.

Table 12.1. ICARDA's social science human resources and research agenda for 1978–2002.

Period	Full-time senior scientists (person-years)	Disciplines	Types of studies
1978–1982	1.3	Agricultural economics	Systems diagnosis
		Demography	
1983–1987	2.7	Agricultural economics	Diagnosis, technology evaluation
		Agricultural extension	
		Demography	
1988–1992	2.4	Agricultural economics	Diagnosis, technology evaluation, adoption
		Applied anthropology	
		Geography	
1993–1997	4.25	Agricultural economics	Technology evaluation, adoption, impact assessment, economics of seed systems, policy, property rights, water management, participatory research
		Applied anthropology	
		Geography	
		Rural development and gender	
1998–2002	3.30	Agricultural economics	Impact assessment,

(*continued*)

Table 12.1. (*continued*)

Period	Full-time senior scientists (person-years)	Disciplines	Types of studies
			economics of seed systems, policy, property rights, water management, poverty, participatory research, community development action research, human nutrition, gender
		Applied anthropology	
		Rural development and gender	
		Human nutrition	
2003	2.75	Agricultural economics	Impact assessment, economics of seed systems, policy, property rights, water management, poverty, participatory research, community development action research, human nutrition, gender
		Applied anthropology	
		Rural development and gender	
		Human nutrition	

projects has been increasing recently, and social science staff resources again rose to 4.25 senior staff-years during 1993–1997 but dropped to 3.30 during 1998–2002. About 2.3 senior staff-years are assigned to restricted projects. One senior economist was committed entirely to the economics of seed production. Therefore, only one full-time senior scientist was left for the centre-wide social science research programme. This situation contrasts with the sharp increase in demand for social science input for almost all ICARDA projects, and in the social science research needs brought about by recent calls to establish clear linkages between research and development, poverty and the environment.

That social science staff in special projects will outnumber core staff is to be expected as special projects are designed to carry out research that cannot be covered by significantly declining core funding. As special projects increase and more staff (usually less experienced, such as postdoctoral fellows, research fellows and PhD students) are recruited, ICARDA's capacity to develop a centre-wide strategy, guide these research activities, develop funding proposals and prepare centre-wide reporting becomes strained. We argue that each of the three Medium-term Plan projects should have at least one core scientist who can guide the research programme.

ICARDA's investment in core senior social science research staff has, therefore, been lower than demand for it in social and economics agricultural research. If ICARDA is to address all these research areas effectively, it must invest more in social science research. ICARDA is at a critical juncture and must use resources more efficiently by prioritizing these research topics based on the needs of farmers in the region, capacity of NARS partners, emerging challenges in development, environmental and natural resource conservation and poverty reduction. The need to deploy additional resources will certainly increase, but can be met by greater involvement of ICARDA's social scientists in designing and formulating restricted-grant proposals and establishing links with advanced research institutions and strong national programmes.

Evolution of the Social Science Research Programme and Outputs

Early work on diagnosis

When ICARDA was founded, the main focus of social science research was on diagnostic and descriptive studies of prevailing farming systems in WANA. In the first decade, the focus was on characterizing farming systems in the region; *ex-ante* socioeconomic evaluation of on-station and on-farm trials; training and capacity building of NARS counterparts; diagnosis studies of production, including cropping and livestock systems; economic analysis of technological options; and evaluation of on-farm trials. The purpose of these studies was to better understand the complex interrelationships within farming systems in the region; identify production problems and the needs and aspirations of farming families; and link agricultural development planners, researchers and extension workers and farmers (ICARDA, 1980). These studies were undertaken as part of an interdisciplinary research effort in collaboration with biophysical scientists (Somel and Cooper, 1985). The results of experimental trials were economically evaluated, including livestock production, fertilizer use, crop rotation and policy issues to ensure that technologies developed from the research pro- gramme met the needs of farming families (ICARDA, 1982).

The main contribution of the social science group in ICARDA's early years was to help understand WANA complex farming systems, allowing the centre to identify and focus on critical elements that could precipitate change (Somel and Cooper, 1985).

Adoption studies

In the late 1980s, when new technologies, particularly new seed varieties, became available to farmers, ICARDA initiated research on technology adoption. Survey methods and informal interviews were used to determine farmers' perceptions of new technologies. Adopted technology was evaluated using farm data. These studies identified different patterns of technology adoption based on location, use of pro- duction and household socioeconomic characteristics (Mazid *et al.*, 1994; Tutwiler *et al.*, 1997). These patterns indicate continuing con- straints on the adoption of improved technologies among certain groups of farmers and suggest strategies to improve the effectiveness and efficiency of technology development and transfer. Some con- straints on the adoption of improved technologies in WANA were iden- tified – for example, for production of winter chickpeas regionwide (Tutwiler, 1994), barley in Syria (Saade, 1991) and wheat in upper Egypt (Aw-Hassan *et al.*, 1995) and Sudan (Faki *et al.*, 1998).

Haddad *et al.* (1997) report on a number of studies within a regional project on crop–livestock integration, which analyse technol- ogy adoption, project impact, as well as constraints encountered by farmers in adopting the new technologies. The adoption of improved barley production technologies increased considerably, and the impact of the project was greatest in increasing the use of improved cultivars and lowering seed rates.

The studies identified the following constraints on technology adoption: (i) information gap – insufficient or unconvincing informa- tion on the recommended technologies, implying an ineffective exten- sion system; (ii) inadequate input supply (seeds, equipment, fertilizers); (iii) inappropriate technology (for example, new wheat varieties with lower bread-making quality than the local variety and low straw yield, and unsuitable for animal feeding and green grazing; small-seed chickpea varieties with a lower market price in Morocco than the preferred large-seed types); (iv) system constraints (labour requirements and availability of family labour and diseases such as *Aschocyta* blight on winter chickpeas); (v) lack of credit; and (vi) pricing policies (low and controlled output prices, and high prices of inputs such as certified seeds) and government input allocation policy (for example, fertilizer allocation in Syria).

Adoption studies also highlighted the importance of farmers' participation in research. In several studies such as Tutwiler *et al.* (1997), farmers participating in on-farm trials and demonstrations had higher adoption rates than non-participating farmers. Farmers' participation in technology evaluation also provided feedback to research and allowed researchers to incorporate farmers' preferences and system knowledge into technology development, reinforcing the need to involve farmers in research and to monitor farmer-to-farmer transfer of information and new agricultural technologies. For example, a 'seed tracer' study was launched in 1994 to monitor farmer-to-farmer exchange of seed of new barley germplasm selected by farmers participating in on-farm germplasm selection trials in north-west Syria. The study concluded that farmers' participation not only helped develop varieties specifically adapted to farmers' preferences, but also increased early adoption through farmer-to-farmer seed distribution (Mazid *et al.*, 2003a). The study also revealed the existence of local commercial seed enterprises, which could provide the basis for strengthening community-based seed systems. More recently, Thomson *et al.* (2003) identified the reproductive rate as the most important factor affecting the productivity of small ruminants in West Asia. However, the authors found little evidence that the reproductive rate has improved over the last 20 years, suggesting the need for a programme of on-farm research on management and feeding practices to increase the fertility of small ruminants. With some support from ICARDA scientists, trained national scientists are carrying out adoption studies and evaluating on-farm technology.

Technology evaluation

In the early 1990s, research priorities shifted from initial diagnostic studies of farming systems and economic evaluation of on-station experimental results to economic assessment of technologies at farm and community levels and impact studies at farm, national and regional levels. Using an econometric approach, the United Nations Economic and Social Commission for West Asia (ESCWA) and the

International Center for Agricultural Research in the Dry Areas (ICARDA) (2000) assessed on-farm water-use efficiency under farm conditions in Syria and Iraq, and found that farmers tend to over-irrigate crops by 25–55%, resulting in a low water-use efficiency (<0.45). Shideed and Hateem (1999) compared the profitability of crop rotations (barley and barley, barley and fallow, barley and forage legumes) considering risk of production, and recommended barley and a mixture of common vetch and barley for mixed crop-livestock systems in Ninawah province, north Iraq, which has low rainfall (200–300 mm annually), as these options had higher returns and lower risks.

Bendaoud *et al.* (1999) and Bachta and Thabet (1999) used community-model prototypes to evaluate the integrated impacts of policy and technological changes on cereal and livestock production, community income, land use and soil erosion. The models, which incorporate private and common resource endowments, were also used to simulate institutional and property right changes and their effects on income and equity.

Impact assessment

During the 1990s, social science research became widely diverse. The research on impact assessment gained new momentum with further support from the Standing Panel for Impact Assessment of the interim Science Council of CGIAR, in addition new research areas such as poverty assessment, human nutrition and gender analysis were given importance. In 1995, research on policy and property rights was initiated in collaboration with IFPRI,[4] and the increased application of participatory research methods needed further research input from social scientists. Some of the highlights of this research work follow.

The demand for quantifying agricultural research impacts beyond technology evaluation has increased. Impact assessment has now become a common feature in all CGIAR work, which is reinforced by the Standing Panel for Impact Assessment. A number of studies on the impacts of germplasm improvement in developing countries were thus completed (Aw-Hassan *et al.*, 1995; Aw-Hassan and Shideed, 2003a,b; Mazid *et al.*, 2003a,b). Brennan *et al.* (2002) also analysed the spill-over impacts of ICARDA's germplasm improvement research on Australian agriculture. Petersen *et al.* (2002) analysed agricultural research priorities in two regions of northern Syria and found improvements in wheat grain yields to have the greatest effect on income, followed by improvements in lentil grain yields.

These studies focused on the impacts of germplasm enhancement research. Less work has been done on the impacts of NRM research,

partly because analysing them is more problematic due to data limitations and accounting and attribution problems. More such impact studies are needed using innovative multidisciplinary approaches that also
include the users' own assessment of these impacts. Less work has also
been done on the impacts of agricultural research on poverty.

Property rights

With an ICARDA-IFPRI appointed position on property rights,
research in this field has progressed. A collection of studies on property rights in WANA is in Chaherli *et al.* (1999). Ngaido (2000),
Ngaido and Kirk (2000) and Ngaido *et al.* (2002) reported additional
research in this field. One main conclusion of these studies was that
whether or not institutional reforms to develop dryland pastoral systems are based on privatization or common property arrangements, it
is crucial that the state provide production strategies and various
market and institutional access options to help pastoralists (Ngaido,
2000). Ngaido *et al.* (2002) also concluded that community participation is necessary for sustainable management of rangelands as local
knowledge is essential for management and enforcement mechanisms. In another study in the Yemeni mountains, Aw-Hassan *et al.*
(2000) found significantly more degraded and unrepaired terraces on
sharecropped public than privately owned land. The study highlighted the importance of strengthening institutional arrangements
(clear and re-enforceable contracts), particularly where power distribution, which favours landlords, has reinforced the lack of clear rules
and made enforcement difficult.

Seed policies and economics

With the appointment in 1996 of a full-time economist specializing in
seed production, research on seed policy and economics has steadily
progressed (Bishaw and Kugbei, 1997; Kahsay and Kugbei, 1998). The
initial focus had been on strengthening capacity in the national seed
programmes to eventually impact on household food security, farm
income and farmers' welfare. One of the main issues addressed was
small-scale seed enterprises: while small-scale seed systems are
appealing for a number of reasons to poor farmers planting marginal
crops in remote areas, which the private sector may not find attractive,
the success of small-scale seed enterprises depends on strong government commitment to introduce favourable policies and encourage
investment (Kugbei and Bishaw, 2002).

Gender analysis

The early Farming Systems Research Programme addressed gender issues. Tully (1990) highlighted the changes in agricultural labour as a result of migration from rural to urban areas and its consequences for agricultural labour supply. Rassam (1985) and Rassam and Tully (1986) observed a decline in the male agricultural labour force in Syria due to mechanization and increased availability of off-farm city work for men, and noted that they were more often involved in mechanized operations, and the women in hand labour. However in 1992, ICARDA's gender research gained impetus from the CGIAR Gender Programme guidelines. Pape *et al.* (1994) then conducted similar work, which found that the work load and responsibilities of Bedouin women in Syria increased due to the migration of men, as did women's contact with the market and therefore, control over household expenditure. Abdelali-Martini (2001) also identified changes in Syrian agriculture work patterns as a result of intensified production systems and migration of male family members to off-farm work in cities and towns. A clear division of labour by gender has developed, and women have participated in informal, but organized, labour gangs led by male or female contractors (Abdelali-Martini *et al.*, 2003a). The success of these labour gangs in filling the gaps created by male migration and intensified agriculture is leading to strong feminization of agricultural labour (Abdelali-Martini, 2003b). Such rural social organizations and other forms of social capital are being recognized as significant in asset access and risk management in dry areas (Abdelali-Martini *et al.*, 2003c).

Khelifi-Touhami (2000) found that women's customary security mechanisms appear to be undermined when women do not claim their parental share of land or do not activate their claim on kinship support, making them vulnerable. Gender-related research with well-defined policy-relevant questions will remain important aspects of ICARDA's social science research, given the vital role that women play in agriculture and livelihood in rural dry areas, and the equity and nutritional implications of changes in rural households' work patterns and social organization.

Participatory research

The increase in client-oriented research as a way to enhance the impact of ICARDA's research has sharply increased the demand for participatory methods and approaches for community-based research and development. Now, virtually every project has some kind of client participation component in its research. As a result, social scientists have provided essential support to the projects such as that to develop participatory barley-breeding research (Ceccarelli *et al.*, 2000). Assessing the impact of these methods is also high in the minds of donors and research managers. Lilja and Aw-Hassan (2003) studied the impact of ICARDA's participatory barley-breeding research as part of the System-Wide Programme on Participatory Research and Gender Analysis. Other studies have highlighted the importance of community participation in NRM research (Aw-Hassan and Sghaier, 1996; Aw-Hassan *et al.*, 2002).

Rural livelihoods

Major attention has been given to rural livelihood analysis, starting with a study characterizing poverty in dry areas (Rodriguez, 1997).[5] Livelihood research received additional impetus from the 2001 EPMR mission, which recommended that:

> ICARDA determine, with its partners, the rural livelihood strategies of the poor in its region to clarify what research options, investments, policies and technologies are most likely to benefit them. Special emphasis should be given to highly vulnerable segments of the population.

> (CGIAR, 2001)

This emphasis on poverty and rural livelihoods has raised researchers' awareness of the importance of explicitly recognizing and including the human dimension in agricultural research, leading to more projects embracing it. For example, Dadi *et al.* (2003) investigated the socio-economic factors affecting grass pea consumption and the incidence of lathyrism (paralysis of lower limbs caused by the consumption of grass pea) in Ethiopia. The study concluded that overall improvement of household incomes and food security would substantially reduce the incidence of lathyrism. The livelihood approach has become essential to integrated NRM research and was recently adopted by NRMP. Several studies analysing livelihood are ongoing in marginal environments (for example, Aw-Hassan *et al.*, 2003; La Rovere *et al.*, 2003).

Impact of Social Science

No formal study assesses the impact of social science research at ICARDA. Its main contributions follow:

- The diagnostic, adoption and technology evaluation studies and collaboration on them with NARS, have been influential in incorporating a social science perspective into national agricultural research. Through training and collaborative research partnerships, facilitated by ICARDA's regional programmes, the NARS of Central and West Asia and North Africa (CWANA) countries have adopted social science research in problem diagnosis, solicitation of farmers' opinions and perceptions and assessment of research results as a standard practice in the research cycle. The adoption studies were instrumental in developing a dialogue between researchers, extension workers and communities, and provided valuable information to generate technology.

- The participatory barley-breeding methodology was developed through the collaboration of breeders and social scientists (Ceccarelli *et al.*, 2000), receiving the CGIAR Chairman's Excellence in Science Award for 2000. The work is expanding to other countries in the region and to other crops. Using the experience and data from that project, a study of the impact of participatory breeding is expected to see how cost-effective it is. As scientists become more aware of participatory research, they increasingly apply it. ICARDA's social scientists are helping other disciplines identify the training needs of research staff in participatory research and community approaches, and seven such training programmes have recently been conducted for different NRMP projects.

Participatory research methods are being used in many ICARDA projects, including the Khanasser Valley Integrated Research Site in Syria, Barani Village Development Project in Pakistan, Integrated Feed-livestock Production Project in Central Asia, Small-scale Sheep Milk Improvement Project in northern Syria, Mountain Terraces Project in Yemen and the Mashreq and the Maghreb Project covering eight WANA countries. Thomas *et al.* (2003) describes in detail the approach used in the last project. The Khanasser Valley Project is another good example of ICARDA's interdisciplinary research. The project team is improving stakeholder collaboration and formalizing farmers' interest groups for participatory technology evaluation. These concepts have become integral to NRMP project development.

Although interdisciplinary research is by its nature challenging and requires a great deal of co-learning, mutual respect and cooperation, lack of discourse space appeared to be insignificant to social research at ICARDA, as is clear from the large number of social science-led publications. The level of cross-disciplinary collaboration in research will certainly increase as the number and types of stakeholders in research grow, which could contribute to defining common problems and understanding constraints and hence, greater likelihood of impact.

- Several studies (such as Saade, 1991; Mazid *et al.*, 1999) have found that fertilizer application in areas of low rainfall was profitable under a range of rainfall variability, which led to a change of government policy on fertilizer allocation in Syria. Before the studies' results were published, this policy restricted the allocation of fertilizer to areas of higher rainfall, and fertilizer use in areas of lower rainfall was thought to be unprofitable. However, after discussions on the studies' results, the government reversed the policy, made fertilizer available to areas of low rainfall and allowed farmers to apply fertilizer as they saw fit. As a result, the use of fertilizer in areas of low rainfall and crop yields has increased.

- Social scientists influenced the development of community-based research in several projects. It is too early to assess the full impact of such research, but it represents a shift from the single-technology farm approach to dialogue with the whole community and its participation in defining problems and evaluating technology. This is particularly important in NRM research, where reversing resource degradation may require communal action. Participatory action research has been used to mobilize the community to rehabilitate indigenous *qanat*[6] systems in a village in Khanasser Valley in Syria (Wessels, 2000). This work led to the rehabilitation of common *qanats* in three more communities (Wessels *et al.*, 2002, unpublished). A television documentary of this work, *Tunnel Vision,* was broadcast on the BBC's Earth Report. ICARDA-IFPRI collaboration in developing community modelling has further raised awareness of the utility of the community approach.

- Ongoing research on child nutrition (ICARDA, 2001; Ghosh and Aw-Hassan, 2003)[7] and food security mapping in Syria, which the government requested, is expected to influence targeting of research and development programmes.

- Impact studies have provided agricultural research managers with important information on the returns to research investment and identified constraints on technology adoption. Many of these studies were requested either by donors or the CGIAR secretariat through the Standing Panel for Impact Assessment.

- ICARDA is the only centre that has a unit dedicated to seed production research and capacity building of national seed systems. The transfer of the benefits of seed system research to farmers requires sustained national efforts with strong backstopping from the international centres. Examples of institutional impact on national seed programmes in the region include the following:
  - creating a multiplier effect of human capacity building by training key national staff members who are now passing on their ideas to other colleagues in structured follow-up programmes, and collaborating in joint seed system research initiatives such as seed policy review in Egypt, Ethiopia, Jordan, Morocco, Pakistan, Syria, Turkey and Yemen;

- creating awareness of alternative, cost-effective approaches to sustainable production of quality seed by smallholders, including food legume seed systems in south-east Anatolia, Turkey; tef and barley seed production in Ethiopia; and forage seed production in north-east Syria;
- participating in joint international seed sector review missions in the region, which formulate recommendations for policymakers to directly impact national policy; and
- conducting seed needs assessment as a basis for project formulation and other forms of development intervention, for example, in Afghanistan.

The Way Forward

Substantial changes have taken place in the agricultural systems of dry areas, particularly in CWANA, over the last 25 years. The traditional cereal-livestock rainfed systems, which were dominant in many countries, have been transformed into more intensive production systems with reduced fallow areas, increased irrigation and expanded tree cultivation. Of the CWANA farming systems that Dixon *et al.* (2001) identified, six are highly relevant to ICARDA's work: irrigated, highland mixed, rainfed mixed, dryland mixed, pastoral and sparse (arid). A high proportion of farmers and pastoralists in these systems depend on agriculture as a primary food and livelihood source but have developed more diversified livelihood options and off-farm (agricultural and non-agricultural) sources of income have gained importance. Increased male out-migration has increased women's role in agriculture (Abdelali-Martini, 2001, 2003). The challenges facing CWANA include high population growth rates, decreasing water and degraded lands (desertification), with loss of natural biodiversity and persistent rural poverty. Food and feed demand has outpaced domestic production in most countries and will continue to do so. The resource bases for traditional livestock raising have come under serious pressure, and large feed deficits are projected (Nordblom and Shomo, 1995). This means that countries are faced with feeding larger numbers of people, with increasingly limited water resources, under highly variable climatic conditions and increasing globalization, while the area of agricultural land per producer decreases, threatening serious food insecurity.

Although increased irrigation from canals and groundwater has resulted in short-term progress in increasing agricultural production and rural incomes, and provides a sense of food security, the long-term sustainability of these gains is questionable. Abstraction of groundwater at rates far greater than its recharge capacity has led to depletion of this resource, which has dried up in some areas and could threaten rural livelihoods. Expansion of canal irrigation may not be sustained in the long term as demand for water by other sectors will increase.

Rural poverty remains a challenge in CWANA. In WANA alone close to 300 million people, or over 40% of the population, are estimated to be living on less than $2 a day.[8] Some countries, particularly those depending largely on imports, may have difficulty financing their food imports. About 42% of consumption needs in North Africa, for example, are met by imports (Meade *et al.*, 2003). Many countries have a highly variable climate, which is likely to be exacerbated by climate change, worsening food insecurity.

Nutrition deficits are predicted to intensify in the vulnerable lower-income countries (Meade *et al.*, 2003), many in North Africa, Central Asia and the Nile Valley, which face highly variable weather and deteriorating land and water resources. Other studies found serious child malnutrition in rural poor households in drier areas of the barley-livestock systems (ICARDA, 2001; Ghosh and Aw-Hassan, 2003).

Lack of investment in human resources such as education (particularly for girls) and health and lack of power to influence policy decisions on service delivery at the local, regional and national levels could further marginalize rural areas and increase poverty (IFAD, 2001). Poverty is also considered to have a 'downward spiral' effect on the environment, because the poor have a short time horizon, little investment capacity and low capacity to tolerate risk, and depend greatly on their environment for their livelihood, for example, for energy and grazing.

Poverty and natural resource degradation can be reduced by adapting a 'pro-poor growth' strategy focusing on investment in human capital of the poor and on agricultural research and development (Senauer, 2002). Agricultural development is a crucial factor in such a strategy. Identifying high-value crops, reducing postharvest losses and improving marketing information and knowledge will also be essential.

ICARDA considers that agricultural research can reduce poverty through four strategic approaches: (i) use of technologies that simultaneously improve productivity and sustain natural resources and can be applied by poor people using low levels of external inputs; (ii) resource management practices that conserve soil, water and vegetation, and do not decrease productivity; (iii) diversified farming systems that reduce economic risk, contribute to greater resource-use efficiency and provide higher returns to the farm community; and (iv) improved vertical integration from producer to consumer, including enhanced quality and added value of farm products, improved postharvest processing and storage and job creation. ICARDA's research agenda has been developed around these strategies, with research projects each addressing one or more of these approaches.

The implication for agricultural research is that methods should be developed to meet challenges with knowledge-based solutions. Such methods should be demonstrated in actual farming systems and transferred to national programmes. The implication for social science research is increased demand for understanding vulnerable segments of rural communities, their characteristics, constraints and options; for establishing the linkages between agricultural research and development and identifying pathways through which agricultural research impacts upon rural livelihoods; and for demonstrating the trade-offs of different options in the use of natural resources and the environment. The development of detailed rural household typologies based on closer analysis of livelihoods in the major farming systems mentioned earlier has been initiated and will intensify. This will allow targeting research to the needs of beneficiaries and provide the basis for anticipating and monitoring the technological and socio-economic impacts of ICARDA research. The 2001 EPMR recognized this as a high priority.

This review suggests clear priorities for ICARDA's social science research: (i) new methods of assessing impacts, particularly of integrated NRM research, and the community-based research process; (ii) analysis of research impacts on rural livelihoods in a comprehensive framework, taking into account non-farm activities and emphasizing gender, social capital, institutional mechanisms, diversification, alternative income-earning opportunities, added value and marketing opportunities; and (iii) economic and policy analysis of NRM (soil, water, natural vegetation and biodiversity). Social scientists are also required to collaborate with biophysical scientists in developing effective stakeholder participation methods to develop and test technological, institutional and policy innovations.

Conclusion

ICARDA's modest investment in social science research has made important contributions to it. However, given the challenges of improving rural livelihoods and reversing natural resource depletion and environmental degradation, the core senior social science staff faces increasing demand for social science research. Priorities have emerged. The first is research on the determinants of rural poverty, and technological, policy and institutional options that can improve rural livelihoods. Rural livelihood studies are required to identify the most vulnerable segments of rural communities, their characteristics, constraints and options. Such studies should also analyse gender, social capital as a means to access assets, risk management, diversification of production, value-added products and market access. The second priority area is research on the linkages between agricultural research and development to identify the pathways through which agricultural research impacts upon rural livelihoods, covering *ex-ante* and *ex-post* impact studies. A third priority is research on the trade-offs between different policy options for the use of natural resources and the environment (land, water and biodiversity).

ICARDA social science research could be rearranged along these priority areas, and at least one senior social scientist maintained for each research area.

Notes

[1]External Programme for Management Review.

[2]Information collected and analysed from the Personnel Services data files.

[3]Staff-years mean the P-level social scientist staff.

[4]This was supported with two IFPRI-ICARDA joint-appointee postdoctoral fellow – Nabil Chaherli (policy) and Tidiane Ngaido (property rights).

[5]This was followed by a presentation by Aden Aw-Hassan on poverty to the board of trustees meeting of 2001.

[6]'A form of subterranean aqueduct or subsurface canal engineered to collect groundwater and direct it through a gently sloping underground conduit to surface canals which provide water to agricultural fields' (Lightfoot, 1996).

[7]The child nutrition work has been initiated with human nutritionist research fellow Shibani Ghosh as a collaborative project between ICARDA and the University of Boston, Massachusetts.

[8]Computed from World Bank (2002).

References

Abdelali-Martini, M. (2001) Female agricultural labour is increasing. In: *ICARDA Annual Report 2001.* ICARDA, Aleppo, Syria, pp. 66–67.

Abdelali-Martini, M. (2003) The impact of agricultural development on the feminization of agricultural labour in Syria. In: *NRMP Annual Report for 1996–2001.* ICARDA, Aleppo, Syria, pp. 215–222.

Abdelali-Martini, M.A., Bailey, E., Jones, G. and Goldey, P. (2003a) Agricultural intensification and female labour in farm production in North-West Syria. In: Hakimian, H. and Nugent, J.B. (eds) *Trade Policy and Economic Integration in the Middle East and North Africa: Economic Boundaries in Flux.* Routledge Curzon, London, pp. 184–204.

Abdelali-Martini, M., Goldey, P., Jones, G.E. and Bailey, E. (2003b) Towards a feminization of agricultural labour in north-west Syria.

Journal of Peasant Studies 30(2), 71–94.

Abdelali-Martini, M., Aw-Hassan, A. and Jones, G.E. (2003c) Social network organization of women's labour gangs in north-west Syria and their impact on the livelihoods of rural households. Paper presented at the Second International Conference of the Middle East Economics Association in cooperation with the Centre for Economics and Ethics, 2–3 June 2003. University of Versailles, France.

Ashby, J., Sperling, L. and Carney, D. (1996) Introduction: Synthesis of discussion working groups in new frontiers in participatory research and gender analysis. In: *Proceedings of the International Seminar on Participatory Research and Gender Analysis for Technology Development*, 9–14 September 1996. Consultative Group on International Agricultural Research (CGIAR) System Programme on Participatory Research and Gender Analysis for Technology Development and Institutional Innovation. Centro Internacional de Agricultura Tropical (CIAT), Cali, Colombia, pp. 1–13.

Aw-Hassan, A. and Sghaier, M. (1996) Participatory natural resources management research in the dry areas: challenges and opportunities in new frontiers in participatory research and gender analysis In: *Proceedings of the International Seminar on Participatory Research and Gender Analysis for Technology Development*, 9–14 September 1996. CGIAR system-wide programme on participatory research and gender analysis for technology devel-

opment and institutional innovation (CAPRI). CIAT, Cali, Colombia, pp. 251–259.

Aw-Hassan, A. and Shideed, K. in collaboration with Ceccarelli, S., Erskine, W., Grando, S. and Tutwiler, R. (2003a) The impact of international and national investment in barley germplasm improvement in developing countries. In: Evenson, R.E. and Gollin, D. (eds) *Crop Variety and its Effects on Productivity. The Impact of International Agricultural Research.* CAB International, Wallingford, UK, pp. 241–256.

Aw-Hassan, A. and Shideed, K. in collaboration with Sarker, A., Tutwiler, R. and Erskine, W. (2003b) Economic impact of international and national lentil improvement research in developing countries. In: Evenson, R.E. and Gollin, D. (eds) *Crop Variety and its Effects on Productivity. The Impact of International Agricultural Research.* CAB International, Wallingford, UK, pp. 275–291.

Aw-Hassan, A., Ghanem, E., Ali, A.A., Mansour, M. and Solh, M.B. (1995) Economic returns from improved wheat technology in Upper Egypt. Social Science Paper No. 1. International Centre for Agricultural Research in the Dry Areas (ICARDA), Aleppo, Syria, pp. 1–31.

Aw-Hassan, A., Alsanabani, M. and Bamatraf, A.R. (2000) Impact of land tenure and other socioeconomic factors on mountain terraces maintenance in Yemen. CGIAR System-wide Programme on Participatory Research and Gender Analysis for Technology Development and Institutional Innovation (CAPRI) Working Paper No. 3. International Food

Policy Research Institute (IFPRI), Washington, DC, 42 pp.

Aw-Hassan, A., Bruggeman, A. and Ebrahim, A.R.Y. (2002) *The Yemeni Mountain Terraces Project: Institutionalizing Community-Based Integrated Natural Resources Management Research.* Caravan No. 16. ICARDA, Aleppo, Syria, pp. 24–26.

Aw-Hassan, A., Mazid, A., La Rovere, R. and Bruggeman, A. (2003) Challenged livelihoods in the dry areas: the case of Khanasser valley in Syria. Paper presented at the workshop of the 25th International Conference of Agriculture Economists, 16–22 August 2003, Durban, South Africa.

Bachta, M.S. and Thabet, B. (1999) Community modelling in Tunisia. In: Chaherli, N., Hazell, P., Ngaido, T., Nordblom, T. and Oram, P. (eds) *Agricultural Growth, Sustainable Resource Management, and Poverty Alleviation in the Low Rainfall Areas of West Asia and North Africa.* IFPRI, ICARDA, National Centre for Agricultural Research and Technology Transfer (NCARTT), and Food and Agriculture Development Centre (ZEL), Amman, Jordan, pp. 188–192.

Bendaoud, M., Boughlala, M., Chaherli, N., Moussaoui, B., Boulanouar, B. and El Mzouri, E. (1999) A community model for evaluating the impact of policy, technology and property rights changes in low rainfall areas of Morocco. In: Chaherli, N., Hazell, P., Ngaido, T., Nordblom, T. and Oram, P. (eds) *Agricultural Growth, Sustainable Resource Management, and Poverty Alleviation in the Low Rainfall Areas of West Asia and North Africa.* IFPRI,

ICARDA, NCARTT and ZEL, Amman, Jordan, pp. 182–187.

Bishaw, Z. and Kugbei, S. (1997) Seed supply in WANA region: status and constraints. In: Rohrbach, D.D., Bishaw, Z. and van Gastel, A.J.G. (eds) *Alternative Strategies for Smallholder Seed Supply. Proceedings of the International Conference on Options for Strengthening National and Regional Seed Systems in Africa and West Asia,* 10–14 March 1997. International Crops Research Institute for the Semi-Arid Tropics (ICRISAT), Harare, Zimbabwe, pp. 18–33.

Brennan, J.P., Aw-Hassan, A., Quade, K.J. and Nordblom, T.L. (2002) Impact of ICARDA research on Australian agriculture. Economic Research Report No. 11. NSW Agriculture, Wagga Wagga, Australia, 84 pp.

Ceccarelli, S., Grando, S., Tutwiler, R., Baha, J., Martini, M.A., Salahieh, H., Goodchild, A. and Michael, M. (2000) A methodological study on participatory barley breeding, I. selection phase. *Euphytica* 111, 91–104.

Chaherli, N., Hazell, P., Ngaido, T., Nordblom, T. and Oram, P. (eds) (1999) *Agricultural Growth, Sustainable Resource Management, Poverty Alleviation in the Low Rainfall Areas of West Asia and North Africa.* Deutsche Stiftung für Internationale Entwickung (DSE), German Foundation for International Development, Washington, DC, 283 pp.

Consultative Group on International Agricultural Research, Technical Advisory Committee (TAC) Secretariat (1993) Report of the Third External Programme and Management Review (EPMR) of ICARDA.

CGIAR Secretariat and World Bank, Washington, DC, 154 pp.

Consultative Group on International Agricultural Research, Technical Advisory Committee (TAC) Secretariat (2001) Report of the Fourth External Programme and Management Review (EPMR) of ICARDA. TAC Secretariat of CGIAR and FAO Dresden, Germany, 139 pp.

Dadi, L., Hailemariam, T., Aw-Hassan, A., Abdel Moniem, A. and Bejiga, G. (2003) The Socio-economic factors affecting grass pea consumption and the distribution of *Lathyrus* in Ethiopia. Integrated Natural Resources Management Research Report Series, No. 4. ICARDA, Aleppo, Syria, 55 pp.

Dixon, J. and Gulliver, A. with Gibbon, D. (2001) *Farming Systems and Poverty: Improving Farmers' Livelihoods in a Changing World.* Food and Agriculture Organization of the United Nations (FAO), Rome and World Bank, Washington, DC, 412 pp.

Faki, H., Aw-Hassan, A., Abdel Moniem, A., Elahmadi, A. and Solh, M. (1998) Adoption of improved wheat technology in the Sudan. Social Science Paper No. 5. ICARDA, Aleppo, Syria, 53 pp.

Ghosh, S. and Aw-Hassan, A. (2003) Poverty, food systems and nutritional well-being of the child. In: NRMP Annual Report for 1996–2001. ICARDA, Aleppo, Syria, pp. 223–234.

Haddad, N., Tutwiler, R. and Thomson, E. (eds) (1997) Improvement of crop-livestock integration systems in West Asia and North Africa. *Proceedings of the Regional Symposium on Integrated Crop-Livestock Systems in the Dry Areas of West Asia and North Africa,* 6–8 November 1995, Amman, Jordan. ICARDA, Aleppo, Syria, 572 pp.

International Centre for Agricultural Research in the Dry Areas (ICARDA) (1980) Research Report No. 2, Farming Systems Programme. ICARDA, Aleppo, Syria, 15 pp.

International Centre for Agricultural Research in the Dry Areas (ICARDA) (1982) Research Report 1982, Farming Systems Programme. ICARDA, Aleppo, Syria, 129 pp.

International Centre for Agricultural Research in the Dry Areas (ICARDA) (1994) Farm Resource Management Programme Annual Report for 1994. ICARDA, Alepppo, Syria, 288 pp.

International Centre for Agricultural Research in the Dry Areas (ICARDA) (2001) *ICARDA Annual Report 2001* ICARDA, Aleppo, Syria, 112 pp.

International Fund for Agricultural Development (IFAD) (2001) *Rural Poverty Report 2001. The Challenge of Ending Rural Poverty.* Oxford University Press, Oxford, UK, 266 pp.

Kahsay, M. and Kugbei, S. (1998) Alternative seed supply systems in Ethiopia. In: Kugbei, S., Turner, M. and Witthaut, P. (eds) *Finance and Management of Small-Scale Seed Enterprises. Proceedings of the Workshop on Finance and Management of Small-Scale Seed Enterprises,* 26–30 October 1998, Addis Ababa, Ethiopia. ICARDA, Aleppo, Syria, pp. 143–149.

Khelifi-Touhami, R. (2000) An examination of the factors affecting women's access to land and implications for livelihood strategies in north-western Syria. MA thesis, Faculty of Graduate Studies of the University of Guelph, Canada.

Kugbei, S. and Bishaw, Z. (2002) Policy measures for stimulating indigenous seed enterprises. *Journal of New Seeds* 4(1/2), 47–63.

La Rovere, R., Aw-Hassan, A. and Arab, G. (2003) Impact of policy and ecological changes on livelihood dynamics on the fringes of Syrian rangelands. *African Journal of Range and Forage Science* 20(2), 202–209.

Lightfoot, D.R. (1996) Syrian *qanat Romani*: history, ecology, abandonment. *Journal of Arid Environments* 33, 321–336.

Lilja, N. and Aw-Hassan, A. (2003) Benefits and costs of participatory barley breeding in Syria. Background paper for a poster presented at the 25th International Conference of Agricultural Economists, 16–22 August 2003. Durban, South Africa.

Mazid, A., Bailey, E. and Seabrook, M.F. (1994) Factors influencing adoption of new technology in dry areas of Syria: fertilizer use on rainfed barley. Farm Resource Management Programme (FRMP) Annual Report for 1994. ICARDA, Aleppo, Syria, pp. 214–229.

Mazid, A., Bailey, E. and Jones, M. (1999) The effect of fertilizer use on rain-fed barley: a case study from Syria. Social Science Paper No. 8. ICARDA, Aleppo, Syria, 28 pp.

Mazid, A., Aw-Hassan, A. and Salahieh, H. (2003a) Analysis of farmers' performance criteria for new barley varieties and their diffusion through farmer-to-farmer seed distribution. NRMP Annual Report for 1996–2001. ICARDA, Aleppo, Syria, pp. 234–243.

Mazid, A., Tutwiler, R., Al-Ahmad, H., Abdelali-Martini, M. and Maya, F. (2003b) Impact of modern agricultural technologies on durum wheat production in Syria. Integrated Natural Resources Management Research Report Series No. 3. ICARDA, Aleppo, Syria, 34 pp.

Meade, B., Rosen, S., Shapouri, S., Andrews, M., Trueblood, M., Nord, M. and Persaud, S. (2003) Food Security Assessment GFA14. Agriculture and Trade Report No. (GFA14), Economic Research Service (ERS), United States Department of Agriculture (USDA), USA, 88 pp.

Ngaido, T. (2000) Can pastoral institutions perform without access options? ICARDA Social Science Paper No. 9. ICARDA, Aleppo, Syria, 25 pp.

Ngaido, T. and Kirk, M. (2000) Collective action, property rights, and devolution of rangeland management: selected examples for Africa and Asia. ICARDA Social Science Paper No. 10. ICARDA, Aleppo, Syria, 34 pp.

Ngaido, T., McCarthy, N. and Di Gregorio, M. (eds) (2002) *International Conference on Policy and Institutional Options for the Management of Rangelands in Dry Areas*. CAPRi Working Paper, No. 23. IFPRI/CAPRI, Washington, DC, 72 pp.

Nordblom, T.L. and Shomo, F. (1995) *Food and Feed Prospects to 2020 in the West Asia/North Africa Region*. ICARDA Social Science Paper No. 2. ICARDA, Aleppo, Syria, vi + 56 pp.

Nour, M.A. (2002) *ICARDA 25: A Promise of Hope*. ICARDA, Aleppo, Syria, 165 pp.

Pape, A., Doppler, W. and Nordblom, T. (1994) The contribution of women to labour and decision making processes in Bedouin families. Pasture, Forage and Livestock Programme (PFLP) Annual Report for 1994. ICARDA, Aleppo, Syria, pp. 245–260.

Petersen, E.H., Pannell, D.J., Nordblom, T.L. and Shomo, F. (2002) Potential benefits from alternative areas of agricultural research for dryland farming in northern Syria. *Agricultural Systems* 72, 93–108.

Rassam, A. (1985) Farm labour by age and sex in northwestern Syria. Implications for two proposed technologies. Paper presented at the Farming Systems Symposium: Farming Systems Research and Extension: Management and Methodology, 13–16 October 1985. Kansas State University, Manhattan, Kansas.

Rassam, A. and Tully, D. (1986) Gender-related aspects of agricultural labour in Northwestern Syria. Discussion Paper No. 20. ICARDA, Aleppo, Syria, 26 pp.

Rodriguez, A. (1997) Rural poverty and natural resources in the dry areas: the context of ICARDA's research. Working Paper. ICARDA, Aleppo, Syria, 20 pp.

Saade, M.E. (1991) An economic analysis of fertilizer allocation and import policies in Syria. A PhD thesis submitted to Michigan State University, Michigan.

Senauer, B. (2002) A pro-poor growth strategy to end hunger. *American Journal of Agricultural Economics* 84(3), 826–831.

Shideed, K. and Hateem, S. (1999) Economic assessment of barley/forage legume rotations within the framework of risk analysis. *Dryland Pasture, Forage and Range Network News* 18, 5–7.

Somel, K. and Cooper, P. (1985) Farming Systems Research at ICARDA. Discussion Paper No. 15. ICARDA, Aleppo, Syria, 40 pp.

Thomas, R.J., El Mourid, M., Ngaido, T., Halila, H., Bailey, E., Shideed, K., Malki, M., Nefzaoui, A., Chriyaa, A., Awawdeh, F., Hassan, S.H., Sweidan, Y. and Sbeita, A. (2003) The development of integrated crop-livestock production systems in the low rainfall areas of Mashreq and Maghreb. In: Harwood, R.R. and Kassam, A.H. (eds) *Research Towards Integrated Natural Resources Management: Examples of Research Problems, Approaches and Partnerships in Action in the CGIAR.* CGIAR, Centre Directors Committee on Integrated Natural Resources Management, Rome, Italy, pp. 97–110.

Thomson, E., Martini, M. and Tutwiler, R. (2003) Sheep management practices in Iraq, Jordan and Syria: the case of reproduction and fertility. Integrated Natural Resources Management, Technical Research Report Series No. 2. ICARDA, Aleppo, Syria, 43 pp.

Tully, D. (ed.) (1990) *Labour and Rainfed Agriculture in West Asia and North Africa.* Klumer, Dordrecht, The Netherlands, vi + 299 pp.

Tutwiler, R. (1994) The great chickpea challenge: introducing winter sowing in the Mediterranean region. Social Science Paper No. 4. ICARDA, Aleppo, Syria, 30 pp.

Tutwiler, R., Martini, M., Kneifis, A., Sweidan, Y. and Haddad, N. (1997) Adoption of improved barley production technologies in Jordan: impact of the Mashreq

Project, 1989–1994. In: Haddad, N., Tutwiler, R. and Thomson, E. (eds) *Improvement of Crop-Livestock Integration Systems in West Asia and North Africa*. ICARDA, Aleppo, Syria, pp. 487–494.

United Nations Economic and Social Commission for West Asia (ESCWA) and ICARDA (2000) *Economic Assessment of On-Farm Water Use Efficiency in Agriculture. Methodology and Two Case Studies*. United Nations, New York, 76 pp.

Wessels, J.I. (2000) Little waterfall: renovating *qanats* in a changing world, a case study in Syria. Paper presented at the International Symposium on *Qanats*, 2–4 May 2000, UNESCO, Yazel, Iran.

Wessels, J.I., Hoogeveen, R., Aw-Hassan, A. and Arab, G. (2002) The potential for renovating qanat systems in Syria through community action. Natural Resources Management Programme, ICARDA, Aleppo, Syria (Unpublished).

World Bank, (2002) *World Development Indicators*. World Bank, Washington, DC, 405 pp.

Agricultural Biodiversity and How Human Culture is Shaping It

13

Pablo B. Eyzaguirre

My role as a social anthropologist at the International Plant Genetic Resources Institute (IPGRI) is to understand how culture, customs, institutions and social relations, including gender, affect the way people use and derive value from plant genetic resources, the biological building blocks of agriculture. Plant genetic resources refer to the genetic material of plants containing traits that can be conserved, characterized, evaluated and used. While plant genetic resources may conjure up images of DNA and genetically modified organisms, its widest use is in the form of germplasm (plants' reproductive material, most often seeds) containing traits that are expressed in the environment and that people can observe, select, propagate and use. The term plant genetic resources became widely used to describe what plant breeders did – passing useful genetic traits between cultivars or wild relatives of a species through cross-breeding to produce an improved variety of a crop. The huge increases in crop production since 1945 are due in large measure to this use of plant genetic resources (Pimentel et al., 1997).

This view of plant genetic resources as the raw material stored in gene banks or breeding collections, while valid, reflects the earlier paradigms within the Consultative Group on International Agricultural Research (CGIAR) and agricultural research and development that focused on technologies rather than people. It now seems obvious, but is none the less worth mentioning, that farmers, particularly small and resource-poor farmers, hold the bulk of the world's agricultural biodiversity in the form of traditional crop varieties and breeds that they depend on for their livelihoods (Eyzaguirre *et al.*, 2001). How farmers identify, classify, exchange, develop and maintain this wealth of agricultural biodiversity can only be understood by knowing their cultures. The fact that humans have evolved so many distinct cultures to adapt to a varied range of environments underpins much of plant genetic diversity in agriculture (Bunting, 1975; Bunting and Pickersgill, 1996). Thus, the study of agricultural biodiversity and plant genetic resources rightly begins with people – the people who first began the process of plant domestication 10,000 years ago and have continued to shape crop and livestock diversity ever since.

Re-introducing culture. Slowly, if not belatedly, there is a growing consensus within rural development around putting people first (Cernea, 1991). The heightened focus on poverty eradication is just as much about local institutions and local knowledge as it is about new introduced technologies. The goal is not technology adoption *per se* but livelihood security comprising all the assets and decisions that people can use to survive and, one hopes, prosper in a given environment (www.livelihoods.org). The role of culture is key to understanding those decisions and to increasing the assets available to the poor. To the anthropologist, culture is the fundamental instrument and process by which humans adapt and evolve. It guides the development of institutions, decisions, social cohesion, rights and collective action. Culture contains and transmits bodies of knowledge. Perhaps it is the very centrality of culture within agri*culture* that made it so difficult for agricultural scientists and development experts to see it for so long. Culture was well hidden right in front of us, all around us, all the time. No wonder we did not see it. Failure to see and consider the role of culture has meant that, in some cases, our agricultural research and development strategies have been the result of blind reckoning and blind luck. But such approaches will no longer suffice. The United Nations Millennium Development Goals and World Food Summit targets to eliminate hunger concur that we are far behind where we ought to be in our fight against hunger and poverty. The Convention of Biological Diversity's global assessments warn of the continued depletion of the biological diversity and plant genetic resources upon which the survival of humanity depends. Despite the continued lack of political will, a major factor in the dire state of affairs, as scientists we have not forged the alliances with the most important actors in the fight against hunger, farmers and the rural poor. To do so we need to return to the main focus of agriculture: people using culture to define and shape their biophysical environment to meet their food and livelihood needs. Culture provides the institutional context to build upon experience and create bodies of knowledge that sustain agricultural production and innovation. As is eloquently set forth in a recent publication by Jules Pretty (2002), the human endeavour and the cultural context of agriculture need to be reaffirmed. If agriculture continues to be seen primarily as a technological process for using soil, water and biodiversity to produce goods and commodities, we will continue to have hunger in the face of overproduction, malnutrition coupled with overnutrition and a growing population that is increasingly dependent upon an ever narrower portfolio of crops and livestock to meet its needs.

How Culture and Knowledge underpin Biodiversity in Agriculture and Development

Anthropological concerns with culture, including customs, values, beliefs, traditional knowledge, social organization and local institutions, are key to focus agricultural development on the needs of the rural poor. Social anthropological research can be used to generate technologies that empower people and increase their access and improve the management of the resources upon which their livelihoods depend. The casting of agriculture as primarily a technical and economic endeavour ignores the way that local cultures developed knowledge systems about plants that generated the thousands of cultivated species that nourished humanity and enabled humans to adapt to a wide range of environments. The break between human cultures and the artefact they produced – agriculture – has led to a decline in the diversity of crops and plant genetic resources upon which humanity depends. While global agriculture now produces more than enough food for all, growing pockets of rural hunger and poverty still exist, and agricultural science and new technologies have not been able to address them. To conserve and optimize agricultural biodiversity and make a more effective effort to reach the hungry and the rural poor and provide them with options to rise out of poverty, the link between local cultures and agriculture needs to be restored.

Culture is the social tool that human communities use to adapt to their environment by the production of knowledge and goods and reproduction (biological and social). Agriculture is one of the most basic and important expressions of culture. As human communities evolved they considered the uses of plants and built up a body of knowledge about how plants behaved when used, disturbed or managed by people. They developed customs and practices on specific uses and interventions in plant reproduction and propagation that made plants more readily accessible and useful. This process of plant domestication has occurred thousands of times across cultures and continues today (Bunting and Pickersgill, 1996).

From an anthropological perspective, the concomitant processes of cultural diversity and the dispersal of human populations across such a wide range of biological and edaphic environments led to the creation of a large number of domesticated crops and livestock, crop varieties and breeds and diverse agroecosystems. These agricultural processes have permitted an explosion of human populations and cultures around the globe; our planet has no major uninhabited land areas. The successful use of culture has extended our presence and drastically increased our impact on the planet to the extent that culture now threatens the biodiversity upon which we depend. The philosophy and ethos of applied anthropological research is to restore the cultural dimensions of agriculture that have been ignored in agricultural science and development.

The neglect of traditional agricultural knowledge systems and the processes of scientific and agricultural innovation embedded in culture is the result of the focus on agricultural development as primarily a technical and economic process (Brush, 1992; Pretty, 2002). This has led to the sorry state of affairs where the world's farmers who maintain the most agricultural diversity within ecologically complex environments do so without the benefit of or despite the efforts of agricultural science and associated social scientists. In many cases, the zones of high agricultural biodiversity are coterminous with zones of high cultural diversity and of rural poverty. These correlations need to be examined and the concentrations of poverty reduced. Social scientists need to define a distinct and central research agenda that addresses the existence of multiple knowledge systems and the fact that the system of agricultural scientific knowledge has remained largely impervious to local knowledge. Instead of looking at scientific and technological innovation as a social process, agricultural development and agricultural scientists (biological and social scientists) all too often considered the problem as one of getting the technology right and considering questions of individual adoption. The persistent pockets of rural poverty and hunger are testimony to the failure of technical approaches to consider the local culture and the knowledge base as a starting point. To change this, some central ideas, hypotheses and techniques can be applied from the work of leading sociologists and anthropologists.

Traditional knowledge and the sociology of science. The CGIAR social science research agenda can be grounded on the insights of great social scientists – or as Robert K. Merton put it, we can 'stand on the shoulders of giants'. Merton developed methods to analyse scientific innovations in general as social and cultural processes whose main construct is a system of knowledge (Merton, 1965, 1973). Anthropologists such as Harold C. Conklin (1957, 1980) and Paul Richards

(1985) applied the cultural understanding of knowledge systems (ethnoscience) to document how agrarian communities classify a plant; patterns and customary uses of plants; and how they imbue plants and crops with values, multiple uses and meaning. The concepts these anthropologists developed on the sociology of science, ethnobotany and indigenous agricultural innovation are current and vital today. The fact that they have been so little used in social science research within CGIAR is unfortunate.

Merton's work on the sociology of science made a major contribution by demonstrating that science and innovation are a social process (Merton, 1973, 1980). His analyses of the scientific process within industrialized societies revealed that institutional disjunctures between the socio-cultural processes of scientific innovation and the social and economic institutions that reward and apply innovation in economic spheres have led to a perverse situation where knowledge is individualized and not shared. Often, Merton notes, the rewards in science are biased to those with established reputations, social status and resources rather than individuals or groups that have contributed original ideas and tested them by iteration with other ideas. The concern with priority of discovery simply does not square with the social process by which new knowledge is created.

Merton affirmed in an elegant and persuasive way that if we are concerned with innovation we ought to focus first on the knowledge systems that are embedded in culture and institutions. This Mertonian insight is crucial for our scientific work with local communities and traditional knowledge. Here the search is not for the 'local expert', the 'progressive' farmer (as opposed to the 'backward' one) or the 'early adopter', and then to focus on him or her. Rather, our focus is to look at the institutional processes by which experience is transformed into knowledge and how it is shared and built upon.

Manifest and latent functions of institutions: the case of seed systems. In the sociological study of institutions, Merton went beyond simplistic views of structural functionalism and raised the fundamental concepts of manifest and latent functions of institutions. This concept is a fundamental principle of social science that is yet to be fully absorbed in agricultural research. In our social science research on agricultural biodiversity we are just now coming to terms with the fact that the latent functions of formal seed systems (whose manifest functions are to provide secure and reliable modern seeds, the certified product of modern plant breeding) may also undermine the traditional seed systems and knowledge of local seed diversity that is particularly important for poor farmers living on marginal lands. In this sense, if the manifest goal is seed security, formal seed systems may undermine it by eroding knowledge and limiting access to local seeds. When formal seed sys-

tems do not function in times of catastrophe or bureaucratic inefficiency, farmers may suffer increased insecurity because their options
and access to local germplasm and seed have been reduced.

The counter argument can be made that formal seed systems and
local biodiversity knowledge and traditional seed systems do not need
to be at odds. Again, the principles set forth in Merton's study of
knowledge systems shows that seed, while a biophysical artefact,
derives most of its value from the knowledge used to identify the
genetic traits it contains, and the knowledge of its viability and performance. Modern and traditional seeds are separated by two knowledge systems that operate according to different principles. The former
operates as an individualized, proprietary knowledge system that
focuses on the priority of innovation, and distributes rewards through
property rights systems such as plant breeders' rights and increasingly,
patents. The latter operates as a collective and open system where priority of innovation is nearly impossible to ascertain, and as a process
for continual iteration and evolution of knowledge (Wilkes, 1995;
Zimmerer, 2003). The reward and value systems of the two are also at
variance. When Bolivian potato farmers in indigenous communities
sought to protect and include their traditional potato varieties, up to 20 or
30 per community, the costs of registering each potato cultivar under
the national seed laws were prohibitive. The culture of traditional
potato farming valued diversity, while the economics of seed legisla-
tion and registration favoured uniformity and dominance of one or two
cultivars as the only way to justify returns to the breeding and registration process.

When considering seed systems in a development and biodiversity
context, three factors are considered. First is understanding that there
are at least two systems of innovation; second, that there are at least
two systems for institutionalizing and sharing knowledge about seed;
and third, that the latent functions of one set of institutions – formal
seed systems – may undermine or contradict others. In such cases, the
latent functions of formal agricultural development institutions and
schemes can be dysfunctional, particularly where biodiversity and
empowerment of the rural poor are concerned. These harmful effects
will not be addressed unless there is a clear method to put people (the
rural poor) at the centre of the agricultural development process
(Cernea, 1996).

Institutions can have several manifest and latent functions, and
some of those latent functions are beneficial. The area of latent functions is one for which anthropological methods are particularly useful
for discerning and assessing their impacts. For example, one may hear
agricultural researchers say that farmers have no institutions for
exchanging seeds, for allocating land access and land rights, for

regulating water use, etc. This fits well with the technocratic development paradigm that calls for the introduction of new technology and
the creation of new institutions as the path to development. I have
heard these statements when discussing traditional crops, where people have maintained a remarkable diversity of cultivars that have
spread and are being maintained over thousands of kilometres, across
cultures, national borders and ecosystems. This is the case of Andean
crops such as quinoa, *cañihua, olluco* and oca. The traditional systems
of classification (folk taxonomies) may change but they have underlying common features that enable varieties to be recognized across communities (Tertazas and   Valdivia, 1998; Zimmerer, 1999, 2003).
Population geneticists confirm that the maintenance of these crop varieties across time and space requires a non-random exchange of seeds
and germplasm. Yet, despite the overwhelming evidence of the existence of an institutionalized system of exchange and maintenance of
crop diversity, some social and biological scientists still fail to see it.
Policymakers and development planners seldom, if ever, recognize
these traditional practices and institutions and try to build upon them
(Cleveland and Murray, 1997; Laird, 2000).

Traditional seed institutions are invisible largely because they are
embedded in a host of cultural institutions and customs. For example,
institutionalized seed exchange is often embedded in the latent functions of many other multipurpose institutions, such as marriages and
community fairs as in the case of Andean crops (Tapia and De la Torre,
1997; Milla, 2003). In other cases institutionalized seed exchange is
embedded in cultural notions of health and well-being, or in the
requirements of spiritual ceremonies and cultural festivals (Tapia and
De la Torre, 1997; Van Kessel and Canasaca, 2003). No one specifies
these institutions as being for the exchange and maintenance of crop
genetic diversity but, in fact, exchange and maintenance of biodiversity
knowledge are one of their important, if latent, functions. Temple gardens, sacred forests, home gardens, property rights, gender roles and
food culture are important topics for social scientists examining how
biodiversity contributes to agricultural development and livelihood
security. The understanding of cultures and the defence of cultural
diversity are increasingly recognized as central to the conservation of
agrobiodiversity (Posey, 2000), and, I argue, at the heart of rural development and agricultural development.

A further tribute to Merton is our rediscovery of the focus group as
a key research method to scientifically document knowledge systems
as the collective knowledge capital of a community. Only now, 30 years
after he elaborated these concepts, have some social scientists begun to
make headway in placing local and traditional knowledge systems at
the core of our social research on how we may help eradicate rural

poverty and hunger. It is also prescient that Merton, himself raised in poverty, pointed out the importance of institutions and social capital as essential assets that enable the poor to improve their condition. Merton's 'family lived above his father's small dairy products shop in south Philadelphia until it burned down, without insurance, and his father became a carpenter's assistant. Merton's family lacked wealth, but he insisted his childhood did not lack opportunity'. Indeed, as Merton described it in 1994, that seemingly deprived slum provided 'a youngster with every sort of capital – social capital, cultural capital, human capital and above all, what we may call public capital – that is, with every sort of capital except the personally financial' (Craig C. Calhoun, president of the Social Science Research Council-USA, recalling Merton's life at the time of his death in 2003).

In summary, social research for agricultural biodiversity and development begins with the study of culture, customs and institutions that shape and distribute knowledge and resources in agrarian communities. The prominence that this approach is given in the new livelihood security paradigm is an indication that it is not just another development fad or buzzword, but the application of the profound thinking of great social scientists, giants, such as Merton, Douglas North, Amartya Sen and Elinor Orstrom, among others.

Ethnobotany and the Social Science of Crop Evolution and Biodiversity

Harold C. Conklin, an anthropologist whose research on the cultural and cognitive systems that traditional societies use in classifying and managing their environment, developed a set of methods to examine these systems rigorously and comparatively. Using this new approach, or ethnoscience, Conklin was able to view agriculture in a new light. The value of fallows, swiddens and marginal patches was documented, providing a rich picture of the resources available and the complex ways that traditional farming cultures managed them (Conklin, 1957). While agricultural scientists only saw the crops, Conklin noted the use of fallows and regenerating swiddens as a conscious management of biological resources. What appeared to be a jumble of crops and crop varieties without elite cultivars of rice, the main staple, was to the ethnoscientist a careful classification and segregation of many different rice varieties to meet the multiple uses, tastes and niches for which rice was grown. Conklin was later honoured by the International Rice Research Institute for having collected some important varieties of rice along with the cultural knowledge and values associated with them.

This type of approach is now being integrated into plant genetic resources collecting and characterization. Expanding this cultural research further, Conklin developed tools for understanding how cultures view the landscapes upon which they depend for their survival (Conklin, 1980). This fundamental approach to human landscapes takes us back to the early human geographers who developed the concept of *landschaft,* or how humans perceive and shape the landscapes that sustain them (Forde, 1932). Now human geographers and social anthropologists are looking at agricultural landscapes from the perspective of local cultures and seeing resources and regenerative processes that have been overlooked and, in some cases, undermined by agricultural development science (Rocheleau, 1995; Fairhead and Leach, 1996; Zimmerer, 1999).

The importance of the cultural perspective on land and biological resources is central to the social research on rural livelihoods. The hard-scrabble life of the rural poor has always been a question of managing many small assets, often dispersed, and of different kinds to make a livelihood. The patchiness of existence coupled with the patchiness of the environment is what typifies poverty as a social and biophysical environment. Reviews of what works in alleviating rural poverty show that it is not the major transformations that work, but rather enhancing the value derived from a particular patch, niche or underutilized crop or species that can then be used to leverage other assets and create a pathway out of poverty (Carney, 2002; Pretty, 2002). Without understanding the social and cultural perspectives of how niches and values are defined and managed, development is not likely to be able to develop technologies that the poor can use or add to the rich knowledge base that farmers already have.

The next section of the chapter will describe how social science research was integrated into IPGRI, an institute that functioned happily and productively for 20 years without it. The starting point for this epistemological marriage was the premise that if social science is to be integrated into agricultural and biological research, it must also be able to transform the agrobiological research agenda in ways that increase the quality of its results and the relevance of its outcomes.

Role of Social Science in Plant Genetic Resources and the Growth of IPGRI

Agricultural science is considered a technical domain about growing better crops more economically. The question that confronts researchers at IPGRI in general is, What does biodiversity conservation have to do with agriculture? A further set of questions confront the anthropologist at IPGRI: What does social anthropology have to do agriculture? What is a social anthropologist doing working with plant genetics? The answers to these questions reveal much about how the work of IPGRI and CGIAR can contribute to sustainable livelihoods of the rural poor and enhance the quality of their natural environments.

The IPGRI 1994 strategy places the human sciences as one of its eight strategic choices:

> Understanding the 'human dimension' is vital to the successful conservation and use of plant genetic resources. IPGRI investigates the socioeconomic factors influencing farmers' management of diversity, including the different roles played by men and women. It also contributes to the international debate on key policy issues affecting the management, availability and use of plant genetic resources worldwide. Understanding the 'human dimension' is vital to the successful conservation and use of plant genetic resources. IPGRI investigates the socioeconomic factors influencing farmers' management of diversity, including the different roles played by men and women. It also contributes to the international debate on key policy issues affecting the management, availability and use of plant genetic resources worldwide.

As noted earlier, when plant genetic resources were primarily seen as inputs to plant breeding held in gene banks, the role of social science was not central. The main issues were: (i) identifying where genetic diversity was found, in nature and in farmers' fields; (ii) measuring and characterizing that genetic diversity; (iii) sampling and collecting it for storage in gene banks where the plant genetic resources would be; and (iv) evaluating and making plant genetic resources available for eventual use in crop improvement. Research focused on the technical issues of sampling and measuring the agro-morphological and ecogeographic distributions of genetic diversity within species. These issues were first defined by N.I. Vavilov, who identified global centres of crop origin and genetic diversity and the need to conserve these plant genetic resources *ex situ* by setting up the first crop gene banks in the Soviet Union's Institute of Plant Industry during the late 1920s (Vavilov, 1997). For the growing and increasingly interconnected system of crop gene banks there were technical issues to be researched as germplasm collections needed continual maintenance, regeneration and research for viable long-term storage. These issues included seed physiology and seed storage and germplasm conservation *in vitro,* including cryopreservation. There was also the issue of safe movement and documentation of germplasm as the various gene banks were increasingly linked in a system of crop gene pools and regions.[1]

The CGIAR system of crop gene banks remains the best example we have of how such systems should be maintained, along with the biological, bio-informatic and economic research that is needed to maintain and expand this system. The global community recognized the value of these collections when, following the establishment of the Convention of Biological Diversity, the collections of over half a million samples of genetic resources of crop, forage and agroforestry species were placed in trust for the world community under the Food and Agriculture Organization of the United Nations (www.singer.cgiar.org/SINGER). Despite the economic importance of these CGIAR collections, it was not what led to the demand for social research. Rather it was the realization affirmed in the Convention of Biological Diversity that the bulk of the world's genetic resources could only be maintained *in situ*; in the case of agricultural genetic resources, that meant in the production systems of the world's small farmers. These genetic resources should continue to evolve *in situ* and, above all, they should meet the development needs of the local communities that maintain them, while contributing to global public goods (Eyzaguirre and Iwanaga, 1996; Brush, 1999; Cleveland and Soleri, 2002; Swaminathan, 2002). In other words, the realization that genetic resources should continue to evolve as biological assets for the livelihoods of the rural poor led to a concern with the social processes by which genetic resources are defined, valued, managed and used. When IPGRI in its new strategy, Diversity for Development (1994), affirmed a commitment to *in situ* conservation and development, the need for social science research became clear and compelling. IPGRI's first social scientist, an anthropologist, was hired at the close of 1994, and the first programme of social research on agricultural biodiversity began in 1995.

Rationale for social science research on agricultural biodiversity. The relationship between the conservation of plant genetic resources and their use is an intimate one. As on-farm, *in situ* and community-level conservation have become integral to the conservation of plant genetic resources, social and cultural factors such as decision-making patterns, local institutions, indigenous knowledge and value systems must be taken into account. Different patterns of access and use of genetic resources can have a variable effect on the genetic diversity and conservation status of useful plant species. Socioeconomic and cultural factors that govern variation within and across communities, especially gender, need to be taken into account when designing plant genetic resources conservation strategies, policies and legal frameworks that promote sustainable uses and effective conservation of genetic resources and the equitable distribution of benefits (Cleveland and Murray, 1997; Laird, 2000).

IPGRI's social science research focuses on livelihoods and institutions and investigates the various ways people use and value genetic resources and how these affect their conservation. There are two main objectives. One is to enhance the contribution of plant genetic resources to the livelihoods and well-being of the rural poor, by understanding and protecting these essential biological assets in their environments. The other is to develop decentralized methods for the use and conservation of plant genetic resources that involve resource users and local communities. Work is also focused on methodology development to assess the economic value of plant genetic resources under diverse conservation and use systems. Initial development of economic theory on plant genetic resources valuation is followed by practical studies in the field to quantify public and private benefits.

How IPGRI's social science research is organized. IPGRI's social science research is coordinated by a project called Livelihoods and Institutions: Social, Cultural and Economic Aspects of Agricultural Biodiversity (www.ipgri.cgiar.org/themes/human). The project applies social science approaches that bring the human aspect to the fore to: (i) identify more of the agrobiodiversity that is managed and used in microenvironments and marginal areas; (ii) increase the value and conserve the diversity of neglected and underutilized species for a broader and more secure agricultural portfolio and more sustainable use of natural resources; (iii) build support for conservation of genetic resources by linking conservation with the economic, social and cultural development of communities that have managed and maintained high levels of agricultural biodiversity; and (iv) support and defend local institutions, customs and cultural practices that serve to maintain biodiversity and local ways of life in unique environments.

Cultural Factors and Crop Genetic Diversity

Over time, humankind has used more than 7000 edible plant species (Wilson, 1992). However, only 150 crops are now commercialized on a significant global scale. Only three crops (maize, wheat and rice) meet 50% of global protein and calorie requirements (Prescott-Allen, 1990). As a result, the base of global security has been narrowed. This limits livelihood options for the rural poor, particularly in marginal areas. Bunting and Kassam (1988) and Bunting and Pickersgill (1996) noted the importance of germplasm choices for poor farmers in marginal areas. To cope with the growing stresses and shocks associated with global environmental change, including growing climatic instability, soil depletion and extreme trends of water scarcity and flooding, the focus of research and development must broaden to include a wider range of crop species and varieties.

Crop science and biotechnology have dramatically increased our ability to use plant genetic resources to increase productivity and value of crops, but do not account for vast amounts of genetic diversity in crops upon which global food security and future crop development depend. Cultural factors are important in maintaining rich genetic resources and associated knowledge of crops that have been neglected by formal crop improvement efforts and by commerce. Food preferences and customs of plant use are deeply embedded in culture. For example, glutinous and starchy varieties of grains, roots and tubers and vegetables arise out of differences in tastes. Migrating people often take crop germplasm (the genetic material for plant reproduction, including seeds, tubers and other plant organs) into new ecosystems or niches. Similarly, migrants introduce genetic resources into new cultures where the plants are used in different ways (Jones, 1959).

Management practices of local farmers enable them to develop and maintain the variation (phenotypes) required to meet their needs. Genetic diversity may be maintained to obtain crucial but diverse traits such as frost or drought tolerance, or disease resistance in highly stressed agricultural environments. Genetic diversity *per se* has been something that scientists observe and study. However, farmers using their own ethnoscience and, to meet their food and livelihood needs, have also observed and shaped diversity. The tools to understand these farmer processes are cultural in nature. Case studies and experiences conducted under the aegis of IPGRI have led to the distillation of a set of ethnobotanical indicators described below and can help us to better understand the mechanisms by which farmers manage genetic resources to obtain the crop traits they need and the qualities they prefer. These indicators are grouped under four rubrics: (i) food culture and folk taxonomy; (ii) multiple uses of species; (iii) deployment of species in diverse niches; and (iv) traditional germplasm management practices. These are described in more detail below (Martin, 1995; Zhu *et al.*, 2000; Martin *et al.*, 2001).

Food culture, folk taxonomy and associated folklore. These are important indicators of diversity relating to how crop populations or ecotypes within a species may be treated differently. For example, a certain variety may have ritual value and uses that cause it to be maintained despite changes in market forces, and perhaps assigned a special place within the cropping system. By developing many names for crop types, farmers are effectively segregating populations and often treating them differently. Over time, this segregation can engender botanically significant distinctions between varieties. Cultural knowledge about a crop variety helps to transmit plant knowledge widely in a community, and specialized knowledge within subsectors of the community. Common examples of this cultural knowledge are recipes and knowledge of associated pests and pathogens.

Multiple uses of a crop species. This is a characteristic of cultures with a long history of coevolution of a local community with a given crop species, resulting in a rich and complex body of associated knowledge about that crop. Identifying multiple-use species does not mean merely noting those of economic importance. In South-east Asia, local communities have developed uses of rice to fit almost all known categories of ingested food, drink, processed snack or medicine; even rice stalks and husks have many important uses. It is in these latter cases of diverse and multiple uses of a crop that we can expect to find a rich body of ethnobotanical knowledge on plant genetic diversity.

Planting a crop in diverse niches and environments. This is another ethnobotanical indicator of diversity. By working with genotype–environment interactions (developing and matching varieties to the niches where they are best adapted), human communities are maximizing the use of ecological niches in their farming systems and the varietal diversity existing within a crop species. The continuing evolution and adaptation of crop varieties to new and diverse environments is a process that contributes to plant genetic diversity and is often managed by farmers growing crops under traditional cultural practices, commonly in marginal areas such as mountains, desert margins, tidal areas or those subject to periodic flooding.

Practices and traditions for managing germplasm (seeds and planting material). These can also be ethnobotanical indicators. Such practices concern the selection of seed and planting materials and the ways to store and exchange seed. They also include the traditions and rules that decide who selects and maintains germplasm. Women farmers often have the most developed criteria for selection of crop varieties – criteria that are not limited to yield, but related to competition with weeds, storability, cooking quality, taste and other desired qualities. We have presented the indicators in a checklist that can be used to compile ethnobotanical information on diversity within crops as they are managed by local peoples. The indicators can also be used to identify ways to support and offer incentives to farmers continuing to manage crops and trees in ways that meet food security needs and maintain cultural and biological diversity.

A growing number of countries are taking steps to meet the obligations of the Convention on Biological Diversity to recognize and promote the role of local people in the maintenance of agricultural biodiversity. Effective use of ethnobotanical approaches is dependent upon participatory approaches and protocols that :

• establish equal partnerships,
• protect the rights of local communities to use plant genetic resources and

- maintain the distinctive cultural practices that help shape the genetic diversity of their crops.

Likewise, ethnobotanical methods allow better understanding of the maintenance of diversity-rich pockets, and microenvironments created and managed by people. These microenvironments can serve as points of introduction for new diversity for crop varieties or wild species that are under threat from commercialization or land-use change.

Increasingly, genetic resources scientists use advanced techniques, including molecular genetics, to measure genetic diversity as it is managed and used by farmers. The growing partnerships between farming communities, ethnobotanists and genetic resources scientists may help ensure that the next advances in agriculture will help maintain the diversity of plant genetic resources under farmer management. Thus, essential biological assets of communities living traditional lifestyles, often in marginal environments or centres of biodiversity, are enriched. In agriculturally marginal areas such as mountains and desert margins, the role of traditional human communities has been shown to be beneficial to the diversity and stability of ecosystems.

Understanding Gender to Empower the Agricultural Biodiversity Decision Makers

A fundamental social and cultural factor that defines resource users is gender. Despite a torrent of pronouncements on gender and the role-of-women-in-development dialogues, gender differences are seldom included as a central organizing principle in research and development. As a result, many opportunities have been missed to support good bio-diversity practices and empower the resource users who are custodians of much of the world's biological and livelihood assets – rural women (Tapia and De la Torre, 1997; Howard-Borjas, 2003). In many countries, women comprise the bulk of the labour in agriculture. Statistics show that women's labour contribution in agriculture ranges from 40% in Latin America to 60 and 80% in Asia and Africa. In sub-Saharan Africa, for example, women produce on average 70% of the food in the region (Food and Agriculture Organization of the United Nations (FAO), 1997). What is often ignored is not only their contribution in terms of labour, but their decision making on how biological resources are used to satisfy the varied needs of rural households. It is rural women's expertise and responsibility for making decisions that make their contribution and participation central to the sustainable management of plant and animal genetic resources in agriculture (Eyzaguirre and Raymond, 1995).

In much of the developing world, the conservation and use of plant genetic resources begins with women. As farmers, they are responsible for growing and collecting food. The processing and storage of food crops is also mainly their responsibility. Women are responsible for the domestic needs of their households, and it is their job to gather and use food, fodder, fuel, medicinal plants and fibre. For this reason, women often determine which crop varieties to grow, which portions of the harvest to keep for home consumption, which portion to keep as seed, and which to sell at the local market (Howard-Borjas, 2003).

Women's special knowledge of the value and diverse uses of plants for nutrition, health and income has important implications for the conservation of genetic resources because the decision to conserve a plant variety largely depends on its usefulness to the farmer and the community. Studies of the different roles of women and men in agriculture show that when women are in a position to choose, they usually adopt a variety of plants, trees and animals, taking into account factors such as processing, flavour and cooking time (Tapia and De la Torre, 1997). Women are also more often than not concerned with how multiple uses of the same plant can add to household income. Women's focus on the household economy provides a balance to market-oriented pressures that emphasize high yield and uniformity.

In many households, women manage components of the farming system containing high levels of biodiversity – such as home gardens – and make extensive use of gathered species and tree products. Often, the home garden is used as an experimental plot, where women tend indigenous and other species as they try them out and adapt them for use. Home gardens also serve as a refuge for less common species and varieties (Watson and Eyzaguirre, 2002; Eyzaguirre and Linares, 2004). Women also make extensive use of wild patches and marginal areas within farm communities. Here they gather traditional vegetables, condiments and medicinal plants that are crucial for the nutritional well-being and health of rural families throughout the world (Howard-Borjas, 2003). Forests are important resources for rural women who harvest leaves, fruits, berries, nuts, seeds, gums and saps, edible roots, tubers and bark. In addition, many rural women rely on the income earned from the sale of forest products such as bamboo and rattan, used for furniture, baskets and mats; other forest products used in medicines; honey; and edible oils.

Rural people's and particularly rural women's concern with intra-species diversity most commonly relates to the differences between traditional varieties of crops such as wheat, maize, rice, potatoes and the improved varieties that are produced intensively by modern agriculture (IPGRI/FAO, 2002a). Many of the characteristics that women farmers have valued and maintained in traditional cultivars are often not present in the improved varieties that favour maximum yields as opposed to multiple uses and stability. Some of these plant characteristics are also important to conserve for future productivity and plant improvement. Because women rely on diverse biological resources to provide food and income for their families, they are reservoirs of knowledge of where useful species are found and maintained (Iriarte *et al.*, 1999). Because women's responsibilities in rural production systems extend from propagation, protection, harvesting, processing, storage and final preparation of food, women may often most understand the uses and usefulness of plants and animals. In all cases, gender is a cultural construct that has to be considered so that the different bodies of knowledge and responsibilities for decisions about agricultural genetic resources are understood. This is essential so that access to resources by the rural poor, and good practices are not undermined (IPGRI/FAO, 2002b). The studies cited are examples of using social and cultural research to contribute to development goals adopted in the Convention of Biological Diversity, which recognizes the vital role that women play in the conservation and sustainable use of biological diversity, and affirms 'the need for the *full participation of women at all levels of policy-making and implementation for biological diversity conservation*' (http://www.biodiv.org/convention/articles.asp).

Social and Institutional Research to Support Community-based Biodiversity Management

To put the pieces together and see the way ahead for social and cultural research in agriculture, we need to stand on the shoulders of giants – R.K. Merton, Harold Conklin, Amartya Sen, Elinor Orstom, Douglas North. A common thread that runs through the work of these seminal thinkers is the primacy of institutions in determining: (i) how people view and shape their environment; (ii) as a crucial element in sustainable resource management; and (iii) as a condition for rising out of poverty. The anthropological perspective of Conklin and the sociology of science as developed by Merton show clearly that agrarian communities have institutions that are effective in classifying and managing biological resources in conditions where modern scientific institutions and scientific culture are ill equipped and socially ill adapted. Sen (1982) has argued persuasively that human and economic development and the fight against poverty and hunger are intimately connected to democracy and empowerment, and local institutions and local ethnoscience are the basis for an equitable and democratic partnership between those working in centres such as IPGRI and the rural poor we aim to help. Finally, as Orstom and North have shown, institutions – particularly local ones – are ultimately the way to build sustainable management of resources and the equitable allocation of resource rights (Orstom, 1990; North, 1990). This is not to say that all local institutions, by their very nature of being embedded in a local culture or a landscape, are inherently fair in their allocation of rights or efficient in the management of biological resources. However, local institutions exist, they are the starting point, they cannot be ignored, and they may even be strengthened and made more effective.

Our new direction for supporting the maintenance of agricultural biodiversity and increasing its value and contribution to the livelihoods of the poor is to focus on community-based biodiversity management.

Notes

[1] The founders of PGR science – Vavilov, Hawkes, Harlan, Frankel, Bennet and Swaminathan among others – have been widely recognized, and in 2000 the global plant genetic resources community came together to take stock of the progress linking *ex situ* and *in situ* plant genetic resources conservation with agricultural development (see Engels *et al.*, 2002; Hawkes, 2002; Jackson, 2002).

References

Brush, S.B. (1992) Reconsidering the green revolution: diversity and stability in cradle areas of crop domestication. *Human Ecology* 20(2), 145–167.

Brush, S.B. (ed.) (1999) *Genes in the Field: On Farm Conservation of Crop Diversity.* Lewis Publishers, International Development Research Centre, International Plant Genetic Resources Institute (IPGRI), Rome, 288 pp.

Bunting, A.H. (1975) Time, phenology and yield of crops. *Weather* 30, 312–325.

Bunting, A.H. and Kassam, A.H. (1988) Principles of crop water use, dry matter production and dry matter partitioning that govern choices of crops and systems. In: Bidinger, F.R. and Johansen, C. (eds) *Drought*

Research Priorities for Dryland Tropics, ICRISAT, Patancheru, India, pp. 43–61.

Bunting, A.H. and Pickersgill, B. (1996) What is a plant genetic resource? *Biologist* 43, 227–230.

Carney, D. (2002) *Sustainable Livelihoods Approaches: Progress and Possibilities for Change.* DFID, UK.

Cernea, M.M. (ed.) (1991) *Putting People First: Sociological Variables in Rural Development.* Oxford University Press, New York, 575 pp.

Cernea, M.M. (1996) *Social Organization and Development Anthropology: The 1995 Malinowski Award Lecture.* Environmentally Sustainable Development Studies and Monographs Series Number 6. The World Bank, Washington, DC, 52 pp.

Cleveland, D.A. and Murray, S.C. (1997) The world's crop genetic resources and the rights of indigenous farmers. *Current Anthropology* 38(4), 477–515.

Cleveland, D. and Soleri, D. (eds) (2002) *Farmers, Scientists and Plant Breeding: Integrating Knowledge and Practice*. CAB International, Wallingford, UK, 338 pp.

Conklin, H.C. (1957) *Hanunoo Agriculture. A Report on an Integral System of Shifting Cultivation in the Philippines*. Food and Agriculture Organization of the United Nations (FAO) Series on Shifting Cultivation XII, Rome, 209 pp.

Conklin, H.C. (1980) *Ethnographic Atlas of Ifugao: a Study of Environment, Culture, and Society in Northern Luzon*. Yale University Press, New Haven, Connecticut, 115 pp.

Engels, J.M.M., Rao, R.V., Brown, A.H.D. and Jackson, M.T. (eds) (2002) Managing plant genetic diversity. *Proceedings of the Conference on Science and Technology for Managing Plant Genetic Diversity in the 21st Century*. IPGRI, Rome, 487 pp.

Eyzaguirre, P.B. and Iwanaga, M. (eds) (1996) Participatory plant breeding. *Proceedings of a Workshop on Participatory Plant Breeding 26–29 July 1995, Wageningen, The Netherlands*. IPGRI, Rome, 164 pp.

Eyzaguirre, P.B. and Linares, O. (eds) (2004) *Home Gardens and Agrobiodiversity*. Smithsonian Books, Washington, DC, 296 pp.

Eyzaguirre, P.B. and Raymond, R. (1995) Rural Women: a Key to the Conservation and Sustainable Use of Agricultural Biodiversity. Paper presented to the Fourth World Conference on Women, Beijing 4–15 September. IPGRI, Rome, 12 pp.

Eyzaguirre, P., Martin, G.J. and Barrow, S. (eds) (2001) Growing diversity, conserving plant genetic resources. *People and Plants Handbook*, no. 7. UNESCO, WWF, IPGRI, Paris, 40 pp.

Fairhead, J. and Leach, M. (1996) Enriching the landscape: social history and the management of transition ecology in the forest savanna mosaic of the Republic of Guinea. *Africa* 66(1), 14–36.

FAO (1997) Gender: the key to sustainability and food security. FAO Sustainable Development Division, Rome, Italy. Available online: http://www.fao.org/WAICENT/FAOINFO/SUSTDEV/WPdirect/WPdoe002.htm

Forde, C.D. (1932) *Habitat, Economy and Society*. Methuen & Co., London, 500 pp.

Hawkes, J.G. (2002) The evolution of plant genetic resources and the work of O.H. Frankel. In: Engels, J.M.M., Rao, Ramanantha V., Brown, A.H.D. and Jackson, M.T. (eds) *Managing Plant Genetic Diversity. Proceedings of the conference on Science and Technology for Managing Plant Genetic Diversity in the 21st Century*. IPGRI, Rome, pp. xvii–xviii.

Howard-Borjas, P. (ed.) (2003) *Women and Plants: Gender Relations in Biodiversity Management and Conservation*. Zed Books Ltd, London, 298 pp.

IPGRI/FAO (2002a) *L'approche participative dans la recherche sur le mode de gestion des espèces cultivées localement en fonction du genre au Mali: méthodologie et techniques; Cas du Mali*. IPGRI and FAO, Rome, 60 pp.

IPGRI/FAO (2002b) *The Role of Women in the Conservation of the Genetic Resources of Maize. Guatemala.* IPGRI and FAO, Rome, 56 pp.

Iriarte L., Lazarte, L., Fernández, J. and Fernández, D. (1999) *El Rol Del Género en la Conservación, Localización y Manejo de la Diversidad Genética de Papa, Tarwi y Maíz.* IPGRI/FAO, Rome, 77 pp.

Jackson, M.T. (2002) Jack Hawkes: plant collector, researcher, educator and visionary. In: Engels, J.M.M.R., Ramanantha V., Brown, A.H.D. and Jackson, M.T. (eds) *Managing Plant Genetic Diversity. Proceedings of the Conference on Science and Technology for Managing Plant Genetic Diversity in the 21st Century.* IPGRI, Rome, pp. xv–xvii.

Jones, W.O. (1959) *Manioc in Africa.* Stanford University Press, Palo Alto, California, 315 pp.

Laird, S.A. (ed.) (2000) *Biodiversity and Traditional Knowledge: Equitable Partnerships in Practice. People and Plants Conservation Manual.* People and Plants Conservation Series, WWF/UNESCO/RBG-Kew, Earthscan Publications, London, 503 pp.

Martin, G. (1995) *Ethnobotany Methods Manual.* Chapman and Hall, London, 268 pp.

Martin, G.J., Barrow, S. and Eyzaguirre, P.B. (eds) (2001) *People and Plants Handbook: Growing Diversity,* Issue 7. WWF/ UNESCO/RBG, Kew, 40 pp.

Merton, R.K. (1965) *On the Shoulders of Giants.* Harcourt Brace and World, New York.

Merton, R.K. (1973) *The Sociology of Science: Theoretical and Empirical Investigations.* University of Chicago Press, Chicago, Illinois, 605 pp.

Merton, R.K. (1980) Social theory and social structure. *Current Contents/Social and Behavioral Sciences* 21, 1–12.

Milla, C. (2003) *Ayni.* Universidad San Martin de Porras, Lima.

North, D. (1990) *Institutions, Institutional Change and Economic Performance (Political Economy of Institutions and Decision).* Cambridge University Press, New York, 152 pp.

Orstom, E. (1990) *Governing the Commons: The Evolution of Institutions for Collective Action.* Cambridge University Press, New York, 280 pp.

Pimentel, D., Wilson, C., McCullum, R., Huang, P., Dwen, J., Flack, Q., Tran, T., Salman and Cliff, B. (1997) Economic and environmental benefits of biodiversity. *BioScience* 47, 750.

Posey, D.A. (ed.) (2000) *Cultural and Spiritual Values of Biodiversity.* ITDG Publishing, 731 pp.

Prescott-Allen, R. (1990) How many plants feed the world? *Conservation Biology* 4, 365–374.

Pretty, J. (2002) *Agri-Culture: Reconnecting People, Land and Nature.* Earthscan, London, 261 pp.

Richards, P. (1985) *Indigenous Agricultural Revolution. Ecology and Food Production in West Africa.* Hutchinson Publishers, London, 192 pp.

Rocheleau, D.E. (1995) Gender and biodiversity: a feminist political ecology perspective. *IDS Bulletin* 26(1), 9–16.

Sen, A. (1982) *Poverty and Famines: An Essay on Entitlement and Deprivation.* Clarendon Press, Oxford, UK, 166 pp.

Swaminathan, M.S. (2002) The past present and future contributions of farmers to the conservation and development of genetic diversity. In: Engels, J.M.M., Rao, Ramanantha V., Brown, A.H.D. and Jackson, M.T. (eds) *Managing Plant Genetic Diversity. Proceedings of the Conference on Science and Technology for Managing Plant Genetic Diversity in the 21st Century.* IPGRI, Rome, pp. 23–32.

Tapia, M.E. and De la Torre, A. (1997) *Women Farmers and Andean Seeds.* IPGRI/FAO, Rome, 45 pp.

Terrazas, F. and Valdivia, G. (1998) Spatial dynamics of *in situ* conservation: handling the genetic diversity of Andean tubers in mosaic systems. *Plant Genetic Resources Newsletter* 114, 9–15.

Van Kessel, J. and Canasaca, F.M. (2003) Contexts, concepts and controversies. *Compas Magazine* 6, 13–14.

Vavilov, N.I. (1997) *Five Continents.* IPGRI, Rome, pp. 198.

Watson, J.W. and Eyzaguirre, P.B. (2002) Home gardens and *in situ* conservation of plant genetic resources in farming systems. *Proceedings of the Second International Home Gardens Workshop,* 17–19 July 2001, Witzenhausen. IPGRI, Rome, 184 pp.

Wilkes, G. (1995) The ethnobotany of artificial selection in seed plant domestication. In: Schultes, R.E. and von Reis, S. (eds) *Ethnobotany: The Evolution of a Discipline.* Chapman and Hall, London, pp. 203–208.

Wilson, E.O. (1992) *The Diversity of Life.* Penguin Press, London, 424 pp.

Zhu, D., Eyzaguirre, P.B., Zhou, M., Sears, L. and Liu, G. (eds) (2000) *Ethnobotany and Genetic Diversity of Asian Taro, Focus on China.* Chinese Society of Horticultural Science, Beijing and IPGRI, Rome, 99 pp.

Zimmerer, K.S. (1999) Overlapping patchworks of mountain agriculture in Peru and Bolivia: toward a regional-global landscape model. *Human Ecology* 27(1), 135–165.

Zimmerer, K.S. (2003) Geographies of seed networks for food plants (potato, ulluco) and approaches to agrobiodiversity conservation in the Andean countries. *Society and Natural Resources* 16, 583–601.

Studying Property Rights and Collective Action: a Systemwide Programme

14

Ruth Meinzen-Dick

Social research plays a pivotal role in the Consultative Group on International Agricultural Research's (CGIAR) Systemwide Programme on Collective Action and Property Rights (CAPRi) in two ways. First, the programme's focus on collective action and property rights requires social research capacity. Indeed, strengthening it within CGIAR centres and national agricultural research systems (NARS) and promoting the study of property rights and collective action were two main reasons for developing the programme. Second, insights from collective action have been used to develop the collaborative programme.

I discuss how a programme with strong social science content has developed within a mostly technically oriented network of international and national agricultural research organizations. I begin with background on the programme and the priority research themes, present the conceptual framework used to relate the study of collective action and property rights to the mandate of CGIAR, then discuss how property rights and collective action are defined and studied, highlight some key findings and show how the programme strengthens social research capacity within CGIAR. I conclude with challenges faced and lessons learned.

Background

The CAPRi programme had its origins in discussions in the mid-1990s between the International Food Policy Research Institute (IFPRI) and

©CAB International 2006. *Researching the Culture in Agri-Culture:*
Social Research for International Development
(eds M.M. Cernea and A.H. Kassam)

several other CGIAR centres about collaboration on bilateral research programmes dealing with property rights, with special reference to rangelands and trees. As CGIAR was starting to encourage systemwide initiatives, IFPRI proposed to convene an inter-centre initiative on property rights and collective action to improve communication among centres on these issues. The idea behind this initiative was to formulate a common conceptual framework and even common research methods, so that empirical research conducted under the programme would be cumulative.

By 1997, all 16 CGIAR centres had joined the initiative, although their level of commitment and involvement in the different themes was still uneven. The CAPRi programme has grown rapidly, despite limited funding in the first few years. While shortly after the programme began, the CGIAR centres that addressed property rights and/or collective action had a total of 13 projects, by 2002 CAPRi identified some 110 such projects involving over 400 institutional partners, including universities in developing and industrialized countries, agricultural research institutes and non-governmental and government organizations. A slight shift in emphasis was also noticeable: in the early years, property rights received more attention, but by 1999 more centres recognized the importance of collective action for their work.

Conceptual Framework and Definitions

The CAPRi programme developed a heuristic device to show how social institutions of collective action and property rights are of relevance to CGIAR's mandate (Knox *et al.*, 1998; Meinzen-Dick *et al.*, 2002). Agricultural technologies and NRM practices can be approximately placed according to their temporal and spatial characteristics (Fig. 14.1). On the temporal scale (horizontal axis), those that have a short time frame between investment and returns (e.g. within a season) are on the left, and those that have longer time frames, on the right. On the spatial scale (vertical axis), those that can be adopted on a single plot are near the bottom, with those operating in larger areas, e.g. community or landscape level, placed higher. For example, high-yielding varieties would be at the bottom left corner because they can be adopted by a single farmer and give short-term returns; thus, even tenants can adopt them. As the time between investment and return increases, property rights become more important to provide incentive and authorization to invest. For example, planting trees can be done on a single plot, but tenants are often precluded from such agroforestry investments. As the spatial scale increases beyond a single farm, col-

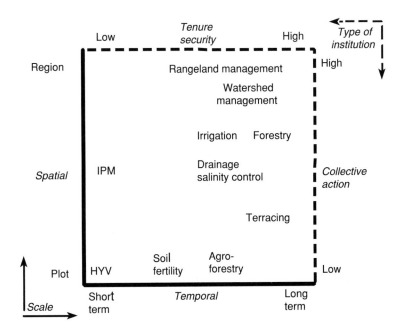

HYV = high-yielding varieties, IPM = integrated pest management.

Fig. 14.1. Time, space and institutional options for innovation in agricultural practice and natural resources management.

lective action is needed to adopt a practice. Many types of integrated pest management, for example, give returns within a season but are not effective if adopted by a single farmer alone. This framework indicates that much of what CGIAR does relates to at least one of these key institutions. In particular, most NRM relates to collective action and property rights.

Recognizing the importance of institutions is not tantamount to understanding how they perform. As with many other social concepts, collective action and property rights are widespread terms that are often used loosely and imprecisely. In particular, collective action is often simplistically equated with formal organizations, and property rights with formal, state-issued legal title or ownership. One of the CAPRi programme's initial activities has, therefore, been to develop a glossary of terms to promote precision in communication across disciplines.

Collective action, as defined by the *Dictionary of Social Sciences*, is 'action taken by a group (either directly or on its behalf through an organization) in pursuit of members' perceived shared interests'

(Marshall, 1998). This includes adopting rules for use (or protective non-use) of resources, as in irrigation systems, watershed management, range-lands or fisheries. Collective action can also facilitate joint investment by small farmers, dissemination of technologies through farmers' groups and even empowerment. Collective action, however, does not always occur, and it may or may not include organizations. One of the topics of research is, therefore, the premises and determinants of collective action, includ-ing the extent to which the many programme organizations – set up by governments, non-governmental organizations and even CGIAR centres – actually contribute to collective action or exist on paper only.

To study this topic has required us to develop measures of collect-ive action. For example, factor analysis of a range of indicators such as number of groups, membership and rule making in agropastoral com-munities in Burkina Faso found that network capacity (related more to organizational density) and implementation capacity (related more to rules and performance) had different determinants and different effects on rangeland management (McCarthy *et al.*, 2002).

Drawing upon the literature on property rights from the social sci-ences and economics (e.g. Wade, 1988; Ostrom, 1990; Schlager and Ostrom, 1992), property rights should be understood not just as own-ership, but as complex bundles of rights – to use, manage and dispose of a resource. Employing these concepts is more useful to understand-ing the types of property rights found, especially in developing coun-tries, than imposing Western concepts of title and ownership that may not fit local situations. Employing concepts of legal pluralism, we rec-ognize that property rights do not derive only from state law but also from multiple bases for claiming property rights, including inter-national, state, religious and a range of customary or local law and traditional entitlements (Meinzen-Dick and Pradhan, 2002). Legal pluralism, while widely accepted by anthropologists and even lawyers, challenges simplistic policy analysis that seeks to identify one 'policy lever' that will effect the desired changes, and state-centred perspec-tives that assume that national cadastres or other titling programmes are necessary to provide secure tenure. In some cases state law, although important, is not as relevant as village or ethnic communities or users' groups in determining property rights on the ground. Property rights do change over time, but legislative reform alone is unlikely to change the manifestation of property rights on the ground. Rather, change occurs through the social and power relations and negotiations between different groups (Ostrom, 1990; Baland and Plateau, 1996).

Although early CAPRi work on property rights focused on the importance of property rights to provide incentives for investment, especially in agriculture and NRM, subsequent research has also dealt with the importance of property rights in providing authorization and control over resources, especially as NRM authority has devolved from governments to communities and users' groups. Property rights are also fundamental for welfare, empowerment and poverty reduction – aspects that are gaining greater attention in the CAPRi programme.

Key Findings

The CAPRi programme first addressed issues regarding the adoption of agricultural technologies and of NRM, both of central importance for the research of most CGIAR centres. Findings from on-going studies on the devolution of NRM in different sectors were next brought together and analysed for factors contributing to effectiveness. The third topic of major synthesis work was on property rights and collective action dimensions of watershed management, followed by rangeland management and most recently, genetic resources (Dennis *et al.*, 2003).

Although the programme has identified the importance of tenure security as an incentive to invest in resources, studies have also shown that government interventions do not always increase it (Meinzen-Dick *et al.*, 2002). The state has often taken land away from tribal institutions managing the rangelands, thereby decreasing local users' involvement in management (Ngaido *et al.*, 2002). Rigid boundaries on the land of different individuals and groups, which are often suggested and even imposed by the state to avert a 'tragedy of the commons', are often not the best approach for rangelands, where resource availability fluctuates a great deal. Instead, access options are important to allow communities to use the land and water resources of other groups under certain conditions, to increase survival during droughts. Understanding the complexity of property rights in practice is needed to prevent unintended negative outcomes of policies in resource management or equity.

In many cases, collective action is needed for technology adoption, but CGIAR centres, NARS and many government or non-governmental organization programmes have not given it due attention. The International Livestock Research Institute had a programme using centres to apply pour-on treatments that would control tsetse and other insects. The treatments would be most effective if all cattle were treated, but there was a potential free-rider problem. Analysis of cooperation patterns identified that crossing land of a different ethnic group to reach a treatment centre was a local cultural problem, which the programme solved by opening treatment centres in areas of each ethnic group (Swallow *et al.*, 2002).

These issues also come to the fore in watershed management, which generally requires the coordination of agricultural and resource management practices across a large area (Swallow *et al.*, 2000). While many technical agencies want to organize management units along hydrologic boundaries, it may be better to build on existing social and administrative institutions, which have different boundaries. Coordination is further complicated because many of the watersheds' land and water resources have multiple uses, and so the rights and interests of many different categories of users need to be considered. Community organizations play a major role in such coordination but most do not include all users, and the issue of who participates needs to be taken into account in developing participatory watershed management programmes.

When the CAPRi programme began, several CGIAR centres were involved in research on the interaction between state and users' groups in managing irrigation, forestry, fisheries and rangelands (Rasmussen and Meinzen-Dick, 1995; Scherr *et al.*, 1995). Bringing these separate areas of research together, and discussing them with policymakers from different countries and sectors, highlighted the importance of collective action for successful devolution programmes (Meinzen-Dick *et al.*, 2001). Unless communities were willing and able to take on a larger role in NRM, transferring it from the state to users' groups might lead to further resource deterioration. At the same time, the state was often eroding local capacity or incentives for collective action, either through attitudes of government agencies or transfer of responsibilities for the resource without corresponding rights to the benefits, thereby reducing people's incentives to participate. Bringing together evidence on these issues from different countries and resource sectors was helpful in identifying cross-cutting lessons and policy implications.

Strengthening Social Research Capacity

When the CAPRi programme began, it was working with social researchers who often felt isolated at the more biophysically oriented CGIAR centres. Strengthening the linkages to other social researchers was one of the original impetuses for centres to approach IFPRI to develop joint projects in this area, and a motivation for researchers to become active in the programme. Many CGIAR centres – and especially their national research partners – did not have strong social science libraries, particularly before internet-based resources became more readily available. Thus, one of the first services provided by the CAPRi programme was producing an annotated bibliography of key literature on the subject and making it available on request from CAPRi members. The bibliography has been placed on the CAPRi web site and CD, in an easily searchable format. Key reading lists, literature reviews and conceptual framework documents proved popular services.

Working in semi-isolation, researchers have difficulty knowing and employing best-practice methods for studying complex institutions such as collective action or property rights. While some in CGIAR were doing leading research in this field, others were simply asking survey questions about land ownership or organizational membership and using them as variables in regression equations – techniques that did not capture these institutions' essential aspects. After the first CAPRi workshop on technology adoption in 1997, Place and Swallow (2000) provided a useful best-practice guide to methods for studying how property rights might affect technology adoption. A key message was the need to collect data at the right level of aggregation. To test how tenure security affects technology adoption on particular pieces of land, property rights data need to be collected at the plot level and associated with individual household members who manage the plot, which requires sub-household-level data collection. For questions of the effect of alternative tenure systems that vary between communities but not within them, data must be collected at the community level, with a sufficient sample size to compare outcomes.

The CAPRi programme has been able to support several innovative empirical studies to examine collective action. One problem with much of the literature on collective action is that it is based on case studies, which may each identify particular factors affecting people's willingness to cooperate. Game theory may identify particular individual incentive structures that make it rational for people to participate, but often do not address cultural and other factors that also play a role. However, little empirical testing has been done to verify the factors suggested by different case studies and game theory. In 2002, a workshop on methods for studying collective action discussed those used in these studies and others by CGIAR centres and outside experts. The approaches included the following:

- case studies of action research with innovative processes to mobilize collective action (e.g. Sultana and Thompson, 2003);
- experimental games that can be played with people in field situations to assess the likelihood of cooperation among people in different communities, and how it is likely to change as a result of different rules, e.g. on communication between participants, repeated interactions and monitoring (Cardenas, 2003); and
- empirically testing what factors affect collective action, by developing community-level data collection instruments and 'institutional survey' methods to identify the full institutional landscape, and quantitative analysis of a large number of communities (e.g. McCarthy *et al.*, 2002; Place *et al.*, 2002).

In addition to the working papers and journal articles discussing the methods and findings of these particular studies, the CAPRi programme has collected and made available the data-generation instruments. Many of these studies found that it is not just formal organizations that matter: in many cases, irrigation, rangelands and genetic resources are influenced at least as much by informal organizations and other social institutions, and each study has enriched the understanding of the institutional framework for resource management.

Above all, the CAPRi programme connects researchers. Early Steering Committee meetings were held in conjunction with International Association for the Study of Common Property meetings, so that participants could benefit from their discussions. Since 1997, CAPRi has held its own workshops on a range of topics covering different priority themes and reaching out to different interest groups within CGIAR and its NARS and other partners:

- gender and property rights (e-mail, hosted by IFPRI, 1996);
- technology adoption (ICARDA, Syria, 1997);
- devolution of NRM (WorldFish Center, Philippines, 1999);
- watershed management (International Center for Tropical Agriculture, Nicaragua, 2000);
- institutions for rangeland management (ICARDA, Tunisia, 2001);
- methods for studying collective action (World Agroforestry Centre, Kenya, 2002); and
- local management of genetic resources (International Plant Genetic Resources Institute, Rome, 2003).

The workshops build capacity by connecting CGIAR researchers not only with each other but also with outside academic experts and practitioners. Most workshops had a research focus, but those on devolution and rangeland management were international policy workshops, bringing together researchers and policymakers from developing countries to examine the results of CGIAR research and foster feedback from policymakers. These workshops have resulted in a variety of CAPRi working papers and other publications, but the discussions and connections among participants have been most valuable in building a community of practice on CAPRi issues.

The CAPRi programme's other activities are also designed to strengthen capacity for applied research on these topics. The programme has been able to fund from its budget eight empirical research projects carried out by CGIAR centres and national partners through a competitive research grant process.[1] These projects have produced innovative and policy-relevant research on a wide range of topics in sub-Saharan Africa, West Asia and North Africa, South-east Asia, Central Asia and the Americas.

Lessons from Social Research for Programme Governance

The first meeting of the interim Steering Committee set out an ambitious research agenda, which was proposed to CGIAR's Technical Advisory Committee, for new empirical research to address each priority theme in turn. Although we had hoped for a large funding base to carry out the CAPRi agenda, such funds were not forthcoming. The initiative received $200,000 in start-up funds – not enough to be divided among different centres. Indeed, many inter-centre initiatives were experiencing much more tension over resource allocation, even with much more money. Drawing upon principles from social science, the programme decided to focus on 'public goods,' i.e. activities that would benefit any interested CGIAR centre and researcher without diminishing the benefits available to others.

Instead of funding new research, the programme sponsored workshops on the priority themes that had broad applicability across CGIAR. These workshops served a number of key functions, drawing together the various researchers who were working separately on these topics at different CGIAR centres to share findings and experiences and to learn from the leading international experts. This process provided peer review of the work, built a network among the researchers at the various centres and increased interaction between CGIAR centres and top academic social researchers. The output of each workshop was also reviewed, edited and published – first as CAPRi working papers and then assembled into books (e.g. Meinzen-Dick *et al.*, 2001, 2002) or special journal issues (Swallow *et al.*, 2000). This refined and publicized the research being done by the CGIAR centres, and provided an incentive for participating in the programme.

As the programme grew, the Steering Committee structure became too large to function effectively, with high turnover of the CGIAR liaisons from one meeting to another. We therefore created a new Executive Committee consisting of only three CGIAR liaisons plus two external Steering Committee members from developing countries. Reducing the committee size increased interaction with the governing body and, as the Executive Committee showed a strong interest in the programme activities, made the secretariat more accountable to the members.

As it developed a track record, the programme attracted more funding, which enabled us to consider funding research projects. However, observations of fund-allocation difficulties in other systemwide programmes called for careful attention to the process of allocating research grants. We were also able to draw upon the study of NRM organizations. Analysis of irrigators' associations indicated that getting cooperation to increase the resource base is often easier than dividing a fixed pool, and that cooperating to obtain the resource can build trust and shared understanding, facilitating subsequent resource allocation (Coward, 1986; Subramanian *et al.*, 1997). Governance studies pointed to the need for transparent decision-making criteria to allocate funds.

To develop a competitive grant programme, the Executive Committee identified clear criteria for selection. An independent proposal review panel was selected, composed of three non-CGIAR experts, with different disciplinary, geographic and resource-base skills. The panel reviewed the proposals according to the criteria and made its recommendations, and the Executive Committee awarded the grants, asking for revisions to proposals when necessary to increase quality.

By accommodating a wide range of levels of interest, the CAPRi programme has developed a community of practice in which a core group of CGIAR people interacts with other experts in the field. Other CGIAR liaisons and other researchers at centres with strong CAPRi activities then pick up these ideas and use them in interactions with relevant 'communities', providing the CAPRi programme with information about other researchers' related work such as on programmes on integrated NRM and alternatives to slash-and-burn, or participatory research and gender analysis. Although much of this work was developed without specific attention to the knowledge-management literature, in recent years we have been expressly using it to increase the flow of tacit and explicit knowledge (Song, 2001). Finally, to ensure the effectiveness of our research, we have involved policymakers in the CAPRi programme and various research programmes we sponsor.

Conclusions

The CAPRi programme is one of the few on-going full-scale CGIAR social research programmes, which has been both a challenge and an advantage. In the early years, the major challenge lay in demonstrating how a programme focusing on institutional issues was relevant to CGIAR's mandate and biophysical research, and in securing funding for such a research agenda. Highlighting the linkages, conceptually and through empirical research, provided the key to gaining CGIAR and donor support. We have identified a number of key areas in CGIAR's mandate and the research agenda of various centres that relate to collective action and/or property rights, including technology adoption, devolution of NRM, watershed management, agro-enterprises and genetic resources. As CGIAR has become more poverty oriented, the number of identified linkages keeps growing.

The CAPRi programme has been able to expand its research agenda by drawing upon non-economics social science (including sociology, anthropology, political science, law) as well as upon institutional economics, and particularly by making linkages across disciplines, regions and resource bases (e.g. land, water, fisheries, forestry). Involving outside experts has been crucial. In turn, expertise within CGIAR is growing and many of our national partners also carry out research that is methodologically innovative, with direct policy and practical application.

Social research has not only contributed to the substance of CAPRi research, but also to the management of the programme itself. We have given explicit attention to developing an inclusive and transparent governance structure, to building trust and social capital among the members and between the members and convening centre and to adapting the evolving programme to challenges at each stage. The 2002 external review found the following:

> The links established with other Centres, and especially with IASCP (International Association for the Study of Common Property), have given CAPRi access to the latest developments in CA (collective action) and PR (property rights) research. This has strengthened CAPRi's activities at modest cost, led to mutual sharing of concepts, methods and analysis, and created a critical mass of social and interdisciplinary scientists working on CA and PR in NRM.
>
> (Interim Science Council, 2002: xiii)

The Review Panel concluded that CAPRi has provided added value in terms of the relevance and quality of its outputs and impacts in:

> **1.** Increased awareness of the role of property rights and collective action on the uptake of technologies by farmers as a result of studies by the CGIAR and NARs;
> **2.** Specific policy findings for certain technologies that can facilitate their adoption and feedback into the design and/or dissemination of the technologies;
> **3.** Improved research practices by the centres in the priority themes;
> **4.** Enhanced policy analysis capacities in this area by the CGIAR and NARS, and in some cases, by government agencies.
>
> (Interim Science Council, 2002: 25)

Based in part on this evaluation, the CAPRi programme won the 2002 CGIAR Scientific Award for Outstanding Partnership.

Social research on collective action and property rights has found a place in CGIAR, but the CAPRi programme may also offer lessons for other CGIAR systemwide programmes and the Global Challenge Programmes. In retrospect, the CAPRi programme's experience of

obtaining only seed funds, and having to demonstrate what the programme could do with them before earning money to distribute in
research grants, was also an advantage. Too much money coming too
quickly can generate a 'feeding frenzy' of expectations that are not met.
Specific attention to the programmes' governance structure, building
social capital and trust among participants and ensuring transparency
in programme management are all crucial for cooperation among
researchers, as well as among groups for agricultural extension, NRM
or other development activities.

Acknowledgements

The CAPRi programme is a collective activity with many key participants, but I wish to especially acknowledge Monica Di Gregorio, Anna
Knox and Lee Ann Jackson for their role in coordinating the programme; the Steering Committee, and especially the Executive Committee (Brent Swallow, Nancy Johnson, Tidiane Ngaido, W. Kisamba
Mugerwa, Narpat Jodha, Pablo Eyzaguirre and Ahmed Herzenni) for
their many contributions; and the governments of Norway, Italy and
Germany; the Ford Foundation; and the Swedish International Development Agency (SIDA) for their financial support.

Notes

[1]At $125,000 each, these grants leveraged up to seven times the amount in
matching funds from other sources.

References

Baland, J.-M. and Platteau, J.-P.
(1996) *Halting Degradation of
Natural Resources: Is there a Role
for Rural Communities?* Clarendon Press, Oxford, UK, 423 pp.
Cardenas, J.C. (2003) Bringing the lab
to the field: more than changing
subjects. Paper presented at the
Meeting of the International
Economic Sciences Association,
19–22 June 2003. Pittsburg,
Pennsylvania.

Coward, E.W. Jr (1986) Direct and
indirect alternatives for irrigation
investment and the creation of
property. In: Easter, W.K. (ed.) *Irrigation Investment, Technology
and Management Strategies for
Development: Studies in Water
Policy and Management, 8.* Westview Press, Boulder, Colorado,
270 pp.
Dennis, E., Ilyasov, J., Van Dusen, E.,
Treshkin, S. and Lee, M. (2003)

The role of local institutions in the conservation of plant genetic diversity. Paper presented at the International Workshop on Property Rights, Collective Action and Local Conservation of Genetic Resources, 29 September–2 October 2003. Rome, Italy.

Interim Science Council (2002) Report of the First External Review of the Systemwide Programme on Collective Action and Property Rights (CAPRi). Food and Agriculture Organization of the United Nations, Rome, 106 pp.

Knox, A., Meinzen-Dick, R.S. and Hazell, P.B.R. (1998) Property Rights, Collective Action and Technologies for Natural Resources Management: A Conceptual Framework. CAPRi Working Paper No. 1. International Food Policy Research Institute (IFPRI), Washington, DC, 63 pp. Available online: http://www. capri.cgiar.org/pdf/capriwp01.pdf

Marshall, G. (1998) *A Dictionary of Sociology.* Oxford University Press, New York, 710 pp.

McCarthy, N., Dutilly-Diané, C. and Drabo, B. (2002) Cooperation, Collective Action and Natural Resources Management in Burkina Faso: A Methodological Note. CAPRi Working Paper No. 27. IFPRI, Washington, DC, 56 pp. Available online: http://www. capri.cgiar.org/pdf/capriwp27.pdf

Meinzen-Dick, R.S. and Pradhan, R. (2002) Legal Pluralism and Dynamic Property Rights. CAPRi Working Paper No. 22. IFPRI, Washington, DC, 41 pp. Available online: http://www.capri.cgiar. org/pdf/capriwp22.pdf

Meinzen-Dick, R.S., Knox, A. and Di Gregorio, M. (2001) *Collective Action, Property Rights and Devolution of Natural Resource Management: Exchange of Knowledge and Implications for Policy. Proceedings of the International Conference, 21–25 June 1999*, Puerto Azul, Philippines. DSE/ZEL, Feldafing, Germany, 293 pp.

Meinzen-Dick, R.S., Knox, A., Place, F. and Swallow, B.M. (eds) (2002) *Innovation in Natural Resources Management: the Role of Property Rights and Collective Action in Developing Countries.* Johns Hopkins University Press and IFPRI, Baltimore, Maryland, 317 pp.

Ngaido, T., McCarthy, N. and Di Gregorio, M. (2002) International Conference on Policy and Institutional Options for the Management of Rangelands in Dry Areas: Workshop Summary Paper. CAPRi Working Paper No. 23. IFPRI, Washington, DC, 74 pp. Available online: http://www. capri.cgiar.org/pdf/capriwp23.pdf

Ostrom, E. (1990) *Governing the Commons: the Evolution of Institutions for Collective Action.* Cambridge University Press, Cambridge, Massachusetts, 280 pp.

Place, F. and Swallow, B. (2000) Assessing the Relationships between Property Rights and Technology Adoption in Smallholder Agriculture: A Review of Issues and Empirical Methods. CAPRi Working Paper No. 2. IFPRI, Washington, DC, 52 pp. Available online: http://www. capri. cgiar.org/ pdf/ capriwp02.pdf

Place, F., Kariuki, G., Wangila, J., Kristjanson, P., Makauki, A. and Ndubi, J. (2002) Assessing the Factors Underlying the Differences in Group Performance: Methodological Issues and Empirical Findings from the Highlands

of Central Kenya. CAPRi Working
Paper No. 25. IFPRI, Washington,
DC, 47 pp. Available online:
http://www.capri.cgiar.org/pdf/ca-
priwp25.pdf

Rasmussen, L. and Meinzen-Dick,
R.S. (1995) Local Organizations
for Natural Resources Management: Lessons from Theoretical
and Empirical Literature. IFPRI
Environment and Production
Technology Division (EPTD) Discussion Paper No. 11. IFPRI,
Washington, DC, 40 pp. Available
online: http://www.ifpri.org/divs/
eptd/dp/papers/eptdp11.pdf

Scherr, S.J., Buck, L., Meinzen-
Dick, R.S. and Jackson,
L.A. (1995) Designing Policy
Research on Local Organization in
Natural Resources Management.
EPTD Workshop Summary Paper
No. 2. IFPRI, Washington,
DC, 136 pp. Available online:
h t t p : / / w w w . i f p r i . o r g /
divs/eptd/ws/eptws02.htm

Schlager, E. and Ostrom, E. (1992)
Property-rights regimes and natural
resources: a conceptual analysis.
Land Economics 68(3), 249–262.

Song, S. (2001) Knowledge Management: Origins and Implications for
Integrated Natural Resources Management. Paper presented at the
CGIAR Conference on Integrated
Management for Sustainable Agriculture, Forestry and Fisheries,
28–31 August, Cali, Colombia.

Subramanian, A., Jagannathan, N.V.
and Meinzen-Dick, R.S. (eds)
(1997) User Organizations for Sustainable Water Services. World
Bank Technical Paper No. 354.
World Bank, Washington, DC,
162 pp.

Sultana, P. and Thompson, P. (2003)
Methods of Consensus Building
for Community-Based Fisheries
Management in Bangladesh and
the Mekong Delta. CAPRi Working
Paper No. 30. IFPRI, Washington,
DC, 49 pp. Available online:
http://www.capri.cgiar.org/pdf/
capriwp30.pdf

Swallow, B., Johnson, N. and
Meinzen-Dick, R.S. (eds) (2000)
Special issue on watershed management. *Water Policy* 3(6),
449–572.

Swallow, B., Wangila, J., Mulatu, W.,
Okello, O. and McCarthy, N.
(2002) Collective action in space:
assessing how collective action
varies across an African landscape. In: Meinzen-Dick, R.S.,
Knox, A., Place, F. and Swallow,
B.M. (eds) *Innovation in Natural
Resources Management: the Role
of Property Rights and Collective
Action in Developing Countries.*
Johns Hopkins University Press
and IFPRI, Baltimore, Maryland,
pp. 24–256.

Wade, R. (1988) *Village Republics.*
Cambridge University Press, Cambridge, Massachusetts, 238 pp.

Crafting Food Policy with Social Science Knowledge

15

Ruth Meinzen-Dick, Michelle Adato, Marc Cohen, Curtis Farrar, Lawrence Haddad and Agnes Quisumbing[1]

The research staff of the International Food Policy Research Institute (IFPRI) has always been composed principally of social scientists. However, economics was the main discipline, with neoclassical economics predominant. Over the years, IFPRI has had just one or two non-economist social scientists at any one time (a sociologist or an anthropologist, a political scientist or a social geographer). Moreover, they often needed to adapt their methods and approaches to economics or else risk marginalization.

Growing recognition of the importance of institutional aspects in much of IFPRI's work has translated into slowly expanding appreciation for the contributions of other disciplines. Some divisions have responded to the increasing salience within the international development field of socio-political and cultural issues – e.g. such as power and empowerment, gender and ethnicity, cultural factors, social capital and relationships and others – that are difficult to measure using only economic methods and perspectives.

This chapter reviews discussions on the disciplinary mix at IFPRI over time, then highlights some research areas where non-economics social sciences have made a major contribution, either through in-house scientists or external collaborators, and directions for the future, such as the following substantive areas:

- institutional analysis of property rights and collective action (PRCA), which brings together the disciplines of sociology and institutional economics, and has developed innovative community and institutional survey methods;

- gender and intra-household research, involving anthropology, economics and sociology, with iterative qualitative and quantitative research;
- research on poverty, including understanding the behaviour of the poor and their responses to a variety of safety nets and other programmes to help them; studies of the dynamics of poverty and inequality; and convening of an inter-centre research programme on the impact of agricultural research on poverty, using the sustainable livelihoods framework;
- greater use of political science and political sociology to analyse governance, linkages between food security and peace, getting poverty on the agenda, policymaking and implementation, and helping IFPRI identify how information is used by policymakers so that our research has the greatest impact; and
- institutional learning and change, including how to develop appropriate partnerships between research, government and civil society, and how to learn from experiences and impact studies to develop more appropriate research and development programmes.

This chapter examines challenges to interdisciplinary research, including understanding of and regard for the different perspectives and concerns of other disciplines, technical languages, research methods and standards of evidence. The chapter also discusses the trade-offs of bringing capacity in-house and through collaborators.

A Historical Perspective

The first CGIAR external programme review of IFPRI, conducted in 1984, 9 years after its founding, devoted three and a half densely written pages to the consideration of staff composition by discipline (Technical Advisory Committee (TAC), 1985). The review panel was headed by a distinguished plant scientist, supported by three economists and an ecologist. They identified an 'IFPRI approach' implemented by staff economists representing a narrow band within the profession, who emphasized 'incentives and inputs rather than power, interest groups, structures or institutions'. IFPRI's economists had sought to make up for their lack of breadth through various palliative measures, which the external review panel rejected as insufficient. While it considered IFPRI research to be of high quality, the panel identified areas where the research was harmed by its narrow approach and lack of attention to structural variables that would concern structuralist anthropologists, political scientists and political economists. The panel also feared damage to specific research projects, particularly those that compared issues across countries, without considering sufficiently how the social, political and biological circumstances of those countries might differ.

The criticisms extended to the six questions that provided the outline of the institute's first long-term research strategy. One, for example, assumed that a combination of farm producer incentives was the aspect of food policy most likely to affect the chances of simultaneously achieving growth and equity. The question as formulated failed to direct attention to agro-climatic, family-structural or economic power-based causes of growth, stagnation, equity or poverty, which would seem more important to an agricultural scientist, social anthropologist or sociologist. A further argument for broadening the presence of the social sciences at IFPRI was to give more support to incorporating political science, anthropology and the full scope of economics in the CGIAR system as a whole.

The review panel recommended that over the coming 5 years IFPRI broaden the approach to economics among its staff, and over the coming 2 years appoint a senior anthropologist and a senior political scientist. While thinking that the natural sciences should inform IFPRI's research, the panel recognized that it would be difficult to establish a suitable research environment for natural scientists and suggested forming a small advisory group. The IFPRI board at the time lumped together this and several other suggestions to expand or improve the institute's programme as steps that could only be considered if additional funding, particularly unrestricted grant funding, were forthcoming.

Suitably involving disciplines other than economics remained an issue in the 1990s, during the second external programme review. The panel noted that the institute had failed to broaden the cadre of social scientists on its senior staff, but did not press the matter. The panel warned against a superficial multidisciplinary approach and concentrated on working relationships between physical and natural scientists; nutrition and the environment were strongly represented on the panel. The members were concerned that isolated scientists could not maintain disciplinary quality. To achieve the long-desired diversity in the social sciences, the panel, whose chair and two team members were economists, urged IFPRI to search for researchers with double majors in economics and another discipline, but not at the cost of second-rate knowledge of economics (TAC, 1991).

In 1996, in preparation for its third CGIAR external evaluation, IFPRI initiated its own internally commissioned external review (ICER), conducted by nine external scholars focusing on the methodology of research and outreach. In a major move toward disciplinary diversity, the team included three economists, two political scientists, an anthropologist, a sociologist and two specialists in public affairs.

There were only two broad recommendations, one of which was 'movement toward methods diversity' (Paarlberg, 1996). This was an extended and encouraging analysis of the process, detected in IFPRI, of movement away from relying principally on conventional analysis of markets and households to being sensitive to the importance of institutions of all kinds, public and private. The ICER team pointed out that this was a direction increasingly favoured within economics, but cautioned against the difficulties of learning to effectively use multiple methodologies together.

ICER stressed the importance of IFPRI conducting research on state institutions, particularly the processes by which research results come to influence governmental policy decisions. There were sensitivities and risks involved but not as great as the risks of IFPRI failing to examine and test generalizations about state behaviour. One suggestion was that more research about successful cases of policy implementation might have greater influence with political leaders than inferences drawn from statistical correlations.

The ICER team noted with approval the gradual inclusion of social scientists of other disciplines in IFPRI research staff, but thought that a major shift in this direction would be unwise, partly because of critical-mass problems. The team suggested instead systematically involving short-term visitors from other disciplines and collaborating with research institutions where economics was not the dominant discipline. In contrast with the universities and their rigid disciplinary departments, and the World Bank with its growing social science presence and multidisciplinary approaches but declining technical agricultural staff, IFPRI was well placed to pioneer and set standards in a multidisciplinary approach to food and agricultural policy.

At the time of the third external review by CGIAR, six out of 52 senior research staff were not primarily economists: two in geography (both since departed), and one each in nutrition, epidemiology, rural sociology and political science. The review foresaw a need for the institute to experiment with different approaches before finding the right combination (TAC, 1998).

These external reviews initiated by TAC and supported by IFPRI senior management, along with the work by IFPRI non-economists and changes within the economics profession itself, have gradually expanded the scope for social research within the institute. The following sections present some of the notable areas in which non-economics social research has found a niche within IFPRI, particularly in the multi-country programmes (MPs) and global and regional programmes that form the building blocks of the institute's research agenda.

Property Rights and Collective Action: Social Research on Institutional Issues

When IFPRI reorganized its research around MPs, one of the first was on Property Rights and Collective Action (PRCA), in 1993. Although the research was designed around two interrelated institutions that cut across a number of resources, it proceeded largely along separate tracks, with an economist leading research on the role of property rights in forest management and a sociologist conducting research on collective action in water management. However, both employed largely econometric analysis, with an emphasis on how these institutions affected productivity and sustainability of resource systems.

As this work progressed, IFPRI began collaborating on these topics with a number of other CGIAR centres, notably International Center for Agricultural Research in the Dry Areas (ICARDA), International Livestock Research Institute (ILRI) and WORLD AGROFORESTRY CENTRE (ICRAF). Rather than just engage in bilateral projects, IFPRI proposed a systemwide programme on PRCA, which got under way in 1995. By 1996 all 16 CGIAR centres had signed on to the programme, which led to greater diversity in the topics and approaches taken to research in these institutions (see Meinzen-Dick, Chapter 14 this volume). Joint appointments between IFPRI and ICARDA on one side, and IFPRI and ILRI on the other, brought in a land policy specialist and an institutional economist to the MP team.

Growing awareness and popularity of institutional economics provided another bridge for improved communication between economics, sociology and other disciplines involved in this research. For example, where once 'culture' was a 'variable' viewed with suspicion by economists, institutional economics' emphasis on 'norms' elevated many aspects of culture to key factors to be investigated. Notions of path dependence from institutional economics similarly challenged narrow econometric assumptions of predictability and extrapolation of how institutions would develop based on regressions, and gave greater credence to more historical and qualitative research on processes of change.

Further mixing of the different disciplines came about as the sociologist's research on water drew her into more work on property rights over water, while the economists within IFPRI and in the systemwide programme began to devote more attention to collective action to manage rangelands and other natural resources. The work on water rights (Bruns and Meinzen-Dick, 2000; Meinzen-Dick and Pradhan, 2002) drew heavily on anthropological work on legal pluralism, and many of these ideas were picked up by those of other disciplines working on other resources, especially rangelands.

The interaction of disciplines led to methodological innovations, particularly in cross-site comparison of institutions. Much of the literature on the role of property rights or factors affecting collective action in natural resources management has been based on case studies. Theoretical work has drawn upon a wide range of case studies by sociologists, anthropologists and political scientists to develop a range of (sometimes inconsistent) hypotheses regarding 'determinants' of collective action (Ostrom, 1990; Baland and Platteau, 1996; Berkes and Folke, 1998). Early IFPRI work on property rights under this MP went significantly beyond case studies, by using what was termed a 'community survey', or modified rapid rural assessment, to collect information on property rights systems and on production and environmental outcomes from a large enough sample of communities and households within them so that econometric analysis could be used to test the strength of community and household relationships (Otsuka and Place, 2001). A similar quantitative approach was taken to studying collective action in canal irrigation in India (Meinzen-Dick *et al.*, 2002). That research protocol, developed by a sociologist, was further refined and adapted by an institutional economist and applied to pastoral management in Burkina Faso, with the addition of more qualitative analysis of the collective action institutions themselves (McCarthy *et al.*, 2002). Other research on management of pastoral resources in West Asia and North Africa has been done in strong collaboration with ICARDA and natural scientists from national agricultural research systems (NARS), as well as policymakers in the countries. The resulting collaboration has resulted in much stronger policy impact and capacity building than if the research had been conducted exclusively by social scientists (Bruce *et al.*, 2002).

Looking outside the Box: Gender and Intrahousehold Research

The objective of IFPRI's gender and intrahousehold research programme, established in 1993, is to test whether or not intrahousehold allocation by families affects the outcomes and consequences of state policies, and to generate information that will help develop high-performing policies, programmes and projects. Central to the objective of this MP is understanding better how households work – whether they make decisions as one, or whether individuals in the household have different preferences, rights, resources and responsibilities. At the outset, it was clear that the processes of household decision making varied enormously across cultures and were affected by processes outside the domain of the traditional focus of economics. Indeed, a conference on intrahousehold analysis that preceded the formal establishment of the MP included papers from sociologists and anthropologists (Haddad *et al.*, 1997). The MP methodology document clearly acknowledged the lead of other social science disciplines, but also that economics research on household decision-making processes had grown tremendously in recent years, stimulated by advances in economics models, econometric techniques and the quantity and quality of household and individual data (Strauss and Thomas, 1995).

The MP proposal developed a convincing argument regarding the inability to anticipate individual responses to economic incentives if intrahousehold allocation processes are neglected. MP documents have also argued that research on the link between intrahousehold allocation and policy depends on: (i) development of household models that can accommodate individual preferences; (ii) development of innovative methods of data collection; (iii) establishment of good dialogue with policymakers in developing countries; and (iv) opportunity to test the relevance of intrahousehold issues for policy in a number of countries, for a number of policy instruments, using common data and modelling methodologies. Qualitative methods were initially introduced in the context of developing innovative (for economists!) methods of data collection, but eventually became appreciated as important methodological tools in their own right.

Qualitative methods were especially important in coming up with culturally relevant definitions of variables that could proxy for bargaining power within marriage. Economics models of the household that allowed for different preferences of individuals within it, predicted that one's share of resources would depend on one's bargaining power. But since bargaining power is an elusive concept, indicators need to be developed for specific cultural settings. At this time, the team was composed primarily of economists. It considered hiring a staff anthropologist or sociologist but thought, given the country-specificity of many indicators of bargaining power, that in-country collaborators would serve the purpose better.

A large outside grant (from the Office of Women in Development of the US Agency for International Development (USAID)) eventually gave IFPRI the means to include inputs from other social sciences. The MP undertook four high-concentration country studies (in Bangladesh, Ethiopia, Guatemala and South Africa) and eight supplemental studies. The countries were chosen so that the research team could: (i) generalize about the relevance of intrahousehold issues to a wide range of policy outcomes in a broad range of countries; and (ii) make specific policy recommendations in each country, with more depth and emphasis in the four high-concentration countries. Each high-concentration country study had a quantitative household survey and qualitative study. The qualitative studies in Bangladesh, Guatemala and South Africa were designed jointly by in-country social scientist collaborators and IFPRI researchers, and were extremely valuable in informing the design of the quantitative survey modules, especially on assets at marriage (the indicator chosen to measure bargaining power in all the countries), social capital and measures of women's empowerment. For Ethiopia, existing qualitative village studies conducted by sociology and anthropology graduate students were available to IFPRI researchers. Rather than treating this qualitative research only as input into the design of surveys, all the qualitative studies were considered research outputs in their own right.

One valuable source of inputs from non-economists was the External Advisory Committee (EAC) of the USAID-funded project. The committee had 11 external members, including three anthropologists and one nutritionist, from universities, international organizations, research institutions and non-governmental organizations (NGOs), who were among the most senior members of their respective professions. The remainder of the group consisted of economists. USAID staff and associated programme staff (most of whom were sociologists and anthropologists) also attended EAC meetings regularly. This group met yearly to review research plans and progress. IFPRI researchers followed most of the suggestions made during EAC meetings. The IFPRI research team also made an effort to include non-economist grantees in its supplemental studies programme. The grantees included two sociologists, three anthropologists and four economists.

Due to the valuable lessons learned from working with social scientists in this and other projects, IFPRI's Food Consumption and Nutrition Division (FCND) included quantitative and qualitative components in its proposal to evaluate the effect of Mexico's Programa Nacional de Educacion, Salud y Nutricion (PROGRESA), including a component on women's status and intrahousehold relations (Adato *et al.,* 2000b). Follow-up work to the Bangladesh study conducted under a project for CGIAR's Standing Panel for Impact Assessment built on the work of the intrahousehold programme and included qualitative studies in the community. In both cases, having a rural sociologist on staff was valuable to the studies' design and analysis. In the case of PROGRESA, relying on the quantitative study results alone would have led to a lack of appreciation of the effects of the programme on women's empowerment, because the quantitative survey questionnaire did not lend itself to capturing many of the subtle attitudinal changes that occurred because of the programme. The involvement of a sociologist also revealed some of the subtleties of how decisions are actually made between men and women in the household, and raised the problem of potential differences between formally recognized (and thus reported) decision makers and actual decision makers (Adato *et al.,* 2000b). However, she also concluded that neither the survey nor this qualitative work, which had a fairly limited mandate, was sufficient for understanding these complex and changing gender dynamics adequately, and that a more in-depth qualitative study drawing on ethnographic methods would be required.

Our positive experience with PROGRESA made team members appreciate the value of having a non-economist social scientist on staff starting from the upstream stage of a research project rather than pulling one in when the research project had already been designed (usually by economists). A lesson learned regarding the challenges to interdisciplinary work is that extra time is needed to carefully integrate the research. Because of the tight time frame of this study, as well as IFPRI's limited experience with interconnecting disciplines and methods, the economic and sociological components were carried out in a parallel, rather than in an integrated and iterative, manner. Neither part of the study had the benefit of learning from the other before being designed. Instead, the value of the mixed method work was reaped during data analysis by each team considering the results of the other. However, write-ups were again done as two separate reports rather than an integrated report. This experience taught us about the need for adequate time and planning to integrate findings and allow each approach to benefit from the other.

The MP also made an effort to reach non-traditional (non-economist, non-academic) audiences in its outreach efforts. The MP sponsored an e-mail listserver to discuss gender issues in development research. One explicit objective of the listserver was to draw social scientists and other policy analysts into the sphere of gender and intrahousehold analysis. Using the listserver as a springboard, the research team organized an electronic conference moderated by two economists, a sociologist and an anthropologist. After the completion of the research, the team wrote a technical guide to including gender in development projects, which was field-tested in Nepal, Kenya and Guatemala, with a multidisciplinary audience of practitioners.

Research on Safety-net Programmes and Poverty

In over 6 years, IFPRI's FCND has carried out five major projects that integrated sociology in its study of safety-net programmes and poverty dynamics. These include studies of urban food security in Ghana in 1996, public works programmes in South Africa, the PROGRESA programme in Mexico, factors explaining movements in and out of poverty in South Africa and the impact of agricultural research on poverty (the last in collaboration with the Environment and Production Technology Division (EPTD)).

The integration of sociology into the public works study in South Africa (Adato *et al.*, 1999) was initially enabled by a Rockefeller Foundation Social Science Research Fellowship in Agriculture placing postdoctoral social scientists (including economists) for a 2-year period at a CGIAR centre. The project was one of the few IFPRI experiences where the non-economics studies were not an add-on but rather drove the project. Given IFPRI's primary function as an economics policy research institute, most of its interdisciplinary projects are driven primarily by economic questions and methods. Non-economics disciplines are often seen as complements, but not the centre, of the studies, and are not given equal weight or funding. In the case of the public works study, the project leader was a sociologist based in South Africa and thus had more freedom to design the study around sociological as well as economic concerns. This did not mean a neglect of economics, which had an equal status in the data collection given the importance of quantifying factors such as job creation, training and costs.

This study represented a turning point in the division's work, because it introduced a focus on several issues of interest to economists but which usually are not in their domain: local institution; community participation and empowerment; the importance of power relationships outside the household; and institutional dynamics at local, regional and national levels, involving politics and culture, helping to explain successes and failures in development programmes. These are now on-going interests in the division, designed into a range of new projects. Methodologically, the public works study was one where time was taken to collect qualitative and quantitative data iteratively. An appreciation of the respective contributions of each approach led to careful consideration of the findings of the other in data analysis and in the write-up of reports and journal articles.

It is important to note that economics does not always use quantitative research, nor do non-economic social sciences always use qualitative research. Some economists use qualitative methods, and mainstream sociology is dominated by survey methods. Economists using qualitative methods usually draw on focus groups, rapid appraisal and key informant interviews (although IFPRI economists rarely use qualitative methods except in collaboration with non-economists), while sociologists and anthropologists in IFPRI projects have combined these and quantitative analysis with ethnographic methods using participant observation, systematic semi-structured interviews using a stratified random or purposive sample, social network analysis and other methods. The contribution of sociology, anthropology, political science and other non-economics social sciences is not just in the orientation toward certain data collection or analytical methods, but in the questions of interest and the variables used. Answering these questions often requires different methods – which, in turn reflect, different epistemologies – than those of economists.

In the public works study, for example, while the economists were interested in labour intensity and jobs created per dollar, the sociologists were interested in the nature of institutional culture and constraints on institutional change to understand why government departments were not changing to labour-intensive methods in the context of public works programmes intended as poverty safety nets (Adato, 1998). While the economists were interested in how community participation affected project outcomes (e.g. costs, jobs created), the sociologists wanted to understand local forms of decision making, conflict and conflict resolution and race- and class-based historical relationships to explain the interactions of local governments, community-based organizations and the private sector in joint project design and management as mandated by the government, and most often confounded institutional arrangements and blocked them from working as intended (Adato *et al.,* 1999). Answering these questions required different variables, methods and epistemological perspectives on reliability and validity. These questions could not have been answered using surveys, although surveys could complement the qualitative findings by testing certain narrower propositions on a broader scale. For example, the qualitative work found that community-based project management committees sometimes made decisions regarding wages and materials that lowered costs, and explored why they were able to do this. Quantitative analysis then tested whether community-managed projects had lower costs across the universe of projects in the study (Hoddinott *et al.,* 2001).

The PROGRESA study followed the public works study. Qualitative work was a small component of the study, given that its primary objective was to measure changes in consumption, health and education as a result of participation in the programme. The value of interdisciplinary work is found in the contributions to the understanding of facilitating and constraining factors and processes in programme operations, intrahousehold dynamics and perceptions of girls' education and the impact of the programme on intracommunity social relationships (Adato, 2000; Adato *et al.,* 2000a). These studies revealed impacts of the programme that would not have been revealed through the surveys alone.

Several challenges to interdisciplinary work emerged in the PROGRESA evaluation. First, while a qualitative component was described in the project proposal, actual funds were not set aside for this in the project budget – an oversight reflecting the division's limited experience with mixed methods – and later had to be realigned for this purpose. This brought to people's attention that qualitative data collection, particularly analysis, are time-consuming and not inexpensive undertakings. Subsequently, although Mexican government officials originally requested qualitative work, they later had to be convinced that they should support the fieldwork once the surveys were under way and dominated the officials' daily concerns. Several FCND safety-net programme evaluations make clear that the ability to carry out qualitative research depends significantly on the training and experience of government officials. (Are any of them sociologists? Have they worked in interdisciplinary teams and used mixed methods?)

Qualitative and quantitative work was not done iteratively but separately, because of the time-famine on the part of study researchers and the tight timeline of the studies. The operations study's findings were integrated in the write-up of the final report. No papers integrating the quantitative and qualitative data have been written, reflecting the problem that professional rewards come from publishing in journals specific to one discipline or the other.

Despite the recognized value of integrating methods demonstrated in the PROGRESA study, two evaluations of similar conditional cash transfer programmes (in Honduras and Brazil) did not budget any funds for qualitative work. However, the evaluation of a similar programme in Nicaragua has allocated substantial funds for a qualitative component, using ethnographic and other qualitative methods, building and expanding on the PROGRESA research. Inclusion or exclusion of the qualitative work depended on two factors, providing insight for future integration efforts. The first is external pressure – whether or not donors require or request non-economics social sciences and mixed methods – and the background of the government officials for whom the work is being done. The second is the orientation of the principal researchers on the project – the extent to which they recognize the potential value of an interdisciplinary approach, reflected by how it is prioritized in the budget.

This points to what may be one of the largest obstacles to increasing non-economics social science in IFPRI projects. When a group of economics researchers sits down to plan a project and staffing, it is economist positions that are designed into the project. Lack of experience working on multidisciplinary research teams and related lack of recognition of the potential value of this contribution leads to the allocation of scarce funds among senior and junior economists (and sometimes a nutritionist), and the problem is perpetuated. A policy of multidisciplinary project proposal planning so that the relative contributions are considered and debated could help to break this circularity.

At the other end of the spectrum is a study of poverty dynamics in South Africa, a qualitative follow-up study led by sociologists and intended to complement and aid in analysis of findings from a large panel survey (of which the intrahousehold work discussed in the previous section was a part). A rigorous sampling framework was used in the qualitative study for selecting clusters and households, stratifying across a set of key variables. Qualitative work was conducted within the same households that were part of the panel survey to understand what lay behind the numbers and regression results, to compare results of different methods and to explore several issues that could not be addressed well through survey methods (Adato *et al.,* 2003). In this case the qualitative research has been well funded, and the teams of economists and non-economists have dedicated time to data integration and joint papers. Iteration has occurred, with this qualitative work informing the next round of the survey scheduled for early 2004, and a subsequent round of qualitative research scheduled for mid-2004.

Finally, since 2000, IFPRI has been leading an experiment in interdisciplinary project design and implementation that involves five projects in four countries and four CGIAR centres. This is a study of the impact of agricultural research on poverty, with each project team including several economists and several sociologists and/or anthropologists. In this project, the UK's Department for International Development required as a condition of funding that the original case study proposals, which had originally been proposed as purely economics studies, be redesigned to become integrated economic and social analysis; that international and national social analysis researchers be hired for each project; and that mixed methods be used. Although most of the case studies are led by economists and dedicate more funding to economics data collection and analysis, the project budgets were substantially increased for social analysis, which showed that it was taken seriously. The result was that researchers from both disciplines experienced first-hand the value of the others' contributions. Use of the sustainable livelihoods approach also provided a common framework for team members to see the contributions of the different disciplines and analytic approaches (Adato and Meinzen-Dick, 2003). This was an interesting case of a donor-driven approach to enabling institutional change, resisted at first but later recognized to have contributed to better studies and a valuable learning process. Indeed, one of the outcomes of this study was the convening of a new CGIAR initiative on institutional learning and change (Mackay and Horton, 2003).

Lessons learned from this experience were that largely separate budgets for the economic and social analyses can also separate rather than integrate components, and that sufficient time is needed for the optimum iterative approach to mixed-method research and for integration during data analysis and write up. Clearly, while bringing in 'outside' capacity for non-economics social science made an immense contribution to the projects, ultimately capacity to undertake interdisciplinary work is to be lastingly strengthened by having more disciplines represented 'inside', on staff, within the CGIAR centres.

Food from Peace Project

In 1994, IFPRI's 2020 Vision Initiative[2] contracted with two external partners – Brown University World Hunger Programme (WHP) and Bread for the World–USA (BFW) – to research the link between conflict and hunger. These partners were not chosen on the basis of the disciplinary backgrounds of their researchers (a nutritional anthropologist and a political scientist, respectively) but because of previous work they had done on the topic. BFW's main researcher on this project later joined IFPRI as special assistant to the director general, which undoubtedly raised the project's profile somewhat at IFPRI, although the topic was also already of great interest to IFPRI's then director general.

In 1995, WHP and BFW assembled a joint team of two political scientists, two anthropologists, a geographer and specialists on community development in the Horn of Africa, and organized three expert consultations of academic and relief and development specialists. These consultations included IFPRI researchers from the FCND, EPTD and the 2020 Vision Initiative.

The project team posed the following questions for the study: What difference would peace make for food security in countries affected by conflict? To what extent is food insecurity a cause of conflict? And, finally, what sorts of policies could break the links between conflict and hunger, in preconflict, conflict and postconflict situations? To explore the first question, one team member developed the 'food from peace' methodology to calculate conflict-induced food production losses (using Food and Agriculture Organization (FAO) data for African countries). The next two questions were answered primarily through an extensive multidisciplinary literature review and case studies, also drawn primarily from Africa.

In addition to numerous conventional academic publications and policy briefs (e.g. Cohen, 1999; Cohen and Pinstrup-Andersen, 1999; Messer and Cohen, 2001; Messer *et al.*, 2001), project outputs include an opinion article in a leading US newspaper (Messer and Cohen, 1998); and numerous conference presentations to scholars and policymakers around the world. The project's results and policy recommendations are frequently cited by donor agencies, CGIAR centres, Future Harvest, United Nations Standing Committee on Nutrition, relief and development NGOs and the development research community. FAO has done additional analysis of 'food from peace' using the methodology developed by the project (FAO, 2000). The project has also attracted attention from a non-traditional audience for IFPRI work – the peace studies community (Environmental Change and Security Project at the Smithsonian Institution's Woodrow Wilson Center, Oslo Peace Research Institute and Essex University's Armed Conflict Unit).

'In-reach' results from the project have been incorporated in varying degrees into the FCND's work on the causes of child malnutrition, EPTD's and 2020 Vision's global food outlook work and the globalization synthesis led by the Trade and Macroeconomics Division (e.g. Pinstrup-Andersen *et al.*, 1999; Smith and Haddad, 2000; Messer and Cohen, 2001).

Beyond the original contract ($15,000 for 1994–1995), the only funding for this work is the time of one researcher in the Director General's Office at IFPRI, which came from core resources. An effort to obtain more funding from the US Institute of Peace was unsuccessful. There has been some discussion with the IFPRI team working on less-favoured areas about looking at conflict in resource-poor areas, and the new IFPRI strategy document (IFPRI, 2003) identifies 'food systems in disaster prevention and relief and rebuilding after crises' as a priority theme, but work in these areas has not yet begun.

Governance

Over 1999–2001, IFPRI's 2020 Vision initiative commissioned two studies on governance issues: a study of governance mechanisms in selected developing countries with respect to transgenic crop technology; and a more general study of governance with respect to food security in globalization. Both studies were carried out by Robert Paarlberg, a political scientist at Wellesley College and long-time IFPRI collaborator, who also chaired ICER.

The work on governance of genetically modified crops looked at policies in four developing countries in key areas: intellectual property rights, biosafety, trade, food safety, consumer choice and public research investment (Paarlberg, 2000, 2001). In each instance, the study explored the forces that shaped the particular policy outcome. For each policy area, the policies of each country were then classified along a spectrum consisting of promotional, permissive, precautionary and prohibitive. The study was based on interviews of policymakers and the actors inside and outside the governments who sought to influence policy. The tools employed are widely utilized by political scientists in qualitative comparative studies of politics and policymaking. As the first comprehensive effort to assess and compare the policies related to crop biotechnology in developing countries, the work has attracted much attention in the international development community, and remains a standard reference on the relevant policies in developing countries.

The more general study of governance and food security conceptualized 'governance' with respect to food security as the assurance that essential public goods are provided. That is to say, the study took a political economy approach and employed a lens that economists would find familiar. Political scientists traditionally are concerned with 'the authoritative allocation of values for society'. The notion of 'good governance' as commonly employed in contemporary development discourse includes public goods provision but is broader, embracing participation, voice, transparency, human rights and subsidiarity as well. The study lays out a case that food security-relevant public goods provision is primarily the purview of national governments (with some important exceptions), and challenges the conventional wisdom (e.g. Mathews, 1997; Smith and Naím, 2000) that transnational and supranational forces (NGOs, multinational corporations, the World Trade Organization, international financial institutions) are the main ones affecting food security (Paarlberg, 2002).

The work has attracted considerable interest in the larger development research and practitioner community and is one of the most popular downloads from the IFPRI website, and controversial for challenging the conventional wisdom that the nation state is becoming obsolete. Spillover effects at IFPRI, although modest so far, appear somewhat more robust than shown by the biotechnology governance study. A presentation by Paarlberg based on the paper was prominently featured at IFPRI's 2001 Conference on Sustainable Food Security for All, and the paper's perspective influenced the subsequent action plan.

In 2003, the adoption of IFPRI's new strategy and the reorganization of the research divisions have given new prominence to governance issues. The strategy identifies food system governance as an overarching objective, dealing with 'policies improving global and national governance, political participation and institutions for pro-poor food, agriculture and natural resources management systems' (IFPRI, 2003: ix). A priority theme deals with 'appropriate roles of state, market and civil society in food, agriculture, nutrition and natural resources management policy'. In a 2002 senior staff retreat to develop the strategy document, this theme was ranked the most important and elicited the most enthusiasm. In 2003, the Development Strategies and Governance Division was formed and has hired a new governance and institutions expert to take the lead on this theme, but will also draw together research in the other three research divisions relating to governance and institutions.

A Missed Opportunity to Undertake Cutting-edge Political Analysis

Much policy research rests on the assumption that an exclusive focus on measuring the narrowly defined costs and benefits of different intervention options is sufficient to produce good policy analysis. An IFPRI research project in Egypt in the late 1990s, which was determined not to fall prey to this assumption, did so nevertheless – due in large part to the absence of a political scientist on the staff.

The mid-1990s spike in the world price of wheat made the Egyptian bread price subsidy programme much more expensive for the government of Egypt to maintain. It was receptive to an analysis of how to make the subsidy system more efficient. IFPRI and its Egyptian collaborators conducted a national household survey in 1996/97, which showed that the government transfer as represented by the bread subsidy was spread evenly across income groups. The poorest 20% of the population captured 20% of the subsidy, as did the richest 20% of the population. Some type of targeting mechanism of the bread price subsidy was an obvious way of improving efficiency. The government had successfully targeted the overall food price subsidy system toward the poor by restricting the application of universal subsidies to a smaller, lower-income elasticity set of foods: sugar, oil, wheat, flour and bread. The government had done so quietly over 15 years partly because previous attempts to reduce the cost of the food, and non-food price subsidies had met with considerable unrest.

The research team therefore suspected that politicians would be sceptical of policy alternatives that included the targeting of bread price subsidies. Policymakers clearly thought the public would have a low tolerance for any targeting scheme, making any recommendation to target the bread price subsidy unlikely to get onto a government agenda. The subsequent technical analysis produced about 20 options to reduce the costs of the bread price subsidy while protecting the welfare of the poor. Seven of those options were further pursued by conducting research to: (i) measure public reaction to the idea of targeting bread price subsidies; and (ii) compare those reactions with policymakers' perceptions of the public's reaction.

At the time, IFPRI did not have a political scientist on the staff, as the funds were insufficient to hire one. So we temporarily employed a political scientist from a local US university to join the team. Looking back, the political science work done under the project certainly had value but it was insufficient: we were left with a sense of a missed opportunity to do some groundbreaking work that might have re-defined the policy space within which policy research on bread price subsidies was constrained to work.

There were several reasons for failing to seize this opportunity, but not having a political scientist on IFPRI staff was a major factor. A polit-ical scientist on the staff would have: (i) made it easier to find a con-sultant in the first place, as even if the political scientist were fully booked with other projects and knew nothing about Egypt, he or she would have been none the less a relevant professional counterpart con-nected to the external political science community and would have known the context within which the political science consultant would have to operate; (ii) been able to serve as an in-house sounding board for an outside consultant; (iii) known about the Egypt project from the pro-posal stage and could have expertly built political analysis into the research plan and research budget, instead of having economists try to do the same thing (economists ought to think what it would be like for them to have a nutritionist design their research outline and budget); (iv) in the eyes of our field collaborators, had more credibility than a (nevertheless technically credible) consultant; (v) had the incentive structure to take a long-term perspective on the research; and (vi) pro-vided opportunities for the other Egypt team members to learn about political analysis due to day-to-day interactions.

A major lesson for the research division at IFPRI was: do not wait for a large project on political science to come along if you do not have a political scientist in-house. Rather, take a leap of faith and set up a search process that ensures the hire of a first-rate political scientist and then give him or her the space to develop a research programme within the institute's medium-term priorities. IFPRI did so in 2004.

Social Research on the Policy Process: is it Worth it?

The 'policy process' describes how policymaking occurs. It has been described as 'a social dynamic that determines how the good and bad in life are meted out' (Clark, 2002). By taking on problems (policy) and interacting with people with varying perspectives and interests in the problem and in the potential solutions (process), one becomes a par-ticipant (Clark, 2002). Yet, research on the policy process in conjunc-tion with 'conventional' policy research is rarely undertaken. It is conventional because it takes a technical and economic perspective towards the framing of a problem, analysis of the causes of the problem and generation and evaluation of policy alternatives to solve it.

Does the absence of systematic inquiry into the policymaking process undermine the quality of policy research? Many would answer 'yes'. Clark (2002), for example, suggests that a limited view of the policy process generates an overreliance on 'lack of resources', 'lack of political will' and 'lack of conventional research' as explanations for lack of progress in reducing, say, malnutrition. While the policy process cannot be described in tidy stages or steps (Sutton, 1999), it is not immune to systematic research (Grindle and Thomas, 1991; Kingdon, 1995).

Why is there not more research on the policy process to test the hypothesis that such a focus would improve the quality of policy alternatives? One factor is that policy processes are often seen as idiosyncratic, and often caught up in particular power issues and players. Therefore, questions are raised about how much the findings from one policy case study may apply to others.[3] This is particularly an issue for organizations such as IFPRI that attempt to be seen as 'neutral' providers of international public goods and to stay above the fray by not becoming too involved in issues of local conflicts and personalities.

Perhaps the most frequent explanation advanced for the lack of research on the policy process is the inability of policy researchers to attain a multifaceted perspective of a policy issue. The policy process involves people with different perspectives or 'rationales' (Table 15.1). These rationales can be technical, economic, political, social, legal or normative.

Table 15.1. Different rationales underlying public policy formation.

Rationality	Examples of key focus
Technical	Cause and effect, efficacy, effectiveness
Economic	Efficiency, market failures, cost-effectiveness, distribution of costs and benefits
Social/normative	Fairness, ethics, rights, justice, participation, accountability
Political	Alliances, interests, compromises
Administrative/ organizational	Rules, capacity, management
Legal	Laws, precedents, rights, enforcement

Source: Pelletier (2001).

Good policy research, it is argued, involves an appreciation and integration of several of these perspectives (Pelletier, 2001; Kanbur, 2002).[4] Yet, the training and subsequent careers of most policy researchers involve immersion in one rationale. The dominant rationale is often technical and economic (perhaps reflecting the dominance of finance ministries in most governments). Professional incentives reward specialization, and many organizations are not willing to cover the initial fixed costs of fostering an interdisciplinary approach because the potential benefits are not clear.

How can this circle be broken? Is it even worth attempting to break it? These questions can only be answered by undertaking research that integrates these multiple rationales. If successful, better policy research questions will be posed, better analysis undertaken, better alternatives generated. Ultimately, the policy research will have more impact on the lives of malnourished people.

IFPRI is developing a research programme to test the hypothesis that analysis of the nutrition policy process will improve nutrition policy research. The hypothesis will be tested by setting up an *ex-ante* evaluation of the new research programme, laying down baselines on the state of research in this area, current perceptions about the value added of this work and current thoughts about how research is best conducted. Only by explicitly articulating the benefits and costs of an integrative rationale approach to research for the policy process can we (sceptics and converts alike) learn how best to conduct policy research.

Lessons: Challenges and Factors Affecting Success

While the need for non-economist social scientists to fulfil IFPRI's mandate of policy research has been conceptually recognized at various points of IFPRI's history, the practical measures to acquire the necessary social research expertise have varied from time to time. In many cases expertise has been 'outsourced' from collaborators from northern universities, on the premise that they were the leading experts in the field. In many other cases expertise was 'outsourced' from NARS collaborators or professionals from southern academic institutions, who were expected to have more understanding of local contextual factors. Both these approaches are valid, but the 'outsourcing' does not provide an effective and enduring representation of social research capacity within the institute. As a result, the social researchers are left to collect data, to answer questions framed by others (often economists) and opportunities to identify where social research can make a major contribution are often missed. A third approach has been to hire social researchers for short durations, often as postdoctoral fellows. This approach gives social research a voice within the institute, but because of their lower status, transitional presence and the fact that they are brought in on projects developed by others, the researchers are still often unable to frame the questions. When appointments of some of these social researchers have been renewed, and they have risen through the system to more senior status, they have been able to demonstrate the contribution of social research to both issues and methods and to create greater institutional ownership for the results of the research.

Even having social researchers on the staff, however, is not in itself sufficient. One or two 'token' social researchers can easily become isolated from their own disciplinary peers and 'go native', adopting the language and methods of economics to gain acceptance. The alternative is to maintain one's disciplinary identity but to work alone with little interaction with colleagues and to depend on external collaborations. Having a critical mass of non-economist social researchers would be ideal, but even the chance to interact with one other person within the institute in one's field can make an enormous difference. Other resources, such as scientific conferences, which offer the chance to interact with others in one's discipline, are also critical to prevent atrophy of specific social research skills and perspectives. Most research assistants at IFPRI have been trained in economics, even when working for a non-economist. Research support from other social research disciplines can provide a sounding board and improve the quality of analysis for non-economist research staff. Having few non-economists on staff also means that those staff members can become overburdened when their expertise is requested, and that these researchers end up working in regions unfamiliar to them – a tension, given that contextual knowledge is particularly important for high-quality sociology and anthropology.

A more elusive, but perhaps ultimately more important, resource to make researchers (of any discipline) effective is receptivity of colleagues and respect within the institute. While some debates between disciplines give rise to a creative tension that sharpens thinking on both sides, a feeling of rejection of one's disciplinary contribution is demoralizing. Related to this is the more practical issue of how proposals are developed and the self-perpetuating effect of having proposals written by teams of economists who will write economics proposals that require the hiring of economists. This happens when staff economists often have little or no experience of working in such interdisciplinary teams and thus do not make such inclusion a priority in their projects. Without the participation of non-economist social scientists in proposal development, the isolation is likely to continue.

A particularly contentious issue concerns the rules of evidence in research. IFPRI economists tend to favour quantitative evidence (if not mathematical proofs), whereas other social researchers may favour qualitative data and analysis. This distinction should not be overdrawn; many non-economist social researchers also use quantitative methods. IFPRI has had some success in recent years in research projects that manage to combine qualitative and quantitative approaches, either in an integrated manner from the beginning (as in some of the work on property rights and collective action) or iteratively (as in the case of intrahousehold studies in Bangladesh). Even with the best of intentions to combine methods and disciplinary perspectives, however, this combination will not happen unless two very scarce resources – time and field work expenses – are devoted to the inclusion of both types of research, as well as to an integration of the findings.

A related matter is the question of peer review. IFPRI's publications review policy calls for internal and external reviewers. Because economists make up the overwhelming majority of social scientists at IFPRI, virtually all internal publications by non-economists are reviewed by economists, but non-economists are rarely invited to review their economist colleagues. Even identifying suitable external reviewers is difficult if only economists are on the review committees. In recent years, the publications review committee has become more sensitive to this issue, although the pool of non-economist reviewers is still not very large.

Finding a common framework or language across disciplines has been helpful. Two particularly useful examples are institutional economics and the sustainable livelihoods framework, which are important because they help each discipline recognize the need for contributions from the others. Social scientists of different disciplines working together on a project, where the problem to be addressed is complex and transgresses the need for disciplinary boundaries, are most valuable. At the same time, it is important to preserve disciplinary integrity and not seek the smallest or simplest common denominator, leading to useless generalities. Although it may be a struggle to learn each other's language and methods, this leads to a better appreciation of what each discipline can do.

IFPRI's experience has shown that it is not enough to have research staff of varying disciplines: it is also important to have social researchers in positions of authority – on review teams, advisory committees, boards of trustees and donor organizations. The disciplinary biases on review panels may be as important as what they advise, and the reaction of boards to the research of the institute and the findings of review panels is similarly conditioned by such boards' disciplinary composition. Donors play a key role, not only in providing funds for social researchers, but in insisting on their inclusion in projects and in the institute as a whole. Without the involvement of other disciplines at all levels, the institution would not be as sensitive or receptive to the need for social research.

Some Closing Thoughts

It will be apparent from the relatively selective discussion above that IFPRI has made considerable progress over recent years in incorporating the contributions of the broader fields of economics (e.g. institutional economics), as well as some contributions from anthropology, sociology and political science into its research. It is also apparent from the above, and from many informal discussions among researchers that there is still a long way to go, from the point of view of dominant group psychology as well as research momentum. The described steps have taken place in the context of a broader move toward a multidisciplinary approach at IFPRI, involving nutrition, macro modelling, geographic information systems and global food models inside, and plant breeding, livestock and irrigation engineering outside, where the issues of multidisciplinary collaboration are similar in many respects, but have complexities of their own.

All of this also takes place in the context of the continued competition between maintaining the cutting-edge quality of research while striving for the greatest possible impact on the lives of poor people. The social researchers at IFPRI, like their economist colleagues and the other scientists at other CGIAR centres, must demonstrate the relevance of their research to the CGIAR mandate. However, as this mandate moves from emphasis on increasing agricultural productivity to reducing poverty, the contribution of social researchers who can help understand power relations and other issues of relevance to poor people becomes more apparent. IFPRI has expressed a growing commitment to including social research inside the institute, not only on an 'outsourcing' basis, and is harvesting results from this inclusion. It is not without costs in terms of financial resources and investment of effort. However, IFPRI's new strategy and the 2003 reorganization of the research divisions places strong emphasis on issues of institutions and governance. There will be additional recruitment of non-economist social scientists for this work.

We hope that this portrait of an ongoing process is relevant to the concerns of other CGIAR institutions, both as potential collaborators of IFPRI and as research organizations struggling with comparable problems in their own work.

Notes

[1]Michael Cernea and Alain de Janvry provided helpful comments for the revision of this chapter. Responsibility for any errors rests with the authors.

[2]A high-profile research and communications programme at IFPRI that aims to develop and promote a shared vision and consensus for action to meet food needs while reducing poverty and protecting the environment.

[3]The question of generalizability is frequently raised by economists for qualitative research by non-economic social scientists. Interestingly, however, business schools greatly emphasize case study research.

[4]In the World Bank, similarly, social scientists who were pushed only to do project fix-ups successfully proved the multiplier value of doing policy research and incorporating social variables (knowledge) in development policies.

References

Adato, M. (1998) *Transforming Institutions for Social Development: the National Public Works Program in South Africa.* Annual Meeting of the African Studies Association, Chicago, Illinois, October 1998.

Adato, M. (2000) The impact of PROGRESA on community social relationships. Final Report, International Food Policy Research Institute, Washington, DC, 46 pp.

Adato, M. and Meinzen-Dick, R.S. (2003) Assessing the impact of agricultural research on poverty and livelihoods. *Quarterly Journal of International Agriculture* 42 (2), 149–166.

Adato, M., Haddad, L., Horner, D., Ravjee, N. and Haywood, R. (1999) From works to public works: labour-intensive public works in Western Cape Province, South Africa. Final Report, International Food Policy Research Institute, Washington, DC, 297 pp.

Adato, M., Coady, D. and Ruel, M. (2000a) An operations evaluation of PROGRESA from the perspective of beneficiaries, *promotoras*, school directors and health staff. August. Final Report, International Food Policy Research Institute, Washington, DC, 194 pp.

Adato, M., de la Brière, B., Mindek, D. and Quisumbing, A. (eds) (2000b) Final Report, The Impact of PROGRESA on Women's Status and Intrahousehold Relations. International Food Policy Research Institute, Washington, DC, 114 pp.

Adato, M., Lund, F. and Mhlongo, P. (2003) Innovations in mixed methods to understand poverty dynamics: a multidisciplinary approach to longitudinal research in Kwa Zulu-Natal, South Africa. Paper presented at the joint DPU-ODI-DFID-World Bank Workshop on Urban Longitudinal Research Methodology, 28–29 May 2003, University College London, London.

Baland, J.M. and Platteau, J.-P. (1996) *Halting Degradation of Natural Resources: Is There a Role for Rural Communities?* FAO and Clarendon Press, Oxford, UK, 440 pp.

Berkes, F. and Folke, C. (1998) *Linking Social and Ecological Systems.* Cambridge University Press, Cambridge, Massachusetts, 476 pp.

Bruce, J., Valdivia, C., Tan-Kim-Yong, U. and Keya, S.O. (2002) Report of the First External Review of the System-Wide Programme on Collective Action and Property Rights (CAPRi). Consultative Group on International Agricultural Research interim Science Council, Rome, 106 pp.

Bruns, B.R. and Meinzen-Dick, R.S. (eds) (2000) *Negotiating Water Rights.* Intermediate Technology Press, London and Vistaar, New Delhi, 394 pp.

Clark, T. (2002) *The Policy Process: A Practice Guide for Natural Resource Professionals.* Yale University Press, New Haven and London, 224 pp.

Cohen, M.J. (1999) Famine prevention during armed conflict: the humanitarian challenge. In: Krach, U. and Schulz, M. (eds) *Food Security and Nutrition: The Global Challenge.* Lit Verlag and St Martin's Press, Münster and New York, pp. 397–417.

Cohen, M.J. and Pinstrup-Andersen, P. (1999) Food security and conflict. *Social Research* 66(1), 377–416.

Food and Agriculture Organization of the United Nations (FAO) (2000) *The State of Food and Agriculture 2000.* FAO, Rome, 329 pp.

Grindle, M. and Thomas, J. (1991) *Public Choices and Policy Change: The Political Economy of Reform in Developing Countries.* Johns Hopkins University Press, Baltimore, Maryland, 222 pp.

Haddad, L., Hoddinott, J. and Alderman, H. (1997) *Intrahousehold Resource Allocation in Developing Countries: Models, Methods, and Policy.* Johns Hopkins University Press, Baltimore, Maryland, 341 pp.

Hoddinott, J., Adato M., Besley T. and Haddad L. (2001) Participation and Poverty Reduction: Issues, Theory and New Evidence from South Africa. FCND Discussion Paper 98. International Food Policy Research Institute, Washington, DC, 96 pp.

International Food Policy Research Institute (IFPRI) (2003) *IFPRI's Strategy Toward Food and Nutrition Security.* International Food Policy Research Institute, Washington, DC, 48 pp.

Kanbur, R. (2002) Economics, social science and development. *World Development* 30(30), 477–486.

Kingdon, J.W. (1995) *Agendas, Alternatives and Public Policies.* 2nd edn. Harper Collins College Publishers, New York, 254 pp.

Mackay, R. and Horton, D. (eds) (2003) Institutional Learning and Change in the CGIAR: Summary Record of the Workshop held at IFPRI, Washington, DC, February 4–6, 2003. Impact Assessment Discussion Paper No. 18. International Food Policy Research Institute, Washington, DC, 63 pp.

Mathews, J.T. (1997) Power shift. *Foreign Affairs* 76(1), 50–66.

McCarthy, N., Dutilly-Diané, C. and Drabo, B. (2002) Cooperation, Collective Action and Natural Resources Management in Burkina Faso: A Methodological Note. CAPRi Working Paper No. 27. International Food Policy Research Institute, Washington, DC, 48 pp.

Meinzen-Dick, R.S. and Pradhan, R. (2002) Legal Pluralism and Dynamic Property Rights. CAPRi Working Paper No. 22. CGIAR System-Wide Programme on Collective Action and Property Rights, Washington, DC. Available online: http://www.capri.cgiar.org/pdf/capriwp22.pdf

Meinzen-Dick, R.S., Raju, K.V. and Gulati, A. (2002) What affects organization and collective action for managing resources? Evidence from canal irrigation systems in India. *World Development* 30(4), 649–666.

Messer, E. and Cohen, M.J. (1998) The hunger-war link in Sudan. *Providence Journal.* 19 July. (Reprinted as Hunger and civil war rage in Sudan, *Joplin Globe*, 24 July.)

Messer, E. and Cohen, M.J. (2001) Conflict and food insecurity. In: Díaz-Bonilla, E. and Robinson, S. (eds) *Shaping Globalization for Poverty Alleviation and Food Security.* 2020 Vision Focus 8, Brief 12 of 13. International Food Policy Research Institute, Washington, DC, 26 pp.

Messer, E., Cohen, M.J. and Marchione, T. (2001) Conflict: A Cause and Effect of Hunger. Environmental Change and Security Project Report 7. Woodrow Wilson Center, Smithsonian Institution, Washington, DC, 16 pp.

Ostrom, E. (1990) *Governing the Commons: the Evolution of Institutions for Collective Action.* Cambridge University Press, Cambridge, Massachusetts, 280 pp.

Otsuka, K. and Place, F. (2001) *Land Tenure and Natural Resources Management: A Comparative Study of Agrarian Communities in Asia and Africa.* Johns Hopkins University Press, Baltimore, Maryland, 389 pp.

Paarlberg, R. (1996) Internally Commissioned External Review (ICER): Research and Outreach Methodologies at IFPRI. International Food Policy Research Institute, Washington, DC, 20 pp. (Plus appendix consisting of 16 sections by MP number each paged separately.)

Paarlberg, R. (2000) Governing the GM Crop Revolution: Policy Choices for Developing Countries. 2020 Vision for Food, Agriculture, and the Environment Discussion Paper No. 33. International Food Policy Research Institute, Washington, DC, 36 pp.

Paarlberg, R. (2001) *The Politics of Precaution: Genetically Modified Crops in Developing Countries.* The Johns Hopkins University Press for IFPRI, Baltimore, Maryland, 181 pp.

Paarlberg, R. (2002) Governance and Food Security in an Age of Globalization. 2020 Vision for Food, Agriculture, and the Environment Discussion Paper No. 36. International Food Policy Research Institute, Washington, DC, 58 pp.

Pelletier, D. (2001) Research and policy directions. In: Semba, R. and Bloem, M. (eds) *Nutrition and Health in Developing Countries.* Humana Press, Totowa, New Jersey, 569 pp.

Pinstrup-Andersen, P., Pandya-Lorch, R. and Rosegrant, M.W. (1999) *World Food Prospects: Critical Issues for the Early Twenty-First Century.* 2020 Vision Food Policy Report. International Food Policy Research Institute, Washington, DC, 32 pp.

Smith, G. and Naím, M. (2000) *Altered States: Globalization, Sovereignty, and Governance.* International Development Research Centre, Ottawa, Ontario, 78 pp.

Smith, L.C. and Haddad, L. (2000) Explaining Child Nutrition in Developing Countries: A Cross-Country Analysis. IFPRI Research Report No. 111. International Food Policy Research Institute, Washington, DC, 112 pp.

Strauss, J.A. and Thomas, D. (1995) Human resources: empirical modeling of household and family decisions. In: Srinivasan, T.N. and Behrman, J. (eds) *Handbook of Development Economics*. Elsevier, Amsterdam, pp. 1883–2023.

Sutton, R. (1999) The Policy Process: An Overview. Working Paper 118 Overseas Development Institute, London, 35 pp.

Technical Advisory Committee (TAC, CGIAR) (1985) Report of the external programme review of the International Food Policy Research Institute. TAC Secretariat, FAO, Rome, xxiii pp. and 82 pp. (plus Annexes 1–VIII each paged separately).

Technical Advisory Committee (TAC, CGIAR) (1991) Report of the second external programme review of the International Food Policy Research Institute. TAC Secretariat, FAO, Rome, xxii pp. and 95 pp. (plus Annexes I–X, each paged separately).

Technical Advisory Committee (TAC, CGIAR) (1998) Report of the third external programme and management review of the International Food Policy Research Institute. TAC Secretariat, FAO, Rome, 94 pp.

Part III The Outsiders' View: Issues, Expectations and Agendas

Not Just One Best System: the Diversity of Institutions for Coping with the Commons[1]

16

Elinor Ostrom

As an outsider to the Consultative Group on International Agriculture Research (CGIAR), I cannot contribute to the internal organizational questions of direct relevance to its network. Rather, I will focus on the content of important social science questions that many of us have been exploring in recent years. We all need to address these questions in the future. The CGIAR network cannot continue to make a major impact on agricultural and resource policy without addressing the social science foundations of agricultural resource policy. Many CGIAR reports have been extremely valuable in my own research. However, the CGIAR network has undertaken substantially less social science than biophysical research. Affecting the institutions that enhance productivity in developing countries is impossible without extensive social science research. Thus, I will review the issues that I think should be on the CGIAR research agenda.

We have witnessed a number of policy failures in natural resources management in the last century (Sussman *et al.*, 1994; Wunsch and Olowu, 1995; Liu *et al.*, 2003; Myers and Worm, 2003; Curran *et al.*, 2004). If the theories used to propose new policies are faulty, then the policies based on these theories will fail (Dietz *et al.*, 2003). We need to learn from past errors but unfortunately, some of our errors have been repeated unnecessarily. The substantial investments in biophysical research of recent decades, inside and outside the CGIAR network, are not matched by investments in social science research. Thus, even after a variety of donor agencies

©CAB International 2006. *Researching the Culture in Agri-*Culture:
Social Research for International Development
(eds M.M. Cernea and A.H. Kassam)

have spent large sums to assist development, we are faced with the following tragic results:

- Food sufficiency is now lower in some countries, particularly in Africa, than it was multiple decades ago.
- Poverty has remained constant or worsened in many countries.
- The number of authoritarian regimes in regions such as Africa has increased over time.
- Multiple civil wars have plagued the world over the last several decades, with millions of people killed.

All in all, development assistance has had too many failures, which should warn us that our underlying theories require some serious rethinking (Gibson *et al.*, 2005).

The Commons and International Development Research

Since the publication of Hardin's (1968) powerful metaphor on the 'tragedy of the commons', scientists and policymakers have searched for the 'one best system' to overcome the incapacity of resource users to devise their own effective institutions. Hardin recommended that government impose solutions on the trapped users of pasture lands, forests, irrigation systems, lakes and other commons. He argued that only two externally imposed systems could sustain natural resources in the long run – centralized government or private property.

Multiple reasons exist to recommend facilitating a diversity of governance solutions rather than to presume that, with enough research, we will be able to find the one best system. As social scientists continue to do rigorous research they consistently find that the resources to be governed in a sustainable manner are complex, as are the people and organizations that use them. While field and laboratory research demonstrates that not all users of common-pool resources are trapped in tragic overuse – as Hardin earlier argued – research also demonstrates the wide variety of specific rules and policies that work effectively in some settings and fail in others.

Some scholars find it frustrating that the best social science can do is to urge the importance of multiple institutional arrangements to solve collective-action problems. When hearing that the advantages and limits of multiple systems, rather than one best system, should be understood, some colleagues become impatient. We are familiar with the large number of medical remedies that have been developed over time. One best medicine does not exist for the multiplicity of biophysical ailments that affect an individual. Why we should expect a magic 'aspirin' for all social policies is a mystery. The sooner we learn that there is no one best system, the easier it will be to recognize the importance of a diversity of institutional solutions and to allow experimentation at multiple levels to continuously search out more efficient solutions. We need to resist the donors' frequent requests to provide blueprints. Often, they are plans for failure.

Common-pool Resources

Most natural resource systems used by multiple individuals can be classified as common-pool resources. They generate finite quantities of resource units such as fish, water or timber. The harvesting activities of one person lessen the resource units available to others (E. Ostrom *et al.*, 1994). Most common-pool resources are sufficiently large that multiple actors can simultaneously use the resource system, and efforts to exclude some potential beneficiaries are costly.

When the resource units are highly valued and many actors benefit from appropriating (harvesting) them for consumption, exchange or as a factor in production, one individual's appropriations are likely to create negative externalities for others. An unregulated, open-access common-pool resource generating highly valued resource units is likely to be overused and even destroyed if the stock or the facility generating the resource flow is destroyed.

Conventional Theory of Common-pool Resources

Since the important early studies of open-access fisheries by Gordon (1954) and Scott (1955), most theoretical studies by political economists have analysed simple common-pool resource systems using similar assumptions (Feeny *et al.*, 1996). The resource is assumed to generate a highly predictable, finite supply of one type of resource unit (one species, for example) in a time period. Appropriators are assumed to have homogeneous assets, skills, rates and cultural views, and to be short-term, profit-maximizing actors who possess complete information. In this theory anyone can enter the resource and appropriate resource units. Appropriators gain property rights only to what they harvest, which they then sell in an open, competitive market. Open access is a given. The appropriators make no effort to change it. Appropriators act independently and do not communicate or coordinate their activities in any way.

In this setting, as Gordon and Scott incisively demonstrated, each fisher will take into account only his own marginal costs and revenues and ignore the fact that increases in his catch lessen other fishers' returns as well as harm the health of future fish stocks. The possible long-term economic returns to resource users are dissipated, and economic overfishing, which may also lead to ecological overfishing, is the result (Feeny *et al.*, 1996: 189).

Until recently, much of the economics literature has not seriously considered the possibility that appropriators would find ways to organize themselves. Organizing to define participants' rights and duties creates a public good for those involved. All users benefit from this public good, whether they contribute or not. Thus, getting 'out of the trap' is a second-level dilemma. Investing in monitoring and sanctioning activities to encourage participants to follow the agreements they have made also generates a public good. These investments, therefore, represent a third-level dilemma. Since much of the initial problem exists because the individuals are supposed to be stuck in a setting where they generate negative externalities on one another, their solving second- and third-level dilemmas to address the first-level dilemma is not consistent with conventional theory.

Many textbooks in resource economics and law and economics present this conventional theory of a simple common-pool resource as the only one needed to understand common-pool resources more generally. (However, for a different approach, see Baland and Platteau, 1996 and Kaimowitz and Angelsen, 1998.)

Until the work of the National Academy of Sciences' Panel on Common Property (National Research Council, 1986), this basic theory was applied to all common-pool resources regardless of appropriators' capacity to communicate and coordinate their activities. The growing evidence from many studies of common-pool resources called for a serious rethinking of the theoretical foundations for resource analysis (see Berkes, 1986, 1989; McCay and Acheson, 1987; Berkes *et al.*, 1989; Bromley *et al.*, 1992; Meinzen-Dick *et al.*, 2002). These studies challenge not the empirical validity of the conventional theory but rather its generalizability. Recent research has provided a strong empirical foundation for the study of a variety of governance mechanisms to make common-pool resources more sustainable (National Research Council, 2002; Dietz *et al.*, 2003).

Self-organized Resource Governance Systems in the Field

Most common-pool resources are more complex than the base theory of homogeneous appropriators taking one type of resource unit from a resource system that generates a predictable flow of units. Small to medium-sized irrigation systems come closer than many biological resources to approximating the conditions of the formal models and are thus an appropriate setting in which to examine these patterns of relationships quantitatively (Coward, 1979, 1985). One resource unit, 'water', is the focus of efforts to organize and coordinate activities. Recent research on small to medium-sized irrigation systems in Nepal has found substantial differences in performance between those systems owned and governed by the farmers themselves in contrast to those owned and operated (but, in some cases, not governed) by a national governmental agency (Shivakoti and Ostrom, 2001).

While most farmers own land in Nepal, most own very small parcels of less than 1 ha. The farmers are relatively homogeneous, preferring to obtain water for rice production during the monsoon and winter seasons and for various crops during the spring. Farmers in Nepal have long had the authority to create their own water associations, construct and maintain their own systems and monitor and enforce conformance to their rules (see Benjamin *et al.,* 1994; Lam *et al.,* 1997). The irrigation systems constructed and maintained by farmers tend to rely on low-technology construction techniques, including building non-permanent headworks from mud, trees and stones. International aid agencies have considerably funded government agencies to upgrade engineering standards.

In a detailed analysis of data from 150 farmer-governed and national government irrigation systems in Nepal, W.F. Lam (1998) develops three performance measures: (i) physical condition of irrigation systems; (ii) quantity of water available to farmers during different seasons; and (iii) agricultural productivity of the systems. Using multiple regression analysis techniques to control for environmental differences among systems, Lam finds several variables strongly related to these dependent variables. One is the form of governance of the system. Holding other variables constant, irrigation systems governed by the farmers themselves perform significantly better on all three performance measures. This variable has the greatest explanatory power of any in Lam's analysis, including the physical size of the system, terrain characteristics and number of farmers.

Thus, farmers with long-term ownership claims, who can communicate, develop their own agreements, establish monitors and sanction those who do not conform to their own rules, are more likely to grow more rice, distribute water more equitably and keep their systems in better repair than appropriators using government systems. While the performance of Nepali systems varies, few perform as poorly as government systems, holding other relevant variables constant. Since many of the government systems rely on high-technology engineering, farmers' capability to increase agricultural production of their 'primitive systems', while also providing the labour to maintain and operate the systems, is particularly noteworthy. The extensive field studies demonstrate both the feasibility and the vulnerability of democratic governance (V. Ostrom, 1997).

On the Origin of Self-governed, Common-pool Resources

Evidence from field research challenges the generalizability of conventional theory (Feeny, 1988; Alcorn and Toledo, 1998; Arnold, 1998; Arnold and Stewart, 1991; Gibson *et al.*, 2000). While it is generally successful in predicting outcomes where appropriators are alienated from one another or cannot communicate effectively, conventional theory does not explain settings where appropriators are able to create and sustain agreements to avoid serious problems of overappropriation. Nor does conventional theory predict well when government ownership will perform appropriately or how privatization will improve outcomes. A fully articulated, reformulated theory encompassing conventional theory as a special case does not yet exist. Scholars familiar with the results of field research, however, substantially agree on a set of variables that enhance the likelihood of appropriators organizing themselves to avoid the social losses associated with open-access, common-pool resources (Schlager, 1990; E. Ostrom, 1990, 1992; Cernea, 1992; ; McKean, 1992, 2000; Tang, 1992; E. Ostrom, *et al.*, 1994; Wade, 1994; Baland and Platteau, 1996). Drawing heavily on E. Ostrom (1992: 298–299) and Baland and Platteau (1996: 286–289), considerable consensus exists that the following attributes of resources and appropriators increase the likelihood that self-governing associations will form (see also Meinzen-Dick and Knox, 2001).

Attributes of the resource:
R1. Feasible improvement: resource conditions are not at a point of deterioration where it is useless to organize or so underutilized that little advantage results from organizing.
R2. Indicators: reliable and valid indicators of the condition of the resource system are frequently available at a relatively low cost.

R3. Predictability: the flow of resource units is relatively predictable.
R4. Spatial extent: the resource system is sufficiently small, given the transportation and communication technology in use, that appropriators can develop accurate knowledge of external boundaries and internal microenvironments.

Attributes of the appropriators:
A1. Salience: appropriators are dependent on the resource system for a major portion of their livelihood.
A2. Common understanding: appropriators have a shared image of how the resource system operates (attributes R1–R4 above) and how their actions affect each other and the resource system.
A3. Low discount rate: appropriators use a sufficiently low discount rate in relation to future benefits to be achieved from the resource.
A4. Trust and reciprocity: appropriators trust one another to keep promises and relate to one another with reciprocity.
A5. Autonomy: appropriators are able to determine access and harvesting rules without external authorities countermanding them.
A6. Prior organizational experience and local leadership: appropriators have learned at least minimal skills of organization and leadership through participation in other local associations or how neighbouring groups have organized.

It is important to stress that many of these variables are, in turn, affected by the type of larger regime in which users are embedded. Larger regimes can facilitate local self-organization by providing accurate information about natural resource systems, providing arenas in which participants can engage in discovery and conflict resolution and providing mechanisms to back up local monitoring and sanctioning efforts. The probability of participants adopting more effective rules in macro regimes that facilitate their efforts over time is higher than in regimes that ignore resource problems entirely or at the other extreme, presume that all decisions about governance and management need to be made by central authorities (see for example, Acheson, 2003). How these variables jointly affect benefits and costs is discussed in E. Ostrom (1999).

Theoretical Puzzles

In addition to the consensus concerning the variables most likely to enhance self-organization, many theoretical issues about self-governance of common-pool resources remain unresolved. Two major issues are the effects of size and heterogeneity.

Size

The effect of the number of participants facing problems of creating and sustaining a self-governing enterprise is unclear. Drawing on the early work of Olson (1965), many theorists argue that group size is negatively related to solving collective-action problems in general (see also Buchanan and Tullock, 1962). Many results from game theoretical analysis of repeated games conclude that cooperative strategies are more likely to emerge and be sustained in small groups (see synthesis of this literature in Baland and Platteau, 1996). Scholars who have studied many self-organized irrigation and forestry institutions in the field have concluded that smaller groups will more likely be successful (see for example, Barker *et al.,* 1984; Cernea, 1989; Hilton, 1992).

A problem with focusing on group size as a key determining factor is that many other variables change as it increases (Chamberlin, 1974; Hardin, 1982). If the costs of providing a public good related to the use of a common-pool resource, say a sanctioning system, remain relatively constant as group size increases, then increasing the number of participants brings additional resources that could be drawn upon to benefit all. Marwell and Oliver (1993: 45) conclude that when a 'good has pure jointness of supply, group size has a positive effect on the probability that it will be provided'. However, if one is analysing the conflict levels over a subtractable good and the transaction costs of arriving at acceptable allocation formulas, group size may well exacerbate the problems of self-governing systems. Since there are tradeoffs among various impacts of size on other variables, a better working hypothesis is that group size has a curvilinear relationship to performance.

Heterogeneity

Many scholars conclude that only very small groups can organize themselves effectively, because they presume that size is related to a group's homogeneity and that it is needed to initiate and sustain self-governance. Heterogeneity is also a highly contested variable. For one thing, groups can differ along a diversity of dimensions, including their cultural backgrounds, interests and endowments (see Baland and Platteau, 1996). Each group may operate differently.

If groups coming from diverse cultural backgrounds share access to a common resource, the key question affecting the likelihood of self-organized solutions is whether the views of the multiple groups concerning the structure of the resource, authority, interpretation of rules, trust and reciprocity differ or are similar. In other words, do the groups share a common understanding of their situation? New settlers may simply learn and accept the rules of the established group, and their cultural differences do not affect their participation in governing a resource. New settlers, however, are frequently highly disruptive to the sustenance of a self-governing enterprise when they generate higher levels of conflict over the interpretation and application of rules and substantially increase enforcement costs.

When the interests of appropriators differ, achieving a self-governing solution to common-pool resource problems is particularly challenging. Appropriators who possess more substantial economic and political assets may have similar interests to those with fewer assets or differ substantially on multiple attributes. When they have similar interests, the more powerful may greatly enhance the probability of successful organization if they invest their resources in organizing a group and devising rules to govern it. Those with substantial economic and political assets are more likely to be members of the group that makes rules and thus have a bigger impact on decisions about institutional changes. Olson (1965) long ago recognized the possibility that some sufficiently affected members of a privileged group would bear a disproportionate share of the costs of organizing to provide public goods (such as organizing a collective).

Some fisheries where local subsistence fishers have a strong interest in sustaining an inshore fishery have this problem, while industrial fishing firms have many other options and may be more interested in the profitability of fishing in a particular location than its sustained yield. The conflict between absentee livestock owners versus local pastoralists has also proved difficult to solve in many parts of the world.

Differential endowments of appropriators can be associated with extreme levels of conflict as well as smooth and low-cost transitions to a sustainable, self-governed system. Johnson and Libecap (1982) reason that the difference in the skills and knowledge of different kinds of fishers frequently prevents them from agreeing on how to allocate quantitative harvesting quotas (see also Scott, 1993). In this case, heterogeneity of endowments and of interests coincide. Heterogeneity of wealth or power may or may not be associated with a difference in interests. When those who have more assets share similar interests with those who have fewer, groups may be privileged by having the more powerful take on the higher initial costs of organizing while crafting rules that benefit a large proportion of the appropriators. They may design institutions that cope effectively with heterogeneities. Thus, when such appropriators adopt rules that allocate benefits using the same formulas used to allocate duties and responsibilities, appropriators who have significantly different assets will tend to agree to and follow such rules.

What Kinds of Systems do Appropriators Design?

With this change in perspective, we can think of appropriators trying to understand the biophysical structure of a common-pool resource and how to affect each other's incentives to increase the probability of long-term sustainable and more efficient use.[2] Instead of being given a set of instructions fully specifying the transformation function, appropriators have to explore and discover the biophysical structure of a particular resource that will differ on key parameters from similar resources in the same region (Shepherd, 1992; Thomson *et al.*, 1992; Wilson, 1997). Appropriators also have to cope with considerable uncertainty related to the weather, complicated growth patterns of biological systems that may at times be chaotic and external price fluctuations affecting the costs of inputs and value of outcomes (see Wilson *et al.*, 1991, 1994). In addition to the physical changes that appropriators can make in the resource, the tools they can use to change the structure of the action situations they face consist of seven clusters of rules that directly affect the components of the action situations. Specifically, the rules the appropriators can change include the following:

- boundary rules, affecting the participants' characteristics;
- authority rules, affecting the actions that participants in positions may, must or must not do;
- payoff rules, affecting assigned costs and benefits to actions and outcomes;
- position rules, differentially affecting the capabilities and responsibilities of those in positions;
- information rules, affecting the kind of information present or absent in a situation;
- scope rules, affecting the outcomes that are allowed, mandated or forbidden; and
- aggregation rules, affecting how individual actions are transformed into final outcomes.

Given that action situations are non-linear and complex, the effect of changing a particular rule is rarely easy to predict. For example, changing a boundary rule to restrict the entry of appropriators simultaneously reduces the number of people who are tempted to break authority rules, but also reduces the number of people who monitor what is happening or contribute funds to hire a guard. Thus, opportunities for rule breaking may increase. The cost of a rule infraction will be spread over a smaller group of appropriators and thus, the harm to any individual may be greater. Assessing the overall effects of a change in boundary rules is a non-trivial, analytical task (for examples, see Weissing and Ostrom, 1991a,b). Instead of conducting such a complete analysis, appropriators are more apt to use their intuitive understanding of the resource and each other to experiment with different rule changes until finding a combination that seems to work.

To better understand the types of tools available to appropriators, let us examine in some detail the kinds of boundary, authority, payoff and position rules used in field settings. These four clusters of rules are the major tools used to effect appropriation situations in many common-pool resources, while information, scope and aggregation rules are used to complement the induced changes.

For the past 20 years, colleagues at or associated with Indiana University have studied a large number of irrigation systems, forests, inshore fisheries and groundwater basins, as well as other common-pool resources (see Schlager, 1990; E. Ostrom, 1990, 1996; Tang, 1992; Schlager *et al.,* 1994; Lam, 1998; Gibson *et al.,* 2000). We have collected an immense archive of original case studies conducted by many different scholars associated with the CGIAR centres as well as with other research groups in all parts of the world (Hess, 1999; http://www.indiana.edu/~workshop).

We developed a coding manual with structured coding forms to help us identify specific kinds of action situations faced in the field, as well as the types of rules that users have evolved to try to govern and manage their resource effectively (E. Ostrom *et al.,* 1989). To develop standardized coding forms, we read hundreds of cases describing how local common-pool resources were or were not regulated by a government agency, the users or a non-governmental organization (NGO).

Affecting the Characteristics of Users through Boundary Rules

The most frequent recommendation concerning boundary rules in the policy literature is to limit the number of people allowed to appropriate from a common-pool resource to reduce the level of appropriation, or to require users to obtain a licence before harvesting. Boundary rules affect the types of participants with whom other participants will be interacting. If contingent cooperation is perceived to be a possibility, then one of the most important ways to enhance the likelihood of using reciprocity norms is to increase the proportion of participants who are well known in a community, have a long-term stake in that community and would find it costly to have their reputation for trustworthiness harmed. Reducing the number of users, but opening the resource to strangers willing to pay a licence fee but lacking a long-term interest in the sustainability of a particular

Table 16.1. Variables used in boundary rules to define who is authorized to appropriate from a resource.

Residency or membership	Personal characteristics	Relationship with resource
National	Ascribed	Continued use of resource
Regional	Age	Long-term rights based on:
Local community	Caste	
Organization (e.g. cooperative)	Clan	Ownership of a proportion of annual flow of resource units
	Class	
	Ethnicity	Ownership of land
	Gender	Ownership of non-land asset (e.g. berth)
	Race	
	Acquired	Ownership of shares in a private organization
	Education level	
	Skill test	Ownership of a share of the resource system
		Temporary use-rights acquired through:
		Auction
		Per-use fee
		Licenses
		Lottery
		Registration
		Seasonal fees
		Use of specified technology

Source: E. Ostrom (1999: 510).

resource, may reduce the level of trust and willingness to use reciprocity and thus substantially increase enforcement costs.

We identified 26 boundary rules described by case-study authors as having been used in at least one common-pool resource (Table 16.1) (E. Ostrom *et al.*, 1989). While some systems use only a single boundary rule, many use two or three in combination. Boundary rules can be broadly classified into three general groups defining how individuals gain authority to enter and appropriate resource units from a common-pool resource. The first type of boundary rule relates to an individual's citizenship, residency or membership in a particular organization. Many forestry and fishing user groups require members to have been born in a particular location. A second broad group of rules relates to ascribed or acquired personal characteristics. Other user groups may require that appropriation depend on ethnicity, clan or caste. A third group of boundary rules relates to the relationship of an individual with the resource. Using a particular technology or acquiring appropriation rights through an auction or a lottery are examples of this type of rule. About half the rules relate to the users' characteristics. The other half involve diverse relationships with the resource.

In a systematic coding of those case studies for which sufficient information existed about rules related to inshore fisheries in many parts of the world, Schlager (1990, 1994) coded 33 user groups out of the 44 identified as having at least some rules on resource use. All 33 groups depended on a combination of 14 boundary rules (Schlager, 1994: 258). None of these groups relied on only one boundary rule. Of the 33 groups, 30 (91%) limited fishing to people from a nearby community, while 13 also required membership in a local organization. Consequently, most user-organized inshore fisheries restrict fishing to people who are well known to each other, have a relatively long-term time horizon and are connected to one another in multiple ways (see Taylor, 1982; Singleton and Taylor, 1992).

After residency, the next most frequent type of rule, used by two-thirds of the organized subgroups, involves the type of technology that a potential fisher must be willing to use. This kind of rule is often criticized by policy analysts, since gear restrictions reduce the 'efficiency' of fishing. However, gear restrictions have many consequences. Used in combination with authority rules that assign fishers using one type of gear to one area and fishers using another type of gear to a second area, gear restrictions solve conflicts among non-compatible technologies. Many gear restrictions also reduce the load on the fishery and thus help sustain its long-term use.

Other rules were also used. A scattering of groups used ascribed characteristics: two groups used age, three used ethnicity and five used race. Three types of temporary use rights included government licences (three groups), lottery (five groups) and registration (four groups). Seven groups required participants to have purchased an asset such as a fishing berth, while three required ownership of nearby land. Schlager did not find that any particular boundary rule was correlated with higher performance levels, but she did find that the 33 groups that had at least one boundary rule were able to solve common-pool problems more effectively than the 11 groups that had not crafted boundary rules.

In a closely related study of 43 small to medium-sized irrigation systems managed by farmers or by government agencies, Tang (1992) found that a smaller variety of rules was used in irrigation than among inshore fisheries. The single most frequently used boundary rule, used in 32 of the 43 systems (74%), was that an irrigator must own land in the service area of an irrigation system (Tang, 1992: 84–85). All of the government-owned and -operated irrigation systems relied on this rule alone. Many of the user-organized systems relied on other rules or on land ownership combined with other rules. Among the other rules used were ownership of a proportion of the flow of the resource, membership in a local organization and a per-use fee. Tang (1992: 87) found a strong negative relationship between reliance on land as the sole boundary requirement and performance. Over 90% of the systems using other boundary rules or a combination of rules, including land ownership, were rated positively in the level of maintenance achieved and of rule conformance, while less than 40% of systems relying solely on land ownership were rated at a higher performance level ($P = 0.001$). Many government systems are designed on paper to serve an area larger than they are actually able to, due to a variety of factors, including the need to show as many posited beneficiaries as possible to justify the cost of construction (see Palanisami, 1982; Repetto, 1986; Meinzen-Dick *et al.,* 2002). After construction, authorized irrigators find water to be scarce and are unwilling to abide by authority rules or help maintain the system.

Thus, many of the richly diverse boundary rules used by appropriators in the field attempt to ensure that they will be relating to others who live nearby and have a long-term interest in sustaining the productivity of the resource. One way of coping with the commons is thus changing the composition of who uses a common-pool resource to increase the proportion of participants who have a long-term interest, are more likely to use reciprocity and who can be trusted. Central governments use a smaller set of rules and some of these may open up a resource to strangers without a long-term commitment to the resource.

Affecting the Set of Allowable Actions through Authority Rules

Authority rules are also often used to regulate common-pool resources. In the coding manual (E. Ostrom *et al.,* 1989), we identified a diversity of authority rules used in field settings. Some rules involve a simple formula. Many forest resources, for example, are closed to all forms of harvesting during one part of the year and open for extraction by all who meet the boundary rules during the open season. However, most authority rules have two components. Table 16.2 shows the eight allocation formulas used in the field in the left column. A fisher might be assigned to a fixed location (a fishing spot) or a fixed rotational schedule, a member of the founding clan may be authorized to cut timber anywhere in a forest, while an irrigator might be assigned to a fixed percentage of the total water available during a season or to a fixed time

Table 16.2. Types of authority rules.

Allocation formula for appropriation rights	Basis for allocation formula
Percentage of total available units per period	Amount of land held
	Amount of historical use
Quantity of resource units per period	Location of appropriator
Location	Quantity of shares of resource owned
Time slot	
Rotational order	Proportion of resource flow owned
Appropriate only during open seasons	Purchase of periodic rights at auction
Appropriate only resource units meeting criteria	Rights acquired through periodic lottery
Appropriate anytime and anywhere	Technology used
	Licence issued by a governmental authority
	Equal division to all appropriators
	Needs of appropriators (e.g. type of crop)
	Ascribed characteristic of appropriator
	Membership in organization
	Assessment of resource condition

Source: E. Ostrom (1999: 512).

slot. In addition to the formula used in an authority rule, most rules require a basis for the assignment. For example, a fisher might be assigned to a fixed location based on a number drawn in a lottery, on the purchase of that spot in an auction or on the basis of his or her historical use. An irrigator might be assigned to a fixed rotation based on the amount of land owned, amount of water used historically or specific location of the irrigator.

If all the bases were combined with all the formulas, 112 different authority rules would result (eight allocation formulas × 14 bases). A further complication is that the rules for one product may differ from those for another in the same resource. For example, children may be authorized to pick fruit from any tree in a forest for their own consumption, women may be authorized to collect a certain number of headloads of dead wood for domestic firewood and certain plants for making crafts, while only shaman are authorized to collect medicinal plants from a particular location in a forest (Fortmann and Bruce, 1988). Appropriation rights to fish are frequently related to a specific species. Thus, the exact number of rules used in the field is difficult to compute since not all bases are used with all formulas, and many rules focus only on specific products. A further complication is that the rules may regularly change over the course of a year, depending on resource conditions.

Schlager (1994: 259–260) found that all 33 organized subgroups used one of the five basic formulas in their authority rules. Every user group she studied assigned fishers to fixed locations using a diversity of bases, including technology, lottery or historical use. Thus, spatial demarcations are a critical variable for inshore fisheries. Nine user groups required fishers to limit their harvest to fish of a specific size, while seven groups allocated fishers to fishing spots using a rotation system and seven others only allowed fishing locations to be used during a specific season. Four groups allocated fishing spots for a particular time period (a fishing day or season).

An important finding – given the puzzles addressed in this chapter – is that the authority rule most frequently recommended by policy analysts (see Anderson, 1986, 1992; Copes, 1986) is not used in any of the coastal fisheries included in Schlager's study. Thus, no attempt was made 'by the fishers involved to directly regulate the quantity of fish harvested based on an estimate of the yield. This is particularly surprising given that the most frequently recommended policy prescription made by fishery economists is the use of individual transferable quotas based on estimates on the economically optimal quantity of fish to be harvested over the long run' (Schlager, 1994: 265; see also Anderson *et al.*, 1988). In an independent study of 30 traditional fishery societies, Acheson and colleagues also noted the surprising absence of quota rules.

All of the rules and practices we found in these 30 societies regulate 'how' fishing is done. That is, they limit the times fish may be caught, the locations where fishing is allowed, the technology permitted, and the stage of the life cycle during which fish may be taken. None of these societies limits the 'amount' of various species that can be caught. Quotas – the single most important concept and tools of scientific management – is conspicuous by its absence.

(Acheson *et al.*, 1998: 397; see also Wilson *et al.*, 1994)

Local inshore fishers, when allowed to manage a riparian area, thus use rules that differ substantially from those recommended by advocates of scientific management. Just to succeed, fishers have to know a great deal about the ecology of their inshore region, including spawning areas, nursery areas, migration routes of different species and seasonal patterns. Over time, fishers learn how 'to maintain these critical life-cycle processes with rules controlling technology, fishing locations and fishing times. Such rules in their view are based on biological reality' (Acheson *et al.*, 1998: 405).

In the irrigation systems studied by Tang (1992: 90–91), three types of authority rules are used most frequently: (i) a fixed time slot is assigned to each irrigator (in 19 out of the 37 cases for which data are available); (ii) a fixed order for a rotation system among irrigators (13 cases); and (iii) a fixed percentage of the total water available during a period of time (five cases). A variety of bases were used in these rules such as 'amount of land held, amount of water needed to cultivate existing crops, number of shares held, location of field, or official discretion' (Tang, 1994: 233). Three poorly performing systems with high levels of conflict use no authority rule at all.

Farmers also do not use rules that assign a specific quantity of water to irrigators other than in the rare circumstances where they control substantial amounts of water in storage (see Maass and Anderson, 1986). Fixed time-slot rules allow farmers considerable certainty as to when they will receive water, without an equivalent certainty about the quantity of water that will be available in the canal. When the order is based on a share system, simply owning land next to an irrigation system is not enough. A farmer must purchase one or more shares to irrigate for a particular time. Fixed time allocation systems, which are frequently criticized as inefficient, do economize greatly on the amount of knowledge farmers need about the entire system and on monitoring costs. Spooner (1974) and Netting (1974) described long-lived irrigation systems in Iran and Switzerland, where there was perfect agreement on the order and time allotted to all farmers in a segment of the system, but no one knew the entire sequence for the whole system.

Tang (1992) also found that many irrigation systems use different sets of rules depending on the availability of water. During the most abundant season, for example, irrigators may be authorized to take water whenever they need it. During a season when water is moderately available, farmers may use a rotation system where every farmer is authorized to take water for a fixed time during the week based on the amount of land to be irrigated. During scarcity, the irrigation system may employ a special water distributor who is authorized to allocate water to those farmers who are growing crops authorized by the irrigation system and are most in need.

The diversity of rules devised by users greatly exceeds the limited authority rules recommended in textbook treatments of this problem. Appropriators thus cope with the commons by using a wide variety of rules affecting the actions available to participants and thus their basic set of strategies. Given this wide diversity of rules, it is particularly noteworthy that rules assigning appropriators a right to a specific quantity of a resource are used so infrequently in inshore fisheries and irrigation systems. These rules are used more frequently when allocating forest products where the quantity available, as well as the quantity harvested, are much easier to measure (Agrawal, 1994). To assign an appropriator a specific quantity of a resource unit requires that those making the assignment know the total available units. Where water is stored from one season to another and reliable information about the quantity of water is available, such rules are more frequently utilized (Blomquist, 1992; Schlager *et al.*, 1994).

Affecting Outcomes through Payoff and Position Rules

One way to reduce or redirect the appropriations made from a common-pool resource is to change pay-off rules to penalize prohibited actions. Many user groups socially ostracize or shun rule breakers, and individual appropriators monitor each other's behaviour intensively. Three broad types of payoff rules are used extensively in the field: (i) imposition of a fine; (ii) loss of appropriation rights; and (iii) incarceration. The severity of each starts from very low and ranges up to very high. Inshore fisheries studied by Schlager (1990) relied heavily on shunning and other social norms and less on formal sanctions. Of the 43 irrigation systems studied by Tang (1992, 1994), 36 used one of these three rules and also relied on vigorous monitoring of each other's behaviour and shunning of rule breakers. The seven systems that did not self-consciously punish rule infractions all performed poorly. Fines were most typically used (21 cases), and incarceration was used the least (two cases). Fines start out very low for the first and second offenses and are graduated depending on the seriousness of the infractions and the number of prior infractions.

Passing rules that impose costs is relatively simple. The difficult task is monitoring behaviour to ascertain if rules are being broken. Self-organized fisheries rely on self-monitoring more than on creating a formal guard position. Most inshore fishers now use shortwave radios that allow instant monitoring as a routine part of their day-to-day operations. An official of a West Coast Indian tribe reports, for example, that 'it is not uncommon to hear messages such as "Did you see so-and-so flying all that net?" over the short-wave frequency – a clear reference to a violation of specified gear limits' (cited in Singleton, 1998: 134). Since most fishers will be listening to their shortwave radio, 'such publicity is tantamount to creating a flashing neon sign over the boat of the offender. Such treatment might be preceded or followed by a direct approach to the rule violator, advising him to resolve the problem. In some tribes, a group of fishers might delegate themselves to speak to the person'. (cited in Singleton, 1998: 134).

Among self-organizing, forest governance systems, creating and supporting a guard position is frequently essential, since resource units are highly valuable and a few hours of stealth can generate substantial illicit income. Monitoring of rule conformance among forest users by officially designated and paid guards may make the difference between a resource in good condition and one that has become degraded. In a study of 279 forest *panchayats* (councils) in the Kumaon region of India, Agrawal and Yadama (1997) found that the number of months a guard was hired was the most important variable affecting forest conditions. The other variables included the number of meetings held by the forest panchayats (when infractions are discussed) and the number of villagers.

The analysis shows that a forest council's capacity to monitor and sanction rule breakers is paramount to maintaining the forest in good condition. The presence of a guard should not be taken simply as a formal mechanism that ensures greater protection but also an indication of the commitment of the panchayat and village to protect their forests. Hiring a guard costs money. The funds have to be generated within the village and earmarked for protection of the resource. If interest in protecting the forest is scant, villagers will not contribute the money necessary to hire a guard (Agrawal and Yadama, 1997: 455).

Whether the monitors of irrigation systems create a formal guard position depends on the type of governance and size of the system. Four-fifths of the government-owned irrigation systems included in Tang's study (1992) have established a guard position. Stealing water was a problem in most government-owned systems, but it was endemic in the systems without guards. Of the 28 farmer-organized systems, 17 (61%) have a water distributor or guard. Of the 11 farmer-organized systems that do not employ a guard, farmers in five systems (45%) are vigilant enough in monitoring each other's activities that rule conformance is

high. This means, of course, that self-monitoring is not high enough in
the other six systems to support routine conformance with their rules.

A study by de los Reyes (1980a,b) of 51 communal irrigation systems in the Philippines illustrates the effect of size on the presence of
guards. Of the 30 systems that are less than 50 ha, only six (20%) have
established a guard position; of the 11 that serve 50–100 ha, five (45%)
have formal guards; and of the 10 that serve over 100 ha, seven (70%)
have created guard positions. She also found in a survey of over
600 farmers served by these communal irrigation systems that most
farmers also patrol their own canals even when these are patrolled by
guards accountable to the farmers for distributing water. The proportion of farmers who report patrolling the canals serving their farms
increases to 80% in the largest self-organized systems, compared to
60% in the smallest systems.

Creating a guard position also requires a change in payoff rules to
be able to remunerate a guard. Several formulae are used. On government-owned irrigation systems, guards are normally paid a monthly
wage that is not dependent on the performance of a system or farmers'
satisfaction. In South India, Wade (1994) describes self-organized systems where the water distributor-guard goes to each farmer to collect
his share of the harvest based on the amount of land owned by the
farmer. Sengupta (1991: 104) describes another system where immediately after appointment, the guards 'are taken to the temple for oath
taking to remain impartial. With this vow, they break a coconut. They
are paid in cash at the rate of Rs10/acre per month by the cultivators.
The *neerpaichys*[3] themselves collect the money'. With such subtle
ways of changing how the payment is made to this position, farmers
are able to monitor the situation more effectively.

Boundary and authority rules also affect how easy or difficult it is
to monitor activities and sanction rule infractions. Closing a forest or
an inshore fishery for a substantial amount of time, for example, has
multiple impacts. It protects particular plants or fish during critical
growing periods and allows the entire system time to regenerate without disturbance. During the closed season, rule infractions are highly
obvious to anyone, as any appropriator in the resource, e.g. forest or
fishing area, is almost certainly breaking the rules. Similarly, requiring
appropriators to use a particular technology may reduce the pressure
on the resource, help resolve conflicts among users of incompatible
technologies and make it easy to ascertain if rules are being followed.
Many irrigation systems are set up with rotations so only two people
need to monitor actions at any one time, thus keeping monitoring costs
low. Changing payoff rules is the most direct way of coping with commons dilemmas. In many instances, dilemma games can be transformed into assurance games – a much easier situation to solve.

Affecting Outcomes through Changes in Information, Scope and Aggregation Rules

Information, scope and aggregation rules are used in ways that complement changes in boundary, authority, payoff and position rules. Individual systems vary radically in regard to the information they require. Many small and informal systems rely entirely on a voluntary exchange of information and on mutual monitoring. Where resource units are valuable and the group is large, more and more requirements are added regarding the information that must be kept by appropriators or their officials. Scope rules are used to limit harvesting activities in some regions that are treated as refugia. Prohibiting appropriation from these locations enhances the regenerative capacity of a system. Aggregation rules are used extensively in collective-choice processes and less extensively in operational settings, but one aggregation rule found in diverse systems is that harvesting should be done in teams to increase the opportunity for mutual monitoring and reduce the need to hire special guards.

We have not yet found any rule to have a statistically positive relationship to performance. The absence of any boundary or authority rules is consistently associated with poor performance. Relying on only a single type of rule for an entire set of common-pool resources also does not improve performance. Self-organized irrigation systems do perform better than government-organized systems, controlling for physical terrain, but not due to any specific rules or set of rules that we have identified.

Policies as Experiments

Searching for better rules

The search for rules that improve the outcomes obtained in commons dilemmas is an incredibly complex task involving a potentially infinite combination of specific rules that could be adopted. To ascertain whether a set of rules will improve the outcomes achieved in a single situation, one would need to analyse how diverse rules from the seven clusters affect the components of such a situation and, as a result, the likely effect of a reformed structure on incentives, strategies and outcomes. Since multiple rules affect each component, conducting such an analysis would be extremely time and resource consuming.

How these changes affect the outcomes achieved in a particular location depends on its biophysical characteristics and the type of community relationships. No set of policy analysts (or even all the game theorists in the world) could ever have sufficient time or resources to analyse all the combinations of rule changes and resulting situations, let alone all the variance in these situations due to bio-physical differences.

Experimenting with rule changes

Instead of assuming that designing rules that approach optimality, or even improve performance, is a simple analytical task that can be undertaken by distant, objective analysts, we need to understand the policy design process as involving an effort to tinker with a large num-ber of component parts (see Jacob, 1977; V. Ostrom *et al.*, 1993). Those who tinker with any tools – including rules – are trying to find combin-ations that work together more effectively than others. Policy changes are experiments based on more or less informed expectations about potential outcomes and their distribution for participants across time and space (Campbell, 1969, 1975). Whenever individuals agree to add a rule, change a rule or adopt someone else's proposed rule set, they are conducting a policy experiment. The complexity of the ever-changing biophysical world combined with the complexity of rule systems means that any proposed rule change faces a nontrivial probability of error (Holland, 1995).

When only a single governing authority exists, policymakers have to experiment simultaneously with all the common-pool resources within their jurisdiction with each policy change (Pinkerton, 1989). Once a change has been made and implemented, further changes will not be made rapidly. The process of experimentation will usually be slow, and information about results may be contradictory and difficult to interpret. Thus, an experiment that is based on erroneous data about one key structural variable or one false assumption about how actors will react, can lead to a large disaster (see Wilson *et al.*, 1999). In any design process with substantial probability of error, having redundant teams of designers has repeatedly been shown to have con-siderable advantage (see Landau, 1969, 1973; Bendor, 1985). The important point is: if the systems are relatively separable, allocating responsibility for experimenting with rules will not avoid failure, but will drastically reduce the probability of immense failures for an entire region.

Conclusion

The conventional theory of common-pool resources, which presumed that external authorities were needed to impose new rules on those appropriators trapped into producing excessive externalities on themselves and others, has now been shown to be a special theory of a more general structure. For appropriators to reformulate the institutions they face, they have to conclude that the expected benefits from an institutional change will exceed the immediate and long-term expected costs. When appropriators cannot communicate and have no way of gaining trust through their own efforts or with the help of the macro-institutional system within which they are embedded, the prediction of the earlier theory is empirically supported. Ocean fisheries, the stratosphere and other global commons come closest to the appropriate empirical referents. Devising new institutions to govern global commons, while not impossible, is the greatest challenge facing international actors.

If appropriators can engage in face-to-face bargaining and have autonomy to change their rules, they may attempt to organize themselves. Whether they do depends on the relative net benefits (or costs) they perceive. These benefits and costs depend, in turn, on the attributes of the resource system and the appropriators. Whether their self-governed enterprise succeeds over the long term depends on whether the institutions they design are consistent with design principles underlying robust, long-living, self-governed systems (E. Ostrom, 1990, 2005).

Social scientists within the CGIAR network and at related institutions interested in these questions have substantially contributed to our general knowledge about how diverse institutions enable appropriators and government officials cope more effectively with diverse types of common-pool resources. These social scientists will also help solve the puzzles.

As an outsider who has also interacted repeatedly with CGIAR scholars, I have always been impressed with the overall quality of work of CGIAR centres, even though they have not undertaken as much social science as I think will be necessary to make a theoretical and empirical contribution to understanding social problems as important as the contribution to understanding the genetics of major agricultural crops.

Two CGIAR programmes are particularly noteworthy. One is the imaginative as well as rigorous inter-centre programme on Collective Action and Property Rights (CAPRi) organized by Ruth Meinzen-Dick of International Food Policy Research Institute (IFPRI). Participants in the programme – well known to scholars outside the CGIAR network (see CGIAR, 2003) – have undertaken a steady stream of careful and important research. The other programme is the effort by David Kaimowitz at Center for International Forestry Research (CIFOR) to understand how institutions and economic processes affect tropical deforestation. I keep his monograph with Angelsen (Kaimowitz and Angelsen, 1998) on my desk and refer to it frequently. Their conclusion that 'there are few modeling exercises that explicitly take institutions into account, and the little work to date has been confined almost exclusively to look at the effect of different property regimes' (Kaimowitz and Angelsen, 1998: 104–105) is an important call to action to include institutional arrangements in the frameworks, theories and models we use to analyse forests and other common-pool resources.

All social scientists – those working outside and inside the CGIAR network – face a challenging future. Much research requires the work of social scientists as well as multidisciplinary teams. We need to be working on nested sets of frameworks, theories and models. Frameworks allow scholars from multiple disciplines to begin to identify the range of biophysical and social variables that need to be taken into account consistently when designing research. Theories posit how some of these variables are linked and enable scholars to derive specific propositions that can be tested. Models represent formal efforts to state part of broader theories as a set of mathematical relationships that can be fully analysed or as an agent-based model or other form of simulation that enables one to derive conclusions about complex systems characterized by considerable uncertainty. More work is needed to include institutions overtly in the frameworks, theories and models used to understand the governance (or lack of governance) of common-pool resources (see E. Ostrom, 2005).

Empirical research continues to need case studies of processes used by local appropriators as they may be assisted by NGOs and various levels of government to develop rules to govern and manage common-pool resources. Case studies that follow developments over a long time and those that study failed efforts are particularly important. Studying failures helps us understand why some groups are stymied when others establish initial systems that they adapt over time. Case studies allow scholars to record complex interactions that occur within a particular setting over time and find out why some systems are robust and others collapse after initial efforts to govern them. While theory is not tested by a single case, multiple cases undertaken to examine theoretical questions are still a useful form of social science research. Case studies that do not address theoretical questions are no longer as useful as when theories had not yet been developed (Poteete and Ostrom, 2004).

A second important research approach is laboratory and field experiments (E. Ostrom *et al.*, 1994; Cardenas *et al.*, 2000). Many CGIAR researchers do undertake important experiments – but more often in regard to agricultural processes, rather than the human ones, that enable appropriators to use natural resources sustainably over time. Experimental research enables scholars to examine the impact of one variable while controlling other variables in a simple setting. Social scientists at CGIAR centres would do well to collaborate with experimental researchers at neighbouring universities to develop sequences of experiments to examine the specific combination of variables of most theoretical relevance to a particular research programme.

Studies that collect data from a large number of user groups as they relate to resources enable scholars to test the relative importance of different variables in field settings. Large N studies are among the more expensive that CGIAR centres undertake and need to be carefully designed. Panel studies are particularly valuable in studying how systems respond to external and internal changes.

This is an interesting time in the study of how institutions affect the sustainability of irrigation systems, forests, pastures and other natural resources closely tied to agriculture. All of us have to do much research and make our findings relevant to the appropriators – the extensive world of NGOs working with local irrigators, pastoral peoples and forest users around the world – and to government officials at all levels. No blueprint solutions can be used in all. This is a disappointment to many who want to solve these difficult problems with quick panaceas. Instead, a rich set of institutional options needs to be matched to ecological and cultural conditions. CGIAR colleagues can greatly help avoid a monocultural approach in recommending institutional innovations and understanding the diversity of institutional arrangements that can be considered relevant for any particular environment.

Notes

[1] I wish to thank the National Science Foundation for its support of the Center for the Study of Institutions, Population and Environmental Change, and the CGIAR for the opportunity to participate in this collaborative publication. Thanks to Joanna Broderick, Sarah Kantner, Patty Lezotte and Nicole Todd for helping me with this manuscript.

[2] This section draws on E. Ostrom (1999).

[3] *Neerpaichy* is a locally selected official who monitors the distribution of water according to a set of rules and is responsible for collecting locally assessed irrigation fees.

References

Acheson, J.M. (2003) *Capturing the Commons: Devising Institutions to Manage the Maine Lobster Industry.* University Press of New England, Hanover, New Hampshire, 264 pp.

Acheson, J.M., Wilson, J.A. and Steneck, R.S. (1998) Managing chaotic fisheries. In: Berkes, F. and Folke, C. (eds) *Linking Social and Ecological Systems: Management Practices and Social Mechanisms for Building Resilience.* Cambridge University Press, Cambridge, Massachusetts, pp. 390–413.

Agrawal, A. (1994) Rules, rule making, and rule breaking: examining the fit between rule systems and resource use. In: Ostrom, E., Gardner, R. and Walker, J.M. (eds) *Rules, Games, and Common-Pool Resources.* University of Michigan Press, Ann Arbor, Michigan, pp. 267–282.

Agrawal, A. and Yadama, G.N. (1997) How do local institutions mediate market and population pressures on resources? Forest *panchayats* in Kumaon, India. *Development and Change* 28(3), 435–465.

Alcorn, J.B. and Toledo, V. (1998) Resilient resource management in Mexico's forest ecosystems: the contribution of property rights. In: Berkes, F. and Folke, C. (eds) *Linking Social and Ecological Systems: Management Practices and Social Mechanisms for Building Resilience.* Cambridge University Press, Cambridge, Massachusetts, pp. 216–249.

Anderson, L.G. (1986) *The Economics of Fisheries Management.* Revised edition. Johns Hopkins University Press, Baltimore, Maryland, 296 pp.

Anderson, L.G. (1992) Consideration of the potential use of individual transferable quotas in US fisheries. *The National ITQ Study Report* 1, 1–71.

Anderson, P.W., Arrow, K.J. and Pines, D. (eds) (1988) *The Economy as an Evolving Complex System.* Addison-Wesley, Redwood City, California, 317 pp.

Arnold, J.E.M. (1998) Managing Forests as Common Property. FAO Forestry Paper No. 136. Food and Agriculture Organization of the United Nations, Rome, 67 pp.

Arnold, J.E.M. and Stewart, W.C. (1991) Common Property Resource Management in India. Tropical Forestry Papers No. 24. Oxford Forestry Institute, Oxford, UK, 51 pp.

Baland, J.-M. and Platteau, J.-P. (1996) *Halting Degradation of Natural Resources: Is There a Role for Rural Communities?* Clarendon Press, Oxford, UK, 423 pp.

Barker, R., Coward Jr, E.W., Levine, G. and Small, L.E. (1984) *Irrigation Development in Asia: Past Trends and Future Directions.* Cornell University Press, Ithaca, New York, pp. 79.

Bendor, J.B. (1985) *Parallel Systems: Redundancy in Government.* University of California Press, Berkeley, California, 322 pp.

Benjamin, P., Lam, W.F., Ostrom, E. and Shivakoti, G. (1994) Institutions, Incentives and Irrigation in Nepal. Decentralization: Finance and Management Project Report. Associates in Rural Development, Burlington, Vermont, 154 pp.

Berkes, F. (1986) Local-level management and the commons problem: a comparative study of Turkish coastal fisheries. *Marine Policy* 10, 215–229.

Berkes, F. (ed.) (1989) *Common Property Resources: Ecology and Community-Based Sustainable Development.* Belhaven Press, London, 302 pp.

Berkes, F., Feeny, D., McCay, B.J. and Acheson, J.M. (1989) The benefits of the commons. *Nature* 340 (6229), 91–93.

Blomquist, W. (1992) *Dividing the Waters: Governing Groundwater in Southern California.* Institute for Contemporary Studies Press, Oakland, California, 415 pp.

Bromley, D.W., Feeny, D., McKean, M., Peters, P., Gilles, J., Oakerson, R., Runge, C.F. and Thomson, J. (eds) (1992) *Making the Commons Work: Theory, Practice, and Policy.* Institute for Contemporary Studies Press, Oakland, California, 339 pp.

Buchanan, J.M. and Tullock, G. (1962) *The Calculus of Consent.* University of Michigan Press, Ann Arbor, Michigan, 361 pp.

Campbell, D.T. (1969) Reforms as experiments. *American Psychologist* 24(4), 409–429.

Campbell, D.T. (1975) On the conflicts between biological and social evolution and between psychology and moral tradition. *American Psychologist* 30(11), 1103–1126.

Cardenas, J.C., Stranlund, J. and Willis, C. (2000) Local environmental control and institutional crowding-out. *World Development* 28(10), 1719– 1733.

Cernea, M.M. (1989) User Groups as Producers in Participatory Afforestation Strategies. World Bank Discussion Papers No. 70. The World Bank, Washington, DC, 80 pp.

Cernea, M.M. (1992) A sociological framework: policy, environment, and the social actors for tree planting. In: Sharma, N.P. (ed.) *Managing the World Forests: Looking for Balance between Conservation and Development.* Hunt Publishing Company, Kendall, Iowa, pp. 301–355.

Chamberlin, J. (1974) Provision of collective goods as a function of group size. *American Political Science Review* 68(2), 707–716.

CGIAR Interim Science Council (2003) Report of the First External Review of the systemwide Programme on Collective Action and Property Rights (CAPRi). CGIAR Secretariat, World Bank, Washington, DC, 19 pp.

Copes, P. (1986) A critical review of the individual quota as a device in fisheries management. *Land Economics* 62(3), 278–291.

Coward, E.W. Jr (1979) Principles of social organization in an indigenous irrigation system. *Human Organization* 38, 28–26.

Coward, E.W. Jr (1985) Technical and social change in currently irrigated regions: rules, roles and rehabilitation. In: Cernea, M.M. (ed.) *Putting People First: Sociological Variables in Rural Development.* Oxford University Press, New York, pp. 27–51.

Curran, L.M., Trigg, S.N., McDonald, A.K., Astiani, D., Hardiono, Y.M., Siregar, P., Caniago, I. and Kasischke, E. (2004) Lowland forest loss in protected areas of Indonesian Borneo. *Science* 303, 1000–1003.

de los Reyes, R.P. (1980a) *47 Communal Gravity Systems: Organization*

Profiles. Institute of Philippine Culture, Ateneo de Manila University, Quezon City, Philippines, 360 pp.

de los Reyes, R.P. (1980b) *Managing Communal Gravity Systems: Farmers' Approaches and Implications for Program Planning*. Institute of Philippine Culture, Ateneo de Manila University, Quezon City, Philippines, 125 pp.

Dietz, T., Ostrom, E. and Stern, P. (2003) The struggle to govern the commons. *Science* 302 (5652), 1907–1912.

Feeny, D.H. (1988) Agricultural expansion and forest depletion in Thailand, 1900–1975. In: Richards, J.F. and Tucker, R.P. (eds) *World Deforestation in the Twentieth Century*. Duke University Press, Durham, North Carolina, pp. 112–143.

Feeny, D.H., Hanna, S. and McEvoy, A.F. (1996) Questioning the assumptions of the 'tragedy of the commons' model of fisheries. *Land Economics* 72(2), 187–205.

Fortmann, L. and Bruce, J.W. (1988) *Whose Trees? Proprietary Dimensions of Forestry*. Westview Press, Boulder, Colorado, pp. 341.

Gibson, C., McKean, M.A. and Ostrom, E. (eds) (2000) *People and Forests: Communities, Institutions, and Governance*. The MIT Press, Cambridge, Massachusetts, 274 pp.

Gibson, C., Andersson, K., Ostrom, E. and Shivakumar, S. (2005) *The Samaritan's Dilemma: the Political Economy of Development Aid*. Oxford University Press, Oxford, UK, 320 pp.

Gordon, H.S. (1954) The economic theory of a common property resource: the fishery. *Journal of Political Economy* 62, 124–142.

Hardin, G. (1968) The tragedy of the commons. *Science* 162, 1243–1248.

Hardin, R. (1982) *Collective Action*. Johns Hopkins University Press, Baltimore, Maryland, 248 pp.

Hess, C. (1999) A Comprehensive Bibliography of Common-Pool Resources. (CD-ROM). Workshop in Political Theory and Policy Analysis, Indiana University, Bloomington, Indiana.

Hilton, R. (1992) Institutional incentives for resource mobilization: an analysis of irrigation schemes in Nepal. *Journal of Theoretical Politics* 4(3), 283–308.

Holland, J.H. (1995) *Hidden Order. How Adaptation Builds Complexity*. Addison-Wesley, Reading, Massachusetts, 185 pp.

Jacob, F. (1977) Evolution and tinkering. *Science* 196(4295), 1161–1166.

Johnson, R.N. and Libecap, G.D. (1982) Contracting problems and regulation: the case of the fishery. *American Economic Review* 72(5), 1005–1023.

Kaimowitz, D. and Angelsen, A. (1998) *Economic Models of Tropical Deforestation. A Review*. CIFOR, Bogor, Indonesia, 139 pp.

Lam, W.F. (1998) *Governing Irrigation Systems in Nepal: Institutions, Infrastructure, and Collective Action*. Institute for Contemporary Studies Press, Oakland, California, 275 pp.

Lam, W.F., Lee, M. and Ostrom, E. (1997) The institutional analysis and development framework: application to irrigation policy in Nepal. In: Brinkerhoff, D.W. (ed.) *Policy Studies and Developing Nations: An Institutional and Implementation Focus*. Vol. 5. JAI

Press, Greenwich, Connecticut, pp. 53–85.

Landau, M. (1969) Redundancy, rationality, and the problem of duplication and overlap. *Public Administration Review* 29(4), 346–358.

Landau, M. (1973) Federalism, redundancy, and system reliability. *Publius* 3(2), 173–196.

Liu, J., Ouyang, Z., Pimm, S.L., Raven, P.H., Wang, X., Miao, H. and Han, N. (2003) Protecting China's biodiversity. *Science* 300 (May 23), 1240–1241.

Maass, A. and Anderson, R.L. (1986) *And the Desert Shall Rejoice: Conflict, Growth and Justice in Arid Environments*. R.E. Krieger, Malabar, Florida, 447 pp.

Marwell, G. and Oliver, P. (1993) *The Critical Mass in Collective Action: a Micro-Social Theory*. Cambridge University Press, New York, 206 pp.

McCay, B.J. and Acheson, J.M. (1987) *The Question of the Commons: the Culture and Ecology of Communal Resources*. University of Arizona Press, Tucson, Arizona, 439 pp.

McKean, M.A. (1992) Management of traditional common lands (*Iriaichi*) in Japan. In: Bromley, D.W., Feeny, D., McKean, M., Peters, P., Gilles, J., Oakerson, R., Runge, C.F. and Thomson, J. (eds) *Making the Commons Work: Theory, Practice and Policy*. Institute for Contemporary Studies Press, Oakland, California, pp. 63–98.

McKean, M.A. (2000) Common property: What is it, what is it good for and what makes it work? In: Gibson, C.C., McKean, M.A. and Ostrom, E. (eds) *People and Forests: Communities, Institutions, and Governance*. The MIT Press, Cambridge, Massachusetts, pp. 27–56.

Meinzen-Dick, R.S. and Knox, A. (2001) Collective action, property rights, and devolution of natural resources management: a conceptual framework. In: Meinzen-Dick, R.S., Knox, A. and Di Gregorio, M. (eds) *Collective Action, Property Rights, and Devolution of Natural Resources Management: Exchange of Knowledge and Implications for Policy*. Zentralstelle für Ernährung und Landwirtschaft, Feldafing, Germany, pp. 40–72.

Meinzen-Dick, R., Raju, K.V. and Gulati, A. (2002) What affects organization and collective action for managing resources? Evidence from canal irrigation systems in India. *World Development* 30(4), 649–666.

Myers, R.A. and Worm, B. (2003) Rapid worldwide depletion of predatory fish communities. *Nature* 423, 280–283.

National Research Council (1986) *Proceedings of the Conference on Common Property Resource Management*. National Academy Press, Washington, DC, 631 pp.

National Research Council (2002) *The Drama of the Commons. Committee on the Human Dimensions of Global Change*. Ostrom, E., Dietz, T., Dolsak, N., Stern, P., Storich, S. and Weber, E. (eds) National Academy Press, Washington, DC, 521 pp.

Netting, R.McC. (1974) The system nobody knows: village irrigation in the Swiss Alps. In: Downing, T.E. and Gibson, M. (eds) *Irrigation's Impact on Society*. University of Arizona Press, Tucson, Arizona, pp. 67–75.

Olson, M. (1965) *The Logic of Collective Action: Public Goods and the*

Theory of Groups. Harvard University Press, Cambridge, Massachusetts, 176 pp.

Ostrom, E. (1990) *Governing the Commons: The Evolution of Institutions for Collective Action.* Cambridge University Press, New York, 280 pp.

Ostrom, E. (1992) The rudiments of a theory of the origins, survival and performance of common-property institutions. In: Bromley, D.W., Feeny, D., McKean, M., Peters, P., Gilles, J., Oakerson, R., Runge, C.F. and Thomson, J. (eds) *Making the Commons Work: Theory, Practice and Policy.* Institute for Contemporary Studies Press, Oakland, California, pp. 293–318.

Ostrom, E. (1996) Incentives, rules of the game and development. In: *Proceedings of the Annual World Bank Conference on Development Economics, 1995.* The World Bank, Washington, DC, pp. 207–234.

Ostrom, E. (1999) Coping with tragedies of the commons. *Annual Review of Political Science* 2, 493–535.

Ostrom, E. (2005) *Understanding Institutional Diversity.* Princeton University Press, Princeton, New Jersey, 376 pp.

Ostrom, E., Agrawal, A., Blomquist, W., Schlager, E. and Tang, S.Y. (1989) *CPR Coding Manual.* Workshop in Political Theory and Policy Analysis, Indiana University, Bloomington, Indiana, 120 pp.

Ostrom, E., Gardner, R. and Walker, J.M. (1994) *Rules, Games and Common-Pool Resources.* University of Michigan Press, Ann Arbor, Michigan, 369 pp.

Ostrom, V. (1997) *The Meaning of Democracy and the Vulnerability*

of Democracies: a Response to Tocqueville's Challenge. University of Michigan Press, Ann Arbor, Michigan, 329 pp.

Ostrom, V., Feeny, D. and Picht, H. (eds) (1993) *Rethinking Institutional Analysis and Development: Issues, Alternatives, and Choices.* 2nd edn. Institute for Contemporary Studies Press, Oakland, California, 486 pp.

Palanisami, K. (1982) Managing tank irrigation systems: basic issues and implications for improvement. Presented at the workshop on Tank Irrigation: Problems and Prospects. Center for International Forestry Research, Bogor, Indonesia.

Pinkerton, E. (ed.) (1989) *Cooperative Management of Local Fisheries: New Directions for Improved Management and Community Development.* University of British Columbia Press, Vancouver, British Columbia, 299 pp.

Poteete, A. and Ostrom, E. (2004) Heterogeneity, group size and collective action: the role of institutions in forest management. *Development and Change* 35(3), 435–461.

Repetto, R. (1986). Skimming the Water: Rent-Seeking and the Performance of Public Irrigation Systems. Research Report No. 4. World Resources Institute, Washington, DC, 47 pp.

Schlager, E. (1990) Model specification and policy analysis: the governance of coastal fisheries. PhD dissertation, Indiana University, Bloomington, Indiana, 247 pp.

Schlager, E. (1994) Fishers' institutional responses to common-pool resource dilemmas. In: Ostrom, E., Gardner, R. and Walker, J.M. (eds) *Rules, Games, and Common-Pool*

Resources. University of Michigan Press, Ann Arbor, Michigan, pp. 247–265.

Schlager, E., Blomquist, W. and Tang, S.Y. (1994) Mobile flows, storage, and self-organized institutions for governing common-pool resources. *Land Economics* 70(3), 294–317.

Scott, A.D. (1955) The fishery: the objectives of sole ownership. *Journal of Political Economy* 63, 116–124.

Scott, A.D. (1993) Obstacles to fishery self-government. *Marine Resource Economics* 8, 187–199.

Sengupta, N. (1991) *Managing Common Property: Irrigation in India and the Philippines*. Sage, New Delhi, 283 pp.

Shepherd, G. (1992) *Managing Africa's Tropical Dry Forests: a Review of Indigenous Methods*. Overseas Development Institute, London, 121 pp.

Shivakoti, G. and Ostrom, E. (eds) (2001) *Improving Irrigation Governance and Management in Nepal*. Institute for Contemporary Studies Press, Oakland, California, 282 pp.

Singleton, S. (1998) *Constructing Cooperation: the Evolution of Institutions of Co-Management in Pacific Northwest Salmon Fisheries*. University of Michigan Press, Ann Arbor, Michigan, 165 pp.

Singleton, S. and Taylor, M. (1992) Common property economics: a general theory and land use applications. *Journal of Theoretical Politics* 4, 309–324.

Spooner, B. (1974) Irrigation and society: the Iranian plateau. In: Downing, T.E. and Gibson, M. (eds) *Irrigation's Impact on Society*. University of Arizona Press, Tucson, Arizona, pp. 43–57.

Sussman, R.W., Green, G.M. and Sussman, L.K. (1994) Satellite imagery, human ecology, anthropology and deforestation in Madagascar. *Human Ecology* 22, 333–354.

Tang, S.Y. (1992) *Institutions and Collective Action: Self-Governance in Irrigation*. Institute for Contemporary Studies Press, Oakland, California, 151 pp.

Tang, S.Y. (1994) Institutions and performance in irrigation systems. In: Ostrom, E., Gardner, R., and Walker, J.M. (eds) *Rules, Games and Common-Pool Resources*. University of Michigan Press, Ann Arbor, Michigan, pp. 225–245.

Taylor, M. (1982) *Community, Anarchy and Liberty*. Cambridge University Press, New York, 184 pp.

Thomson, J.T., Feeny, D. and Oakerson, R.J. (1992) Institutional dynamics: the evolution and dissolution of common-property resource management. In: Bromley, D.W., Feeny, D., McKean, M., Peters, P., Gilles, J., Oakerson, R., Runge, C.F. and Thomson, J. (eds) *Making the Commons Work: Theory, Practice, and Policy*. Institute for Contemporary Studies Press, Oakland, California, pp. 129–160.

Wade, R. (1994) *Village Republics: Economic Conditions for Collective Action in South India*. Institute for Contemporary Studies Press, Oakland, California, 238 pp.

Weissing, F.J. and Ostrom, E. (1991a) Crime and punishment: further reflections on the counterintuitive results of mixed equilibria games. *Journal of Theoretical Politics* 3 (3), 343–350.

Weissing, F.J. and Ostrom, E. (1991b) Irrigation institutions and the games irrigators play: rule enforcement without guards. In:

Selten, R. (ed.) *Game Equilibrium Models II: Methods, Morals, and Markets.* Springer-Verlag, Berlin, pp. 188–262.

Wilson, J.A. (1997) Maine fisheries management initiative. In: Palsson, G. (ed.) *The Social Impacts of Individual Transferable Quotas.* TemaNord, Copenhagen, pp. 335–533.

Wilson, J.A., French, J., Kleban, P., McKay, S.R. and Townsend, R. (1991) Chaotic dynamics in a multiple species fishery: a model of community predation. *Ecological Modelling* 58, 303–322.

Wilson, J.A., Acheson, J.M., Kleban, M. and Metcalfe, M. (1994) Chaos, complexity and community management of fisheries. *Marine Policy* 18, 291–305.

Wilson, J.A., Low, B., Costanza, R. and Ostrom E. (1999) Scale misperceptions and the spatial dynamics of a social-ecological system. *Ecological Economics* 31 (2) (November), 243–257.

Wunsch, J. and Olowu, D. (eds) (1995) *The Failure of the Centralized State,* 2nd edn. Institute for Contemporary Studies Press, San Francisco, California, 334 pp.

Social Research and Researchers in CGIAR: an Underused Potential

17

Robert Chambers

This chapter will identify and explore some potential gains from social research and social researchers in the Consultative Group on International Agricultural Research (CGIAR). Social science includes economists, while social researchers and social research refer to non-economist social scientists and their work. The thrust is that new and changing perceptions, priorities and conditions open up new needs and potential. These are for practical theory, for being in touch with realities, for developing and spreading methodologies, for institutional learning and change and for questions and directions to sharpen the focus on poverty.

Realities: the Context of Accelerating Change

In many dimensions affecting CGIAR and its centres, change is rapid and often accelerating. At the same time, the challenges have become more complex and more combined with local diversity.

The most significant change has been the redefinition of CGIAR's mission. The simple aim of increasing production is history. CGIAR is now guided by the goals of poverty reduction, which is to be demand driven, with the primary demand from poor people, and of environmental sustainability. Work undertaken is also meant to be of global significance. These guidelines are made more challenging by the following:

- the powerlessness, lack of voice, dispersal and diversity of poor people;

©CAB International 2006. *Researching the Culture in Agri-Culture:*
Social Research for International Development
(eds M.M. Cernea and A.H. Kassam)

- the multidimensionality of poverty, defined in the *World Develop-ment Report 2000/2001: Attacking Poverty* (World Bank, 2001) as 'pronounced deprivation of well-being', and including at least material lack, health, vulnerability, social relations and powerless-ness (Alcamo *et al.*, 2003: 73–76);
- rapid and often accelerating, rural change, as with, for example, migration, farming systems and cropping patterns, markets, femi-nization of agriculture, labour shortages (due to HIV/AIDS), social relations and climatic conditions;
- changing perceptions, aspirations and priorities of rural people, not least through the spread of mass communications, literacy, the work of non-governmental organizations (NGOs) and social movements; and
- the increasing complexity, diversification and local variations of livelihoods, livelihood strategies and agroecosystems.

The new mandate and tasks of the CGIAR impel a quantum leap to a new level of complication and difficulty. They demand a heightened awareness of the realities of poor people, their lives and livelihoods, and of potential causal pathways between what international agricul-tural research centres (IARCs) do and benefits to poor people. These are tall orders. Moreover, they are aggravated by the need to work with increasing numbers of partners, by the transaction costs implied and by a funding squeeze. Taking the aims together with the conditions, the challenges are formidable and make a case for a radical rethink.

Paradigms and Practical Theory

Rethinking can be approached through practical theory about research and process.

The word 'paradigm' is overused but does fit this context. Para-digm refers to a pattern of concepts, beliefs, values, methods and behaviours that are mutually reinforcing. In this sense, the new mandate and tasks of CGIAR shift its dominant older and simpler paradigm of controlled and reductionist pipeline research to the new, more com-plex paradigm of the learning process.[1] This shift can be characterized in many ways, for example, from Newtonian to post-Newtonian sci-ence (Uphoff, 1992). Comparing the two, pipeline research is more planned and executed in controlled conditions, with measurements to test hypotheses, with a beginning, middle and an anticipated end; less expected to fail; and aimed to lead to technologies that will then be dis-seminated. Learning-process research is more a voyage or journey in which errors and false leads, adaptations and changes of direction are expected, and learning and adapting are continuous and contextual.

Learning-process research is underpinned by the practical theories of complexity and chaos. Characteristics of complexity theory and postmodern biology (Reason and Goodwin, 1999) make sense for learning-process research. These include rich interconnections, reflecting the complexity of networks and relationships; iteration, including repeated cycles of action, reflection and learning; and holism in the sense of inclusiveness in the universe considered relevant. There are resonances with edge-of-chaos theory and a zone of creativity in which a few principles of behaviour and interaction generate emergent self-organization and insights.

The contrast is far from absolute, there are many exceptions, and much depends on individual personality and predispositions. To a degree, however, the approaches, methods and training of social research fit and are more comfortable with open-ended learning processes, and the approaches, methods and training of economics and the physical and biological sciences are more comfortable with the discipline of pipelines. This means that social researchers are generally better placed to catalyse and support the reorientation of CGIAR research to deal with the complexity, diversity and dynamism of the realities toward which it is pointed by its new mandate.

Comparative Disadvantages of the CGIAR System

In facing these challenges, the IARCs have disadvantages:

- *Isolation.* Physical, social and political isolation distances many (although not all) IARC scientists from poor people. The centres' mandates have sometimes been interpreted as to do 'upstream' research, with contact with the messy world of actual farms and farmers the proper domain of national agricultural research systems.
- *Public relations.* Some at the February 2001 Costa Rica conference on 'Why has impact evaluation not had more impact?' attributed the funding problems of CGIAR in part to failures of presentation. The defensive reflex was not to change what was done and how, but to communicate better. With some hyperbole it was remarked that CGIAR was 'surfing continuously on the froth of its own rhetoric'. Surf soon hits shallow water and the shore. As Peter Matlon said, 'Donors are not stupid'. It is substantive achievements, not presentation, that matter and convince.
- *Language and litanies.* When repeated too often, these lose credibility or induce complacency. In CGIAR's new strategy statement, *A Food Secure World for All: Toward a New Vision and Strategy for*

the CGIAR (TAC Secretariat, 2000) phrases such as 'efficient and effective' begin to lose force with repetition and can even become self-defeating. To describe IARCs, as is customary, as 'centres of excellence' is a form of self-indulgent hubris.

* *Professional mindsets.* Ways of seeing things threaten to be a deep problem for the new directions. Powerful policy narratives can point research projects in wrong directions. The linearity of pipeline research thinking impedes iterative learning but persists as in the 2000 strategy statement, which sees the system as 'research suppliers' who 'deliver customized technologies'. Logframe thinking, with its emphasis on time frames, targets and verifiable preset indicators, is more appropriate for infrastructure and physical things than for people, and narrows the space for creativity, serendipity and opportunism. The earlier 'piles-of-grain' orientation persists, with poverty and livelihoods less the starting point and core than add-ons that top and tail documents without challenging and changing the basic frames and modes of thinking.

This is not to say that such mindsets are entirely unreasonable or wrong. In almost all contrasts drawn here, the question is not of 'either–or' but of a better balance of 'both–and'. But we have to ask whether commonly dominant ways of seeing and doing things represent and reinforce a momentum in what has now become a wrong direction, and whether the need is for more flexible and creative ability to identify and respond to opportunities.

* *Inflexible and reduced core funding.* The great value of core funding is the flexibility it allows to respond to changing realities, perceptions and opportunities. It is a sad paradox that precisely when CGIAR's mandate and context demand greater adaptability and opportunism, CGIAR's core funding should be shrinking.[2]

Impudent imagery of the old CGIAR comes to mind: of a supertanker whose weight and speed slow its change of direction, even when tugs push its bows; or of slow-moving dinosaurs, declining and doomed, when the future lies with the small and nimble protomammals at their feet (especially some of the younger and innovation-seeking professionals?).

Comparative Advantages through Social Researchers

The comparative advantages of CGIAR are many and well known, not least its global reach, the positive aspects of its professional competence, its lack of rivals for producing certain global goods and the status that means that it can set norms and an example that others will emulate. These are usually considered in relation to the work of biophysical scientists and economists.

Less well recognized is CGIAR's comparative advantage through the work of social researchers, despite their low numbers in most IARCs (see Rathgeber, Chapter 3 this volume).

Much of this comparative advantage stems from the discipline of having to be relevant and make a difference. Unlike their academic counterparts, social researchers in CGIAR have to justify their work in practical terms, ultimately now toward achieving the system's poverty and environmental goals.

Social researchers have had a significant handmaiden role to biophysical scientists, as a sort of add-on or service provider to examine and deal with the social side of things. With the new mandate this role has to become wider and deeper, and no longer secondary but equal. This has perhaps already been achieved, or largely so, in centres such as the International Water Management Institute (IWMI) and the Center for International Forestry Research (CIFOR), which are concerned with the collective management of natural resources, and where the proportion of social researchers is higher than in other IARCs. But it is difficult to see how this can occur in IARCs that have more of a commodity orientation and very few social researchers (and astonishingly, in some cases – International Center for Agricultural Research in the Dry Areas (ICARDA) is one – none at all).

Seeing, thinking about and trying to strengthen this significant service role can obscure the big contributions social researchers have made and can make in other ways and more in their own right. Here we cannot deny that they have already contributed outstandingly and on a considerable scale. An example is the generation and dissemination of practical theory through work on collective property rights (as through the CGIAR Systemwide Programme on Collective Action and Property Rights (CAPRi) network).

Social researchers have a comparative advantage in contributing to achieving the mandate in three other areas, which have strengths and potentials:

- methodologies, as through the innovation and spread of forms of participatory action research (as through the Participatory Research and Gender Analysis network);
- institutional learning and change; and
- the questions social researchers ask and the directions they point to.

Methodologies

First, the importance and potential influence and impact of new and better ways of doing things are almost everywhere overlooked or underestimated. Across the disciplines, this is a strange blind spot. Yet, new methodologies have great potential. New ways of doing things lead to new insights and new outcomes. Much has already been achieved by social researchers in CGIAR.[3] An illustration is the early work of social anthropologists in the International Potato Center (CIP) (Rhoades, 1982 and Chapter 20 this volume). Six areas now stand out for their potential for methodological pioneering and spread. These can be thought of as potential high-yielding methodologies (HYMs).

- *Bottom-up demand.* Those whose demand is to provide the drive for 'demand driven' are in various combinations poor, vulnerable, excluded, voiceless and powerless. They are also diverse in their social relations, aspirations and livelihood strategies. To enable these groups to analyse and express their needs and priorities presents a special challenge. It requires sensitive research for them to help identify their research needs, to link these with what appears 'do-able', and to generate pro-poor innovations.
- *Social innovations.* These are institutions in the sense of rules, norms and accepted ways of doing things. One opportunity here is to learn how better to search for good social institutions. Another is to innovate ways of doing things, as already with farmer field schools, Integrated Pest Management, the comité de investigación agrícola local, or local agricultural research committee (CIAL) and many institutions in natural resources management. There should be potential for more social innovations and then for their spread.
- *Attitudes, behaviour, power and relationships.* Little attention has been paid to attitudes, behaviour, power and relationships as components of good science, yet these are now recognized as significant dimensions of development, not least now that partnerships are such an important part of good practice (Groves and Hinton, 2004). The potential here would seem huge. The dimensions are personal, professional and institutional. Behaviours and relationships for 'learning alliances' with partners are an example.
- *Reflection and learning.* Many methodological innovations and lessons pass unnoticed, unrecorded and unlearned from for two reasons: they are not recognized as significant; and professionals have no time for reflection, writing and sharing. Yet, social researchers in CGIAR, especially, produce a great deal of valuable innovation.[4] Beyond this, all professionals need time and space for reflection, learning and writing. There is scope here to adopt, adapt, invent,

practise and evolve approaches and methods. Examples are the write-shops of the International Institute for Rural Reconstruction in the Philippines, the reflection and review and downward accountability initiatives of ActionAid (ActionAid, 2000, 2001), immersion practices (Eyben, 2004; Irvine *et al.,* 2004) and reflection retreats. A vital part of this is learning through the reflexivity of self-critical awareness.

- *Learning about learning, innovation, adapting and creativity.* This is in part linked with the sociology of science and innovation, and includes learning about processes of innovation and change through reflection on experience. A contribution here could be a series of histories of innovation (see, for example, Douthwaite, 2002).
- *Spread and influence.* This area has perhaps the greatest potential, encompassing processes described as scaling up, scaling out, diffusion, dissemination, adoption, adaptation and impact. Practical theory about the spread and influence of methodologies is lacking, yet the CGIAR system already has much experience. This area offers a wonderful opportunity to better understand how good methodologies can be spread faster and better, and how HYMs can be self-spreading and self-improving, with greatly augmented influence and impact.

Several of these opportunities for HYMs are linked. Resolutely seized together, they might be powerfully transformative. Nor are they necessarily a full list. Development and spread of good HYMs might have an immense influence and impact on reducing poverty and enhancing livelihoods.

It would be a start to recognize clearly what has already been achieved. More could then be done to further evolve and spread the HYMs already developed. Space and resources could (and in my view, should) be made available for this. But beyond that, I sense a need for radical changes of thinking and practice in CGIAR if future potentials are to be exploited, and that such changes are latent, feasible and incipient in several centres.

Institutional Learning and Change in CGIAR

The second area where social researchers have a special new contribution to make is institutional learning and change (ILAC).

'CGIAR can't learn. It is not a learning organization', and 'The challenge proposals have galloped back to the 1980s', may be harsh remarks, and in conversation things are said with a sharpness that is rare in print. But they give pause for reflection on how CGIAR should change to become a learning organization, how the pressure of preparing challenge proposals can avoid regression to reductionist pipeline research and how CGIAR can look forward resolutely with vision and imagination. For learning, as donors pointed out at the Costa Rica conference in February 2002, it would be good to analyse what has not worked, the dead ends and lessons that can be learned from these as well as from successes.

Creative and radical reflection, review and change have not been hallmarks of the CGIAR system. Rathgeber's survey of scientists (Chapter 3, this volume) is one of the rare pieces of research on CGIAR. That the mandate of International Service for National Agricultural Research (ISNAR) should have been management of national agricultural research systems, but not including the CGIAR centres themselves, was a bizarre and even arrogant omission. 'They need it, we don't', is self-negating. Physician, heal thyself. Therapists need therapy as learning to help them help others. With ISNAR now submerged into International Food Policy Research Institute (IFPRI), this may be a good time to correct this omission for the sake of substantive gains to CGIAR.

ILAC is a promising initiative in this direction. A small informal group began to coalesce around this theme at the Costa Rica conference. The IFPRI research on poverty impacts of CGIAR research (Adato and Meinzen-Dick, 2003) also pointed toward the potential for continuous reflection and learning during research processes. A workshop at IFPRI in 2003 took this further, and a Rockefeller grant made space for the ideas to be developed as a pilot initiative (Horton and Mackay, 2003; ISNAR, 2003; Watts *et al.*, 2003). Key elements are accelerated institutional innovation and critical self-awareness. 'Shortened, self-reflective learning cycles exploring the effectiveness particular approaches and processes could drive the rapid institutional change that CGIAR centres need to improve the contribution of science to poverty reduction and environmental sustainability' (Watts *et al.*, 2003: 7). Four synergistic approaches have been proposed:

- developing a supportive external environment, especially among donors;
- fostering a culture of innovation, learning and change;
- reorienting management systems to encourage and celebrate risk-taking, innovation and learning; and
- developing and enhancing individuals' awareness, knowledge and skills.

As a start, ILAC for CGIAR might include the following list, which is far from fully thought out:

- identification of initiatives already taking place;
- recruiting of more social researchers, including from management science;

- research, especially reflective and participatory action research, on the system and centres;
- reflection by social and biophysical scientists on the histories of research programmes and relating them to follow through what they find out in the field;
- documentation and sharing of experience and networking; and
- provision of regular opportunities for self-critical reflection, learning and writing, especially about processes and methodologies.

Social researchers have no monopoly of ability and orientation for these activities, but their skills and leavening, with the diversity of insights they can bring, will make a major contribution. Social researchers' collegial participation, facilitation and at times, leadership will be essential ingredients.

Questions, Systems and Directions

A third gain from social researchers is the questions they can and should ask, and the directions and content of research that follow from them. These questions relate not only to methodologies and ILAC but also to aspects of reality that other disciplines may overlook, underestimate or be unable to research and take adequately into account. These questions apply to much that concerns people rather than things, organisms and ecosystems. Arguably, the human, institutional and political dimensions are so important that social researchers should be as many as other kinds of researchers. IARCs that are most concerned with collective action and management of natural resources – notably International Center for Living Aquatic Resources Management (ICLARM, fisheries); International Water Management Institute (IWMI, water); and CIFOR (trees) – do, and properly so, have higher proportions of social researchers. But their numbers are low, derisory or nil in other centres, and in consequence the critical questions that have to be asked and answered, with the pro-poor mandate and the context of complexity, diversity and dynamism noted above, may not be asked. At a general level, social scientists (including economists) have a special responsibility with the pro-poor orientation to keep on again and again asking the questions they are best placed to ask, and which enlarge the agenda of relevance to make it more realistic.

There are many questions, but one is overarching and has to be asked again and again, the answers probed and researched and the findings acted upon with frequent iterations: who gains and who loses?

Following on from this, how can poor people gain more and lose less? The question leads straight into the messy, complex realities of people, social institutions, bureaucratic dynamics, corruption and politics. These realities are part of the holism of complexity and chaos theory. They cannot be left out, and they are where the special skills and insights of social researchers are needed.

The cost of not asking this question would be a degree of wild aiming and blind lottery in the relevance and impacts of biophysical research. Perceptive donors will always be asking the question. The CGIAR system needs the capacity to answer it, *ex-ante* and especially iteratively during research processes, and not just *ex-post*. Only then can the CGIAR system approach its huge potential for reducing poverty.

Conclusion

In addition to their accepted roles in support of biophysical scientists, CGIAR social scientists should be augmented for an additional reason: to increase effectiveness and efficiency in achieving the system's mandate. This reason relates to paradigms, practical theory, methodologies, ILAC, questions, systems and directions. Social researchers do not have a monopoly of expertise in these areas. Leadership and contributions can come from professionals in any discipline if they have the personal orientation and commitment. All the same, social researchers, from the nature of their disciplines, training and the questions they ask, do have a comparative advantage. The marginal gains from having more good social researchers in the CGIAR system should, therefore be high and, subject to personality and personal orientation, higher than the marginal gains from more biophysical scientists or economists. The question is not of alternatives, but of case-by-case realism. Unfortunately, for many reasons, when funds are short the social researchers are the ones axed, not least because their contributions are less tangible and visible. Conversely, when funds are more abundant, social researchers are not necessarily given priority in recruitment. If the CGIAR system is to fulfill its new mandate, and achieve anything like its potential, this has to change. If it is serious about poverty, the system has to better balance the disciplines.

Taking these ideas as starting points (and surely to be modified and augmented in ongoing processes of learning), increasing the number of social researchers would enable the CGIAR centres to do the following:

- play to their comparative advantage and better fulfill their comparative responsibility;
- better reduce poverty and enhance the livelihoods of their poor clients;

- be more credible (and to support the chorus, effective and efficient) by becoming self-critical learning organizations;
- be more exciting, and so able to recruit and keep more creative and innovative professionals; and
- be more likely to be funded.

For many years it has been a mystery to me why donors do not fund the CGIAR more generously. Now more than ever, with the poverty focus, the benefits of additional funding should be high indeed. This view is being reinforced and substantiated by the evidence presented in this volume of what social researchers have been doing and the contributions they have made. The potential for social research in the CGIAR system remains vastly underrealized. The likely benefits of additional funding to CGIAR would be considerably higher if this meant more good social researchers encouraged and enabled to work creatively with a pro-poor orientation on the themes outlined above.

To be serious about poverty, CGIAR has to be serious about social research.

Notes

[1] For other related dimensions, described as frameworks for development practice with two columns under the headings of *from things* and *expanded to include people*, see Watts *et al.* (2003: 8).

[2] In the Participation Group in the Institute of Development Studies (IDS), Sussex, UK, we and our work have benefited from the willingness of our consortium of donors to include a budget head of 10% for 'unanticipated opportunities'. This has encouraged and allowed us to see and seize the unexpected opportunities that can be anticipated in our rapidly changing world. CGIAR does not seem to have equivalent flexibility.

[3] I became more aware of these during the first 2 days of the conference and will not list them here. But the contribution over the years has been remarkable, and the impact on how national agricultural research system, non-governmental organizations and others work has been immense, not least in participatory approaches and methods.

[4] This became more evident than ever in the first 2 days of the conference, in almost every presentation.

References

ActionAid (2000) *ALPS: Accountability, Learning and Planning System.* ActionAid, London, 28pp. Available online: www.actionaid.org/ resources/ pdfs/alps.pdf

ActionAid (2001) *Notes to Accompany ALPS.* ActionAid, London, 105pp. Available online: www.actionaid.org/resources/pdfs/ alps_notes.pdf

Adato, M. and Meinzen-Dick, R. (2003) Assessing the impact of agricultural research on poverty and livelihoods. *Quarterly Journal of International Agriculture* 42(2), 149–166.

Alcamo, J. *et al.* (2003) *Ecosystems and Human Wellbeing: a Framework for Assessment.* Island Press, Washington, DC, 245 pp.

Douthwaite, B. (2002) *Enabling Innovation: a Practical Guide to Understanding and Fostering Technological Change.* Zed Books, London and New York, 266 pp.

Eyben, R. (2004) *Learning from Poor People's Experience: Immersions, Policy Briefing.* IDS Sussex, Brighton, UK, 4 pp.

Groves, L. and Hinton, R. (eds) (2004) *Inclusive Aid: Changing Power and Relationships in International Development.* Earthscan, London, 237 pp.

Horton, D. and Mackay, R. (2003) Innovative approaches for evaluating agricultural research and development, Special Issue, *Agricultural Systems* 78(2), 119–336.

Irvine, R., Chambers, R. and Eyben, R. (2004) *Learning from Poor People's Experience: Immersions,* Lessons for Change Series No. 13. Institute of Development Studies, Sussex, UK, 35 pp.

ISNAR (2003) *Institutional Learning and Change: a CGIAR Pilot Initia-*tive. ISNAR, The Hague, Netherlands, 6 pp. Available online: d.horton@cgiar.org

Reason, P. and Goodwin, B.C. (1999) Toward a science of qualities in organizations: lessons from complexity theory and postmodern biology. *Concepts and Transformations* 4(3), 281–317.

Rhoades, R. (1982) *The Art of the Informal Agricultural Survey.* International Potato Center, Lima, Peru, 40 pp.

TAC Secretariat (2000) *A Food Secure World for All: Toward a New Vision and Strategy for the CGIAR.* TAC Secretariat, FAO, Rome, 40 pp.

Uphoff, N. (1992) *Learning from Gal Oya: Possibilities for Participatory Development and Post-Newtonian Social Science.* Cornell University Press, Ithaca, New York, 448 pp.

Watts, J., Mackay, R., Horton, D., Hall, A., Douthwaite, B., Chambers, R. and Acosta, A. (2003) Institutional Learning and Change: An Introduction. ISNAR Discussion Paper 03–10, International Service for National Agricultural Research, The Hague, Netherlands, 19 pp.

World Bank (2001) *World Development Report 2000/2001: Attacking Poverty.* The World Bank, Washington, DC, 335 pp.

The Rockefeller Foundation and Social Research in Agriculture

18

Gordon Conway, Akin Adesina, John Lynam and Joyce Moock

The green revolution was one of the great technological success stories of the 20th century, greatly increasing cereal yields in developing countries, bringing down cereal prices and feeding millions of people. However, many did not benefit, especially in Africa, and the green revolution had other undesirable consequences (Conway, 1999; Hazell, 2002). Most of the successes can be attributed to the application of biological knowledge, however, marketing arrangements, credit, input supply, price policy and rural infrastructure provided the sufficiency conditions for the new varieties to have an impact. These conditions do not exist in much of Africa.

Many of the shortfalls in achieving food security today are due not to a failure of the biological sciences *per se*, but to a lack of understanding and application of social sciences, especially to market strengthening and policy formulation. In part, this has resulted from the compartmentalization of the natural and social sciences, both in training and research.

Such intellectual differentiation is particularly detrimental in dealing with agroecosystems, defined as biological processes managed by farmers who pursue their social, cultural and economic objectives (Conway, 1987). These systems are strictly codependent in that the density of the world's human population requires intensively managed agricultural systems for food supply and at the same time, most of these biological processes are dependent on human agency. Modern crops such as maize or cassava could not exist in the wild, and agriculture has radically shifted the species distribution within the globe's

©CAB International 2006. *Researching the Culture in Agri-Culture:*
Social Research for International Development
(eds M.M. Cernea and A.H. Kassam)

overall biological diversity. This codependency was essential to the evolution and development of agricultural systems.

It is therefore paradoxical that the study of biological processes and the study of human agency have not developed interactively within modern agricultural research. Rather, research has principally been the preserve of the biological scientist, while social sciences were late arrivals to the enterprise and have had to justify and articulate a role within international agricultural research institutes.

We briefly chart the history of that process within the Consultative Group on International Agricultural Research (CGIAR), evaluate the role of the Rockefeller Foundation's Social Science Fellowship Programme within a rapidly changing research environment, and finally, look forward to how social sciences might be developing within CGIAR in the immediate future.

Social Sciences in International Agricultural Research

The roots of social science in international agricultural research go back to the tail end of the colonial period. The British colonial agricultural research institutes were organized and staffed along strict disciplinary lines. Most of the officers came with degrees in specialized sciences such as chemistry, botany and entomology, followed by an applied orientation, first through the Department of Agriculture at Cambridge University and then at the Imperial College of Tropical Agriculture in the West Indies. Officers received strong disciplinary training in the various core sciences and then applied it to plant breeding, soil science, plant protection and crop management. Research institutes were organized along these disciplinary lines.

When the International Rice Research Institute (IRRI) was established in 1959, it was also compartmentalized in this way. In 1963, Vernon Ruttan arrived as the first economist in the new Department of Agricultural Economics. As he notes, 'neither the director nor the associate director of the IRRI conveyed to me a very clear idea of why they needed an agricultural economist or what contribution they expected from the economics unit at the IRRI' (Ruttan, 1982). In 1965, the Ford Foundation supported the creation of the Rural Economy Research Unit at the Institute for Agricultural Research at Ahmadu Bello University in Nigeria, headed by David Norman. In 1961, Michael Collinson was appointed as the first economist in the agricultural research institutes in East Africa at Ukiriguru in Tanzania. As Norman (2000) noted, 'since the experiment station had been there for almost

50 years, the question that immediately came to my mind was why none of the results had "rubbed off" on neighboring farms'.

The incorporation of social science within agricultural research institutes in the tropics is thus relatively recent. Its origins are related to the movement away from research on export and plantation crops to a focus on food crops within smallholder farming systems. As a result, the need for an interdisciplinary framework to carry out research became more obvious.

In the early 1960s, system research was developing both as a conceptual model for understanding the constraints on productivity in smallholder farms and as a framework for organizing research. This notion, pioneered by Richard Bradfield at IRRI, was central to the creation and organization of the International Center for Tropical Agriculture (CIAT) and the International Institute of Tropical Agriculture (IITA) in the late 1960s. The timing dovetailed with the application of farm management and modelling in agricultural economics to smallholder agriculture. The social sciences were debating whether theories developed in the North could be applied to African and Asian farmers. To answer this question, researchers first needed to understand why peasant farmers managed their systems the way they did. Social science and agricultural sciences in the 1960s were thus focusing on the same research problems and finding some common ground in research approaches.

The green revolution in the late 1960s and early 1970s changed the dynamics of the evolving incorporation of social sciences into the expanding number of international agricultural research centres:

- First, the green revolution shifted the organizational impetus from farming systems to multidisciplinary commodity-focused research programmes that organized much of the research around centralized breeding programmes. That is, the green revolution put the biological sciences back at the core of technology development, but now with concerns about whether alternative designs of that technology might have different economic and social outcomes.
- Second, the transformation and growth potential unleashed by widespread adoption of new agricultural technology moved agricultural research from being one among a number of investments in rural development to being, instead, an instrument of development policy, with a corresponding expansion in the range of societal goals that motivated public investment in research. Agricultural technology thus became a central feature of development studies and therefore, a focus of research by social scientists in the North.
- Finally, the green revolution coincided with the arrival of Robert McNamara at the World Bank and a shift in development policy

towards growth with equity. The immediate concerns about the green revolution's equity impacts moved social science research into a more critical mode. Those concerned about technology design argued for placing social scientists within commodity research programmes, while those who critically evaluated social and economic impacts argued for more independent research enquiry; for a social science research agenda aligning with emerging enquiry within the social sciences; and for separate social science departments, more often than not purely agricultural economics.

Over the past 30 years, the intellectual horizons of the international agricultural research system have broadened. Recognition of the multitude of farming systems and institutional and policy environments unfavourable to green revolution approaches, along with increasing concern over the depletion of natural resources, has evoked demand for new criteria to assess viable technology. Added to the traditional tests of productivity and stability are such considerations as diversification of food products for nutritional security, potential for income generation, improvements in the well-being of the poor and excluded and more recently, conservation of natural resources and the sustainability of production systems over time. Together they illustrate the trend in agricultural research to move analysis of social factors in technology development to the forefront of scientific concerns.

The 'Rocky Doc' Programme

The Rockefeller Foundation is one of several funding agencies supporting the integration of the human factor into agricultural research and technology development. Through its Social Science Fellowship Programme in Agriculture, launched in 1974, the Foundation helped produce a new breed of economists, anthropologists, geographers and cultural ecologists versed in multidisciplinary research and knowledgeable about the human and biological complexities of agricultural transformation. Over 22 years, the programme placed 114 exceptional young scholars ('Rocky docs') from North America and Africa in CGIAR and its associate centres for 2-year assignments and in the process helped those centres enhance their outreach to national agricultural research systems and incorporate farmer knowledge into problem identification and research strategy formulation.

By focusing on the links between farmer knowledge, technology development and sustainable food systems, the fellows had a visible impact on the objectives and strategies of the international agricultural centres, most of which now include programme alumni in their lead-ership. Assignments featured integrated work with plant breeders and crop and animal production scientists at various stages of technology development. Overall, the programme combined a problem-solving, human capital development strategy with a systematic field-based effort to incorporate farm-level reality into the research priorities of national and international scientific organizations.

This initiative was in many ways a platform to deepen and expand the range of social science in the CGIAR system. Several features of the programme were geared to optimize its value. Maximum attention was paid to the qualifications and screening of candidates, with particular focus on excellence of disciplinary skills and beyond this, to solid field experience that allowed the social scientists to hit the ground running. The centres had to compete for the limited pool with good research ideas and for appropriate placement within the institution – thus facili-tating the centres' ability to expand the research frontier. Nearly every assignment was designed to enable the social scientist fellow to inter-act on the technology design question in collaboration with the biological scientist.

The work of the young postdoctoral fellows changed over time as two factors – recognition of the multitude of farming systems and insti-tutional and policy environments unsuited to green revolution approaches, and rising alarm over the degradation of natural resources – mandated new criteria to assess technology. An expanded set of evalu-ation criteria applied throughout technology generation helped move analysis of its human factor to the forefront of scientific concerns and provide the programme fellows with research space. Typical research issues concerned potential economic incentives for the producer; pro-jections about who stands to gain or lose from a given technology; and the balance between a genetic or varietal solution to a problem and an agronomic, management or policy solution. Typical research strategies recognized the contribution of male and female farmers as active experimenters – plant experts, soil scientists and local economists – in their own right. The Rocky docs often helped the international and national agricultural research centres talk and listen to farmers.

Under the programme, the host centre contributed at least 50%, often 75%, of the total cost of each posting. Examples of assignments are an investigation of farmer participatory research for improved soil, crop and pest management in bean cropping systems in East Africa (CIAT); building of capacity at the Kenya Agricultural Research Insti-tute to set national priorities in resource management (International Service for National Agricultural Research); and a study of food secu-rity and household nutrition under urban stress in Ghana (Interna-tional Food Policy Research Institute (IFPRI)). In each case the assignment emphasized environmental concerns and building the capabilities of national agricultural systems and staff.

Biennial conferences in collaboration with the host centres brought the fellows and alumni together to discuss aspects of biological or resource management research that have benefited from social analysis (Moock and Rhoades, 1992). Fellowships thus resulted in translating social perspectives into tangible technological outcomes affecting, for example, the use of living mulches in hillside maize production in Central America, genetic diversity in bean-breeding programmes in Rwanda, generation of *la papa simpática* (the friendly potato) in the Peruvian Andes, cassava production and utilization in Nigeria and Colombia and cassava-chip processing and marketing in Ecuador. By mobilizing farmers' experiential knowledge about their production base while broadening their comprehension of the full range of available technology opportunities emerging from world science, the fellows helped make the concept of sustainable agriculture a reality.

Nearly half of the programme alumni remained for at least 3 years on the core staff of the international centres or were hired by donor agencies, while the remainder turned to the training of others. All of the African alumni were retained by the international centres with the exception of one who returned to become assistant director of the Kenya Agricultural Research Institute. The programme also had the distinction of long being the single major source for channelling female scientists (43) into the international agricultural research establishment.

By approaching technology assessment as the totality of multiple economic, socio-cultural and biological system interactions, many of the fellows carried their research skills into largely uncharted waters. However worthy the recent broad-based objectives of the international agricultural research system, the danger continues of producing social research that has little direct relevance to biological science and producing findings impossible to implement. As their research objectives broaden and become more sophisticated, international centres are likely to request national systems to carry out social research tasks for which they have little finance and few human resources. A key challenge then, is to enhance staffing patterns that reinforce operationally oriented practical approaches to critical social research and to build on and strengthen existing local capacities.

The Future

The change in funding of CGIAR from core contributions to project-based funding had a dissembling effect on programme structures in the centres. Organization of research programmes moved towards matrix structures of projects and thematic programme areas.

More than anything else this change served to integrate social scientists into an expanding range of projects and themes, breaking down traditional disciplinary boundaries. Most of the centres found project organization too fragmentary, with large transaction costs in effective management. Recently, most have amalgamated projects into broad themes, in many ways significantly different from the previous organization along disciplinary, commodity or technology lines, and reflecting much more the human factor in agricultural technology. Thus, for example, the World Agroforestry Centre (ICRAF) now has four principal research themes: land and people, trees and markets, environmental services and strengthening of institutions. Biological and social scientists are integrated within each theme, in many ways achieving an interdisciplinarity that was not possible in CGIAR's history.

The other principal change defining the future role of the CGIAR social scientist is the notion that while agricultural technology is integrally embedded in farming systems, these are equally embedded in larger social and economic structures that influence their performance. As agricultural technologies moved into rain-fed or marginal agro-ecologies and then from varietal and input components to system technologies such as integrated pest management, agroforestry or integrated soil management, the speed and extent of such technologies' adoption were constrained, limiting the growth linkages through which the green revolution had its transformative impacts. Removing these constraints and freeing up the adoption and spread of new technologies depended as much on the institutional frameworks as the technology adaptation to farming systems. Institutional innovations in marketing, extension, credit, farmer collective action and information delivery were essential complements to improved technologies in generating sustained growth in agricultural productivity.

Policy changes in the 1990s, particularly structural adjustment and market liberalization, eliminated public sector institutions but without a compensatory replacement by private sector institutions. Farmers thus face a number of market failures in selling crops, which in turn, dampen uptake of new technologies. Nowhere is this more serious than in sub-Saharan Africa, slowing the growth of agricultural productivity and worsening food insecurity and rural poverty.

Poor farmers face many market failures and missing markets, high transaction costs and high risks, worsened by the lack of appropriate regulations and contract enforcement and by poor public market infrastructure. Yet, unless they are able to better participate in markets, farmers will not be able to improve their incomes and find pathways out of poverty and food insecurity. These market imperfections mean that new institutional innovations are required to improve the functioning of markets, lower the transaction costs faced by the poor and raise their level of participation and returns from markets. With globalization and trade, additional challenges confront the poor, especially those related to market and trade information, grades and standards, precluding the poor's access to the market as well as to capital for investing in storage facilities. Markets should be made to work better for the poor. Many international agricultural research centres such as ICRAF now have emerging agricultural market improvement programmes, led principally by social scientists.

While the biological revolution with genetically modified crops is receiving a lot of attention, the less noticed revolution in information and communication technology has huge implications for the poor. With rapid globalization, access to information is now more important as it allows farmers to take advantage of new market opportunities. With the deregulation of the communication sector in many countries, the use of cell phones is rapidly expanding. Some countries require companies to expand their rural access as a condition to obtain a licence, offering untapped opportunities for the poor.

Efforts to assist farmers in harnessing these 'non-traditional' technologies could be strengthened with better linkage to those with skills in information and communication technologies. CGIAR needs a new mix of 'non-traditional social scientists', especially those with skills in information and communication technologies. These 'non-traditional social scientists' can work with biological researchers to develop and adapt new information and communication technologies to rapidly diffuse new agricultural technologies to farmers, and help rural organizations access information to improve their farm decision making and market access.

While CGIAR has done much on policy research, a huge gap still exists between policy research and policy action. Closing this gap will require stronger links between centralized policy research and work on the ground by national institutions.

Enriching and expanding creative social science research in CGIAR and pointing it in directions where it can be most productive is essential to promote sustainable agricultural systems. This includes placing policy analysts and social scientists with legal, organizational and management expertise within national and regional agricultural institutions, and linking them to IFPRI or similar institutions to enhance the relevance of national and regional agricultural policy frameworks.

References

Conway, G.R. (1987) The properties of agroecosystems. *Agricultural Systems* 24, 95–117.

Conway, G.R. (1999) *The Doubly Green Revolution: Food for All in the 21st Century.* Penguin Books, London, and Cornell University Press, Ithaca, New York, 335 pp.

Hazell, P. (2002) *Green Revolution: Curse or Blessing?* International Food Policy Research Institute, Washington, DC, 3 pp.

Moock, J.L. and Rhoades, R. (eds) (1992) *Diversity, Farmer Knowledge, and Sustainability.* Cornell University Press, Ithaca, New York, 278 pp.

Norman, D. (2000) FSR: a personal evolution. In: Collinson, M.P. (ed.) *A History of Farming Systems Research.* CAB International, Wallingford, UK, 432 pp.

Ruttan, V.W. (1982) *Agricultural Research Policy.* University of Minnesota Press, Minneapolis, Minnesota, 369 pp.

A Donor Perspective: Accomplishments, Limitations and Opportunities for Social Research

19

Scott Bode and Deborah Rubin*

The contributions of the social sciences[1] to the process and outcomes of international agricultural research are well documented elsewhere in this volume and in the broader literature. Participatory methodologies and consideration of gender and the environment are built on the intersection of the social and biological sciences and have improved development interventions around the world. Less well recognized, but potentially more important, are the contributions of social scientists in leadership roles in the Consultative Group on International Agricultural Research (CGIAR)[2] and of social science research to policy discussions and policymaking. In recent years, social science research has significantly contributed to the broad framing of development questions and analysis. Social research has helped change the fundamental questions addressed by international agriculture research – from primarily maximizing yields to the even more difficult goal of increasing factor productivity in an environmentally and socially sustainable manner.

Turning the social research lens on to the process of social research itself, we aim to raise awareness of the significant contributions of social science research to broad development debate and policy discussions. We briefly review contributions of social science to development efforts that received significant donor support and were carried out or formulated within the CGIAR system. We then discuss the recent influence of social science research on several new policy directions. We conclude by suggesting how donors can continue to support social science research within the CGIAR system as well as in its linkages with key development stakeholders.

382   *The views expressed are the authors' and not necessarily those of USAID.

Despite the achievements by social researchers in some CGIAR centres, we need to be careful not to paint too rosy a picture. Meeting in Cali, Colombia, social scientists from inside and outside the CGIAR system pointed out some systemic problems related to its overall ability to maintain a critical mass of social scientists who could accomplish the system's objectives and mandate.

Donors fund social research for many reasons: they expect to find better ways to help poor farmers, to increase the effectiveness of their resources by identifying the most appropriate constraints to study, to improve adoption of new approaches, to reduce development's unintended consequences and to achieve better results. Expectations of donors from social research and the support they provide to social research in the CGIAR system make up a two-way street, not only improving the work of the biological scientists and the farmers they serve, but also ultimately feeding back into the donors' own programmes and policies.

Past Efforts

One of the best-known efforts to insert social science perspectives into the biologically oriented work at the heart of the centres' original mission has been the Rockefeller Social Science Fellowship Programme in Agriculture and Rural Development. Over its lifetime (1974–1997) the programme[3] had two broad purposes: to support the interaction of social science perspectives in the centres and to help forge better links between the international centres and the national agricultural research networks. These objectives were gradually refined toward improving the identification of research problems, creating well-crafted interdisciplinary research strategies and finally, 'translating social perspectives into tangible technological outcomes' (Moock, 1992: 3). Initially designed to place US and Canadian social scientists in the centres, the programme was augmented in 1985 to place African social scientists in international agricultural centres in Africa (Moock, 1992: 3, fn 3).

This programme and its recipients had many successes: it led to several significant innovations in research methods and in agricultural technologies, and created a group of agriculturally oriented social scientists. Some provided in-house capacity for sociocultural research in the centres, becoming research leaders. Others carried their insights and experience into other development organizations and into the academic community (Conway *et al.,* Chapter 18 this volume). In some cases, the contributions of the non-economist social scientists permanently

altered the research practice of some centres' programmes.[4] The programme's biennial research conferences permitted exchanges of ideas
and experiences and created a stable network of interdisciplinary, agriculturally oriented professional social researchers.

The involvement of social scientists at CGIAR centres, and more
broadly in international agricultural research, led to the development
or refinement of several new approaches:

- *Farming systems research.* The anthropological origins of the
  'farmer-back-to-farmer' approach developed by Robert Rhoades,
  Robert Werge and colleagues at the International Potato Center (CIP)
  have been well documented (Rhoades and Booth, 1982; Rhoades,
  1984; 2000; Cernea and Guggenheim, 1985). The central tenet of
  this approach required that the problems that agricultural
  researchers selected to study had to be based in conditions of the
  farmers and their communities, and that they had to be active participants in the research process throughout its four-step cycle of
  diagnosis, interdisciplinary team research, on-farm testing and
  adaptation and farmer evaluation and adaptation (Rhoades, 1984).

Reflecting on his 10 years at CIP, when the 'farmer-back-to-farmer'
model was developed, Rhoades (2000: 161) noted that 'anthropological
thinking (was incorporated) into the very values of the centre itself'. Others are less satisfied with the progress achieved. Fujisaka (1993), who
favours including farmers in agricultural research from its earliest phases
of design, found that an increasing emphasis on biotechnology
approaches in centres may limit the institutionalization of farming systems research. Becker (2000: 1) states that biological scientists remained
'sceptical and untouched' by farming systems research until later, in the
1990s, when donors began to demand greater farmer integration into
research as part of a broad quest for accountability and results and a
renewed interest in poverty reduction. Bellon and Morris (2002: 9) note
that the emerging institutionalization of participatory plant breeding
promises to make 'varietal development efforts more responsive to the
needs of technology users,' and argue that the physical and subjective
traits (e.g. taste, texture and indirect uses) of plants need to be assessed in
breeding programmes by natural and social scientists working together.

The close attention to the farming household pioneered by social
researchers had many spin-offs such as greater interest in intrahousehold dynamics, including gender, refinements of participatory methodologies and rising awareness of the importance of natural resources
management and collective action.

- *Gender analysis.* Interest in women and food security emerged as an
  important line of research in agricultural production and natural

resources management in several CGIAR centres as an outgrowth of women's presence as farmers in farming systems research, the examination of women's roles in the household as part of intra-household research and the growing interest in women's part in economic development. An early review was carried out at a high-level conference held at the International Service for National Agricultural Research (ISNAR) addressing women's roles in agricultural technology.[5] The conference concluded that additional interdisciplinary research and new methodologies on gender issues were needed, particularly as linked to technology generation.

The CGIAR Gender Programme[6] was formed in 1991 to strengthen gender analysis in research as well as address gender inequalities in staffing and training (Feldstein and Merrill-Sands, 1996; Feldstein and Slack, 1995). Donor support for specific projects, however, was the key to broadening the impact of gender research. International Food Policy Research Institute's (IFPRI) current research theme, gender and intra-household aspects of food policy, for example,[7] was enhanced by significant support from the US Agency for International Development (USAID)[8] to investigate gender issues[9] and to fund outreach efforts[10] to link scientists at different CGIAR centres with each other and with researchers at other international institutes and academic institutions, practitioners and policymakers, and is now funded by several donors.[11] This grant 'gave IFPRI the means to include inputs from other social sciences' (Meinzen-Dick *et al.*, Chapter 15 this volume). The government of Norway supported a synthesis of the work as a guide to practitioners. As in the case of farming systems research, attention to gender has reshaped centre methodologies and is increasingly visible in the identification of centre objectives.

- *Participatory and institutional approaches.* Participatory research methodologies are an outgrowth of or elaboration on farming systems research. These efforts initially borrowed heavily from social anthropology methodologies, stressing the importance and relevance of using a qualitative approach and of capturing the local perspective in 'getting the overall picture right' when doing analysis at the local level (Rennie and Singh, 1996).

In 1997, the inter-centre initiative on Participatory Research and Gender Analysis was created to provide more structure and focus in promoting and developing gender-sensitive participatory analysis. The programme has been supported by several donors: Kellogg Foundation; Ford Foundation; and the governments of Italy, Norway, Sweden and Canada. The systemwide programme on Collective Action and Property Rights (CAPRi) is another inter-centre collaborative effort that links research on institutional and social issues to agriculture development and natural resources management. The programme has successfully demonstrated improved agricultural and natural resources management technology development and adoption through analysis of social processes. CAPRi support has come from the Swedish International Development Agency (SIDA), Ford Foundation, and the German Federal Ministry for Economic Cooperation and Development (BMZ).

- *Integrated rural development and sustainable livelihoods.* One of the recognized shortcomings of farming systems research was its lack of attention to aspects of environmental sustainability, even though its formulation paralleled a period when development agencies began to formally incorporate environmental analysis into their programming approaches.[12] By requiring an environmental filter, development agencies recognized and supported the social benefits of clean water and air, and better environmental stewardship.

Sustainable livelihood is the latest iteration of a development approach that emerged in the 1970s, known initially as integrated rural development, and was essentially a policy response to the limits of crop productivity research. Integrated rural development for the first time recognized the complexities of the farmer's life. Problems with the approach led it to be discredited by the 1980s. One concern was that despite heavily subsidized programmes, most farmers remained unable to receive the world market price for their products (often less than 50% of that value). Conceptually, the sustainable livelihood framework enhanced integrated rural development by recognizing the importance of resource ownership and access, basic needs and livelihood security. Sustainable livelihood also embraced a participatory approach and defined 'livelihood' to include all the means, activities, entitlements and assets by which people make a living. This approach made the focus on the rural household more inclusive of existing off-farm income-earning strategies and their impact on agricultural production systems.[13]

In the early 1990s, reflecting these wider developments, CGIAR expanded the number of research institutions to include centres whose research mandate focused on some of the larger issues that the sustainable livelihood framework encompasses, including sustainable forest management, soil and water conservation, coastal zone conservation and management, fisheries research and agroforestry.[14]

Sustainable livelihoods is an approach that at its heart is cross-sectoral and more than other approaches, reflects the realities that development practitioners face in the field. The approach borrows from social science analytical frameworks and addresses issues that are not typically addressed in agricultural development circles. The United Nations Development Programme, CARE, Ford Foundation and the Department of International Development–UK (DfID–UK) all have strong conceptual models related to sustainable livelihoods.

Shaping Donor Development Policy through Social Research

Achieving food security through agricultural research and harnessing its power for the poor has always been CGIAR's mission. Today, 'poverty reduction is the guiding principle of CGIAR-supported research.'[15] As the new strategy document articulates, 'CGIAR's greater focus on poverty reduction will entail increasing the role of socioeconomic research to augment understanding of people and their agricultural and technological needs' (Technical Advisory Committee, 2002: xiv, 33–34) as well as expanded attention to policy research. CGIAR can improve its contribution to poverty reduction by reorienting its research agenda, criteria and approaches to identifying and addressing the socioeconomic determinants of poverty.

By reframing CGIAR's goals in terms of poverty reduction, the role of social research shifts from one that serves technological adoption to one that helps define research priorities and policies. While it is not yet clear whether the management of each centre has incorporated this message into research programmes and staffing levels, since the numbers and qualifications of CGIAR social researchers have not improved, renewing attention to the status of social research is critical.

Social science researchers must reduce poverty, through their own research and by working in conjunction with biological scientists to develop creative synergies. Social science researchers also contribute to shaping the policies that centres provide to governments for agricultural development and sustainable management of natural resources, as well as the policies that development institutions adopt. Three such areas are discussed below.

- Development of a holistic understanding of poverty. The publication of two documents – *World Development Report 2000/2001: Attacking Poverty* World Bank, (2001) and *Guidelines on Poverty Reduction* (OECD/DAC, 2001) – marked a major shift in the conceptualization of poverty. This multidimensional definition of poverty included reference to various measures of 'well-being,' including health, food security and empowerment, and ended the measurement of poverty as simply a defined level of income. The work on which these reports were based largely depended on the work of economists and non-economist social scientists, and grew out of ethnographic and survey work on the lives of poor people, including their movements in and out of poverty, as well as studies of the impact of microfinance lending on vulnerability. Illuminating these social aspects of poverty can reframe the importance of social research in CGIAR's mandate to address the role of agriculture in reducing poverty.

- *Sustainability and sustainable development.* The concept of sustainability includes environmental, social, economic and financial[16] sustainability, and draws much from social science research in its conceptualization and approach.[17] Growing out of the 'Brundtland Report' (1987),[18] the term 'sustainable development' is defined as 'development that meets the needs of the present without compromising the ability of future generations to meet their needs' (WCED, 1987: 43). A key international event that enabled the concept of sustainability to become mainstreamed into the rhetoric and, in some cases, into donor policymaking was the first Earth Summit in 1992 in Rio de Janeiro, Brazil. Attempts to integrate provisions to ensure sustainability into development programmes are improved by including social science research frameworks and methodology.[19] Today, most development agencies accept sustainability as a key policy condition.

One of the most important contributions of social science research is the concept that agricultural research should not be carried out by CGIAR centres as if they operated in a social or cultural vacuum. Over the past 10–15 years, much CGIAR research is moving off the research station on to farmers' fields, and is now sometimes being managed and even designed by 'farmer researcher' organizations. These trends reflect the agricultural research community's recognition that, for their research to have a lasting impact, the determinants of sustainability should be explored and highlighted so as to inform all the centres' research.

As sustainability relies on aspects of the social and natural worlds, and on their interdependence, the concept of social capital has gained increasing importance for the agenda of social science research in CGIAR. Social capital refers to the norms and networks that enable collective action. Increasing evidence shows that social capital is critical for poverty alleviation and sustainable human and economic development.[20]

A different task is the formalization of social impact assessments that capture the concerns, issues and alternative analyses that non-economist social scientists have raised over the years. For example, negative environmental impacts (externalities in the neoclassical economic framework) often tend to have a stronger impact on the poor and the weak than on the wealthier and more powerful. By mainstreaming environmental considerations, other social concerns such as health, equity and cultural values are simultaneously addressed. Another strategy would be to better link environmental concerns to other areas or sectors such as health, cultural survival and economic livelihood to move beyond the routine thinking about the types of contributions and analysis of the social sciences.

- *Institutionalizing gender analysis.* The work on gender carried out by numerous bilateral and multilateral donor agencies is now voluminous. Initially, because of recognition of women's critical role in agricultural production, processing and marketing, the agriculture sector was one of the first in which studies were carried out and literature written. As a result, gender has been a central feature in the development and elaboration of participatory methodologies and in investigation into intrahousehold decision making and the importance of social networks.

CGIAR has partially institutionalized gender analysis in research questions. What remains to be done is to work within individual centres' programmes to ensure that the goals of gender equality that have been adopted by the governments of most donors under the 1995 Beijing Declaration on Women are translated into research design, implementation and analysis.

Strengthening Social Research and its Role in CGIAR

There is little doubt that significant support to integrating social science into the method and policies of CGIAR, such as that initiated by the Rockefeller Foundation's postdoctoral fellow programme, and the creation of several inter-centre initiatives to bring together biological and social scientists to work on particular development issues, have had positive results. Such efforts need to be continued and expanded, and sufficiently funded to maintain their effectiveness and productivity. The following table (see Table 19.1) indicates the scale and scope of some recent donor support to activities with significant social science components. The table does not attempt to be comprehensive but only illustrative of the variety of donors (14) that have funded social science research over the last few years. The Swiss Development Cooperation, DfID–UK, SIDA, European Union and Ford Foundation are strong recent supporters of social science research. Many donors, including USAID, have explicitly funded social science research over the years. In addition, donors such as the Swiss Development Corporation, CIDA and SIDA have official policy statements regarding social research.

At the same time, attention should be paid to smaller but also effective interventions. Drawing on the work of social and biological researchers, Malcolm Gladwell's (2000) stimulating book, *The Tipping Point*, documented many cases in which relatively small changes in how information is transmitted caused large shifts in human behaviour. Much like the wings of the fabled butterfly whose movements in one part of the world create a hurricane elsewhere (Lorenz, 1972), small but critical changes in information and knowledge sometimes have a large impact.

Table 19.1. Illustrative topics and levels of donor support for social research in CGIAR at three centres (All figures are US$ equivalents).

Centre	Dates	Activity	Funding
CIAT	Jan 2003	Mejorando los servicios locales de apoyo para Agroempresas en Yorito y Sulaco en Honduras y Caldono en Colombia (Improving the local support services for agribusinesses in Yorito and Sulaco in Honduras and in Caldono in Colombia)	New Zealand/ LADAF (US$17,821)
CIAT	Mar 2003	Enhancing the contribution of crop-livestock systems and agro-processing to sustainable livelihoods in peri-urban areas, Hanoi (interim phase II)	CGIAR (US$13,750)
CIAT	Oct 2003	Diversified livelihoods through effective agro-enterprise interventions	IDRC (US$421,234)
CIAT	Dec 2003	Small-scale agro-enterprise development in the uplands of Laos	SDC (US$2,523,000)
CIAT	Mar 2002	Building the agricultural assets and marketing opportunities of rural women and the poor, through participatory research in a resource to consumption framework	DGIC (US$203,030)
CIAT	Sep 2002	Participatory monitoring and evaluation for rural innovation	DfID–UK (US$462,405)

		in Bolivia to articulate poor farmers' demand for agricultural research with supply, and to increase the accountability of research providers to the poor	
CIAT	Dec 2002	Extending the lessons of participatory research from Africa and Latin America	Rockefeller Foundation (US$327,100)
CIAT	Mar 2003	Building capacity in social and gender analysis in the eastern Himalayas	IDRC (US$177,170)
CIAT	Apr 2003	Participatory research and gender analysis – Africa	CIDA (US$316,001)
CIAT	Jun 2003	Participatory research and gender analysis for technology development and institutional innovation	New Zealand (US$100,000)
CIFOR	1999–2001	Testing of criteria and indicators methodology Publications and translations	USAID/Jakarta USAID/EGAT (US$100,000) Ford Foundation (US$17,250)
CIFOR	2001–2003	People managing forests	USAID/Bolivia (US$300,000)
CIFOR	2000–2005	Legal literacy policy	Ford Foundation (US$475,000)
CIFOR	2001–2004	Adaptive collaborative management of forests in Asia (Indonesia, Nepal, Philippines) and in Africa (Cameroon, Ghana, Malawi, Zimbabwe)	Asian Development Bank (US$1.2 million over 3 years) European Community (US$1 million plus) DfID–UK (over US$526,000 in Africa, and US$500,000 in Indonesia)
CIFOR	2001–2003	Community forestry, criteria and indicators, gender and participation	IDRC (US$216,700)

(Continued)

Table 19.1. (*continued*)

Centre	Dates	Activity	Funding
CIFOR		Policy dialogue	SIDA (US$1 million)
CIFOR	2002–2004	Forest-poverty links	DfID–UK (US$510,000)
IFPRI		Strengthening development policy through gender analysis	USAID (US$3 million)
IFPRI	1999	CAPRi	SIDA (US$200,000)
IFPRI	2000–2003	CAPRi	Ford Foundation (US$1.2 million)
IFPRI	2003	CAPRi	BMZ (US$1 million)

BMZ, German Federal Ministry for Economic Cooperation and Development;
CAPRi, Collective Action and Property Rights;
CGIAR, Consultative Group on International Agricultural Research;
CIAT, International Center for Tropical Agriculture;
CIDA, Canadian International Development Agency;
CIFOR, Center for International Forestry Research;
DFID–UK, Department of International Development–UK;
DGIC (now called DGDC), Directorate-General for International Cooperation/Directorate-General for Development Cooperation, Belgium;
USAID/EGAT, United States Agency for International Development/Economic Growth, Agriculture, and Trade;
IDRC, International Development Research Centre;
IFPRI, International Food Policy Research Institute;
SDC, Swiss Agency for Development and Cooperation;
SIDA, Swedish International Development Agency;
USAID, US Agency for International Development.

Imagine for a moment that social science research was like that butterfly. What conditions would maximize its impact? According to Gladwell, three factors determine whether behavioural changes will grow dramatically or die away without notice: having the right agents to pass on information, having the right message and creating a context conducive to replicating the message. The agents include those who create the message (the 'mavens'), those who pass it on (the 'connectors') and those who persuade (the 'sales people'). The message itself must be 'sticky,' and the environment receptive. Gladwell argues that small details in the environment can either facilitate or impede the spread of information in ways that hugely affect the result. For change to occur, all of these factors must work together, but the process, once understood, can be manipulated for success.

Drawing from this brief review of social research efforts and impacts on policy, what conclusions can be drawn about how donor support can enhance these efforts? Many suggestions were put forward at the Cali conference and are presented in the chapters in this volume. Clearly there is no dearth of good ideas emerging from social science work for international agricultural research. But, following Gladwell's framework, have these ideas benefited from the right messengers' shaping a sticky message and sending it into an appropriately receptive environment? With few exceptions, what has been lacking is a systematic analysis of the process by which successful social research methods and conclusions are incorporated into the institutional context of CGIAR, and how to thoughtfully manipulate that process to improve the end results. Now we look at areas that donors might support to enhance the use and absorption of social research in the CGIAR system.

Do the Right 'Agents' Spread the Message about the Relevance of Social Research?

Three types of messengers are needed to promote the right message: those who discover or create the knowledge, those who connect the information to the right people and those who persuade them to take action. All scientists work to discover new knowledge, and they form the bulk of the professional CGIAR staff. Donors, in turn, need to consider changes in recent staffing patterns and commit to keep a diverse disciplinary mix active among centres' staff so that sufficient numbers of mavens of all types are in the system. In this volume, Paris *et al.* raise concerns about the number of non-economist social scientists at the International Rice Research Institute (IRRI), which they demonstrate is now 'below any definition of a 'critical mass', although economist positions are being maintained. Samad and Merrey at the International Water Management Institute (IWMI) make a similar point about the importance of maintaining an adequate presence of non-economist social scientists. The authors state that the share of social scientists in the institution has been fairly stable, but has declined and is currently at about 35% of all internationally recruited research staff, from an earlier level of 40%. As Meinzen-Dick *et al.* point out in this volume, numbers alone can be misleading: having senior staff, rather than post-doctoral fellows or junior staff, on board in one area of expertise, makes it easier to recruit additional specialists as needed for short-term consultancies. In addition, unless the interdisciplinary work starts at the design phase with a diverse staff, the social researchers always have to adapt to a plan created under a different paradigm and risk being marginalized.

Some key staff members, particularly those in charge of the cross-centre initiatives, can be considered connectors. Building networks of various sorts across the CGIAR centres and among groups of CGIAR researchers, by problem and discipline, is important. A 'sociology of CGIAR research networks' (J. Kathy Parker, Delaware, 2004, personal communication) could increase effectiveness of research inside CGIAR and is a task ready for initiation. This is a category that could easily benefit from donor support. Funding might be made available to support the work of several social researchers who connect people within and across centres as well as between centres and other organizations to boost cross-disciplinary synergies, whether in a particular country context or by a particular subject, as well as to study the process of networking and interdisciplinarity. It is also critically important to connect CGIAR social researchers to the global social science research community.

Structural changes, such as the creation of cross-sectoral funding mechanisms can strengthen the approaches discussed above. Indeed, dialogue across disciplinary sectors has increased over the past years; many development programme officers and researchers now express genuine interest in these alternative approaches, but actual integrated work remains in the minority because the funding mechanisms are limited to supporting a single sector. Providing institutional space and in this case, a funding mechanism, would allow realization of more substantive collaboration.

Wide dissemination of information alone is still not enough. CGIAR social researchers also need to cultivate enthusiastic advocates who can help persuade others of the need for a holistic approach to agricultural research. Ideally, those advocating social research would have a range of disciplinary backgrounds. Social and biological scientists must share responsibility for advocating effective integration of social research.

It is not only within CGIAR that social science capabilities should be bolstered by adding qualified staff. Samad and Merrey (Chapter 7 this volume) note that the number of social scientists within national partner organizations is too low, and is unlikely to improve quickly, limiting the social scientists' ability to work effectively through partnerships on complex development topics. An important role for significant donor support would be to build social science capability within the national agricultural research and extension systems, much as the Rockefeller Foundation sought to do within CGIAR through the postdoctoral fellow programme.

Have Social Researchers Crafted the Right Message?

Many agricultural researchers and extension agents have thought deeply about how to convey their technical advice to farmers to enhance adoption, and about communicating science to policymakers. Some excellent work on the relationship between science and policy illuminates how the different characteristics of the worlds (e.g. different vocabularies and time frames, different incentive structures and different audiences and different orientations to 'truth' or to 'compromise') each inhibit clear communication between them, and complicate the creation of science-based policy (Tabor *et al.*, 1998). Little institutional effort, however, has been exerted to put some of these findings into practice; this has been left to individuals. Social researchers have not made the effort to reshape the messages they want to convey to their other disciplinary colleagues or vice versa.

Paris *et al.* (Chapter 4 this volume) remark that 'social scientists are often perceived to be the "bearers" of bad news (when they report findings critical of centres' research) rather than the "drivers" of research for technology development and diffusion.' Clearly, the positive contributions of social research to the CGIAR mandate need to become better known. Donors could support efforts to identify what characteristics would make social research ideas likely to make a difference in the work of biologically oriented scientists.

How Should Centres Change to Enhance the Success of Social Research?

Although many specific examples for halting the erosion of social science expertise in the CGIAR system and for improving the ability of current staff to carry out social research have already been presented elsewhere in this volume and earlier in this chapter, we propose two ways to create a different environment for integrating social science perspectives that could have a marked impact:

- *Include social science as the default position for new research proposals.* A proposal for new research programmes in CGIAR will need to explain the social aspects of the research and how they will be carried out, or else justify why the activity did not require such attention. Paris *et al.* (Chapter 4 this volume) note that many donors require positive social impact, and some already require proposals to 'explicitly state that social (including gender) concerns are addressed in the process as well as by the impact of the research project'. Among the donors mentioned that are prioritizing social concerns in research are the Swiss Agency for Development and Cooperation, DfID–UK, Australian Council of Agricultural Research, Danida, Asian Development Bank, International Fund for Agricultural Development and CGIAR Global Challenge Programme (see Paris *et al.,* Chapter 4 this volume). Including the social science perspective would become the default, rather than the unusual, condition. This approach has been taken by advocates of gender integration with growing success.[21] Thinking through whether or not a new research idea needs to consider the economic, cultural or political context could be a stimulating process that could lead to new solutions to old problems.

- *Include social science in every centre.* To maintain the gains and benefits that social science research has provided to CGIAR as a whole, the system also must clearly recognize the concerns raised at the Cali conference. Several centres have seen a marked decline in the number and quality of social science researchers. For example, several recent External Programme Management Reviews (EMPRs) have recommended hiring more researchers and improving support to social science research within various centres. Most recently, EMPRs have recommended additional support from centres for social science research (i.e. International Center for Agricultural Research in the Dry Areas (ICARDA), International Crops Research Institute for the Semi-Arid Tropics (ICRISAT), International Institute of Tropical Agriculture (IITA) and/or commended other centres (i.e. Centro Internacional de Agricultura Tropical or the International Center for Tropical Agriculture (CIFOR), CIP and International Center for Tropical Agriculture (CIAT)) for providing good institutional support to social science research centres.'[22]

The following quote from ICARDA's 2001 EMPR (TAC, 2001) captures the general sense from most EMPRs across the CGIAR system: 'There is high demand for the time of the social scientists by the national agricultural research system as well as other scientists in ICARDA.' However, and unfortunately, ICARDA's social science research numbers have declined since 2001.

As several assessments have pointed out, the number, level and type of social science researchers have varied across the years and across the centres. The first step is a commitment for centres to hire qualified social scientists for research programmes. Creating positions for postdoctoral fellows is an important step, especially if there is room for their promotion and maintenance at the centre after they have recovered from their culture shock and begun to function as team members. Maintaining senior staff positions for social researchers is also key, as noted earlier, since not only do they have greater legitimacy within a centre but also greater access to larger pools of other experts with social science expertise.

Building on the findings of the Technical Advisory Committee and Science Council assessments and the Cali conference, donors can support a comprehensive analysis of current staffing patterns to identify which subdisciplines would be most useful in which centres. Donors could link new programmes to revitalize university systems and training efforts, such as the ongoing Partnership for Higher Education in Africa and the new long-term training programmes being initiated by USAID, to recruitment of new staff in the centres. Donors might also choose to support postdoctoral programmes and senior positions, particularly for regionally recruited staff, to expand the number and diversity of social researchers in the system and help centres find ways to finance these positions.

Conclusion

Ten years ago, most of the papers and commentary in the *Social Science in the CGIAR* (Collinson and Platais, 1992) emphasized the key role of social science research in what Jock Anderson of the World Bank called the 'human factors' of international agricultural research. Anderson as well as others in the volume also called for greater involvement of social scientists in policy work, an area that remains a challenge for centres and social researchers. We have argued that this area has grown in importance over the past 10 years.

The status of social science research and social research in CGIAR remains, in Anderson's (1992: 116) term, 'mixed,' although there have been areas of real advance. Consistent systemwide institutional support is lacking. We feel that support for social science knowledge as a public good (see Dalrymple, Chapter 22 this volume) could be better coordinated and funded, making donors' efforts more effective and helping build stronger social research in CGIAR.

Acknowledgements

Many CGIAR staff members (too numerous to list individually) responded to our requests for information about the type of social research each had undertaken, and their thoughts on ways to enhance donor support in this arena. Special thanks to Dana Dalrymple and Michael Cernea for their willingness to read successive drafts of this piece and to provide thoughtful commentary on each one.

Notes

[1]In this chapter, we include economics and non-economics social sciences (anthropology, sociology, geography and political science) under the umbrella of 'social

research'. We indicate where we are referring to economics or the non-economics social sciences, as appropriate.

[2]A few social scientists have moved into positions of leadership within the CGIAR system. In 2000, Joachim Voss, a social anthropologist, was named director general at the International Center for Tropical Agriculture (CIAT). Agricultural economists have a broader record of appointment, including Joachim von Braun at the International Food Policy Research Institute (IFPRI) (since 2002), Carlos Seré at the International Livestock Research Institute (ILRI) (since 2002), Peter Hartmann at the International Institute of Tropical Agriculture (IITA) (since 2001), David Kaimowitz at the Center for International Forestry Research (CIFOR) (since 2001) and John Mellor at IFPRI (1977 to 1990). Others head research programmes at individual centres.

[3]The programme, whose grantees were informally known as 'Rocky docs', is described in more detail elsewhere in this volume (Conway *et al.*, Chapter 18,).

[4]From 1975 to 1984, 21 of 33 of the postdoctoral fellows were anthropologists (Rhoades, 1984: 5). Several innovative programmes at CGIAR centres and their partners were initially designed with the direct involvement of Rockefeller postdoctoral fellows either during or after their fellowship, including the farmer-back-to-farmer model at the International Potato Center (CIP), a shift to institutional analysis of property rights and collective action at IFPRI, an approach that has since grown into an inter-centre initiative, and the Social Science Interface Project at the International Centre for Insect Physiology and Ecology (ICIPE) among others. Currently, 23% of social researchers are either anthropologists or sociologists, and 61% are economists (referenced in the write-up of the Cali conference).

[5]See the joint ISNAR and Rockefeller Foundations reports on a CGIAR Inter-Center Seminar on Women and Agricultural Technology held in Bellagio, Italy, in March 1985. The conference sought to review efforts by the centres and to improve their integration of women's concerns and participation into development and adoption of new agricultural technologies.

[6]The programme was originally funded through special project funds contributed by the Australian Council for International Agricultural Research (ACIAR), US Agency for International Development (USAID), Canadian International Development Agency (CIDA), Dutch Ministry of Foreign Affairs, Ford Foundation, International Development Research Centre (IDRC) in Canada, Overseas Development Administration (UK) and the Norwegian Royal Ministry of Foreign Affairs.

[7]See http://www.ifpri.org/themes/mp17.htm.

[8]The Strengthening Development Policy through Gender Analysis Project was supported by USAID's Office of Women in Development, formerly with the Bureau of Economic Growth and Agricultural Development, from 1995 to 2001, with US$3 million.

[9]Field studies involving primary data collection were conducted in Bangladesh, Ethiopia, Guatemala and South Africa; a small-grant programme funded additional

work in Brazil, Ecuador, Ghana, Indonesia, Nepal, Peru, the Philippines and Zimbabwe.

[10]More information on the GENDEV Network is available at http://www.ifpri.org/themes/mp17/gender/gender.htm. USAID funds supported a seminar series in Washington, DC, an electronic list-serve, electronic forum on gender and property rights (1995–1996) and a published newsletter (1994–1999).

[11]The programme also received funds from other donors: Department of International Development–UK (DfID–UK), the governments of Japan and Mexico, the Danish International Development Agency (Danida) and the Swedish International Development Agency (SIDA), as well as the World Bank and the World Health Organization (WHO).

[12]For example, USAID established the environmental review process in 1984, known as Regulation 216 (Title 22, Part 216 of the Code of Federal Regulations). It requires that all USAID-funded activities undergo an environmental review to avoid or lessen any potential adverse impacts on the environment. CIDA in 1986 'adopted an environment policy that led to the application of procedures for routine environmental screening and assessment of projects'. Other donors, including the World Bank and Asian Development Bank, require environmental analysis through national processes such as national environmental action plans, or provide funds to directly support policy analysis, technical assistance on conservation and sustainable development projects and institutional strengthening.

[13]Singh, N. and Wanmali, S. (1998) 'Sustainable Livelihoods Concept Paper' (http://www.undp.org/sl/Documnets/Strategy-papers/Concept_Paper/Concept_of_SL.htm)

[14]The Center for International Forestry Research (CIFOR), International Agroforestry Research Centre (ICRAF), WorldFish Center (ICLARM), and International Water Management Institute (IWMI).

[15]www.cgiar.org

[16]CIDA identifies four types of sustainability: economic, social, cultural, and political.

[17]United Nations Department of Social and Economic Affairs, http://www.un.org/esa/sustdev/

[18]The official title of the 'Brundtland Report' is *Our Common Future* (World Commission on Environment and Development, 1987).

[19]See, for example, a recent statement by a group of agricultural scientists: 'For any technology to be successful, social scientists should be an integral part of new technology development and use' (Miller, Hanson, Fretz and Weismiller, 2004: 57).

[20]See http://www.worldbank.org/poverty/scapital/whatsc.htm

[21]At USAID, a gender analysis is required to prepare any new strategic plan. A new activity design is also required to demonstrate that gender issues have been identified or that a waiver has been granted.

[22]CGIAR provides an oversight mechanism to insure transparency and accountability through EPMRs. These are the joint responsibility of the Science Council and CGIAR secretariat and are conducted for each centre approximately every 5 years.

References

Anderson, J. (1992) Social science in agricultural research: implications and issues for IARCs. In: Collinson, M. and Platais, K.W. (eds) *Social Science in the CGIAR. Proceedings of a meeting of CGIAR social scientists held at the International Service for National Agricultural Research (ISNAR), The Hague, The Netherlands, August 1992.* Study Paper No. 28. World Bank, Washington, DC, pp. 88–104.

Becker, T. (2000) Participatory Research in the CGIAR. Paper prepared for the NGO workshop, Food for All – Farmer First in Research. Available online: http://www.agrecol.de/dokumente/1TBECKER.pdf

Bellon, M.R. and Morris, M.L. (2002) Linking Global and Local Approaches to Agricultural Technology Development: The Role of Participatory Plant Breeding Research in the CGIAR. Economics Working Paper 02–03. International Maize and Wheat Improvement Center, Mexico, DF, 30 pp.

Cernea, M.M. and Guggenheim, S.E. (1985) Is anthropology superfluous in farming systems research? *Farming Systems Research. Kansas State University Research Series* 4(9), 504–517. (Also reprinted in the World Bank Reprint Series No. 367, Washington, DC, World Bank.)

Collinson, M. and Platais, K.W. (eds) (1992) *Social Science in the CGIAR. Proceedings of a meeting of CGIAR social scientists held at the International Service for National Agricultural Research (ISNAR), The Hague, The Netherlands, August 1992.* Study Paper No. 28. World Bank, Washington, DC, 160 pp.

Feldstein, H.S. and Merrill-Sands, D. (1996) Gender and the renewal of the CGIAR, *CGIAR News* 3(2), May.

Feldstein, H.S. and Slack, A. (1995) Inventory of Gender-related Research and Training in the International Agricultural Research Centers, 1990–1995. CGIAR Gender Program, Working Paper No. 8. CGIAR Secretariat, Washington, DC, 74 pp.

Fujisaka, S. (1993) Will Farmer Participatory Research Survive in the International Agricultural Research Centres? *Gatekeeper Series No. 44.* International Institute for Environment and Development, Sustainable Agriculture and Rural Livelihoods Programme, London, 13 pp.

Gladwell, M. (2000) *The Tipping Point: How Little Things Can Make a Big Difference.* Little, Brown and Co., New York, 301 pp.

Lorenz, K. (1972) Predictability: Does the Flap of a Butterfly's Wings in Brazil Set Off a Tornado in Texas? Talk presented at the American Association for the Advancement of Science meetings in Washington, DC. Available online: http://www.cmp.calttech.edu/~mcc/chaos_nes/Lorenz.html

Miller, R.J., Hanson, J., Fretz, T. and Weismiller, R. (2004) Science and education: necessary conditions for successful agriculture and rural development. *Outlook on Agriculture* 33(1), 55–58.

Moock, J.L. (1992) Introduction. In: Moock, J.L. and Rhoades, R.E. (eds) *Diversity, Farmer Knowledge, and Sustainability*. Cornell University Press, Ithaca, New York, pp. 1–10.

Organisation for Economic Co-operation and Development (OECD) (2001) *Guidelines on Poverty Reduction*. OECD, Paris, 127 pp.

Rennie, J.K. and Singh, N.C. (1996) *Community Adaptation and Sustainable Livelihoods Program Guidebook on Participatory Research for Sustainable Livelihoods: A Guide for Field Projects on Adaptive Strategies*. International Institute for Sustainable Development, Winnipeg, Manitoba, 122 pp. Available online: http:// www.iisd. org/casl/caslguide/GuideBook-home.htm

Rhoades, R.E. (1984) *Breaking New Ground: Agricultural Anthropology*. International Potato Center, Lima, Peru, 71 pp.

Rhoades, R. (2000) New disciplinary blood in an International Research Organization. In: Higgins, P.J. and Paredes, J.A. (eds) *Classics of Practicing Anthropology 1978–1998*. Society for Applied Anthropology, Oklahoma City, Oklahoma, pp. 159–162.

Rhoades, R.E. and Booth, R.H. (1982) Farmer-back-to-farmer: a model for generating acceptable agricultural technology. *Agricultural Administration* 11(2), 127–137.

Rockefeller Foundation and International Service for National Agricultural Research (1985) *Women and Agricultural Technology: Relevance for Research*. Vol. 1: *Analyses and Conclusions*. ISNAR and the Rockefeller Foundation, The Hague, The Netherlands, 79 pp.

Singh, N. and Wanmali, S. (1998) Sustainable Livelihoods Concept Paper. Available online: http:// www.undp.org/sl/Documnets/ Strategy-papers/Concept_Paper/Concept_of_SL.htm

Tabor, S.R., Faber, D.C., Meijerink, G. and Duiker, S. (1998) The research-policy interface. In: Tabor, S.R. and Faber, D.C. (eds) *Closing the Loop: From Research on Natural Resources to Policy Change. Policy Management Report No. 8*. European Centre for Development Policy Management, Maastricht, The Netherlands, pp. 8–21.

Technical Advisory Committee Report (2000) *A Food Secure World for All: Toward a New Vision and Strategy for the CGIAR*. SDR/TAC:IAR/00/14.1 Rev. 2. CGIAR, Washington, DC, p. xiv.

Technical Advisory Committee (2001) Report of the Fourth External Programme and Management Review – ICARDA. TAC Secretariat, FAO, Rome.

World Bank (2001) *World Develop-ment Report 2000/2001: Attack-ing Poverty.* The World Bank, Washington, DC, 335 pp.

World Commission on Environment and Development (WCED) (1987) *Our Common Future.* Oxford University Press, Oxford, 343 pp.

Seeking Half our Brains: Constraints and Incentives in the Social Context of Interdisciplinary Research

20

Robert E. Rhoades

Almost from the dawn of the 'age of development' after World War II, insightful biological or 'natural' scientists and practitioners have realized that technical solutions alone are inadequate for effective change. Dart (1963), a physicist working in Nepal in the early 1960s, wrote:

> We (technical people), in our turn, are puzzled and exasperated, yet in our puzzlement we ourselves doubt the relevance or competence of our own social science. The very development of Western science which should help us the most we are unwilling to use, bravely we struggle ahead without it, as though to show the world that we can do it anyway...even with half our brains tied behind us.

Four decades later, as we examine the contributions of the social sciences in interdisciplinary efforts to improve the livelihoods of the poor in developing countries, we have to ask whether or not we are anywhere close to becoming Dart's 'half our brains' of agricultural research and development. As we begin a new century of scientific improvement of agriculture, do social scientists still inspire doubt among, and appear irrelevant to, their biological science colleagues? If this is the case, as some observers argue, what are the historical and structural reasons for our continuing inability to incorporate analysis of the human dimension into the technical challenges of feeding the world and protecting the environment? Given the widespread agreement over Dart's argument that social science is relevant, what can be done to overcome the under-utilization and marginality of the human sciences in agricultural and environmental research?

The converse of biological scientists' doubt is the perception of social scientists that they work in institutional settings that either do not value their input or wish to channel their contributions into less-than-professionally satisfying roles (e.g. *ex-post facto* impact or adoption analysis). In short, social scientists feel like 'second-class citizens' in a world dominated by biological scientists or economists. I analyse my experiences in distinct institutional contexts to point to commonalities of experience that grow from the broad structural issues of how the social sciences are positioned and rewarded within research organizations, whether applied or academic. I argue that the status of social research in many Consultative Group on International Agriculture Research (CGIAR) centres, regardless of the organizational setting or personality of the researcher, lessens the potential of social science to help develop agriculture. This ascribed status of social scientists is not unique but part of a larger institutional problem of scientific prestige and a reward system that cuts across a range of organizations and contexts. A better understanding of the 'sociology (or politics) of knowledge' will more clearly reveal the problems faced by social scientists and can give enlightened managers a better way of balancing the interdisciplinary process so that technical, economic and socio-cultural dimensions are accounted for through research and effectively utilized in application and policy.

The analysis is based on personal 'participant observation' of interdisciplinary dynamics since the early 1960s. In-depth immersion in a wide range of social science roles within agricultural organizations allows me to compare problems of interdisciplinary research and development. Social science hats I have worn include those of farm extension worker (Nepal, 1962–1964); graduate student researcher (Philippines, International Rice Research Institute (IRRI), 1967); consultant (various); team leader and member (Peru, International Potato Center (CIP), 1979–1999); agricultural administrator (Philippines, Users' Perspectives with Agricultural Research and Development (UPWARD), 1988–1991); board member (various international centres); and university professor (USA, 1991–present). However, I will focus mainly on my 12 years in CGIAR from the late 1970s to the early 1990s and subsequently, as an anthropology professor in a US land-grant university. Although a CGIAR centre and a university are distinct settings, I show that many problems social scientists face in agricultural research are recurring. A comparison of the two settings will reveal differences but also structural commonalities, which can lead to deeper insights about social research in agriculture.

Interdisciplinary teams involving biological and social scientists make good sense. Real-world problems – hunger, low production, polluted water or genetic erosion – are by their nature interdisciplinary since they involve biology, ecology, economics and social questions. Sustainability science is ideally a collective venture based on the creed that no one discipline can fully understand the scope of the problem and provide all the answers. The idea is that problem solving, especially collaboratively with farmers, is more than a juxtaposition of specialized knowledge or simply placing one discipline alongside another. If joint problem solving is desirable, which the propaganda of CGIAR centres and universities advertises, an institution proclaiming that creed should provide the setting, resources and rewards for scientists who identify, formulate and resolve a commonly perceived problem. Each discipline needs opportunity and encouragement to appreciate the knowledge and language of the other so that the team can transgress boundaries and challenge them. Donors have seized on the rationality of interdisciplinary teamwork by insisting on the inclusion of some amount of social science research on relevant social and cultural variables in projects, even in the most reductionist efforts such as biotechnology.

How is this ideal played out in the institutional reality of attempting to combine and transcend disciplines in solving problems? What political and social dynamics of working on teams unfold in the trenches? How do the various disciplines perceive each other and how are roles assigned and rewards distributed? How do perceptions and rewards ultimately affect the outcomes of research for effective problem solving? While I cannot answer all these questions here, comparing my experiences might offer some insights and a few suggestions for using 'all our brains' in agricultural research and development. I will begin by looking back on my experiences as one of the first anthropologists to work in CGIAR. I will analyse these experiences within the social context of the centre's different disciplines and compare these experiences to similar efforts to incorporate social science into agricultural projects in a large US land-grant university. Finally, I will point to possible institutional innovations useful for crafting new perspectives on improving communication between those who deal with the 'agri' and those who deal with the 'culture' of agriculture.

Status and Rewards for Social Science in the CGIAR: the International Potato Center Experience

From around 1975 to 1990, CIP was a hotbed of experimentation in using social scientists on interdisciplinary teams. The reasons for this development and its successes and failures have been extensive documented in a number of publications (Rhoades and Booth, 1983; Rhoades, 1984; Thiele *et al.*, 2001). CIP was founded and directed for more than two decades by an innovative director general (Richard Sawyer) who wanted to prove his uniqueness in a system dominated by grain-based centres such as IRRI or the International Maize and Wheat Improvement Center (CIMMYT). While economics was the dominant human science in all CGIAR centres, in defining its differentness within the centres CIP also saw a potential role for anthropologists and sociologists. In Peru, where CIP is headquartered, anthropology is a strong academic discipline on par with economics in the universities as well as in civil-society organizations, especially those that work with or represent Andean or Amazonian indigenous peoples. Douglas Horton, who headed CIP's Social Science Department in the 1970s and 1980s, was a Cornell University economics graduate and a friend of many well-known Peruvian anthropologists. These personal contacts and the creation in 1975 of the Rockefeller Foundation postdoctoral programme in the social sciences allowed CIP to bring in outside anthropologists such as myself, and also to staff many of its Peru-based teams with 'non-economists', as sociologists and anthropologists were defined in those days.

Despite the willingness to experiment with non-economists, however, CIP was typical of the biological science-dominated crop institute of that era. When I first arrived in 1979 as a recent PhD in anthropology, I was immediately and constantly reminded that I was a suspected newcomer admitted with extreme reservation into a house of hallowed potato scientists. The first test for acceptance was to demonstrate what one knew about the potato plant which, in my case, was next to nothing. CIP in its early years had a clear hierarchy that ran from the breeder to the plant physiologist to the agronomist to the economist and finally to the lowly bottom – the anthropologist. This pecking order was reflected in virtually every aspect of the centre's formal and informal operations, from cocktail parties to the distribution of funds. The all-important 'show your stuff' annual review meeting began with prime-time presentations by the breeding programme and ended days later with a few rushed minutes by the social scientists. Everyone knew exactly where one stood in the disciplinary hierarchy. Tongue in cheek, beleaguered CIP social scientists used to compare the social dynamics to the Hindu caste system.

The social inequity also translated into fewer core resources for social scientists, who largely existed on special-project 'soft' funds and were typically released when these ran out. Social scientists were employed at CIP and other international agriculture centres in the late 1970s and early 1980s mainly because donors (e.g. Rockefeller Foundation) provided earmarked funds for issues such as gender, social impact assessment or nutrition. It was unlikely that any international centre, *circa* 1975, would have hired an anthropologist or sociologist on its own, using core funds.

The antagonism towards social scientists from the institutionally more powerful biological scientists and economists was perhaps less a matter of Dart's 'doubting the relevance or competence' of social science than it was turf guarding and protection of status and its rewards, underpinned by a philosophical misconception about social versus technical research. I believe that few of my biological science colleagues understood enough social science to doubt its 'relevance or competence'. The soft-money social scientists were constantly reminded that they had to 'prove themselves' before they would be accepted. The proving ideally had to involve a unique contribution to the centre's potato technology mandate. Proving one's uniqueness, however, was difficult since each higher-ranked discipline thought it could do whatever the next discipline in the hierarchy could do, and better. The breeder claimed that a good variety would create its own 'suction' force (projects were described by CIP's largely male scientific staff in metaphorical sexual symbolic language such as suction, thrusting, fathering, birthing pains). So why did we need an agronomist standing between him and the farmer? The agronomist argued that an 'economically aware' agronomist could do farm budgeting, so why did he need an economist? The economist, in turn, said he could make 'social observations', so why did we need an anthropologist? The questioning ended with the anthropologist, who had no one below him or, worse, her. Disciplinary ethnocentrism was strong and the social stratification clear and painful for those at the bottom of the social ladder.

There was an overall scepticism of the value of social science research, especially 'pure' research, which did not focus narrowly on technology generation. This, too, was understandable given that biological scientists were under strong pressure (both self-motivated and institutionally fostered) to accomplish the centre's short-run technical goals. The director general told me on the first day I arrived in Lima that he did not want his social scientists hanging like a nest of angry hornets outside CIP, but to be integrated into the business of producing more and better potatoes for developing countries. Economists and social scientists (anthropologists and sociologists) in those days were largely relegated to two narrow 'service roles': technology adoption studies ('Tell us how many farmers are adopting CIP technologies') and generation of statistical information that would elevate the potato's image, especially in comparison to grains. Anthropologists generally inherited the 'mop-up' role of identifying what went right or wrong (the last being a very unpopular finding) in adoption. Economists crunched potato statistics to put the centre in a good light *vis-à-vis* other centres competing for the same resources. In retrospect this too, was comprehensible given the struggle for resources within a globally competitive agricultural research context. However, the assigned roles for social scientists also highlighted how different disciplines were perceived, used and incorporated within CGIAR during its early years.

Fresh out of graduate school, where I had been immersed in the great debates of dependency theory, systems theory, cybernetics and neo-functionalism, doing 'mop-up' analysis of Dr Breeder's breeding lines or Ing. Agronomo's planting technique was hardly what I had in mind as an anthropological research career. I had yet to learn that performance in CGIAR was evaluated in terms of how individuals or teams served the narrow and clearly focused goals of the employer, not what they contributed to the theory of the discipline. Given the emphasis on managed teamwork and crop impacts, the first several years of anthropologists' efforts in CGIAR were far from successful. There were many early resignations, early releases and – for those who stayed – rebellion or on-the-job resistance. There were success stories, such as CIP's diffused-light potato storage, but these were far and few between. Young anthropologists had been ill-prepared by their academic programmes to work on interdisciplinary teams, where they had to blend and modify anthropological methods and skills to match the focused research agendas. Rural sociologists might have been better trained but their field was undergoing a crisis of being eliminated in its university homes and few found their way into the early CGIAR. Anthropologists did not have a 'client' relation with society in the same way as economists, agronomists or even plant breeders, and were reluctant to service a technical research mandate. Netting (1974) pointed to a problem with anthropology and its application to agriculture:

> Agriculture was considered too basic for the ambitious new science of man, the suspicion still lingers that it is intellectually *'infra dig'*. The supposed simplicity, concreteness and lack of system in most non-Western farming techniques did not attract minds stimulated by the complex, abstract order of kinship terminology, descent groups or ritual patterns.

At the same time, administrators, biological scientists and economists held stereotypical views of social scientists and what they should be doing (which rarely corresponded to what anthropologists thought they should be doing). Most agricultural scientists, however, had little idea about what anthropology or sociology did or what they could contribute.

Despite management's proclamations that CIP was 'one big family', social scientists there and in the rest of CGIAR were clearly considered 'outsiders' in Merton's conceptual dualism of 'insider–outsider'. In building up the field of the sociology of knowledge, Merton (1972) argued that, based on their social status, certain groups claim to have privileged access to new knowledge and its production. Although

Merton was in the main writing about scholarly interpretation of issues such as race and gender, he would have certainly approved of applying his theory to the international centres where 'insiderism' characterized the biological science-dominated CGIAR. When social scientists baulked at being defined by insider values – naïvely believing they were free to contribute a distinct set of knowledge and methods – insiders tended to describe social scientists as difficult, alienating, rule break-ers, negative and having a number of other personality disorders. Despite the fact that biological science is not homogeneous, Merton would have seen similarities in the way that disciplines group under a single definition and impose their ethnocentrism on those not con-sidered fully legitimate or proven in terms of institutional values. The centre's doctrine was defined by the biological and technical mandates, and a social scientist had to surrender to them to gain acceptance as a full colleague.

As in all human groups, however, participants in CIP's activities did not interpret day-to-day social interactions in an objective, intel-lectual fashion. Rather, social status was not only understood in terms of budgets, salaries and perks, but was also played out in the centre's halls, offices and fields in conversations, jokes, gossip and ridicule. In laboratories and the field, jokes abounded among biological scientists about 'their' esoteric anthropologist who behaved strangely. For exam-ple, one anthropologist (the 'Lone Ranger' type) was rumoured to refuse rides in institute field vehicles for fear of being identified with the centre's officials, and was not considered a 'team player' because he insisted on walking to the village alone and interacting there unac-companied. Women anthropologists and sociologists were even more prone to be stereotyped. They were accused of carrying the 'gender thing' too far through emotional outbreaks and verbal haranguing of patriarchal male colleagues. Methods of anthropologists were put down as too qualitative, and ethnographic research as taking too long. Social scientists were portrayed by their colleagues as vocal anti-change 'naysayers' who preached about how technical people had gone wrong. While some insiders explained the behaviour of social scien-tists in psychological terms (uppity, temperamental, sensitive, emo-tional), a better explanation perhaps lay in understanding their position within the centre's status sets.

Criticism of early social scientists in CGIAR may have had less to do with substantive matters of social science theory, methods or poten-tial knowledge than the 'new kid on the block' syndrome. Anthropolo-gists and sociologists were vulnerable to scrutiny, especially from economists who were still marginal in their newly won 'insider' status and thus felt most threatened by the newcomers. 'Murder occurs more frequently inside the family', observed one biological science participant after witnessing a nasty confrontation between economists and anthropologists at CIP.

My point is that the fate of many early social scientists, which was more institutional failure than success, was in large part unavoidable and a natural process of social dynamics. Merton's 'insiders' felt they shared the group's deepest concerns, and all efforts had to be relevant and subservient to them. To succeed and gain acceptance, social scientists had little choice but to redefine their methods, theories and subjects as well as discard most of what they had learned about holism, systems thinking and interrelatedness of human cultures. The socio-historical context had delivered to biological science a monopolistic and highly privileged status based on access to knowledge and control.

Despite an almost universal agreement as to its importance, interdisciplinary research as a group dynamic has rarely been described. One exception is a reflective paper from that era co-authored by Horton (economist), Robert Booth (biological scientist) and me (anthropologist), using the humorous metaphor of the Three Stooges (comic movie figures of the 1950s) to describe how our team really worked, as opposed to the way farming systems research manuals said it should (Rhoades *et al.*, 1986). We independently described our own views of team dynamics and interaction at CIP and why the chances of failure were high for such teams. We were all aware of the institutional context of differential resources and rewards accorded the disciplines.

Horton and I wrote about the strong pressures we felt to water down our disciplines to support the narrow technical knowledge produced by the elite biological scientists. Anything that looked like holism, policy and a non-technical matter was declared interesting but basically irrelevant to technological priorities. The pressure to leave behind social science theory and methods took place not only through rejected work plans or reduced funding but also informally in the centre's work culture. I wrote (Rhoades *et al.*, 1986: 24):

> There was a sort of ritualized form of 'insults' which were passed back
> and forth between members of different disciplines. I was totally
> unprepared for the intense questioning that I as an anthropologist had to
> face...the issue was constantly forced on me; 'prove what anthropology
> can contribute' or 'why does agricultural research need anthropology?'

Like Marx's divided working classes, economists and anthropologists were more threatened by each other than by the powerful biological scientists they both wanted to please. Again, I wrote (Rhoades *et al.*, 1986: 24):

> the problem that anthropologists and economists have with each other
> probably arises less from subject matter competition than from problems
> of rewards and recognition. At least in my own case, when I perceived
> that I might be destined for a service role to economics, I balked. It was

better to form alliances with biological scientists than to become a 'pet anthropologist' to an economist. Economists, on the other hand, had their own problem of becoming 'pet economists' to agronomists or other biological scientists.

Horton (Rhoades *et al.*, 1986: 30) also zeroed in on the institutional context of rewards and statuses. For brevity, he called economists 'cons', anthropologists 'ants', and biological scientists 'bios'. He wrote:

> Within agricultural research institutes such as CIP, biologists maintain higher status and more authority than social scientists. As a consequence, there is a latent tendency to consider 'ants' and 'cons' as assistants to the technologists. In this role, which both ants and cons fiercely fight against, the actual contribution of social scientists to the applied research process is far below its potential.
> CIP's first social scientist was a con, and the head of the Social Science Department has always been a con. Hence, ants are not only newcomers but they are a kind of third-class citizen, below both the bios and cons. Especially in the early years, ants tended to feel that cons like to keep them down, rather than share second-class status with them.
> Consequently, in order to break out of their third-class status and get 'out from under' the cons, ants have been eager to establish strong ties with powerful members of CIP's bio-elite. This situation was further complicated by a 'divide and conquer' approach of some bios (page 31).

Booth criticized the anthropologist and economist for their tendency to stray from the centre's technical mandate. Anthropologists, he said, are apt to think they know all about farmers (but little about technological needs) while economists cannot communicate their basic concepts to non-economists. Claims of discrimination, he said, arise from 'sour grapes', especially among economists who had lost control to technical scientists. Booth notes (Rhoades *et al.*, 1986: 36):

> (the team's) attention should not be allowed to drift away from the team's objective, and the potential **technological solution.** All team members must **service the defined objective** and not be tempted into side studies unless these are agreed to be necessary to the accomplishment of the objective. Anthropologists appear to be particularly prone to the above, and, **if not controlled**, are commonly tempted into complex and complete studies of particular communities or situations. While such a study may be interesting, it may go well beyond what is required for the generation and **transfer of the specific agricultural technology** which is the objective of the team efforts (emphasis mine).

Booth was by far the most open at CIP to working with social scientists, and much social science success was due to his collaboration and leadership. His statement, however, is clear as to expectation of how teamwork was to proceed: entirely in the service of potato technology generation.

It should not be assumed from my 'looking back' that the CIP experience was a failure for social scientists. The same experience is considered one of the biggest successes of social science in the entire CGIAR. CIP has been described as nothing less than 'world renowned as a centre for participatory research' (Thiele *et al.*, 2001). The impacts derived from CIP's use of anthropologists and sociologists even inside the box of technology generation were widespread. The 'farmer-back-to-farmer model' (Rhoades and Booth, 1982) was a close precursor to participatory action research in CGIAR, Michael Cernea's (1984) broader model of 'putting people first' in development projects at the World Bank and elsewhere, and Robert Chambers's (Chambers and Ghildyal, 1985) 'farmer-first-and-last' model. The 'farmer-back-to-farmer model', with its premise of beginning and ending technology generation with the farmer's knowledge and guidance, has been adopted by dozens of projects, including the pan-Asian UPWARD, which was a spin-off of social science learning from CIP. The diffused-light technology generated by the CIP postharvest team reached over 30 countries and was adopted by thousands of farmers, reducing losses and improving seed production. Writings on the CIP experience are considered classics, such as the *Three Stooges Paper* (Rhoades *et al.*, 1986), *The Art of the Informal Survey* (Rhoades, 1986) and *Breaking New Ground: Agricultural Anthropology* (Rhoades, 1984), and have inspired a generation of young social scientists interested in working in agriculture. Much to the chagrin, and despite protests, of biological scientists, CIP may be as well known globally for its social science innovations as its potato technology. Giving such credit to social scientists might be perceived as undermining the status of biological research at the centre.

My point is not that CIP's social science experience was weak, as it clearly was not, but rather that it still left most of Dart's 'half brains' tied behind. The full potential of social science was only partly realized due to its restricted and narrow role in the centre. Cernea (1996) insightfully discussed the core biases in development towards reductionism, which he classifies into three types. 'Econocentric' models foreground economic and financial variables to the exclusion of almost everything else. 'Technocentric' models deal with the technological variables 'dis-embedded and disembodied from their contextual social fabric'. 'Commodocentric' models focus on 'the thing', such as potatoes, 'more than on the social actors that produce it'. CIP in the 1980s was clearly a 'techno-commodocentric' research centre in the extreme. Social scientists argued forcefully against such reductionist thinking, but found that the social production of knowledge within CIP was hostile to integrated approaches that would emphasize potato farmers as much as the potato.

Ironically, CIP's research management rejected as irrelevant early arguments by social scientists for researching farmers' strategies and roles in preserving potato genetic resources or for placing potato research within the ecological framework of mountains. Today both themes have become mainstream within the centre as well as the entire CGIAR system. At that time, however, the then CIP director of research not only publicly declared he had rarely talked to a farmer who knew much but also rejected any suggestion that strayed from the narrow potato focus: 'This place is about potatoes, not about anything else.' For job security and basic peace on the job (doing daily battle with one's colleagues is tiresome), the successful CIP social scientist had to play down the differences in theory, methods and conceptualization in favour of doing anthropology that addressed CIP's techno-commodity focus.

Before I return to a discussion of a broader view of interdisciplinary research in the CGIAR, allow me to turn to a comparative case of social science in the US university.

Status and Rewards for Social Science Agriculture Research in the US University

A university, especially in the USA, is a very different place than an international agriculture research centre. First, a US university's primary mission is teaching and basic scholarship, not technology development and applied research. Second, the US university is organized along lines of general colleges (e.g. arts, science, agriculture, medicine, law) and conical departments of academic disciplines (e.g. genetics, anthropology, agronomy, economics), not along 'problem'-focused areas as are many CGIAR centres. In the academic departments one normally only finds individuals with advanced degrees in that particular field. Third, the sheer complexity and size of a large US land-grant college dwarfs in all respects even the largest CGIAR centres in terms of scientists and staff. A typical land-grant university may have 100 times the number of scientists that work in an international centre. Fourth, rewards are given for individual effort, and teamwork is not a normal part of academic culture. Everything in the university is structured against teamwork, especially across disciplines. Despite differences, however, one commonality between the US university and CGIAR centres is the prestige and resources given to colleges, departments and faculty excelling in basic research in the natural or biological sciences. Such privileged positioning is not necessarily based on achievement but on an ascribed social status embedded in the history of the US university.

In 1991 I accepted the post of professor and head of the Department of Anthropology at the University of Georgia in the USA. Among the reasons for my decision was the opportunity to expand my research beyond the narrowly managed technological mandate of a CGIAR centre. After 12 years, I was running out of interesting social science angles on the potato plant. I looked forward to joining my anthropological colleagues in a disciplinary setting where anthropology could be practised and debated with some depth of analysis. However, I soon learned that 'big science' interdisciplinary research was a growing trend among US academics as well as in international development. While most faculty still pursued their independent disciplinary work, bigger rewards were awaiting those who joined large-scale, complex research projects that brought in millions of grant dollars to the university.

Soon after arrival at the university, I was pleased to learn that my new academic colleagues, especially those in the agricultural college, valued my experience in CGIAR and even considered it 'cutting edge'. Before long I was invited as a social scientist to planning meetings to discuss preparing large grant proposals for work in sustainable agriculture and natural resources management. While my agriculture colleagues were still prone to write proposals along narrow production lines, I was able to provide new trends of thinking gleaned from the international sphere. Instead of production *per se*, donors were interested in environmentally friendly production. Instead of annual cropping cycles on plots, donors were interested in long-term studies on multiple scales such as landscapes or watersheds. This was the heyday as well of participatory research and action, indigenous knowledge and involvement of non-governmental organizations (NGOs). To my university colleagues' credit, they listened and engaged me to help our university win a $20-million 10-year project called Sustainable Agriculture and Natural Resources Management (SANREM). It is one of the nine Collaborative Research Support Programs (CRSPs) funded by the US Agency for International Development (USAID), which aim to link developing-country scientists with US universities. All CRSPs are managed and controlled by the college of agriculture where they are headquartered.

As I prepared to devote time to the project, however, similar institutional constraints in applying social science to agriculture reared their heads again. Despite my collaborative work in helping win the grant, I soon learned that social scientists in the university are not considered equal partners with biological scientists in research. Although 'big science' demands social science participation, few institutional rewards or resources are to be gained from participation in these team endeavours. A social scientist in a US university is first and foremost assigned the service role of teaching undergraduates. For my biological science colleagues, it was the reverse: their primary role was research, with undergraduate teaching secondary or non-existent. Despite lip service that teaching is a noble activity, far more prestige and resources are credited to scientists who engage in research and do their teaching with advanced graduate students. If a social scientist wants to work on a research grant, the more fundamental resource of time could be captured only after the teaching service was fulfilled. My biological science colleagues in the project were typically required to teach no more than one or two courses a year, while social scientists taught four and sometimes five. With up to 300 students in many social science courses, teachers had precious little time to do much else.

The few social scientists who have acquired grants or principal investigator status under large grants have frequently pressed the university administration on the issue of differential resources and time released based strictly on one's discipline as opposed to one's achievement. Not only is time an issue, but the university also spends millions of dollars each year in 'start-up' funds for biological science laboratories ($100,000 is usual for a new genetics assistant professor), while an assistant professor in the social sciences will typically receive a $3500 computer and printer. The official response from the dean's office is that the difference in treatment is 'historical'. At some point in the past the university administration decided to elevate and support basic research in the natural sciences, leading to a corresponding problem of who would do most of the day-to-day classroom teaching of the sons and daughters of the State of Georgia. Once established, the reward system became rigid, with social scientists defined as service teachers regardless of performance in obtaining grants or publishing. It did not matter if a social scientist brought in record grants, and a biological science colleague none – the statuses stayed the same. The social scientist teaches, the biological scientist does research. In the minds of the people who run the university, the statuses of social and biological scientists have always been that way and will stay that way. As in CGIAR, the role of the social scientists is ascribed – it cannot be escaped regardless of achievement.

Another telling example of discrimination between social and biological scientists working on the same interdisciplinary team has to do with a university performance indicator called 'academic credit'. Promotion, and individual and department resources are mainly based on number of students taught and bringing in external research dollars. The university keeps a tally sheet (called 'the book'), which shows how much in grants ('academic credits') a professor has brought to the university. Despite my role in the writing teams of a number of external grants (even designated principal investigator for one major component), neither my department nor I have ever received any 'academic credit' in 'the book' for the millions of grant dollars we raised. The credit was fully claimed by the agriculture college, which in its processing of the paperwork, did not see any need to recognize the team's social science members. Ongoing protests have only partly resolved the problem. This is not an insignificant issue although to the outsider it may seem so. Academics are not normally highly paid so their self-worth is determined in part by peer recognition and institutional awards. The 'academic credit' indicator is used during budget negotiations to support or cut programmes, hire or fire staff, award or deny promotion and tenure. Social scientists in land-grant colleges are rarely given the coveted title of research professor despite acquiring lucrative grants and performing excellently. Academic administrators, who buy into the academic caste system by separating biological and social scientists, seem to be oblivious to the inequities. Like racial segregation in the pre-civil-rights era or unequal opportunities for women, such differential treatment is seen as the natural order of things. Again, as in CGIAR, social scientists have to complain loudly and bitterly. Again, they are labelled difficult and untrustworthy.

Is a university-based interdisciplinary agriculture project more open to non-economics social science even if the university itself is not? On the surface, yes. At a more fundamental level, not necessarily. A university-based project, especially one on sustainable agriculture and natural resources management, is by content broader and more accepting of diverse disciplines. Academics, in my experience, are less prone to the 'cowboy' verbal aggression and positioning I experienced in the 1980s CIP. By the 1990s, political correctness had more or less eliminated the patriarchal anti-female jokes and comments (although they continue in private discussions). Another difference in research culture between the CGIAR and a university has to do with the size of staff and departmental organization of the university where aggression within, not between, disciplines is rancorous. The SANREM project was open to input from social science, and the grant was won largely on the strength of the new perspective it offered on participation, multiple-actor and -scale research, social capital and gender and of the project's comparative ecoregional framework. However, although more subtly than at CIP, the mind-set of the donor's administrators still remained within Cernea's 'technocentric' and 'econocentric' models in important ways.

Despite SANREM's original framework of examining systemic interactions of biological and human interactions at the landscape scale, subtle and not so subtle reviews and funding decisions constantly reminded social scientists of their lesser value to the project. Regular pressure was exerted by the technical committee (through time it had fewer and fewer social science members) and the donor to return SAN-REM to 'business-as-usual' component techno-economic perspectives like other CRSPs. Over the 10 years of the project, social research was gradually diminished, leading to the same phenomena I witnessed in CGIAR of early termination of projects, cutting of budgets and unilateral replacement of activities involving social science, by those with an emphasis on economics and biological science. Gender, participation and NGOs had virtually disappeared by the end of the programme while economics, agricultural sector modelling and biological research all increased in funding and number of scientists. Despite enormous interest on the part of local communities, an ethno-ecology project to document indigenous knowledge of plants was put-down in one review as 'little more than documenting the demise of traditional agriculture'. Given the project's strong interest in participatory action research, a belief circulated in USAID that SANREM was little more than a social science programme. This was despite the fact that the most passionate proponents of participatory action research were biological scientists who had become caught up in the participatory fetish. However, when the tide turned against participatory action research, one biological scientist said, 'We tried social science, and it did not work', despite previous outcries from seasoned social scientists as to the pitfalls of the methodology. Social scientists were constantly asked to re-write repeatedly their writing and proposals and reports since they contained too much 'social science jargon'. A corresponding 'dumbing down' to match the limited visions of bureaucrats was never required of biological scientists and economists, who regularly used totally incomprehensive bio-jargon or equations in their reports. This was considered rigorous science, not jargon. Since landscape-scale research was new and experimental, USAID also became more and more nervous that the project was drifting away from producing short-term impacts as measured by a log-frame (which had also become popular about this time). The more anxious the managers became, the more they obsessively micromanaged and controlled the project (e.g. by requiring detailed quarterly progress reports). Getting the project 'back on track' in terms of conventional agriculture research took many forms, including technical evaluations, shifting resources, redefining success indicators and constantly changing the project's overall goals to accommodate the technocentric and econocentric approaches. In one effort to save SANREM, USAID made a mysterious decision to reallocate a full one fourth of SANREM's budget to do agriculture sector modelling, although no scientific review had demonstrated its need. Finally, despite a tremendous outpouring of excellent research and methodological breakthroughs by the original SANREM team, the University of Georgia programme was cancelled by USAID in early 2004. While there were many reasons for

SANREM's termination, it was no secret in Washington that the project simply had strayed too far from the expected approach of a CRSP and had become a 'social science' programme.

Conclusion

I have compared two experiences of social scientists working on interdisciplinary agricultural research teams with biological scientists. Although a CGIAR centre and a US university are distinct contexts, they have similarities.

The differences, however, diminish the closer the social scientists come to working on real-world problems with technical scientists. The problems of achieving a robust interdisciplinarity are largely social, not narrowly scientific. How problems are defined, who controls the process, which rewards are given to whom are not scientific or even negotiated 'processes'. The problems grow from ingrained biases in favour of those who address short-term objectives and technical and economic impacts, which are measurable, giving rise to expressed displeasure and impatience with social science research that foregrounds culture and society and gives human meaning to agriculture. Social science is channelled largely into a service field working on problems identified by biological and technical agriculture, not by the ultimate clients of that effort.

I have argued, drawing on Merton's concept of 'insider–outsider', that privilege and control over the production of knowledge in agriculture research are part of a social process that has historically favoured the biological and economic science perspectives. I can already see my technical colleagues leaping up to argue that I have overstated my case. Merton would simply chuckle at such an exchange since it is inherent in the 'insider–outsider' social dynamic that both sides see the same phenomenon distinctly.

I have to deny that my description is based on bitterness or 'sour grapes'. Far from it. I have great respect for my many colleagues in CGIAR and the university. My aim here is not to demean but to open needed dialogue on the role of social science in the interdisciplinary process. Despite my portrayal of knock-down drag-out fights (some humourous, some serious) with biological, technical or economics colleagues, I would not trade a single one for the secure smugness of doing pure disciplinary research. Interdisciplinarity – or better yet, transdisciplinarity – is the future, and those of us who have already engaged in it are on the cutting edge. The CGIAR centres are light-years ahead of the university.

I also deny that I believe 'insider' biological science knowledge should be replaced by 'outsider' social science knowledge. Merton (1972: 36) says it better:

> The cumulative point of this variety of intellectual and institutional cases is not – and this needs to be repeated with all possible emphasis – is *not* a proposal to replace the extreme Insider doctrine by an extreme and equally vulnerable Outsider doctrine. The intent is, rather, to transform the original question altogether. We no longer ask whether it is the Insider or the Outsider who has monopolistic or privileged access to social truth; instead, we begin to consider their distinctive and interactive roles in the process of truth seeking.

What we know is that after years of interdisciplinary work in the international centres, and now in the universities, the boundaries between the social and biological sciences are far more permeable than we realized back in the mid-1970s. A recent article about CIP points to how biological scientists themselves have taken steps to break down barriers of conventional thinking (Thiele *et al.,* 2001). As we have struggled together on common problems, competition and conflict have led to a circumstance in which individuals and groups take over ideas and procedures from one another. The wholesale adoption of participatory research methods by biological scientists in the early 1990s is one example. It might have not worked well, and distant managers may have found it inappropriate, but the process of borrowing and synthesizing moved agriculture research and development to new plateaus.

What new steps might be taken to further balance interdisciplinary work in agriculture? For starters, those who hold administrative power in the university and CGIAR need to immediately correct the distorted reward structure to give equal resources and credit to the social sciences. As long as the powers-that-be see social scientists as marginal 'outsiders', there will be no chance to capture a holistic view of agricultural change. Second, we need to create more opportunities and partnerships for training in interdisciplinarity at the university level before students become scientists and carry their biases to CGIAR. Courses, exchanges of staff and students and honest discussions of the reality of teamwork (the Three Stooges) instead of ideal step-by-step blueprints (farming systems research manuals) are needed. Finally, we need everyone's humility and insights to lay to rest forever the fallacy that agricultural development is primarily economic and technological. Along with these conventional 'agri' elements, the element of 'culture' must assume an equal and proper role. Scientists and administrators who let go of orthodoxy will find abundant new and divergent possibilities in new agriculture research – and we will use our entire brain, not just half.

References

Cernea, M.M. (1984) *Putting People First. Sociological Variables in Rural Development Projects.* Oxford University Press, London and New York, 575 pp.

Cernea, M.M. (1996) *Social Organization and Development Anthropology. The 1995 Malinowski Award Lecture.* World Bank, Washington, DC, 38 pp.

Chambers, R. and Ghildyal, B.P. (1985) Agricultural research for resource poor farmers: the farmer-first-and-last model. *Agricultural Administration and Extension* 20, 1030.

Dart, F.E. (1963) The rub of cultures. In: Dean, V.M. and Harootunian, H.D. (eds) *West and Non-West: New Perspectives.* Hold, Rinehart and Winston, New York, pp. 34–42.

Merton, R. (1972) Insiders and outsiders: a chapter in the sociology of knowledge. *The American Journal of Sociology* 78(1), 9–47.

Netting, R. (1974) Agrarian ecology. *Annual Review of Anthropology* 3, 21–56.

Rhoades, R. (1984) *Breaking New Ground. Agricultural Anthropology.* International Potato Center, Lima, 71 pp.

Rhoades, R. (1986) The art of informal survey. In: Hildebrand, P.E. (ed.) *Perspectives on Favoring Systems Research and Extension.* Lynne Rienner Publishers, Boulder, Colorado, pp. 83–93.

Rhoades, R. and Booth, R.H. (1982) Farmer-back-to-farmer: a model for generating acceptable agricultural technology. *Agricultural Administration* 11, 127–137.

Rhoades, R. and Booth, R.H. (1983) Interdisciplinary teams in agricultural research and development. *Culture and Agriculture*, 1–7.

Rhoades, R., Horton, D. and Booth, R.H. (1986) Anthropologist, economist and biological scientist: the three stooges or three musketeers of farming systems research. In: Jones, J. and Wallace, B. (eds) *Applying Science in Farming Systems Research.* Westview Press, Boulder, Colorado, pp. 21–40.

Thiele, G., van de Fliert, E. and Campilan, D. (2001) What happened to participatory research at the International Potato Center? *Agriculture and Human Values* 18, 429–446.

Roots: Reflections of a 'Rocky Doc' on Social Science in the CGIAR

21

Scott Guggenheim

I spent 3 years on a Rockefeller post-doctoral fellowship and loved every minute of it. My initial assignment was to the International Fertilizer Development Corporation (IFDC) based in Muscle Shoals, Alabama; however, for all but a month of the time I was stationed in Cali, Colombia. Of course the biggest blessing was being able to work with such a smart and dedicated staff, and in particular my project supervisor, Jacqueline Ashby, taught me many lessons that I continue to draw on throughout my work in the World Bank.

Four lessons proved to be particularly significant: the importance of interdisciplinarity, the organizational trade-offs faced in deciding how best to use social scientists in technical organizations, the social scientists' need to strike a balance between applied social science and technical literacy and why social scientists will ultimately need to complement their 'mainstreaming' into sectoral fields with better integration into policy formation and management. What was most interesting was that while each of these points may seem obvious in the abstract, working at an agricultural research centre taught me just how complicated they are to put into practice. I would like to explain why these four lessons are more complex than they seem.

Introduction to CIAT

The journey that brought me to Centro Internacional de Agricultura Tropical or the International Center for Tropical Agriculture (CIAT) did not follow a very direct path. I had had a fair amount of international experience first, doing fieldwork in Mexico and the Philippines, and then apprenticing under Michael Cernea on social issues within the World Bank, before applying to the Rockefeller programme. Like most anthropology graduate students, my training was heavily theoretical and pretty much focused on joining a future department of anthropology rather than a community of professional practitioners.

IFDC's crash course for Rockefeller social science post-docs was both fascinating and intimidating. IFDC staff were uniformly friendly and their explanations so down to earth and so clear that after 2 weeks I thought I understood what they were talking about. In fact I had only the most superficial understanding of what were very sophisticated technical presentations.

Yet, while I could not follow the detailed explanations, I quickly appreciated the power of applied science to induce major and generally positive changes to farm practices. For many social scientists, this is an important corrective. Most of us finish our fieldwork with pretty sceptical views of rural development: to this day we still see just too many cases of failed extension, top-down directives and mistaken assumptions about input availability and marketing outlets. Seeing the potential of some of these technologies was not just sobering but, at least in my case, also led to a more reflective view of what it might take to make these new ideas work.

I also appreciate to this day the value of clear explanation. If the head of IFDC could take the time and care to explain why different kinds of phosphate were differentially absorbed by tropical plants in ways that made perfect sense even to a technical neophyte like me, then surely it is incumbent upon me and other social scientists to use our professional vocabularies to communicate to others as transparently and clearly as we can than to limit discussion to the charmed circle of fellow PhDs.

As much as I enjoyed the learning at Muscle Shoals, the transfer to CIAT was a relief. At the time it was just starting to ramp up its programme of on-farm and farmer-managed research, so a big part of our orientation there consisted of visits to the different farms and demonstration plots where the research teams were setting up their on-farm trials. Now this was an environment I felt more comfortable in. Even I knew – razzle-dazzle soil science modelling or not – that fertilizer trials planted on a recently abandoned tomato field would have the scientific validity of treating cancer by casting a horoscope.

My team leader for the next 2 years was Jacqueline Ashby. A better team leader would have been hard to find. She was brilliant, innovative and an excellent teacher. But what impressed me the most throughout the 3 years was her grasp of the entire process of rural development, from economic policy environments to how to measure edge effects in the trials. It took another 2 years to realize that she *did not* know everything about every bit of her fertilizer trials, but enough to support an interdisciplinary team by preparing a well-formulated research programme, dividing up each specialist's skills and making sure that the results would all fit together into an innovative and technically sound story.

In social science circles, CIAT at the time was an outlier, much less known outside the Consultative Group on International Agricultural Research (CGIAR) circles than, say, the International Potato Center (CIP). CIP had taken the path-breaking step of forming a freestanding social and economic unit. CIP's socioeconomic unit published a great deal of exciting work, work that did an excellent job documenting the indissolubility of socioeconomic and technical aspects in agricultural research. CIP was particularly interesting because it would routinely enter into what for the time were unusual partnerships with Andean universities, non-governmental organizations, activists and other groups that were as concerned with culture as they were with agriculture.

Within our CIAT group, we frequently discussed the merits and drawbacks of forming a freestanding unit. CIP itself provided the best argument in favour of going this route: the centre's strong publication record of well-thought-through applied research showed the advantages that accrue by encouraging social scientists to work together as a group. In the end, though, we concluded that more long-term benefits would come from distributing social scientists into each commodity team. Too many social scientists in one place can all too easily produce inbreeding, with social people responding to each other's problems rather than providing solutions to the shared problem of increasing farmer yields and incomes. On the other hand, what we might have lost through that decision was the ability to focus fully on social or cultural variables that are not just important for agriculture, but which require and justify distinct social research: that is, research done 100% by social scholars, not necessarily through interdisciplinary collaboration.

By contrast, CIAT's strategy of making sure that each commodity team had a social scientist appeared, at least superficially, to produce fewer publications but bigger impacts on core breeding programmes. Research groups each have a social life of their own, regardless of structural and disciplinary loyalties. Social scientists who worked every day with the agronomists and soil scientists were automatically part of 'their' group – 'insiders' – but, as Merton insightfully theorized, were able to be simultaneously 'outsiders' as well, thus gaining and exercising a hard-to-grasp but important intellectual comparative advantage (Merton, 1973).

CIAT's social scientists, because they were core parts of interdisciplinary teams, seemed to play a central role in which problems were first proposed for novel research, not just for assessing the impacts of already designed technologies. I have seen this same choice repeat itself in the World Bank, where successive reorganizations have produced a shift towards groups of similarly skilled specialists and away from the interdisciplinary model used at CIAT. To this day, however, I still defend the merits of the alternative CIAT model.

If the first lesson was about organizational alternatives, the second was about just how technically proficient – that is truly *technical* – a social scientist should be. As with any culture, social scientists coming in cold to the international agricultural research system clearly need to become proficient in the language of their intellectual hosts. Acquiring basic literacy in agricultural development, biophysical sciences, genetics and even in agricultural economics makes scientific communication much easier for everybody. The most successful social scientists I met during my post-doc knew quite a bit more than the basics of these non-social sciences.

Even so, I think this can be overdone. One criticism that I would commonly hear from my agronomist friends was not that social scientists did not know enough about agronomy, but that they did not know enough social science. I found such comments very telling. The gap between social science as doctoral programme and social science as an applied science is quite large. Most of my professional career since leaving CIAT has consisted of trying to bridge that gap. For anthropologists, at least, the root of the problem probably lies in a deeply held belief that every society has a unique history and culture, whereas most modern sciences are predicated on the assumption that a small number of common laws and practices can explain a great deal of superficial diversity.

In practice, both sides of this debate yield. Most contemporary social scientists will agree that a number of mechanisms can be generalized that allow rural communities and their constituent farmers to make culturally informed choices. Most agriculturalists and economists now recognize that cultural and economic preferences should enter the crop development cycle earlier rather than later.

What did my agronomist friends mean when they said they preferred solid social science to technical proficiency? They gave two reasons, to which I would like to add another that I think they would agree with but did not mention at the time. The first was clearly the result of Ashby's entirely convincing experiments. The scientists were learning something important from her trials – about social structure and cultural behaviour – that they were not learning from their own forays into the field. The combination of ethnographic fieldwork and an ability to work with groups of farmers in a structured way mattered a lot to them. This was more than just a matter of Ashby and her team being 'nice guys' who enjoyed fieldwork. The substantive part of their work mattered. Preparing a social map that could distinguish homogeneous (i.e. all poor farmers) from heterogeneous (i.e. primarily subsistence versus commercial growers) groups was one activity they all thought was useful.

Another was to identify different fora and interview contexts that would provide a channel for farmer participation, of which perhaps the most difficult was to create contexts in which farmers would feel sufficiently comfortable to give open feedback. We all knew what the problem was: the 'official' interview that confirms that the preferred trial really was the best, only to find out later that the response showed little more than the fact that rural people are wise enough to tell drop-in visitors whatever it is they most want to hear. But the CIAT team's sustained engagement between the research team and the local communities meant that the researchers could count on reliable feedback and not just polite nods.

One aspect of this engagement was very surprising, at least to me. While it would be a mistake to over-generalize, I was repeatedly taken aback by how difficult it was for full-time scientists not trained in social specialties to avoid carrying out leading interviews when they did interview farmers. Even when the questions were of the 'so what did you really think?' sort, researcher's body language nearly always gave away the politically correct answer. At first I thought this was just an aberrant perception on my part, but we later confirmed it by re-interviewing farmers after the research teams had left. I have no doubt that, to some extent, we too succumbed to this tendency, but at least, in my case, it probably helped somewhat that I genuinely did not know what the right answer was.

The second domain where social science thinking helped the research teams was in shifting the basic unit of analysis away from the farm and towards the farm household. That meant taking an important step closer to grasping the 'culture' part of agriculture. Thinking domestic development strategies, household asset collections and family divisions of labour opened up many new angles for our research at a time when people close to CGIAR still thought that anthropology was superfluous in farming systems research (e.g. Norman Simmonds' study on farming systems research in CGIAR[1]). For example, the natural tendency for on-farm research was to work with farmers, but in many areas of Latin America and Africa, the real farmer was actually the farmer's wife, who would decide which varieties of seeds to grow, cook or sell. Very few experiment designs included structured ways to involve these household decision makers even though the primary purpose of setting up on-farm research was to get direct feedback from the end-user. Similarly, while it was no surprise to find that households with many sources of income had a different view of cropping options than families entirely dependent on farming, it was a bit disconcerting to see how rarely this variable made it into the specification of who the 'average' farmer was.

The third social science contribution, that I think my agronomist colleagues much appreciated even when they were not able to 'name' it as such, was what our social literature calls 'types of socio-cultural integration'. This is, in fact, an umbrella term that covers a broad range of concepts. In practice, the term referred to getting the general picture of how farming fits into the general rural economy. Were farm families growing crops as their main source of livelihood, or were they doing so primarily as an insurance strategy just in case off-farm income sources suddenly dried up? Do farm families have large networks of family members and friends who provide them with information, or do they rely primarily on extension services and private providers? Who were the real 'actors,' and their motives, who could open for us new windows to understand why agriculture was done the way it was done? To use Cernea's words, what are the sociological entry points for agricultural development and how might social research teams best work their ways through them into the inner junctures of the processes placed under our research lens?

One other big lesson I took from my CIAT experience was the importance of a final product. Like many social scientists, my proclivities are towards process. Give people voice. Understand culture. Promote dialogue and negotiation. Increase participation. In both CIAT and in the World Bank, social scientists for the most part focus their attention on improving the quality of baseline social assessments and on ensuring that development programmes become more socially inclusive and participatory. They focus a lot on the quality of inputs.

My time in CIAT, however, was one big lesson in how important an end product is. Farmers loved to enlighten me about the fine points of ethno-botanical classification, but what would really make their eyes light up was finding out how better seeds and fertilizers could double their yields (without their prices being halved). How important a tangible product was for farmers was an eye-opener for me, too. While I will never be a full-fledged technocrat, over time I have only deepened my appreciation for the contribution that technology and engineering can make to farmers' well-being.

If keeping an eye on the technological ball was a key virtue of CIAT's excellent biophysical scientists, their trained inattention to the sociological and organizational determinants of what makes technology useful to poor farmers was an eye-opening experience of a different sort. 'Just how are farmers supposed to get this?' sort of questions all too often seemed to elicit a bland mush of expectations that non-existent agricultural extension systems would somehow disseminate the fine products of the research programmes to the poor.

CIAT and CGIAR seemed generally aware of the problem, but they were and remain stuck between a rock and a hard place. The gap between global research to find better crops and national systems to disseminate them is enormous and it is unequal. Tackle the national dissemination problems and CIAT's comparative advantage dilutes into a mishmash of quasi-research on 'local' microenvironments. No CGIAR centre can make up for the weaknesses of rural extension services and national agricultural policymaking. Restricting research to core biological research, however, would keep CGIAR centre products limited to national elites and those peri-urban areas with reasonable access to information – hardly a good outcome for organizations committed to improve food security and reduce poverty. Bringing end-users into the design process seemed to be a good entry point to correct some of these structural problems, but the overall lack of an institutional focus in the general CGIAR strategy and in its dialogue with its funders and counterparts was striking.

The World Bank and CGIAR: a Brief Comparison

Although I did not continue my career within the CGIAR system, I did stay involved in international development. For the past 8 years, I have been the World Bank's social coordinator for its Indonesia assistance programme, a role that has included being project officer for a billion-dollar nationwide community development programme. That experience provides a useful perspective for reviewing certain aspects of my time in CIAT. As I hope that even this cursory discussion shows, there are some patterns and contrasts to draw by comparing the experience of being a social scientist in CIAT and in the World Bank.

The two institutions provide some useful comparisons. Both have global mandates. Both have gone through a number of far-reaching reorganizations and introspective examinations of their role, reorganizations whose objective has been to align institutional mandates and procedures to make them more in line with a global objective of poverty reduction. Both institutions first began experimenting with using social scientists in the mid-1970s (World Bank) and in the 1980s (CGIAR, through agreement with the Rockefeller Foundation to 'prime the pump' by financing a post-doctoral programme, that would, in principle, later be taken up by CGIAR core budgets).[2]

However, the trajectory of social scientists in the two institutions has diverged somewhat. In the World Bank the leading social scientists have moved from only supporting operational projects towards playing a growing role in policy formulation, and development strategies, so much so that even IMF-World Bank macro-level adjustment programmes increasingly incorporate social science team members. Social scientists have also come to play a bigger role in rural development programmes, where the traditional focus on farm production and technology transfer is now supplemented by much more interest in household production systems and improvements in the capacity of local formal and informal institutions.

By contrast, CGIAR does not appear to have capitalized well on the splashy start enabled by its generous Rockefeller support. While there are still some top social scientists working within the CGIAR system, total numbers appear to have held constant for a while, but then started to decline. New entrants have also declined significantly. Of course, overall decreasing budgets make a bad situation worse, but shrinking budgets alone cannot explain why social research is what gets sacrificed first. In addition, while the World Bank has funded a social development network at the World Bank's centre to offer guidance across the system, CGIAR has nothing of the kind at its 'headquarters'.

I think that the CGIAR is paying a fairly heavy price for this situation. In my work first as coordinator for the World Bank's poverty work in Indonesia and then subsequently as project officer for a nationwide community development project, we had few if any contacts with CGIAR. Perhaps even more ominously, neither our government counterparts nor Indonesian civil-society groups ever suggested to the World Bank's resident mission that such contacts would be relevant for our work. I doubt that this would have been the case had the agricultural centres been able to analyse the social policy environments of rural producers or been more deeply engaged in developing cropping packages that could better suit changing socioeconomic circumstances and farmer demands.

A second comparative observation between CGIAR and the World Bank refers to where social scientists are placed in the system's institutional hierarchy and organizational structure. Here the comparison highlights more similarities than differences. In my experience in CIAT and the World Bank, I noticed a clear difference between what social scientists can achieve when they are providing support services to so-called 'core' teams and what they can achieve when they have independent resources and more autonomy. Clearly there is a need for both functions. But in CGIAR, by far more than in the World Bank, non-economic social scientists have been overwhelmingly located in the position of support service. Very few have had the autonomy to set the agenda rather than support it.

One or another exception in CGIAR only clinches the argument. Watching Jacqueline Ashby or, later, Joachim Voss, develop their farmer participation programme in CIAT gave me more than an inkling that it was both possible and necessary for a social scientist to be in control of a programme and yet do it in ways that would also support the institutional agenda in non-threatening ways. Jacqueline Ashby was lucky in that the senior agricultural scientists working with her were soon convinced that her collaborative approach was producing unexpected and valuable results. But at least to me it was soon clear that without the managerial and economic freedom she had, her wings would have quickly been clipped from within the team whenever it came time to choose between just one more microscope and supervising the field trials.

My later work with Michael Cernea at the centre of the World Bank on involuntary population resettlement fortified this view that social scientists should not remain confined to the support service roles, if development institutions wish to use them well. Theoretically guided applied social science will challenge big blocks of received development wisdom, particularly when it comes to poor people's involvement in decision making. Applied social science does have a great deal to offer development, but without access to the policy arena and to enough independent resources to be able to promote a policy agenda, it will always be playing catch-up to agendas set elsewhere. While responding to institutionally defined priorities is a good thing, unless there are ways to challenge and reform institutional procedures, social scientists will always be working within excessively narrow constraints. Social scientists at their best bring a bottom-up, participatory perspective to development that will require a number of significant policy and organizational adjustments. Robert Rhoades at CIP, Jacqueline Ashby and Joachim Voss at CIAT, Douglas Vermillion and Douglas Merrey at IWMI, Carol Colfer at CIFOR and others, have pioneered opportunities for such change in CGIAR centres but, for the most part, the CGIAR system as a whole seems to be letting this opportunity slip away.

Conclusions

The Rockefeller post-doctoral programme for social scientists was an exciting challenge both for the social scientists who joined it and the institutions that received them. While criticisms of the green revolution have been overdone, even then it was clear that growth in rural production through new farm production technology was reaching limits set by unfamiliar socioeconomic environments and missing institutional linkages. Rockefeller's programme to restore culture and society to agriculture and soil science was one effort to bypass these constraints, by providing channels to introduce local actors' voices into agricultural research in scientifically respectable ways. Today the need for this type of contribution is even greater. Much has been written about globalization, protectionist subsidies in developed countries and the need for policy environments that favour growth among poor people rather than impede it, for us to ever return to the belief that another round of technological miracle work will be sufficient. But making closer links between global policies and agricultural research only strengthens the need to ensure that rural producers can quickly adapt and use new varieties. The original argument for incorporating more sophisticated understanding of local cultural and economic demand, and of institutional constraints, into agricultural technology's design and transfer still holds.

Notes

[1]The study, commissioned by the World Bank's Agricultural Research Advisor, triggered a debate not only in CGIAR but also inside the World Bank, where social scientists reviewing the manuscript objected strongly to the underestimation of anthropology. Eventually, the internal memos became an article critical of the published study. See Michael Cernea and Scott Guggenheim (1985) Is Anthropology Superfluous in Farming Systems Research? *Farming Systems Research.* Kansas State University Research Series 4 (9).

[2]However, except for a small number of centres, by and large, CGIAR did not follow through on the implicit deal, and the Rockefeller Foundation's initiative to introduce research capacity in the social disciplines was not continued.

Reference

Merton, R.K. (1973) The perspectives of insiders and outsiders. In: *The Sociology of Science.* University of Chicago Press, Chicago and London, pp. 99–136.

Social Science Knowledge as a Public Good

22

Dana G. Dalrymple*

There is much merit in economic progress, but there is also
an overwhelming role for intelligent and equitable social policies.

(Amartya Sen, 2001)

Social science research might well be expected to make a major contribution to the formulation of policies that combine the pursuit of economic growth with social policy concerns. Within international
agricultural research, this task logically falls primarily to social science
researchers in the public sector who – like other researchers in this sector – are expected to produce international public goods. While the
concept of public goods has its roots deep in history and has been
specifically articulated by economists and philosophers during the
past 50 years, it does not appear to have been widely adopted by the
other social sciences.

This is paradoxical for several reasons. The first is that the concept
would seem to be a natural for social scientists. It should, on the basis
of its name alone, appear to have considerable relevance to all their
work and provide a common medium of communication. Second,
social science knowledge is produced in the public sector and is relatively pure in that it is not embedded in a patented product, has no or
few inherent or imposed constraints on its spread or availability and is
not diminished by use.

Given these circumstances, it may be useful to provide some
notions and information that could help stimulate a more widespread
awareness of public goods among social scientists. I start from the
point of view of economics and then move to some other components
of the social sciences. I also start with an orientation to the importance
of the biological and physical sciences in increasing productivity and

*The views expressed are the author's and not necessarily those of USAID.   431 stimulating economic growth, particularly as shaped by my long experience with the Consultative Group on International Agricultural Research (CGIAR) (Dalrymple, 2003a,b).

Definitions and Dimensions

The key categories are social science and public goods.

Social science

While the chapers in this book focus largely on 'social research' – essentially in anthropology and sociology – I will try to encompass the broader meaning of social science and also include economics, political science, geography and demography. While these and other areas deal with, and/or enlighten, the social process, they generally have not been highly interwoven with social research.[1]

The role of social scientists in the economic growth process has varied over time. Ruttan (2004: xv) notes that before World War II, social science interest in non-Western societies was dominated by applied anthropologists in the service of colonial administration. During the 1950s, disciplinary subfields rapidly emerged such as development sociology, political development and development administration. Members of other disciplines such as history, geography and law also began to explore possible contributions to the development process or practice. 'The early expectation that these several streams of inquiry might merge to enrich each other has failed to materialize.'

This gap has been widest between anthropologists and economists. Ruttan (1988: S250) noted that 'almost no attention has been devoted by economists to the role of cultural endowments'. Cernea (1987: 239), however, states, 'Sociology and anthropology have endeavoured primarily to describe and explain past or existing social structures rather than to look towards the future and plan for purposeful change.' After examining some of the potential contributions of anthropology to development economics, Ruttan (1988: S264) concluded, 'The response must be ambiguous.' He also notes (Ruttan, 2004: xv) that the rapid pace of national development in the 1960s and 1970s 'seemed to confirm the perspective that development could be left to the economists'.[2] This faith began to erode in the 1980s, and by the early 1990s 'institutional and cultural explanations for stagnation or distorted development again emerged as important themes'.

Just as the place of economics in all of this has varied, views of economists have differed. Shortly after the appearance of economics in the late 1700s, Edmund Burke (1790/1986: 170) was moved to write: 'But the age of chivalry is gone. That of sophisters, economists, and calculators, has succeeded; and the glory of Europe is extinguished for ever'. Similarly, in 1943 Sir Albert Howard (1943: 198) lamented that 'economics has done a much greater disservice to agriculture than the collection of useless data. Farming has come to be looked at as if it were a factory'. More recently, Kenneth Arrow – a Nobel laureate in economics – made a key distinction.

> The market is one system; the polity another. Use of the market and its language leads to results which offend our intuitions; so does the use of political language. Looking at policy issues from the point of any one system is likely to lead to unsatisfactory conclusions somewhere.
>
> (Arrow, 1997: 765)

Public goods

The general notion behind public goods was first, or at least most famously, stated by Adam Smith (1776/2000: 779) in 1776 when he wrote that:

> the third and last duty of the sovereign or commonwealth is that of erecting and maintaining those public institutions and those public works, which, though they may be in the highest degree advantageous to a great society, are, however, of such a nature, that the profit could never repay the expense to any individual or small number of individuals, and for which it therefore cannot be expected that any individual or small number of individuals should erect or maintain.

Current interpretations of public goods tend to follow Smith's intent, but vary by discipline. Economists focus on two characteristics: (i) public goods are freely available to all; and (ii) they are not diminished by use. The first is usually expressed as 'non-excludability' and the second as 'non-rival'. Excludability is usually an imposed constraint, as through intellectual property rights. Non-rivalry is usually an innate characteristic and is exemplified by knowledge. Lawyers tend to speak of the public domain rather than public goods and then in terms of public availability and lack of legal restraints. Sociologists use the term collective goods when public goods are produced through collective action. At the international level, public goods are often viewed as being freely available, meeting some public need or concern, and requiring collective action to be provided. The interrelationships of some of these interpretations are presented in Fig. 22.1.[3]

In most cases, public goods are, by the economist's definition, *impure public goods* (Dalrymple, 2003d). They are not completely non-excludable or non-rival – usually because the public and private sectors are, or have been, involved in some way in their generation. The private sector is clearly most interested in activities that will generate a profit. This means knowledge that can be embedded in a saleable product, preferably one subject to some type of intellectual property rights.

In agriculture these products usually fall into the category of purchased inputs, and sometimes public institutions hold intellectual property rights to such products. This fact also means that the private sector has little or no interest in products for which there is little effective demand – such as developing agricultural and natural resource policy (unless appropriate for private sector use or done under a contract funded by the government) or other even less marketable forms of social science research. The private sector entities (excluding private foundations), therefore, usually leave social science of a public good type out of their portfolios, resulting in a 'market failure'. Thus, most social science research, partly by default, remains a relatively *pure public good*, to be supported by the public sector.

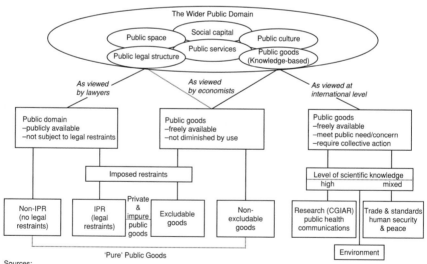

Sources:
'Wider Public Domain.' Adapted from Daniel Drache, *The Market and the Public Domain*, Routledge, New York, 2001, p. 39.
'As viewed by...' Drawn in part from 'Background Note', International Task Force on Global Public Goods, Stockholm, May 25, 2003.
IPR, Intellectual property rights.

Fig. 22.1. The public domain and public goods: conceptual relationships (with emphasis on knowledge-based public goods).

Characteristics of Public Social Science Research

Social science represents a broad range of topics and disciplines. It is far from homogeneous and may not have the expected degree of inter-action and communication between the various components. Still, the role of social science in international development is vital. Ruttan (1982: 42, 307–308) observed over 20 years ago, 'As the technical con-straints on the growth of agricultural productivity become less binding, there is an increasing need for institutional innovation that will result in a more effective realization of the new technical potential'.[4]

Just how one most efficiently employs social science in view of its heterogeneity and its varied homes in the public sector is another ques-tion. At the academic level, individual components are to be found all over the campus, including museums. At the governmental level, a similar dispersion is found, with perhaps a greater variation in the degree to which various branches of the social sciences are to be found. In each case, the degree of interaction between the social sciences and the biological and physical sciences is also variable but probably limited. In total, Ruttan (1982: 298) wrote, 'The social sciences have been junior partners in the agricultural research enterprise.'

From the start, the CGIAR centres focused on what later came to be recognized as global public goods,[5] and attempted to build an interdis-ciplinary structure that would blend social and biological and physical sciences. The centres' view of social science was initially limited to that of agricultural economists: primarily to support production pro-grammes (or policy research at the International Food Policy Research Institute (IFPRI)). However, this view broadened over time, especially with the advent of the Rockefeller Foundation's postdoctoral fellow-ship programme in the social sciences; many of the 'Rocky docs' were stationed at CGIAR centres.[6] With this programme's end and increased financial difficulties for many centres, some weakening of the social science dimension was to be expected, despite increased donor emphasis on policy and poverty alleviation.[7]

Most social science research, as suggested earlier, would qualify as a public good in definitional terms, but this only sets the threshold. Whether the research ever becomes more than academic knowledge and finds useful application is another matter. At the university level, such questions are probably of less concern for departments in the col-lege of arts and sciences, where the emphasis is on teaching, than for those in the college of agriculture, where research and extension and outreach functions are part of the department's task (also see Ruttan, 1982: 313–316). Yet, Ruttan (1982: 319) stated that leadership of experi-ment stations in the USA 'has rarely been able or willing to utilize social science research capacity in its own decision-making processes'. Whether this is still the case has not been analysed recently.[8]

Even where social science research has been utilized, its value is difficult to demonstrate or quantify.[9] Norton (1987: 177) observed, 'Few studies...have attempted to quantitatively measure impacts of social science research...including agricultural economics research (AER).' He went on to acknowledge that while other forms of research provide new information that is eventually embedded in new inputs or products that can be identified in a tangible way, 'In the case of AER we do not have such imbedding' (Norton, 1987: 179). Since then, there have been a number of attempts at developing and/or measuring the impact of the social sciences in the CGIAR system, including a special effort at IFPRI that is under way.[10]

Funding and Prioritizing Public Social Science Research

While the public-good status of most of social science research in the public sector is not in question, this does not necessarily mean that all of the research is worth doing or that it should be funded from public sources. This is true of all types of research, but the question is often complicated by the degree to which the research involves an impure public good and whether it should be handled by the private sector. The fact that social science research will normally be taken up by the private sector only under special circumstances – as market failure is normal – does not necessarily mean that the research is worth doing by the public sector. The answer to this question involves *ex-ante* and *ex-post* impact assessment but also brings us to other questions relating to the funding and priority-setting process for public social science research.

In this case we are not dealing with the market process referred to by Arrow, but with the polity or a political process. Decisions relating to public goods and services, as Buchanan (1968: 5) puts it, 'are made through political, not market institutions and there is no analogue to competitive order that eases the analytical task'. While often having considerable influence on funding for agricultural research and the uses to which it is put, the political process in developed nations often seems preoccupied by biological and physical types of research. The extent to which the political process specifically promotes social science research is uncertain; some better-known cases refer to instances where the political side expressed its displeasure.

Several of the clearest and fully reported examples of the latter have occurred in the USA. Hardin (1955/1976) has documented the political pressures brought to bear on social science research in the US Department of Agriculture (USDA) and in the state colleges of agriculture from the mid-1920s to the early 1950s. Ruttan (1982: 325–326) summarized some of the USDA instances and added, 'Efforts to develop and to maintain social science research capacity in the USDA continue to be subject to considerable stress', partly arising from tension between the professional criteria involved in conducting the research and 'the political and bureaucratic desire to use social science analysis to legitimize programme activity'.

Political forces are probably most influential at the state and national levels (Hadwiger, 1982; Huffman and Evenson, 1993: 219–241), but likely to be less so at the international level, except as they influence the choice of programmes to be supported by foreign assistance, which, however, can work both ways. Many donors' interest in policy and poverty alleviation has influenced the orientation of CGIAR centres and increased their attention to social science research.[11] However, the US Agency for International Development (USAID) has long been enjoined from working on certain commodities that might compete with US exports, although so far this has not had any particular effect on CGIAR or on social science research.

Aside from political forces, which vary sharply in their nature and influence, what else sets the research agenda for social sciences? The answer is not clear. In most CGIAR centres, the agenda is shaped by the overall CGIAR mission and goals and, in turn, by the centre's leadership and the nature of the research (principally biological) being done by the other scientists. In many cases in the social sciences, however, the agenda may be heavily influenced by the researchers themselves.[12] Some may be thinking of real-life problems and needs, but others may be influenced by personal curiosity and still others by possible professional advancement or standing. Increasing attention is being given to demand-driven research, by which is meant a bottom-up approach involving farmers and the rural community. Supply- and demand-driven approaches have their advantages and limitations; the challenge is to develop a balance, which may vary with research organization and geographic level (Dalrymple, 2003c).

A further issue might concern the allocation of research resources among the various social sciences, which is not a centralized decision but made at the individual institution level. About the only aggregative information on this relates to CGIAR for 1999–2001, and indicates that 58% of the total social science staff members were economists, 17% anthropologists and sociologists, 11% from related fields, and 13% 'other' (Cernea and Kassam, 2002: Table 1).[13] More details on the last two categories would be interesting, in part to see what other disciplines were included. My suspicion is that political scientists in particular may – given the political nature of the public research process – be under-represented in the CGIAR system and generally.[14]

A Broad View of the Landscape for Public Goods

While most of the output of social science research would qualify as a public good, partly by default on the part of the private sector, and partly because the research is unembedded knowledge (and the two reasons can be closely related), there is more to the story in terms of development. Two issues come to mind.

First, different groups have different views of what public goods are or should be. The Office of Development Studies at the United Nations Development Programme (UNDP), which has done the most to expand international understanding of public goods, has recently suggested an enlargement of the theory to encompass four provision-related policy issues (Kaul and Mendoza, 2003: 89–94):[15]

- Re-envision public choices, which would call for a close matching of the circle of stakeholders in the benefits from a particular public good with the circle of participants in negotiations on its provision. This might involve expanding across fiscal or political jurisdictions.
- Differentiate between publicness in consumption and publicness in utility. The latter would entail publicness in decision making and in distribution of net benefits, creating a triangle of publicness.
- Pay more attention to the role of other groups beyond the state in providing public goods.
- Expand the theory of public goods beyond market-failure cases to give more weight to their contributions to enhancing people's well-being and stimulating economic growth on a global basis.

These are substantial proposals and necessitate considerably more study by a number of social science disciplines.

Second, UNDP (Kaul and Mendoza, 2003: 94–104) emphasizes the need for a better understanding of global public goods with respect to the geographical extent of their benefits, noting that some goods are global naturally and others have become global by policy choice, and whether aspects of the provision of global public goods are specific to their political decision making and production. This leads the authors to two main findings: (i) globalized national public goods are an important class of global public goods; and (ii) the expansion of public good theory becomes even more important when considering global public goods because they 'require and create commonality in a world of extreme disparities' (Kaul and Mendoza, 2003: 95).

This issue raises a central question about where the different disciplines and different types of research fall in the local-to-global continuum. Galison (2003: 38–39), a historian of science, observed: 'It has become habitual to divide history into separate scales: intellectual history for ideas that are or aim to be universal; social history for more localized cases, groups, and institutions; biography or micro-history for individuals and their immediate surround'. Generalizing about social science research is hazardous, but placing it within Galison's social history category seems safe. Some social science research, however, might be viewed as providing building blocks of knowledge that could be used at broader geographic levels, such as in the nationalized public-good case noted above. These broad types of knowledge could then, in turn, be used in other more localized situations.

Some Implications for Social Research in CGIAR

What other specific implications might be suggested for social research conducted by sociologists, anthropologists and others in the centres? One key factor is that social research may exist as a public good in a variety of geographic and political divisions: local, national and global. The need is equally great for such knowledge at each level, but the degree of public support for such research may vary by jurisdiction and level. Social research, like social science or biological research generally, operates in a political milieu and is probably more dependent on public funding than many other areas.

The Technical Advisory Committee (TAC) vision and strategy paper for CGIAR (TAC, 2000b: 38) stated that, with respect to socio-economic research,

> The CGIAR's enhanced mandate and strategic focus on poverty reduction will entail an increased role of socioeconomic research within the CGIAR Centres. Research of this nature is expected to build the body of knowledge on understanding people, the agricultural and technology needs, assessing adoption and the impact of innovations... Additional socioeconomic research by the CGIAR, in collaboration with others, should focus on the sociocultural and agricultural dimensions of rural and urban poverty.

Since the product of social research meets the standard criteria for public goods, viewing it in this context is logical. As noted, however, public goods have wide geographic gradations – from local to global. Much of the work of anthropologists and sociologists may fall closer to the local than the global end. The recent meta-review of CGIAR by the Operations Evaluation Division of the World Bank (2003b: 94) noted that one of the two main tasks of social research is 'considered to focus on household and community-level issues'. Yet, social researchers are working in centres with a predominantly global public-good orientation.

Two major issues then are the degree to which: (i) social researchers can scale up the significance of their work; and (ii) social research of this type helps improve the relevance, efficiency and effectiveness of the centre research programmes, and those of related organizations at the country level. The last issue could be addressed, for example, by clearly identifying and defining social problems (rural and urban), developing relevant research methodologies and measuring impact (which was noted in the meta-review). The newly established Science Council can help raise social issues and consciousness to CGIAR donors, but the decisions on allocating staff resources have traditionally been largely made at 'home' by centre management.[16]

Another issue then is the degree to which the social researchers should become part of teams composed of other centre scientists or left alone to pursue professional interests that may lead to other knowledge-oriented public goods. As noted earlier and argued elsewhere (Dalrymple, 2003c), the last step, which I term a supply-driven element, is essential to stimulate knowledge generation and enlighten the research process. The difficulty is finding the time and resources (particularly as unrestricted funding decreases) to be able to maintain a balance in an environment that is, as the meta-review put it (World Bank, 2003a: 3; World Bank, 2003b: 43–44, 155–158), becoming less science driven and more service oriented.

All of this may encourage social researchers at centres to pay more attention to the wider public-good dimensions of their work and the more specific patterns of change under way within the CGIAR system.

Conclusion

The concept of public goods has essentially been developed by economists and has not spread much further among other social scientists.[17] Even among those familiar with it, the concept has not been extended to the global level until recently. Yet it is particularly appropriate for public-supported international agricultural research such as that conducted in CGIAR because it is focused, to a greater degree than virtually any other major organization, on the production of public goods. Thus the concept could well play a useful role in the tool kit of social scientists working in this area.[18]

Social science research itself is generally conducted in the public sector and produces relatively pure public goods. The importance of specific international development efforts is likely to vary, depending in part on the degree of 'globalness' of their findings. Even though the pattern has varied, Ruttan (1984: 550; 1988: S247, S263; 2004: xvi, 271) asserts that 'advances in social science knowledge represent a powerful source of economic development', in part because they help lower the costs of institutional innovation by reducing trial and error.

A further dimension, however, is that the decisions on funding public goods are made in a political arena, where not all the social sciences are equally comfortable or useful. This leads Ruttan (1982: 327–328) to state, 'A question that the social science disciplines must ask is whether they will respond to rising demand or whether their past alienation from the policy process will limit their capacity to respond.'

Another question will be whether the social sciences would be willing or able to think in terms of a broader geographic context in conducting their research or interpreting the results. Spillovers of useful knowledge at wider and wider levels multiply the payoff from research and have been useful in arguing for support for international research in the biological and physical sciences (which, in some cases, may carry related social science research along with them).

In any case, the importance of significant social problems that require international and global attention continues to increase. If efforts, such as those of UNDP and the new International Task Force on Global Public Goods, are successful in expanding interest in global public goods, and even enlarge their scope, the call for social science could well expand. Are the social sciences ready to think and act in this broader context?

This brings me back to where I started, Sen's (2001) statement that there is clearly 'much merit in economic progress', but also a great need for 'intelligent and equitable social policies'. Both are within the scope and grasp of social science research but should not be independent enclaves. In the case of agricultural research, Sen's concerns are also not independent of biophysical science issues or the political process. A more integrative approach is needed, and that may be facilitated by viewing social science research fully in the context of public goods.

Notes

[1]Bernal (1969: 1019), a historian of science, refers to archaeology, anthropology and sociology as the descriptive social sciences, and economics, law and political science as analytic social sciences. He also includes much of psychology and philosophy with social science. The role of agricultural history in policy is discussed by Cochrane (1993: 461–466).

[2]Further information on this period in development economics is provided in Ruttan (1988: S250–S256). He noted, 'Professional opinion in economics has not dealt kindly with the reputations of those development economists who have made

serious efforts to incorporate cultural variables into development theory or into the analysis of the development process' (Ruttan, 1988: S225).

[3]A further dimension is provided by Bobbitt (2002: 17, 337, 814), a constitutional lawyer and historian: 'The State needs to produce public goods – which engender the qualities of reciprocity, justice, solidarity, empathy, and civility – because such goods are, by definition, what the market does not produce on its own... The markets (and new market-state situations) do not provide these processes unaided by the State and its laws'.

[4]Ruttan (1982: 311) also referred to some early research at the International Rice Research Institute relating to biological and socioeconomic constraints on yield. These were also described as '(t)he institutional constraints imposed by the economic, social, and cultural environment in which the farmer lives and works' (Ruttan, 1982: 312).

[5]In the priorities and strategies report prepared by the Technical Advisory Committee (TAC) (1987: 126–127) in 1986, one of the principal sets of criteria was grouped under 'international character of the commodity or research programme' and included 'transferability' and comparative advantage. In 1991, TAC (1992: 43) stated, 'In planning and determining priorities in international research, consideration will be given to the maximization of spillover effects that will result from research activities.' Public goods were perhaps first explicitly mentioned in 1997 (TAC, 2000a: 30).

[6]The programme was formally known in its later years as the Social Science Research Fellowships in Agriculture. The first appointments were made in 1975 and the last in 1997. Altogether 115 fellows were drawn from anthropology, demography, economics and agricultural economics, geography and sociology. There was also a parallel programme in population (information forwarded by Jocelyn Penna of Rockefeller Foundation, 30 July and 4 August 2003). Unfortunately, no general review or evaluation of this vital programme seems to have been done (which in itself would have been a useful piece of social science research).

[7]Much further detail on social science research in CGIAR is provided in Cernea and Kassam (2002), Kassam (2002) and Kassam *et al.* (2002). As Kassam notes, Baum gave only one sentence to 'socio-economic research' in his early history of CGIAR, and then in terms of formulating national policy (Baum, 1986: 94).

[8]A recent study by the National Research Council (NRC) of the National Academies on frontiers in agricultural research in the USA (NRC, 2002: 54–55) recognized the importance of agriculture as a system 'that links many biologic, physical, social, and economic processes'. NRC's first recommendation included, 'A greater emphasis on multidisciplinary work that engages all relevant disciplines will be needed to address many new research frontiers.'

[9]However, for example, 'It is quite clear...that lack of economic knowledge has at times imposed very heavy costs on American farmers and the American economy' (Ruttan, 1984: 557). This is undoubtedly true, although to a differing degree in other economies.

[10]Information on publications and discussion papers issued as part of the IFPRI effort may be obtained from www.ifpri.org/impact/impact.htm. Others are forth-

coming, including some thematic evaluations (e.g. Pardey and Smith, 2004). One long-standing and ongoing question is the degree of emphasis that the centre should place on country case studies vs. multi-country studies and syntheses of broader and more global public-good value. The two may be linked, with the former providing building blocks for the latter, but experience has been mixed. Determining the appropriate balance at this point is more art than science (partly based on e-mail from James Ryan, 4 August 2003).

[11]The poverty focus may not come without some opportunity costs for an internationally and globally oriented biological research organization (Dalrymple, 1999; Alston, 2002: 336–337). The causes of poverty, which are in part an income distribution problem, are many and complex. Their alleviation involves a broad array of often localized efforts, and research is only part of the answer (see Gardner, 2003). The type of research deemed best for poverty alleviation may not maximize international spillovers of technology and knowledge. Complicated and delicate questions are involved in appropriately balancing resource allocation in the poverty area.

[12]This appears to have been, for instance, the case in the Economic Research Service of USDA from 1981 to 1993 (phone conversation with John Lee, former administrator of the Economic Research Service, 25 July 2003). For a broader and more quantitative assessment of sources of influence, see Goldberger (2001).

[13]Further information about social science research in CGIAR is provided in TAC (1997), Kassam (2002) and Kassam *et al.* (2002).

[14]See Orstrom and Orstrom (1991) for an example of the political science dimension.

[15]UNDP is being joined by a newly established International Task Force on Global Public Goods, which was created as a joint effort of the governments of France and Sweden, and has its secretariat in Stockholm. Friends of the Task Force held its first meeting in Paris in July, and the task force held its first meeting in New Haven, USA, in September 2003. See www.gpgtaskforce.org for details.

[16]This process, however, is changing due to two exogenous forces: (i) a steady decline in unrestricted funding to centres and a corresponding increase in restricted funding; and (ii) the establishment of Challenge Programs, which have assumed the size and character of semi-independent centres with complex management structures. The degree to which these developments have influenced the extent and nature of social research, or are likely to do so, is uncertain. (At a seminar on the meta-review held at IFPRI in September 2003, it was suggested that funding has largely been aimed at downstream projects in the case of natural resources.)

[17]The social scientists are not alone in this instance. Less surprisingly, the biological and physical sciences have also given little attention to public goods (Dalrymple, 2003b). Henry Wallace (1934: 4), former US Secretary of Agriculture, once commented that 'It is difficult to see how the engineer and the scientist can much longer preserve a complete isolation from the economic and social world around them.'

[18]Gardner and Lesser (2003) have, for example, recently provided some helpful economic perspectives on the concept in the context of the CGIAR. Further such contributions from other social scientists would be highly useful.

References

Alston, J.M. (2002) Spillovers. *The Australian Journal of Agricultural and Resource Economics* 46(3), 315–346.

Arrow, K.J. (1997) Invaluable goods. *Journal of Economic Literature* 35 (June), 757–765.

Baum, W.C. (1986) *Partners against Hunger: The Consultative Group on International Agricultural Research.* World Bank, Washington, DC, 337 pp.

Bernal, J.D. (1969) *Science in History (Vol. 4: The Social Sciences, Conclusion).* The MIT Press, Cambridge, Massachusetts, 1328 pp.

Bobbitt, P. (2002) *The Shield of Achilles: War, Peace, and the Course of History.* Alfred Knopf, New York, 919 pp.

Buchanan, J. (1968) *The Demand and Supply of Public Goods.* Rand McNally and Company, Chicago, Illinois, 214 pp.

Burke, E. (Conor Cruise O'Brien (ed.)) (1790/1986) *Burke's Reflections on the Revolution in France.* Penguin Books, London, 404 pp.

Cernea, M.M. (1987) The 'production' of a social methodology. In: Eddy, E.M. and Partridge, W.L. (eds) *Applied Anthropology in America.* Columbia University Press, New York, pp. 237–262.

Cernea, M.M. and Kassam, A. (2002) Brief Notes on the Social Research Conference. Interim Science Council, Consultative Group on International Agricultural Research (CGIAR), Rome, 10 pp.

Cochrane, W.W. (1993) *The Development of American Agriculture: a Historical Analysis.* University of Minnesota Press, Minneapolis, Minnesota, 500 pp.

Dalrymple, D.G. (1999) *Donor Bandwagons and the CGIAR: the Case of Poverty Alleviation.* Office of Agriculture and Food Security, Global Bureau, US Agency for International Development (USAID), Washington, DC, 4 pp.

Dalrymple, D.G. (2003a) *International Agricultural Research as a Global Public Good: a Review of Concepts, Experience, and Policy Issues.* USAID, Bureau for Economic Growth, Development and Trade, Office of Environment and Science Policy (USAID/ EGAT/ ESP), Washington, DC, 30 pp.

Dalrymple, D.G. (2003b) Scientific knowledge as a global public good: contributions to innovation and the economy. In: Esanu, J. and Uhlir, P. (eds) *The Role of Scientific Data and Information in the Public Domain: Proceedings of a Symposium.* National Academies Press, Washington, DC, pp. 35–51. Available online: www.nap.edu/ catalog/10785.html

Dalrymple, D.G. (2003c) *Demand- and Supply-Driven International Agricultural Research: Setting the Agenda for Global Public Goods.* USAID/EGAT/ESP, Washington, DC, 20 pp.

Dalrymple, D.G. (2003d) *Impure Public Goods and Agricultural Research: Some Concepts, Views, and Issues.* USAID/EGAT/ESP, Washington, DC, 14 pp.

Drache, D. (2001) *The Market and the Public Domain.* Routledge, New York, 39 pp.

Galison, P. (2003) *Einstein's Clocks, Poincaré's Maps: Empires of Time.* W.W. Norton & Co., New York and London, 389 pp.

Gardner, B.L. (2003) Causes of rural economic development. Elmhirst Lecture and the 25th Conference of the International Association of Agricultural Economists, 18 August 2003, Durban, South Africa. Department of Agricultural Economics, University of Maryland, College Park, Maryland, 41 pp.

Gardner, B. and Lesser, W. (2003) International agricultural research as a global public good. *American Journal of Agricultural Economics* 85(3) (August), 692–697.

Goldberger, J.R. (2001) Research orientation and sources of influence: agricultural scientists in the US land-grant system. *Rural Sociology* 66(1) (March), 69–92.

Hadwiger, D.F. (1982) *The Politics of Agricultural Research.* University of Nebraska Press, Lincoln, Nebraska, 230 pp.

Hardin, C.M. (1955) *Freedom in Agricultural Education.* University of Chicago Press, Chicago, Illinois, (reprinted by Arno Press, New York, 1976), 275 pp.

Howard, A. (1943) *An Agricultural Testament.* Oxford University Press, New York and London (reprinted by Rodale Press, Emmaus, Pennsylvania, 1972), 253 pp.

Huffman, W.E. and Evenson, R.E. (1993) *Science for Agriculture: a Long-Term Perspective.* Iowa State University Press, Ames, Iowa, 268 pp.

International Task Force on Global Public Goods (2003) *Background Note.* Stockholm.

Kassam, A. (2002) *An Overview of Social Science Research in the CGIAR.* Interim Science Council Secretariat, CGIAR, Food and Agriculture Organization of the United Nations (FAO), Rome, 28 pp.

Kassam, A., Barat, S. and Moreddu, E. (2002) *A Compilation of Excerpts on Social Science Research in the CGIAR from TAC-Commissioned External Reviews of Centers and Systemwide Programs Since 1995.* Interim Science Council Secretariat, CGIAR, FAO, Rome, 38 pp.

Kaul, I. and Mendoza, R.U. (2003) Advancing the concept of public goods. In: Kaul, I., Conceicao, P., Le Goulven, K. and Mendoza, R.U. (eds) (2003) *Providing Global Public Goods; Managing Globalization.* Published for the United Nations Development Programme by Oxford University Press, New York and Oxford, 646 pp.

National Research Council (NRC) (2002) *Frontiers in Agricultural Research: Food, Health, Environment, and Communities.* National Academies Press, Washington, DC, 239 pp.

Norton, G.W. (1987) Evaluating social science research in agriculture. In: *Evaluating Agricultural Research and Productivity. Proceedings of a symposium, 29–30 January 1987, Atlanta, Georgia.* University of Minnesota, Minnesota Agricultural Experiment Station, St Paul, Miscellaneous Publication 57-1987, Minneapolis, Minnesota, pp. 177–193.

Ostrom, V. and Ostrom, E. (1991) Public goods and public choices. In: Ostrom, V. (ed.) *American Federalism: Constitution a Self-Governing Society.* Institute for Contemporary Studies Press, San Francisco, California, pp. 163–197.

Pardey, P. and Smith, V. (eds) (2004) *What's Economics Worth? Valuing*

Policy Research. Johns Hopkins University Press, Baltimore, Maryland.

Ruttan, V.W. (1982) *Agricultural Research Policy.* University of Minnesota Press, Minneapolis, Minnesota, 369 pp.

Ruttan, V.W. (1984) Social science knowledge and institutional change. *American Journal of Agricultural Economics* 66(5) (December), 549–559.

Ruttan, V.W. (1988) Cultural endowments and economic development: what can we learn from anthropology? *Economic Development and Cultural Change* 36(3) (April), S247–S271.

Ruttan, V.W. (2004) *Social Science Knowledge and Economic Development.* University of Michigan Press, Ann Arbor, Michigan.

Sen, A. (2001) Economic progress and health. In: Leon, D.A. and Walt, G. (eds) *Poverty, Inequality, and Health.* Oxford University Press, Oxford and New York, pp. 333–345.

Smith, A. (1776/2000) *The Wealth of Nations.* The Modern Library, New York, 1154 pp.

Technical Advisory Committee (TAC) (1987) *CGIAR Priorities and Future Strategies.* TAC of CGIAR, TAC Secretariat, FAO, Rome, 245 pp.

TAC (1992) *Expansion of the CGIAR System.* TAC/FAO, Rome, 337 pp.

TAC (1997) *Policy and Management and Institution Strengthening Research and Service in the CGIAR.* TAC/FAO, Rome, 193 pp.

TAC (2000a) *CGIAR Priorities and Strategies for Resource Allocation during 1998–2000 and Centre Proposals and TAC Recommendations.* TAC/FAO, Rome, 89 pp.

TAC (2000b) *A Food Secure World for All: Toward a New Vision and Strategy for the CGIAR.* TAC/FAO, Rome, 50 pp.

Wallace, H.A. (1934) The social advantages and disadvantages of the engineering-scientific approach to civilization. *Science* 79(2036) (January 5), 1–5.

World Bank (2003a) The CGIAR at 31: celebrating its achievements, facing its challenges, *Précis,* World Bank Operations Evaluation Department, Washington, DC, Spring, No. 232, 6 pp.

World Bank (2003b) The CGIAR at 31: An Independent Meta-Evaluation of the Consultative Group on International Agricultural Research, World Bank Operations Evaluation Department, Washington, DC, 230pp. Available online: http://www.worldbank.org/oed/ cigar/

Contributors

Malika Abdelali-Martini is a graduate of law and economics from the University of Algeria and has a PhD degree in rural development from the University of Reading, UK. Her research has focused on adoption and impact of new technologies developed by the International Center for Agricultural Research in the Dry Areas (ICARDA), and on mainstreaming gender analysis. Her broader research interests include building social capital through local networks dealing with women's agricultural labour, livestock dairy production, processing and marketing and their effectiveness in reducing poverty and improving people's livelihoods.

Michelle Adato, a research fellow at the International Food Policy Research Institute (IFPRI), received a PhD in development sociology from Cornell University, and an MA in public administration from Harvard University. She focuses primarily on human capital-based safety-nets and social protection programmes, employment and work and regional and community-based institutions. She co-leads two multi-country research programmes, one on evaluating nutrition-related programmes and another on evaluating the impact of agricultural research on poverty. She has done extensive fieldwork in South Africa and Mexico, and more recent work in Kenya and Nicaragua.

Akin Adesina is an agricultural economist, with several years of professional experience in African agriculture. He holds a BSc in agricultural economics from the University of Ife, Nigeria, and in 1988 obtained a PhD in agricultural economics from Purdue University, USA. He won the Rockefeller Foundation Social Science Research

447

Fellowship in 1988, which initiated his career in international agricultural development. He has worked in various senior research positions in the International Agricultural Research Centres of the Consultative Group on International Agricultural Research (CGIAR), including as senior economist and social science research coordinator for IITA (1995–1998). He joined the Rockefeller Foundation, New York, as a senior scientist for Africa in 1998, and later served as the representative for Southern Africa, based in Harare, Zimbabwe. Currently, he is an associate director (food security) at the Rockefeller Foundation, based in Nairobi, Kenya. He has published extensively on issues of agricultural development in Africa. His primary research interests are technology development, capacity building and institutional development and improvement of agricultural policies and markets to enhance food security and incomes for the rural poor.

Mahfuzuddin Ahmed is principal scientist (fisheries economist), programme leader and member of the Senior Management Team of the WorldFish Center. He leads the WorldFish research team for fisheries policies in developing countries. His professional career began in the late 1970s as researcher and economics lecturer at the University of Chittagong, Bangladesh. He is president of the International Institute for Fisheries Economics and Trade. A founding member of the board of governors of Grameen Fisheries Foundation, he is scientific adviser to the International Foundation for Science and associate editor of *Asian Fisheries Science*. He received the Dr Elvira Tan Memorial Award 2002 for his work on milkfish fry resources in the Philippines. He recently co-authored *Fish to 2020 – Supply Demand in Changing Markets*.

Jacqueline Ashby is a development sociologist, whose work has made a vast contribution to the introduction of social science knowledge and sociological research methods in Centro Internacional de Agricultura Tropical or the International Center for Tropical Agriculture (CIAT) and CGIAR at large. Her current work focuses on action research to promote organizational change and innovation in natural resources management and food systems, both global and local. She recently took on new responsibilities as director of the Rural Innovation Institute at CIAT, having been, since 1996, Director of Research, Natural Resources Management, and leader for the CGIAR Systemwide Participatory Research and Gender Analysis Programme.

Mauricio R. Bellon is senior scientist for the Economics Programme with the International Maize and Wheat Improvement Center (CIMMYT) in El Batán, Mexico. He received his BSc in agronomy from the Universidad Autonoma Metropolitana, Mexico, and his

MSc and PhD in human ecology from the University of California, Davis. At CIMMYT he is responsible for participatory research and the social and cultural aspects of crop biodiversity research. He is the principal investigator in several projects that deal with on-farm conservation, gene flow in traditional farming systems and the impact of improved germplasm in the livelihoods of poor farmers. He has carried out field work in Mexico, the Philippines, Vietnam and Zimbabwe. Before joining CIMMYT in 1997, he was affiliate scientist at the Genetics Resources Center, International Rice Research Institute (IRRI) (1995–1997), and *investigador asociado* 'C' at the Centro de Ecologia, Universidad Nacional Autonoma de Mexico (1990–1995). He is a member of the Mexican Academy of Sciences.

Scott Bode is a natural resources advisor at United States Agency for International Development (USAID) Office of Environment and Science. His main responsibility is working with CGIAR. He has a BA in anthropology (1987) from Beloit College, USA, and an MSc in forestry (1997) from North Carolina State University, USA. He began his career with the Peace Corps in Sierra Leone as an agroforestry extension agent (1989–1991), and subsequently has worked and consulted in a number of countries in Africa and Asia: Cape Verde, Cameroon, Kenya, Liberia, Sierra Leone, Tanzania, Uganda, Malawi, Zambia, Mozambique, the Philippines and India. He served as the Africa programme coordinator for a non-governmental organization, Trees for the Future (2000–2001), and also worked as a research associate (1995–1999) for several institutions in North Carolina, including the US Forest Service, Water Resources Research Institute and North Carolina State University.

Dindo Campilan is a sociologist and communications specialist at the International Potato Center (CIP). He received a PhD in communications and innovation studies from Wageningen University in 1994, joined the International Potato Center in 1995 as a post-doctoral fellow, and in 1997 became coordinator of CIP's participatory research network in Asia – Users' Perspectives with Agricultural Research and Development. He has been involved in potato and sweet potato research projects in China, Indonesia, Laos, Nepal, Pakistan, the Philippines and Vietnam. His specialities include participatory research, sustainable agricultural livelihoods, monitoring and evaluation and capacity development. He is the CIP liaison scientist for the CGIAR Systemwide Programme on Collective Action and Property Rights.

Michael M. Cernea, anthropologist and sociologist, is Research Professor of Anthropology and International Affairs, George

Washington University, and Honorary Professor of the Hohai University, Nanjing, China. During 1974–1997 he served as the World Bank's Senior Sociologist and senior Adviser for Social Policies and Sociology, and from 1998–2003 as Member of TAC and the interim Science Council of the CGIAR. He was elected to Romania's Academy of Sciences, is Chief Scientist of the Science Board of the Social Development Institute, Hohai University, China and was Vice President of the European Society for Rural Sociology. Cernea contributed to defining some of the World Bank's key social and agricultural/rural development policies, particularly on agricultural extension, population resettlement, indigenous populations, irrigation and social forestry. For his social research and social policy work, he was awarded prizes by the Romanian Academy of Sciences, and also the Solon T. Kimball Award (1988) and the Bronislaw Malinowski Prize (1995) in the USA. He has written or edited numerous books, including *Putting People First – Sociological Variables in Rural Development*, translated in many countries, *The Economics of Involuntary Resettlements* (1999) and *Risks and Reconstruction* (2000, with C. McDowell). His most recent book is *Cultural Heritage and Development: a Framework for Action in the Middle East and North Africa* (2001, 2003).

Robert Chambers is a research associate of the Institute of Development Studies at the University of Sussex, UK, where he is a member of the Participation Group. He has a background in natural sciences, history and public administration. He has worked as a manager of rural development, trainer, university teacher, evaluation officer in the United Nations High Commissioner for Refugees (UNHCR), programme officer at the Ford Foundation and field researcher in East Africa and South Asia. He co-edited *Seasonal Dimensions to Rural Poverty* (1981) and *Farmer First: Farmer Innovation and Agricultural Research* (1989), and co-authored *To the Hands of the Poor: Water and Trees* (1989) and *Voices of the Poor: Crying out for Change* (2001). He wrote *Rural Development: Putting the Last First* (1983), *Challenging the Professions: Frontiers for Rural Development* (1993), *Whose Reality Counts? Putting the First Last* (1997) and *Participatory Workshops* (2002). His current work is concerned with poverty and its perceptions; participation; and professional, institutional and personal change, including institutional learning and change in CGIAR.

Marc Cohen earned his BA at Carleton College, USA, and his MA and PhD in political science at the University of Wisconsin, Madison, USA. A US citizen, he joined the International Food Policy Research Institute in 1998, and is special assistant to the director general. In addition to serving as secretary of IFPRI's Board of

Trustees, he assists the director general in research, writing and outreach activities. His research focuses on the world food situation and outlook, biotechnology and food security, conflict and food security and the right to adequate food.

Carol J. Pierce Colfer is a principal scientist and anthropologist at the Center for International Forestry Research in Bogor, Indonesia. Her long-term fieldwork has been in the US Pacific north-west, various islands in Indonesia and the Sultanate of Oman. She has also been involved in cross-cultural studies spanning 15 countries around the world. She has specialized in working with other disciplines with communities on development and conservation issues, with special emphasis on gender concerns. Her PhD is in cultural anthropology from the University of Washington in Seattle (1974); and she also has a master's degree in public health and international health from the University of Hawaii (1980). She has worked on education, health, agriculture, engineering, ecology and forestry projects.

Gordon Conway, a world-renowned agricultural ecologist, served as the 12th President of the Rockefeller Foundation between 1998 and 2004 and currently is senior scientific advisor to DfID–UK. Before joining the Rockefeller Foundation, he was Vice Chancellor of the University of Sussex in Brighton and chair of the university's Institute of Development Studies. Conway received his PhD in agricultural ecology from the University of California, Davis, USA, and also honorary degrees from the University of Sussex, UK and the University of the West Indies, Trinidad. A former Ford Foundation representative for India, Nepal and Sri Lanka, he spent 12 years as an administrator, director and professor at the UK's Imperial College of Science, Technology and Medicine. He pioneered integrated pest management in Sabah, North Borneo, Malaysia, in the 1960s; developed agroecosystems analysis in Thailand in the 1970s; and in the 1980s was one of the first to define the concept of sustainable agriculture. He developed interdisciplinary centres of environmental education at London University in the 1970s, and helped set up similar centres in the Sudan, Indonesia, the Philippines and Thailand. Conway has written many papers, monographs and books on applied ecology, resource and environmental management and international development. His most recent book was *The Doubly Green Revolution: Food for All in the 21st Century* (1999). For his services to international development, science and agriculture, he was appointed Knight Commander of the Order of St Michael and St George (KCMG).

Dana G. Dalrymple is senior research advisor, International Research and Biotechnology Team, Office of Environment and Science

Policy, US Agency for International Development (USAID), Washington, DC; and agricultural economist, Foreign Agricultural Service, US Department of Agriculture. He has helped administer US government involvement in, and support of, CGIAR and its network of centres for over 30 years. Dalrymple received his BSc and MSc from Cornell University, and his PhD from Michigan State University, USA. He is a long-time student of the development and adoption of agricultural technology in agriculture and has published widely on this subject. He has served as an analyst on studies of agricultural research sponsored by the National Academies of Science and the Office of Technology Assessment of the US Congress. He has also studied and written about the development of Soviet agriculture and the Soviet famine of 1933. His recent analytical work has focused on the public-goods dimension of agricultural research and the role of maintenance research.

Hugo De Groote is a senior scientist and regional economist with CIMMYT in Kenya. He received an MSc in tropical agriculture from the University of Ghent, Belgium, and a PhD in agricultural economics from the University of Wisconsin, USA. His research activities include the economic analysis and participatory evaluation of new technologies and analysis of policies and institutions relevant to them (such as seed systems, credit and extension and biotechnology policies). Previously, he was coordinator of the biological control project at the International Institute for Tropical Agriculture (IITA), in Benin, conducting economic analysis and participatory evaluation of biological control of pests such as the water hyacinth, locusts and mango mealybug. He also worked in farming systems research, developing and evaluating new technologies and evaluated group-based credit and loan associations in the International Food Policy Research Institute, in Mali. He worked as an agriculturalist in rural development for non-governmental organizations in Togo and Thailand.

Madan Mohan Dey is a senior research scientist at the WorldFish Center. A PhD in agricultural economics, he has 20 years of experience in agricultural research and development in tropical countries. His areas of expertise include food sector modelling, agricultural and trade policy analysis, impact assessment, community-based natural resource management, economics of development and diffusion of agricultural technologies and poverty analysis. Over the last 9 years, he has been leading and implementing a number of pioneering research projects at the WorldFish Center and has helped in developing and disseminating pro-poor aquaculture technologies in developing Asian countries. Before joining the WorldFish Center, he worked for two other CGIAR centres – IRRI and IFPRI. He has also conducted collaborative research with other advanced research institutes including Yale University and the International Service for National Agricultural Research (ISNAR). He served the government of Bangladesh for 10 years in different capacities.

Edmond Dounias is a scientist at the French Research Institute for Development (IRD) and a seconded scientist at the Center for International Forestry Research (CIFOR). He has been working in Cameroon since 1984, as student in a research programme on anthropology of food of Cameroonian populations living in constraining environments. He finished his doctoral dissertation in 1993 on the contrasted land-use systems of Yasa coastal fishermen, Mvae farmers and trappers and Bakola hunter–gatherers – three ethnic groups living in the same ecological environments in southern coastal Cameroon. In the early 1990s, he conducted postdoctoral research on the effects of the management of wild yams by the Baka Pygmies of Eastern Cameroon on the demography of these tuber plants. In IRD from 1994, he supervised a research programme on the human ecology of the Tikar, living in the forest and savannah of Central Cameroon. During the late 1990s, he coordinated the Cameroonian component of the Future of Rainforest Peoples, a programme of the European Commission. At CIFOR now, he conducts research on diet and disease among the Punan hunter–gatherers of the Tubu watershed in Eastern Kalimantan.

Javier M. Ekboir is a consultant with FAO, evaluating agricultural policies in Mexico. Previously he was an economist at CIMMYT (1998–2003) studying agricultural innovation systems, innovation networks and development and diffusion of appropriate sustainable technologies for small farmers. In 1984–1990, he also worked at INTA, Argentina, as a researcher, organizer and manager of an MSc programme in agricultural economics. He received a BSc in economics from the Universidad de Buenos Aires, Argentina; an MSc in agricultural economics from the Hebrew University of Jerusalem, Israel; and a PhD in agricultural economics from the University of California, Davis, USA. In 1984–1990 he taught in several undergraduate and graduate programmes in Argentina.

Pablo Eyzaguirre, a Chilean national, has been senior scientist in anthropology and socioeconomics in the Genetic Resources Science and Technology Group (GRST) of International Plant Genetic Resources Institute (IPGRI), Rome, since 1995. A specialist in social and ecological anthropology, tropical farming systems and agrarian institutions, he is also President of the International Society of Ethnobiology. He has a PhD (1986) in anthropology from Yale University, has taught anthropology in the USA and conducted long-term field research on ecology and livelihoods in West and Central Africa. He has also carried out many short research missions throughout Africa, Asia and Latin America on the integration of social, ecological and institutional research approaches to agricultural development and biocultural conservation. Before joining IPGRI, he was senior officer in the International Service for National Agricultural Research (ISNAR) in The Hague, Netherlands. He has published several books and many articles on agriculture and environmental research and biodiversity, including *Agricultural and Environmental Research in Small Countries* (1996) and *Home Gardens and Agrobiodiversity* (2004) with Olga Linares.

Curtis Farrar is writing a history of the International Food Policy Research Institute focused on the content and relevance of the institute's research. He was executive secretary of CGIAR (1982–1989), and has served in executive positions at IFPRI and at the US Agency for International Development (USAID). With the Asia Foundation, he spent 5 years in Pakistan, and 3 in Cambodia. He has a PhD in economics from the London School of Economics. His research interests include research institutions, particularly IFPRI and CGIAR; global policy issues; and assessment of the impact of agricultural research in developing countries.

Marina Goloubinoff, anthropologist, has worked as a consultant for several French, Mexican and international institutions, including the Center for International Forestry Research and the International Agroforestry Research Center. Her PhD dissertation at the University of Paris (1994) was about trade and social relations among the Nahua Indians of Guerrero, Mexico. In Mexico, she also worked on traditional medicine, rituals and indigenous political strategies. Since 1997, she has been working in Indonesia on environmental issues and trade of forest products. She is co-editor of several books on the anthropology of climate.

Scott Guggenheim has a long career in development studies. Before receiving his PhD in social anthropology from the Johns Hopkins University, USA, in 1984, he worked for the applied research centre of the Anthropology Museum in Mexico City on a study of regional industrialization. After completing his PhD, he joined CGIAR as a Rockefeller postdoctoral fellow assigned to the International Fertilizer Development Centre and the International Center for Tropical Agriculture (CIAT). Beginning in 1988, he worked with Michael Cernea on the issues associated with involuntary resettlement caused by World Bank-funded development projects, which culminated in the 1994 World Bank-wide review of projects entailing forced resettlement. Since finishing the review, Scott has been based in the Jakarta office of the World Bank in Indonesia, where he is the lead social scientist and the head of a nationwide community development programme. In 2003, he was a fellow at Yale University's Center for International Areas Studies. His development interests focus on the changing patterns of integration between rural communities and national governments, and on how 'models of' and 'models for' development appear, change and adapt to a world that resists planning.

Lawrence J. Haddad joined the International Food Policy Research Institute as a research fellow in 1990 and since 1994 has been director of the Food Consumption and Nutrition Division. His research focus is on the design and impact of policies and programmes to reduce poverty and malnutrition. His research interests include how decisions are made within families and the role of individual status; links between agriculture, poverty and nutrition; role of social capital in protecting income levels and promoting income growth; role of community participation in the performance of poverty programmes; implications of the human rights movement for food policy research; and challenges faced by households and policymakers in areas of the developing world where rapid urbanization is worsening poverty and malnutrition. Before joining IFPRI, he was a lecturer in quantitative development economics at the University of Warwick, UK. A UK citizen, Haddad received a BSc from the University of Reading, UK; an MSc from the University of Massachusetts, USA; and an MSc and a PhD in food research from Stanford University, USA.

Aden A. Aw-Hassan is a graduate of agricultural science from Somali National University (1982). He received his PhD in agricultural economics at the Oklahoma State University, USA (1992) and postgraduate education at the Utah State University and the University of Wisconsin, USA. He is research project manager in socioeconomics at ICARDA, responsible for research planning, implementation and reporting, coordination with other disciplines and research projects, research collaboration with national programmes, training and mentoring young researchers and reporting for donors. He has worked extensively in agricultural extension at different levels. His research interests include production systems characterization for targeting research and development interventions, research impact, poverty and livelihoods analysis, process monitoring, participatory research methods and gender analysis.

Dean Holland originally trained as an agricultural entomologist, but jumped ship to the social sciences to study adult learning and participatory approaches to agricultural research. He has studied action-learning systems for farmers and researchers in the Philippines, and with CIAT, in the forest margins of Peru. He works for the not-for-profit non-governmental organization Greening

Australia in Queensland. In a country where an organized private
sector is the main driver of environmental change, he is exploring
ways to link the private sector with civil society and the public
sector to better manage natural resources.

Mahabub Hossain joined IRRI in 1992 as head of its Social Sciences
Division. Since 2000, he also became leader of IRRI's Research and
Development Linkage Programme. He began his career in 1970 as
a staff economist at the Pakistan Institute of Development Economics, which was renamed the Bangladesh Institute of Development Studies (BIDS) after the civil war in 1971, where he rose
through the ranks and became the director general of BIDS in 1989.
His research interests include the role of technology, credit and
infrastructure in rural development; income distribution and
poverty analysis; land tenure and land reforms; research prioritization; supply and demand projections for policy formulations;
rural non-farm economy; hybrid rice; and the economics of
biotechnology. He has a PhD in economics, University of
Cambridge (1977); a diploma in development economics, University
of Cambridge (1973); an MA in economics, University of Dhaka
(1969); and a BA (Honours) in economics, University of Calcutta
(1966).

Amir H. Kassam, served as Executive Secretary of the CGIAR Science
Council at FAO, Rome, from 2003–2004, and as Senior Agricultural Research Officer in the CGIAR Technical Advisory Committee
Secretariat at FAO, Rome, from 1990–2003 where he was responsible
for facilitating the Council's work on research priorities and strategies, and on performance monitoring and evaluation. He is
currently Visiting Professor in the School of Agriculture, Policy and
Development at the University of Reading, UK. He received his
BSc (Hons) in Agriculture and PhD in Agricultural Botany (agroecology) from the University of Reading, UK, and MSc in Irrigation
from the University of California, Davis. During the 1970s and
'80s, he worked with several national agricultural research systems
(including Nigeria, Mozambique, Kenya and Bangladesh), and
with several CGIAR centres and UN agencies in the fields of crop
physiology and agronomy, crop improvement, natural resources
management, agroecology and land resources evaluation for development planning. During 1998–2000 he was Deputy Director General
for Programmes at West Africa Rice Development Association
(WARDA), Cote d'Ivoire. He also served as the Chairman of the
Aga Khan Foundation (UK) from 1985–1989, and as Chairman of
the FOCUS Humanitarian Assistance Europe Foundation from
1995–1998. He has worked in the NGO sector in rural development in Pakistan and India, and in humanitarian assistance in

Central Asia. He is co-editor of the *Irrigation Science Journal* and a Fellow of the Institute of Biology, London. For his services to tropical agriculture and to rural development, he was appointed Officer of the Order of the British Empire (OBE).

Citlalli López was born in Mexico, where she worked for 6 years as anthropologist in several rural development projects in the State of Veracruz. She completed her PhD in development studies in the Netherlands in 2003. Her particular research interests are ecology and society relations. She has worked with CIFOR on a range of research and information dissemination projects which relate to non-timber forest products (NTFPs); this has included editing three volumes (Asia, Africa, Latin America) of collected case studies on NTFPs. Her personal interest is in returning information to communities where research scientists work by providing examples of NTFP use in other regions.

John Lynam has been associate director in the Food Security Programme of the Rockefeller Foundation, Nairobi, Kenya for 16 years. Over that time he has been involved in a number of programmes developing capacities in national, regional and international agricultural research systems in east and southern Africa. He holds a PhD in agricultural economics from the former Food Research Institute at Stanford University, USA, from where he was selected as one of the first 'Rocky docs', joining CIAT in Cali, Colombia. That turned into an 11-year tenure as economist in the Cassava Programme, where he helped integrate social science work into biological research programmes.

Ruth Meinzen-Dick, sociologist, is a senior research fellow at IFPRI, and coordinator of the CGIAR Systemwide Programme on Collective Action and Property Rights (CAPRi). She received her PhD in development sociology from Cornell University, USA. Much of her work has been interdisciplinary research on policies for water and natural resources management. This includes work on water rights, gender analysis, local organizations, comparative analysis of irrigation system performance, operation of water markets, relations between farmers and government agencies, impact of agricultural research on poverty and sustainable livelihoods. Her field work has been primarily in India, Zimbabwe, Pakistan, Nepal and Sri Lanka. She serves on several professional bodies, including the steering committee of the Global Water Partnership, and the Executive Council of the International Association for the Study of Common Property.

Mariano Mejía M. has been an associate of information and documentation at CIAT, since 1972, providing technical information to CIAT staff and their partners in research and development institutions in

Latin America and the Caribbean, Asia and Africa. With an undergraduate degree in education from Santiago de Cali University, and an MA in adult education from San Buenaventura University in Cali, Colombia, Mariano specializes in training researchers, teachers, students, agribusinesses and smallholder farmers to access information through the Internet. Mariano is involved in a pilot project on distance education.

Erika C.H. Meng is a scientist with the economics programme at CIMMYT in Mexico. She holds a dual BA in international relations and political science from the University of Pennsylvania, as well as an MSc and PhD degree in agricultural and resource economics from the University of California, Davis, USA. Her primary areas of research are the economics of genetic diversity in wheat production systems, including *in situ* conservation incentives and effects of diversity on productivity; wheat and maize production systems in Central Asia and the Caucasus (CAC), West Asia and North Africa, and China; application of household-level modelling techniques; analysis of technology adoption; and research priority setting. She has field experience in China, Turkey, numerous CAC countries and Afghanistan. She was an international affairs specialist with the US Department of Agriculture, Office of International Cooperation and Development, Washington, DC (1988–1990).

Douglas J. Merrey, social anthropologist, is director for Africa at the International Water Management Institute (IWMI) and has worked on water and irrigation institutional issues since the mid-1970s. He holds a PhD from the University of Pennsylvania, USA. Before joining IWMI in 1985, he worked for Colorado State University, USA, USAID, and a private consulting firm. His research is focused on institutional arrangements at local, river basin and national levels to manage water resources, especially irrigation. He was deputy director general for programmes in 1998–2000, when he was appointed director of IWMI's new Africa regional office. He lived and carried out social research in Pakistan, India, Sri Lanka, Indonesia and Egypt before moving to South Africa. He has done short-term assignments in Nepal, the Philippines and other developing countries.

Bruno Minjauw has worked in Africa for more than 10 years and at the International Livestock Research Institute since 1997. His basic background is in animal production science, and he received a PhD from the Veterinary Epidemiology and Economic Unit of the University of Reading, UK, for his work on the epidemiology and control of East Coast fever. As a livestock scientist, he has a special interest in developing links between research and development, using biological and social sciences, to increase the impact of live-stock research. He has extensive field experience in rural African production systems, using participatory and conventional research methodologies. Keen to increase the impact of research on the livelihood of poor farmers, he is now leading the livestock Farmer Field School (FFS) Project. The FFS methodology is based on an innovative, participatory and interactive learning approach and has proved successful for integrated pest management and soil fertility issues in many countries.

Joyce Lewinger Moock, anthropologist, is associate vice president of the Rockefeller Foundation, where she serves as principal programme officer for higher education and human capacity building in Africa. She has been the Foundation's assistant director for social sciences, associate director for agricultural sciences and acting director for global environment. In 1995–1996, she was appointed special advisor to the president of the Social Science Research Council, New York, to redesign its international programme, with attention to the conceptualization of human capital against the challenges of the 21st century. She serves on the board of governors at the Rockefeller Archive Center, board of directors for the African Economic Research Consortium and steering committee of the Association for the Development of Education in Africa, among others, and is an elected member of the Council on Foreign Relations. In Africa, she has served in the US Peace Corps in Malawi and has conducted extensive field research on agriculture and education in Kenya. She received her PhD in anthropology from Columbia University, USA, in 1975, and has written extensively on international development.

Steve Morin is an anthropologist with a PhD in applied cultural anthropology from the University of Kentucky, USA, with a major in anthropology and minor in environmental systems (1989); and an MA in anthropology from the University of Nebraska, USA (1989). He joined IRRI at Los Baños in 1997 as affiliate scientist-anthropologist at the Genetic Resources Centre. In 1999–2001, he worked as an anthropologist at the Social Sciences Division, IRRI. His research mainly focused on agrodiversity, *in situ* conservation and preservation of rice genetic resources, understanding farmers' beliefs and practices regarding management of soil fertility, rodent pests and common property resources. He left IRRI in 2002 and is now an agricultural development officer at USAID in Washington, DC.

Michael Morris is a principal economist with CIMMYT in El Batán, Mexico. He holds a BA in anthropology from Amherst College, USA, and an MSc and PhD in agricultural economics from Michigan State University, USA. At CIMMYT, he served as director of the Economics Programme and, following CIMMYT's reorganization, recently was appointed director of the Global and Strategic Issues Programme. His research interests include agricultural development policy, technology adoption and impacts analysis, agricultural research priority setting and the economics of biotechnology. A US citizen, Morris has spent most of his life outside of the USA and has lived for extended periods in Latin America, sub-Saharan Africa, South-east Asia and Western Europe.

Oscar Ortiz received his BSc in agronomy, and his MSc in crop production and agricultural extension from the Universidad Agraria La Molina, Peru. After working with Nestlé-Peru in its Agricultural Extension Department, he joined CIP in 1992 as a research assistant in the Social Sciences Department, with responsibilities in participatory research and impact evaluation related to integrated pest management. Out of this work, he developed a PhD research programme to work on the subject of agricultural knowledge and information systems for integrated pest management. He received a PhD in agricultural extension and rural development from the University of Reading, UK, in 1997. In 1998 he rejoined CIP to coordinate special project activities in participatory research, including the adaptation of the farmer field school approach to potato-related problems such as the control of potato late blight. He is the leader of CIP's Integrated Crop Management Division.

Elinor Ostrom is the Arthur F. Bentley Professor of Political Science and co-director of the Workshop in Political Theory and Policy Analysis, and the Center for the Study of Institutions, Population and Environmental Change, Indiana University, Bloomington, USA. She was elected to the National Academy of Sciences in 2001; is a member of the American Academy of Arts and Sciences; and received the Frank E. Seidman Prize in Political Economy, Johan Skytte Prize in Political Science and the Lifetime Achievement Award (with Vincent Ostrom) from the Atlas Economic Research Foundation. Her books include *Governing the Commons: The Evolution of Institutions for Collective Action*; *Rules, Games, and Common-Pool Resources* (with Roy Gardner and James Walker, 1990) and *Local Commons and Global Interdependence: Heterogeneity and Cooperation in Two Domains* (with Robert Keohane, 1995).

Florencia G. Palis is an assistant scientist at the Social Sciences Division, IRRI, Los Baños, Philippines. She joined the division in 1987, and there, studied the economics of integrated pest management on rice. Her research interests include the role of culture in technology development and dissemination; integrated pest management, social capital; indigenous knowledge and rice biodiversity; and common property resources management. She has a BSc and MSc in statistics from the University of the Philippines, Los Baños; and a PhD in anthropology from the University of the Philippines, Diliman.

Thelma R. Paris is a socioeconomist and gender specialist at the Social Sciences Division, IRRI, Los Baños, Philippines. She joined IRRI in 1976 and worked as research assistant until 1997, as an affiliate scientist in 1998–2000 and as gender specialist in 2001–2003. She has received numerous international and local awards in recognition of her achievement, including CGIAR's Chairman's Excellence in Science Award for Outstanding Local Professional in 1996. Her research interests include socioeconomic issues in cropping and farming systems research; human nutrition; gender issues in agriculture; labour out-migration; and shifting gender roles and farmer participatory research for technology development, including plant breeding, biodiversity and natural resources management. She has an MSc in agricultural economics from the University of the Philippines, Los Baños, and a PhD in social ecology from the University of Western Sydney, Australia.

Gordon Prain received his PhD in social anthropology from Cambridge University in 1984. Following periods as a postdoctoral researcher with the British Overseas Development Administration and the Swiss Development Corporation, he joined CIP's Social Science Department as an anthropologist in 1988. He led research projects on rootcrop agriculture in Latin America (1988–1991), taking over as acting department head in 1990. In 1991 he moved to South-east Asia to coordinate a participatory research and development network, Users' Perspectives with Agricultural Research and Development (UPWARD). The network combined a small-grants programme with capacity development in participatory approaches to agricultural research in China, Indonesia, Nepal, the Philippines and Vietnam. In 1998–2000 he was CIP's regional representative for South-east Asia and the Pacific. Since 2000 he has been global coordinator for the newly established CGIAR Systemwide Initiative on Urban and Peri-urban Agriculture, URBAN HARVEST, which has established research sites in cities in Asia, sub-Saharan Africa and Latin America.

Agnes Quisumbing is a senior research fellow in the Food Consumption and Nutrition Division of IFPRI, Washington, DC. Her research examines how resource allocation within households and families may affect the design and outcome of development policies. Her research interests include intrahousehold allocation, interventions to increase women's incomes and food security, intergenerational transfers, property rights and land reform. She led a study on intrahousehold allocation and development policy in Bangladesh, Ethiopia, Guatemala and South Africa, and also worked on women's land rights in Ghana, the Philippines and Sumatra. She has started a new research programme analysing the factors that enable individuals, households and communities to move out of poverty, with field sites in Bangladesh, Guatemala and the Philippines.

Eva Rathgeber is a Canadian sociologist of education. During a long career with the International Development Research Centre (IDRC-Canada) she worked as a programme officer in science and technology policy, as founder and coordinator of IDRC's Gender and Development Programme, and in 1992–2001 as regional director for Eastern and Southern Africa, based in Nairobi, Kenya. Since 2002 she has been the joint chair of Women's Studies at Carleton University and Université d'Ottawa, Canada. She has published widely on science and technology policy, natural resources management, knowledge production and gender and development.

Robert E. Rhoades is professor of anthropology, University of Georgia, USA. He has spent 40 years as a social scientist in agriculture research, beginning in 1962 as a Peace Corps volunteer in Nepal. In the late 1960s, he was an East-West Center Fellow at IRRI in the Philippines, where he worked on the adoption of 'miracle rice' (IR-8). In 1979–1991, he worked at CIP as one of the first anthropologists in CGIAR. In addition to teaching, he manages an interdisciplinary programme in the Ecuadorian Andes, Sustainable Agriculture and Natural Resources Management (SANREM). He is considered a founder of agricultural anthropology as well as a pioneer in farming systems research and participatory methods. He co-authored with Robert H. Booth, *Farmer-Back-to-Farmer* (1982), which became a classic in anthropology and agriculture. He has published over a dozen books and 120 scientific papers.

Dannie Romney has worked for ILRI as a collaborator since 1995, joining the organization in 1999. Since completing a PhD in ruminant nutrition, she has developed her research interests to consider the multiple roles of livestock within the farming systems at different levels of intensification. She focused on the contribution of livestock to sustainable livelihoods relative to other activities and sources of income, analysing socioeconomic factors contributing to farm management and farmer decisions and working closely with social scientists, including livestock economists. Incorporation of participatory approaches using appropriate modes, from contractual to collegiate, has been crucial in identifying research questions and developing and evaluating interventions. Recently she has been involved in a small task team, developing ILRI's new theme – 'Enabling innovation'. An important objective of this theme is to effect institutional change to allow ILRI research to be more responsive to development needs and engage directly with development partners.

Deborah Rubin is the co-owner of the consulting firm *Cultural Practice, LLC*, in Washington, DC. She contributes to policies, strategic planning and research programme evaluation in the areas of agriculture, economic growth and gender for organizations such as USAID and the World Bank. She received a PhD in anthropology (1986), and held a Rockefeller Foundation postdoctoral fellowship in agriculture and rural development at IFPRI in Washington, DC and at the International Centre for Insect Physiology and Ecology in Nairobi, Kenya. She was the field director for the IFPRI study in Kenya on the impact of cash cropping on household nutritional status and income levels (1985–1987). Returning to academia, she taught at Stanford University and then at the University of the Pacific in California, USA, leaving as associate professor. She is affiliated as a senior research scientist at George Washington University, Washington, DC, teaching occasionally on development anthropology, and is a founding member of the research and policy programme, Culture in Global Affairs. She is conducting research on the use of the concept of culture in international development, an outgrowth of a MacArthur Foundation grant for *Accounting for Culture: Investigating Diversity in Development* (2000–2003).

Gustavo E. Saín is an independent consultant specializing in measuring results and impacts of technological change. Previously he worked in the Economics Programme at CIMMYT (1982–2003), as the senior economist responsible for research and management of the Economics Programme for Central America and the Caribbean. He was a key person in the development and diffusion of participatory research methodology as well as a leader in several projects on the adoption and impacts of new maize technologies. He received his BSc in agronomy from the Universidad Católica de Mar del Plata, Argentina, and his MSc and PhD in agricultural economics from the University of California-Davis, USA. Before joining CIMMYT, he was assistant professor at the University of Puerto Rico (1981–1982).

Madar Samad is principal researcher and theme leader for water resources, institution and policies, at IWMI in Colombo. He is an agricultural economist and has over 25 years' research experience on a wide range of issues relating to agriculture and rural development. He has worked extensively in formulating agricultural development policies, irrigation and water management, institutional reforms in the irrigation sector, agrarian reforms, farming system research development and issues relating to poverty and food security. He has been

extensively involved in capacity-building activities and has provided academic supervision and guidance to students studying for
MA and PhD degrees. Samad has managed several research projects
and organized several successful national and international
workshops and conferences. He graduated from the University of
Peradeniya, Sri Lanka. He did his postgraduate studies at
Cambridge University and the University of London.

Parvin Sultana is a specialist in participatory natural resources management, with experience in rural development and impact assessment. She received her PhD in natural resources management in
1985 from Colorado State University, USA; her MSc in zoology
(entomology) in 1975 from the University of Dhaka, Bangladesh;
and BSc (Honours) in zoology in 1973 from the same university. Her
work has included enabling poor fishing communities and farmers
to organize for resources management; networking with community
organizations; developing methods for consensus building for natural resources management; assessing household consumption patterns, determining farmers' agricultural extension needs. She has
worked in Bangladesh, Vietnam, Laos, Cambodia, Sri Lanka, the
USA and the UK.

William Sunderlin works as researcher in the Forests and Livelihoods
Programme at CIFOR in Bogor, Indonesia. He got his PhD in rural
sociology at Cornell University, USA, in 1993. In 1994–1999 he
conducted research at CIFOR on the underlying causes of deforestation in developing countries, with a focus on case studies in
Cameroon and Indonesia. In 2000 he took a sabbatical from CIFOR
to write *Ideology, Social Theory, and the Environment* (2003).
Since returning to CIFOR in 2001, he has been focusing on theoretical development on the use of forest resources for poverty alleviation, and has begun case studies on this topic in Cambodia,
Lao People's Democratic Republic and Vietnam.

Graham Thiele completed his social anthropology PhD at Cambridge
University on the impacts of villagization in Tanzania. In 1984, he
joined the Overseas Development Administration (ODA), now the
Department for International Development (DfID–UK) as an associate professional, after earning an MSc in agricultural economics.
He was posted to the agricultural marketing department in lowland
Bolivia. Subsequently, he worked in a farming system team looking for alternatives to slash-and-burn farming. This led to the setting up of a liaison unit between research and extension
organizations and a major study of collaboration between non-
governmental organizations and the public sector. In 1994 he
moved to CIP, Bolivia, to incorporate small-farmer perspectives
into the agricultural research institution. This led to work in par-

ticipatory variety selection and seed systems. Since 1998 he has worked in the Papa Andina Project in Bolivia, Peru and Ecuador, developing platforms and participatory methods for technological and institutional innovation, especially helping small farmers to link with markets.

Paul Thompson is a social scientist with the WorldFish Center, specializing in natural resources issues, particularly community management of fisheries and floodplain resources management in Bangladesh. He was the project leader of the community-based fisheries management projects in Bangladesh during 1996–2004. He is a consultant for the Forth Fisheries Project, a large fisheries development project in Bangladesh funded by the World Bank and DfID–UK.

Magnus Torell holds a PhD in economic geography (fisheries in Thailand) from the University of Gothenburg, Sweden, and also a law degree from the University of Lund, Sweden. After a year of work with the South-east Asian Programme in Ocean Law, Policy and Management (SEAPOL) in Bangkok, he joined the Swedish International Development Agency (SIDA) in 1988, and was a senior programme officer until 1996. Responsibilities mainly related to fisheries, natural resources management and the environment. In 1996 he joined ICLARM, (now the WorldFish Center), seconded by SIDA, and its Policy Research and Impact Assessment Programme (PRIAP) until 2003. Later in 2003 he was appointed senior advisor to the South-east Asian Fisheries Development Centre (SEAFDEC), where he is still employed.

K. Kuperan Viswanathan is a senior social scientist with the WorldFish Center, with 20 years experience as a natural resources economist in development projects. He led the Global Fisheries Co-Management Project at the WorldFish Center in 1999–2003. The project involved the systematic documentation of co-management initiatives through case studies in Indonesia, Thailand, the Philippines, Cambodia, Vietnam and Bangladesh in Asia; and in Malawi, Mozambique, Zambia, Zimbabwe and South Africa in Africa. He has also conducted training on fisheries co-management for fisheries managers, policymakers and researchers from Asia and Africa. He is on the technical advisory board of the Marine Stewardship Council, UK. He has a particular interest in community-based fisheries projects and in the use of collective action-based institutions for development in the fisheries sector. He is the project leader for a community-based fisheries management project in Bangladesh, and the director of the Bangladesh and South Asia office of the WorldFish Center.

Joachim Voss, a citizen of Canada, holds a PhD in economic anthropology from the University of Toronto and an MA in rural sociology from the University of Guelph. He joined the CGIAR as a 'Rocky doc', worked as a senior scientist for CIAT's Central Africa Programme during 1984–1988, and became CIAT's Director General in January 2000. In 1988–1999 he worked with the International Development Research Centre (IDRC) in Canada, where his last post was as senior research manager of IDRC's Research Division. Voss has been a board member or chair of several international initiatives such as the Consortium for Sustainable Andean Development (CONDESAN), the CGIAR Gender Committee, the CGIAR Integrated Natural Resource Management Task Force and the Multi-Stakeholder Forum on Intellectual Property and Access Rights in Plant Genetic Resources (CRUCIBLE). He chairs the Latin America and Caribbean Sub-committee and the Millennium Development Goals task force of the CGIAR's Centre Directors' Committee. He has conducted research and published extensively on soil fertility management, farming systems, participatory breeding, indigenous knowledge and social-cultural aspects of development.

Abbreviations

ACIAR	Australian Council for International Agricultural Research
ACM	adaptive collaborative management
AER	agricultural economics research
BFW	Bread for the World – USA
BMZ	Bundesministerium für wirtschaftliche Zusammenarbeit und Entwicklung (German Federal Ministry for Economic Cooperation and Development)
C&I	criteria and indicators
CAPRi	Collective Action and Property Rights
CGIAR	Consultative Group on International Agricultural Research
CIAL	comité de investigación agrícola local (local agricultural research committee)
CIAT	Centro Internacional de Agricultura Tropical (International Center for Tropical Agriculture)
CIDA	Canadian International Development Agency
CIFOR	Center for International Forestry Research
CIMAT	Criteria and Indicators Modification and Adaptation Tool
CIMMYT	International Maize and Wheat Improvement Center
CIP	International Potato Center
CRSP	Collaborative Research Support Program

CTBS	community trap barrier system
CWANA	Central, West Asia and North Africa
Danida	Danish International Development Agency
DfID–UK	Department for International Development – UK
DGDC	Directorate-General for Development Cooperation – Belgium
DSE	Deutshe Stiftung für Internationale Entwicklung (German Foundation for International Development)
EAC	External Advisory Committee
EGAT	Economic Growth, Development and Trade
EPMR	external performance management review
EPTD	Environment and Production Technology Division
ESCWA	United Nations Economic and Social Commission for West Asia
ESI	extra-sectoral influences
ESP	Environment and Science Policy
FAO	Food and Agricultural Organization of the United Nations
FCND	Food Consumption and Nutrition Division
FFS	farmer field school
FMIS	farmer-managed irrigation system
FPP	Forest Products and People
FSP	Farming Systems Programme
FSP	forests, society and people
FSR	farming systems research
GIS	geographic information systems
HYM	high-yielding methodology
HYV	high-yielding variety
IARC	international agricultural research centre
IASCP	International Association for the Study of Common Property
ICARDA	International Center for Agricultural Research in the Dry Areas
ICER	internally commissioned external review
ICLARM	International Centre for Living Aquatic Resources Management (now WorldFish Center)
ICRAF	International Centre for Research in Agroforestry (now WORLD AGROFORESTRY CENTRE)
ICRISAT	International Crop Research Institute for the Semi-Arid Tropics
IDE	International Development Enterprises
IDRC	International Development Research Centre
IDS	Institute of Development Studies, Sussex, UK

IFAD	International Fund for Agricultural Development
IFDC	International Fertilizer Development Corporation
IFPRI	International Food Policy Research Institute
IIMI	International Irrigation Management Institute
IITA	International Institute of Tropical Agriculture
ILAC	institutional learning and change
ILCA	International Livestock Centre for Africa
ILRAD	International Laboratory for Research on Animal Diseases
ILRI	International Livestock Research Institute
IMT	irrigation management transfer
IPGRI	International Plant Genetic Resources Institute
IPM	integrated pest management
IPRA	Proyecto de Investigación Participativa en Agricultura (Participatory Research in Agriculture Project)
IRRI	International Rice Research Institute
IRS	Internationally Recruited Staff
iSC	interim Science Council
ISNAR	International Service for National Agricultural Research
IWMI	International Water Management Institute
IWRM	integrated water resource management
LADAF	Latin America Development Assistance Facility
MP	multi-country programme
NARES	national agricultural research and extension system
NARS	national agricultural research systems
NGO	non-governmental organization
NRC	National Research Council
NRM	natural resources management
NRMP	Natural Resources Management Programme
NTFP	non-timber forest product
OFR	on-farm research
PRA	participatory rural appraisal
PRCA	property rights and collective action
PRGA	Participatory Research and Gender Analysis
PRIAP	Policy Research and Impact Assessment Programme
PROGRESA	Programa Nacional de Educacion, Salud, y Nutricion
PROINPA	Promoción e Investigación de Productos Andinos
SANREM	Sustainable Agriculture and Natural Resources Management
SDC	Swiss Agency for Development and Cooperation
SGRP	Systemwide Genetic Resources Programme

SIDA	Swedish International Development Agency
SPEA	Systemwide Programmes with an Ecoregional Approach
SPSS	Statistical Package for the Social Sciences
SSD	Social Sciences Division
TAC	Technical Advisory Committee
TPS	true potato seed
UCD	underlying causes of deforestation
UNDP	United Nations Development Programme
UPWARD	Users' Perspectives with Agricultural Research and Development
USAID	United States Agency for International Development
USDA	US Department of Agriculture
WANA	West Asia and North Africa
WARDA	West Africa Rice Development Association – the Africa Rice Centre
WFC	WorldFish Center
WHO	World Health Organization
WHP	World Hunger Programme

Index

Note: CGIAR refers to Consultative Group on International Agricutural Research. As the principal institution discussed throughout the book, it does not have a main entry, but where mentioned in other topics, is referred to as CGIAR. Page numbers in *italics* refer to figures and tables. Page numbers with suffix 'n' refer to notes.

socioeconomics 48n, 49n
    farmer-managed irrigation
        system profiling 144–145
socioeconomist–gender specialist 94
    IRRI 82–83
sociological factors, agricultural
    productivity 33
socio-political dimension of social
    research 184, 185–186, 187
Somel, K. 246
Song, S. 294
South Africa
    public works 308, 309
    river basin management 155
    water institutions 152
South Asia, treadle pumps 156–157
SPEA (Systemwide Programmes
    with an Ecoregional
    Approach), social science
    capacity 40
Spooner, B. 345
Sri Lanka, irrigation 146–147, 150
Staal, S.J. 199
staffing
    Cali Conference report 17–18,
        24, 44–45
    CGIAR system 52
    CIAT 13, 221, *222,* 230–231
    CIFOR 13
    CIP 13, *14,* 167–170
        trends *14*
    connectors 394
    CYMMIT 14
    depletion 11–18
    ICARDA 13, 14, *15,* 241–242,
        243–244, 244–245
    ICRISAT 13, 14
    IITA 13, 15
    ILRI 13–15, *16,* 194–195
    IRRI 13, 14, 15, *16,* 393
    social research 35
    social science research 35
    WARDA 14, 15
    World Bank 17, 28n–29n
stakeholders
    forest management 105, 106
    river basin management
        152, 153

Statistical Package for the Social
    Sciences (SPSS) 52
Stegner, W. 235
strategic research 32–39, 40,
    42, 45, 47
strategic stripe review 43, 47, 49n
Strauss, J.A. 305
Sudan, irrigation 147
Suherman, R. 177
Sultana, P. 209, 291
Sunderlin, W.D. 100, 108
supply-driven approaches 437
Sussman, R.W. 329
sustainability 21, 388
    land 201
    livelihoods 311
    livestock 201
    natural resources 42
    science 405
sustainable agriculture,
    grant proposals 414
Sustainable Agriculture and Natural
    Resources Management
    (SANREM) 414–418
sustainable development 11, 388
sustainable food security 33
sustainable forest management
    criteria and indicators
    101–102
sustainable livelihoods framework
    311, 320, 386–387
sustainable rural livelihood
    framework (CIAT) 234
Sutton, R. 317
Svendsen, M. 153
Swallow, B. 289, 290, 293
Swaminathan, M.S. 274
sweet potato crops 171, 177–178
    integrated pest management 172
    postharvest storage 182
swiddens 271
Syria, ICARDA projects 252, 253
system level research 5, 33, 375
Systemwide Genetic Resources
    Programme *see* SGRP
Systemwide Programmes with an
    Ecoregional Approach
    see SPEA

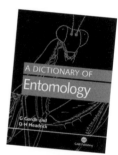

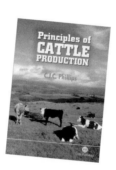